The New International Lesson Annual

1995–96

September—August

THE NEW INTERNATIONAL LESSON ANNUAL

1995–96

September—August

Abingdon Press
Nashville

The New International Lesson Annual

Copyright © 1995 by Abingdon Press

Scripture quotations, unless otherwise indicated, are from the New Revised Standard Version Bible, Copyright
© 1989, by the Division of Christian Education of the National Council of the Churches of Christ in the USA.
Used by permission.

Scripture quotations noted NIV are taken from the Holy Bible: New International Version. Copyright © 1973,
1978, 1984 by the International Bible Society. Used by permission of Zondervan Bible Publishers.

Scripture quotations noted KJV are taken from the King James Version of the Bible.

The song, "Here I Am, Lord," on page 181 is copyright © 1981, Daniel L. Schutte and New Dawn Music, P.O.
Box 13248, Portland, OR 97213. All rights reserved. Used with permission.

The Psalm 63 adaptation on page 198 appears in *The Upper Room Worshipbook: Music and Liturgies for Spiritual
Formation*. It is adapted from the Good News Bible, copyright © 1976. Used by permission.

The prayer on page 227 is from *A Book of Uncommon Faith*, by Kenneth G. Phifer. Copyright © 1989 by Dorothy
Johnson Marchal. Used by permission of Upper Room Books.

The Lord's Prayer on page 364 is Ecumenical Text from the English translation of the Lord's Prayer. Used by
permission of The International Consultation on English Texts.

ISBN 0-687-19159-9

ISSN 0074-6770

94   95   96   97   98   99   00   01   02   03 —10   9   8   7   6   5   4   3   2   1

MANUFACTURED IN THE UNITED STATES OF AMERICA

Preface

This edition of *The New International Lesson Annual* marks a transition in its life as a new general editor receives the baton from Dr. William Willimon, who has so capably overseen this publication for the last three years. We assume this awesome new responsibility both with gratitude for the solid foundation that has been laid before us and with dreams for adding our own imprint to this important educational publication.

Our continuing goal is to make *The New International Lesson Annual* a flexible tool for teachers and students in a wide variety of Sunday school settings. We know that our readers represent at least twenty denominations. You belong to small, medium, and large membership congregations. Your churches are located in the cities, rural towns, and suburbs across North America. You use different teaching strategies, ranging from lecture to discussion to creative interactive activities, or combinations of all three. Your students prefer differing translations of the Bible. Some of your classes have a full hour for the lesson while others have only thirty-five or forty minutes. Some of you gather in lovely church parlors whereas others pull up a stool in the church kitchen. In short, you are a diverse group who are bound together by the common thread of serious, systematic Bible study based on the Uniform Lesson Series. You are interested in becoming faithful disciples of Jesus Christ and are willing to invest your time and your talents in learning and sharing with others what Jesus expects of us.

Meeting such diverse needs and expectations is a major challenge, but together we can do it. The Abingdon staff and skilled writers will continue to work hard to bring you an easy-to-use publication, based on sound biblical scholarship, that will provide you scriptural information and a host of ideas for leading each session. As you prepare to teach, you will be able to select from among those ideas the ones that seem most suited to your class. We encourage you to experiment with options that perhaps you have never used before. Different teaching strategies have an amazing way of bringing new vitality to a class. You will want to plan to introduce change gradually and to enlist the class support in trying unfamiliar types of activities.

You can help shape this publication by letting us know what works well for your class, what you wish we would add, and what you could happily live without. While we can make no guarantees about changes—since some teachers invariably dislike features that others adore—we will make every effort to respond to requests from a large contingent of our readers. Please send your ideas to: Dr. Nan Duerling, Abingdon Press, 201 Eighth Avenue South, P.O. Box 801, Nashville, TN 37202. We will do our best to respond to each letter because your input is extremely important to us.

The opportunity to serve and be in dialogue with you will be a real blessing to us, and we trust for you as well. The work that you do as a teacher of adults is critically important, both to the individuals you lead and to the continuing vitality of your congregation. Research conducted by Search Institute has concluded that Christian education is the most important factor in promoting spiritual maturity among teens and adults. Your work enables persons to be more intimately related to God and more willing to reach out to other persons in Jesus' name. May God richly bless and guide you in this important ministry of teaching God's people, for in doing so, you touch eternity.

Dr. Nan Duerling, *General Editor*

Contents

SECOND QUARTER

God's Promise of Deliverance

UNIT 1: THE COMING OF A NEW DAY
(December 3–31)

UNIT 2: THE MINISTRY OF THE SUFFERING SERVANT
(January 7–28)

UNIT 3: GOD'S LOVE FOR ALL PEOPLE (JONAH, RUTH)
(February 4–25)

THIRD QUARTER

Teachings of Jesus

UNIT 1: TEACHINGS ABOUT THE KINGDOM OF HEAVEN
(March 3–31)

UNIT 2: TEACHING ABOUT GOD
(April 7–28)

UNIT 3: TEACHINGS ABOUT LIVING
(May 5–26)

FOURTH QUARTER

UNIT 1: A PRACTICAL RELIGION (JAMES)
(June 2–30)

God Is with Us (Psalms)

UNIT 2: PRAISING GOD
(July 7–28)

UNIT 3: RESPONDING TO GOD
(August 4–25)

FIRST QUARTER

SEPTEMBER 3—NOVEMBER 26, 1995

During the fall quarter, we will be studying *The Story of Christian Beginnings: The Acts of the Apostles*. This story could also be called The Acts of the Holy Spirit, for it is by the power and inspiration of the Spirit that the church grows and thrives. The book of Acts picks up the story where its author, Luke, left it at the close of his gospel. The scene opens just prior to the ascension when the resurrected Jesus promises his followers that the Holy Spirit will come upon them in power. After this outpouring, Jesus' followers were expected to witness for him in Jerusalem, Judea and Samaria, and to the ends of the world. The rest of the Acts story is the fulfillment of that promise. As a result of this powerful witness, Jews and Gentiles respond to the life-transforming work of the Holy Spirit. The church grows and spreads, just as Jesus had envisioned.

Unit 1, *Beginnings in Jerusalem*, is a four-week study of the earliest days of the church. The first lesson, based on Acts 1, looks at Jesus' promise of power to his disciples. On September 10, we will examine the Pentecost experience, as recorded in Acts 2. The third lesson focuses on the saving, life-changing power of Jesus as seen in the healing of a man who had been lame since birth. This unit closes with the spine-tingling account of Peter and John's miraculous release from prison and their boldness in returning to the temple to teach after being forbidden to do so.

The second unit, *Witnessing in Judea and Samaria*, traces the movement of the church as it extends into Gentile territory. "Becoming a Servant," the lesson for October 1, considers the selection and consecration of seven men to serve the church by overseeing food distribution to the Hellenist widows. The following week, we will follow Philip as he preaches to receptive Samaritans and to an Ethiopian eunuch who chooses to be baptized in response to the Word. The lesson for October 15 will be familiar, for it investigates Saul's Damascus road experience, as told in Acts 9. Then we will read the fascinating story of Cornelius, the first Gentile convert, who responds to a God-given vision to send for Peter, who was also given a vision in preparation for this unexpected event. This unit ends with a lesson based on Acts 11:19-30 and 12:24-25, concerning the purposeful work of the church in Antioch.

Unit 3, *Spreading the Gospel into All the World*, opens with an account of Paul and Barnabas's missionary travels in Gentile lands. The lesson for November 12, "Grace on Trial," concerns the successful attempt by the Jerusalem Conference to resolve a serious church conflict. Acts 15:36–16:40 is the background scripture for the next class, which follows Paul and Silas as they win the first European convert, Lydia. They also nearly cause a riot and wind up in jail because they cast a demon from a slave woman. The quarter closes with a lesson based on Acts 18:18–19:41, which demonstrates the power of the gospel to overcome other gods and demons.

MEET OUR WRITER

DR. NAN DUERLING

Currently the general editor of *The New International Lesson Annual*, Dr. Duerling has written church curriculum for youth and adults since 1984. She has served as a voting member of the Curriculum Resources Committee of The United Methodist Church, as well as the Curriculum Consultant in the Mid-Atlantic region for The United Methodist Publishing House. A former secondary and university level English teacher, Nan teaches in the Course of Study School at Wesley Theological Seminary in Washington, D.C. She also enjoys teaching adult classes at Linthicum Heights UMC where she and her husband Craig are both active laypersons. The Duerlings live in Crownsville, Maryland.

PROMISE OF NEW POWER

PREVIEWING THE LESSON

Lesson Scripture: Acts 1:1-14
Background Scripture: Acts 1
Key Verse: Acts 1:8

Focus of the lesson:
Jesus' promise to his disciples that they would receive the power of the Holy Spirit in order to witness for him

Main question(s) of the lesson:
(1) What did this promise mean to Jesus' first followers?
(2) What does it mean to me today as I seek to live my life as a faithful follower of Jesus?

This lesson will enable adult learners to:
(1) identify the Holy Spirit as the power that Jesus promised to send in order to enable his followers to be faithful witnesses
(2) enter into the fear and anxiety Jesus' followers experienced as they saw their Lord ascend and waited for the promise to be fulfilled
(3) respond by becoming more faithful witnesses, both as individuals and as a church body.

Today's lesson may be outlined as follows:
(1) Introduction
(2) New Power Is Promised (Acts 1:1-8)
(3) Jesus Ascends into Heaven (Acts 1:9-11)
(4) The Disciples Wait for the Promise to Be Fulfilled (Acts 1:12-14)

FOCUSING ON THE MAIN QUESTION

Do you remember a time in your life when you eagerly anticipated a special event? Perhaps you had worked hard for a college degree and looked forward to graduation. Maybe you could hardly wait until your wedding day. Perhaps you were so anxious to cuddle a new child or grandchild that you felt the nine months of waiting would never end. Or maybe the prospect of a new job or promotion raised your enthusiasm for work to new heights. Whatever the event was, you likely experienced a wide range of feelings as you waited: hope, expectation, anxiety, and excitement.

Jesus' disciples found themselves in a similar situation. After the crushing defeat of the crucifixion, they had seen their beloved master—alive! He continued to teach them about the kingdom of God as he sojourned with them for forty days. Then, as they watched from the Mount of Olives, Jesus ascended into heaven. Before he left them, he promised that the baptism of the Holy Spirit, which John the Baptist had also spoken of, would be given to them. This promised power would enable them to be witnesses to the good news of Jesus.

Imagine how the eleven disciples, as well as the women who had accompanied Jesus during the days of his ministry, must have felt. In fact, a band of one hundred twenty believers waited in eager anticipation for the fulfillment of this promise. They prayed constantly as they waited together.

This same power is promised to us as well. We have the indwelling presence of God's Holy Spirit within us. God's Spirit has the power to change the direction of our lives, just as it changed the lives of Jesus' first followers. Like them, we face daily challenges. We may feel timid about accepting certain responsibilities or inadequate to meet the challenges before us. We may keep that Spirit hidden under a basket because we believe we are unwilling or unable to let it shine as a witness of light and hope to a world that desperately needs to hear the good news of our risen Lord. As we begin our study of Acts, we must ask ourselves: **What did this promise mean to Jesus' first followers? What does it mean to me today as I seek to live my life as a faithful follower of Jesus?**

READING THE SCRIPTURE

NRSV
Acts 1:1-14

1 In the first book, Theophilus, I wrote about all that Jesus did and taught from the beginning ²until the day when he was taken up to heaven, after giving instructions through the Holy Spirit to the apostles whom he had chosen. ³After his suffering he presented himself alive to them by many convincing proofs, appearing to them during forty days and speaking about the kingdom of God. ⁴While staying with them, he ordered them not to leave Jerusalem, but to wait there for the promise of the Father. "This," he said, "is what you have heard from me; ⁵for John baptized with water, but you will be baptized with the Holy Spirit not many days from now."

6 So when they had come together, they asked him, "Lord, is this the time when you will restore the kingdom to Israel?" ⁷He replied, "It is not for you to know the times or periods that the Father has set

NIV
Acts 1:1-14

1 In my former book, Theophilus, I wrote about all that Jesus began to do and to teach ²until the day he was taken up to heaven, after giving instructions through the Holy Spirit to the apostles he had chosen. ³After his suffering, he showed himself to these men and gave many convincing proofs that he was alive. He appeared to them over a period of forty days and spoke about the kingdom of God. ⁴On one occasion, while he was eating with them, he gave them this command: "Do not leave Jerusalem, but wait for the gift my Father promised, which you have heard me speak about. ⁵For John baptized with water, but in a few days you will be baptized with the Holy Spirit."

⁶So when they met together, they asked him, "Lord, are you at this time going to restore the kingdom to Israel?"

⁷He said the them, "It is not for you to know the times or dates the Father has set

Key
Verse

by his own authority. **⁸But you will receive power when the Holy Spirit has come upon you; and you will be my witnesses in Jerusalem, in all Judea and Samaria, and to the ends of the earth."** ⁹When he had said this, as they were watching, he was lifted up, and a cloud took him out of their sight. ¹⁰While he was going and they were gazing up toward heaven, suddenly two men in white robes stood by them. ¹¹They said, "Men of Galilee, why do you stand looking up toward heaven? This Jesus, who has been taken up from you into heaven, will come in the same way as you saw him go into heaven."

12 Then they returned to Jerusalem from the mount called Olivet, which is near Jerusalem, a sabbath day's journey away. ¹³When they had entered the city, they went to the room upstairs where they were staying, Peter, and John, and James, and Andrew, Philip and Thomas, Bartholomew and Matthew, James son of Alphaeus, and Simon the Zealot, and Judas son of James. ¹⁴All these were constantly devoting themselves to prayer, together with certain women, including Mary the mother of Jesus, as well as his brothers.

by his own authority. **⁸But you will receive power when the Holy Spirit comes on you; and you will be my witnesses in Jerusalem, and in all Judea and Samaria, and to the ends of the earth."** ⁹After he said this, he was taken up before their very eyes, and a cloud hid him from their sight.

¹⁰They were looking intently up into the sky as he was going, when suddenly two men dressed in white stood beside them. ¹¹"Men of Galilee," they said, "why do you stand here looking into the sky? This same Jesus, who has been taken from you into heaven, will come back in the same way you have seen him go into heaven."

¹²Then they returned to Jerusalem from the hill called the Mount of Olives, a Sabbath day's walk from the city. ¹³When they arrived, they went upstairs to the room where they were staying. Those present were Peter, John, James and Andrew; Philip and Thomas, Bartholomew and Matthew; James son of Alphaeus and Simon the Zealot, and Judas son of James. ¹⁴They all joined together constantly in prayer, along with the women and Mary the mother of Jesus, and with his brothers.

Key
Verse

UNDERSTANDING THE SCRIPTURE

Introduction to Acts. This exciting book chronicles the spread of Christianity under the direction of the Holy Spirit. Scholars disagree on the date of this work, but it was likely written in the last quarter of the first century C.E. While the author of both Acts and the Third Gospel are acknowledged to be the same person, commentators disagree over whether the writer is actually Paul's traveling companion, as suggested in Colossians 4:14; 2 Timothy 4:11; Philemon 1:24, or an unknown writer using Luke's name. Much of Acts records Paul's missionary journeys. Numerous speeches enable the reader to feel a part of the action of the narrative. Summaries at many points show the continuing numerical growth and geographical spread of the church (see for example Acts 2:41; 4:4; 14:1).

Acts 1:1-5. This preface to the book of Acts links it to the Gospel of Luke, referred to in verse 1 as "the first book." Both the Gospel and its sequel are written for Theophilus, an unknown person also mentioned in Luke 1:3 whose name means "lover of God." Theophilus may have been a Roman official who wanted to know more about Jesus. Luke reminds Theophilus that "the first book" recounted Jesus' life from the beginning until his ascension.

During the forty days between the crucifixion and the ascension, Jesus appeared to his disciples and offered "many convincing proofs," as recorded in Luke 24:13-53, that he was alive. Since Jerusalem was the center of Jesus' activity, Jesus commanded the disciples to remain there until the promised baptism with the Holy Spirit occurred. This "promise of the Father" likely refers to Joel 2:28-32 (quoted in Acts 2:17-21) wherein the coming of the Holy Spirit is described.

Acts 1:6-8. This section records an important discussion between the disciples and Jesus. The site where "they had come together" was probably the Mount of Olives mentioned in Acts 1:12. The disciples question Jesus about the time of the restoration of the kingdom of Israel. They expected him to assume the throne of David, as foretold in Luke 1:32, and want to know when that event will occur. Jesus' answer indicates that only God knows the time of that restoration. This matter is not to concern the disciples. Instead, they are to be witnesses for Jesus first in Jerusalem (the center of his ministry), then in all Judea and Samaria (neighboring areas), and finally "to the ends of the earth" (as symbolized by Rome, the seat of the Roman Empire). This geographic scheme serves two purposes. First, it emphasizes the movement of the church as recorded in Acts from Jerusalem (Acts 3:1—8:3) to Judea and Samaria (Acts 8:4—12:25), and then "to the ends of the earth" (Acts 13:1—28:31). Second, this geographic blueprint for ministry underscores the importance of witnessing to all persons. The church begins in Jerusalem but quickly moves into Gentile territory. The Greek word for witness, *martus*, comes into English as the word martyr.

Acts 1:9-11. The disciples are witnesses to the ascension of Jesus into heaven. Jesus is transported by a cloud. The event is interpreted by "two men in white robes," who seem similar in appearance to the "two men in dazzling clothes" who appeared to the women at the tomb (see Luke 24:4). Just as these angelic beings asked the women why they sought the living among the dead, they ask the disciples, "why do you stand looking up toward heaven?" These two men promise that Jesus will return "in the same way" as he went into heaven. Luke's account of the transfiguration of Jesus (Luke 9:28-36) includes similar elements. Luke 24:50-51 provides another account of the ascension.

Acts 1:12-14. The eleven disciples return to Jerusalem after having witnessed the ascension. They had come "a sabbath day's journey," about a half a mile, from the Mount of Olives. When they arrived in Jerusalem, they went to an upper room to pray. Their company also included women who had been close to Jesus (Acts 1:14). Likely they huddled together, afraid of the Roman authorities who had crucified Jesus. The list of the eleven disciples given in Acts 1:13 is the same as the one in Luke 6:14-16, but the order is different and the name of Judas Iscariot is missing.

Acts 1:15-26. In Acts 1:15, Peter takes leadership responsibility for the one hundred twenty persons who believed in Jesus. He gives an account of Judas's activities and final end, though this account is different from the tradition recorded in Matthew 27:5. Peter quotes Psalm 69:25 [in Acts 1:20*a*] and Psalm 109:8 in Acts 1:20*b* to call for a replacement for Judas. Acts 1:21-22 sets forth criteria for Judas's successor: he must have been with Jesus from his baptism, which marked the beginning of Jesus' public ministry, and he must have seen the ascension, which marked the end of his earthly mission. The most important event to which the additional apostle must bear witness to, according to verse 22, is the resurrection. Two men, Joseph (known also as Barsabbas and Justus) and Matthias met these criteria. The eleven apostles prayed and cast lots, according to the practice set forth in Leviticus 16:7-10 in which God chooses a sacrificial goat by lots. Matthias, whose name means "gift of the Lord," is chosen by lot but never mentioned again. The number of apostles has been restored to twelve so as to correspond to the twelve tribes of Israel.

INTERPRETING THE SCRIPTURE

New Power Is Promised

The writer of Acts, who also wrote the Gospel of Luke, opens his sequel by referring back to the post-resurrection events attested to in the closing verses of his Gospel. In doing so, the author moves from an account of the life and work of Jesus to the story of the early church, its mission, and its challenges. Luke demonstrates that Jesus' death on a crude wooden cross is definitely not the end of the story. The disciples must have experienced hope, joy, amazement, and fear as their master convincingly appeared to them not once but many times over the course of forty days. In his resurrected state, Jesus continued to teach his followers about the kingdom of God, though the exact content of this teaching is not recorded (Acts 1:3).

Jesus was with his disciples in Jerusalem—the scene of much of his ministry, as well as his trial and crucifixion (Acts 1:4). Likely, the disciples were anxious to leave this city and its painful memories. They certainly had no guarantees that they would not be arrested and crucified as their beloved Lord was. Peter had already been identified a follower but denied the allegation (Luke 22:54-62). The charge against Jesus was that he was a political rebel, a threat to the Roman Empire—the King of the Jews (Luke 23:1-3, 38). Although neither Pilate nor Herod could substantiate this accusation, they caved in to pressure to have Jesus executed. Surely the Roman government was not about to allow Jesus' followers to create an uprising. Their lives were in jeopardy, their futures uncertain.

What had become of their dream? Was Jesus now going to "restore the kingdom to Israel?" the disciples asked (Acts 1:6). He replied that such authority rested solely with the Father, who would act according to his own schedule. Jesus announced to the disciples that they would play an important role: they would be witnesses for him first in Jerusalem, then in the surrounding territories of Judea and Samaria, and finally throughout the world. Jesus clearly had great expectations for his followers! How could these expectations be fulfilled, especially when one of the strongest, most vocal members of the group had already denied even knowing Jesus for fear that he, too, would be hauled before the Roman court?

Jesus knew of their weaknesses, but he also knew of God's strength. Through the power of the Holy Spirit the disciples would be able to do great things for the kingdom of God. This power was not something that they could earn or attain by their own efforts but was a gift promised to them by the Father. "(N)ot many days from now," (Acts 1:5) the disciples would be baptized with the Holy Spirit. Jesus knew that their timidity would be transformed into boldness. Their recollections about Jesus, now discussed behind closed doors in an upper room, would be shouted from the housetops when the Holy Spirit descended. For the moment, however, Jesus told the disciples simply to wait for this precious promise to be fulfilled.

Jesus Ascends into Heaven

Immediately after Jesus announced the coming of the promised Holy Spirit (Acts 1:8), he ascended into heaven. Luke gives a short description of the ascension in his Gospel (Luke 24:50-51), though it is different from the account reported in Acts. The story of the ascension found in Acts 1:9-11 bears greater similarity in its details to Luke's description of the first Easter morning (Luke 24:1-7).

We do not know where Luke, who did not witness the ascension, got his specific information regarding this event. Mark 16:19 simply records that Jesus "was taken up into heaven and sat down at the right hand of God." The Gospel prologue (Luke 1:1-4) indicates that Luke had done careful research, talked with eyewitnesses, and read accounts written by others. Possibly Luke based his accounts on traditions that existed within the early church, though Matthew and John do not refer directly to the ascension.

Elijah's ascension may have influenced the early church's understanding of Jesus' departure. Elijah was transported amid a whirlwind into heaven by a chariot and horses of fire (see 2 Kings 2:9-13). Non-biblical accounts also record that Moses was taken into heaven. During the transfiguration (Luke 9:28-36), Jesus was seen in "dazzling white" clothes. Two men, Elijah and Moses, were with him. The cloud of God overshadowed the three disciples. These elements appear again in the ascension story. Luke portrays Jesus as being lifted up by a cloud. As his astonished disciples stare heavenward, "two men in white robes stood by them" (Acts 1:10), explaining that Jesus will come again in the same manner that he is ascending.

When the promised Spirit comes upon them, the disciples will be able to witness not only to Jesus' teaching, death, and resurrection but also his ascension into heaven. The one whom they had believed to be the Messiah—the heir of David's throne who would restore the kingdom of Israel—is now perceived to be the Lord of heaven. Surely they will have great news to tell when they are empowered by the Holy Spirit.

The Disciples Wait for the Promise to Be Fulfilled

After witnessing this spectacular event, the disciples walk about a half mile back to Jerusalem. Jesus had commanded them not to leave the city until after they had received the promised Holy Spirit (Acts 1:4). Obediently, they returned to the upper room where they had been lodging. The disciples, except Judas Iscariot, are named. Note that Peter, John, and James, who are mentioned at the head of the list, will be key players in the unfolding story of the fledgling church as recorded in Acts. The eleven men are not alone, however. They are in the midst of a larger community of faith that includes the women who traveled with Jesus, Jesus' family, and other believers—one hundred twenty in all. Luke portrays this group as living harmoniously, dedicating themselves to the spiritual discipline of prayer as they await the coming of the Holy Spirit.

We can only imagine the emotions of these followers as they waited. They knew that God had called them—and continues to call. Soon their lives would move in a new direction. The waters were uncharted but by the grace of the Holy Spirit's leading they would be able to fulfill great expectations as witnesses.

How often have we found ourselves in a similar situation? That still small voice within us, words from those who care about us, and external circumstances seem to be saying to us, just as clearly as Jesus spoke to the disciples, "Hang on. You will soon be changing course. Don't worry, though. By my Spirit, I will guide and direct you."

I have had several such experiences in my own life. Following my first year as a high school teacher, I felt God calling me to go into another school district to teach in a small school for students with very special needs. Some persons closest to me thought that I had taken leave of my senses for wanting to go into this difficult situation. The school official responsible for teacher placement was also having trouble understanding why I was turning down "choice" assignments, especially since the school I had requested had no openings in my subject area. Waiting was hard. The summer was almost over. I needed a job but God's promise of a position at this school kept me from saying yes to other offers. Finally, with less than two weeks remaining before the beginning of school, a slot unexpectedly opened for me. The placement official was dumbfounded. I was overjoyed. God had been faithful. God had not only called me to a task but had provided the means for me to fulfill that calling. All I had to do was wait.

Waiting is difficult, though. It can be exciting as we anticipate a change of course or a special event. It can also produce a great deal of anxiety. In our do-it-now society, waiting seems especially agonizing. People expect us to act, and we want to be in control of our own destinies. "What if I'm wrong?" we wonder. "Sup-

pose God did not really tell me to wait here in Jerusalem or Topeka or Sacramento? Even if I am right about the waiting, will I be able to meet the challenge God has set before me?"

As we look back on a period of waiting for God to fulfill a promise, we will likely be able to view that time and the lesson that it taught us as a gift. God does have challenges for us to meet here on earth. We can meet them, not in our own strength but through the power of the Holy Spirit. We dare not move ahead, however, until God gives us what we need to do the task at hand. Like the disciples, we can practice the spiritual disciplines and surround ourselves with the community of faith. We can also recognize that waiting for God to lead us is crucial to the success of whatever we have been called to do. As he considered how he would serve God when he was nearly blind, the poet John Milton wrote in the closing of Sonnet XIX: "They also serve who only stand and wait."

SHARING THE SCRIPTURE

PREPARING TO TEACH

September 3 marks the first day of the new Sunday school year in most churches. You may want to make some special preparations for this Sunday such as: (1) contacting all members on the roll to let them know that a new quarter is beginning and inviting them to return from vacation; (2) contacting adults who are new to the church and inviting them to be a part of this class; (3) doing whatever you can to make your teaching space as attractive, comfortable, and accessible to adults as possible; (4) checking with the superintendent to see if any special Rally Day or school-wide event will be held that your class will be participating in; and (5) possibly planning, in consultation with several regular members, a

kick-off event such as a fellowship evening at the church or someone's home.

Our study this quarter will focus exclusively on The Acts of the Apostles. You will need to read today's background scripture, Acts 1, but you may also want to read the entire book if you have not done so recently. As you read, jot down any questions you have. If you are asking them, class members will likely want to know the answers too.

Check in your church library, with your pastor(s), and resource catalogues (such as the Cokesbury catalogue) for commentaries or other books that can supplement your preparation this quarter. Later in the quarter you will likely want to have maps that show Paul's travels. Order these now if your church does not already have them available.

Prepare yourself spiritually to teach these lessons each week by: (1) praying for all your class members; (2) asking for God's wisdom and guidance as you prepare and later lead the lesson; and (3) keeping a spiritual journal.

Develop each week's lesson by: (1) carefully reading and studying each lesson and background scripture; (2) doing additional research as necessary; and (3) selecting and adapting activities that seem best suited to the format of your class (for example: lecture, discussion, small groups, activity oriented) and most appropriate for the class members' level of biblical knowledge.

If your class prefers a lecture format, the points made under "Understanding the Scripture" and "Interpreting the Scripture" could serve as the basis for your lecture.

LEADING THE CLASS

Introduction

Read or retell the first paragraph under "Focusing on the Main Question." Ask class members: **(1) What are some special events that you have anticipated? (2) What kinds of emotions did you experience while you waited for these events to occur?** At this point, you are looking for short answers, not lengthy stories.

Finish this introduction by reading or retelling the rest of the information under "Focusing on the Main Question." To help the class focus on today's topic, you may want to write these questions on a chalkboard or newsprint: **(1) What did this promise mean to Jesus' first followers? (2) What does it mean to me today as I seek to live my life as a faithful follower of Jesus? We will try to answer these questions during the session.**

New Power Is Promised

Choose a volunteer to read Acts 1:1-8.
Use the information for these verses under "Understanding the Scripture" to set the stage for study. Give special attention to the key verse, Acts 1:8, by pointing out the importance of Jerusalem, Judea and Samaria, and ends of the earth as they relate (1) to the way Luke tells his story and (2) to the spread of the gospel in Gentile territory. If you have a map available, point out Jerusalem, Judea, Samaria, and the entire Roman Empire. Note the connection between Acts and the Gospel of Luke.

If your class enjoys a lecture format, read or retell the information in the section "New Power Is Promised" under "Interpreting the Scripture."

In discussion or activity classes, draw out the information in this section from the class by asking:

(1) How might the disciples have felt about seeing Jesus in his resurrected state?

(2) How might they have felt about being commanded by Jesus to stay in Jerusalem? Explain the reason(s) for your answer.

(3) What seems to be the disciples' concern when they ask about the restoration of the kingdom of Israel?

(4) What is God's purpose in promising to send the Holy Spirit?

(5) How are you called to be a witness at home (in Jerusalem), in the larger community (Judea and Samaria), and to all the world?

Jesus Ascends Into Heaven

Direct attention to Acts 1:9-11. Do a brief Bible study with the class on the ascension by referring to passages mentioned under this heading in "Interpreting the Scripture" and under "Understanding the Scripture."

If the class likes to work in groups, ask one group to research the images in Luke's Easter story (Luke 24:1-7); another group to look at Elijah ascending into heaven (2 Kings 2:9-13); a third group to review the transfiguration as recorded by Luke

(Luke 9:28-36); and a fourth group to look at the ascension stories in Luke (Luke 24:50-51) and Mark (Mark 16:19). Give each group an opportunity to report to the entire class.

The Disciples Wait for the Promise to Be Fulfilled

Read aloud Acts 1:12-14. Share the biblical information under "Understanding the Scripture."

Ask the class: **(1) Have you ever felt called to do something for God but knew that you had to wait until God's time was right? (2) How do you feel about having to wait?** Encourage class members to share several stories. Tell your own experience or the one I recounted under this heading above if you need to get the discussion started.

Note that the disciples had to wait but they continued to be spiritually disciplined. Acts 1:14 shows them praying together. Luke 24:52 shows them in the temple praising God. Also, they stayed in community, waiting together for God's promise of power to be fulfilled. Then ask: What do you do as you wait for God to act?

HELPING CLASS MEMBERS ACT

Challenge class members to read and meditate on today's key verse, Acts 1:8, throughout the week. Encourage them to find a way to be a witness to someone each day. Brainstorm ideas for witnessing, which you can record on a chalkboard or newsprint. Possibilities include: (1) saying a word in the midst of a conversation about how God has been working in your life; (2) doing an unexpected good deed; (3) acting in a Christ-like way in a difficult situation; or (4) inviting an unchurched friend or neighbor to accompany you to class and worship next week.

Invite class members to evaluate the kind of witness that your congregation is giving by taking one or more of the following actions this week:

Look at this week's bulletin or a current newsletter to see what kinds of activities are available to members and to the community.

Become familiar with missions or outreach projects that your church supports. Suggest additional projects if the church does not seem to be heavily invested (in terms of financial and time commitments) in programs that share the gospel by means of word (preaching and teaching) and deed (caring for the poor, the hungry, the prisoner, the neglected).

Check with your membership secretary to get the names of new members. Call or write and introduce yourself. If no one has joined recently, talk with the pastor and/or appropriate committee chairs to find out why they think few persons are joining. See what can be done to change this pattern.

Consider ways in which your congregation has joined with other churches, both within and across denominational lines, to be a witness for Christ in your community. Begin to talk with friends and neighbors who belong to other churches to see what could be done.

PLANNING FOR NEXT SUNDAY

Ask students to read Acts 2. Next week's lesson will focus on the fulfillment of the promise as the Holy Spirit comes with power on Pentecost. Some students may want to research Pentecost, a major Jewish agricultural festival known as the Feast of Weeks or Festival of Harvest. Bible references include Exodus 23:16, 34:22, Leviticus 23:15-21, Numbers 28:26, and Deuteronomy 16:9-12.

RECEIVING NEW POWER

PREVIEWING THE LESSON

Lesson Scripture: Acts 2:1-4, 14*a*, 29-33, 37-39, 44-45
Background Scripture: Acts 2
Key Verse: Acts 2:38

Focus of the lesson:
the gift of the Holy Spirit that enables baptized persons to live together as a Christian community

Main question(s) of the lessons:
(1) What happens when the Spirit of God comes in power to persons who are ready to receive it?

This lesson will enable adult learners to:
(1) recognize that the power of the Holy Spirit is available to all persons who repent of their sins and are baptized
(2) experience the excitement and hope of Jesus' promise as fulfilled in the coming of the Holy Spirit on Pentecost
(3) respond to the power of the Holy Spirit by witnessing with bold words and deeds.

Today's lesson may be outlined as follows:
(1) Introduction
(2) The Gift of New Power (Acts 2:1-4)
(3) Peter Preaches the Word in Power (Acts 2:14*a*, 29-33, 37-39)
(4) Life Together in the Church (Acts 2:44-45)

FOCUSING ON THE MAIN QUESTION

Our society craves power. Business tycoons exercise power to control money and Wall Street. Advertisers use their power to entice buyers. Military leaders require powerful weapons to win a war. The media wield their power to shape public opinion. Politicians use the power of their offices to enact legislation. Athletes train powerful bodies to defeat their opponents. Drivers choose cars with powerful engines to display their prowess on the road. Scientists work to harness nuclear power. Everywhere we turn we are confronted by power. Some uses of power are beneficial, while other uses are harmful or corrupting.

God too has power. We need not have money, strength, education, perfect bodies, or any special equipment to receive and use this power. We do not need to work late hours or compete with anyone to get it. God offers it to us as a free gift. Sounds too good to be true, doesn't it? Why would God want to give power to us? Moreover, what would we do with it? We have enough problems with the power we earn or wrest from others.

The gift of the Holy Spirit, unlike some other types of power, is not for our personal benefit. It does not move us higher up the ladder of prestige, status, or wealth. It does not empower us to control other persons or circumstances as we choose. In fact, this gift of power comes not as we exert control but as we surrender unto God by repenting of our sins and receiving forgiveness. To use this gift of power

aright, we must respond to it by witnessing to others about God. This gift, given to us, is meant to work through us so that other persons may come to know of God's acts and of Jesus. In other words, it is a gift bestowed on individuals to increase and build up the entire church.

Before his ascension, Jesus had promised this gift to us. It is indeed a gift of power. Unlike most power, the Holy Spirit is not in limited supply, held tightly by a few persons. No, God is willing to pour out this gift on all persons so that everyone may experience the reality of God's grace and love. As we study today's lesson we may ask: **What happens when the Spirit of God comes in power to persons who are ready to receive it?**

READING THE SCRIPTURE

NRSV
Acts 2:1-4, 14*a*, 29-33, 37-39, 44-45

1 When the day of Pentecost had come, they were all together in one place. ²And suddenly from heaven there came a sound like the rush of a violent wind, and it filled the entire house where they were sitting. ³Divided tongues, as of fire, appeared among them, and a tongue rested on each of them. ⁴All of them were filled with the Holy Spirit and began to speak in other languages, as the Spirit gave them ability.

Acts 2:14*a*

But Peter, standing with the eleven, raised his voice and addressed them.

Acts 2:29-33

29 "Fellow Israelites, I may say to you confidently of our ancestor David that he both died and was buried, and his tomb is with us to this day. ³⁰Since he was a prophet, he knew that God had sworn with an oath to him that he would put one of his descendants on his throne. ³¹Foreseeing this, David spoke of the resurrection of

NIV
Acts 2:1-4, 14*a*, 29-33, 37-39, 44-45

1 When the day of Pentecost came, they were all together in one place. ²Suddenly a sound like the blowing of a violent wind came from heaven and filled the whole house where they were sitting. ³They saw what seemed to be tongues of fire that separated and came to rest on each of them. ⁴All of them were filled with the Holy Spirit and began to speak in other tongues as the Spirit enabled them.

Acts 2:14*a*

Then Peter stood up with the Eleven, raised his voice and addressed the crowd.

Acts 2:29-33

²⁹"Brothers, I can tell you confidently that the patriarch David died and was buried, and his tomb is here to this day. ³⁰But he was a prophet and knew that God had promised him on oath that he would place one of his descendants on his throne. ³¹Seeing what was ahead, he spoke of the resurrection of the Christ, that he was not

the Messiah, saying,
　'He was not abandoned to
　　Hades,
　　nor did his flesh experience
　　　corruption.'
[32]This Jesus God raised up, and of that all of us are witnesses. [33]Being therefore exalted at the right hand of God, and having received from the Father the promise of the Holy Spirit, he has poured out this that you both see and hear.

Acts 2:37-39

37 Now when they heard this, they were cut to the heart and said to Peter and to the other apostles, "Brothers, what should we do?" [38]Peter said to them, "Repent, and be baptized every one of you in the name of Jesus Christ so that your sins may be forgiven; and you will receive the gift of the Holy Spirit. [39]For the promise is for you, for your children, and for all who are far away, everyone whom the Lord our God calls to him."

Acts 2:44-45

44 All who believed were together and had all things in common; [45]they would sell their possessions and goods and distribute the proceeds to all, as any had need.

abandoned to the grave, nor did his body see decay. [32]God has raised this Jesus to life, and we are all witnesses of the fact. [33]Exalted to the right hand of God, he has received from the Father the promised Holy Spirit and has poured out what you now see and hear.

Acts 2:37-39

[37]When the people heard this, they were cut to the heart and said to Peter and the other apostles, "Brothers, what shall we do?"

[38]Peter replied, "Repent and be baptized, every one of you, in the name of Jesus Christ for the forgiveness of your sins. And you will receive the gift of the Holy Spirit. [39]The promise is for you and your children and for all who are far off—for all whom the Lord our God will call."

Acts 2:44-45

[44]All the believers were together and had everything in common. [45]Selling their possessions and goods, they gave to anyone as he had need.

Key
Verse

K
Ve

UNDERSTANDING THE SCRIPTURE

Acts 2:1. The Greek word translated "had come" in the NRSV actually means "is fulfilled." The time of waiting is ended and the promise made by Jesus in Acts 1:5-8 is about to be fulfilled. This fulfillment comes on the day of Pentecost, which is celebrated seven weeks after Passover. Pentecost was an agricultural festival that was also thought to be the day on which the law was given. The purpose of Pentecost was to offer unto God the first fruits of the wheat harvest. According to Deuteronomy 16:10, this feast was to be observed by "contributing a freewill offer-

ing in proportion to the blessing that you have received from the Lord your God." As part of this holy celebration, grain was brought to the altar to acknowledge God as the owner of the land and the source of its products. Exodus 23:16, 34:22, Leviticus 23:15-21, Numbers 28:26, and Deuteronomy 16:9-12 give detailed information concerning this feast.

Acts 2:2-4. The wind and fire, often used as symbols for God, are reminiscent of an appearance of God before Elijah (1 Kings 19:9-12). The ability to speak in foreign languages, which are unknown to the disciples, accompanies the infilling of the Holy Spirit.

Acts 2:5-13. Since Pentecost was one of three festivals that all Jewish males were required to attend, the city of Jerusalem was likely packed with devout Jews from around the world. Throngs of onlookers were startled by the sound of the wind, the sight of the tongues of fire, and the cacophony of identifiable languages being spoken by persons with Galilean accents. According to the list of nations in verses 9-11, the announcement of "God's deeds of power" is heard simultaneously by persons from around the known world. Some commentators note that this experience is the reversal of the confusion of languages at Babel (Genesis 11:1-9).

Acts 2:14-36. Filled with the Holy Spirit, Peter responds to the snide comment that the speakers are drunk by preaching a powerful sermon. After getting the audience's attention, Peter quotes from Joel 2:28-32. This prophecy refers to the coming of the Spirit to all persons in "the last days." Peter preaches to his Jewish listeners about Jesus, noting that all that happened to him was according to God's plan. Again demonstrating his intimate knowledge of Jewish Scriptures, Peter quotes Psalm 16:8-11 in Acts 2:25-28 and Psalm 16:10 in Acts 2:31, both concerning the resurrection. Peter refers to Psalm 132:11 in Acts 2:30 regarding God's oath to David that his heir would occupy the throne. Psalm 110:1, seen in Acts 2:34-35, indicates that David perceived Jesus to be his Lord. Peter marshals this evidence to make his point in Acts 2:36: Jesus, whom God raised from the dead, is both the promised Messiah and the Lord.

Acts 2:37-41. The confused, jeering crowd (Acts 2:12-13) now responds to the word preached in power. Peter calls the crowd to repentance and baptism so that they might receive the Holy Spirit. This sequence of repentance-water baptism-Holy Spirit does not become a formula, however. Luke writes of conversions with no mention of baptism (Acts 9:35, 13:12, 48), water baptism that does not include the Spirit's coming (Acts 8:14-17), and the reception of the Spirit prior to water baptism (Acts 10:44-48). As described in Acts 2:39, the promise of forgiveness and the gift of the Holy Spirit are universal ("everyone whom the Lord our God calls to him"), transcending both time ("for you, for your children") and space ("for all who are far away"). In response to Peter's message, three thousand persons chose to be baptized immediately and were added to the growing church.

Acts 2:42-47. These verses provide a thumbnail sketch of life in the community of faith. The believers' religious acts include participation in education, fellowship, partaking of a common meal and communion, and an active prayer life both at home and in the temple. The people lived in complete unity and harmony, bearing responsibility for one another. While personal property was allowed (Acts 5:4), believers would sell what they had to provide for those in need. At this point Christianity was not a religion separate from Judaism but a group within it. Therefore persons worshipped in the temple. These Jewish-Christians continued the tradition of the festival meals served at home. As Luke showed Jesus growing in favor with humanity (Luke 2:52), he also recorded that the fledgling church had the "goodwill of all the people" (Acts 2:47). Luke concluded this summary of early church life by noting that the church grew daily.

INTERPRETING THE SCRIPTURE

The Gift of New Power

As the scene opens in Acts 2, crowds of Jews are participating in dances, feasts, and processions that marked the celebration of Pentecost. In contrast, the disciples are cloistered in a home waiting expectantly for Jesus' promise to be fulfilled (Acts 1:5-8), though they had no clue as to how or when this power would be given to them.

Without warning, familiar signs of God's presence—wind and flame—descend on each of the disciples. Miraculously, they begin to speak in languages that they do not know. Confused, timid disciples, now empowered by the Holy Spirit, are speaking boldly. Though these languages are foreign to them, they are well known to the crowds in the streets. The word of God is truly being poured out on all flesh. Astonished listeners can identify their native languages. Somehow the hearers knew that the speakers were from Galilee. Perhaps they had a distinctive Galilean accent that betrayed their origins.

Many of the listeners reacted as twentieth-century skeptics might. They could not believe that a supernatural event was occurring. Instead, they chalked up the experience to drunkenness on the part of the speakers. Other listeners, equally unable to explain this strange phenomenon, simply wanted to know what this spectacular display of power meant.

Perhaps we too are like those scoffers. We may want to believe that God continues to pour out the gift of the Holy Spirit upon us, but our rational understanding of what is possible gets in the way of acknowledging and receiving this priceless gift. We may be like the man in a familiar story who is confident that God will save him from the midst of a raging flood. This man refuses the offer of a boater making his way down a flooded street to rescue victims. The man insists that God will save him. Giving the same reason, the man also turns down help from a crew in a bigger boat and finally from a helicopter rescue team who wants to pluck him off his roof as he clings to the chimney. Of course, the man drowns. Arriving in heaven, he angrily confronts God about failing to save him. God replies that he had sent two boaters and a helicopter crew, but the man refused them all. Is it possible that we too are missing the power of God's Spirit in our lives because we fail to see it in our midst?

Peter Preaches the Word in Power

The same Peter who had denied even knowing Jesus (Luke 22:54-62) for fear of reprisals now steps forth boldly to proclaim the word of truth. With the newly imbued power of God's Spirit, Peter is able to put this morning's miraculous events into perspective for the Jewish listeners. What is happening is not that strange or confusing. Instead, it is the fulfillment of a promise God made long ago through the prophet Joel. In the last days—the age of the Messiah—God's Spirit will be poured out upon all persons. Men, women, young, old, free, and slave: they will all receive this gift and have the opportunity to experience salvation simply by calling on the name of the Lord. Peter's eloquent sermon draws upon numerous references from the Jewish Scriptures to demonstrate that Jesus, the crucified one, was now risen in power according to God's own plan. This man Jesus is both the earthly Messiah who had been promised to the Jews and the Lord of the heavens.

Peter's sermon marks the beginning of the fulfillment of Jesus' words in Acts 1:8. Those persons who receive the Holy Spirit are indeed called to be witnesses, first in

Jerusalem. And what a witness Peter was! His words had a life-changing effect on his listeners. They responded to this powerful message by asking Peter how they could be saved. The way to salvation was straightforward: "Repent and be baptized . . . and you will receive the gift of the Holy Spirit" (Acts 2:38).

The response to the preached gospel was overwhelming. In the midst of an agricultural holy day that had been held for generations, the pilgrims at this particular festival were confronted with a new vision, new understandings, and new power. The reality of God's love for them had been communicated in a dramatic new way. They responded in droves to the invitation to repent and be baptized. As three thousand persons each made their own decisions about their relationship with Christ, they were drawn into a new relationship with God and with one another.

God's Holy Spirit is still very active in our midst today. Why then do so many modern churches seem so lifeless, dull, and impotent? The example of Acts demonstrates that dynamic preaching of the word of God is crucial. So too is active listening and a willingness to respond to the gospel message with wholehearted repentance and commitment. Is it possible that parishioners and pastors have an unspoken agreement that substitutes comfortable words for life-changing challenges, and lukewarm accommodation for firebrand commitment?

Life Together in the Church

According to Acts 2:44-45, believers were together and took care of one another's needs. This togetherness was marked not only by physical closeness but also by certain activities that melded them into a unified body. In Acts 2:42 we see the fledgling congregation engaged in activities that we still consider crucial to the mission and ministry of the church. First, "(t)hey devoted themselves to the apostles' teaching." Notice that this was not worship but group study led by persons of wisdom and faith. Members of the early church knew instinctively what a major research project by Search Institute has recently demonstrated: namely, that the single most important factor in the development of mature faith is Christian education. We can imagine that persons grew in faith as they increased their knowledge, voiced their doubts, and shared their questions with the group. This avenue for spiritual growth is still available to us through Sunday school classes and other study groups.

The early believers also fellowshipped together. When we fellowship together, we allow ourselves to know and be known by others. We chip away at the barriers that prevent us from sharing our joy and sorrow, from feeling one another's fear and pain, and from entering into a truly caring relationship. Members of the early church recognized the importance of the bonds of fellowship. Too often, modern Christians see the church more as a theater where they just sit adjacent to other persons. They stare at the back of someone's head for an hour and exchange polite greetings as they leave the service. Even when they are crying inside for love and understanding, many parishioners will not take the risk of intimate fellowship with one another. When we perceive ourselves as part of the family of God we are willing to trust one another enough to be vulnerable, to get involved, and to extend our hand in friendship and love.

A third facet of togetherness is the act of eating with one another. Covered dish suppers have a long history! Breaking of bread also refers to the Sacrament of Holy Communion. In the infant church, believers shared a meal and communion at the same time. The sacred and the secular intertwined, for the whole person had made a life-changing commitment to God through Jesus. Neither one's relationship to God nor one's relationship to the church could be compartmentalized or separated from the rest of life.

Being together also includes engaging in corporate prayer, as noted in Acts 2:42. We don't seem to do that as much anymore. Instead, it seems that many modern churches have substituted committee meetings for prayer meetings. We need to risk openness with one another as we offer prayers of praise, thanksgiving, confession, petition, and intercession. Through prayer, Christians of any era bond themselves to God and to each other.

Luke goes on in Acts 2:44-45 to describe the communal nature of the church. Although first-century Christians were not required to sell all of their property and pool their resources, they did so willingly to meet the needs of other church members. These early Christians had captured the understanding of stewardship that Jesus so often taught in his parables. The steward recognized that everything came from God, and that the role of a trustee was to be sure that the needs of God's household were met.

In Acts 2:46, we learn that the first Christians went daily to the temple to worship. They also met in homes, experiencing small group relationships that nurtured their faith.

Their witness to the world must have been impressive, for Luke records that they had "the goodwill of all the people" (Acts 2:47). Luke also notes that new members were joining the family of faith each day. Perhaps the signs and wonders done by the apostles drew new believers into the fellowship, but it is doubtful that they would have stayed had they not felt the power of God in their midst and experienced a sense of belonging and well-being within the church.

Luke's description of the early church provides a crisp snapshot of the activities and relationships within the first congregation. As we look at the photo album of our own churches, do we see the same kind of purpose, commitment, devotion to God, and care for one another, or are these pictures simply faded images of what was once a dynamic, growing church?

SHARING THE SCRIPTURE

PREPARING TO TEACH

Review the general suggestions under this section in Lesson 1.

Focus your study on Acts 2 this week. Be sure to look up the Old Testament references referred to in this chapter, as noted in the "Understanding the Scripture" section.

If your class prefers a lecture format, the points made under "Interpreting the Scripture" could serve as the basis for your lecture.

Since a sermon is meant to be heard, not read silently, consider asking your pastor, an effective speaker within the church or class, or someone else you know to open the middle segment of the lesson by read-

ing, as if preaching, Peter's sermon. If the person cannot be present, consider using a tape made earlier in the week. The entire sermon is found in Acts 2:14-36, though only verses 29-33 are printed. You will need to decide in advance whether to use the entire sermon or these portions. Contact the person you have chosen and make arrangements.

Numerous persons today attest to a powerful experience with the Holy Spirit, often accompanied by speaking in unknown tongues or other signs. Likely class members will have heard of this charismatic experience (also known as the baptism of the Holy Spirit) and may have questions. Perhaps you and/or some class members will have firsthand knowledge of this experience. If not, try to talk with a friend or member of the congregation who has had this experience to find out more about it.

LEADING THE CLASS

Introduction

If your class prefers a lecture, read or retell the information found under "Focusing on the Main Question."

Otherwise, ask the class:

(1) **When you hear the word** *power*, **what images come to mind?**
You may want to record their answers on a chalkboard or newsprint. Probe further by asking:

(2) **Does God have power?**
(3) **Is God's power available to us?**
(4) **If so, how do we receive it?**

Point out that the main question for today's lesson is: **What happens when the Spirit of God comes in power to persons who are ready to receive it?**

The Gift of New Power

Set the stage for the reception of the Holy Spirit by explaining the Jewish feast of Pentecost, which drew thousands of pilgrims into Jerusalem. Information on the feast is given under "Understanding the Scripture," Acts 2:1. The list of nations represented in Jerusalem is found in Acts 2:9-11.

Ask class members to pretend that they are in the midst of this crowd. Prepare them to enter into the scripture reading by telling them to close their eyes and envision themselves in this scene. Ask them to pay attention to what they can see, hear, taste, touch, and smell. Then read aloud Acts 2:1-4. After the reading, ask the class members to share what they sensed. You may want to record their answers on a chalkboard or newsprint.

Point out the reactions of the crowd, as recorded in Acts 2:12-13 (which is not part of the printed scripture reading). Ask the class: **Had you been present, what do you think your reactions might have been to this spectacular display of power?**

To close this segment of the lesson, you may want to use the story in this section concerning the man who drowns because he fails to recognize the gifts that God sends. Like the scoffers in Acts 2:12-13, the man in the story misses salvation because he fails to perceive God's hand in the situation. Ask the class: **(1) Is it possible that we too are missing the power of God's Spirit in our lives because we fail to see it in our midst? (2) How do you see God at work in the world around you?**

Peter Preaches the Word in Power

If you plan to have a guest preacher deliver Peter's sermon, do so now. Otherwise, direct the class members' attention to Peter's sermon, a portion of which is printed.

Ask the class: **What arguments do you hear Peter making on behalf of Jesus in Acts 2:29-33?** (See information under Acts 2:14-36 under "Understanding the Scripture.")

Note that this preaching is so powerful that the crowd responds by wanting to know what they could do. Ask:

(1) **What does Peter say is necessary for salvation? (Acts 2:38, the key verse).**
(2) **What have we added to this list?**
(3) **Have our additions helped or hindered the spread of the gospel?**

Provide a few moments of silence for class members to reflect on actions they regret having done or omitted during the previous week. Assure them that God will offer forgiveness if they repent (that is, turn completely away from) their sin. A brief prayer may be appropriate at this point.

Life Together in the Church

Focus either on the printed text, Acts 2:44-45, which deals with the unity of the new church and the willingness of persons to share their belongings, or on the entire summary of life in the early church provided in Acts 2:42-47.

If you choose to focus on the two printed verses, help the class recognize that common property (as in a commune) was highly regarded, though persons did not have to forfeit all personal property to be Christians (Acts 5:4). Luke's concern here is that people took care of one another. They saw one another as members of the family of God and cared for one another as family.

If you choose to use the summary (Acts 2:42-47) that expands the understanding of what verse 44 means by being "together," make two columns on a chalkboard or newsprint using these questions: How is the first church still a model for us today? on the left side. How has the church changed so as to adapt to our current needs? (on the right side.) Encourage the class to brainstorm ideas related to your own congregation for each column. Additional ideas may be found under "Understanding the Scripture," as well as under this section in "Interpreting the Scripture."

Whichever option you choose, close this portion of the lesson by asking: **What might God do within the modern church if Christian believers saw their relationship to God not simply as a personal matter but as one that demanded their full participation in the life of the community of faith?**

HELPING CLASS MEMBERS ACT

When the disciples received the promised power of the Holy Spirit, the world began to be turned upside down. Ask class members (either individually or collectively) to consider helping someone in the church who needs financial aid and/or assistance with routine chores that he or she cannot do perhaps because of advancing age or illness.

Encourage class members to be alert for current stories that demonstrate the power of God at work in today's world. Miraculous healings, inexplicable escapes from danger, unexpected provision in a time of need are examples of such stories. If you want to devote a few minutes of class time to this topic next week, ask students to be prepared to share what they found.

Consider with the class the possibility of having at least one event this quarter that will strengthen fellowship within the group. A covered dish dinner at a class member's home, a night at a concert or theater, a game night at the church, or a swim party are some activities that you might wish to propose. Begin to plan that event now, perhaps by forming a task force to make recommendations to the entire class.

PLANNING FOR NEXT SUNDAY

Note that next week's lesson, entitled "Christ's Power to Save," will look at Peter and John's transforming encounter with a lame man and the upshot of this episode as the two apostles were called before the Sanhedrin to give an account of their actions. Request that students read and study Acts 3:1–4:31.

CHRIST'S POWER TO SAVE

PREVIEWING THE LESSON

Lesson Scripture: Acts 3:1-8; 4:5-12
Background Scripture: Acts 3:1–4:31
Key Verse: Acts 3:6

Focus of the lesson:
the power of Christ to save persons and radically transform their lives

Main question(s) of the lesson:
(1) How do we encounter Christ's saving power?
(2) How do other persons encounter Christ through us?

This lesson will enable adult learners to:
(1) discern Christ's power to save persons, no matter how hopeless their situation seems
(2) empathize with the plight of the lame man at the temple
(3) react positively to the needs of persons they encounter in their own lives.

Today's lesson may be outlined as follows:
(1) Introduction
(2) Encountering Christ at the Beautiful Gate (Acts 3:1-8 from the lame man's point of view)
(3) A Willingness to Risk (Acts 3:1-8, from Peter and John's point of view)
(4) Preaching the Faith (Acts 4:5-12)

FOCUSING ON THE MAIN QUESTION

Sometimes the stories of the Bible seem so unreal and distant. A man tending sheep is confronted by a burning bush and commissioned by God, or a reluctant prophet finds himself in the belly of a great fish, or fishermen get out of their father's boat when a wandering teacher calls them to follow him.

When we stop to examine these stories carefully, we find ordinary people going about the everyday business of their lives when God comes to them, often in surprising, unanticipated ways. When God does choose to do the unexpected, God usually works through other ordinary people who have heard God's voice, felt empowered by the Holy Spirit, and taken a risk in order to respond to divine leading.

Today's lesson is such a story. Acts 3 opens on an ordinary afternoon as worshipers attend the three o'clock prayer service at the temple. No holy day is being celebrated. No special rituals will be observed. Worshipers are routinely going into the temple. Not everyone is entering, though. As usual, poor and physically impaired persons beg outside the temple, hoping to receive a charitable donation. One man in particular, a forty-year-old lame man, is in his regular place. He searches the eyes of each passerby, hoping for a few coins to sustain him through the day. He asks two men for alms and, to the amazement of everyone, his life is changed forever. Through two obedient, empowered servants, Peter and John, God heals the man in the name of Jesus.

Perhaps we too act with the boldness of Peter. More likely, we are timid about proclaiming the good news of Jesus' saving power. We may miss opportunities to work in Jesus' name. Maybe our problem is that we just see ourselves as ordinary people. We are unaware that God wants to work through us and for us. Consequently, the spiritual power that is available to us may lie dormant deep within us. Similarly, we may not expect God to meet our needs. We ask for coins when God wants to change our entire world. Through the book of Acts, God is calling us to ask: **How do we encounter Christ's saving power? How do other persons encounter Christ through us?**

READING THE SCRIPTURE

NRSV
Acts 3:1-8

1 One day Peter and John were going up to the temple at the hour of prayer, at three o'clock in the afternoon. 2And a man lame from birth was being carried in. People would lay him daily at the gate of the temple called the Beautiful Gate so that he could ask for alms from those entering the temple. 3When he saw Peter and John about to go into the temple, he asked them for alms. 4Peter looked intently at him, as did John, and said, "Look at us." 5And he fixed his attention on them, expecting to receive something from them. 6But Peter said, "I have no silver or gold, but what I have I give you; in the name of Jesus Christ of Nazareth, stand up and walk." 7And he took him by the right hand and raised him up; and immediately his feet and ankles were made strong. 8Jumping up, he stood and began to walk, and he entered the temple with them, walking and leaping and praising God.

Acts 4:5-12

5 The next day their rulers, elders, and scribes assembled in Jerusalem, 6with

NIV
Acts 3:1-8

1 One day Peter and John were going up to the temple at the time of prayer—at three in the afternoon. 2Now a man crippled from birth was being carried to the temple gate called Beautiful, where he was put every day to beg from those going into the temple courts. 3When he saw Peter and John about to enter, he asked them for money. 4Peter looked straight at him, as did John. Then Peter said, "Look at us!" 5So the man gave them his attention, expecting to get something from them.

6Then Peter said, "Silver or gold I do not have, but what I have I give you. In the name of Jesus Christ of Nazareth, walk." 7Taking him by the right hand, he helped him up, and instantly the man's feet and ankles became strong. 8He jumped to his feet and began to walk. Then he went with them into the temple courts, walking and jumping, and praising God.

Acts 4:5-12

5The next day the rulers, elders and teachers of the law met in Jerusalem.

Key Verse

Annas the high priest, Caiaphas, John, and Alexander, and all who were of the high-priestly family. [7]When they had made the prisoners stand in their midst, they inquired, "By what power or by what name did you do this?" [8]Then Peter, filled with the Holy Spirit, said to them, "Rulers of the people and elders, [9]if we are questioned today because of a good deed done to someone who was sick and are asked how this man has been healed, [10]let it be known to all of you, and to all the people of Israel, that this man is standing before you in good health by the name of Jesus Christ of Nazareth, whom you crucified, whom God raised from the dead. [11]This Jesus is

   'the stone that was rejected by
      you, the builders;
     it has become the
     cornerstone.'

[12]There is salvation in no one else, for there is no other name under heaven given among mortals by which we must be saved."

[6]Annas the high priest was there, and so were Caiaphas, John, Alexander and the other men of the high priest's family. [7]They had Peter and John brought before them and began to question them: "By what power or what name did you do this?"

[8]Then Peter, filled with the Holy Spirit, said to them: "Rulers and elders of the people! [9]If we are being called to account today for an act of kindness shown to a cripple and are asked how he was healed, [10]then know this, you and all the people of Israel: It is by the name of Jesus Christ of Nazareth, whom you crucified but whom God raised from the dead, that this man stands before you healed. [11]He is

   " 'the stone you builders rejected,
     which has become the capstone.'

[12]Salvation is found in no one else, for there is no other name under heaven given to men by which we must be saved."

UNDERSTANDING THE SCRIPTURE

Acts 3:1-11. Peter and John went to the temple at 3:00 P.M., also known as the ninth hour, which is the time for evening prayer and sacrifice in the Jewish tradition. Probably located on the east side of the temple, the Beautiful Gate was fashioned of bronze with silver and gold ornamentation. These descriptive details (Acts 3:1-2) set the stage for a miracle story: the description of the affliction (Acts 3:2-3), the meeting between the healer and the healed (Acts 3:4-5), words of healing (Acts 3:6), a healing gesture (Acts 3:7*a*), the healing act (Acts 3:7*b*), proof of healing (Acts 3:8), and the effect of the miraculous healing on witnesses (Acts 3:9-11). The miracle is performed "in the name of Jesus Christ of Nazareth" (Acts 3:6). The power of Jesus is now being appropriated and used by his followers. Since the healed man was well known to the persons who regularly

visited the temple, they wanted to know what happened to him. Their astonishment provides the occasion for Peter's sermon, his second one since the coming of the Holy Spirit.

Acts 3:12-26. In his second sermon Peter clarifies that the man was healed not by some power of Peter or John (Acts 3:12) but by the power of the God who the Jews have come to the temple to worship (Acts 3:13). In his sermon, Peter emphasizes God's saving activity throughout history by calling to mind Abraham, Moses, Samuel, and the prophets. Peter also describes Jesus as the suffering servant, the one "whom God raised from the dead" (Acts 3:15). The apostle points out the role of the Jews in Jesus' crucifixion but insists that this was the means through which God's plan for the suffering Messiah would be fulfilled (Acts 3:18). In verse 19,

Peter calls the crowd to repentance, the key to salvation. In verse 22, Peter quotes Deuteronomy 18:15-16 to create the linkage between the prophet who is to come after Moses and Jesus to show that the man from Nazareth is indeed the Messiah.

Acts 4:1-4. Peter clashes with the Sadducees, just as Jesus had (Luke 22:4, 52). Since the Sadducees do not believe in life after death (Mark 12:18, Luke 20:27-40, and Acts 23:8), they are particularly upset that Peter is preaching that Jesus was resurrected from the dead. As the leading officials of the temple, the Sadducees likely want to ensure that they have authority over healing or other miracles that occur within their territory. A prophecy of Jesus (Luke 21:12) is fulfilled as Peter and John are held in custody overnight. Despite the cost of responding to the call to repentance, five thousand persons decide to believe that Jesus is the Messiah.

Acts 4:5-12. The prisoners, Peter and John, appear before the Sanhedrin, which is a judicial and administrative council headed by the high priest. The role of the Holy Spirit to empower witnesses, announced by Jesus in Acts 1:8, is reiterated in Acts 4:8. Peter's speech includes two major teachings of the early church: Jesus Christ (that is, Jesus the Messiah) was crucified, and God raised the crucified one from the dead. In Acts 4:11 Peter quotes from Psalm 118:22. This passage, which shows a reversal, is frequently associated with Jesus in the New Testament (Matthew 21:42, Mark 12:10, and 1 Peter 2:7). Peter's witness is that salvation is available only through Jesus.

Acts 4 :13-22. Boldness is a hallmark of the witnesses who have been empowered by the Holy Spirit. The reference to Peter and John's lack of education (Acts 4:13) likely means that they have not received a rabbinical education. When ordered not to speak or teach in the name of Jesus, the disciples responded by saying that God impelled them to bear witness. The work that the disciples were called and empowered to do, as foretold by Jesus in Acts 1:8, will continue despite threats from the very persons whose decisions led to Jesus' crucifixion.

Acts 4:23-31. The reunited apostles join in a prayer to the powerful God of all creation. Psalm 2:1-2, quoted here in Acts 4:25-26, is perceived by the apostles as being fulfilled in the person of Jesus. The Gentiles have indeed raged against the Messiah, for it was the Romans who crucified Christ. The kings and rulers, seen in the persons of Herod and Pilate, have gathered against Christ. As the apostles pray for continued boldness to preach and act on behalf of Jesus, the power of the Holy Spirit shakes the very place in which they are gathered, an action reminiscent of the Spirit's display of power at Pentecost.

INTERPRETING THE SCRIPTURE

Encountering Christ at the Beautiful Gate

Imagine yourself in the situation of the man at the Beautiful Gate. You are more than forty years old (Acts 4:22) and have never walked in your life (Acts 3:2). Today is just another ordinary day in your difficult existence. People carry you to this gate near the temple to beg, just as you have been doing for years. You want to work but your lameness prevents you from doing so. Your only option is to depend upon the generosity of others. Perhaps they will give you a few coins. Everyone knows you. They pass by regularly on their way to worship God.

Two men, Peter and John, approach you as they near the temple. You must ask them to take pity on you and contribute alms so that you won't starve to death. They seem responsive. Perhaps they will give a contribution. But no, they announce that they have no money. Rejected again, you think. Wait. They have no money but they are offering you a chance to be healed. They tell you to stand up and walk in the name of Jesus Christ. They reach for your hand. How compassionate! Most people simply turn away, forgetting that you are a human with feelings and a deep desire to be loved and accepted. Before you know what's happening you are on your feet. You can feel tremendous power coursing through your feet and ankles. Suddenly you are walking and leaping—sensations you have never felt before.

You respond by praising God. These two men who had no money have given you a most precious gift: the accident of birth has been reversed and you are restored to the wholeness that the creator God intended. Your life has been totally transformed by this gracious gift. The crowd recognizes you as the familiar beggar but they too are stunned. Clearly, you are a new person as a result of your encounter with the living Christ.

As we put ourselves in the place of this man, we can begin to perceive situations in our own lives that need to be touched by the saving power of Christ. Perhaps we have a physical challenge, an addiction, or an illness that confronts us daily. Or maybe we must confront other adversities that makes us feel trapped. We may feel powerless to act. We can only receive what others are willing to give of their financial resources, time, emotions, love, and support. Instead of helping us, some of those persons who pass by us every day may be making our lives more difficult. Then we recognize—either gradually or as the result of a sudden action—that God's power to save is available to us in the name of Jesus. In that moment, we too begin praising God. Like the healed man, we now have hope.

A Willingness to Risk

Let's consider this same scene from the point of view of Peter and John. Like the man outside the temple they too are going about their daily business. They are on their way to the three o'clock worship, a service that includes the offering of a sacrifice with prayer. As probably had happened before, they are stopped by a beggar. He looked expectantly at the two apostles, hoping they would respond generously to his plea. Peter and John could have thrown a few coins in his cup, or they could have walked by, pretending not to notice this man's need. Peter and John did not give the man what he asked for, but they did not turn aside from him either. Instead, they offered this man healing in the name of Jesus Christ. Through the power of the Holy Spirit these two apostles did what they had often seen their Lord do.

Perhaps Peter had acted as his old, impetuous self, not stopping to consider the consequences. Or perhaps he had not realized that a miraculous act of healing would put him in the same kind of jeopardy with temple officials that Jesus faced. Maybe he thought no one would notice the change in this man. Perhaps Peter did not really know what to expect when he took the lame man by the hand and called him to rise up and walk. Then again, maybe Peter was very aware of what he was doing and the potential consequences of his actions but chose to act anyway. The power of the Holy Spirit may have stirred so strongly within him that he had to take a risk and minister in Jesus' name.

Peter and John may have been just as stunned as the healed man and the other persons who saw him. Their beloved Jesus was no longer in their midst, but God's power was working through them. What an exhilarating but humbling experience! The response that this action generated provided an opportunity for further witness as the astonished crowd wanted to know what had happened.

Our experiences, though different from those of the apostles, may bear great similarities. How many times have we found ourselves engaged in our normal routine—even our regular church work—only to be interrupted by an urgent need? God calls us. Perhaps the timing is inconvenient. The task may seem overwhelming. Or maybe the possible consequences force us to give careful consideration before we will respond. Suppose the Spirit prompts us to take action that requires us to change our job or profession, or to be reconciled with someone we have pushed to the corners of our life, or to simplify our lifestyle, or to make an unreserved commitment to God? What do we do? Do we take the risk, trusting that God will lead and uphold us by the power of the Holy Spirit? Or do we play it safe by just making a token gesture or ignoring the call altogether? The lesson of this story in Acts is clear: we must take the risk, for it is as we act in the Spirit's power that other persons encounter Christ and the world is transformed.

Preaching the Faith

The astonished crowd wanted to know what had happened. The familiar was now new and different. The man before them was the same one they had seen for years, yet he was totally changed. What had occurred? Seeing their astonishment, Peter launched into a sermon (Acts 3:12-26). He witnessed boldly to this group of Jewish worshipers, calling them to repentance. The God of their ancestors was the same God of the suffering Jesus. This crucified man from Nazareth was indeed the Messiah foretold by the prophets. In his name this miracle had been done. In his name, they too would be blessed if they turned from their evil ways (Acts 3:26). Peter's message was compelling: five thousand persons believed (Acts 4:4).

Word of this unusual event and its electrifying effect upon the crowd quickly reached the temple officials. They wasted no time in taking Peter and John into custody, holding them overnight until the council, known as the Sanhedrin, could be convened to investigate the matter.

The temple officials have only one question for Peter and John: "By what power or by what name did you do this?" (Acts 4:7). The Holy Spirit empowers Peter to speak a strong word of witness on behalf of the saving power of Jesus the Messiah. Peter tells the council, which could imprison him or have him executed, that they are responsible for the crucifixion of Jesus, the very one whom God raised from the dead. Peter quotes a familiar passage from Psalm 118:22 to demonstrate a tremendous reversal: builders rejected the stone that was to become the cornerstone. The temple leaders whom Peter addressed were those builders. They had rejected Jesus, but God had a crucial role for him to fill. He was the cornerstone of God's plan of salvation.

How do we share this witness of faith with others? Do we share it at all, especially if we think we may put ourselves at risk by doing so? Perhaps you have heard some Christians say that they do not need to give a verbal witness. They claim that their actions speak for them. That certainly may be true in some instances. Peter and John certainly acted. In fact, their action precedes their words. But when both a curious crowd and a group of powerful leaders with a vested interest in the status quo want to know what happened, Peter does not hesitate to give a thorough account. His unflinching words land him and his partner in ministry in jail. We cannot imagine that such bold deeds and words would be possible were it not for the mighty presence of the Holy Spirit. The deeds cannot be hidden. Neither can the words be silenced. The witness must go forth.

SHARING THE SCRIPTURE

PREPARING TO TEACH

After you have read Acts 3:1—4:31, try putting yourself in the shoes of the characters involved. Imagine how you would have felt had you been the lame man, Peter, John, or the temple leaders. What concerns would you have had in this situation? How would you have reacted?

Think about the times when God has come to you in ways that you might later define as miraculous. Try to reconstruct the circumstances, either through meditation or by means of spiritual journaling. As you look back on the encounter with God, would you say that God came to you in the midst of your ordinary life? If not, how was this encounter extraordinary?

Think about how you witness to others. Peter acted and preached. You are called to teach in Jesus' name. What implications does this understanding have for you in terms of your preparedness to teach? How do you witness to others through your teaching?

If your class prefers a lecture format, become familiar with the information under "Interpreting the Scripture." You can use this information as a basis for the lecture by helping class members see the meaning of this story in Acts from the perspectives of several different persons.

Draw up a list of ordinary activities for the Introduction to "Leading the Class." Have paper and pens on hand.

If you plan to have several class members do a pantomime of the healing story in Acts 3:1-8 during the "Encountering Christ at the Beautiful Gate" segment, contact them early in the week.

If you plan to ask two persons to play Peter and John for an interview during the "A Willingness to Risk" segment, contact them early in the week.

LEADING THE CLASS

Introduction

Draw up a checklist of ordinary activities. Write them on a chalkboard or newsprint before class. Here are some examples:

(1) A parent stays up all night with a sick child.
(2) A shopper loads groceries into a car for a stranger.
(3) A neighbor lends a tool to another neighbor.
(4) A hospital visitor strikes up a conversation with a patient who has no visitors.
(5) A church member brings an unchurched neighbor's child to Sunday school.

As the session begins, ask the class to identify any activities in which they might encounter Christ. Then ask them to identify any activities that would provide an opportunity for persons to encounter Christ through the actions of someone else. This exercise may be done orally, or you may want to have people write answers first and then discuss them with the total group.

Briefly discuss their answers and the students' reasons for them. Be sure to point out that we encounter Christ in the ordinariness of our daily activities. Similarly, we provide many opportunities for other persons to encounter Christ through us in the midst of our regular activities.

You may want to read or retell the information under "Focusing on the Main Question." Be sure to close this portion of the class by identifying the main questions for today's lesson: **How do we encounter Christ's saving power? How do other persons encounter Christ through us?**

Encountering Christ at the Beautiful Gate

Choose a volunteer to read aloud Acts 3:1-8. If the class enjoys active involvement in the lesson, arrange with several persons ahead of time to play the parts of the lame man, Peter, and John. As the story is being read aloud, have these three class members (who may be men or women) pantomime the action, beginning at verse five.

Tell the class to put themselves in the lame man's situation. Ask these questions:

(1) How did you feel about having to beg?

(2) How did you feel about the religious people who passed by you on their way to worship?

(3) What did you expect God to do for you? (Help the class see that the man only expected to receive enough to subsist. He had no inkling of the power that God was willing to pour out in Jesus' name.)

(4) What were your physical and emotional responses to the gift of healing that you so unexpectedly experienced?

Read or retell the last paragraph in the section under "Interpreting the Scripture." Ask the class to think silently about how they have experienced Christ's power in their own lives. If time permits and if your class members feel comfortable sharing personal stories, a few volunteers may be willing to bear witness to an unexpected, life-changing encounter they had with the risen Christ.

A Willingness to Risk

Use the information under Acts 3:1-11 in "Understanding the Scripture" to point out the elements of this miracle story.

If the class prefers a lecture, read or retell the section on Acts 3:1-11 as found under "Interpreting the Scripture."

If the class enjoys lively interaction, arrange for one or two persons to play the roles of Peter and John who are being interviewed on a newscast. The rest of the class becomes the investigative reporters who want to find out what these two men did, where they got the power to act, why they took such a risk, and what really happened to the lame man. If the class is large, you may want to ask several persons to play witnesses to this event.

If the class prefers traditional discussion, ask the following questions:

(1) Peter and John were on their way to the temple to pray. Likely they assumed that they could be witnesses to Christ by worshiping. What does the fact that their religious routine was interrupted say to us about how God might use us?

(2) Peter and John knew they were on the territory of the very leaders whose actions ultimately led to Jesus' crucifixion, but they did not hesitate to heal the lame man. What does their action say to us about our own willingness to take risks for Jesus' sake?

(3) What risks do you think your congregation should be taking to minister to those in need?

Preaching the Faith

You may want to bridge the gap between Acts 3:1-8 and the second portion of scripture by giving background information about the crowd's response and Peter's sermon, as found under "Understanding the Scripture." Make sure that the class understands that Peter and John were taken into custody and held overnight until the Sanhedrin could be convened the next day.

Choose a volunteer to read Acts 4:5-12 aloud.

Ask the class two questions: (1) What question do the temple officials ask? (See Acts 4:7). (2) How does Peter respond? (See Acts 4:10, noting that Jesus' crucifixion and resurrection are both important parts of Peter's answer.)

Move the discussion to a more personal level by asking class members how they feel about witnessing to others, especially when the listeners may be hostile. Try to consider some real life situations that may be meaningful to your class members.

Here are some examples:

(1) Suppose you are a tax preparer or accountant faced with a client who wants you to cheat on the tax return.

(2) Suppose an adult son has returned home to live but he refuses to take responsibility for supporting his children who are now living with his estranged wife.

(3) Suppose an employer suddenly insists that you work every Sunday morning.

Conduct this discussion by asking:

(1) What risks are you willing to take in these situations?

(2) As you make this witness, how do you experience the Holy Spirit empowering you?

(3) Give an example of a situation in which you know that your willingness to take a risk produced a positive outcome.

Close this discussion with a prayer that each person might be empowered to show forth the saving power of Christ in both words and deeds.

HELPING CLASS MEMBERS ACT

Challenge the class members to think of someone they regularly encounter, particularly someone in need. What does this person ask of them? What do they provide for this person? Ask students to make a deliberate effort to give or do something special for this person.

Ask the class to think about the accessibility of your church to persons who are physically challenged. Can they enter the sanctuary, move to a Sunday school classroom, use rest rooms and other facilities? If not, what changes does the congregation need to institute to make the building more accessible? What changes might be needed to make the church more user-friendly for persons with handicapping conditions? Are there sign language interpreters or hearing enhancing devices available? Are large print hymnals, Bibles, and Sunday school materials available? If not, what can this class do to bring these problems to the attention of the church leadership?

PLANNING FOR NEXT SUNDAY

Ask class members to read the background scripture for next Sunday, found in Acts 4:32–5:42. The focus of the lesson will be on Acts 5:17-32, the story of the Lord sending an angel to open the prison door and setting the apostles free so that they could return to the temple to preach again. Encourage the class to think seriously about the boldness required not only to endure imprisonment for their faith but also to continue preaching after a miraculous release.

BOLDNESS TO OBEY

PREVIEWING THE LESSON

Lesson Scripture: Acts 5:17-32
Background Scripture: Acts 4:32–5:42
Key Verse: Acts: 5:29

Focus of the lesson:
uncompromising courage to obey God resists pressure to submit to human authority

Main question(s) of lesson:
(1) Am I willing to boldly obey God even in the face of real pressure to conform to the orders and expectations of some earthly power?

This lesson will enable adult learners to:
(1) comprehend the risks that Peter and the other apostles took to be faithful to God's will
(2) acknowledge the limits of earthly power and its claim on their lives
(3) stand firm when threatened by pressure to conform to socially expected behaviors that are in tension with Christian beliefs
(4) speak out when a word of witness is called for, despite pressure to remain silent.

Today's lesson may be outlined as follows:
(1) Introduction
(2) The Limits of Earthly Power (Acts 5:17-21*a*)
(3) Resisting Pressure to Conform (Acts 5:21*b*-29)
(4) Witnessing to God's Work Through Christ (Acts 5:30-32)

FOCUSING ON THE MAIN QUESTION

Our world is filled with pressures to conform. A boss orders us to do certain tasks that seem ethically questionable to us. Legal covenants in our community require us to paint our home a certain color, whether we like it or not. We echo a teacher's perspective on a test in order to earn a high grade, even though we disagree with the point of view espoused.

The media set forth standards of behavior and attitude that many find acceptable, and they expect us to adhere to as well. We feel pressured to vote against a potential member of an organization to which we belong because of discriminatory attitudes among certain members. A medley of authoritative voices sings in our heads.

Sometimes a lone voice impels us to stand

in opposition to these siren calls for conformity, especially when knuckling under to pressure requires us to disobey God. Such opposition is difficult, often costly. Whistle blowers who expose waste, fraud, or illegal activities risk find themselves without a job. A witness who comes forward to testify in a criminal case may be in jeopardy, perhaps putting his or her life on the line for speaking the truth. Politicians who vote their consciences rather than support a huge special interest group may become the victims of a smear campaign designed to unseat them in the next election. Persons who contest certain religious views may be branded as heretics and ousted from a church.

In today's lesson from Acts 5:17-32 the apostles find themselves in a similar bind. The temple officials have pressured them to stop teaching about Jesus and his resur-rection from the dead. Their first encounter ended with a stern warning to Peter and John "not to speak or teach at all in the name of Jesus" (Acts 4:18). Logically, we would expect these apostles to heed this warning. The Sanhedrin, after all, were the authority figures in the temple. The apostles could not obey, however, because they were impelled to witness by a higher authority. Without concern for personal safety or the potential consequences of disobedience, Peter announced that the apostles would obey God (Acts 5:29). His boldness was rewarded with a flogging and a second warning not to speak in Jesus' name. The lesson prompts us to ask: **Am I willing to boldly obey God even in the face of real pressure to conform to the orders and expectations of some earthly power?**

READING THE SCRIPTURE

NRSV
Acts 5:17-32

17 Then the high priest took action; he and all who were with him (that is, the sect of the Sadducees), being filled with jealousy, [18]arrested the apostles and put them in the public prison. [19]But during the night an angel of the Lord opened the prison doors, brought them out, and said, [20]"Go, stand in the temple and tell the people the whole message about this life." [21]When they heard this, they entered the temple at daybreak and went on with their teaching.

When the high priest and those with him arrived, they called together the council and the whole body of the elders of Israel, and sent to the prison to have them brought. [22]But when the temple police went there, they did not find them in the prison; so they returned and reported, [23]"We found the prison securely locked and the guards standing at the doors, but when we opened them, we found no one inside." [24]Now

NIV
Acts 5:17-32

[17]Then the high priest and all his associ-ates, who were members of the party of the Sadducees, were filled with jealousy. [18]They arrested the apostles and put them in the public jail. [19]But during the night an angel of the Lord opened the doors of the jail and brought them out. [20]"Go, stand in the temple courts," he said, "and tell the people the full message of this new life."

[21]At daybreak they entered the temple courts, as they had been told, and began to teach the people.

When the high priest and his associates arrived, they called together the San-hedrin—the full assembly of the elders of Israel—and sent to the jail for the apostles. [22]But on arriving at the jail, the officers did not find them there. So they went back and reported, [23]"We found the jail securely locked, with the guards standing at the doors; but when we opened them, we found no one inside." [24]On hearing this when the captain of the temple and the chief priests heard these words, they were perplexed about them, wondering what might be going on. ²⁵Then someone arrived and announced, "Look, the men whom you put in prison are standing in the temple and teaching the people!" ²⁶Then the captain went with the temple police and brought them, but without violence, for they were afraid of being stoned by the people.

27 When they had brought them, they had them stand before the council. The high priest questioned them, ²⁸saying, "We gave you strict orders not to teach in this name, yet here you have filled Jerusalem with your teaching and you are determined to bring this man's blood on us." ²⁹But Peter and the apostles answered, "We must obey God rather than any human authority. ³⁰The God of our ancestors raised up Jesus, whom you had killed by hanging him on a tree. ³¹God exalted him at his right hand as Leader and Savior that he might give repentance to Israel and forgiveness of sins. ³²And we are witnesses to these things, and so is the Holy Spirit whom God has given to those who obey him."

report, the captain of the temple guard and the chief priests were puzzled, wondering what would come of this.

²⁵Then someone came and said, "Look! The men you put in jail are standing in the temple courts teaching the people." 26 At that, the captain went with his officers and brought the apostles. They did not use force, because they feared that the people would stone them.

²⁷Having brought the apostles, they made them appear before the Sanhedrin to be questioned by the high priest. ²⁸"We gave you strict orders not to teach in this name," he said. "Yet you have filled Jerusalem with your teaching and are determined to make us guilty of this man's blood."

²⁹Peter and the other apostles replied: "We must obey God rather than men! ³⁰The God of our fathers raised Jesus from the dead—whom you had killed by hanging him on a tree. ³¹God exalted him to his own right hand as Prince and Savior that he might give repentance and forgiveness of sins to Israel. ³²We are witnesses of these things, and so is the Holy Spirit, whom God has given to those who obey him."

Key
Verse

K
V

UNDERSTANDING THE SCRIPTURE

Acts 4:32-37. This section, like Acts 2:42-47, summarizes the activities of the community of faith in Jerusalem. Acts 4:34*a* echoes Deuteronomy 15:4 by stating that "there was not a needy person among them." The distribution of funds is clearly based on need. Old Testament law requires care for the poor but does not require communal property. The Essenes, a Jewish sect, did hold property in common. A Greek proverb, "friends have all things in common," is cited in *The Republic of Plato* (4.424*a*). The New Testament community described here in Acts holds common property on a voluntary basis (Acts 5:4). Acts 4:36-37 uses the example of one

person, Joseph, to show how the community functioned.

Acts 5:1-11. In contrast to Joseph, who shared his possessions, Ananias and Sapphira held back on theirs (Acts 5:2). Their failure to share all of the proceeds from the sale of their property is not, however, the sin for which they are punished. Peter notes that they are allowed to do as they choose with the money (Acts 5:4). This husband and wife sinned because they lied before God. They also deceived other members of the Spirit-filled community into thinking that they had contributed all they earned from the sale. Furthermore, the couple had conspired together to create this illusion and "put the Spirit of the Lord to the test" (Acts 5:9). Independently questioned, Ananias and Sapphira both gave the same false information about the price of the land. This miracle story of punishment understandably caused great fear to come upon the church members.

Acts 5:12-16. This section forms the third major summary of the activities and progress of the infant church. The prayer for "signs and wonders" (Acts 4:29-30) comes to fruition in Acts 5:12. A group of believers gathered at Solomon's Portico, likely located on the east side of the temple, but the reference is unclear as to whether the group included the whole church or just the apostles. Even though non-believers did not dare join this group, as noted in Acts 5:13, they have a very high opinion of the Christians. Peter remains the focal point of the church. His shadow, like the fringe of Jesus' cloak (Mark 6:55-56), is thought to be powerful enough to cure the sick. The number of believers, both male and female, continues to multiply (Acts 5:14). Just as Jesus had commanded (Acts 1:8), the witness of the good news is beginning to move from the spiritual center of Jerusalem, the temple, into "the towns around Jerusalem" (Acts 5:16).

Acts 5:17-21a. The apostles are again persecuted by the Sadducees who control the temple. The church leaders' actions are understandable in light of the fact that the apostles are witnessing and healing persons after they have been forbidden to do so (Acts 4:18). Again the Sadducees, led by the high priest, have the apostles arrested. This time all of the apostles, not just Peter and John, are rounded up (Acts 5:18, 29,

40). Led by an angel, the apostles miraculously escape from the guarded prison (Acts 5:19). They follow the orders of the angel, which are in opposition to the orders of the Sanhedrin, and return to the temple to continue their teaching (Acts 5:21a).

Acts 5:21b-32. None of the temple officials, including their police force, knows what has happened to the prisoners until an unnamed person arrives and reports the apostles' whereabouts (Acts 5:21b-25). Recaptured without incident or ado (Acts 5:26), the apostles are brought before the Sanhedrin. Unlike the gentle inquiry and dismissal of Acts 4:7-21, the apostles face angry accusations (Acts 5:28) and flogging (Acts 5:40). Speaking for the group, Peter reiterates their need to obey God above all, the saving work that God was doing through Jesus, and the apostles' role as joint witnesses with the Holy Spirit (Acts 5:32).

Acts 5:33-42. Gamaliel, a well respected Jewish scholar, intervened on behalf of the apostles. Unlike the Sadducees, Gamaliel would have believed in the possibility of the resurrection, for he was a Pharisee. Gamaliel is a historical figure, but Luke's record contains inaccuracies possibly gleaned from the work of the Jewish historian, Josephus. Theudas led a revolt, but it occurred about ten years after Gamaliel's speech (Acts 5:36). Judas revolted about the time of the census in 6 C.E., which was much earlier than Theudas (Acts 5:37). Gamaliel's counsel is accepted, though the apostles are beaten and again enjoined to keep quiet about Jesus, an injunction they will not follow.

INTERPRETING THE SCRIPTURE

The Limits of Earthly Power

Who would have thought that a wall as solid and heavily guarded as the one that

cut an ugly gash in the city of Berlin would have fallen during our life times? It did, though, partly in response to the work of Christians trying to bring peace and unity in their German homeland. We are witnesses to this momentous change.

Who could have guessed that the churches in Russia, marginalized for decades by a government that claimed atheism as its official religion, would again become vibrant places, flinging wide their doors to welcome worshipers? Christians can now come together without threat of reprisals. We too are witnesses to this awesome reversal.

Who could have imagined that a religious community's writings, hidden in caves under threat of siege, would have been discovered centuries later by some young Bedouins in search of their sheep? They were. These Dead Sea Scrolls are slowly helping us to learn more about our own religious roots around the time of Jesus. We have witnessed this significant discovery and continue to be influenced by its findings.

In each of these examples, an earthly power has done its best to control the course of human history. Admittedly, those powers did succeed, at least for a season. But they did not have the final word. In some way known only to God events occurred that sharply altered history, just as a volcanic eruption changes the face of the surrounding landscape. The human powers who thought they were in charge, who thought they could control the events, ultimately found that their powers had limits.

The Sadducees in today's story from Acts 5:17-32 find themselves in such a limited position. They are hardly bad people. In fact, they have been charged with the important task of the administration of the temple. Wanting to do a good job, they try to uphold the religious teachings of their faith as they understand them. The problem they face is that God is doing a new thing in their midst. Walls are being torn down, doors are being thrown open, and new teachings rooted in ancient prophecies are being revealed. The temple officials cannot, however, recognize that God is the one who is bringing about these transformations.

After having chastised Peter and John for healing the lame man and preaching in the temple, the Sadducees again must confront these religious upstarts who are winning converts by the thousands. Jesus' apostles have to be silenced. The temple leaders decide that the best way to do that is to imprison them. This seems like a good plan, but God clearly has other ideas. An angel of the Lord appears to the apostles and leads them out of a securely locked, heavily guarded prison—without anyone even noticing!

Dumbfounded, the temple officials are at a loss to explain this strange occurrence or pinpoint the apostles' whereabouts. They didn't have to look far. The apostles had returned to the temple and, in obedience to the angel's order, were boldly proclaiming the words of life. God's power had won out. The earthly authorities, who probably seemed to other persons to be taking appropriate measures to avoid division and confusion among the covenant community, found themselves in conflict with the surprising power of God.

Resisting Pressure to Conform

The temple officials had warned these followers of Jesus once. No more polite warnings or kid glove treatment for these stubborn apostles of a dead man who, according to the Sadducees' beliefs, could not have been resurrected because no one can be resurrected. This time the high priest and his men would have to say or do something to make sure that Jesus' apostles stopped teaching this heretical nonsense.

In Acts 5:28, the high priest reminds the prisoners of his injunction against teaching in Jesus' name. Apparently these fellows had not gotten his message, for they continued to preach throughout Jerusalem. Furthermore, their straightforward talk pinned the blame for Jesus' death on this council. The council members were enraged; they demanded that this kind of preaching stop immediately.

Without hesitation, Peter and the other apostles answer the high priest's charges decisively: "We must obey God rather than any human authority" (Acts 5:29). These men have no questions about where their loyalty lies. Nor do they question the source of their authority. Through the power of the Holy Spirit, they resist the pressure to conform to the expectations of the Sanhedrin. They cannot tone down, alter, or back away from their message. No, they will boldly obey, regardless of the consequences.

These courageous apostles set a high standard of Christian discipleship for us. We recognize that many persons around the world do not enjoy religious freedom. In fact, they may face hardship or even death because of their beliefs. Yet most North Americans have never had to be concerned about such threats.

Instead, we face pressures to conform to the ethics of the business world. We are enticed by the alluringly packaged entertainment shipped to our home via airwaves. After watching or listening to assorted sitcoms, docu-dramas, and talk shows that glorify old sins as the new morality, we may feel out of the mainstream. Sports figures who cheat, die of drug overdoses, or demand astronomical sums of money for their athletic prowess are no longer oddities but part of the everyday fabric of American life.

We feel pressured from all sides. People assure us that "everybody else is doing it," but these words have a hollow ring for persons of faith who are committed to live in contrast to the rest of the world. We find ourselves in an even more difficult position if we have children or grandchildren who insist that our beliefs are simply old fashioned and outmoded.

Peter's words and actions can lead us to new heights, to more faithful discipleship. He not only talked about the premier importance of God's authority but he acted on it. Through the power of the Holy Spirit, Peter and the other disciples were able to stand firm in their convictions, despite compelling pressure to change their minds. Their example can serve as a reminder to us that such bold obedience to God is possible in any situation.

Witnessing to God's Work Through Christ

In Acts 5:30-32, Peter powerfully preaches the word to the council. He testifies to the fact that God has raised up to an exalted life the very Jesus whom they had raised up to a cursed death on a tree (see Deuteronomy 21:22-23). Jesus had come offering repentance and forgiveness. Surely Peter's word of witness is not intended only as information but as an invitation to the council to repent and believe.

Peter speaks eloquently about the role of Jesus in salvation history. Jesus is the leader of Israel. He is also its savior, for he came offering opportunities for persons to repent and be forgiven of their sins. The teacher from Nazareth, known and loved by the apostles, is now exalted in glory at the right hand of God the Father. As Jesus had commanded them to be witnesses (Acts 1:8), so Peter boldly proclaims that they are witnesses to the events that surrounded Jesus' life, death, and resurrection. Following the Jewish tradition of calling upon two witnesses, Peter notes that the Holy Spirit is also a witness.

In response to their bold speech, as well as to the irrefutable evidence of lameness of a man who had recently been healed, the Sanhedrin decides that it has no case against the apostles. Gamaliel, a respected Pharisee scholar, reminds the council of other movements that disintegrated when their leaders died. Moreover, he warns his colleagues that if this movement is from God they cannot stop it and, worse yet, would be fighting against God if they tried to do so. Before the apostles are freed, they are beaten and again admonished not to teach in Jesus' name. They return home, not chastened or fearful, but rejoicing that they were found worthy to suffer for the precious name. Well aware of the consequences, they resume their teaching, boldly proclaiming Jesus as the promised Messiah.

We too are called to be witnesses. Guided by the Holy Spirit, our efforts must be as enthusiastic and wholehearted as those of the apostles. We must be willing to take a stand and then to stand our ground. The sad reality, however, is that most of us lack the courage of the apostles. Though we are not likely to face life-threatening persecution, we often back away from cherished beliefs rather than face ridicule or censure. Sometimes our beliefs, if we took them seriously, would force us to make difficult choices. We could not continue to engage in behaviors or hold attitudes that do not measure up to the highest ideals of biblical teaching. What choices do we make, though, when changing these actions and opinions would put us at odds with significant persons in our lives? Usually we stick with the status quo, letting the light of our witness burn dim, rather than summon the courage to act decisively for Jesus. The choice, of course, is ours. Peter and the other apostles have shown us that the difficult choice is not only possible but far more rewarding personally and of immeasurable worth in the upbuilding of the kingdom of God.

SHARING THE SCRIPTURE

PREPARING TO TEACH

As you study the scripture and this lesson, pray for yourself and your students that each of you may, by the power of the Holy Spirit, have the courage to witness for Jesus by word, deed, and attitude.

Be on the lookout for any news articles that show either the persecution or lifting of persecution against Christians. Plan to include this information during the "Limits of Earthly Power" discussion, showing if possible how believers remain bold in their witness.

If you plan to have several members stage the scene between the Sanhedrin and police as recorded in Acts 5:21b-26, invite them early in the week. Assign each one a role: member of the Sanhedrin, police, temple captain, and the unnamed person who reports on the whereabouts of the apostles.

If you plan to do the discussion of denominational positions on issues, but are unsure of what these positions are, ask your pastor for materials to guide you or invite your pastor to attend the class as a resource person during the "Resisting Pressure to Conform" segment.

Have paper and pencils on hand if you choose to use the optional writing activity under "Witnessing to God's Work Through Christ."

LEADING THE CLASS

Introduction

Begin the class by asking members to brainstorm answers to this question: **What examples of pressure to conform to society's ideals do you experience or see around you? List their answers on a chalkboard or newsprint.**

If your class prefers a lecture format, use the information under "Focusing on the Main Question" to open the session.

Whether you choose the lecture or the brainstorming, close this segment of the class with the main question for today's study: **Am I willing to boldly obey God even in the face of real pressure to conform to the orders and expectations of some earthly power?** Note that the story of the arrest and witness of the apostles before the Sanhedrin, which is the focus of our lesson, will help class members see how they can be obedient to God even under crushing pressure to conform to a different standard.

The Limits of Earthly Power

Ask the class members to think of modern or historical examples of Christians being persecuted either by an unfriendly government or by other Christians. List these ideas on a chalkboard or newsprint. Examples may include: the former communist regime, tensions between Roman Catholics and Protestants in Northern Ireland, persecution of Quakers and other religious groups in colonial America, and Middle East tensions that (as of this writing) are forcing Christian minorities to leave the area.

Then ask: **What do you think caused (or may cause) these persecutions to cease?** If possible, move the discussion to an understanding that God had worked, perhaps in a miraculous way as seen in Acts 5:19 or more likely through the intervention of Christians who were keeping the faith alive.

Select a volunteer to read Acts 5:17-21a (through "their teaching"). Follow the reading with information on this passage from the "Understanding the Scripture" portion.

Close this segment by asking class members to put themselves in the place of the apostles. They have been arrested, imprisoned, and miraculously freed with the mandate to, "Go, stand in the temple and tell the people the whole message about this life" (Acts 5:20). Ask:

(1) **What would you honestly do under these circumstances?** If the class is large, you may want to ask partners or small groups to discuss their answers so that everyone will have a turn.

(2) **If you think you would return, what would motivate you to do so?**

(3) **What would you expect to happen?**

Resisting Pressure to Conform

If your class enjoys drama, invite several members to stage the scene between the Sanhedrin and police as recorded in Acts 5:21b-26. Otherwise, choose a volunteer to read this passage.

Select three persons to read Acts 5:27-29. One reader is the narrator, one the high priest, and one Peter. The use of several readers, especially if they are expressive persons, will show the heightened tension between the temple officials and the apostles.

Point out that the high priest is trying to make the apostles conform to the teachings and standards of the temple. If you did not discuss society's pressures to conform (see "Introduction" under "Leading the Class") do so now for a few moments.

The biblical situation involves persons of differing religious viewpoints. Ask class members to share examples of issues, preferably from their own denomination, where they disagree with a position taken by the church at large. This discussion can be very helpful if persons are respectful of other opinions and recognize that two conflicting points of view may both have biblical support. The discussion could be harmful if a few persons with strong opinions either dominate it or try hard to convince the other class members that they are unerringly correct. If you need help in understanding what your denomination's positions are, see your pastor for suggested resources, or ask your pastor to sit in with the class.

Close this segment by reading the key verse, Acts 5:29. Note that dissenters are important in the life of the religious community, provided that they are led by the Holy Spirit and not their own vain ideas or aspirations.

Witnessing to God's Work Through Christ

Choose a volunteer to read Acts 5:30-32. If your class members are willing to bear witness to what God is doing in their own lives, open the floor for a few testimonies. Request that these be relatively current events and brief so that more persons can share.

For a class that prefers quiet reflection, provide some silent time so that persons can meditate on these questions that you have written on the chalkboard or newsprint:

(1) **What is Jesus doing in my own life?**

(2) **How can I share this witness with others, even in situations where I feel timid or pressured?**

(3) **What difference might my witness make in the life of someone who need to experience God's love?**

An alternative way to do this activity would be to provide paper and pencil so that persons can write their answers and take them home for review.

Close this segment by summing up the outcome of the encounter between the apostles and the Sanhedrin using information for Acts 5:33-42 from "Understanding the Scripture" and/or the last paragraph under this section in the "Interpreting the Scripture" portion.

Offer a prayer that class members, like the apostles, may be empowered by the Holy Spirit to go forth boldly as witnesses to the love and saving grace of Jesus the Messiah.

HELPING CLASS MEMBERS ACT

Challenge class members to identify one situation this week in which a word or deed of witness is needed and then respond to that need even if they feel pressured to keep silent or act in ways that are not in keeping with their understanding of the Bible.

Encourage class members to look for current situations in which Christians are threatened or persecuted. Have them do whatever they can, including praying, financially supporting missionaries or other Christian workers in that situation, or writing to elected U.S. officials regarding their concerns and offering suggestions as to how this country could act. Suggest that some adults may want to read stories of modern or historical figures who have been persecuted, such as Dietrich Bonhoeffer or Corrie ten Boom.

Ask class members to think about how their own church and/or denomination handles differences of opinion that seemed to be based upon differing interpretations of the Scripture. Suggest that they give a word of witness to someone with whom they disagree, while respecting that person's understanding.

PLANNING FOR NEXT SUNDAY

Our study of Acts continues next week with a look at the selection and work of the deacons, found in Acts 6:1-14. Ask the class to read all of the background scripture, Acts 6:1–8:3. Point out that we will be beginning a new unit entitled "Witnessing in Judea and Samaria." In this unit, we will investigate the movement of the new church out of its Jerusalem center and into a wider outreach that includes Gentiles.

BECOMING A SERVANT

PREVIEWING THE LESSON

Lesson Scripture: Acts 6:1-14
Background Scripture: Acts 6:1–8:3
Key Verse: Acts 6:6

Focus of the lesson:
the selection and consecration of faithful persons to serve the community of faith

Main question(s) of the lesson:
(1) What kinds of services are needed by the church?
(2) How can we choose and support those persons who are willing to serve?

This lesson will enable adult learners to:
(1) understand why and how the seven men were appointed to serve
(2) identify with Stephen as a model of servant ministry
(3) respond by discerning needs that the church is called upon to meet today
(4) offer support and encouragement to church workers who act as servants.

Today's lesson may be outlined as follows:
(1) Introduction
(2) Discerning the Need (Acts 6:1)
(3) Choosing and Supporting the Servants (Acts 6:2-7)
(4) Stephen: A Model Servant (Acts 6:8-14)

FOCUSING ON THE MAIN QUESTION

I'm number one! What's in it for me? I may give a small monetary donation, but my time is my own. As long as I'm okay, I don't worry about the rest of the world. I want to get to the top, and I don't care who I have to step on to do it. These phrases and ideas permeate our society. Sometimes they are spoken; other times the effects of these attitudes are reflected in people's behaviors.

The church of Jesus Christ operates by a different standard. Instead of lifting our-

selves up, Christians bend low to serve others. Service may take many forms. A retired couple delivers meals to elderly homebound persons. A teenager volunteers to baby-sit for a single parent who cannot afford to pay her. A gifted musician takes time from his busy schedule to work with poor children who otherwise would have no access to music lessons. A homemaker bakes bread for new neighbors or those who are sick or experiencing a family crisis. A medical student decides to serve a rural community in need rather than establish a more lucrative practice in another area. The list goes on and on. Whether persons are volunteering in their spare time or engaged full time in service professions, they are offering themselves and their talents in service to others. This service may be done through the church, or it may be done outside the church and its programs. In either case Christians who willingly become servants are putting their God-given talents to work in Jesus' name.

In today's lesson we see the example of seven men who were chosen to serve the church. The church does not choose just anyone, but sets criteria as to the character and witness of those who will be consecrated to minister as servants. Their work complements and expands the work of the apostles, leaving them free to do the work of preaching and teaching to which they have been called. The church also becomes more faithful to its mission of caring for the needy. Today's lesson prompts us to ask two questions: **What kinds of services are needed by the church? How can we choose and support those persons who are willing to serve?**

READING THE SCRIPTURE

NRSV
Acts 6:1-14

1 Now during those days, when the disciples were increasing in number, the Hellenists complained against the Hebrews because their widows were being neglected in the daily distribution of food. [2]And the twelve called together the whole community of the disciples and said, "It is not right that we should neglect the word of God in order to wait on tables. [3]Therefore, friends, select from among yourselves seven men of good standing, full of the Spirit and of wisdom, whom we may appoint to this task, [4]while we, for our part, will devote ourselves to prayer and to serving the word." [5]What they said pleased the whole community, and they chose Stephen, a man full of faith and the Holy Spirit, together with Philip, Prochorus, Nicanor, Timon, Parmenas, and Nicolaus, a proselyte of Antioch. [6]They had these men stand before the apostles, who prayed and laid their hands on them.

7 The word of God continued to spread; the number of the disciples increased greatly in Jerusalem, and a great many of the priests became obedient to the faith.

8 Stephen, full of grace and power, did great wonders and signs among the peo-

NIV
Acts 6:1-14

1 In those days when the number of disciples was increasing, the Grecian Jews among them complained against the Hebraic Jews because their widows were being overlooked in the daily distribution of food. [2]So the Twelve gathered all the disciples together and said, "It would not be right for us to neglect the ministry of the word of God in order to wait on tables. [3]Brothers, choose seven men from among you who are known to be full of the Spirit and wisdom. We will turn this responsibility over to them [4]and will give our attention to prayer and the ministry of the word."

[5]This proposal pleased the whole group. They chose Stephen, a man full of faith and of the Holy Spirit; also Philip, Procorus, Nicanor, Timon, Parmenas, and Nicolas from Antioch, a convert to Judaism. [6]They presented these men to the apostles, who prayed and laid their hands on them.

[7]So the word of God spread. The number of disciples in Jerusalem increased rapidly, and a large number of priests became obedient to the faith.

[8]Now Stephen, a man full of God's grace and power, did great wonders and miraculous signs among the people. [9]Opposition

Key Verse

Ke Ver

ple. ⁹Then some of those who belonged to the synagogue of the Freedmen (as it was called), Cyrenians, Alexandrians, and others of those from Cilicia and Asia, stood up and argued with Stephen. ¹⁰But they could not withstand the wisdom and the Spirit with which he spoke. ¹¹Then they secretly instigated some men to say, "We have heard him speak blasphemous words against Moses and God." ¹²They stirred up the people as well as the elders and the scribes; then they suddenly confronted him, seized him, and brought him before the council. ¹³They set up false witnesses who said, "This man never stops saying things against this holy place and the law; ¹⁴for we have heard him say that this Jesus of Nazareth will destroy this place and will change the customs that Moses handed on to us."

arose, however, from members of the Synagogue of the Freedmen (as it was called)—Jews of Cyrene and Alexandria as well as the provinces of Cilicia and Asia. These men began to argue with Stephen, ¹⁰but they could not stand up against his wisdom or the Spirit by whom he spoke.

¹¹Then they secretly persuaded some men to say, "We have heard Stephen speak words of blasphemy against Moses and against God."

¹²So they stirred up the people and the elders and the teachers of the law. They seized Stephen and brought him before the Sanhedrin. ¹³They produced false witnesses, who testified, "This fellow never stops speaking against this holy place and against the law. ¹⁴For we have heard him say that this Jesus of Nazareth will destroy this place and change the customs Moses handed down to us."

UNDERSTANDING THE SCRIPTURE

Acts 6:1-7. As the church grew, two factions, the Hebrews and the Hellenists, apparently developed. The Hebrews were Jewish, Aramaic-speaking Christians from Palestine. Scholars have proposed several theories concerning the Hellenists. They may have been Jewish Christians who spoke only Greek. Possibly the Hellenists interpreted the Torah (first five books of our Old Testament) more liberally than the Hebrews did. In any event, the seven servants named in Acts 6:5 are all Hellenists who were selected by their peers, at the request of the apostles, for the purpose of caring for the Hellenist widows. One of the seven, Nicolaus, was a proselyte, which means that he was a Gentile who converted to Judaism and then joined the Christian movement.

Acts 6:8-15. Curiously, Luke does not show Stephen in his role as a servant to the widows. Instead, he is portrayed as one who performs signs and wonders by

the power of the Holy Spirit. He is opposed by other religious persons who see his ministry as a threat. The opposition parties mentioned in Acts 6:9 are Hellenists, but it is unclear as to whether they all belonged to one synagogue, or whether there were five different groups, or two different groups (the Freedmen and a group from Asia and Cilicia). The Freedmen may have been "Libyans," a name which refers to the area from which the Cyrenians and Alexandrians come. Other scholars believe the name Freedmen refers to Jews who have been redeemed from slavery. Historical records show that several Greek-speaking synagogues did exist in Jerusalem during the first century. Stephen's opponents cannot refute what he says and does (Acts 6:10), though they disagree. As was the case with Jesus' accusers, they trump up charges based on the testimony of false witnesses. The charges focus on Stephen's teachings concerning the law and the temple. Confronted by a hostile Sanhedrin, Stephen is composed and angelic looking, as if he has been in the presence of God.

Acts 7:1-53. In response to the high priest's question regarding the truth of the charges, Stephen launches into a sermon. Here he demonstrates his intimate knowledge of Jewish Scriptures, though he is very selective in what he chooses to include. This sermon reminds the reader of Old Testament summaries recounting how God has dealt with Israel (see Joshua 24:1-15; Nehemiah 9:6-38; and Psalm 78, 105, 106, 135, 136). The sermon's tone is similar to that of Psalm 78, for like the psalmist, Stephen is decrying the people's faithlessness. Stephen begins by focusing on three major figures of Jewish history: Abraham (Acts 7:2-8), Joseph (Acts 7:9-16), and Moses (Acts 7:17-43). This historical survey ends in Acts 7:42-43 with a quote from Amos 5:25-27, concerning idolatry. Stephen abruptly changes the subject to the tabernacle/temple (Acts 7:44-50). He quotes from Isaiah 66:1-2 in Acts 7:49-50 to argue that a temple constructed by humans cannot house God. He closes the sermon with a scathing attack on his listeners who, like their ancestors, resisted the law, the Holy Spirit, and the prophets (Acts 7:51-53).

Acts 7:54–8:3. Stephen's listeners likely agreed with him until he quoted scripture to speak against the temple (Acts 7:48-50) and then criticized them for persecuting God's chosen agents (Acts 7:51-53). The crowd's predictable response to his vigorous speech was rage. Luke sharply contrasts the look of the listeners who "ground their teeth" with the calm assurance of Stephen, who has a vision of Jesus with God in glory. The grinding or gnashing of teeth is a familiar image (Psalm 35:16, 37:12, 112:10) used to describe a hostile response of evil persons against the righteous. The crowd pounces on him when he announces the vision. Stephen sees Jesus "at the right hand of God," just as Jesus had foretold (Luke 22:69) with a minor variation. Stephen sees Jesus standing, whereas Jesus said he would be seated. The point is clear despite the variation: Jesus, shown as the glorified judge in heaven (Son of Man) is to be recognized as the risen Lord. Hearing Stephen's words as blasphemy, the crowd drags him out of the city to stone him. Witnesses were required by Jewish law to cast the first stones (Deuteronomy 17:2-7). Like Jesus (Luke 23:46, 34), Stephen commends his spirit to God and prays that his tormentors be forgiven. As a result of his death, the Christian church is persecuted. Saul (later Paul), first seen at Stephen's execution, opposes and imprisons Christians (Acts 8:3). Persecution forces adherents to move into Judea and Samaria where they will become witnesses, just as Jesus had commanded them to be in Acts 1:8.

INTERPRETING THE SCRIPTURE

Discerning the Need

Many churches are very intentional about keeping their collective eyes open to the needs of their members, the community, and the wider world. A member sees a need and suggests a way to fill it. Often a committee or task force is formed to investigate the matter and report back to a larger voting body. Plans are made, action is implemented, and the need is addressed. Such churches are constantly discerning new avenues of ministry.

Other congregations, located in the same community and just as aware of the need, respond with the familiar seven last words of the church: "We've never done it that way before!" Or the finance committee reports that no money is available for such a project. An important, innovative idea for ministry falls flat to the ground because no one is willing to explore creative options to enable it to happen.

In yet other churches, parishioners keep their spiritual blinders on, fearful that they may be called to new arenas of service that are beyond their narrow range of vision. The trustees insist, for example, that the building is not available for non-church purposes such as a soup kitchen. Or the Sunday school may be unwilling to accept students from a nearby shelter because the children are perceived as somehow different from those of church members.

Effectively meeting the spiritual and physical needs of all persons has been a mandate for Christians since Jesus walked the earth. Caring for the poor, the hungry, the sick, the imprisoned, and other needy persons is not an option. Such care is at the heart of ministry. The four Gospels record numerous instances of Jesus' associating with society's outcasts, healing the sick, liberating those held captive to demons, and lifting up the fallen.

Sometimes, despite our best intentions, we fail to meet these needs. Perhaps we have not recognized the need or grasped its magnitude. Acts 6:1 records such an instance in the early church. For the first time Luke mentions two groups of Christians, the Hellenists (who may have been Greek-speaking Jews) and the Hebrews (who were from Palestine and probably spoke Aramaic). Thus far, Luke's portrait of the fledgling church has been idyllic. The people are living together in peace and harmony, sharing as persons have needs. Suddenly, however, a conflict breaks out because the Hebrew widows were being cared for while the Hellenist widows lacked food. Since widows, especially those who were older and childless, had no means of support, the church had to straighten out this problem immediately. The need had been discerned; now the apostles had to figure out a way to meet it.

One way, of course, would be to increase the workload of the apostles, but they have enough to do. They see their primary mission as preachers (Acts 6:2). Other servants are needed. Their work is in no way inferior to the work of the apostles, but it is different. The base of ministry begins to expand as the early church realizes that the preachers cannot be responsible for doing everything. Nor should they be. God provides other persons with different talents to serve the church in a wide variety of ways.

Choosing and Supporting the Servants

Once we have discerned a need, the question becomes: How do we select and support persons whose ministry will be to meet that need? Many churches use the begging technique: "We've asked fifteen other people to do this job and if you don't take it we don't know who will." Another familiar strategy is the it-won't-take-much-time technique. Churches desperate for Sunday school teachers or persons to spearhead a finance campaign often resort to minimizing the work and commitment involved. Others use a committee nominations process, which is useful, provided the persons who are elected to offices have the gifts and talents to do the job. The problem inherent in this process is that the persons who are selected may not have the talents, time, or interest to do the job. Consequently, someone's name is listed on the church's roster of officials, but the work is left undone and the need remains unmet.

The early church had a better idea, one that enabled vital ministry by drawing more persons into the work of the church. The apostles told the congregation to select seven men—not just anyone—but persons "of good standing, full of the Spirit and of wisdom" (Acts 6:3). In other words, the seven were to be spiritually mature persons whose lives gave evidence of their relationship with God.

The seven, named in Acts 6:5, were chosen by their peers. These newly appointed men were responsible for meeting the needs of the widows. Exactly how they did this is unclear from the Bible reference. To "wait on tables" or "serve tables" (KJV) may refer to the actual serving of a meal at a common table (Acts 6:2). It may also refer to the keeping of accounts for the church at the money tables. In either case, the seven men were called to do a particular task that was different from the apostles' task of devoting themselves "to prayer and to serving the word" (Acts 6:4). Together, the twelve and the seven would share responsibility for the oversight of the church.

The seven servants were not only called but consecrated by the apostles with the laying on of hands (Acts 6:6). This public installation service surely left no doubt in anyone's mind that these Christians had been duly chosen and authorized to serve the church. They understood what their role was. The church members also knew what to expect of them. As a result of the addition of these persons to the "staff," the church continued to grow numerically and help persons, including temple priests, become obedient disciples of Jesus (Acts 6:7).

Stephen: A Model Servant

Described as "full of faith and the Holy Spirit" (Acts 6:5), Stephen finds himself embroiled in increasing resistance to the Christian movement. The "great wonders and signs" he performs (Acts 6:8) apparently spark the controversy. He faces opposition from his own people, the Hellenistic Jews, who had tried to argue with Stephen but could not compete with his wisdom and spiritual insight (Acts 6:9-10). His opponents instigate a plot to have him hauled up before the Sanhedrin on charges of speaking against the temple and the law. In Acts 6:14, Stephen's words are linked to those of Jesus (Mark 14:58 and John 2:19). As the council stares at Stephen, his face seems to be like that of an angel, an image that reminds us of Moses when he came down from the mountain after being in the presence of God (Exodus 34:29-35).

What would it mean if members of the modern church were to take Stephen as a model for their own servant ministry? Perhaps we would be called to follow Stephen to martyrdom, but this path is unlikely. A more probable scenario is that we find ourselves in the midst of controversy if we are faithful to the kind of highly committed discipleship to which we are called. Servant-leaders of the church may have to do a lot of teaching, praying, and communicating to help others see the importance of undertaking a particular ministry that fills a specific need. Some leaders have difficulty getting the congregation to open the church's doors to important ministries within the community. The servant-leader may be criticized for wanting to let "those people" use "our building." Excuses abound as to why the kind of ministries that Jesus engaged in cannot be done in certain congregations.

Empowered by the Holy Spirit, Stephen apparently spoke with wisdom that was rooted in a thorough knowledge of the teachings of the Bible (Acts 7). Such teaching tends to upset persons, especially when it flies in the face of their preconceived ideas or challenges them to grow beyond an immature level of spirituality. For example, during a finance campaign you may have taught that God is the owner and creator of all that exists. Therefore, when we give money to God through the church, we are only returning a portion of what already belongs to God. Possibly an angry listener snapped back with: "It's my money and I'll do as I please." Like Stephen, we may be opposed by persons who prefer a comfortable discipleship that requires little or nothing from them. They want to control their lives, allowing God only limited access to areas they carefully choose.

We are all called to use our own talents—

whether they be preaching the word or waiting on tables—to undertake and expand the ministry of the church. Some members will gladly undertake servant and/or servant-leadership roles, just as Stephen did. Others, like the crowd that persecuted him, prefer to criticize those persons who dare to be bold in their faith. Just as Jesus forgave his executioners, so too did Stephen (Acts 7:60). We may need to learn to forgive, without shrinking back from, those critics who perhaps are misinformed about what we are doing and why we are doing it. Despite the risks, criticisms, and costs, we must persevere to the end in our service. Stephen paid the ultimate price for his servanthood. Yet, the persecution that followed his martyrdom forced Christians to move beyond Jerusalem. In doing so, they had the opportunity to take the Word into all the world, which was just what Jesus wanted them to do.

SHARING THE SCRIPTURE

PREPARING TO TEACH

Today's lesson, which focuses on Acts 6:1-14, concerns the selection of servants to assist the apostles with ministry. Although Stephen's eloquent sermon, his death, and the impact of his death on the Christian community is not covered in the lesson, be sure to read and study this background scripture for your own enrichment.

For the "Introduction" activity, secure church brochures and/or newsletters, or make your own complete list of church ministries by talking with the pastor or several church leaders.

Depending on how you choose to do the "Discerning the Need" segment, you will need to have on hand pencils and writing paper or magazines, scissors, glue, and paper or poster board.

LEADING THE CLASS

Introduction

If your church has a brochure listing its activities (such as might be given to new or prospective members) or a newsletter, try to get enough copies of at least one of these publications for the entire class. Distribute these and ask the class: **(1) What kinds of ministries does our church engage in? (2) What kinds of talents or traits are needed to do these ministries?** Record their answers on a chalkboard or newsprint.

Even if you do not have printed resources available, brainstorm answers to the two questions above. You may want to talk with the pastor or several knowledgeable church leaders during the week to be sure you have a complete list of ministries to which you can refer.

Close this segment by noting that we will focus on the story of the selection of seven servants of the church, as found in Acts 6:1-14. This account prompts us to ask two main questions: **What kinds of services are needed by the church? How can we choose and support those persons who are willing to serve?**

Discerning the Need

Ask the class: How do we as a church decide which ministries we will perform? If the class is large, you may want to break into small discussion groups. You may want to use the information in the first three paragraphs under this heading in "Interpreting the Scripture" to spark discussion, or in lieu of discussion if the class prefers a lecture. Likely, each church will see itself in all three of the categories mentioned, though they may lean toward one or think of another alternative.

Then ask the class members to complete this sentence:

I wish our church could . . . (fill in the blank with a need that they would like to see met). Do this activity orally by going around the room so that everyone has a turn. You may want to record their answers. Or ask students to write their answers first and then share them orally. If you choose the second option, consider passing the papers on to a church leader or the pastor for discussion at a committee responsible for making decisions regarding programs.

If the class enjoys activities, bring assorted magazines. Let each person complete the sentence: *I wish our church could . . . by cutting out a picture representing a need (such as hunger, shelter, healing for the ill, friendship for the lonely) and pasting it to a poster board to form a collage.* As they work, talk about the kinds of needs that Jesus met and how the church is called to meet those needs as well.

Close this portion by asking someone to read Acts 6:1. Identify the need in the early church (Hellenist widows needed to be cared for). Use the information under "Understanding the Scripture" to help the class understand the conflict between the Hebrews and Hellenists and who comprised these two groups.

Choosing and Supporting the Servants

Direct the class's attention to Acts 6:2-7. Ask the class: What process does the early church use in choosing and supporting its servants? Paragraphs two and three of the "Choosing and Supporting the Servants" section under "Interpreting the Scripture" give information that may supplement the class answers or be used as the basis for a lecture on this topic.

Compare and contrast the early church's process to your own church's process by asking: How do we choose and support persons who lead and serve our church? Depending on their answers, class members may want to continue the discussion by suggesting ways in which the process could be improved. If so, focus on the process, not on individual leaders.

The early church identified seven persons whom they believed had the talents to do the job that needed to be done. If your class members feel comfortable with one another, spend some time allowing them to identify each other's gifts and talents. You may want to do this activity in small groups. One way of doing it would be to have one person say to another, "Jay, I really appreciate the way you are able to. . . ." Such an exercise not only relates to the Bible lesson but helps class members feel valued and supported within the community of faith.

Stephen: A Model Servant

Ask a volunteer to read aloud Acts 6:8-14.

Provide information from the "Understanding the Scripture" portion to help the class understand who the key players are and why they are upset with Stephen.

Discuss Stephen as a model for ministry by reading or retelling the information in the first paragraph of this section under "Interpreting the Scripture."

Like Stephen, most servant-leaders in the church find themselves in conflict with others because of something they have said or done. Provide a time of quiet meditation for the class to reflect on the following two scenarios. You may want to: (a) read the questions aloud, allowing an interval of silence; (b) write the questions on a chalkboard or newsprint before class; or (c) reproduce them as handouts for each member of the class.

Scenario I:

(1) Recall a time when you as a church member criticized a church leader (either a volunteer or paid professional) for something he or she said or did. Think about the situation.

(2) Why did you hold your point of view?

(3) Do you think the way you handled your concern helped or hindered the leader?

(4) Did your words or deeds help or hinder the church?

(5) What would you do if a similar situation arose again?

Scenario II:

(1) Recall a time when you were working as a servant in the church and someone criticized you for something you said or did.

(2) How did you feel about the critic?

(3) How did you feel about yourself and the job you were doing?

(4) Did the critic's actions cause you to back away from what you were doing or stop using your talents for the church?

(5) How would you respond if a similar situation arose in the future?

Close this segment of the lesson by offering a prayer that: (1) God will help us as we are being served to be sensitive to those who are working on our behalf; (2) God will enable us to be effective servants who persevere in the power of the Holy Spirit even in face of hurtful criticism.

HELPING CLASS MEMBERS ACT

Ask class members to keep their eyes open for needs within the church, community, or world that your congregation could address. Challenge them to contact the appropriate church official or the pastor to raise their concern and, if possible, suggest specific ways that the church could begin to meet this need. Challenge class members to consider volunteering their time to a church or community organization that helps persons in need.

Encourage each class member to select someone who serves the church in a paid or volunteer position. As a way of supporting this person, have them write a thank you note this week, describing how much his or her work means to them.

PLANNING FOR NEXT SUNDAY

Next Sunday's session will focus on another one of the seven servants, Philip, who witnesses about Jesus to a man considered an outcast. In preparation for this lesson, ask the class to read Acts 8:4-40. They may want to consider ways in which they reach out to persons who are struggling to know and understand the good news.

THE WORTH OF A PERSON

PREVIEWING THE LESSON

Lesson Scripture: Acts: 8:5-6, 26-38
Background Scripture: Acts 8:4-40
Key Verse: Acts 8:35

Focus of the lesson:
Philip's witness of good news to persons considered to be outcasts

Main question(s) of the lesson:
(1) How does our witness by word and deed demonstrate to others that they are persons of worth in God's sight?

This lesson will enable adult learners to:
(1) appreciate the scope of Philip's mission to all persons who are willing to listen
(2) affirm the value of all persons as worthy recipients of God's good news
(3) respond by seeking opportunities to share God's love with strangers.

Today's lesson may be outlined as follows:
(1) Introduction
(2) Philip Preaches in Samaria (Acts 8:5-6)
(3) Philip Meets the Ethiopian Eunuch (Acts 8:26-34)
(4) Philip Preaches the Good News of Jesus (Acts 8:35-38)

FOCUSING ON THE MAIN QUESTION

How do we measure the worth of a person? Do we value one person more highly because he drives an expensive sports car or another because she wears designer label clothes? Do we check to see whether a new acquaintance lives in the right neighborhood before pursuing a friendship? Do we value well-educated or financially secure persons more than we esteem others? Do we evaluate persons of a particular race, class, sex, age bracket, religion, or nationality as being better than others?

We humans have many criteria by which we determine how valuable another individual is. God's criteria are quite different. Genesis 1:27 tells us that all of humanity was created by God in God's own image. Psalm 24:1 reminds us that all who dwell on the earth are the Lord's. God values us—each and every one of us—more highly than we will ever be able to comprehend. That value is affirmed for us in God's gracious gift of Jesus. If God loves us this much, who are we to limit our concern to certain persons? We are called to go not only to those whom we think merit our attention but to the outcast as well. Jesus is clearly our model, for he reached out to the hated tax collectors, the Samaritan woman, the leper, the demon-possessed, and a host of other persons who lived on the fringes of society. He did this so that they too might hear the good news of the kingdom of God.

In today's lesson we follow Philip, one of the seven Hellenist servants we met last week, as he preaches the words of life to bitter enemies of the Jews, the Samaritans. He is also led by God to travel a wilder-ness road where he meets a resident of the biblical Nubia (known then as Ethiopia) who is reading the Scriptures and hungry to learn more about what they mean. Although this man held a high royal posi-tion, he would have been an outcast at the Jewish temple because he was castrated. Through Philip's Spirit-led witness in words and deeds, this eunuch hears and responds to the news of Jesus Christ. He is a person of worth. As we study this lesson from Acts 8, we will consider the question: **How does our witness by word and deed demonstrate to others that they are persons of worth in God's sight?**

READING THE SCRIPTURE

NRSV
Acts 8:5-6

5 Philip went down to the city of Samaria and proclaimed the Messiah to them. ⁶The crowds with one accord listened eagerly to what was said by Philip, hearing and seeing the signs that he did.

Acts 8:26-38

26 Then an angel of the Lord said to Philip, "Get up and go toward the south to the road that goes down from Jerusalem to Gaza." (This is a wilderness road.) ²⁷So he got up and went. Now there was an Ethiopian eunuch, a court official of the Candace, queen of the Ethiopians, in charge of her entire treasury. He had come to Jerusalem to worship ²⁸and was returning home; seated in his chariot, he was reading the prophet Isaiah. ²⁹Then the Spirit said to Philip, "Go over to this chariot and join it." ³⁰So Philip ran up to it and heard him reading the prophet Isaiah. He asked, "Do you understand what you are reading?" ³¹He replied, "How can I, unless someone guides me?" And he invited Philip to get in and sit beside him. ³²Now the passage of the scripture that he was reading was this:

NIV
Acts 8:5-6

⁵Philip went down to a city in Samaria and proclaimed the Christ there. ⁶When the crowds heard Philip and saw the miraculous signs he did, they all paid close attention to what he said.

Acts 8:26-38

²⁶Now an angel of the Lord said to Philip, "Go south to the road—the desert road—that goes down from Jerusalem to Gaza." ²⁷So he started out, and on his way he met an Ethiopian eunuch, an important official in charge of all the treasury of Candace, queen of the Ethiopians. This man had gone to Jerusalem to worship, ²⁸and on his way home was sitting in his chariot reading the book of Isaiah the prophet. ²⁹The Spirit told Philip, "Go to that chariot and stay near it."

³⁰Then Philip ran up to the chariot and heard the man reading Isaiah the prophet. "Do you understand what you are reading?" Philip asked.

³¹"How can I," he said, "unless someone explains it to me?" So he invited Philip to come up and sit with him.

"Like a sheep he was led to the
    slaughter,
  and like a lamb silent before
    its shearer,
    so he does not open his
     mouth.
³³In his humiliation justice was
    denied him.
  Who can describe his
    generation?
    For his life is taken away
     from the earth."
³⁴The eunuch asked Philip, "About whom, may I ask you, does the prophet say this, about himself or about someone else?" ³⁵Then Philip began to speak, and starting with this scripture, he proclaimed to him the good news about Jesus. ³⁶As they were going along the road, they came to some water; and the eunuch said, "Look, here is water! What is to prevent me from being baptized?" ³⁸He commanded the chariot to stop, and both of them, Philip and the eunuch, went down into the water, and Philip baptized him.

³²The eunuch was reading this passage of Scripture:
"He was led like a sheep to the slaughter,
    and as a lamb before the shearer is silent,
    so he did not open his mouth.
³³In his humiliation he was deprived of justice.
  Who can speak of his descendants?
  For his life was taken from the earth."

³⁴The eunuch asked Philip, "Tell me, please, who is the prophet talking about, himself or someone else?" ³⁵Then Philip began with that very passage of Scripture and told him the good news about Jesus.
³⁶As they traveled along the road, they came to some water and the eunuch said, "Look, here is water. Why shouldn't I be baptized?" ³⁸And he gave orders to stop the chariot. Then both Philip and the eunuch went down into the water and Philip baptized him.

Key Verse

UNDERSTANDING THE SCRIPTURE

Acts 8:4-8. As Jesus had commanded in Acts 1:8, the preaching of the gospel now moves beyond Jerusalem. Christians in Jerusalem were persecuted following Stephen's stoning and scattered into Judea and Samaria (Acts 8:1). Philip, a Hellenist who was one of the seven servants (Acts 6:5), goes to Samaria as an evangelist. The city is unidentified but may have been Sebaste or Shechem. The Samaritans were a mixed blood remnant of the northern tribes that had been conquered by the Assyrians in 721 B.C.E. Although they were hated by the Jews, the Samaritans believed in the same God and accepted the first five books of the Jewish Scriptures (Torah) as authoritative. Philip's mission was to proclaim that Jesus was the Messiah. Philip's words and deeds of exorcism and healing were well received by an enthusiastic crowd.

Acts 8:9-13. This crowd had also "listened eagerly" to Simon (compare Acts 8:6, 10, and 11). Magicians, astrologers, and soothsayers were common, but Simon acclaimed himself as "someone great." The wording of Acts 8:10 hints that he may have been worshiped as a god. Everyone in Samaria from the least to the greatest revered him. Despite this elevated status, Simon chose to be baptized, along with many others, when he heard Philip preach "the good news about the kingdom of God and the name of Jesus Christ" (Acts 8:12). Perhaps Simon was more intrigued by the signs and wonders than the words, for he became a companion (perhaps a disciple) of Philip's.

Acts 8:14-25. Two apostles, Peter and John, were dispatched from Jerusalem to confirm Philip's work in Samaria. Their role was to supervise the growing mission of the church and link the new church to the mother church in Jerusalem. Although Philip had baptized Samaritans in the name of Jesus, these new believers had not received the Holy Spirit. (A similar example of time lag between baptism and the conferring of the Holy Spirit is recorded in Acts 19:1-6.) When the apostles prayed and laid hands on the converts, the Spirit fell upon them. Simon the magician was so impressed by the power of the apostles that he wanted to buy it. Peter became angry, pronouncing a curse on Simon for believing that he could buy a gift that only God can give. (Our word *simony* refers to the attempt to purchase a church office.) Simon apparently had not committed an unpardonable sin because the apostle called him to repent and pray for forgiveness. Simon asked Peter to pray for him. As they returned to Jerusalem, Peter and John continued to witness to the Samaritans.

Acts 8:26-38. The story returns to Philip as he is called by an angel of the Lord to travel a wilderness road to Gaza, the southernmost Philistine city, located on the route to Egypt. Philip obeys. En route he meets a eunuch who holds a very responsible position as the overseer of the treasury of the queen of Ethiopia. Candace was her title, not her name. Although the eunuch "had come to Jerusalem to worship" (Acts 8:27), his status is unclear. Deuteronomy 23:1 strictly forbade eunuchs from being a part of the congregation. Yet, the prophet Isaiah (56:3) foretold a time when foreigners and eunuchs would be able to participate in worship. Whether the Nubian (Ethiopian) eunuch is a Gentile or a proselyte converted to Judaism is not stated, though Luke's depiction of Cornelius as the first Gentile convert (Acts 10:1-48) suggests that Luke thinks of the eunuch as a proselyte. When his chariot passes, the Spirit prompts Philip to join it, which he does. As was customary in the ancient world, the eunuch was reading aloud rather than silently. Philip knew therefore that he was reading from Isaiah. In Acts 8:32-33 Luke quotes a portion of Isaiah's fourth servant song, found in 53:7b-8, stopping short of Isaiah's words "stricken for the transgression of my people." Philip boldly asks if the man understands what he is reading. Instead of being offended, the eunuch asks Philip to join him in the chariot. He questions the evangelist to learn who Isaiah is speaking about. Philip had won converts by signs and wonders in Samaria. This time he wins a convert from Africa who responded to his preaching and requested water baptism.

Acts 8:39-40. As soon as Philip and the Ethiopian rise from the water, the Spirit again intervenes, miraculously transporting Philip. He finds himself in Azostus, formerly called Ashdod, a town just a few miles inland from the Mediterranean in northern Judah. He moves on to his home in Caesarea, preaching the word as he travels.

INTERPRETING THE SCRIPTURE

Philip Preaches in Samaria

Like many other Christians, Philip had left Jerusalem because of the persecution that followed Stephen's martyrdom. Stephen and Philip had been co-workers chosen by the Jerusalem church to supervise the daily food distribution to the Hellenist widows (Acts 6:5). Had we been in the position of seeing a friend stoned, we probably would have thought seriously about denying our faith or at least keeping our beliefs to ourselves. But not Philip!

A Jewish-Christian from Caesarea (Acts

21:8), Philip willingly goes into a Samaritan city to proclaim the Word of God. The power to heal and exorcise unclean spirits that was seen first in Jesus' ministry and then in the ministry of the apostles (Acts 3:1-11) is now manifested in Philip. He assumes the role of an evangelist in Samaria. His preaching marks the first recorded movement of Christianity into non-Jewish territory.

Samaria, a region to the north of Jerusalem, had been the home of ten of the tribes of Jacob until the Assyrians overran them in 721 B.C.E. Following this conquest, many Jews were deported and foreign colonists settled the area (2 Kings 17). The Samaritans worshiped the same God as the Jews, though at Mount Gerizim, not in Jerusalem. They accepted the Torah (the first five books of the Old Testament) but none of the other Jewish writings as sacred scripture. Tensions between Jews and Samaritans developed and continued to grow over time into bitter hostility.

We can only imagine how Philip, a Jew, felt about being among persons he had been taught to consider inferior. Likewise, we have to wonder what the Samaritans thought about Philip coming into their midst to proclaim that the promised Messiah had come. In some mysterious way the Spirit of God must have been at work preparing Philip to speak and act in power and the Samaritan people to listen receptively and respond with joy.

Philip's story challenges us to confront our own willingness to witness to others, especially those whom we perceive to be quite different from ourselves. Who are the Samaritans in our day? Perhaps they are persons who share a religious heritage, such as the Roman Catholics and Protestants of Northern Ireland, but who nonetheless are bitter enemies. Maybe our Samaritans are persons we have stereotyped as inferior or unworthy, such as drug addicts or the homeless, without recognizing their inestimable worth before God. Maybe our Samaritans are family members from whom we are estranged because of a feud or disagreements regarding lifestyles. Whoever these persons are, we are called to speak and act in ways that will let them know that God truly loves them. Our actions, like those of Philip, should offer health and wholeness to persons. We are called to minister in ways that will open the channels of God's grace and love to all persons. In recent years, a poster proclaimed the message that we are all special because God made us, and God doesn't make junk. No, God does not make junk. We are all priceless treasures in God's sight.

Philip Meets the Ethiopian Eunuch

Philip is having a successful evangelistic campaign. His work is confirmed and authenticated by two representatives of the apostles, Peter and John. His ministry is going well when an angel of the Lord suddenly calls him to leave this fruitful field and head south toward Gaza, near the Mediterranean coast. Philip obeys, but he surely must have wondered about this strange turn of events. In Samaria throngs are coming to listen to his message. Their lives are being changed. Yet, the angel wants him to move south of Jerusalem, traveling along a wilderness road.

In an unexpected place Philip encounters another marginalized person whose life will be changed by the news Philip brings. A eunuch with great responsibility for the Nubian queen's treasury is reading a portion of the fourth servant song from Isaiah 53. We are not certain of his status. He may have been a Gentile or a proselyte who converted to Judaism. In either case, he was both a foreigner and a castrated male, making it unlawful for him to worship in the temple. Yet he wants to have a relationship with God. He is reading and searching for answers. At the Spirit's prompting, Philip volunteers to help. The eunuch eagerly invites the evangelist to join him.

How do we respond when persons ask us to help them understand more about God? Perhaps the inquirer does not point to a specific Bible passage and ask for a direct explanation, though that situation does occur. More likely we are asked by friends or neighbors, family members or co-workers to help them find God in the midst of difficult or unexplainable circumstances. They want to know where God was when their loved one was suffering with cancer. Or why their teenager began to experiment with drugs. Or how a loving God would allow major disasters such as floods or earthquakes to devastate communities. Or when God was going to enable them to find a new job. Or how they can find peace in their troubled existence.

Philip's encounter offers us some clues as to how we can effectively witness to persons, even those who are strangers. First, Philip followed the leading of the Spirit, here depicted as an angel. Logically, one would not leave a city while engaged in a fruitful ministry. Yet Philip made the illogical move and quickly discerned why he was sent there. Sometimes we may feel the Spirit prompting us to do or say something, but we remain silent and passive, fearful of appearing foolish. Second, Philip was not timid about asking the eunuch if he needed help in understanding the Scripture. Probably most of us would shy away from volunteering assistance to someone, especially a stranger whose means of travel may have suggested the responsible court position he held. We may assume that the person does not want help or that we may be rebuffed. We may discover, as Philip did, that the stranger is yearning for someone to help him find answers to his questions. We can only guess how many persons around us are searching for the meaning, truth, and love that only God can provide. If we do not let these persons know that they are precious to God, who will tell them?

Philip Preaches the Good News of Jesus

Philip arrives on the scene at a teachable moment. The eunuch is ready to hear what the evangelist has to say. He wants to know and is diligently seeking answers. Although Luke only records that Philip "began to speak, and starting with this scripture, he proclaimed to him the good news about Jesus" (Acts 8:35), we can make some guesses about the content of Philip's teaching. The evangelist must have linked Isaiah's portrait of the suffering servant (Isaiah 52:13–53:12) with Jesus. He must have told the eunuch about Jesus' crucifixion, resurrection, and ascension. Philip also must have proclaimed Jesus' innocence of wrongdoing, for "justice was denied him" (Acts 8:33).

Since the eunuch's response to Philip's message is a request to be baptized, we must assume that Philip told him that the way to accept Jesus was to repent and be baptized. Some late biblical manuscripts include a verse to make this idea more explicit: "And Philip said, 'If thou believest with all thine heart, thou mayest.' And he answered and said, 'I believe that Jesus Christ is the Son of God' " (Acts 8:37 KJV). This verse is not included (except as a footnote) in the NRSV, NIV, or other modern Bible translations because the verse does not appear in the oldest manuscripts. The Western church made the addition so that the eunuch did not appear to be baptized without proper instruction and a confession of faith. We know for certain the eunuch is so eager to be baptized that he implores Philip to do so in some water that they pass along the road. Philip baptizes him and as the two rise from the water, Philip is miraculously transported to another city.

The Bible text makes no further mention of the eunuch, except to say that he "went on his way rejoicing" (Acts 8:39). Surely he returned to his Nubian homeland, south of Egypt. He likely told other members of the royal court about his powerful religious experience. Thus the gospel witness extended much further geographically than the area where the encounter between Philip and the eunuch occurred. Jesus' command to be witnesses (Acts 1:8) was being fulfilled in surprising ways.

As we think about the potential outreach of Philip's one meeting with a stranger, we can only wonder about our own opportunities to reach persons with the good news of Jesus' love. Admittedly, we will not likely be led by an angel to a particular location, or picked up and deposited in another city when our task is finished. The absence of such supernatural events does not mean, however, that God is not working through us to reach other persons.

We may be very surprised to hear someone tell us how much a small act of kindness meant in a time of need. In fact, we may not have even been aware of the need, but God knew and prompted us, perhaps through a still small voice within, to say or do something that let another one of God's precious creations know of their worth and of God's love for them.

SHARING THE SCRIPTURE

PREPARING TO TEACH

You may want to read the fourth servant song, Isaiah 52:13–53:12 in its entirety. Parts of 53:7-8 are quoted in Acts 8:32-33. If you compare these verses with the Isaian verses you will notice that, in addition to being selectively shortened, they are translated differently. The reason for this difference is that Luke, like most of the early church members, relied on a Greek translation of the Hebrew Scriptures known as the Septuagint. This version often reads differently from the translation we have directly from the Hebrew in our Bibles.

If you choose to lecture, become familiar with the scripture and the information above, which can serve as the basis for your presentation.

Notice that the Ethiopian was very eager to have someone dialogue with him. One of the great values of adult education is that we have opportunities to learn and share with one another in interactive ways. If your class has been solely accustomed to a lecture format, see if you can begin to include a few of the questions, especially those that call for opinions, in the lesson. By slowing introducing discussion, you may begin to draw out class members and make them feel more comfortable about offering their

opinions at first and later, raising their doubts and questions or sharing their own needs for help as they relate to the topic at hand.

If you plan to sing, select the hymn and be sure to have hymnals on hand.

LEADING THE CLASS

Introduction

Prior to class, write the following information on a chalkboard or newsprint: Think of a time when someone said something to you or did something for you that made you feel very special.
(1) What was this word or deed?
(2) Why did you feel so uplifted by it?
(3) Describe the effect that word or deed had on your relationship with the other person or with God.

As the class convenes, allow time for meditation on the questions above. Invite a few volunteers to share their thoughts with the class. Or, if the class is large, ask students to share their responses with a partner, if they choose.

Wrap up the discussion by indicating that we know from our own experiences how special a kind word or deed can make us feel. Similarly, our supportive words and actions indicate to other persons that they are persons of worth. As we study today's lesson in which Philip witnesses to persons, we want to ask ourselves: **How does our witness by word and deed demonstrate to others that they are persons of worth in God's sight?**

If you prefer to omit discussion, use the information under "Focusing on the Main Question" to introduce today's topic.

Philip Preaches in Samaria

Remind the class of the events studied last week, especially of Stephen's stoning that led to the persecution of Christians in Jerusalem. As a result, many persons fled Jerusalem and scattered throughout Judea and Samaria, taking their beliefs and witness to persons who otherwise would not have heard the gospel.

Direct the class's attention to Acts 8:5-6. Ask: **What do you know about the Samaritans?** Use the information under "Understanding the Scripture" to fill in gaps.

Then ask: **Who do you perceive to be the Samaritans in our day?** List their ideas on a chalkboard or newsprint. You will find information—perhaps additional ideas—in the last paragraph of this section under "Interpreting the Scripture."

Close this segment by asking:

(1) **How did the Samaritans receive Philip's words and deeds of witness?**

(2) **What do you think might be the response of the Samaritans in our day if we were willing to let them know that they were loved and valued by God?**

(3) **What can we do now to begin to reach these persons?**

Philip Meets the Ethiopian Eunuch

Choose a volunteer to read Acts 8:26-34. Invite the class to put themselves in Philip's place and ask them:

(1) **How would you have felt about being called away from Samaria?**

(2) **Why would you feel this way?**

(3) **Would you have gone, or would you have assumed that you must have been mistaken about the direction to leave a fruitful ministry?**

Ideas suggested in the section under "Interpreting the Scripture" may be added to this discussion.

Ask the class: **How do we respond when persons ask us to help them understand more about God?** You may need to remind them that some persons will bring direct biblical questions to them, but others will want help in seeing God in difficult situations, such as the loss of a loved one, illness, unemployment, natural disasters, or a divorce.

The class may profit from doing one or both of the following case studies as a group, or in small groups if the class is large. Their purpose is to think of words or deeds that could show the individual in each case that he or she is a person of worth who is loved by God.

Case I: As a result of verbal and physical abuse, Margie left home with her two children to seek refuge in a shelter. She thought she had been a good wife but her self-esteem was at an all time low. Her husband's repeated criticisms had hurt deeply. She feels she has nowhere to turn. You are a volunteer at this shelter. What can you say or do to help Margie know that she is a person of worth before God?

Case II: Victor's son was killed last year by a drunk driver. Although Victor occasionally attended church, he did not have a close relationship with God before the accident. In a way, he wants nothing to do with God. He feels God does not care about him. On the other hand, he would like to feel that his son is at peace with God in an afterlife. You are a neighbor and member of the church Victor attends. How can you let Victor know that God does love and care for him?

Philip Preaches the Good News of Jesus

Focus attention on Acts 8:35-38.
Note that Luke does not tell us much

?

about the content of Philip's witness. Ask the class: **(1) What do you think Philip must have said to the Ethiopian? (2) How do you think the eunuch responded?** Ideas for answering this question are found in the first and second paragraph of this section under "Interpreting the Scripture."

If the students enjoy creative activities, two members of the class may be willing to role play a discussion between Philip and the Ethiopian. The class could respond by questioning their remarks or adding ideas.

Note that the eunuch continued homeward thrilled about having heard such good news. Philip had not gone to Ethiopia, but by his words and interaction with this one man the gospel likely spread there in surprising ways. Ask the class to give some examples of ways that their influence spreads to other persons.

If appropriate in your setting, sing a rousing hymn of witness, such as "We've a Story to Tell to the Nations," found on page 569 in *The United Methodist Hymnal*.

HELPING CLASS MEMBERS ACT

Encourage each class member to help a child or an adult to understand a Bible passage this week. A parent or grandparent may want to make a special effort to purchase or borrow a book of Bible stories to use with a child.

Challenge each person to invite at least one guest to attend class next week. Ask them to think especially about inviting an unchurched person, perhaps one who is new to the community or who is facing difficult problems and needs to become aware of God's love.

Encourage students to find at least one opportunity to share Christ's love with a stranger this week. They may do so in a conversation (perhaps in a doctor's office or school lobby) or by performing an act of kindness that lets the stranger know that he or she is a person of worth.

PLANNING FOR NEXT SUNDAY

Next week we will read a familiar passage from Acts 9:1-31, Saul's life-changing encounter with Jesus on the road to Damascus. Ask the class to read this material, paying particular attention to verses 1-6 and 10-20. Encourage them to think about the ways in which the risen Christ has confronted them.

CONFRONTED BY JESUS

PREVIEWING THE LESSON

Lesson Scripture: Acts 9:1-6, 10-20
Background Scripture: Acts 9:1-31
Key Verse: Acts 9:15

Focus of the lesson:
Saul's life-changing experiences as a result of Jesus' confrontation and Ananias's role as mediator

Main question(s) of the lesson:
(1) How does Jesus confront me in my own life and enable me to meet the challenge he sets before me?

This lesson will enable adult learners to:
(1) relate the story of the Damascus road experience to its transforming effect on Saul
(2) envision themselves in Saul's position as persons whom Jesus confronts
(3) respond by mediating God's grace to others, as Ananias did.

Today's lesson may be outlined as follows:
(1) Introduction
(2) Saul Becomes a Disciple (Acts 9:1-6)
(3) Ananias Has a Vision (Acts 9:10-16)
(4) Overcoming Obstacles (Acts 9:17-20)

FOCUSING ON THE MAIN QUESTION

Have you ever been faced with a challenge so difficult that you were not sure you would be able to meet it? The odds seemed overwhelmingly stacked against you. Fear gripped you as you struggled to cope with the situation. Perhaps you felt that you had failed as a parent because your child was so unruly. Or maybe you worried that you were in over your head at work because of a promotion that you felt ill-equipped to handle. Possibly a nasty neighbor's behavior made you so uncom-fortable that you seriously considered moving. Whatever the circumstances, you knew that somehow you had to overcome your anxieties and press ahead. And you did.

As difficult as these kinds of situations are, most of us have learned that we can grow as we face these challenges squarely and seek God's guidance in meeting them. We are victorious because God is present with us. We are not alone. The image of Shadrach, Meshach, and Abednego in Nebuchadnez-zar's fiery furnace is a helpful reminder of

God's presence. As the king looked into the fire, he saw four persons walking unhurt in the middle of the fire, though only three had been thrown in (see Daniel 3, especially verses 24-25). That fourth was God, as even this Babylonian king recognized.

In today's lesson from Acts 9:1-6 and 10-20 we see another example of a person who dreaded a difficult challenge. Ananias had been called by God to restore the sight of Saul after he had been blinded on the road to Damascus. Well aware of Saul's reputation, Ananias understandably did not want to become involved in a potentially life-threatening situation. Ananias trusts God and enables Saul to regain his sight and be filled with the Holy Spirit. Similarly, the disciples in Jerusalem were afraid of Saul, not knowing if this feared persecutor of Christians had really had a change of heart or was only pretending to be a disciple so as to capture them. Because of his transforming confrontation with Jesus, Saul too finds himself in a situation where both Christians and Jews want to kill him. If he is going to become God's emissary to the Gentiles, Saul must be willing to meet difficult challenges head on. As a result of these experiences, we are compelled to ask: **How does Jesus confront me in my own life and enable me to meet the challenges he sets before me?**

READING THE SCRIPTURE

NRSV
Acts 9:1-6

1 Meanwhile Saul, still breathing threats and murder against the disciples of the Lord, went to the high priest ²and asked him for letters to the synagogues at Damascus, so that if he found any who belonged to the Way, men or women, he might bring them bound to Jerusalem. ³Now as he was going along and approaching Damascus, suddenly a light from heaven flashed around him. ⁴He fell to the ground and heard a voice saying to him, "Saul , Saul, why do you persecute me?" ⁵He asked, "Who are you, Lord?" The reply came, "I am Jesus, whom you are persecuting. ⁶But get up and enter the city, and you will be told what you are to do."

Acts 9:10-20

10 Now there was a disciple in Damascus named Ananias. The Lord said to him in a vision, "Ananias." He answered, "Here I am, Lord." ¹¹The Lord said to him, "Get up and go to the street called Straight, and at the house of Judas look for a man of Tarsus named Saul. At this moment he is praying, ¹²and he has seen in

NIV
Acts 9:1-6

1 Meanwhile, Saul was still breathing out murderous threats against the Lord's disciples. He went to the high priest ²and asked him for letters to the synagogues in Damascus, so that if he found any there who belonged to the Way, whether men or women, he might take them as prisoners to Jerusalem. ³As he neared Damascus on his journey, suddenly a light from heaven flashed around him. ⁴He fell to the ground and heard a voice say to him, "Saul, Saul, why do you persecute me?"

⁵"Who are you, Lord?" Saul asked.

"I am Jesus, whom you are persecuting," he replied. ⁶"Now get up and go into the city, and you will be told what you must do."

Acts 9:10-20

¹⁰In Damascus there was a disciple named Ananias. The Lord called to him in a vision, "Ananias !"

"Yes , Lord," he answered.

¹¹The Lord told him, "Go to the house of Judas on Straight Street and ask for a man from Tarsus named Saul, for he is praying.

a vision a man named Ananias come in and lay his hands on him so that he might regain his sight." ¹³But Ananias answered, "Lord, I have heard from many about this man, how much evil he has done to your saints in Jerusalem; ¹⁴and here he has authority from the chief priests to bind all who invoke your name." ¹⁵But the Lord said to him, "Go, for he is an instrument whom I have chosen to bring my name before Gentiles and kings and before the people of Israel; ¹⁶I myself will show him how much he must suffer for the sake of my name." ¹⁷So Ananias went and entered the house. He laid his hands on Saul and said, "Brother Saul, the Lord Jesus, who appeared to you on your way here, has sent me so that you may regain your sight and be filled with the Holy Spirit." ¹⁸And immediately something like scales fell from his eyes, and his sight was restored. Then he got up and was baptized, ¹⁹and after taking some food, he regained his strength.

For several days he was with the disciples in Damascus, ²⁰and immediately he began to proclaim Jesus in the synagogues, saying, "He is the Son of God."

¹²In a vision he has seen a man named Ananias come and place his hands on him to restore his sight."

¹³"Lord," Ananias answered, "I have heard many reports about this man and all the harm he has done to your saints in Jerusalem. ¹⁴And he has come here with authority from the chief priests to arrest all who call on your name."

¹⁵But the Lord said to Ananias, "Go! This man is my chosen instrument to carry my name before the Gentiles and their kings and before the people of Israel. ¹⁶I will show him how much he must suffer for my name."

¹⁷Then Ananias went to the house and entered it. Placing his hands on Saul, he said, "Brother Saul, the Lord—Jesus, who appeared to you on the road as you were coming here—has sent me so that you may see again and be filled with the Holy Spirit." ¹⁸Immediately, something like scales fell from Saul's eyes, and he could see again. He got up and was baptized, ¹⁹and after taking some food, he regained his strength.

Saul spent several days with the disciples in Damascus. ²⁰At once he began to preach in the synagogues that Jesus is the Son of God.

Key Verse

UNDERSTANDING THE SCRIPTURE

Acts 9:1-9. First introduced at the stoning of Stephen (Acts 7:58, 8:1), Saul has been relentlessly persecuting followers of the Way, which was one of the earliest names for Christianity. Likely Saul was looking for Jewish Christians who attended the synagogue in Damascus. Though Luke's text would indicate that the high priest from the synagogue in Jerusalem had authority over Diaspora communities, this authority cannot be documented by other writings. Saul is on his way to the Damascus synagogue to round up Christians when he sees a light and hears a voice. Jesus' question and reply in Acts 9:4-5 indicate that to persecute the

people of the Way is the same as persecuting Jesus himself. Although heavenly light is usually a symbol of divine revelation, Saul does not seem to understand what is happening, for he asks who the voice is. Saul's traveling companions see no one, but they can witness to this extraordinary encounter. Saul's blindness was probably the result of the brilliance of the vision. The account of Paul's confrontation by Jesus on the road to Damascus (Acts 9:3-19) is retold with minor variations in Acts 22:4-11 and 26:9-18.

Acts 9:10-20. Ananias is simply referred to in verse 10 as "a disciple in Damascus." In Acts 22:12 Paul refers to Ananias as "a devout man according to the law and well spoken of by all the Jews living there." In a vision, Ananias hears the voice of God calling him and he responds. God's directions are very specific. Ananias is to go to the home of Judas on Straight Street, the main east-west road in Damascus, and lay hands on Saul so that he will regain his sight. God says that Saul is similarly receiving a vision that Ananias will be coming to him. Ananias understandably resists, citing Saul's reputation. God tells Ananias that Saul is a chosen vessel. Luke shows Saul being healed, filled with the Holy Spirit, and baptized in preparation for the role he will play. The result of the transformational experience on the road to Damascus is a reversal of Saul's behavior. The detractor now becomes the witness; the persecutor, the persecuted. He begins his ministry by proclaiming that Jesus is the Son of God.

Acts 9:21-25. Saul's ministry is eyed with great suspicion by everyone. Some recurring patterns of Saul's ministry are set up here. He taught in the synagogue (see also Acts 13:14), met with resistance and controversy (see also Acts 13:45-46, 50; 14:2, 4-5, 19), faced death threats (see also Acts 14:19; 20:3, 19), and was delivered from death or vindicated (Acts 9:27, 30; 14:20). The story of his escape from Damascus is also told by Paul in 2 Corinthians 11:32-33. In that account, Paul says that the governor under King Aretas wanted to kill him. Aretas IV, king of Nabataea, located southeast of Palestine, apparently had authority in Damascus. According to Luke's account, a plot against Saul is discovered by his disciples who lower him through an opening (window, in 2 Corinthians 11:33) in the city wall. Saul had been placed in a basket such as would have been used to haul cargo over land.

Acts 9:26-31. As was the case in Damascus, Christians in Jerusalem also eyed Saul suspiciously, unconvinced that he was a disciple. Barnabas intercedes by taking Paul to the apostles. Luke's account seems to be in conflict with Paul's own version of his first trip to Jerusalem as recorded in Galatians 1:18-23. Paul does not mention Barnabas, says that the trip occurred three years after his conversion, and that he was unknown by sight. In Acts, Saul makes the trip soon after his Damascus road confrontation, is commended to the apostles by Barnabas for his bold witness in Damascus, and seems to be accepted into the church at Jerusalem. Acts 9:29 indicates that Saul is opposed by Hellenists, likely the same group that stoned Stephen. Saul is again saved from death as Christians take him from Jerusalem to Caesarea and send him home to Tarsus. Paul stays in his hometown until Barnabas comes to get him (Acts 11:25). In Acts 9:31 Luke summarizes the state of the church in the regions of Palestine. Empowered by the Holy Spirit, the church was growing numerically and members were living in peace and harmony.

INTERPRETING THE SCRIPTURE

Saul Becomes a Disciple

Change is a normal part of our modern lives. Today's older adults have seen the development of cars and superhighways, airplanes and space shuttles, telephones and telecommunication satellites. We experience change in our personal lives as well. Many middle aged adults who began their careers expecting to work for one company all of their lives are being forced to change employers, perhaps even their vocations, in response to a dramatic shift in U.S. business and industry. Today's generation of young adults faces the prospect of being the first group of Americans who will likely fare less well financially than their parents did. Change is inevitable. How we cope with change and integrate it into our lives dramatically affects our attitude toward life. Positive responses generally enable us to grow and develop into more mature persons. Negative responses to change often create bitterness and anger, causing us to be stuck in a rut.

Saul of Tarsus was a man who knew much about change and its affect on one's life. By his own account he was a devout Pharisee who was righteous under the law (Philippians 3:5-6). The Christian movement surely was upsetting to his secure frame of reference concerning who he was and how he related to God. Believing that he was doing the work of the Lord, Saul zealously persecuted the Christian church. He went so far as to obtain letters from the high priest so that he could extradite Jewish Christians from Damascus and bring them to Jerusalem (Acts 9:1-2). He was certainly intent on doing his best to stamp out this renegade movement known as the Way.

God, however, had other plans. As Saul approached the city where he hoped to round up suspects, God intervened in a surprising way. Saul would not have listened to the voice of preachers, but he was forced to listen to a supernatural voice that called his name and asked, "Why do you persecute me?" (Acts 9:4). Saul was blinded by a heavenly light, possibly caused by the radiance of the divine presence and certainly to be understood as a symbol of divine revelation. From this voice, Saul comes to understand that to persecute the church is tantamount to persecuting the Lord himself. Jesus instructed him to go into Damascus and wait for further directions.

Not only have Saul's plans been radically altered but his whole life has been changed. The God that he thought he knew so well was different than Saul had understood God to be. This powerful man who had access to the high priest and the power of life and death over Christians was reduced to a helpless wanderer who had to be led by the hand into Damascus.

We can only guess what Saul must have been thinking as he humbly stumbled toward an unknown future. Yet, if we are honest, we might have to admit that we are stumbling along with him. Changes in the world around us and in our own lives cause us to act and react. We rely on familiar teachings and responses only to find that, at times, we are persecuting Jesus himself. God called Saul to change radically. We need to listen carefully. God may be speaking to us as well, calling us to a new kind of life that we cannot even imagine.

Ananias Has a Vision

Often God's work requires the cooperation of a group of persons to fulfill his plan. Ministry is not the work of lone rangers but of the community of faith. Surely God could have healed Saul's eyesight and sent him on his way just as miraculously as God stopped Saul in his tracks. But God chose another way. Through a vision, God called a devout follower to serve as a mediator. God gave Ananias specific directions as to how to find Saul, who was staying in a home on a main street in Damascus. Ananias's task was to go to Judas's home and lay hands on Saul so that his sight would be restored. Ananias would be expected, for God had also sent Saul a vision that Ananias would come to heal his eyes.

Ananias responds to this vision with an understandable protest. In essence he says: "You've got to be kidding, God. You want me to go to help a man who is creating havoc among the Christian church—a man who has the power to arrest Christians—and heal him?" But God insists that this is the plan. God tells Ananias that Saul is a chosen vessel, the one who will confess God's name before the Gentiles and kings and the people of Israel (Acts 9:15). Like Jesus, Saul too will suffer. These words of God come to fruition over time.

First, however, Ananias must act. He has heard the reports and knows that his life is in danger and yet God's own self has called him. Despite his fear, Ananias knows that he must obey. He has to meet this challenge if God's purposes are to be fulfilled through Saul. What choice will he make?

What choice do we make when confronted by God and called to intervene in a situation that we would prefer to run from? Some Christians have always been called to make choices that put their lives at risk. During World War II, for example, some Christians put their lives and the lives of their families on the line by protecting Jews in their homes or helping them to escape. Christians in the United States risked the potential violence of bigots by standing against racism. Some, including the Baptist minister Dr. Martin Luther King Jr., paid the ultimate price for their commitment.

The challenges with which God confronts us are probably not as dramatic as these, but God calls us to overcome our fears and take action. We can accomplish unimaginably difficult tasks because God not only places them before us but gives us the strength and wisdom, by the power of the Holy Spirit, to accomplish them.

Overcoming Obstacles

Ananias not only overcame his own anxiety but was able to graciously greet this feared enemy as "Brother Saul." Imagine how those words must have sounded to Saul who just three days earlier would have gladly bound Ananias and hauled him back to Jerusalem! Ananias identified the Lord Jesus as the one who appeared to Saul on the Damascus road and appeared to him. As soon as Ananias spoke, Saul

was again changed. His eyes were healed; he was filled with the Holy Spirit. After being baptized, he broke his fast and his strength returned.

Ananias certainly must have been changed too. God had confronted him, just as God had confronted Saul. God called and used this servant in such a transforming way that his life was probably never the same. When other challenges presented themselves, he could look back on this experience and say with assurance that God would indeed guide and direct him.

Saul also must overcome a major obstacle: the reorganizing of his understandings about God. A few days after Saul's second dramatic encounter with the power of God, he began to do the work to which he had been called. Saul went into the Damascus synagogue—the place where he had expected to nab Jewish Christians—and proclaimed that Jesus is the Son of God. He knows this in his heart. Yet we cannot help but wonder how difficult it must have been for him to make a statement that a few days ago would have been heresy to his own ears.

Finally, those who hear Saul, both in Damascus and in Jerusalem, must overcome their suspicions about this man. Old images die hard. The believers find it difficult to imagine that someone could have such a powerful experience that his life would be totally changed. They cannot truly hear what he has to say. Christians hear Saul's proclamation as an insincere attempt to infiltrate the Christian fellowship and persecute believers. Some are so convinced of this that they plot to kill Saul. Saul's Jewish colleagues are incensed by his attempts to prove to them that Jesus is the Messiah. They too want to kill him. God provides ways for Saul to escape his own persecutors, but they still need to overcome the barriers that separate them from hearing the Word of God through Saul.

Most adults have obstacles in their lives that need to be overcome as well. Like Ananias, we may be fearful about meeting the difficult challenges of life. Or like Saul we may find that changes, though ultimately for the best, cause confusion and disorientation in our lives until we can grasp what is happening to us. Or like the Jews and Hellenist Christians, we may be unable to relate to someone whose behavior does not meet our expectations. We cannot fathom such a change and do not know how to deal with this person. In each of life's situations, though, Jesus is there to confront us and move us in the direction that he would have us to go through the power of the Holy Spirit. We can choose to say yes or no to God, but we must decide knowing that our own future and the future of a far wider community may hang in the balance of our decision.

SHARING THE SCRIPTURE

PREPARING TO TEACH

As you study the Scripture and the lesson for this week, think about times in your life when Jesus has confronted you. How did you respond? In retrospect, do you think your response was the one that God wanted you to make? You may want to record your thoughts in your spiritual journal.

As you read and study this week's lesson, try to put yourself in the place of Ananias. How would you have felt and reacted if you believed God was calling you to a task that made you fearful or seemed to be beyond your ability to do? Also try to put yourself in the place of Saul who truly believed that he was doing God's will by rounding up Christians until a powerful spiritual experience caused him to change his point of view. How would you go about trying to reorganize your beliefs, now that you realized you had been wrong?

Be sure to look up all of the accounts of Saul's conversion experience: Acts 9:1-6; 22:4-11; 26:9-18; and Galatians 1:13-17. Make notes on the similarities and differences of these accounts. Class members will be asked to do a comparative Bible study under the section "Saul Becomes a Disciple." Unless you plan to lecture, students will be searching their own Bibles for this information. You will, however, want to be prepared to supplement their remarks if necessary. Have paper on hand if students will write a diary entry.

LEADING THE CLASS

Introduction

Read the first paragraph under "Focusing on the Main Question." Provide a few moments of silence for class members to think about a challenging time in their own lives. What was the situation? How did they overcome it? How did they feel God's presence during that difficult period?

You may want to ask a few class members to briefly relate such an incident to the class.

Conclude the opening by reading or retelling the rest of the information under "Focusing on the Main Question." If you choose to retell it, be sure to include the main question for today's study: **How does Jesus confront me in my own life and enable me to meet the challenges he sets before me?**

Saul Becomes a Disciple

Invite students to share briefly, either with the whole class or in a small group, stories of changes in their own lives. Perhaps some will tell of dramatic religious conversions. Others may report on new understandings that helped them view the world in a different way. Some people may have experienced physical changes, such as blindness, that have forced them to readjust. Still others may have changed careers.

You may want to have class members do a comparative Bible study. Luke tells the story of Saul's experience three times: Acts 9:1-6, Acts 22:4-11, and Acts 26:9-18. Paul himself makes reference to this experience in Galatians 1:13-17. Some discrepancies exist among these conversion accounts, but students will pick up additional details by doing this comparative study. To do this activity, be sure that everyone reads the story from Acts 9:1-6. Ask one group to look at the account in Acts 22, a second to consider the one in Acts 26, and a third to examine Paul's own account. Allow time for each group to share their findings with the class. If the class is too small to divide into groups, choose to look at two or more accounts as time permits.

If your students enjoy activities, you may want to have them write a diary entry of the Damascus road experience. Some may choose to tell the story from Saul's point of view, while others may want to write as if they are the witnesses accompanying him. Set a time limit. Encourage several volunteers to read their accounts. You may want to note that Luke focuses on the external events, though a diary entry will include how Saul or the witnesses felt about the event. Therefore, the students will have to imagine themselves in the situation along the Damascus road.

Ananias Has a Vision

Choose a student to read Acts 9:10-16. If three students can be enlisted to read the parts of a narrator, Ananias, and the Lord, this passage will come alive for the class.

Ask the class these questions: **(1) What does the fact that God sent two visions, one to Ananias and one to Saul, suggest to you about how God works in human**

affairs? **(2) Have you ever had an experience where you felt God was calling you to do something only to learn later that another person also felt God's leading? If so, briefly describe what happened.**

Point out that Ananias was willing to take action that would benefit not only Saul but also the larger community of faith. He had to take a risk and act in spite of his fears in order to accomplish God's purpose. Ask the class:

(1) What visions for ministry does your church currently have?

(2) Recall how these ideas were brought to the attention of the church at large. Was one person responsible for sharing this vision and helping the church to begin a new ministry or program?

(3) If so, what risks did that person have to take to share this vision and work to have it implemented?

Direct the class's attention to the key verse, Acts 9:15. Here God tells Ananias that Saul is a chosen vessel for ministry. Ask the class:

(1) What seem to be the expectations for ordained clergy in your denomination or congregation?

(2) Are there members in the church (or in the class) who seem to be prime candidates for the pastorate?

(3) Are there members in the church (or in the class) who seem to have the talents for other ministries in the church, such as directors of music or Christian educators or medical missionaries?

(4) If so, how can we begin to let these members know that God may have a role for them to play as church leaders?

Overcoming Obstacles

Select a volunteer to read Acts 9:17-20.

Ask the class these questions concerning the biblical text: **(1) How might Ananias's attitude have helped or hindered Saul? (2) What happened to Saul as a result of Ananias's visit?** (Be sure to note that Saul experienced a spiritual change in that he was baptized and received the Holy Spirit. He also experienced a physical change, for his eyes were healed, he broke his fast, and his strength was restored.)

On a chalkboard or newsprint make two columns. Label one side: "Obstacles That Ananias Had to Overcome." Label the other side: "Obstacles That Saul Had to Overcome." If you have time and want to include background scripture from Acts 9:21-31, create a third column labeled: "Obstacles Other Persons Had to Overcome in Dealing with Saul." Conduct a discussion about what these obstacles might have been. List the class members' suggestions in the appropriate columns. Information under this section in "Interpreting the Scripture" may supplement the students' suggestions.

Ask the class to consider the following situations that may be similar to the ones Ananias and Saul experienced:

(1) **Ananias.** Perhaps you have been called to act as a mediator to bring a word of healing or reconciliation to someone whose actions harmed or created problems for a family or a group. How did you feel about assuming that challenging role, especially if you questioned how this person would respond to your overture?

(2) **Saul.** Perhaps at some time you believed that God has been working to change the direction of your life. If you did change directions, how do you feel God worked through you and others to help guide you in the right path? Did you come to this new direction in a relatively painless way, or did you find yourself backed into a corner before you finally said yes to God?

HELPING CLASS MEMBERS ACT

Challenge class members to be aware of at least one opportunity at home, at work, in the church, or in the community where they can bring a word or action from God that will heal or encourage someone. Maybe they would prefer not to get involved in the situation, just as Ananias wanted to stay away from Saul. Encourage students to trust God to lead them.

Ask class members to read Acts 9:15, the key verse for this lesson, at least once each day and ask themselves: How can I be an instrument for God today? Challenge them to act in whatever way seems appropriate.

Encourage each class member to think of someone he or she knows who is trying to make a change for the better. Perhaps previous broken promises or unpredictable behavior make it difficult for the student to trust this person. Challenge the members to take a step this week to show this person that the change in his or her behavior is being recognized and affirmed.

PLANNING FOR NEXT SUNDAY

Next week's lesson, entitled "No Partiality," shows the Roman soldier Cornelius accepting Christ. The witness to Jesus Christ is now extending into the Gentile community. Ask the class to read Acts 10:1–11:18, looking especially at Acts 10:30-39 and 44-48, in preparation for next week's class. Encourage them to think about how the modern church may show partiality and what differences would exist in congregations if Christians welcomed everyone without partiality.

No Partiality

PREVIEWING THE LESSON

Lesson Scripture: Acts 10:30-39, 44-48
Background Scripture: Acts 10:1–11:18
Key Verses: Acts 10:34-35

Focus of the lesson:
God's impartiality as demonstrated by the pouring out of the Holy Spirit on the Gentiles

Main question(s) of the lesson:
(1) What did the surprising revelation that God shows no partiality mean to the early Jewish Christians?
(2) What does it mean to us today?

This lesson will enable adult learners to:
(1) recognize that all persons are invited to come to God
(2) experience the challenge to traditional understandings and cherished beliefs that Peter must have faced
(3) respond by being open to spiritual truths that are new to them.

Today's lesson may be outlined as follows:
(1) Introduction
(2) Cornelius Welcomes His Guest (Acts 10:30-33)
(3) Peter Preaches a Sermon (Acts 10:34-39)
(4) God Gives the Spirit to the Gentiles (Acts 10:44-48)

FOCUSING ON THE MAIN QUESTION

Surprise! Have you ever walked into a banquet hall, a restaurant, or a friend's home and heard this word shouted as flash-bulbs nearly blinded you? Perhaps you stood still, momentarily disoriented about what was going on. Your escort had told you that you were coming for a quiet dinner, or to honor another friend. You had no idea that such a surprise was in store for you. When you finally got your bearings, perhaps you could see in retrospect that preparations were being made right under your nose, but you hadn't realized it at the time. In any case, you had to quickly read-just your expectations for the evening, step into the spotlight, and see what was about to happen.

Peter may have understood our feelings, for he was surprised by God in a very unique way. Imagine Peter as a guest in the home of his friend, Simon, a fellow tradesman who tanned leather. It's noon when Peter goes to the flat roof of Simon's house to offer prayer. He may be expecting a call for lunch, but instead he is surprised by a call from God. An angel of the Lord appears with a vision of a wide variety of animals, some clean and others unclean according to Jewish law. Peter recoils when a voice tells him to kill and eat these animals. Three times this heavenly voice tells him not to call impure what God has made clean. Yet, like the guest of honor at a surprise party who seems baffled, Peter is unsure about what is happening. Who would ever expect God to change a teaching that Peter—and generations of ancestors before him—had so rigorously observed? But dietary laws were not what this vision was all about.

Thirty miles away in Caesarea a Roman soldier had also been surprised by the inbreaking presence of an angel of the Lord. He too had a puzzling vision that ordered him to send for Peter. Cornelius did as he was told and hastily issued invitations for friends and family to gather at his home to hear what Peter had to say.

When Peter and his associates arrived and heard about Cornelius's vision, the pieces of God's surprising puzzle could finally be fit together. Something new was happening. God was not only the God of the Jews but of the Gentiles as well. The work and message of Jesus was to be shared universally with all, for "God shows no partiality" (Acts 10:34). **What did the surprising revelation that God shows no partiality mean to the early Jewish Christians? What does it mean to us today?** These two questions will help us to focus this week's lesson.

READING THE SCRIPTURE

NRSV
Acts 10:30-39

30 Cornelius replied, "Four days ago at this very hour, at three o'clock, I was praying in my house when suddenly a man in dazzling clothes stood before me. [31]He said, 'Cornelius, your prayer has been heard and your alms have been remembered before God. [32]Send therefore to Joppa and ask for Simon, who is called Peter; he is staying in the home of Simon, a tanner, by the sea.' [33]Therefore I sent for you immediately, and you have been kind enough to come. So now all of us are here in the presence of God to listen to all that the Lord has commanded you to say."

34 Then Peter began to speak to them: "I truly understand that God shows no partiality, [35]but in every nation anyone who fears him and does what is right is acceptable to him. [36]You know the message he sent to the people of Israel, preaching peace by Jesus Christ—he is Lord of all.

NIV
Acts 10:30-39

[30]Cornelius answered: "Four days ago I was in my house praying at this hour, at three in the afternoon. Suddenly a man in shining clothes stood before me [31]and said, 'Cornelius, God has heard your prayer and remembered your gifts to the poor. [32]Send to Joppa for Simon who is called Peter. He is a guest in the home of Simon the tanner, who lives by the sea.' [33]So I sent for you immediately, and it was good of you to come. Now we are all here in the presence of God to listen to everything the Lord has commanded you to tell us."

[34]Then Peter began to speak: "I now realize how true it is that God does not show favoritism [35]but accepts men from every nation who fear him and do what is right. [36]You know the message God sent to the people of Israel, telling the good news of peace through Jesus Christ, who is Lord of all. [37]You know what has happened throughout

Key Verses

ey rses

³⁷That message spread throughout Judea, beginning in Galilee after the baptism that John announced: ³⁸how God anointed Jesus of Nazareth with the Holy Spirit and with power; how he went about doing good and healing all who were oppressed by the devil, for God was with him. ³⁹We are witnesses to all that he did both in Judea and in Jerusalem.

Acts 10:44-48

44 While Peter was still speaking, the Holy Spirit fell upon all who heard the word. ⁴⁵The circumcised believers who had come with Peter were astounded that the gift of the Holy Spirit had been poured out even on the Gentiles, ⁴⁶for they heard them speaking in tongues and extolling God. Then Peter said, ⁴⁷"Can anyone withhold the water for baptizing these people who have received the Holy Spirit just as we have?" ⁴⁸So he ordered them to be baptized in the name of Jesus Christ. Then they invited him to stay for several days.

Judea, beginning in Galilee after the baptism that John preached— ³⁸how God anointed Jesus of Nazareth with the Holy Spirit and power, and how he went around doing good and healing all who were under the power of the devil, because God was with him. ³⁹"We are witnesses of everything he did in the country of the Jews and in Jerusalem.

Acts 10:44-48

⁴⁴While Peter was still speaking these words, the Holy Spirit came on all who heard the message. ⁴⁵The circumcised believers who had come with Peter were astonished that the gift of the Holy Spirit had been poured out even on the Gentiles. ⁴⁶For they heard them speaking in tongues and praising God.

Then Peter said, ⁴⁷"Can anyone keep these people from being baptized with water? They have received the Holy Spirit just as we have." ⁴⁸So he ordered that they be baptized in the name of Jesus Christ. Then they asked Peter to stay with them for a few days.

UNDERSTANDING THE SCRIPTURE

Acts 10:1-8. Cornelius is a member of the Italian regiment stationed at Caesarea. He is a God-fearer, meaning that he had engaged in Jewish religious practices such as alms-giving "to the people" (that is, to Jews) and prayer, but he has not converted to Judaism. While observing a customary Jewish prayer time at three in the afternoon, he is confronted by an angel of God who announces that God has remembered what Cornelius has done. The soldier immediately responds to the angel's order by calling three men and sending them to Joppa, about thirty miles to the south, to find Peter.

Acts 10:9-16. The next day Peter is praying, just as Cornelius had been, when an angel of the Lord unexpectedly appears to

him at noon while Peter is waiting for lunch. In a trance he sees a vision of a sheet containing animals that are both clean and unclean. God calls him to kill and eat this food, but Peter refuses on the grounds that it is unclean as specified in the dietary laws (see Leviticus 11). His words echo Ezekiel 4:14. God's words in Acts 10:15, "What God has made clean, you must not call profane," were stated three times to emphasize the message that God has cleansed them. This vision does not concern food restrictions but is meant to prepare Peter for the inclusion of all into the household of God, though Peter is not yet aware of the meaning.

Acts 10:17-23a. Peter is obviously puzzled by this vision for it is contrary to what he has learned and practiced, though Jesus "declared all foods clean" according to Mark 7:14-19. As he tries to make sense of it, Cornelius's men arrive and ask for Peter. The Spirit directs Peter to meet them. The men repeat Cornelius's vision to Peter, but he makes no mention to them of his own vision. Although he is a guest in the home of Simon the tanner (Acts 10:6), Peter extends hospitality to Cornelius's men. Luke's account enables the reader to make the connection between the two visions, but Peter apparently does not yet see the relationship.

Acts 10:23b-33. Peter, Cornelius's men, and six Jewish Christians from Joppa (see Acts 11:12) set out for Caesarea, a Hellenistic port city, the next day. Without knowing if or when Peter would come, Cornelius has invited relatives and friends to listen to the apostle. When the contingent arrived from Joppa the following day, they were met by a full household, a group that would soon become the nucleus of the church in Caesarea. Rebuffing Cornelius's attempt to worship him as a god, Peter reminds the group that his presence in a Gentile assembly is improper. He came, however, because of God's vision. Note that the vision itself concerned animals, whereas in Acts 10:28 Peter's use of "anyone" refers to persons, perhaps indicating that Peter is seeing the connection between his vision and his visit to this Gentile home. Cornelius states his visionary experience and tells Peter that he and his company are waiting expectantly for a word from the Lord through him.

Acts 10:34-43. Peter opens his sermon with words of understanding regarding the visions: "God shows no partiality." This insight opens the way for evangelism among the Gentiles. As commanded by Jesus in Acts 1:8, Peter does bear witness. He sums up the gospel message by recounting the baptism, work, death, and resurrection of Jesus, as well as his role as the universal judge of all. Peter mentions "forgiveness of sins through his name" in Acts 10:43, though he does not explicitly call Cornelius and his guests to repent.

Acts 10:44-48. Peter's message seems to be complete, though he "was still speaking" when the Spirit fell upon the listeners. The Jewish Christians who had accompanied Peter are astounded that God's gift of the Spirit is poured out on Gentiles. Yet there can be no mistaking the Spirit's presence; the new believers speak in tongues, praising God, just as Jews had done on Pentecost. This situation is unique, for the believers receive the Holy Spirit before they are baptized. The apostle orders that these believers "be baptized in the name of Jesus Christ" (Acts 10:48), though the text does not indicate that Peter himself performed the sacrament.

Acts 11:1-18. News of this event traveled quickly. When Peter reached Jerusalem, he was confronted by conservative Jewish colleagues who demanded an explanation for his behavior among Gentiles. He recounts his own vision, Cornelius's vision, and the events that occurred in Cornelius's home. Peter defends himself against his critics by arguing that since these believers had received the Holy Spirit he would be hindering God if he withheld baptism from them. The matter of including Gentiles in the Christian movement who have not first converted to Judaism seems to be put to rest with the critics praising God. This matter is far from resolved, however, and will continue to be a problem in the church.

INTERPRETING THE SCRIPTURE

Cornelius Welcomes His Guest

Picture yourself in Cornelius's place. You are a centurion in the Roman army, a commander with about one hundred soldiers in your company. Your position places you in a relatively small, elite group of military personnel. As such, you have power and status, along with a handsome retirement package. You are attracted to Judaism, perhaps because of its belief in one God (known as monotheism), rather than the many gods (known as polytheism) of your own Roman culture. You have been practicing the Jewish religion by offering prayers and giving alms to persons in need. You have a good reputation among the Jewish people, yet you have not moved from the position of a God-fearer to a proselyte. For some reason you have not chosen to convert to Judaism.

At three in the afternoon, while praying at the customary time of the Jewish evening prayer, you are suddenly confronted by a heavenly vision. An angel tells you that, as a result of your devotion, God plans to take action on your behalf. You have no idea what that might mean, and the angel certainly does not give you any details, except that you are to send men to fetch a man named Peter who is in Joppa. Being accustomed to giving orders, you immediately dispatch two slaves and a devout soldier with directions on how to find Peter.

At this point, most of us would have waited to see if this person who was as unknown to us as we were to him would even show up. Not you! You must have been dispatching other servants in all directions, for by the time Peter arrives—as you somehow knew he would—you have a house full of company. You have invited your relatives and friends to hear this man Peter. What a risk! Suppose he hadn't come. Or suppose his words would

have caused you pain or embarrassment. But he does come and you, along with those you care about, are there and ready to hear what Peter has to say.

When he arrives, after a gaffe in which you bow down as if he were a god, you recount in front of everyone the vision that prompted you to send for him. You recognize that you and your guests are in God's presence as you listen to the words God has given to you through Peter.

Can you really picture yourself in a position such as Cornelius was in? If God were to surprise you by sending a heavenly messenger to you today, would you take bold action as he did? Or would you ask God for an instant replay to be sure that you understood what was going on? Or would you just ignore the entire episode, assuming that you had been dreaming?

Cornelius welcomed Peter because he believed that he would be taught more about God through Peter's ministry. Do we do likewise, invite our friends to worship, Sunday school, church activities, or other opportunities where we feel God will be powerfully present to us? The church in Caesarea began because one man was faithful. What might we accomplish if we listen for God's voice and respond decisively to it?

Peter Preaches a Sermon

Now try putting yourself in Peter's place. While in prayer at a friend's home, you've had a puzzling vision that makes no sense to you. A Noah's-ark variety of animals has appeared to you in a sheet and a voice tells you to kill and eat these animals. This seems like a revelation from God, complete with an angel. But can this be? Is God really telling you that it is okay to eat anything, that God has made all things clean?

While you're pondering this disturbing revelation, several strangers arrive. The Holy Spirit prompts you to go with them as they request to the home of a Gentile. You leave with them the next day and arrive at this Roman soldier's home the following day. By this time you are probably asking yourself, "What am I doing here?" You have carefully observed the ways of your Jewish religion in the past. Now you are in the home of a man who is bowing down as if you were a god. Listening to his story, though, you know God has given both of you visions. You belong here. You have work to do, and that work is to preach the gospel. Again you are reminded of Jesus' words before his ascension that you are to be a witness.

You begin your witness by boldly proclaiming that God shows no partiality. People of every nation who fear and obey God are God's people. That vision you had wasn't about food, but about people! All people are pure in God's sight. Since the messengers had already told you that Cornelius was a God-fearer who was spoken well of by the Jews, you know that he knows that Jesus Christ was sent to the nation of Israel. That message began to be spread in Galilee when Jesus was baptized by John. Jesus himself went about doing good, healing the sick, and liberating those who were oppressed by demons. You and others can bear personal witness to these facts. Furthermore, this same Jesus was crucified, resurrected, and even ate and drank with you in his resurrected state. You announce that those who believe in him will receive forgiveness of sins through his name.

Now picture yourself in the audience listening to Peter. This information is very exciting, but you have always been excluded from a relationship with God because you were not Jewish. Is this man Peter really saying that God is impartial? Does he mean that anyone—even a Gentile like me—who fears and obeys God can enter into a reconciled relationship? This idea is completely overwhelming.

God Gives the Spirit to the Gentiles

Just when you think you have misunderstood Peter's message, everyone in the room begins speaking in tongues. The Holy Spirit has come upon all of you in power. It's true! You can be one of God's own people. You have never been offered such an invitation before. Your own response is one of praise and thanksgiving to God.

As you look around the room, you notice that not only are your friends and family members speaking in ecstatic utterances, but the Jewish Christian friends that Peter brought from Joppa seem to be in a state of shock. They cannot fathom that a group of Gentiles has received a gift that they thought was reserved for God's own people, the Jews. These Jewish Christians may already be wondering how the leaders in the mother church in Jerusalem are going to react to news like this. But there is no denying what is happening. Everyone is praising God, and you are a witness to this miraculous scene.

Peter recognizes that God is indeed inviting Gentiles into the fold. They are no longer to be seen as impure people who should be avoided. Instead, they are brothers and sisters in the faith. "Can anyone withhold the water for baptizing these people who have received the Holy Spirit just as we have?" Peter asks (Acts 10:47). No, they cannot be denied baptism in Jesus' name, for God has decided that they too are part of God's household.

As you imagine this scene in Caesarea from the point of view of a twentieth-century Christian in North America, what relevance does the story have in your own life? Perhaps you are like Peter, who had his religious beliefs so well in hand that he could not make sense of a surprise visit from God that announced, in essence, that what he had believed and practiced all his life was incorrect. Or can you picture yourself as someone who feels excluded from the church because of a bad habit or addiction or a fear that people won't think you are good enough to join them? Suddenly you are surprised to learn that God has a word for you. God loves you and has sent Jesus the Christ to care for you physically, mentally, and spiritually.

Finally, perhaps you are an upstanding church member who, like Peter's friends, also assumes that you know what God is willing to do. Suddenly you are confronted by an amazing example of God at work among people you didn't even think knew or cared about God. Yet the evidence is clear. God is working in their lives, and who can deny such people a place in the church? To recognize this possibility likely means that the church will need to open its doors wider to receive those who come. It likely means that the church will have to adjust its thinking, its programs, and its ministry. But who knows? That may be exactly the vision that God is trying to send to the church today. Are we responding with the joy, excitement, and openness to new possibilities that marked the scene in Cornelius's home, or do we have other agenda that makes such a scene impossible for us to imagine?

SHARING THE SCRIPTURE

PREPARING TO TEACH

Note that this week's lesson includes much background scripture. Become familiar with that material, which is discussed in the "Understanding the Scripture" section, so that you can fill in gaps between the parts of the story that are included in the body of the lesson.

You may want to have a map on hand so that class members can visualize where Caesarea and Joppa are in relation to each other. Such a map can be found on page 147 of *The Bible Teacher Kit* (Abingdon Press). Joppa, now a suburb of Tel Aviv, was an important harbor in ancient Palestine. Caesarea, about thirty miles north of Joppa, was a Hellenistic port city that served as the capital of Palestine for nearly six hundred years after a new city was constructed by Herod the Great. This geography may be of interest to the class since Cornelius's men had to make the trip to Joppa and return to Caesarea with Peter and his associates.

Think about a time when you learned something, perhaps a religious truth, that seemed contrary to what you had previously believed or understood. You may want to write in your spiritual journal about how this surprising development took place and what affect it had on your behavior and attitudes.

Have paper and pencil on hand if you choose to do the writing activity under "Peter Preaches a Sermon."

If your class prefers a lecture format, look carefully at "Interpreting the Scripture." This section can be used as the basis for your talk, but it is written in such a way as to draw the reader or listener into the action. This approach may be different from what the class is accustomed to, but it can be a helpful means of opening up the Bible story if you are willing to try it.

LEADING THE CLASS

Introduction

If your class prefers a lecture, use the information under "Focusing on the Main Question" to introduce the lesson.

If the class enjoys discussion, ask these questions: **(1) Have you ever been the guest of honor at a surprise party? (2) If so, how did you feel when you first recognized that what you expected to happen was different from what was really going on?**

Link this discussion to today's lesson by pointing out that two characters, Peter and Cornelius, were surprised by God through heavenly visions. Cornelius was given specific directions, which he fulfilled. Peter was given a vision that was contrary to what he had been taught and understood to be appropriate behavior. Like the honored guest, Peter had difficulty in comprehending what was happening.

Announce that we will be looking at the following two questions as we study our lesson from Acts today: **What did the surprising revelation that God shows no partiality mean to the early Jewish Christians? What does it mean to us today?**

Cornelius Welcomes His Guest

Use the information from Acts 10:1-33 found under "Understanding the Scripture" to set the stage for this portion of the lesson. Be sure to spend some time helping the class understand that Cornelius exercised Jewish piety (prayers and alms-giving), but he had not formally converted to Judaism. Also be certain that the class understands that the content of Cornelius's vision was basically a direction from God. He was told that God was pleased by his prayers and alms. He was also told to send for Peter. Point out that Cornelius had apparently never met Peter, so he had no way of knowing if Peter would even come, or what Peter might say or do when he arrived. Nonetheless, Cornelius acts immediately in response to the vision. While his servants are en route to Peter's lodging in Joppa, Cornelius invites friends and family to join him to hear what Peter has to say.

If you plan to use a map to show Joppa and Caesarea, this would be an appropriate time in the lesson to do so.

Select a volunteer to read aloud Acts 10:30-33, which picks up with Peter's arrival at Cornelius's home.

Ask the class to answer the following questions as if they were Cornelius:
(1) Why did you act on this vision by sending for Peter? After all, you are not a converted Jew.
(2) How did you convince all these other people to come? What did you tell them?
(3) What do you expect to receive from Peter?
If the class enjoys activities, use the three questions above to create a role-play between Cornelius and one or more of the men who accompanied Peter from Joppa.

Peter Preaches a Sermon

Select several volunteers to read aloud Acts 10:34-39 from different Bible translations. End with the word "Jerusalem."

Ask members to state what Peter is saying according to Luke's account. List their responses on a chalkboard or newsprint.

Then point out that Peter's preaching is recorded here in very summarized form. Invite the class to be more specific about what Peter might have said. Consider doing this exercise in one of two ways. One way is to distribute paper and pencils and ask each student to write his or her own speech. Set a time limit, after which you call for volunteers to read what they have written. Another way is to divide into partners or teams. Ask these groups to talk about the most important points they would make to someone who had never heard the good news of Jesus. Either way, the students are acting as witnesses to what they believe about Jesus.

God Gives the Spirit to the Gentiles

Choose someone to read Acts 10:44-48.
Point out that Luke notes the astonishment of the Jewish Christians who accompanied Peter when God gives the Holy Spirit to these Gentiles (Acts 10:45). Ask the class members to give examples from church history or their own experience

when persons that certain Christians did not expect to be included in the church were clearly brought into the fellowship by God. One such example would be the laborers, such as coal miners, who had no place in the established church but accepted Christ as a result of John Wesley's preaching in eighteenth-century England. Another example might be the inclusion of women in ordained ministry and other positions of authority from which they were excluded (and still are in some denominations).

Ask the class:

(1) **How do you believe that the church is enriched by the inclusion of those who formerly had no place in it?**

(2) **In Peter's day, the Gentiles were the ones who had no place in the church. What groups of people seem to be forgotten in the mission and ministry of many modern churches?**

(3) *Target the question more specifically to your own congregation by asking:* **Are people from all age groups, differing racial and ethnic groups, varying socioeconomic classes, vastly different educational backgrounds and careers, and differing family situations and lifestyles welcomed and made to feel a part of our church?**

(4) **What implications do God's words to Peter, as recorded in today's key verses from Acts 10:34-35, have for modern Christian mission and evangelism outreach efforts in general and for our congregation in particular?**

HELPING CLASS MEMBERS ACT

Encourage students to be aware of situations this week in which God speaks to them in unexpected or surprising ways. Perhaps they learn a spiritual truth as a result of an interaction with a child or a sick friend. Maybe they find new meaning in a familiar Bible verse or story. Or perhaps an incident causes them to recognize God at work in ways they had not previously experienced.

Challenge class members to make an intentional effort to share a word or deed of witness this week with someone they would not expect to find in church, such as a grumpy store clerk who is always fussing, or the homeless person who approaches them for money as they go to work, or an alcoholic neighbor.

PLANNING FOR NEXT SUNDAY

Ask the class to prepare for next Sunday's session by reading Acts 11:19-30 and 12:24-25. This lesson concerns a revival at Antioch that began after believers were scattered as a result of persecution. As students read, ask them to be especially aware of insights concerning purposeful living that can be drawn from these passages.

PURPOSEFUL LIVING

PREVIEWING THE LESSON

Lesson Scripture: Acts 11:19-30; 12:24-25
Background Scripture: Acts 11:19-30; 12:24-25
Key Verse: Acts 11:23

Focus of the lesson:
loving service offered in God's name

Main question(s) of the lesson:
(1) How can I live purposely as a Christian?

This lesson will enable adult learners to:
(1) learn how Paul and Barnabas worked tirelessly as servants of God on behalf of
    the fledgling church in Antioch
(2) identify their own mission or purpose in life
(3) respond by serving others.

Today's lesson may be outlined as follows:
(1) Introduction
(2) Mission in Antioch (Acts 11:19-26)
(3) Relief for the Hungry (Acts 11:27-30)
(4) The Church Continues to Grow (Acts 12:24-25)

FOCUSING ON THE MAIN QUESTION

Who am I? What is my purpose in life? These questions confront all of us, usually in our teen years. Changes in our life situations may cause us to revisit these questions at different stages in our lives, perhaps prompting a career change or a refocusing of our time and talents.

People who are clear about their own purpose in life strike us as having well integrated personalities. We use such phrases as "his walk matches his talk" or "she certainly has her act together" to describe those who live purposefully. Often these individuals have strong convictions that they fearlessly voice, regardless of the cost. Criticism, ridicule, or other obstacles do not deter them from living according to the purpose they have identified for their own lives. They set a course for their lives and appear to move unerringly in that direction.

Often we admire such people because they seem to know how to do the right thing at the right time. A need arises and they meet it. Leadership is called for, so they provide it. A problem or conflict must be solved, and they step in to offer a creative solution. Purposeful adults are willing to serve as role models for others.

Of course, the purpose that one identifies may be for good or for evil. Mother Teresa has a clear purpose for her life, but so did Adolph Hitler. As we study the Bible we see that God has an overarching purpose for our lives: loving service in God's name to others. Depending on our God-given talents, that service may take many forms, but its purpose is to build up the kingdom of God. Perhaps we are called to witness to the good news at home or in a far country. Maybe God calls us to respond to specific needs of others. Or maybe we have the gifts to mentor a young person.

The main figures in today's lesson from Acts—Barnabas, Saul, Agabus, John Mark, and countless unnamed believers in Antioch—all lived purposeful lives unto God. Through their witness and work other converts were brought into a new relationship with God in Jesus Christ. As we study their stories today, we will want to examine our own lives by asking: **How can I live purposefully as a Christian?**

READING THE SCRIPTURE

NRSV
Acts 11:19-30

19 Now those who were scattered because of the persecution that took place over Stephen traveled as far as Phoenicia, Cyprus, and Antioch, and they spoke the word to no one except Jews. 20But among them were some men of Cyprus and Cyrene who, on coming to Antioch, spoke to the Hellenists also, proclaiming the Lord Jesus. 21The hand of the Lord was with them, and a great number became believers and turned to the Lord. 22News of this came to the ears of the church in Jerusalem, and they sent Barnabas to Antioch. 23When he came and saw the grace of God, he rejoiced, and he exhorted them all to remain faithful to the Lord with steadfast devotion; 24for he was a good man, full of the Holy Spirit and of faith. And a great many people were brought to the Lord. 25Then Barnabas went to Tarsus to look for Saul, 26and when he had found him, he brought him to Antioch. So it was that for an entire year they met with the church and taught a great many people, and it was in Antioch that the disciples were first called "Christians."

27 At that time prophets came down from Jerusalem to Antioch. 28One of them named Agabus stood up and predicted by

NIV
Acts 11:19-30

19Now those who had been scattered by the persecution in connection with Stephen traveled as far as Phoenicia, Cyprus and Antioch, telling the message only to Jews. 20Some of them, however, men from Cyprus and Cyrene, went to Antioch and began to speak to Greeks also, telling them the good news about the Lord Jesus. 21The Lord's hand was with them, and a great number of people believed and turned to the Lord.

22News of this reached the ears of the church at Jerusalem, and they sent Barnabas to Antioch. 23When he arrived and saw the evidence of the grace of God, he was glad and encouraged them all to remain true to the Lord with all their hearts. 24He was a good man, full of the Holy Spirit and faith, and a great number of people were brought to the Lord.

25Then Barnabas went to Tarsus to look for Saul, 26and when he found him, he brought him to Antioch. So for a whole year Barnabas and Saul met with the church and taught great numbers of people. The disciples were called Christians first at Antioch.

27During this time some prophets came down from Jerusalem to Antioch. 28One of them, named Agabus, stood up and

Key Verse

Key Vers

the Spirit that there would be a severe famine over all the world; and this took place during the reign of Claudius. ²⁹The disciples determined that according to their ability, each would send relief to the believers living in Judea; ³⁰this they did, sending it to the elders by Barnabas and Saul.

Acts 12:24-25

24 But the word of God continued to advance and gain adherents. ²⁵Then after completing their mission Barnabas and Saul returned to Jerusalem and brought with them John, whose other name was Mark.

through the Spirit predicted that a severe famine would spread over the entire Roman world. (This happened during the reign of Claudius.) ²⁹The disciples, each according to his ability, decided to provide help for the brothers living in Judea. ³⁰This they did, sending their gift to the elders by Barnabas and Saul.

Acts 12:24-25

²⁴But the word of God continued to increase and spread.

²⁵When Barnabas and Saul had finished their mission, they returned from Jerusalem, taking with them John, also called Mark.

UNDERSTANDING THE SCRIPTURE

Acts 11:19-21. Luke begins this section by referring to the persecution described in Acts 8:1. As a result of this persecution, Christians fled Jerusalem along the Mediterranean coast to Phoenician cities, Antioch, and the island of Cyprus. According to verse 19, these believers witnessed only to Jews. Verse 20 indicates that believers from the island of Cyprus and the city of Cyrene in northern Africa proclaimed Jesus to the Gentiles, marking the first widespread attempt to reach non-Jews. The efforts of the witnesses result in explosive church growth. This success is attributed to the "hand of the Lord," a familiar Old Testament image of God's supportive power found, for example, in Exodus 9:3 and Joshua 4:24.

Acts 11:22-26. To authenticate the work, Barnabas was sent by the Jerusalem church to Antioch. His role there would have been similar to the one played by Peter and John in Samaria (Acts 8:14-24). Barnabas, whose name means "son of encouragement," was a native of Cyprus (Acts 4:36), "a good man, full of the Holy Spirit and of faith" (Acts 11:24). The grace of God was clearly evident among the Christians at Antioch, so Barnabas

exhorted them to remain steadfastly devoted to the Lord. The potential for ministry was so great in this major Syrian city that Barnabas left for a while to find Saul and bring him there. The church in Antioch grew to such an extent that followers of Christ were called Christians. Scholars debate as to whether the name was given by outsiders or whether Christians took this name for themselves. This title may signal the first time that the believers were seen as separate from Judaism. Originally it may have been a negative title for it means "partisans of Christ," but scholars disagree as to whether it was used derogatorily.

Acts 11:27-30. The prophet Agabus is mentioned only here and in Acts 21:10-11 where he makes a prediction about Paul. In response to his prophecy concerning a severe famine, Christians in Antioch took up a collection to benefit believers living in Judea. The famine, predicted to occur worldwide during the reign of Claudius (41–54 C.E.), is probably one that happened in 46–48 C.E. in Palestine. Luke records that Saul accompanied Barnabas to Jerusalem to turn over the offering. While the collection was likely an accurate fact, scholars question whether Saul went at this time because Luke seems to contradict Saul's own record of his travels. This passage mentions two groups in the church—prophets and elders. Luke often referred to Old Testament prophets, whose writings he quotes, but this is the first mention of New Testament prophets whose major purpose was to exhort others to live righteously. Agabus is one of the charismatic prophets in the New Testament church. Similarly, this is Luke's first reference to elders in the Christian church. Perhaps these persons functioned in local congregations, though Luke never defines this office as he understands it.

Acts 12:24-25. Despite persecution that includes the martyrdom of James, the son of Zebedee, and Peter's miraculous escape from prison (see Acts 12:1-23), people still continue to join the Christian movement in response to the witness of the gospel. Acts 12:24 is a typical Lucan summary of the growth of the church. Acts 12:25 refers to Barnabas and Saul. They were last mentioned in Acts 11:30 as they were on their way from Antioch to Jerusalem with money for famine relief. Based on that previous information, the reader would con-

clude that Barnabas and Saul should be returning from Jerusalem to the church in Antioch. The word "from" is used in some English translations, including the KJV and NIV. The best ancient manuscripts, however, say "to Jerusalem," which is the translation seen in the NRSV. If these usually reliable manuscripts are correct, the reader is left to wonder whether Saul and Barnabas had already returned to Antioch and were going again to Jerusalem. In any event, a young man named John Mark is with them. Later known as Mark, the gospel writer, John Mark was the son of Mary, a devout woman who hosted prayer meetings in her home (Acts 12:12). In the year 46 C.E., John Mark accompanies Saul and Barnabas on a missionary tour from Antioch to Cyprus to Perga. Later, when the two were ready to embark on a second missionary journey, Saul and Barnabas argue over whether John Mark should be included. Saul argues against taking him because John Mark had "deserted them in Pamphylia" (Acts 15:38). Barnabas wants to include him. Since the dispute could not be resolved, Barnabas took Mark and went to Cyprus, while Paul chose another companion, Silas, and headed for Syria.

INTERPRETING THE SCRIPTURE

Mission in Antioch

In Acts 11:19-26, Luke records a mission to the Greeks in Antioch. The impetus for this mission is the persecution that took place in Jerusalem after Stephen was stoned. While some Christians in Antioch went exclusively to the Jews, others preached to the Hellenists. The people referred to in Acts 11:20 may have been Greek-speaking Jews, but more likely they were Gentiles. Those who witnessed were from Cyrene, located in the modern African country of Libya, and from the Mediterranean island of Cyprus.

God moved mightily in this area, though the church in Jerusalem had not commissioned any missionaries to go there. Apparently the spontaneous witness of Christians brought new sheep into the fold. These unnamed witnesses had experienced a profound change in their own lives, which they obviously shared with others. Although they were forced to flee from Jerusalem, they remained undeterred by the threat of persecution.

Only after news of the great number of converts reached Jerusalem did the mother church send an emissary to confirm the work. Barnabas, a Cypriot Jew (Acts 4:36), was chosen to go to Antioch where he became a key figure in the life of the growing church. When he reached Antioch, he knew that God's grace was at work. Acting in accordance with his name—which means "son of encouragement"—Barnabas encouraged believers "to remain faithful to the Lord with steadfast devotion" (Acts 11:23).

Throngs of people became believers. The church was growing so rapidly that Barnabas sought Saul's assistance. Together they spent a year in Antioch witnessing and teaching others about Jesus. The Christian presence was being felt to the extent that believers were first called Christians in Antioch.

Such a scene causes us to reflect on the size and zeal of the Christian community in our own area. Are people so enthusiastically telling others about Jesus that denominational leaders have to rush to found a new congregation? Do church leaders need to hire additional staff to meet the needs of growing congregations with diverse ministries? These are exciting thoughts! More likely, though, leaders are concerned about how to fill existing buildings and pay the bills. In many cases, leaders are striving to revitalize congregations that only want to hear soothing words from the pulpit and engage in programs that require only minimal commitment. Such congregations are no longer taking the risks and challenges necessary to bring others to Christ.

Perhaps what many of our church members are lacking—both individually and collectively—is a focused purpose. Maybe our problem is that church is just another menu item on our smorgasbord of opportunities. We go to church when we have a need or when its demands do not conflict with other priorities. Possibly we feel foolish or insecure about speaking on behalf of Christ because the reality of Christ's pervasive love is not the real center of our lives. We know Christ as an object of academic study but not as the very core of our being.

If modern North American Christians are going to live with the zeal and purpose of our first-century counterparts, we must begin to see ourselves in mission and service to others. We must be willing to make an unshakable commitment to God that is lived out through a vital, active church that is drawing others unto itself and sending each member into the world to fulfill the purpose to which God calls us.

Relief for the Hungry

Concerns for hungry persons permeate the Bible. From God's provision of food in the garden (Genesis 1:30), and manna in the wilderness (Exodus 16:31-35), to Joseph's stewardship of food in Egypt (Genesis 41:25-36), to the laws regarding gleaning (Deuteronomy 24:21), to the prayer of Hannah (1 Samuel 2:5), to Mary's Magnificat (Luke 1:53), to Jesus' feeding the multitudes (Matthew 14:16-21), to Jesus' words of commendation for those who have fed the hungry (Matthew 25:35), it is clear that God has great concern for those who do not have enough to eat.

During the first century most workers earned only a denarius a day—if they had work at all. Hunger was a very real issue. "Give us this day our daily bread" was not just a gratuitous comment; it was the cry of those who knew what is was like to be hungry. The poor masses lived, as we would say, on the edge. Being able to afford bread was one problem. Scarcity of bread due to a famine was another threat to poor and rich alike.

Consequently, when a charismatic prophet known as Agabus told the church at Antioch that a severe famine would strike, they wasted no time in taking an offering to help the victims. This was a freewill offering, given by each one according to his or her financial means. Although the prophet had said this famine would be worldwide, historical accounts do not support that prediction. They do, however, record a famine in Palestine beginning in 46 C.E. during the reign of Claudius. Barnabas took the proceeds from this offering to the church leaders in Jerusalem. Although Luke records that Saul went with Barnabas, scholars debate this point because it does not jibe with Paul's own account of his travels, as pieced together from his letters. Whether Saul accompanied Barnabas or not, relief was sent to Jerusalem to aid victims of the famine.

Such aid was—and continues to be—a major expectation in the Christian church. We are called to feed the hungry whether they live in our neighborhood, our larger community, our nation, or across the globe. Many countries experience hunger as a result of famine. In other nations, political strife prevents much needed food supplies from reaching the victims of hunger. In other countries, including our own, some are hungry at least several days during the month because they cannot afford to buy food.

As Christians we are called to be purposeful in addressing the profound issue of hunger. We can do so by supporting denominational, ecumenical, or other nonprofit organizations devoted to fighting hunger. Some of these groups, such as Bread for the World, take political action to end or ease hunger in the long term. Others use their resources to feed the hungry on a short-term basis, perhaps with a meal today or a three day supply of food from a pantry. Still other organizations try to take both a short-term and long-term approach. Christians need to be involved, as the church at Antioch was, in whatever ways possible to ensure that all, regardless of who they are or where they live, have access to an adequate supply of nutritious food.

The Church Continues to Grow

The spontaneous witness to Jesus Christ, which began as a result of persecuted Christians fleeing Jerusalem to live in Antioch, has mushroomed into a vibrant church. Some modern skeptics may say that such growth could not happen today, especially not in large, often troubled urban areas. Yet, Antioch in Syria was the third largest city in the Roman Empire. Home to Jews, Jewish and Gentile Christians, and a large population of adherents of mystery cults, this commercial hub on the Orontes River had a cosmopolitan population of about 800,000. Good access to communication and transportation made it an ideal site for missionary work. Christianity flourished here, even without any well planned blitz of the city or church growth gimmicks that we might consider necessary today.

Why was this church so vital? Luke answers this question for us in Acts 12:24. Neither church planners nor growth ploys were operative here. The church grew because of the Word of God. It alone was responsible for the large influx of believers into the newly forming church. Luke's description may slightly echo Isaiah 55:11 that states that God's word will not return empty. When God's word is sent forth in power, amazing results are bound to occur.

The Antiochene church was also vital because leaders such as Saul and Barnabas taught the new converts over an extended period of time (Acts 11:26). Christian education was a crucial component in the life of the early church. One reason that our modern churches may be experiencing decline is that we relegate Christian education to children. That notion would have been unfathomable in the early church. Yet far too many modern adults assume that whatever they learned in third grade Sunday school will support their spiritual journey throughout life. As is the case with reading or math skills, elementary education lays a foundation, but spiritually mature believers must continue to build upon that foundation.

The mature believers were expected to help and mentor younger believers. Barnabas acts a mentor for his cousin, John Mark (Colossians 4:10), whom he involves in ministry (Acts 12:25). When we look around our churches today, do we see enthusiastic, mature Christians acting as role models and mentors for family members, children, and teens? We need to take a cue from the early church and begin to draw more of our young people into active leadership roles. Not all attempts will be successful, as Saul found with John Mark (Acts 15:38). But Saul did not give up on mentoring, for he took Silas with him to Syria (Acts 15:40-41). If we want to see our own churches grow, we need to be purposeful in including our youth in ministry.

SHARING THE SCRIPTURE

PREPARING TO TEACH

Today's lesson mentions numerous places: Phoenicia and two of its major cities, Tyre and Sidon; Cyprus, an island in the Mediterranean; Antioch, the third largest city in the Roman Empire, located on the Orontes River in Syria; Cyrene, located on the northern coast of Africa; Tarsus, a prosperous commercial city on the Cydnus River; Judea, Caesarea, and Jerusalem. Try to secure a map of the Roman Empire during the New Testament period to help the class visualize how the gospel is spreading out from its center in Jerusalem. If your students are particularly interested in geography, you may want to locate additional information on these areas. *Bible Teacher Kit*, available through Cokesbury, is an excellent resource for maps and other information.

Keep an eye out for written or broadcast articles concerning hunger this week. Clip them or be prepared to retell them so that the class understands that the issue of hunger is ever present, even in our agriculturally fertile and economically prosperous country.

Also be prepared to offer class members a list—even a short one—of agencies that they can support in the fight against hunger. Your pastor should be able to identify denominational and perhaps ecumenical groups that are involved in this issue. Some communities publish resource directories, often available at public libraries, that list agencies in the area involved in hunger-related issues. Your church itself may offer a soup kitchen or food pantry. Perhaps an involved class member could talk about such a program.

If students normally do not have paper and pencils, have some available for use in the "Introduction" activity.

LEADING THE CLASS

Introduction

Before class, write these sentence stems on a chalkboard or newsprint. Keep them covered until the class has assembled. Then distribute slips of paper and pencils and ask each person to complete the sentences:

(1) The purpose or main goal of my life is. . . .
(2) Persons who know me can figure out that this is my purpose or goal because. . . .
(3) I think God's purpose or main goal for my life is. . . .
(4) The reason that my purpose matches/ does not match what I believe to be God's purpose for me is that. . . .

Spend a few moments talking generally about the topic of living with purpose. Allow a few volunteers to share what they have written, but do not press for response on this personal issue. Announce today's main question: **How can I live purposefully as a Christian?**

If your class would not be comfortable doing this kind of activity, open the class by reading or paraphrasing "Focusing on the Main Question."

Mission in Antioch

Select a volunteer to read aloud Acts 11:19-26.

Use a map if possible to locate the places referred to in this segment.

Ask the class to give you words or phrases that describe the state of the forming church in Antioch. Although Luke does not provide such words, students should be able to deduce from his comments that the church is lively, vital, growing, filled with God's grace, witnessing to those who are outside the church, faithful, devoted, purposeful, connected to a mother church that will provide leadership, distinctive from the rest of the society around it (as evidenced by its new name, "Christian"), and engaged in teaching. As answers are suggested write them on a chalkboard or newsprint.

Personalize the discussion by asking class members to describe their own congregation. Do not let the discussion degenerate into a critique on the pastor or church leadership, but do allow class members to voice honest, constructive criticisms if they arise.

Close this segment by asking class members, **"What do you understand the purpose of our own congregation to be."** If they cannot articulate a purpose or mission that is undergirded by funding and programs, then you may want to talk with the pastor and lay leadership about creating and publicizing such a focus.

Relief for the Hungry

Choose someone to read Acts 11:27-30.

Use the information in this section under "Interpreting the Scripture" and "Understanding the Scripture" to set the stage regarding hunger and the impor-

tance of the church's response to the threat of a famine.

Ask the class: **What is being done by our church, our community, or our government to fight hunger locally and globally?** Supplement students' answers with any news articles you have gathered and/or with lists of agencies that you have been able to compile.

The issue of hunger needs to be discussed, but more importantly, it needs to be addressed. At this point, be sure to lift up the suggested activity regarding hunger under "Helping Class Members Act." If your class is very action oriented, they may be willing to investigate the possibility of starting a soup kitchen or food pantry in your church building or in regularly supporting a nearby established program. They may also be willing to become involved in an organization that takes political action, such as making calls or writing letters to elected officials, to end hunger.

The Church Continues to Grow

Direct the class's attention to Acts 12:24-25.

Ask the class: **Why was the ministry in Antioch so fruitful?** Use the information under this section in "Interpreting the Scripture" to supplement their answers.

Relate the church in Antioch to your own congregation by asking:

(1) **Are we experiencing growth as a congregation? If not, why not? If so, what is it about our church that is drawing persons to it?**

(2) **Are we offering a well-rounded program of adult education? If not, what kinds of classes do we need to add? If so, what kinds of members are participating? What kinds of members are not involved? Is there anything we can do to invite them into the educational ministry?**

(3) **What opportunities do our children and teenagers have to work with an adult mentor in our church? If we have**

no such formal or informal arrangement, who among our class might be
interested in volunteering as a mentor,
perhaps for a limited time to work
with a confirmation class student?
(4) **Five years from now, what would you
like to be able to say regarding numerical and spiritual growth in your congregation over the ensuing five years?**

HELPING CLASS MEMBERS ACT

Challenge class members to become
involved in the fight against hunger. Jesus'
expectation that we feed the hungry
(Matthew 25:35) is still valid today, for
countless thousands of people go to bed
each night hungry or malnourished. One
path to involvement is to join an organization such as Bread for the World that lobbies
Congress and educates people about worldwide hunger. For information about this
broadly-based ecumenical group that is supported by individuals and denominations,
write to Bread for the World, 1100 Wayne
Avenue, Suite 1000, Silver Spring, MD
20910. Another means of involvement is
through local soup kitchens or food pantries,
many of which are sponsored by Christian
churches. Class members can provide
hands-on assistance to these organizations.

Encourage class members to serve as
mentors for a new member or younger
person. Some churches use mentors to
work with confirmands. If this is true in
your congregation, suggest it as an option.

PLANNING FOR NEXT SUNDAY

The final unit of our study of Acts
begins next week. Ask class members
to read Acts 13–14, noting that the
focus of our session will be on Acts
13:1-5 and 14:1-7, 24-27. Here we will
again see Saul (now called Paul), Barnabas, and John Mark as they bring the
good news of Jesus to the Gentiles.

A GOSPEL FOR EVERYONE

PREVIEWING THE LESSON

Lesson Scripture: Acts 13:1-5; 14:1-7, 24-27
Background Scripture: Acts 13–14
Key Verse: Acts 14:27

Focus of the lesson:
the continuing mission to share the good news with the Gentiles

Main question(s) of the lesson:
(1) Are we willing, like Paul and Barnabas, to take on new challenges for ministry so that everyone might be invited into God's Kingdom?

This lesson will enable adult learners to:
(1) appreciate the challenges Paul and Barnabas faced in order to invite all people into God's kingdom
(2) evaluate the outreach of their own congregation
(3) respond by actively supporting a mission project or missionary.

Today's lesson may be outlined as follows:
(1) Introduction
(2) Commissioning Missionaries (Acts 13:1-5)
(3) Responding to the Good News (Acts 14:1-7)
(4) Reporting on Ministry (Acts 14:24-27)

FOCUSING ON THE MAIN QUESTION

"Come one, come all to the greatest show on earth." The circus is coming to town! Everyone is invited to this dazzling spectacle of color, pageantry, and daredevil action. Patrons line up to buy tickets. Service clubs solicit contributions so that poor children can go and enjoy the show. Even those who cannot attend may watch outside as the animals and equipment are unloaded. The circus truly offers something for everyone.

Can we say the same thing about our church? Is everyone really invited and made to feel welcomed? Is there something about the church's mission and ministry that attracts people of all ages? Is the church enabling persons, who for whatever reason would not otherwise attend, to come and participate? Do people invite their friends to church, just as they get a group together to go to the circus? Is the gospel preached, taught, and acted upon in such a way that people can easily say yes to Christian discipleship?

Led by the Holy Spirit, the early church began to recognize that the gospel truly was for everyone—including Gentiles. The missionaries went not only into the synagogue but also out into the streets to preach the Word of God. Throngs gathered around Paul and Barnabas, eager to hear what they had to say and see what they would do. Ordinary citizens and political leaders heard the word. People of different races, ethnic groups, and nations were invited into the kingdom of God. Some accepted that invitation.

Unlike the circus, however, one need not pay for a ticket. Yet the cost of discipleship is very high. Paul and Barnabas faced increasing persecution as they went from city to city on their first missionary journey. Harsh words against these two men later escalate into violence. In Lystra,

Paul is stoned and thought to be dead. He perseveres, returning to those same cities that persecuted him because he wanted to strengthen the newborn churches.

When Paul and Barnabas finally return to Antioch in Syria, about eighteen months after they left, they share stories of their encounters with friends at home. Despite the hostility and danger they have faced, these two missionaries recognize that the door to the kingdom of heaven has been opened wider than ever before. Gentiles are now invited to come to what is truly life's greatest experience: a relationship with Jesus. As we study our lesson today, let's ask ourselves: **Are we willing, like Paul and Barnabas, to take on new challenges for ministry so that everyone might be invited into God's kingdom?**

READING THE SCRIPTURE

NRSV
Acts 13:1-5

1 Now in the church at Antioch there were prophets and teachers: Barnabas, Simeon who was called Niger, Lucius of Cyrene, Manaen a member of the court of Herod the ruler, and Saul. ²While they were worshiping the Lord and fasting, the Holy Spirit said, "Set apart for me Barnabas and Saul for the work to which I have called them." ³Then after fasting and praying they laid their hands on them and sent them off.

⁴So, being sent out by the Holy Spirit, they went down to Seleucia; and from there they sailed to Cyprus. ⁵When they arrived at Salamis, they proclaimed the word of God in the synagogues of the Jews. And they had John also to assist them.

Acts 14:1-7

1 The same thing occurred in Iconium, where Paul and Barnabas went into the Jewish synagogue and spoke in such a way that a great number of both Jews and

NIV
Acts 13:1-5

1 In the church at Antioch there were prophets and teachers: Barnabas, Simeon called Niger, Lucius of Cyrene, Manaen (who had been brought up with Herod the tetrarch) and Saul. ²While they were worshiping the Lord and fasting, the Holy Spirit said, "Set apart for me Barnabas and Saul for the work to which I have called them." ³So after they had fasted and prayed, they placed their hands on them and sent them off.

⁴The two of them, sent on their way by the Holy Spirit, went down to Seleucia and sailed from there to Cyprus. ⁵When they arrived at Salamis, they proclaimed the word of God in the Jewish synagogues. John was with them as their helper.

Acts 14:1-7

1 At Iconium Paul and Barnabas went as usual into the Jewish synagogue. There they spoke so effectively that a great number of Jews and Gentiles believed. ²But the

NOVEMBER 5

Greeks became believers. ²But the unbelieving Jews stirred up the Gentiles and poisoned their minds against the brothers. ³So they remained for a long time, speaking boldly for the Lord, who testified to the word of his grace by granting signs and wonders to be done through them. ⁴But the residents of the city were divided; some sided with the Jews, and some with the apostles. ⁵And when an attempt was made by both Gentiles and Jews, with their rulers, to mistreat them and to stone them, ⁶the apostles learned of it and fled to Lystra and Derbe, cities of Lycaonia, and to the surrounding country; ⁷and there they continued proclaiming the good news.

Acts 14:24-27

24 Then they passed through Pisidia and came to Pamphylia. ²⁵When they had spoken the word in Perga, they went down to Attalia. ²⁶From there they sailed back to Antioch, where they had been commended to the grace of God for the work that they had completed. ²⁷When they arrived, they called the church together and related all that God had done with them, and how he had opened a door of faith for the Gentiles.

Jews who refused to believe stirred up the Gentiles and poisoned their minds against the brothers. ³So Paul and Barnabas spent considerable time there, speaking boldly for the Lord, who confirmed the message of his grace by enabling them to do miraculous signs and wonders. ⁴The people of the city were divided; some sided with the Jews, others with the apostles. ⁵There was a plot afoot among the Gentiles and Jews, together with their leaders, to mistreat them and stone them. ⁶But they found out about it and fled to the Lycaonian cities of Lystra and Derbe and to the surrounding country, ⁷where they continued to preach the good news.

Acts 14:24-27

²⁴After going through Pisidia, they came into Pamphylia, ²⁵and when they had preached the word in Perga, they went down to Attalia.

²⁶From Attalia they sailed back to Antioch, where they had been committed to the grace of God for the work they had now completed. ²⁷On arriving there, they gathered the church together and reported all that God had done through them and how he had opened the door of faith to the Gentiles.

Key Verse

UNDERSTANDING THE SCRIPTURE

Acts 13:1-5. A new phase of missionary activity begins as the gospel spreads westward. Acts 13:1–14:28 is generally referred to as Paul's first missionary journey. During a time of worship and fasting at the church in Antioch, the Holy Spirit prompted the church to "set apart Barnabas and Saul for the work to which I have called them" (Acts 13:2). The mission thus begins at the initiative of God, who has appointed these two persons to undertake the work. Their colleagues fast, pray, and lay hands of blessing upon them. The reference to "prophets and teachers" (Acts 13:1) indicates the spiritual vitality of the

Antiochene church. Except for Barnabas and Saul, the persons named are unknown as individuals. Niger means black. Cyrene had a large contingent of Jewish residents. John Mark accompanied them as they sailed out from Seleucia, which was Antioch's seaport, and arrived at the largest city in Cyprus, then called Salamis, located on the eastern side of the island. There they preached to the Jews in the synagogues.

Acts 13:6-12. Saul and Barnabas are summoned westward to the capital city of Cyprus, Paphos, by the proconsul who is interested in hearing their message about

God. There the missionaries are confronted by a false prophet known as Bar-Jesus or Elymas. Led by the Holy Spirit, Paul condemns Elymas and performs a miracle that causes Elymas to become temporarily blind. This miracle not only wins the proconsul, Sergius Paulus, but also demonstrates that Paul's spiritual abilities are on a par with those of Peter. In verse 9, Saul is called by his Roman name, Paul, for the first time in Luke's account.

Acts 13:13-52. As the three missionaries move on toward Antioch of Pisidia, Luke clearly shows that Paul is the leader. John Mark leaves them, a decision that later causes a sharp dispute between Barnabas and Paul (Acts 15:38-39). While attending the synagogue there, which is located in Galatia in Asia Minor, Paul was invited to speak. This gesture was not unusual. Furthermore, Paul's demeanor likely marked him as a Pharisee. Paul summarizes Israelite history from the Exodus to David. Linked to David, Jesus' story is told in Acts 13:23-41, focusing on his death and resurrection. Invited by the people to return the following sabbath, the whole city turns out, but Paul was not well received by the Jewish leaders. The gospel was first preached to the Jews here, but it is the Gentiles who respond positively, thereby increasing the church and advancing the spread of Christianity.

Acts 14:1-7. Driven out of Antioch in Pisidia, Paul and Barnabas move about eighty miles east to Iconium where similar events occur. Jews and Gentiles do believe, but unbelieving Jews stir up hostility against them. Despite the problems caused by animosity, Paul and Barnabas remain "a long time," witnessing both in word and in deed (Acts 14:3). Hostility grows to the point where Paul and Barnabas, threatened with stoning, flee this commercial city.

Acts 14:8-20. Paul and Barnabas go about twenty-five miles southwest from Iconium to Lystra. There Paul heals a lame man, a story reminiscent of Peter's healing of the lame man in Acts 3:2-10. Witnesses to this miracle concluded that Barnabas and Paul were the Greek gods, Zeus and his messenger, Hermes, who Anatolian legend believed had visited the area. The priest of Zeus' temple wanted to offer the usual sacrifices of oxen and garlands, but Paul and Barnabas would have none of it. They tore their clothes in response to what they perceived as blasphemy (compare Mark 14:63). Paul preaches a brief sermon highlighting God as the creator, a preview of the sermon he will preach in Athens (see Acts 17:22-31). Why Jews come from Iconium to Lystra is not explained, but they do arrive and manage to win the crowd. Whereas Paul was threatened with stoning in Iconium, in Lystra he is stoned, dragged from the city, and left for dead (Acts 14:19). Somehow Paul and Barnabas managed to move the next day to Derbe, which is thirty miles southeast of Lystra.

Acts 14:21-28. After proclaiming the good news in Derbe, Paul and Barnabas head back to Antioch in Syria. They stop to strengthen the churches in towns from which they had been ousted, Lystra and Iconium. The two missionaries encourage the new believers and strengthen the church structure by appointing elders. Since Paul never refers to elders in his own letters, it is possible that Luke is assuming that such an office, which did exist in his day, functioned in the earliest period of the Christian church. As the first missionary journey ends in Antioch, Paul and Barnabas call the church there together to report on what God had done through them. A major point of their report is that the door was now open for ministry with the Gentiles.

INTERPRETING THE SCRIPTURE

Commissioning Missionaries

Matthew's Gospel closes with Jesus' challenging words that we call the Great Commission: "Go therefore and make disciples of all nations, baptizing them in the name of the Father and of the Son and of the Holy Spirit, and teaching them to obey everything that I have commanded you" (Matthew 28:19-20a). These words remind us of Jesus' call to his disciples to be witnesses to the ends of the world (Acts 1:8). Clearly, the gospel is meant for all people in all nations.

As Paul argues in Romans 10:14b-15, the challenge is that someone must go and proclaim the message: "But how are they [that is, those who have not heard the good news] to believe in one of whom they have never heard? And how are they to hear without someone to proclaim him? And how are they to proclaim him unless they are sent?" How, indeed, will the gospel be proclaimed unless the church sends forth witnesses?

The sending forth of missionaries, though confirmed by spiritually mature believers within the church, is undertaken at God's initiative. Through the Holy Spirit, God sets apart believers for this important ministry. In Acts 13:1-5 we see teachers, prophets, and others gathered for worship and prayer at the church in Antioch. In the midst of this spiritually vibrant assembly, God calls two persons—Barnabas and Saul—to go into the mission field. After being blessed and sent forth by the Antiochene congregation, they go westward to proclaim the Word of God, speaking first to the Jews and then to the Gentiles.

How is this scene similar to, or different from, the calling and sending forth of missionaries in our day? In part, the answer to this question depends upon your denomination. Some churches, aware of the harm that was historically done by well-intentioned missionaries who forced converts to change their culture as well as their religion, rely more on native missionaries to speak God's word in their own homeland. Actually, this idea is not new, for Barnabas was a Cypriot Jew (Acts 4:36) who returned to his country as a missionary with Saul. More and more indigenous missionaries are being educated to share the good news with their own compatriots in ways that win converts to Christ.

In the story of Acts 13, Saul and Barnabas are called to go forth, but no time limit is set on their work. In our day, increasing opportunities are available for Christians who feel called to the mission field on a short-term basis. Workers are often needed to build or repair churches or other structures, teach, offer medical assistance, and use other specialized skills for anywhere from one week to a year or two. Some of these fields are in exotic places, but others are close to home, perhaps in one of our troubled cities or poor rural regions.

However the call comes, for whatever time period, Christians who answer that call have a rare opportunity to witness the gospel to individuals from all walks of life, including those with whom they would not normally have contact. Missionaries have a chance through their words and deeds to show forth the resurrected power of Christ to people who desperately need to know of God's love for them. Furthermore, missionaries place themselves in a unique position where God can use and teach them, apart from the demands of their daily lives. They have a chance to see the world through new eyes and hear the cries of others through ears that bend low to listen.

Responding to the Good News

"Different strokes for different folks." It's true! One person hears a new idea as a challenge and responds eagerly, while another barely feigns politeness, anxious to get away from ideas that seems blasphemous or offensive. Some persons are quite willing to keep an open mind. They weigh the facts, check alternatives, and see if there is room in their own worldview to include ideas that are new to them. Other persons have their minds utterly and irrevocably made up. The door to their minds is firmly shut and tightly bolted. Their demeanor seems to say, "Don't bother me with the facts or another viewpoint."

Saul and Barnabas encountered both of these responses as they ministered. In fact, there seemed to be a repeated pattern for their work. First, they would go to the local synagogue where Saul would preach at the invitation of church leaders. Such invitations were not unusual, especially when the visitor was trained in Judaism, as Saul the Pharisee was. Next, those attending services responded enthusiastically to the message of Jesus Christ that Saul brought before them. In the midst of this successful witness, those who do not believe begin to stir up resistance. Often the resisters are Jewish leaders. The missionaries continue their work, branching out to Gentiles. Words and deeds, which may include miracles, convince a goodly number of people to follow Christ. The missionaries find themselves at the center of controversy as believers and unbelievers disagree. Due to hostile threats or overt action, Saul and Barnabas must flee the city. In short, Saul (or Paul, to use his more familiar Roman name) and Barnabas experience both success and failure. Some who hear believe, while others turn aside or actively fight against the message.

Paul does not modify his message to win everyone. Instead, he states the gospel story as best he knows how and then leaves the outcome of his witness to God. Everyone is offered the good news, but not everyone chooses to accept it. As we witness the decline of mainline Protestantism

in our day, maybe we need to ask ourselves if part of our problem is our insistence on success. Each congregation tries to be all things to all people. We avoid the demands of the gospel and proclaim a domesticated version that neither challenges nor excites anyone. We're so anxious to sign new names into our membership books that we may forget that there is a price to be paid for discipleship. Paul and Barnabas knew that. On more than one occasion Paul nearly paid with his life. Yet he knew that he had been called to share the story of Jesus Christ with all people, and he was unwilling to let physical hardship, negative responses, or angry leaders deter him from the work to which he was called by God.

Reporting on Ministry

Paul and Barnabas retrace their steps, stopping to strengthen new congregations as they pass through towns for the second time. They return home to Antioch in Syria about eighteen months after they departed. When they arrive, they tell the church what God has been doing in the places they have visited. They particularly point out that God "had opened a door of faith for the Gentiles" (Acts 14:27). While questions remained about how Gentiles could receive salvation (as we shall see next week), the fact that Gentiles were to be evangelized and included in the church seemed indisputable. God was providing opportunities for witness and response to them. The invitation of the gospel was being extended to them and, as Paul was pleased to report, these persons who had been outsiders were now eagerly becoming a part of the household of faith.

We can only imagine the enthusiastic gleam in Paul's eyes as he told of how many people, including Gentiles, responded to his witness. Perhaps the church members at Antioch listened intently and then had asked Paul and Barnabas questions about the people they met and the places they visited. They may have expressed deep concern for the safety of Paul and Barnabas in cities where enthusiastic welcomes gave way to hostile demands to leave. Through this reporting session, the people who had sent Paul and Barnabas forth from Antioch could learn about and appreciate their work. They could also see the hand of God at work in bringing new persons to life in Christ and protecting Paul and Barnabas from death.

One of the problems facing many modern churches is that many members don't know what's going on. Somehow news does not travel. Members in many churches seem to have little awareness of the depth and breadth of their congregation's ministry. They have no idea that the youth group is planning to work with a local Habitat for Humanity group and needs funding. Or that one of the women's groups is doing a mission study on China. Or that the evangelism committee is sponsoring a "Bring a Friend Sunday" next month.

Of course, sometimes members do not hear any news regarding ministry because very little is happening. But they need to know this too. A church that is not engaged in mission and ministry is not a church, no matter what the sign on the door says. If there is no ministry to report on, then the church needs to gather for worship and prayer so as to discern, as the church in Antioch did, what God wanted them to do in order to be witnesses to the good news of Jesus Christ.

SHARING THE SCRIPTURE

PREPARING TO TEACH

Try to locate a map with Paul's first missionary journey charted. You will find one on page 149 of *Bible Teacher Kit* (Abingdon Press) available through Cokesbury. You may also want to find additional information on Cyprus and its cities of Salamis and Paphos, Antioch in Pisidia, Iconium, Lystra, and Derbe.

Check with your pastor or church leader who is responsible for mission projects to obtain information about missionaries and projects your congregation supports, as well as short-term opportunities for class members to go to a mission field themselves.

If you plan to do the writing activity under "Responding to the Good News," have paper and pencils available.

If you plan to invite a guest speaker for one of the "Reporting on Ministry" activities, be sure to contact that person early in the week. Let him or her know what your expectations and time constraints are. Also be certain this person understands that the class is only dealing with Paul's first missionary journey.

If you wish to use a missions-related hymn, such as "Go, Make of All Disciples" (page 571 in *The United Methodist Hymnal*), be sure to have hymnals on hand.

LEADING THE CLASS

Introduction

If your class prefers a lecture, read "Focusing on the Main Question" aloud or retell it in your own words.

Another way to introduce the main question is to ask class members to think about the reading they did for today's lesson. Ask the group: What challenges did Paul and Barnabas take on so that everyone might be invited into God's kingdom? Answers will vary, but students will likely mention the physical hardships of travel, personal danger at the hands of angry crowds, having to deal with feelings of both success and failure, and preaching to Jews and Gentiles who had very different religious backgrounds.

Close this segment by asking the main

question: **Are we willing, like Paul and Barnabas, to take on new challenges for ministry so that everyone might be invited into God's kingdom?** Provide a few moments for silent reflection.

Commissioning Missionaries

Direct the class's attention to Acts 13:1-5. Use the information under "Understanding the Scripture" and a map to clarify what is happening and where Saul, Barnabas, and John Mark are headed.

Ask class members if any of them have been on the mission field, even for a short term. If so, perhaps these persons would be willing to speak briefly about their experiences there.

If you have obtained information about missionaries supported by your church, or available for support through your denomination, share that information now.

Talk with the class about the idea of undertaking a mission project such as:

- participating in a short-term trip to a work camp;
- helping to underwrite the salary of a missionary;
- providing support for a project such as the building of a church or providing Bibles for it;
- sharing the cost of sending some youth from the church to a summer work camp;
- participating in a lay witness ministry.

Responding to the Good News

Locate Iconium on a map if you have not previously done so. Share any information about this commercial city in the Roman province of Galatia that may be of interest to the class.

Choose a student to read Acts 14:1-7.

Note that this passage begins, "The same thing occurred in Iconium," indicating that a pattern for ministry and response exists. Ask the class to see if they can identify the pattern. List it on a chalk-board or newsprint. Information is found in the second paragraph under this heading in the "Interpreting the Scripture" section. This material can serve as a supplement to the discussion or the basis for a lecture.

If you have students who enjoy creative activities, you may want them to write either a newspaper account of the events in Iconium or an editorial about how the presence of Paul and Barnabas has affected the city. They could do this work individually, with a partner, or in a small group.

Reporting on Ministry

Ask a student to read aloud Acts 14:24-27.

Tell the class members to assume that they were part of the congregation in Antioch. Ask them to consider this question: **What would you want to know about the missionary journey?** List their questions on a chalkboard or newsprint.

Proceed to find answers to their questions. Here are two ways you might do this.

(1) For variety, you could arrange with a guest (perhaps your pastor or another person well versed in the biblical story) to recount the details of Paul's first missionary journey as found in Acts 13:1–14:28. Be sure to set a time limit in advance for this person to speak. Or you could do this yourself as an animated lecture from the first person point of view as if you were Paul.

(2) Another way to answer their questions is to provide commentaries, Bible dictionaries, and atlases, and allow them time to work. If you have enough resources and persons, assign one group to the Cyprus mission (Acts 13:4-12), another to the Pisidian Antioch mission (Acts 13:13-52), another to Iconium (Acts 4:1-7), and a final group to Lystra

and Derbe (Acts 14:8-20). If you do not have enough resources, assign each group to several cities. Set a time limit. Ask each group to report back, answering as many of the class's questions as possible. This option is particularly helpful if you believe that most students will have read all of the background scripture during the week.

Spend a few minutes talking about the way news of mission and ministry is reported in your own congregation. Ask the class:

(1) What kinds of missions or outreach projects are going on in our church now?

(2) How do church members find out about them?

(3) If you think the church should be more involved in spreading the gospel both in the community and around the world, what steps do you think the church should take?

(4) What are you willing to do to enable more missions work to be undertaken by your congregation?

If appropriate in your setting, you may want to sing a missions-related hymn, such as "Go, Make of All Disciples" to close today's session.

HELPING CLASS MEMBERS ACT

Challenge students to pray daily for at least one missionary or missions project that your congregation supports. If possible, try to have information available on the work and geographic location of this person or project.

If your church or denomination sponsors short-term mission projects, such as the Volunteers in Mission program in The United Methodist Church, challenge each class member prayerfully to consider becoming involved in a project. Even persons who cannot go to a missions site for a week or two may be able to offer financial support to those who can participate.

Encourage class members to try to talk with a friend or family member this week about differing religious beliefs that they hold. The purpose of this discussion is not to persuade anyone to change his or her mind, or to argue that a particular point of view is better or more enlightened than another. Instead, ask students to approach the discussion with the attitude of trying to understand better the other person's beliefs and to find points on which they can agree.

PLANNING FOR NEXT SUNDAY

Next week we will look at the conference in Jerusalem that was called to determine how Gentiles might be saved. After both sides are heard, James, the brother of Jesus who heads the church in Jerusalem, shares a decision. Ask class members to read Acts 15:1-35. Students who have the time may also want to read Paul's account of this conference, as recorded in Galatians 2:1-10. The latter reading will not be discussed in our lesson, but it may bring some questions to mind.

GRACE ON TRIAL

PREVIEWING THE LESSON

Lesson Scripture: Acts 15:1-2, 6-18
Background Scripture: Acts 15:1-35
Key Verse: Acts 15:11

Focus of the lesson:
the conflict in the early church concerning the means and requirements of salvation

Main question(s) of the lesson:
(1) What do we understand the requirements for salvation to be?
(2) What can the modern church learn from the early church about handling conflict?

This lesson will enable adult learners to:
(1) learn about the reasons for and outcomes of the Jerusalem conference
(2) examine their own feelings about one or more current conflicts in the church
(3) respond by researching opposing sides of an argument and be better prepared to see and understand differing points of view.

Today's lesson may be outlined as follows:
(1) Introduction
(2) The Problem Comes to a Head (Acts 15:1-2)
(3) Stating the Issue (Acts 15:6-12)
(4) Solving the Problem (Acts 15:13-18)

FOCUSING ON THE MAIN QUESTION

"Women are called to ministry just as men are. They should be ordained." "No, they shouldn't." "Abortion is murder." "No, it isn't." "Practicing homosexuals must not be ordained." "Yes, they should." "The Bible is unerringly true, each and every word of it." "No, it isn't."

Such major conflicts, though very regrettable and sometimes downright nasty, seem to be on the front burner in many modern denominations. Most church leaders, lay persons and clergy alike, have been involved in numerous official meetings where important issues such as these are intensely debated. Although both sides usually have scriptural and theological support for their arguments, one side cannot or will not see the other's point of view. Participants often leave meetings angry, shaking their heads in disbelief that their opponents could be so spiritually blind. A few dissidents may even threaten to leave what they consider to be an apostate church. We have difficulty dealing with conflict, especially when we are positive that our way is the right way—the only way—to resolve the problem.

Conflicts are hardly new to the church. Even in its early days, the Christian church had to deal with disputes. These earliest debates focused on the relationship between Gentile Christians and Judaism. Simply put, the question was: Does one have to become a Jew and observe all the laws and rituals of Judaism in order to find salvation through the Jewish messiah, Jesus? Such a question may seem incomprehensible now, since Judaism and Christianity are two separate religions, though both worship the same God. In the early days of the church, how-ever, the Christian movement was a group within Judaism, just as the Pharisees or the Zealots or the Essenes were. Consequently, this question was of paramount importance, especially to Gentiles who wanted to come to Christ and to Jews who wanted to maintain the holiness that they understood God had called them to as a people. To resolve this complex issue, the early church held a conference in Jerusalem and reached a resolution that was embraced by all of the participants.

As we study passages from Acts 15 today, we will continue to ask ourselves these two questions: **What do we understand the requirements for salvation to be? What can the modern church learn from the early church about handling conflict?**

READING THE SCRIPTURE

NRSV
Acts 15:1-2

1 Then certain individuals came down from Judea and were teaching the brothers, "Unless you are circumcised according to the custom of Moses, you cannot be saved." [2]And after Paul and Barnabas had no small dissension and debate with them, Paul and Barnabas and some of the others were appointed to go up to Jerusalem to discuss this question with the apostles and the elders.

Acts 15:6-18

6 The apostles and the elders met together to consider this matter. [7]After there had been much debate, Peter stood up and said to them, "My brothers, you know that in the early days God made a choice among you, that I should be the one through whom the Gentiles would hear the message of the good news and become believers. [8]And God, who knows the human heart, testified to them by giving them the Holy Spirit, just as he did to us; [9]and in cleansing their hearts by faith he has made no distinc-

NIV
Acts 15:1-2

1 Some men came down from Judea to Antioch and were teaching the brothers: "Unless you are circumcised, according to the custom taught by Moses, you cannot be saved." [2]This brought Paul and Barnabas into sharp dispute and debate with them. So Paul and Barnabas were appointed, along with some other believers, to go up to Jerusalem to see the apostles and elders about this question.

Acts 15:6-18

[6]The apostles and elders met to consider this question. [7]After much discussion, Peter got up and addressed them: "Brothers, you know that some time ago God made a choice among you that the Gentiles might hear from my lips the message of the gospel and believe. [8]God, who knows the heart, showed that he accepted them by giving the Holy Spirit to them, just as he did to us. [9]He made no distinction between us and them, for he purified their hearts by faith. [10]Now then, why do you try to test

tion between them and us. ¹⁰Now therefore why are you putting God to the test by placing on the neck of the disciples a yoke that neither our ancestors nor we have been able to bear? ¹¹On the contrary, we believe that we will be saved through the grace of the Lord Jesus, just as they will."

12 The whole assembly kept silence, and listened to Barnabas and Paul as they told of all the signs and wonders that God had done through them among the Gentiles. ¹³After they finished speaking, James replied, "My brothers, listen to me. ¹⁴Simeon has related how God first looked favorably on the Gentiles, to take from among them a people for his name. ¹⁵This agrees with the words of the prophets, as it is written,

¹⁶   'After this I will return,
     and I will rebuild the dwelling of
         David, which has fallen;
     from its ruins I will rebuild it,
     and I will set it up,
¹⁷ so that all other peoples may
       seek the Lord—
     even all the Gentiles over
       whom my name has been
       called.
     Thus says the Lord, who
       has been making these
       things ¹⁸known from long
       ago.'

God by putting on the necks of the disciples a yoke that neither we nor our fathers have been able to bear? ¹¹No! We believe it is through the grace of our Lord Jesus that we are saved, just as they are."

¹²The whole assembly became silent as they listened to Barnabas and Paul telling about the miraculous signs and wonders God had done among the Gentiles through them. ¹³When they finished, James spoke up: "Brothers, listen to me. 14 Simon has described to us how God at first showed his concern by taking from the Gentiles a people for himself. ¹⁵The words of the prophets are in agreement with this, as it is written:

¹⁶" 'After this I will return
     and rebuild David's fallen tent.
   Its ruins I will rebuild,
     and I will restore it,
¹⁷that the remnant of men may seek the
     Lord,
   and all the Gentiles who bear my
     name,
   says the Lord, who does these things'
¹⁸   that have been known for ages."

Key Verse

UNDERSTANDING THE SCRIPTURE

Acts 15:1-2. Although a fruitful ministry to the Gentiles has been underway, a heated conflict regarding the status of Gentile Christians must be resolved by church leaders. Apostles, elders, Paul, Barnabas, and other distinguished leaders gather for a conference in Jerusalem. The major issue that threatens to divide the church concerns circumcision. Unnamed individuals, possibly Pharisee Christians (Acts 15:5), are teaching Gentile converts to Christ that they must be circumcised in order to receive salvation. From their perspective,

this argument has merit because the earliest followers of Christ are part of Judaism, not a separate religion known as Christianity. Circumcision, the sign of God's covenant with Abraham (Genesis 17:9-14), was required of all Jewish males.

Acts 15:3-5. According to Luke's account, Paul, Barnabas, and several other persons are appointed by the church at Antioch to go to Jerusalem to discuss the issue. As they head south, they preach in Samaria and Phoenicia, winning converts along the way. Luke reports that they are welcomed by two groups: the apostles and the elders. Just as they had reported on their missionary work to the church at Antioch, Paul and Barnabas report on what God has accomplished through them on their way to this meeting in Jerusalem. Pharisee Christians insist that persons must come to Christ by means of the laws and rituals of Judaism.

Acts 15:6-12. Peter, who has been the prominent leader of the Jerusalem church thus far, reminds the conference participants of three points concerning ministry to the Gentiles. First, God is the one who initiated the ministry to the Gentiles (Acts 15:8; see also Acts 10:1–11:18). Second, God approved this work, as evidenced by the Holy Spirit falling upon these converts (Acts 15:8; see also Acts 11:15). Finally, God has cleansed the Gentiles so distinctions no longer exist between Jews and Gentiles (Acts 15:9; see also Acts 10:15). Peter argues against testing God (see Deuteronomy 6:16, quoted by Jesus in Matthew 4:7). Noting that the law has been burdensome to their Jewish ancestors, Peter states that salvation will come to both Jews and Gentiles through grace. Although Paul is not shown by Luke as actively involved in the debate, he and Barnabas bear witness to the work of God among the Gentiles. Their testimony supports Peter's claim that God is working at divine initiative among the Gentiles.

Acts 15:13-18. James, the brother of Jesus and head of the church in Jerusalem (see Acts 12:17), has listened carefully and is ready to give an opinion on the matter. He uses a Semitic reference to Peter, calling him Simeon. In Acts 15:16-18, James quotes from several prophets (Amos 9:11-12; Jeremiah 12:15; and Isaiah 45:21). The reference from Amos, though not an accurate translation from the Hebrew, helps James's argument. His point is that recent outreach to the Gentiles should not be seen as a new direction because God had intended such a ministry and announced it through the prophets long ago.

Acts 15:19-21. James continues by offering concrete conditions, rooted in the Holiness Code (Leviticus 17–26, especially in chapters 17–18), which will be put into writing for circulation. Gentile Christians are to abstain from food offered to idols, from sexual immorality (see Leviticus 18:1-30), from whatever has been strangled (that is, meat not ritually butchered, see Leviticus 17), and from blood (see Leviticus 17:10-13). In sum, James is setting forth an ingenious compromise. While circumcision is not required for Gentiles to be saved, they must observe the Jewish ritual requirements that "aliens" have been required to observe since the days of Moses (see for example Leviticus 17:10).

Acts 15:22-29. Representatives are chosen by the conference to take copies of a letter to the churches in Antioch, Syria, and Cilicia. The contents of this letter, found in verses 23-29, explain to the recipients that church leaders are aware that unauthorized persons have been spreading teaching that is troubling these Gentiles. The four essential requirements are set forth, though in a different order from James's speech. Verse 28 clarifies that the leaders are acting in accordance with God's will as expressed to them through the Holy Spirit. The letter also commends the work of Paul and Barnabas.

Acts 15:30-35. Luke's account shows the church at Antioch as joyously receiving it. The mother church in Jerusalem and the church in Antioch seem to be at peace. Scholars question the accuracy of some of the details in this scene. For example, verses 32-33 would indicate that Judas and Silas left Antioch together, while Paul and Barnabas remained. Acts 15:40, however, shows Paul and Silas setting off from Antioch. Some manuscripts added words in verse 34 stating that only Judas left and Silas remained.

INTERPRETING THE SCRIPTURE

The Problem Comes to a Head

Trouble. Big trouble. Trouble serious enough to divide the young church and curtail the emerging Christian mission among the Gentiles. Contrary to the message Paul and Barnabas have been proclaiming, some folks from Jerusalem have taken it upon themselves to teach the Gentiles in Antioch that they cannot be saved unless they have been circumcised.

The issue isn't new. Peter had a lot of explaining to do when he returned from his vision-led meeting with Cornelius (Acts 11:2-3). After Peter described how the Holy Spirit had fallen on those gathered in this Gentile home and how he believed that to withhold baptism from these persons would be hindering God, his critics were silenced and even rejoiced (Acts 11:18).

The silence was only temporary, however. Questions about Jewish-Gentile relationships among persons who professed Christ continued to be heard. The voices were growing louder now that a Gentile church in Antioch had sent Paul and Barnabas off on what turned out to be an eighteen-month missionary trip. More and more Gentiles were coming into a relationship with Israel's God through the person that some Jews believed to be Israel's messiah— Jesus of Nazareth. Yet these new converts were not observing the laws of Judaism. In fact, they were not even participating in its most basic covenantal sign—circumcision.

The problem has come to a head. A heated debate ensues, but no agreement can be reached in Antioch. Action must be taken through established channels of church decision making. To settle the matter, the church at Antioch appoints Paul, Barnabas, and some other unnamed believers to go to Jerusalem and discuss the impasse with the church leadership.

While the modern church does not face this particular question, we are confronted with many other problems that are seething just below the surface, like an active volcano ready to explode.

Some modern questions, such as the ordination of women, have been resolved within particular denominations, but not across denominational lines. Thus, Christian churches are divided over this issue, or at the least find it difficult to meet on common, ecumenical ground. Even within denominations where the issue is supposedly resolved, some Christians have chosen to withdraw from their church or covertly express disapproval.

Other questions, such as the ordination of self-avowed homosexuals and lesbians, continue (as of this writing) to be vigorously contested in most denominations. Church houses are divided against themselves. Time and energy that could be spent reaching out to unchurched persons or assisting persons who need Christian care are consumed by debates that seem to have no end in sight. It's as if the opponents are traveling on parallel train tracks. They lean out of windows, hurling accusations, but will never come to the place where their paths will cross and common understandings can be established.

Like the early church, we certainly have to be honest about voicing our differences and standing for what we believe. But we also have to do so with respect for others' points of view and a firm commitment to seeking God's will. As many early church members discovered, God's solution may be surprising. It may have been God's intended plan all along, but we just hadn't recognized it.

Stating the Issue

Luke does not devote much attention to the opposition. He mentions in Acts 15:5 that some Pharisee believers argued that Gentile believers needed to be circumcised and required to keep the law. The forum in which they set forth their position is unclear, for the assembly does not seem to officially convene until Acts 15:6. In any event, the concerns of these Pharisees are the focus of the conference.

After much debate, Peter rises to state his position. Although we tend to think of Paul as the apostle to the Gentiles, Peter originally held that distinction in the church. He was a respected leader, the head of the church in Jerusalem in its earliest days. Luke's account credits Peter with winning the first Gentile converts, Cornelius and his household. As Peter speaks, making oblique reference to that experience in Acts 15:8-9, participants in the conference surely must have remembered how difficult it was for Peter to go to these Gentiles. Yet he did so because a vision from the Lord had prepared him for this mission. The listeners also must have remembered how he answered criticisms about his fellowship with non-Jews and his willingness to baptize them after the Holy Spirit had fallen rather than risk hindering God.

In today's key verse, Acts 15:11, Peter states the basis for salvation: "We believe that we will be saved through the grace of the Lord Jesus, just as they will." The grace of the Lord Jesus is the key that unlocks the door to salvation. In his letter to the Romans (3:22b-24), Paul makes a very similar statement: "For there is no distinction, since all have sinned and fall short of the glory of God; they are now justified by his grace as a gift, through the redemption that is in Christ Jesus." In other words, both Jews and Gentiles are saved by grace.

Peter's speech prompts us to ask: What are the requirements of salvation? Peter and Paul are both certain that salvation comes by grace. We cannot do anything to earn or merit it. Our good works issue forth as the fruit of salvation, but they are not the seed from which it springs. Salvation is God's gift to us, a gift that we freely

choose to accept or reject. Unfortunately, some Christians attach strings to the gift by adding requirements for salvation that God neither intends nor expects. As was happening in the early church in relation to Gentiles, some believers built barriers, rather than bridges, in front of the church. Self-appointed gatekeepers examined credentials to see if a newcomer could be admitted, rather than leaving the door unlocked and allowing God to make that decision. Perhaps many conflicts in the church could be more amicably and quickly resolved if we would be more intentional about recognizing the centrality of grace in our individual spiritual lives and in the life of the church.

Peter's speech also prompted Paul and Barnabas to witness to God's gracious activity among the uncircumcised. These speakers make no theological or scriptural arguments but simply bear witness to what God has been doing through them among the Gentiles (Acts 15:12). Although Luke records no specific examples of the signs and wonders that are recounted before the conference, they must have been impressive, for the audience listens in rapt attention to these two missionaries.

Solving the Problem

James, the brother of Jesus and the head of the church in Jerusalem, responds to all of the arguments by proposing a creative solution to the problem. He carefully builds his case, using words from a Greek version of the prophet Amos, supplemented by Isaiah 45:21, to show that God intended to gather in all persons—even Gentiles. This perspective casts the entire situation in a different light. Ministry to the Gentiles is not some novel idea being undertaken by dissident Jewish Christians who are flaunting the law of Moses. Instead, as James interprets the Scripture, this ministry is an integral part of the plan God announced centuries ago. This point, in effect, supports Peter's argument that God is the one taking the initiative for the ministry to the Gentiles.

When the problem can be seen from a new angle of vision, the solution becomes more readily apparent. James rules that circumcision is not to be required of Gentiles because this covenantal sign is specific to the Jews. He does, however, set forth four conditions found in the Holiness Code of Leviticus that non-Jews living as "aliens" among Jews have always been required to observe. His proposal, seen as Spirit-led, was readily agreed to by all persons at the conference.

The process that the early church used to resolve the conflict and James's solution to the problem can serve as models for the modern churches. Let's see if we can analyze what happened at the Jerusalem conference. First, all parties were invited to the table. Not only were they present but they were encouraged to air their opinions and engage in spirited debate. Second, Luke's account would indicate that the meeting was orderly and that the partici-

pants were respectful of one another. They rose to speak, each in turn. The audience was silent as Paul and Barnabas presented their testimony. Third, the participants realized that this problem was tearing at the heart and soul of the church, threatening to divide it. No time was available for lengthy studies by committees or outside experts. A definite answer was needed immediately. Fourth, as presenters stated their cases, they demonstrated how God was at work in the current situation or how God's Word through the law or the prophets should be seen as a guide and boundary line for their actions. Fifth, unity prevailed partly because the resolution was not seen as a win-lose situation. Those who had argued against circumcision were satisfied, as were those who had argued in favor of observing the law. Unity was also preserved because the participants affirmed the decision as coming from the Holy Spirit. Finally, the decision was to be communicated in writing so that everyone would know what was expected of them.

SHARING THE SCRIPTURE

PREPARING TO TEACH

In addition to reading the scripture and lesson from Acts, you may also want to read Paul's own account of the Jerusalem conference, found in Galatians 2:1-10, for your own information. The differences between the two accounts of what is believed to be the same event raise questions for scholars.

If you plan to use the first activity under "Helping Class Members Act" and you need your pastor's help in securing information for the research on an issue troubling your denomination, contact him or her as soon as possible.

If you choose to use a checklist option for the activity concerning the require-

ments of salvation under "Stating the Issue," prepare handouts or newsprint ahead of time using the suggested items or others that you prefer.

As you read and study Acts 15:1-35 and the lesson, give some thought this week to the way your own congregation resolves disputes. Does the Jerusalem conference suggest ways to deal with conflict that may be more productive than the ways typically used in your own church?

LEADING THE CLASS

Introduction

Ask class members to identify several major issues that are currently being debated in your denomination or congregation. List these issues on a chalkboard or newsprint. You may want to carry this discussion further by focusing for a few moments on just one issue and asking students to state at least two sides to the argument. Be careful in doing this, since our purpose here is not to spend time debating these issues but simply to show that there is more than one way to frame and resolve the problem.

Point out that church conflicts have existed throughout the history of the church. Indicate that we will be looking at one of the early conflicts regarding the requirements of salvation for Gentiles.

Note that today's lesson will focus on both the issue that created the conflict and the way in which the church tried to handle and resolve the issue. Two questions that will guide us through this session are: **What do we understand the requirements for salvation to be? What can the modern church learn from the early church about handling conflict?**

The Problem Comes to a Head

Choose a volunteer to read aloud Acts 15:1-2.

Ask the class: **(1) What is the issue at stake here? (2) Why would circumcision and adherence to the Jewish law be so intensely debated in the early church?** Use information under "Understanding the Scripture," and from the third paragraph of this section under "Focusing on the Main Question" to supplement the class discussion as needed. Help students see that from a Jewish perspective the issue was of crucial importance.

If the class enjoys activity, stage an informal debate on this resolution: Gentiles must become full-fledged Jews as a prerequisite for salvation in Christ. You may want to choose several persons to represent the pro and con sides, respectively. If the class is large, divide into several groups and stage this debate.

Stating the Issue

Direct the class's attention to Acts 15:6-12.

Ask the class: **What points does Peter make concerning ministry to the Gentiles?** Information on these verses in the "Understanding the Scripture" section may supplement the class's answers.

Consider the requirements for salvation with the class by using one of the methods below.

(1) Conduct a discussion on the question: What do you think are the requirements for salvation? List the answers on a chalkboard or newsprint.

(2) Prepare a checklist that could be distributed to individuals or posted on newsprint. Include items such as: church membership, regular prayer and Bible study, grace, fasting, church attendance, repentance, good deeds, and affirmation of particular beliefs (for example: the virgin birth, inerrancy of the Bible, bodily resurrection). Provide a few moments for students to look over the list and decide which items are necessary for salvation.

Close this activity by reading aloud Acts 15:11, this week's key verse, which indicates that God's grace through Jesus is all we need. Peter does not even speak of repentance, for even that can only come about by the grace of God. (Note that the same idea is expressed by Paul in Romans 3:22b-24). Help the class understand that other actions and beliefs may follow as a result of salvation, but that God's gift of grace is sufficient in and of itself for salvation.

Solving the Problem

Use the information concerning Acts 15:13-18 and 15:19-21 under "Understanding the Scripture" to help the class understand James's solution to the problem and why it would be favorably received by persons on both sides of the issue. The first paragraph under "Solving the Problem" in the "Interpreting the Scripture" section will also be helpful.

Ask the class: **(1) Why was James's solution in reference to the prophets so helpful in resolving the conflict?** *(The people could understand that God had planned to include Gentiles in the Kingdom long before the current dispute arose.)* **(2) What ideas can the modern church gain from this incident about resolving conflicts?**

As an enrichment activity, ask the class to look carefully at the record of the entire Jerusalem conference, Acts 15:1-35 (background scripture), to see how the early church successfully dealt with conflict. Ask the class the following questions. Ideas for answers are found in the last paragraph of this section under "Interpreting the Scripture."

(1) **What sides of the issue were represented and heard at the conference table?**

(2) **How would you characterize the tone of the meeting?**

(3) **How urgent did the need for resolution seem to be? Give reasons for your answer.**

(4) **How did the participants take into account God's role and will in this issue?**

(5) **What factors enabled the participants to feel so unified at the end?**

(6) **How did the conference ensure that its decision would be made known?**

Conclude this activity by asking class members: What can our own denomination or congregation learn from the Jerusalem conference about resolving conflict?

HELPING CLASS MEMBERS ACT

Challenge class members to seek information about a major issue troubling your denomination or congregation. Ask them to look at the issue from at least two opposing angles to try to find a solution. Encourage them to do some independent Bible study related to this issue. To help the class do this activity, you may want to assign one issue. Ask your pastor to assist you in putting together a list of scriptures, several articles or books, or other resources. You may be able to secure position papers or transcripts of official discussions on this issue from your denomination.

Look up the words "salvation" and "grace" in a topical Bible or concordance. Study the biblical references. Write a paragraph or two in your own words stating what these words mean to you.

PLANNING FOR NEXT SUNDAY

Next Sunday's lesson will focus on passages from Acts 16:9-10, 13-15, and 25-34, which give Luke's account of portions of Paul's second missionary journey. We will travel with Paul to Philippi where he meets Lydia, who becomes the first convert in Europe. He also converts a Philippian jailer from whose prison he and Silas could have easily escaped after an earthquake. Ask class members to prepare for this session by reading Acts 15:36–16:40.

HELP WANTED

PREVIEWING THE LESSON

Lesson Scripture: Acts 16:9-10, 13-15, 25-34
Background Scripture: Acts 15:36–16:40
Key Verse: Acts 16:10

Focus of the lesson:
God's call for believers to witness wherever they are sent

Main question(s) of the lesson:
(1) How is each of us called to provide the help God needs in spreading the good news?

This lesson will enable adult learners to:
(1) see the importance of God's plan to spread the gospel into Europe, as revealed to Paul in a vision
(2) consider their own willingness to take risks in order to meet the needs of others
(3) respond by encouraging or supporting others.

Today's lesson may be outlined as follows:
(1) Introduction
(2) A Vision for Ministry (Acts 16:9-10)
(3) The First European Convert (Acts 16:13-15)
(4) Freeing the Jailer (Acts 16:25-34)

FOCUSING ON THE MAIN QUESTION

Help wanted: Enthusiastic self-starter needed as messenger. See the world! Must be willing to travel at any time. Itinerary subject to change on short notice. Opportunities for lots of interaction, perhaps even confrontations, with town residents. No lodging expenses provided. Accommodations available in private homes and local jails. Must be able to act boldly, especially in dangerous circumstances. Unpopularity, physical abuse, and imprisonment are occupational hazards. No vacations. Volunteer position. Employer will be with you at all times.

Who would be crazy enough to answer an ad such as this? We want jobs that guarantee personal fulfillment, offer limitless salary increases, and have benefits that include generous vacations. We may not mind traveling, but we prefer to book reservations in advance to guard against schedule conflicts. Confrontations may occur on our jobs, though we seek to avoid them. If we know the message we have to share will not be well received, we try to put a better spin on it. We want to be popular with everyone.

No, we wouldn't answer this ad. Paul may not have answered it either had he known in advance all that God had in store for him. Paul could not foresee each obstacle in the road, but he was willing to trust God to steer him in the direction that God wanted him to go. Paul was so attuned to God's leading that if he were alive today his car might have a "God Is My Pilot" bumper sticker on it. Not that Paul didn't try to make some arrangements for himself. Remember how he wanted to spread the word in Asia? God had other plans, though. Paul was needed in Europe, so God sent a vision of a man in Macedonia calling for the apostle to come and help the people there. God needed human help to accomplish divine purposes, and Paul responded faithfully.

God still has help wanted ads posted all over the world. People are needed to spread the message of God's grace and love. Some will do that right in their own Jerusalem as they work at home or in an office, factory, store, or school. Others will take the message into the larger community. A few, like Paul, will go anywhere on the globe that they are needed, regardless of political boundaries or geographical features. **How is each of us called to provide the help God needs in spreading the good news?** That is our question for this lesson.

READING THE SCRIPTURE

NRSV
Acts 16:9-10

9 During the night Paul had a vision: there stood a man of Macedonia pleading with him and saying, "Come over to Macedonia and help us." 10When he had seen the vision, we immediately tried to cross over to Macedonia, being convinced that God had called us to proclaim the good news to them.

NIV
Acts 16:9-10

9During the night Paul had a vision of a man of Macedonia standing and begging him, "Come over to Macedonia and help us." 10After Paul had seen the vision, we got ready at once to leave for Macedonia, concluding that God had called us to preach the gospel to them.

Key Verse

Acts 16:13-15

13 On the sabbath day we went outside the gate by the river, where we supposed there was a place of prayer; and we sat down and spoke to the women who had gathered there. 14A certain woman named Lydia, a worshiper of God, was listening to us; she was from the city of Thyatira and a dealer in purple cloth. The Lord opened her heart to listen eagerly to what was said by Paul. 15When she and her household were baptized, she urged us, saying, "If you have judged me to be faithful to the Lord, come and stay at my home." And she prevailed upon us.

Acts 16:13-15

13On the Sabbath we went outside the city gate to the river, where we expected to find a place of prayer. We sat down and began to speak to the women who had gathered there. 14One of those listening was a woman named Lydia, a dealer in purple cloth from the city of Thyatira, who was a worshiper of God. The Lord opened her heart to respond to Paul's message. 15When she and the members of her household were baptized, she invited us to her home. "If you consider me a believer in the Lord," she said, "come and stay at my house." And she persuaded us.

Acts 16:25-34

25 About midnight Paul and Silas were praying and singing hymns to God, and

Acts 16:25-34

25About midnight Paul and Silas were praying and singing hymns to God, and

NOVEMBER 19

the prisoners were listening to them. ²⁶Suddenly there was an earthquake, so violent that the foundations of the prison were shaken; and immediately all the doors were opened and everyone's chains were unfastened. ²⁷When the jailer woke up and saw the prison doors wide open, he drew his sword and was about to kill himself, since he supposed that the prisoners had escaped. ²⁸But Paul shouted in a loud voice, "Do not harm yourself, for we are all here." ²⁹The jailer called for lights, and rushing in, he fell down trembling before Paul and Silas. ³⁰Then he brought them outside and said, "Sirs, what must I do to be saved?" ³¹They answered, "Believe on the Lord Jesus, and you will be saved, you and your household." ³²They spoke the word of the Lord to him and to all who were in his house. ³³At the same hour of the night he took them and washed their wounds; then he and his entire family were baptized without delay. ³⁴He brought them up into the house and set food before them; and he and his entire household rejoiced that he had become a believer in God.

the other prisoners were listening to them. ²⁶Suddenly there was such a violent earthquake that the foundations of the prison were shaken. At once all the prison doors flew open, and everybody's chains came loose. ²⁷The jailer woke up, and when he saw the prison doors open, he drew his sword and was about to kill himself because he thought the prisoners had escaped. ²⁸But Paul shouted, "Don't harm yourself! We are all here!"

²⁹The jailer called for lights, rushed in and fell trembling before Paul and Silas. ³⁰He then brought them out and asked, "Sirs, what must I do to be saved?" ³¹They replied, "Believe in the Lord Jesus, and you will be saved—you and your household." ³²Then they spoke the word of the Lord to him and to all the others in his house. ³³At that hour of the night the jailer took them and washed their wounds; then immediately he and all his family were baptized. ³⁴The jailer brought them into his house and set a meal before them; he was filled with joy because he had come to believe in God—he and his whole family.

UNDERSTANDING THE SCRIPTURE

Acts 15:36-41. Paul suggested to Barnabas that they make a follow-up visit to the churches where they had ministered on their first missionary trip. Luke records that a sharp division between Barnabas and Paul occurred over the question of including John Mark, who had left the two in Pamphylia on their previous trip (Acts 13:13). According to Paul's own account in Galatians 2:13, the rift between himself and Barnabas was actually caused by a disagreement over table fellowship with Gentile Christians. As a result of this conflict, Barnabas took his cousin John Mark and sailed to his homeland, Cyprus. Luke makes no further mention of Barnabas.

Paul took Silas and set off to strengthen the churches in Syria and Cilicia.

Acts 16:1-5. Paul revisited Lystra, where he had been stoned, and Derbe. While in Lystra he met Timothy, a young man with a good reputation among the believers, who may have been won to Christ through Paul (1 Corinthians 4:17). Timothy's parentage is mentioned, possibly to help explain Paul's circumcision of him. While this action seems to be contrary to the decision reached by the Jerusalem conference (Acts 15:19-20), a child born to a Jewish mother was considered Jewish and should therefore be circumcised. Paul's action can also be seen as an attempt to be sensitive to the concerns of Jews whom he would visit. He wanted to present himself as an observant Jew who was building a bridge between Judaism and a worldwide church. Despite Luke's report of Paul delivering the conference's decision to the churches, some scholars feel that such action is historically improbable.

Acts 16:6-10. Luke portrays Paul's itinerary and actions as being led by the Holy Spirit. Paul travels to Troas, a seaport city on the northwest coast of Asia Minor. There he has a vision (dream) of a man beckoning him to come to Macedonia, a European province that includes Philippi, Thessalonica, and Beroea. Paul wasted no time in responding to this vision. Acts 16:10 begins one of four "we" passages found in Acts. While these passages have traditionally been used to show that Luke was a traveling companion of Paul's, perhaps joining him in Troas, some modern scholars believe that Luke did not accompany Paul but was using a travel journal as one source for his account in Acts.

Acts 16:11-15. Taking a direct route, Paul and his associates make their first European stop in Philippi, an important city but not the capital of Macedonia. On the sabbath they meet a woman from Thyatira, named Lydia, at an outdoor meeting place used by the Jews. She was not a Jew but a Gentile worshiper, a God-fearer. After listening to Paul, she and her whole family were baptized. The first European convert, Lydia offered exemplary hospitality to Paul and his companions, which they accepted.

Acts 16:16-24. Paul encountered a slave whose powers of soothsaying and ventriloquism made her a valuable commodity to her owners. She followed Paul and his associates, yelling that they were "slaves of the Most High God," that is, the highest god in the pantheon. After repeated episodes, Paul cast out the spirit of Python from this girl, apparently because he was annoyed by the demon. Her owners had him and Silas hauled up before the magistrates on charges that these Jewish men were creating a public disturbance. The accusers' point may have been that Paul and Silas were proselytizing Romans. The two men were stripped, beaten, and imprisoned. This story shows an example of the power of the gospel over the pagan gods.

Acts 16:25-34. Despite the torture of being in stocks, Paul and Silas are praying and singing hymns, thereby making a witness to other prisoners. An earthquake shakes the doors loose, clearing the way for an escape. Believing that the prisoners had fled, the jailer draws his sword to commit suicide when Paul shouts to stop him. This event sets the stage for the conversion of the jailer. He hears the word of the Lord and is baptized, along with his family. He comforts Paul and Silas by washing their wounds and offering them food. The atmosphere in his home is one of jubilant celebration.

Acts 16:35-40. The next morning, the magistrates send word that Paul and Silas are to be released, though no reason for that decision is given. Paul refuses, saying that the magistrates would need to come and handle the matter themselves because they had beaten Roman citizens, an action that carried a stiff penalty. Paul also noted that he and Silas were uncondemned, which likely means that the incident was not properly investigated before punishment was meted out. Fearful of reprisals from higher authorities, the magistrates came and apologized. Paul takes his time leaving Philippi, stopping first at Lydia's home to encourage the members of the house church there.

INTERPRETING THE SCRIPTURE

A Vision for Ministry

Like an auto club member with a detailed itinerary, Paul has his travel plans all mapped out. He intends to visit the churches that he and Barnabas worked to establish. Barnabas will not be his traveling companion this time though. After a dispute that caused a rift, the two men head in different directions. Silas is Paul's partner on this journey. In Lystra, Paul invites a third member named Timothy to join his party. The three men journey together in Asia Minor, passing through Phrygia and Galatia. Amazingly, the Spirit of God had forbidden them to preach in Asia. Paul tries to head north to Bithynia, but a divine red light stops his progress.

We can only imagine what Paul must have been thinking as these roadblocks continually impeded his progress. We can almost hear him ask: "What am I doing wrong, God? The last trip was so successful. Nothing seems to be going well this time. I'm not sure where I'm going, and when I do arrive somewhere I don't feel led to speak." Likely, we'd ask the same kinds of questions. In fact, most of us would probably give up and go home, assuming that this heavenly messenger business was not for us.

Fortunately, Paul did not give up. He continued to answer God's help wanted ad even though he didn't seem to be accomplishing much. At the seaport of Troas, perhaps having cast an eye across the Aegean toward Macedonia in northern Greece, Paul has a vision during the night. An unidentified man calls Paul to come to Macedonia and help the people there. Macedonia was certainly not on Paul's itinerary. In fact, Paul had not planned to go to Europe at all, but he responds immediately, believing that this is the place where God would have him minister. As Acts 16 makes clear, Paul was definitely going in the right direction.

What kinds of visions do we have for ministry? Where is God calling us to go? What is God calling us to do? Perhaps these questions seem odd to us, for we assume that God has called the clergy to be in ministry. We figure that we can sit back and relax, leaving our pastor to plan the route and do all the driving along our spiritual journey. Nothing could be further from the truth! Although a few of us are called to the ordained ministry, every baptized Christian is a minister. Therefore, we lay persons need to be intentional about addressing questions concerning our own visions for ministry. We need to discern where God wants us to be and what God needs us to do. God may be calling us to heal a sick person, clean up the environment, teach a child, design a safer car, cook food, or do any of a myriad of tasks. The way we do our paid jobs, our volunteer work, or care for our own families bears spoken and unspoken witness as to how we are answering God's help wanted ad.

The First European Convert

In response to the vision he had seen, Paul and his party traveled straightway to Philippi, a Roman colony in northeastern Greece. Philippi was an important point along a major road, the Egnatian Way, which connected Byzantium with ports along the western coast of Macedonia. Travelers could sail from these ports across the Adriatic Sea to Italy. Diverse peoples passed through and lived in Philippi. When Paul arrived here in about 50 C.E., he would have found people worshiping a wide variety of gods, including the God of Israel.

On the sabbath Paul and his party visited the Jewish place of prayer, which apparently was an outdoor gathering area.

There they met Lydia, who had come from Thyatira, located about one hundred miles north of Ephesus. This business woman was not Jewish, but a God-fearer, a Gentile who was attracted to Judaism. According to the Jewish historian, Josephus, a significant number of such women of means were attracted to Judaism. Lydia listened intently to Paul. His words must have touched her deeply, for she and her household were baptized. Lydia and her family were the first Europeans known to convert to Christianity.

As a merchant who dealt in fine cloth, Lydia apparently had the means to offer extended hospitality. She invited Paul and his companions to stay with her, an invitation which they accepted. Her home became their base of operations while in Philippi. After an episode in jail, which began when irate owners had Paul arrested for casting a demon out of their slave girl, the apostle returned to Lydia's home. He wanted to encourage the believers who were gathering there, for this place was the seedbed for the church in Philippi. The Philippian church was so important to Paul that he wrote a letter to it while he was imprisoned.

Lydia's story may be our story as well. Here was a woman who was clearly searching for meaningful religious experiences. She was attracted to Judaism, even in a community that apparently had too few Jewish believers to form a synagogue. Listening to Paul, she must have recognized that a relationship with Jesus was what she was really seeking. Like the Ethiopian eunuch and Cornelius, she wanted to be baptized immediately. Her family was baptized with her, perhaps at the place by the river where she and others had met for prayer. Somehow she immediately caught a vision of Christian service. She did what she could to nurture and tend this church that she invited into her home.

What are we doing? Have our lives been so radically transformed by the grace of God in Jesus that we too are anxious to offer significant assistance? Are we willing to take the initiative to invite others to join us on our faith journey? Lydia's story reminds us that we need not go off into foreign lands in order to serve God. Opportunities abound all around us if we will but open our eyes to the needs of others.

Freeing the Jailer

Traveling with Paul seems to be much like associating with J. B. Fletcher, the heroine of television's popular "Murder, She Wrote" series. No matter where this detective writer goes, someone turns up dead. Likewise, accompanying Paul almost guarantees you accommodations in the local prison. Although he does not intend to stir up a ruckus, the power of the gospel is so great that it threatens people.

The owners of a slave girl were hopping mad when Paul cast a demon out of her. No longer could she tell fortunes. No longer were their pockets lined with the money she made from this spirit of divination. The owners were so incensed that they had Paul and Silas dragged before the authorities, flogged, and thrown into prison.

Most people would consider this situation very discouraging. God had given Paul the power over unclean spirits, and look where the use of that power landed him! Surely he and Silas would be much more comfortable at Lydia's place.

Instead of bemoaning their fate, Paul and Silas recognized that they had a prime opportunity to witness to persons who had a desperate need to hear the good news—a literally captive audience. They prayed and sang. The other prisoners were listening, likely marveling over the kind of God that these men worshiped, a God who enabled them to sing while tortuously pinned in stocks.

As if their behavior were not miracle enough, the jail is suddenly rocked by an earthquake. With a violent rumble, chains fall off the wall and prison doors fling wide open. Everybody's free to go. But no one moves. Paul has to convince the jailer not to commit suicide. His prisoners are all inside. He will not be punished.

The jailer realizes that Paul and Silas hold the keys to salvation. He too can be free. That very night he and his whole household profess their belief in Christ and are baptized. The jailer, like Lydia, offers food and hospitality. Moreover, he dresses the wounds that he himself may have inflicted.

Paul had gone over to Macedonia in response to God's visionary want ad. He had won several new converts, one of which was willing to open her home to a small, but soon to be growing church. Although his exorcism of the demon had landed him in jail, it had clearly demonstrated the power of the gospel of Jesus Christ over the vagaries of fortune telling. In retrospect, that episode laid the groundwork for the conversion of another whole family.

What are our expectations when we answer God's want ad? Do we expect to perform our service in the Garden of Eden where there is neither strife nor pain? In return for our work, do we expect God to make sure that nothing bad happens to us or to those we love? Or do we enter into God's service aware that suffering may be part of the deal? Are we willing to face the risk of unpopularity, discouragement, even physical pain to stand up for the high ideal of the Christian gospel? If so, we are ready to set sail for Macedonia, for God needs us to proclaim the good news there.

SHARING THE SCRIPTURE

PREPARING TO TEACH

As you prepare the lesson, think about how God has called you to come over to Macedonia and help your students. In accepting the challenge of leading an adult class you are indeed helping others to find and strengthen their own relationship with Christ. You are also enabling them to identify new avenues of service. You may want to write your perceptions about your role as a teacher in your spiritual journal.

Have paper and pencils on hand if you plan to do the writing activity under the "Introduction" section.

If possible, have a map on hand so that you can trace Paul's journey.

If you want a student to tell the story of the slave girl with the demon in Acts 16:16-24, be sure to contact that person early in the week.

If your class will be changing teachers at the end of the quarter, you may want to invite the teacher for the winter quarter to sit in with the class next week. If so, be certain to introduce this person.

LEADING THE CLASS

Introduction

If your class prefers a lecture format, read or retell the "Focusing on the Main Question" section.

If the class likes creative activities, distribute paper and pencils and ask class members to write help wanted ads that reflect what they consider to be an ideal job in light of their talents and dreams. Allow a brief period for this activity. Do not discuss students' ideas at this point.

Now read the ad found at the beginning of "Focusing on the Main Question." Ask the class: **How does this want ad for Paul's job differ from the one you wrote for the job you would like to have?** Discuss their answers. You may want to list some of their ideas on a chalkboard or newsprint.

Close this segment by stating or writing the main question: **How is each of us called to provide the help God needs in spreading the good news?**

A Vision for Ministry

Read aloud Acts 16:9-10.

If the class enjoys using their imaginations, ask several persons to describe the scene in this vision. What does this man look like? How does his voice sound? What kinds of gestures or facial expressions does he make?

Ask the class this question: **Where, in figurative terms, is Macedonia today? In other words, where does God need people to go in order to spread the good news of Jesus?** The answers may include: the names of specific countries, especially those in the news because of unrest or natural disaster; groups of persons, such as the homeless or substance abusers; generic place names, such as inner cities or wealthy suburbs. Record the answers on a chalkboard or newsprint.

After the answers have been listed, ask the class to identify as many church programs or missions occurring in the places they have mentioned. Spend a few moments talking about how your church is actively involved in reaching out to one or more of these "Macedonias." If your church is not involved, talk for a brief period about how this class could become the initiators of such an outreach.

The First European Convert

Enlist a volunteer to read Acts 16:13-15.

Encourage a few members to share stories of worshiping in a church that was very different from their own, perhaps even located in a foreign country. Ask them to tell the class how they felt as strangers there. Did anyone offer hospitality to them? If so, how did they feel about that offer?

Ask the class: **How would you describe Lydia?** Information for this passage under "Understanding the Scripture" and "Interpreting the Scripture" may be useful in supplementing their answers. You may want to list the class answers on a chalkboard or newsprint. [?]

Then ask: **Who are the Lydias in our church or community?** The point of this question is to name and affirm men and women who do seemingly insignificant tasks that truly help the church. These may be the folks who duplicate and assemble the newsletter, who pack food bags for the church pantry, who prune bushes, or do minor repairs. Try to list as many of these unsung heroes—especially ones who are members of the class—as possible. Affirm the fact that these persons have also answered God's help wanted ad. [?]

Freeing the Jailer

Since the story of the slave girl's deliverance from demons is not included in the printed scripture you will need to impart this information to the class by (a) telling the story in your own words, (b) reading Acts 16:16-24, or (c) asking a student in advance to be prepared to tell this story. Information under "Understanding the Scripture" will help you. This incident is the reason for Silas and Paul's imprisonment.

Then choose a student to read Acts 15:25-34.

Encourage the class to discuss for a few moments how they would have felt had they been the other prisoners in the jail. Ask these questions:

(1) **What would Paul and Silas's witness have meant to you?** [?]

(2) **After hearing their prayers and songs, would you have understood the earthquake as merely a coincidence or as a sign of divine intervention? Why?**

(3) **Would you have stayed in the prison just because Paul said so, or would you have made an escape? Why?**

Point out that God sometimes allows us to get to the very end of our ropes, to peer over the abyss as it were, before we are ready to seek God. Note that the jailer was standing with sword in hand, ready to commit suicide, when Paul shouted to him. We do not know the rest of the story concerning this man. All we know for certain is that he did accept Christ. Speculate for a few minutes with the class as to how the jailer may have become a different person after that transforming experience. Ask these questions:

(1) **How do you think his life may have changed?**

(2) **What differences would the prisoners have noticed in him?**

(3) **How would his family life be different?**

Invite class members to think of a situation in their own lives or in the life of someone they know that needs to be transformed. Provide a few moments of silence for quiet reflection and prayer. Encourage students to open themselves to God's transforming power. Also encourage them to answer a call from a friend for help or support in a difficult situation.

HELPING CLASS MEMBERS ACT

Encourage class members to pray daily for at least one missionary that your congregation or denomination supports.

Challenge students to make a financial contribution to a mission project this week.

Seek out a friend, neighbor, or church member who has been in difficult circumstances recently, perhaps due to a death, divorce, illness, job loss, or other crisis. Plan to spend some time with this person, even if only by phone. Listen to his or her fears and discouragement. Offer a word of encouragement. If possible, do a helpful deed, such as baby-sitting for a few hours so that a single parent can get out.

PLANNING FOR NEXT SUNDAY

We will conclude our study of Acts next Sunday. Ask the class members to read the background scripture, Acts 18:18—19:41. This portion of scripture shows the conclusion of Paul's second missionary journey. Our focus will be on Acts 19:1-6 and 19:11-20, which describe a portion of Paul's ministry in Ephesus.

THE GOSPEL'S POWER TO OVERCOME

PREVIEWING THE LESSON

Lesson Scripture: Acts 19:1-6, 11-20
Background Scripture: Acts 18:18–19:41
Key Verse: Acts 19:20

Focus of the lesson:
the power of the gospel to overcome evil

Main question(s) of the lesson:
(1) In what ways do we perceive the gospel of Jesus Christ to overcome all other powers?

This lesson will enable adult learners to:
(1) explore Paul's experience in Ephesus
(2) consider their own perceptions of how the gospel challenges evil in today's world
(3) respond by examining the ways in which they handle evil as it confronts them daily.

Today's lesson may be outlined as follows:
(1) Introduction
(2) The Whole Gospel (Acts 19:1-6)
(3) The Gospel's Power Over Evil (Acts 19:11-19)
(4) The Word of the Lord Prevailed (Acts 19:20)

FOCUSING ON THE MAIN QUESTION

We all want to be on the winning team. Whether we're circling the victory lap, or looking at the black ink on our bottom line, or hearing compliments on a job well done, we delight in basking in the glow of our accomplishments. We feel good about ourselves and the world when we know we have done our best and that our work has been noticed by others.

Often we achieve these victories by imitating what other successful persons in our field have done. Business persons, for example, read books and journals, take college courses, and network with others to learn how to operate a profitable enterprise. New teachers observe master teachers to learn their art. Professional sports teams watch videotapes of themselves and their opponents, seeking information that will show them how they can strengthen their own team while capitalizing on the weaknesses of their competitors. Coaches analyze what the athletes are doing and help them improve their performance. In many Olympic sports where hundredths, even thousandths, of a second separate the gold medalist from the fourth place finisher, every contestant trains hard to have that extra edge that distinguishes the winners from the losers.

How do we define success as Christians? Some churches perceive it in terms of numerical growth, or budget increases, or participation in the programs they offer. The early church, however, looked at suc-

cess in terms of the power of the gospel to overcome the claims of competing gods and religious practices. In our scripture lesson today, for example, the name of Jesus challenges the occult arts that were widely practiced in Ephesus. Exorcists of all stripes had been using Jesus' name to cast out demons. Although they were not Christians, these persons had tried to use Jesus' name, just as many other successful exorcists had done. One day, however, the demon that was being cast out turned on the exorcists. The power inherent in this episode caused persons to burn their magic books and become followers of the one who had far greater power than occult practices.

As we examine Paul's ministry in Ephesus in our lesson for today, we will want to ask ourselves: **In what ways do we perceive the gospel of Jesus Christ to overcome all other powers?**

READING THE SCRIPTURE

NRSV
Acts 19:1-6

1 While Apollos was in Corinth, Paul passed through the interior regions and came to Ephesus, where he found some disciples. [2]He said to them, "Did you receive the Holy Spirit when you became believers?" They replied, "No, we have not even heard that there is a Holy Spirit." [3]Then he said, "Into what then were you baptized?" They answered, "Into John's baptism." [4]Paul said, "John baptized with the baptism of repentance, telling the people to believe in the one who was to come after him, that is, in Jesus." [5]On hearing this, they were baptized in the name of the Lord Jesus. [6]When Paul had laid his hands on them, the Holy Spirit came upon them, and they spoke in tongues and prophesied—

Acts 19:11-20

11 God did extraordinary miracles through Paul, [12]so that when the handker-

NIV
Acts 19:1-6

1 While Apollos was at Corinth, Paul took the road through the interior and arrived at Ephesus. There he found some disciples [2]and asked them, "Did you receive the Holy Spirit when you be-lieved?"

They answered, "No, we have not even heard that there is a Holy Spirit."

[3]So Paul asked, "Then what baptism did you receive?"

"John's baptism," they replied.

[4]Paul said, "John's baptism was a baptism of repentance. He told the people to believe in the one coming after him, that is, in Jesus." [5]On hearing this, they were baptized into the name of the Lord Jesus. [6]When Paul placed his hands on them, the Holy Spirit came on them, and they spoke in tongues and prophesied.

Acts 19:11-20

[11]God did extraordinary miracles through Paul, [12]so that even handkerchiefs

chiefs or aprons that had touched his skin were brought to the sick, their diseases left them, and the evil spirits came out of them. [13]Then some itinerant Jewish exorcists tried to use the name of the Lord Jesus over those who had evil spirits, saying, "I adjure you by the Jesus whom Paul proclaims." [14]Seven sons of a Jewish high priest named Sceva were doing this. [15]But the evil spirit said to them in reply, "Jesus I know, and Paul I know; but who are you?" [16]Then the man with the evil spirit leaped on them, mastered them all, and so overpowered them that they fled out of the house naked and wounded. [17]When this became known to all residents of Ephesus, both Jews and Greeks, everyone was awestruck; and the name of the Lord Jesus was praised. [18]Also many of those who became believers confessed and disclosed their practices. [19]A number of those who practiced magic collected their books and burned them publicly; when the value of these books was calculated, it was found to come to fifty thousand silver coins. [20]So the word of the Lord grew mightily and prevailed.

and aprons that had touched him were taken to the sick, and their illnesses were cured and the evil spirits left them. [13]Some Jews who went around driving out evil spirits tried to invoke the name of the Lord Jesus over those who were demon-possessed. They would say, "In the name of Jesus, whom Paul preaches, I command you to come out." [14]Seven sons of Sceva, a Jewish chief priest, were doing this. [15]One day the evil spirit answered them, "Jesus I know, and I know about Paul, but who are you?" [16]Then the man who had the evil spirit jumped on them and overpowered them all. He gave them such a beating that they ran out of the house naked and bleeding. [17]When this became known to the Jews and Greeks living in Ephesus, they were all seized with fear, and the name of the Lord Jesus was held in high honor. [18]Many of those who believed now came and openly confessed their evil deeds. [19]A number who had practiced sorcery brought their scrolls together and burned them publicly. When they calculated the value of the scrolls, the total came to fifty thousand drachmas. [20]In this way the word of the Lord spread widely and grew in power.

Key Verse

UNDERSTANDING THE SCRIPTURE

Acts 18:18-23. Having founded and nurtured a church in Corinth, Paul leaves for Antioch in Syria, his home base. Priscilla and Aquila, who had hosted Paul in Corinth, accompany him as far as Ephesus, where they will stay (see 1 Corinthians 16:19). At Cenchreae, a port in the eastern suburbs of Corinth, Paul shaved his hair (see also Acts 21:24). By taking this temporary Nazarite vow, Paul is portrayed as a loyal Jew. Luke's account seems odd, for the vow was usually ended, not begun, with the shaving of the head (see Numbers 6:5, 13-21). After reaching the important commercial port city of Ephesus, Paul preached in the synagogue, an act that gives him

claim to having founded the church there. Paul left and sailed into Caesarea, a puzzling choice of ports, for his destination in Antioch was three hundred miles to the north. Also unclear is the reference to the church Paul greets. It could have been the one in Caesarea, but was more likely in Jerusalem. The later possibility is supported by some ancient manuscripts that refer to the "feast that cometh in Jerusalem" (Acts 18:21 KJV). In Acts 18:23, Luke records that Paul does return to Antioch and quickly sets off again on what is traditionally known as his third missionary journey.

Acts 18:24-28. A Jewish man who has accepted Christ was enthusiastically teaching in Ephesus. Although well educated in the Scripture, (apparently having learned in a major city of Jewish culture, Alexandria), Apollos' message was incomplete. Priscilla and Aquila, who had studied under Paul, instructed him more thoroughly. With encouragement and a letter of introduction, Apollos went to Achaia and ministered to the Jews there.

Acts 19:1-7. When Paul returns to Ephesus, he finds Christians who have heard an incomplete gospel message, perhaps from Apollos or perhaps from disciples of John the Baptist. They had received the water baptism of John, but through the laying on of Paul's hands in the name of Jesus these twelve persons received the Holy Spirit. They gave outward evidence of the Spirit's presence by speaking in tongues and prophesying. Luke shows Paul incorporating a group on the theological fringes of Christianity into the mainstream of apostolic teaching.

Acts 19:8-10. Paul spends three months in the synagogue at Ephesus teaching about the kingdom of God, the main theme of Jesus' teachings. After detractors spoke against Christianity (the Way), Paul moved to a lecture hall, possibly owned by an otherwise unknown person named Tyrannus. He continued teaching for two years, a period that would have included missions to found churches in cities of Asia Minor such as Colossae, Laodicea, and Hierapolis.

Acts 19:11-20. Luke shows Paul as having extraordinary powers, similar to those of Peter (Acts 5:15). The image of Paul in Acts 19:12 may be legendary, for it is not in keeping with Paul's own description of himself (see for example 2 Corinthians 10:10). Ephesus was well known as an ancient center of magic. Pagan and Jewish sources attest to the use of Jesus' name in exorcisms performed by non-Christians. No Jewish high priest named Sceva is known.

Acts 19:21-22. Paul announces Spirit-directed travel plans that will be fulfilled in the rest of Luke's account. He goes to Macedonia and Achaia (Acts 20:1-2). He travels to Jerusalem (Acts 21:17) to deliver an offering (Acts 24:17 and Romans 15:22-29). Rome is the ultimate goal of his journeys as recorded in Acts.

Acts 19:23-41. Before Paul leaves Ephesus, a conflict breaks out that has both religious and economic significance. A silversmith named Demetrius gathered his colleagues and expressed serious concern that Paul's teachings were threatening their business as well as the reputation of the goddess Artemis. The silversmiths had a thriving business making miniature temples and other souvenirs related to Artemis' temple, located in Ephesus and hailed as one of the seven wonders of the ancient world. Paul's teachings, which caused persons to turn from Artemis, were damaging the silversmiths' business and the greatness of Ephesus. A riot breaks out which is finally quelled by the town clerk who advises Demetrius and others to bring charges, if such exist, against Paul so that the matter can be properly settled in court. Mob action by the townspeople in this provincial capital would have resulted in the Romans charging them with rioting, a very serious offense.

INTERPRETING THE SCRIPTURE

The Whole Gospel

Early in his long ministry at Ephesus, Paul encounters twelve persons who seem to be Christian. They had received the water baptism of repentance as proclaimed by John. Somehow, though, they had not heard the whole story. Perhaps they had been instructed by Apollos, who himself needed instruction from Paul's associates, Priscilla and Aquila, because "he knew only the baptism of John" (Acts

18:25). While it is unlikely that those familiar with the Old Testament would claim that they had "not even heard that there is a Holy Spirit" (Acts 19:2), as these folks did, they certainly had not understood that the Holy Spirit was part of the Christian experience. Baptizing them in the name of Jesus, Paul laid his hands upon them and they received the Holy Spirit.

Certainly Christians of good will and faithful study do not agree on all points of faith and practice. Such disagreements will always exist because none of us has total and absolute information about God. We will always find mysteries of God to ponder. Yet, how often have we seen tragic consequences that result from an incomplete or lopsided understanding of the gospel? Two modern examples—Jonestown and the Branch Davidians in Waco, Texas—underscore the possibility of grievous errors among persons who think they are following Christ.

How can we be on guard against perversions of the gospel that leave us vulnerable? How can we avoid finding ourselves backed into spiritual corners because we don't know the rest of the story? No easy answers exist to these questions, but some directions may be helpful.

First, we have to make a full-time commitment to building our relationship with Jesus. Unfortunately, some Christians assume that an hour or two on Sunday morning will be sufficient to nurture their relationship with Jesus. Just as our relationships with spouses, children, extended family, or friends do not thrive unless they are nurtured, so too our relationship with God must be carefully tended throughout the course of our lives. We must seek to know and be known by the creator of the universe and the Lord of our lives.

Second, we have to be teachable. The twelve persons Paul met were open to hearing new ideas that broadened their horizons about God. We learn about God through worship, prayer, and serious Bible study in private and among other members of the household of faith. When we are teachable, we recognize that other points of view exist, rather than rigidly assume that our way is the only way. However, we always test what we believe against the Scriptures, along with our traditions, reason, and experience.

Third, we need to look for validation of our own understandings. The twelve experienced God in a new, powerful way through the outpouring of the Holy Spirit. They could see signs of the Spirit's presence in their midst. We also have experiences that confirm for us a point that God is trying to teach us or a direction in which God is trying to lead us.

As Christians we need to be constantly seeking the whole gospel. We must undertake this goal with humility, knowing that we can never have access to all knowledge, for only God has that. On the other hand, if we ever decide that we know all we need to know—that we can stop seeking more intimate knowledge of God—then we have allowed ourselves to be lulled into contentment with a partial, impotent gospel.

The Gospel's Power Over Evil

Improper use of the gospel can be as dangerous as having too little knowledge of it. Luke gives an account of Paul's encounter with seven "itinerant Jewish exorcists" who find themselves overcome by the power of the gospel. All seven of them were overpowered by one demon possessed man when the spirit they were attempting to exorcise from him in the name of Jesus replied, "Jesus I know, and Paul I know; but who are you?" (Acts 19:15).

The seven, who claimed to be sons of a Jewish high priest of whom there is no record, were certainly not alone in using Jesus' name to exorcise demons. Even when Jesus was ministering, his disciples reported that an unknown person was casting out demons in his name (Mark

9:38-41 and Luke 9:49-50). Such activity was not unique, for both Jewish and pagan sources attest that non-Christians did indeed use Jesus' name to exorcise demons. Ephesus was a prime place for such activities because of its reputation as a center of magic. In fact, some books on magic were even referred to as "Ephesians scripts."

In using the name of Jesus to cast out demons, the sons of Sceva were following an established, effective pattern. They likely assumed that they too would be successful. This time, though, the exorcists had met their match. The demons turned upon all seven men, forcing them to run from a house "naked and wounded." Luke reports that "everyone was awestruck" (Acts 19:17) when they learned that one demon possessed man was able to overpower seven other men. News of this amazing incident spread quickly.

After seeing evidence of such power, many became Christian believers. The name of Jesus was not to be used lightly, especially by those who had not accepted that name for themselves. Ironically, the name that had been tossed about so casually had now become the name that many persons—including former practitioners of magic—professed. New Christians hauled out books on magic worth a fortune and burned them, not privately, but publicly, thereby openly severing ties to the occult. The sight of such a bonfire of books must have made a deep and lasting impression on those who witnessed this event. Reliance on occult powers had literally gone up in smoke.

Of course, one episode in Ephesus did not curtail occult practices. We know that two thousand years later many people in our society believe in the power of magic and engage in the occult arts. Even some Christians dabble in such practices, apparently assuming that the occult is a form of spirituality that is compatible with biblical religion. These people are seriously in error, but diluting or polluting biblical religion is hardly new. King Saul engaged in an occult practice (1 Samuel 28:1-25), even though it was forbidden by law (Deuteronomy 18:10-11). Neither evil nor examples of disobedience to God's will have disappeared. Yet demonstrations, such as the one seen in Ephesus, continue to remind us of the incomparable power of the gospel over evil.

The Word of the Lord Prevailed

Luke closes this episode in Ephesus by telling us that "the word of the Lord grew mightily and prevailed" (Acts 19:20). This statement may be difficult for us to interpret. After all, we need not look far to see that evil still abounds. Occult powers are still acknowledged, though they are only one form of evil. People are oppressed by evil, systemic social structures—such as racism, sexism, classism, and ageism—to a far greater degree than they are victimized by spells and incantations. Individuals experience evil as personal violence against them, tragically perpetrated by an unknown assailant or someone who is close to them. Entire groups are pushed to the margins of society because they are too powerless to stand against elite people and the formidable structures that these elitists support and which in turn support them. Evil continues to spread over the globe like a cancer.

Despite evidence of the continuing presence of evil, Christianity still affirms that the Word of God prevails. God's Word, as mediated to us through the person of Jesus Christ, will never fail us or be unable to withstand assaults from evil structures or anything else. We may suffer, just as members of the early church did, as we fight against evil powers. But we can be assured that God will be present with us, and that in the end God's word of truth and justice will prevail. We are called, just as surely as the persons to whom Jesus spoke in Acts 1:8, to witness for him and act against such evil. Evil cannot flourish where persons are willing to witness in word and deed to an alternative life rooted in the power of God's love and grace.

That witness, however, must be spoken with conviction and acted upon in a way that is consistent with what we say. We have the power in our hands to illuminate a world of darkness with the light of the Way. We could put on a tremendous fireworks display. Somehow, though, the power of the gospel turns from a breathtaking demonstration rich in spectacular colors to a few ineptly launched duds. Surely the Word of God is not flawed. Nor has it become ineffectual. The problem is that we do not know how to use that power, just as Sceva's sons did not know how to handle it. We have somehow diffused its potency so that what should be a resounding boom that draws people from all walks of life to it has become a barely audible pop.

As an oft repeated car ad intoned: "You have to lead, follow, or get out of the way." Too often we are in the way, blocking the power of God's Word. Our talk may not match our walk, thereby diluting the witness of the gospel's power. In contrast, leaders such as Paul, who un-ashamedly articulated the gospel message and stood for it against all perils, point us in new directions. These Christians give us glimpses of the transforming power that is available to us if we follow Jesus more nearly and boldly proclaim his word in a world that is desperately waiting to hear it.

SHARING THE SCRIPTURE

PREPARING TO TEACH

As you read the scripture lesson and study this week's lesson, think about the evils that exist in our society. Seeing a demon possessed person overcome seven men would likely not occur in our society. What, in your opinion, would be a modern equivalent? What would have to happen for persons to feel that the Word of God was prevailing in our day? You may want to write your ideas in your spiritual journal.

If you plan to set today's lesson within the larger biblical context, as presented in the background scripture, familiarize yourself with Acts 18:18–19:41 and the information under "Understanding the Scripture." Be prepared to retell this information or incorporate it into a lecture.

If you plan to use the activity concerning occult practices under "The Gospel's Power Over Evil," you may want to keep an eye out for current news, movie listings, astrology columns, or other media information that may give the class a better idea of occult practices in their own community.

If you plan to do a closing summary lecture, spend some time pulling together what you and your class have found to be the most important points in this quarter's work.

If you plan to use a closing hymn, have hymnals available.

LEADING THE CLASS

Introduction

Draw a line down the center of a chalkboard or sheet of newsprint. Label one column "Winners" and the other "Losers." Ask the class to list characteristics or traits of these two groups. Students can think of these words as they relate to any endeavor, such as sports, business, academics, human relationships, or whatever. Discuss the kinds of things that winners do to be winners. You may also want to discuss why the class thinks that losers are defeated.

Turn the discussion to today's lesson by talking about how Christians believe that the gospel has the power to defeat the forces of evil. The gospel, in other words, ultimately always wins out over evil.

Present the main question to the class either verbally or by writing it where everyone can see it: **In what ways do we perceive the gospel of Jesus Christ to overcome all other powers?**

The Whole Gospel

Choose a volunteer to read aloud Acts 19:1-6.

Encourage class members to try to summarize and state the problem faced by the twelve persons in this story before they met Paul. A possible response is: They were not fully empowered as Christians because they had heard only an incomplete version of the gospel.

Then ask: **Can you think of any modern examples of persons who were "incomplete Christians" because they had not been taught the whole gospel?** Answers will certainly vary, but two well-known examples are the group at Jonestown, led by Jim Jones, and the Branch Davidians, led by David Koresh.

Help the class to brainstorm ways that they can guard themselves against incompleteness. List their ideas on a chalkboard or newsprint. Three ideas are discussed in this section under "Interpreting the Scripture."

The Gospel's Power Over Evil

Direct the class's attention to Acts 19:11-19.

Use information from "Understanding the Scripture" related to these verses to help the class understand the attitude toward magic in Ephesus and become aware that sources exist, including biblical references, to document the use of the "name of Jesus" by non-Christian exorcists.

Invite class members to suggest occult arts that are practiced in our society at large or in your community in particular. Some

answers may include: astrology, fortune telling, consulting spirits through a medium, witchcraft, and Satanic worship.

Spend a few moments discussing how the class feels these practices:
- are in conflict with Christianity
- are glamorized in the media
- are harmful in that they keep people from making a total commitment to God.

The Word of the Lord Prevailed

Invite the class to read together Acts 19:20. Or ask several members who have different translations to read this verse.

Ask the class: **What evidence do you see today of God's Word spreading?** This question will likely raise comments concerning missions and the translation of the Bible into languages that previously had no Bible.

Then ask: **What evidence do you see of God's word prevailing over evil?** This question may be harder to answer. In fact, some persons may feel that evil is winning. If that sentiment is expressed, ask the class: **How can Christians bear witness to a different way of life that is not rooted in the evils that are so prevalent in our society?**

Since this is the last lesson on Acts, you may want to do a summary or review of this quarter's work in one of two ways.

(1) If your class prefers a lecture, prepare a brief list of highlights from the lessons. Focus your review on the empowerment of the church at Pentecost for the purpose of witnessing to others and spreading the gospel to all people in all places.

(2) If your class prefers discussion, ask these two questions to the total group or to small groups: **(a) What insights have you gained about the early church and the spread of the Christian gospel? (b) How will this study enable you to be a more effective witness in a world that is still filled with evil and sin?**

You may want to sing an Advent hymn, such as "Come, Thou Long-Expected Jesus" or "Hail to the Lord's Anointed" (pages 196 and 203, respectively, in *The United Methodist Hymnal*) to tie the lesson of the gospel's power to overcome evil in Jesus Christ with the beginning of the church year that is marked by the preparation for Jesus' coming.

HELPING CLASS MEMBERS ACT

Ask students to make a list of broad questions they have concerning their Christian faith, or areas where they feel their knowledge is incomplete. Tell them to be prepared to hand their lists in anonymously next week. When they are submitted, read the questions yourself to see if any mesh well with upcoming Sunday school lessons. Pass the questions on to your pastor, who may be able to address them in sermons over the coming weeks. If questions focus on a theme, you may want to talk with the appropriate church leader regarding a short-term study on that topic.

Encourage class members to be especially aware of the actions they imitate and the persons they consciously or unconsciously have adopted as role models. Have them look carefully at the actions they are taking to determine whether they are following someone else's lead just because it is successful, or because they believe that such action truly reflects the gospel's expectations for their lives. If class members find discrepancies between what they are doing and what they profess to believe, challenge them to take steps to change their behavior.

Ask students to identify an evil that they encounter regularly. Challenge them to do something to respond to this problem as a Christian witness. For example, if they must deal with a co-worker who tells inappropriate jokes, encourage them to let the jokester know why they do not appreciate the humor. Another example would be to write to elected officials to let them know of concerns about an unjust or illegal situation.

PLANNING FOR NEXT SUNDAY

Next Sunday you will begin a new quarter that will include study of the books of Isaiah, Jonah, and Ruth. Ask students to read Isaiah 40:1-11 in which the prophet offers comfort to those who hurt. Class members may want to think of times when they needed to hear a word of comfort from God.

Please turn now to the Quarterly Evaluation form on pages 487-88. Complete this form for the First Quarter.

SECOND QUARTER

DECEMBER 3, 1995 – FEBRUARY 25, 1996

During December and January, we will be exploring passages from the book of the prophet Isaiah that focus on the theme of God's promise of deliverance. This promise was surely good news to the Israelites who were living in exile in Babylon. The prophet's words would have provided comfort for today and hope for a better tomorrow. Isaiah also portrays God's suffering servant as one who will bring about deliverance. In February, we will consider the theme of God's love for all people as we study two short, but well-known Old Testament books, Jonah and Ruth.

The five-session unit for December is entitled *The Coming of a New Day*. The first lesson, based on Isaiah 40:1-11, looks ahead to a time of comfort promised to those who are hurting. In Isaiah 51, the Scripture for the second session, God speaks through the prophet to encourage those who are discouraged by the difficult circumstances that confront them. The third week we will reflect on the promise, as recorded in Isaiah 9:1-7, that a time of joy will come to those in despair. The lesson for December 24 includes scripture from Isaiah 11 as well as the beloved Christmas story from the second chapter of Luke. This session will highlight a time of peace and righteousness, an era that will be ruled over by the promised messiah. The final lesson in this unit looks at the prophet's message, found in Isaiah 60–61, that a time will come to share good news.

The Ministry of the Suffering Servant, a four-session unit, focuses particularly on the servant whom Isaiah describes in four different passages. On January 7, we will probe Isaiah 42:1-9, the first of the servant songs, to study the servant's call. Next we will consider the mission of the servant as set forth in Isaiah 49:1-6. Our third session will describe the servant's steadfast endurance, as discussed in Isaiah 50:1-11. Finally, we will celebrate the servant's victory through suffering, as promised in Isaiah 52:13–53:12.

Our four-session unit for February, *God's Love for All People*, opens with two lessons from the book of Jonah. The first, taken from Jonah 1–2, looks at Jonah's flight from God when he was called to go to Nineveh to prophesy. The second portrays God's mercy toward the repentant residents of Nineveh, as seen in Jonah 3–4. In both of these lessons, the emphasis is on the inclusiveness of God's gracious love. On February 18, we turn to the first chapter of Ruth. Her well-known loyalty to her mother-in-law Naomi is covered during this session. Our quarter closes with selected passages from Ruth 2–4 that demonstrate Boaz's kindness. As next of kin, Boaz marries Ruth, whose first husband, Naomi's son, had died. Ruth bears a son to Boaz named Obed, who becomes the grandfather of King David.

MEET OUR WRITER

DR. LYNNE DEMING

Dr. Lynne M. Deming is the publisher for The United Church Board for Homeland Ministries, United Church of Christ, Cleveland, Ohio. She was formerly with the curriculum division of The United Methodist Publishing House and senior editor of Upper Room Books. She has a B.A. from Lycoming College, Williamsport, Pa., and a Master of Divinity degree from Candler School of Theology, Emory University, and a Ph.D. in Hebrew Scripture from Emory University. She has been leading adult church school classes and other adult study groups for many years. She is currently enrolled in The Upper Room's Academy for Spiritual Formation.

FOR THOSE WHO HURT

PREVIEWING THE LESSON

Lesson Scripture: Isaiah 40:1-11*a*
Background Scripture: Isaiah 40:1-11
Key Verse: Isaiah 40:1-2

Focus of the lesson:
the comfort God provides to persons in times of suffering and despair

Main question(s) of the lesson:
(1) How is God there when we are hurting and need comfort?

This lesson will enable adult learners to:
(1) understand how God comforted the Israelites during their exile in Babylon through forgiveness, through removing obstacles, and through the words and actions of others
(2) perceive how God comforts them in their own sufferings
(3) respond by offering the comfort of forgiveness to others.

Today's lesson may be outlined as follows:
(1) Introduction
(2) Forgiveness
(3) Removing Obstacles
(4) Being the Hands of God for Others

FOCUSING ON THE MAIN QUESTION

Is God there when we are hurting and need comfort? The prophet who wrote these words answers this question with a resounding yes. "Comfort, O comfort my people, says your God" (Isaiah 40:1).

When times are tough, when we are hurting, we often ask, like the psalmist did, "My God, my God, why have you forsaken me?" (Psalm 22:1). A man dies just after retirement, leaving his wife to live their golden years alone. A couple agonizes over the illness of their child. A fac-

tory closes down and many people lose their jobs. A flood ravages the Midwest and people lose their homes. In times like these God seems far away from us.

But God is not absent. Many people who have experienced times of grief, despair, or loneliness will say that, looking back, God seemed closer during that time than ever before. This passage from Isaiah says yes to our main question: **How is God there when we are hurting and need comfort?** God does not forsake us when we need comfort. Rather, God is there, comforting us, making our rough places a plain and leading us through the desert like a shepherd leads a flock.

Let's go back to our often-asked question: "God, why have you forsaken me?" That question opens up the dialogue with God. We may begin by asking why God is so far away from us only to conclude that God is nearer than we thought. How do we experience God's presence in times of suffering and despair?

Sometimes we experience comfort when God removes obstacles that stand in our way. When God helps us to clarify and fol-low a particular path, we find comfort in that. Or, we may experience God's comfort in the act of forgiveness. Just as God forgives us, we can forgive and be forgiven by others. When we are hurting, we also experience God's presence through the comfort that others provide. A friend takes the time to listen to our worries. A relative comes to care for other family members so that we can concentrate on the crisis at hand. Church members call and ask what they might do to help. The challenge that today's topic presents is twofold: to find God when we need his comfort and to be God's comfort to others when they need it.

READING THE SCRIPTURE

NRSV
Isaiah 40:1-11
1 Comfort, O comfort my
people,
says your God.
²Speak tenderly to Jerusalem,
and cry to her
that she has served her term,
that her penalty is paid,
that she has received from the
LORD's hand
double for all her sins.

³A voice cries out:
"In the wilderness prepare the
way of the LORD,
make straight in the desert a
highway for our God.
⁴Every valley shall be lifted up,
and every mountain and hill be
made low;
the uneven ground shall become
level,
and the rough places a plain.
⁵Then the glory of the LORD shall
be revealed,
and all people shall see it
together,
for the mouth of the LORD has
spoken."

NIV
Isaiah 40:1-11
1 Comfort, comfort my people,
says your God.
²Speak tenderly to Jerusalem,
and proclaim to her
that her hard service has been completed,
that her sin has been paid for,
that she has received from the LORD's hand
double for all her sins.

³A voice of one calling:
"In the desert prepare
the way for the LORD;
make straight in the wilderness
a highway for our God.
⁴Every valley shall be raised up,
every mountain and hill made low;
the rough ground shall become level,
the rugged places a plain.
⁵And the glory of the LORD will be revealed,
and all mankind together will see it.
For the mouth of the LORD has spoken."

Key
Verses

133

⁶A voice says, "Cry out!"
　　And I said, "What shall I
　　　cry?"
　All people are grass,
　　their constancy is like the
　　　flower of the field.
⁷The grass withers, the flower
　　fades,
　　when the breath of the LORD
　　　blows upon it;
　　surely the people are grass.
⁸The grass withers, the flower
　　fades;
　　but the word of our God will
　　　stand forever.
⁹Get you up to a high mountain,
　　O Zion, herald of good
　　　tidings;
　lift up your voice with strength,
　　O Jerusalem, herald of good
　　　tidings,
　lift it up, do not fear;
　say to the cities of Judah,
　　"Here is your God!"
¹⁰See, the Lord GOD comes with
　　might,
　　and his arm rules for him;
　his reward is with him,
　　and his recompense before
　　　him.
¹¹He will feed his flock like a
　　shepherd;
　　he will gather the lambs in his
　　　arms,
　and carry them in his bosom,
　　and gently lead the mother
　　　sheep.

⁶A voice says, "Cry out."
　　And I said, "What shall I cry?"

　"All men are like grass,
　　and all their glory is like the flowers of the
　　　field.
⁷The grass withers and the flowers fall,
　　because the breath of the LORD blows on
　　　them.
　　Surely the people are grass.
⁸The grass withers and the flowers fall,
　　but the word of our God stands forever."

⁹You who bring good tidings to Zion,
　　go up on a high mountain.
　You who bring good tidings to Jerusalem,
　　lift up your voice with a shout,
　lift it up, do not be afraid;
　　say to the towns of Judah,
　　"Here is your God!"

¹⁰See, the Sovereign LORD comes with power,
　　and his arm rules for him.
　See, his reward is with him,
　　and his recompense accompanies him.

¹¹He tends his flock like a shepherd:
　　He gathers the lambs in his arms
　and carries them close to his heart;
　　he gently leads those that have young.

UNDERSTANDING THE SCRIPTURE

Chapter 40 in Isaiah begins a new section in the book. Isaiah of Jerusalem, whose prophecies are recorded in the first 39 chapters of Isaiah, lived and worked in Judah, the Southern Kingdom, during the eighth century B.C.E. With the opening words of chapter 40, we move ahead approximately 150 years to the time of the Babylonian Exile. The author of the prophecies in Isaiah 40–55, known as Second Isaiah, lived and worked among the exiles in Babylon, and his message reflects that situation throughout.

This passage is divided into four parts: (1) the prophet's message of comfort (Isaiah 40:1-2); (2) the prophet's proclamation of God's intention to remove obstacles (Isaiah 40:3-5); (3) information about the prophet (Isaiah 40:6-8); and (4) the prophet's message of God's constancy (Isaiah 40:9-11).

Second Isaiah lived and wrote in what might be called a very small space between promise and fulfillment. His life and his work were dominated by his conviction that the end of the Babylonian Exile was at hand. He was so certain of this that in his prophecies he often speaks of the return home to Judah as if it had already happened. There is an urgency about this prophet's message that both reflects the situation in which he lived and gives us hope when we are dealing with our own times of crisis.

Isaiah 40:1-2. The first two words we encounter when we begin reading Second Isaiah, "Comfort, comfort," summarize the message of this prophet to his original audience and to us. The prophet is utterly convinced of God's concern for humanity. Just as God will not leave the chosen people languishing in exile, God will not leave us in our own times of despair and desolation. The twofold imperative "Comfort, comfort" parallels and foreshadows the similar imperative near the end of the book: "Depart, depart" (Isaiah 52:11).

"Comfort, comfort" is the first of three cries that form the structure of this section. This first cry is uttered by the prophet, on behalf of God, to the exiles. The message is that the people of Judah, now in exile, have served their term. In other words, the exile is about to come to an end. The people have paid their penalty; they have received not just the punishment they deserved, but double the punishment that would have sufficed. Imagine the response of these exiles when they heard the news that they had already suffered more than enough.

Isaiah 40:3-5. This section constitutes the second of the three cries; this cry is uttered by an unidentified person to an unidentified audience. In these verses the prophet proclaims that it is now time for the road to be built on which the exiles will return to Judah. The year is approximately 538 B.C.E. Cyrus of Persia has just defeated the Babylonian Empire and has declared his intention to release the Judean captives and allow them to return home (see Ezra 1:1-4). Second Isaiah paints a vivid picture of joyful exiles celebrating their release from captivity.

This second cry contains a well-known phrase that the writer of the Gospel of Luke used to describe the coming of John the Baptist: "In the wilderness prepare the way of the LORD." In fact, Luke uses most of these three verses to illustrate his conviction that John's arrival on the scene represents a fulfillment of Second Isaiah's prophecy. As we can see from Luke 3:4-6, the phrase "in the wilderness" takes on a slightly different meaning when Luke repeats these words almost 600 years later. For Second Isaiah, "in the wilderness" referred to the place where the highway was to be built; for Luke, Matthew (3:3), Mark (1:3), and John (1:23), the wilderness was the location of the voice that proclaims the message. However, the essential message remains the same across the years: the fulfillment of the promise is at hand.

Isaiah 40:6-8. Most prophetic books in the Hebrew Scriptures open with what is called a *superscription,* or an introduction to the writer. For examples, look at the opening verses of Amos and Isaiah. These three verses in Second Isaiah provide the only information we have about this prophet who chooses to remain in the background. We read in these verses that he was called to prophesy, that he objected at first to this call on the grounds that he did not know what to say ("And I said, 'What shall I cry?'"), and that his objection was answered with the assurance that God's word is steadfast and will remain forever.

Isaiah 40:9-11. Here we see the third of three cries that form the structure of this section. This cry is addressed to Zion, representing the people of Judah, who are now in exile. The speaker is the prophet, speaking on behalf of God. Again the prophet emphasizes the constancy of God. The message here is that the promise of release from captivity would never be fulfilled if God were not at work in the world. God is pictured here as both powerful and nurturing.

INTERPRETING THE SCRIPTURE

Forgiveness

At times we experience God's comfort through forgiveness. Forgiveness has several facets: we are forgiven by someone else for harm we have inflicted on that person; we forgive ourselves for something we have done; we forgive someone else for hurting us; we feel God's forgiveness for something we have done. Some persons believe that we cannot forgive others until we are able to forgive ourselves. Others maintain that we must first forgive those who have wronged us. Still others think that God's forgiveness is primary and necessary before we can experience human forgiveness.

In today's scripture passage, Second Isaiah begins by proclaiming to the people that God has forgiven them for their sins: "Speak tenderly to Jerusalem, and cry to her that she has served her term, that her penalty is paid, that she has received from the LORD's hand double for all her sins" (Isaiah 40:2). Here the prophet is alluding to the prevailing idea that the people were sent into exile to Babylon partially for political reasons (i.e., Babylon had come to power and was doing what any conquering nation would do) and partly for theological reasons (i.e., the chosen people had sinned and God had punished them).

In this passage, however, we see that God has forgiven the people and intends that they be released from captivity and allowed to return to Jerusalem. Try to imagine the impact of that message on the weary exiles. Not only does the prophet proclaim the promise of release from bondage; the prophet also proclaims that God has forgiven them. They have served their term; they have paid the price and all is forgiven. Not only that, they have paid double the price, so there is no question of more needing to be done. They have suffered more than enough, and it is time to go home. Surely the people who heard these words from the mouth of the prophet experienced God's comfort, for God does, indeed, comfort us through forgiveness.

Some time ago I experienced firsthand the comfort that comes through forgiveness. Through a painful conversation, I discovered that I had inadvertently done something that hurt a good friend. As we talked, I was also hurt by some of the things this friend said to me. The whole conversation was difficult and we parted awkwardly. For a long time afterward we did not speak to one another. Some time later we began to talk again. In the interim we had both been thinking about what had transpired and how we did not want that conversation to erase what had been between us before that point. In that second conversation, which was also difficult, we forgave each other.

The second conversation did not erase the first one; the first conversation and the events that brought it about will always remain with us. But we both experienced a sense of peace and comfort through the forgiveness that we offered to each other.

Acknowledging our need for forgiveness helps us to forgive others for what they have done to us, knowingly or unknowingly, as this story from the desert tradition illustrates:

A brother at Scetis committed a fault. A council was called to which Abba Moses was invited, but he refused to go to it.

Then the priest sent someone to say to him, "Come, for everyone is waiting for you." So he got up and went. He took a leaking jug, filled it with water and carried it with him. The others came out to meet him and said to him, "What is this, Father?" The old man said to them, "My sins run out behind me, and I do not see them, and today I am coming to judge the errors of another." When they heard that they said no more to the brother but forgave him.

Forgiving and being forgiven are powerful expressions of the comfort God can provide.

Removing Obstacles

Another way God comforts people is to remove obstacles for them. Second Isaiah speaks in today's scripture about the many barriers God was about to remove so that the people could be released from captivity and return home to Judah. When God lifts up valleys, makes mountains low, makes rough places smooth, and creates roads in the middle of the desert, God is effectively eliminating obstacles that hinder the homeward journey.

In this passage we also read that God is also at work removing obstacles that stand in the way of the prophet. In verse 6, God summons the prophet to cry, or to proclaim a message to the people. God says, "Cry out!" As Old Testament prophets usually did when first called by God to prophesy, this prophet objects that he is not equal to the task. His response "What shall I cry?" and his protest that all of life (including prophetic messages) is transitory is another way of objecting that there really is nothing to say. How can he prophesy when there is nothing lasting in life to talk about?

God removes this obstacle in verse 8 by saying, in essence, "Yes, you are right. All of life is transitory. Nothing lasts. Nothing, that is, except the most important thing: the Word of God." God's message does indeed endure, and that is the message the prophet is to proclaim.

What does it mean for God to remove obstacles in our lives? What obstacles stand in our way? Sometimes physical or tangible barriers block our way. Sometimes, on the other hand, our obstacles are more like the one this prophet faced when he was called upon to proclaim God's message of comfort.

Recently I was called upon to preach to a community of which I am a part. Like Second Isaiah, I was initially reluctant, but I agreed to preach nevertheless. My agreeing to preach the sermon, however, did not remove the obstacles. As the time to preach approached, I became more and more aware of the thoughts and prayers that were being offered to me by many people. Some of these people were in the community and would be there to hear me preach the sermon; others would not be there but would be with me in spirit. Through these thinkers and prayers, God was removing the obstacle of my fear in the face of my task. When I stood up to preach, I did so in confidence. I was not afraid. The calm that settled in on me was God's comfort, which I felt strongly because fear had left me.

Being the Hands of God for Others

We know that God's comfort often comes to us through the words and actions of those around us like friends, loved ones, members of our congregation, and sometimes those we do not even know. Try to place yourself in the situation of the exiles to whom Second Isaiah was speaking. They were suffering; after fifty or more years in exile, they had likely given up hope of ever returning to their homeland. Into this situation of despair steps the prophet with a message of hope and release from captivity. Surely these exiles experienced the comfort God provides through the words and deeds of this unknown prophet.

In the book *To Be the Hands of God,* Judy Griffith Ransom and James G. Henderson tell the story of Joan Henderson and her battle with cancer. Joan was a middle-aged woman who lived with her family in a suburb of Nashville, Tennessee. A physical education major in college, Joan was the picture of health. She was active in her community and her church, and lived a full life. She seemed to have an inexhaustible supply of energy, which made her illness seem all the more improbable.

When Joan found out she had cancer, she and her family and friends were devastated. Early tests and procedures seemed to indicate that there was a chance she could be cured. But the more the disease progressed the less hope the doctors held out that she would recover. After two years of hard work and struggle, Joan lost her battle with cancer.

This is a story that repeats itself in every city and town every day. But Joan Henderson's story is remarkable because of the congregation that lived through her illness with her, every step of the way. Joan and her husband Jim were members of an active Sunday school class in their United Methodist church. When word spread throughout the church of Joan's diagnosis, members of that Sunday school class went to work. Among other things, they organized food for the family, arranged care for the children, offered support for Jim, and provided financial help for the family. *To Be the Hands of God* is as much a story of the work of Joan's community of faith as it is a story of her courage in the face of her cancer, for the members of Joan's congregation were truly the hands of God for her. Through them, Joan experienced the comfort of God in the face of her crisis. Joan Henderson's story illustrates the truth that we often experience the comfort God provides through the support of others.

SHARING THE SCRIPTURE

PREPARING TO TEACH

Today's lesson focuses on the comfort God can provide during times of suffering, pain, and crisis. The prophet's proclamation in Isaiah 40 centers on three ways God's comfort can be manifested: through forgiveness, through removing obstacles that stand in the way of progress, and through the actions of others.

During the coming week, as you prepare to teach this lesson, think about these three ways that we can experience God's comforting presence in our lives. Ponder these questions:

(1) When in your life have you experienced forgiveness?

(2) Have you forgiven someone lately?

(3) Has someone forgiven you?

(4) Have you felt God's forgiveness as you struggled with how to deal with a situation?

Read the section on forgiveness in "Interpreting the Scripture"; perhaps that will spark your imagination or refresh your memory.

Recall a time when you faced a task or a situation that seemed overwhelming. We look to God during those times to receive the comfort that only God can provide. Focus on one situation or event. Think about how obstacles were removed so that you could either complete the task or move through the situation. What obstacles stood in your way? How have you experienced God's comfort as you faced this task?

Reread the section called "Being the Hands of God for Others." Do you know of a similar situation in your congregation or your community? You might want to talk to your pastor, since he or she is most likely to know about such cases. Perhaps there is someone in your church school class whose family is in crisis. Give some thought to how your class might help this family in the weeks to come.

During your preparation time this week, spend some time reading and rereading the Isaiah 40 passage. Read the section entitled "Interpreting the Scripture." Make a special effort to be aware of instances in your life when you experience God's comfort.

LEADING THE CLASS

Introduction

Read or retell the material under the heading "Focusing on the Main Question." Provide a few moments of silence so that class members can focus on the topic for the morning.

Ask the main question: **How is God there when we are hurting and need comfort?** Then mention again the three ways of experiencing God's comfort that form the outline of this session: through forgiveness, through removing obstacles, and through the words and actions of others. Ask the class members to suggest other ways that we experience God's comfort. Answers may include: praying, reading our Bibles, or singing familiar hymns are other ways many of us experience God's presence in times of crisis. You might want to record these ideas on a chalkboard or on newsprint. Emphasize that this lesson focuses on the three ideas listed above, since they reflect the message of the prophet in today's scripture passage.

Choose a volunteer to read the scripture passage aloud, ending with the words "He will feed his flock like a shepherd." From this point on the discussion will highlight the three ways of experiencing God's comfort that are covered in the material.

Forgiveness

Open this section of the lesson by rereading verses 1 and 2 of Isaiah 40, which focus on the idea of forgiveness. Of the three topics, this is perhaps the most difficult to discuss, since it is the most per-

sonal. Begin by either (1) having someone read aloud the section entitled "Forgiveness" under "Interpreting the Scripture," or (2) relating an incident from your own life related to forgiveness. Pause for a time of reflection.

After class members have had time to think about forgiveness, ask for volunteers to speak of personal experiences of forgiveness. Be sensitive to the fact that this is a very personal topic, and class members (especially if they do not know each other well) may be reluctant to share their own experiences. If you think this may be a problem, be certain to mention the possibility of sharing other situations with which they may be familiar but not directly involved. It is easier to speak of topics like forgiveness with a little objectivity.

Guide the class members into a time of sharing thoughts and experiences related to forgiveness. Keep in mind the various aspects of forgiveness (forgiving, being forgiven, experiencing God's forgiveness), and point out these various aspects as they are mentioned in the discussion. Close the time of discussion by reading aloud the passage from the desert tradition, found in the "Interpreting the Scripture" section.

Removing Obstacles

Begin this discussion by having someone read aloud Isaiah 40:3-8, which are the prophet's proclamation concerning God's intention to remove obstacles that stand in the way of the return to Judah. You might want to use the information provided under "Understanding the Scripture" as background to explain why the prophet was proclaiming these words at this particular time.

After the scripture selection is read and explained, ask class members to list the obstacles that are mentioned here. Write them on a chalkboard or newsprint as they are suggested.

If your class members like to use their imaginations, help them draw a visual picture of what life in Babylon might have been like. They are living in a relatively large city, far away from home. Focus first on what they might see and hear. What sights and sounds come to mind? For instance, what would it be like to live in a city where a different language is spoken? Help the group experience the sense of loneliness and despair that these exiles must have felt.

Ask the class to picture the obstacles that are mentioned in the text. Discuss how their mental picture changes when the mountains are made low, the rough places made smooth, and so forth.

What other obstacles, which are not mentioned by the prophet, might the people have faced? Help class members to suggest ideas such as lack of faith, despair, or loss of hope.

Bring the discussion closer to home by asking for examples of obstacles we must overcome when we face difficult situations. Begin with a time for reflection and then ask group members to share experiences. This discussion time may focus on either a general list of the kinds of obstacles we all face, or specific instances in the lives of group members in which obstacles were removed. Whichever direction the discussion goes, make certain the connection is made between the obstacles we face and the comfort God provides when these obstacles are removed and our path is cleared.

Being the Hands of God for Others

Begin this segment by reminding class members that the topic for today is God's comfort during times of turmoil, and that one way we experience the comforting presence of God during these times is through the help we receive from those who are close to us. Ask the group members to think of examples from their own lives when they have experienced God through others. Be prepared with an example of your own to start the discussion.

After everyone has had a chance to share an incident, have someone read aloud the section from this lesson about Joan Henderson, from the book *To Be the Hands of God*. Then ask the class to brainstorm possible situations in your congregation or community in which this kind of help might be both needed and offered. Record their suggestions on a chalkboard or newsprint.

After a list is generated, take some time to decide which situation your class might address. Discuss how the group might go about organizing an effort to be the hands of God to those persons who need comfort.

HELPING CLASS MEMBERS ACT

Encourage class members to forgive someone this week.

Challenge adults to think about obstacles that are hindering them from completing an important task. Have them ask God to remove these distractions. If your group focused on one individual or family that needs help during a time of crisis, plan to take action in the coming week.

PLANNING FOR NEXT SUNDAY

Encourage class members to prepare for next week's session by reading Isaiah 51:1-8. Tell them that next week's topic is encouragement: the prophet proclaims that we can count on God to fulfill promises because God has worked on our behalf in the past. Ask class members to be aware of instances of encouragement in the face of challenge.

FOR THOSE WHO ARE DISCOURAGED

PREVIEWING THE LESSON

Lesson Scripture: Isaiah 51:1-6
Background Scripture: Isaiah 51:1-8
Key Verse: Isaiah 51:6

Focus of the lesson:
the encouragement that God's promises give to persons who are discouraged

Main question(s) of the lesson:
(1) Is God steadfast in times of crisis and despair?

This lesson will enable adult learners to:
(1) examine God's promises of comfort, steadfast love, and future salvation as proclaimed by the prophet Isaiah
(2) experience hope in their own lives
(3) respond by sharing a word of encouragement with persons who are in difficult circumstances.

Today's lesson may be outlined as follows:
(1) Introduction
(2) God's Past Actions Bring Hope to Present Situations
(3) God's Promise of Comfort
(4) The Permanence of God in the Midst of Change

FOCUSING ON THE MAIN QUESTION

In Psalm 63:3, the psalmist proclaims with confidence that he will praise God because God's steadfast love is better than life itself. In a way, the psalmist is addressing the main question of today's lesson: **Is God steadfast in times of crisis and despair?** Many things in life do not endure through times of trial. We often lose faith.

Friends and loved ones disappoint us. We cannot count on our government. Sometimes even our congregation lets us down when we need help. All these things happen. But God's love is steadfast. God's covenant and promises remain secure through all the chaos that the world brings us. That is the prophet's message to the exiles, and that is the message for us as well.

In today's passage, Second Isaiah has several things to say concerning the steadfastness of God's presence among us. First, we can be certain of God's love because of what God has done for us or for others in the past. The psalmists, who were responsible for recording the hymns of praise used in the worship services of the ancient Israelites, praised God for two main reasons: for who God is and for what God has done. Today's scripture lesson refers to the latter reason. God had been active in the lives of the Israelites even before they existed as a people. Look to your ancestors, the prophet proclaims. Look at what God has done there. Surely that will convince you that God will work in our lives as well.

Second, the prophet proclaims that "this, too, shall pass." Isaiah encourages the people to envision themselves in another place in order to help themselves through their current situation. The prophet believes this, too, shall pass because God is acting on behalf of the exiles to bring their current situation to an end.

Third, the prophet reassures the people that salvation is imminent. He concludes this section by reaffirming his basic message that God remains permanent in the midst of chaos. God's permanence is contrasted to the temporality of earthly things. That contrast gives the discouraged exiles hope that, first, their current situation is temporary, and second, that God's promise to bring about the end of their struggle remains steadfast.

READING THE SCRIPTURE

NRSV
Isaiah 51:1-6
1 Listen to me, you that pursue
        righteousness,
    you that seek the LORD.
    Look to the rock from which
            you were hewn,
        and to the quarry from which
            you were dug.
²Look to Abraham, your father
        and to Sarah who bore you;
    for he was but one when I called
            him,
        but I blessed him and made
            him many.
³For the LORD will comfort Zion;
    he will comfort all her waste
            places,
    and will make her wilderness like
            Eden,
        her desert like the garden of
            the LORD;
    joy and gladness will be found in
            her,
    thanksgiving and the voice of
            song.

NIV
Isaiah 51:1-6
1 "Listen to me, you who pursue
        righteousness,
    and who seek the LORD:
    Look to the rock from which you were cut
        and to the quarry from which you were
            hewn;

²look to Abraham, your father,
    and to Sarah, who gave you birth.
    When I called him he was but one,
        and I blessed him and made him many.

³The LORD will surely comfort Zion
        and will look with compassion on all her
            ruins;
    he will make her deserts like Eden,
        her wastelands like the garden of the
            LORD.
    Joy and gladness will be found in her,
        thanksgiving and the sound of singing.

⁴Listen to me, my people,
  and give heed to me, my
    nation;
  for a teaching will go out from
    me,
  and my justice for a light to
    the peoples.
⁵I will bring near my deliverance
    swiftly,
  my salvation has gone out
  and my arms will rule the
    peoples;
  the coastlands wait for me,
    and for my arm they hope.
⁶Lift up your eyes to the heavens,
  and look at the earth beneath;
  for the heavens will vanish like
    smoke,
  the earth will wear out like a
    garment,
  and those who live on it will
    die like gnats;
  but my salvation will be forever.
  and my deliverance will never
    be ended.

Key Verse

⁴"Listen to me, my people;
  hear me, my nation:
  The law will go out from me;
    my justice will become a light to the
      nations.

⁵My righteousness draws near speedily,
  my salvation is on the way,
  and my arm will bring justice to the
    nations.
  The islands will look to me
    and wait in hope for my arm.

⁶Lift up your eyes to the heavens,
  look at the earth beneath;
  the heavens will vanish like smoke,
    the earth will wear out like a garment
  and its inhabitants die like flies.
  But my salvation will last forever,
    my righteousness will never fail.

Key Verse

UNDERSTANDING THE SCRIPTURE

The passage is divided into three parts: (1) the promise of God's comfort (Isaiah 51:1-3); (2) the promise of God's steadfast love (Isaiah 51:4-6); and (3) the promise of future salvation (Isaiah 51:7-8).

Recall the message of Isaiah 40:8, which was part of last week's scripture: "The grass withers, the flower fades; but the word of our God will stand forever." In a world where everything seems transitory, God remains steadfast. That is Second Isaiah's message in a nutshell, and it is the heart of today's lesson.

Today's passage is a first-person address by God through the prophet to the Babylonian exiles. God speaks through Second Isaiah to those seeking deliverance from their captivity. Scholars call Isaiah 51:1-8 an oracle of comfort.

These verses combine an appeal to God's work in history with a promise of future salvation.

Isaiah 51:1-3. God addresses the exiles directly, calling them "you that pursue righteousness." The prophet uses the word "righteousness" here to mean "salvation," rather than the more common usage of the word, referring to right actions. God knows the exiles' situation, recognizes their need for deliverance, and offers words of comfort and encouragement in the form of a promise of future salvation. Given the conditions under which the Israelites were living in Babylon, their need for salvation is obvious.

"Look to the rock from which you were hewn," says God to the chosen people. A rock is a solid foundation, something that can be counted on. In the case of the exiles, the rock from which they came was their homeland, their place of security. The word "quarry" is an unusual one, found only twice in the Old Testament. The prophet uses this word as a parallel to the word "rock"; it is another way of referring to the solid foundation of their homeland.

God also calls the exiles to, "Look to Abraham your father and to Sarah who bore you." God's dealings with Israel's ancestors attest to the active presence of God in history. In Genesis 12:1-3 God promises Abraham that he and Sarah will be the forebears of a great nation and a blessing to many people. Isaiah refers to Genesis to underscore his point about God's faithfulness in keeping promises: just as God has fulfilled the promise to Abraham and Sarah, God will fulfill the promise to the exiles. God will allow them to return to their homeland.

Ancient Hebrew hymns of praise usually consisted of two parts: a call to praise God and the reasons for praise, which were generally related to God's creating or saving activities. Verse 3 of today's passage sounds like a fragment of a hymn of praise, since it gives a reason for praising God: God will comfort Zion, the chosen people. Note the change from God speaking in the first person in verses 1 and 2 to God being spoken of in the third person here in verse 3. The prophet proclaims that the end will be like the beginning when the time of God's salvation comes. When God's promise of salvation is fulfilled, the return to Judah will resemble the return to the idyllic conditions in the Garden of Eden. Just as Eden was a perfect place, restored Judah will be a paradise compared to the exiles' current living conditions in Babylon.

Isaiah 51:4-6. The message of these verses is that salvation, or deliverance, is surely near. Notice the urgency in the prophet's words, conveyed by the imperatives in these verses: listen, give heed, lift up your eyes, look. Notice also the personal tone of the address. God speaks to the exiles in captivity, referring to them as "my people," and "my nation."

The word "teaching" in verse 4 can also be translated as "law"; the Hebrew word is "torah." The prophet uses the word here as a parallel to justice. He speaks not just of any teaching, but of God's teaching. Torah and justice are also spoken of together in the first servant song in Isaiah 42:1-4. In fact, this whole section in chapter 51 is reminiscent of the themes and language of the servant songs.

In verse 5, God proclaims that salvation will come swiftly. God's "arms" are a symbol of God's power. The arms of God represent the power God will use to bring about salvation for the chosen people. God's power for deliverance comes forth, and the people wait in hope for it.

Again in verse 6 we see a recurring theme of this prophet: Although earthly things are temporary, God's protection for the chosen people will endure forever. Recall the similar proclamation in Isaiah 40:8 "The grass withers, the flower fades; but the word of our God will stand forever." Notice the vivid imagery that the prophet uses to convey his message. The permanence of God is contrasted to: (1) the heavens, which will vanish like smoke as it rises into the sky; (2) the earth, which will wear out like a garment that has been worn until it is threadbare; and (3) those who live on the earth, who will die like gnats.

Isaiah 51:7-8. These verses are a promise of future salvation. The promise of deliverance is offered by the prophet as a means of comfort, as we can see by the phrase "do not fear" in verse 7. With a sense of urgency the prophet addresses these words to "you who know righteousness," a parallel to "you that pursue righteousness" in verse 1. The exiles both pursue righteousness and know it. They live according to God's law, or God's teaching, which provides for them stability in the midst of their chaos.

Notice the sharp contrast in verse 8 between God's protection of the chosen people and the fate of Israel's enemies, described here as those who reproach the people of Israel. The prophet is no doubt speaking of the Babylonians, Israel's captors. In verse 8 the prophet reiterates the affirmation of the steadfastness of God's promise in the face of instability and chaos,

a comforting word for those who have been displaced. Although the prophet's words may seem repetitive to us, for those who were held captive in a foreign land the promise of deliverance is comforting no matter how many times it is proclaimed.

INTERPRETING THE SCRIPTURE

God's Past Actions Bring Hope to Present Situations

In the world of Second Isaiah, ancestors in the faith and family ancestors were the same people. Abraham and Sarah, who were among the patriarchs and matriarchs of the Hebrew faith, were also the common ancestors of the Israelites. God said to Abraham: "I will make of you a great nation, and I will bless you, and make your name great, so that you will be a blessing" (Genesis 12:2). In that promise the writer alludes to relationships that are both religious (the handing down of faith from generation to generation) and physical (parenting offspring to carry on the family name).

When Isaiah encouraged the exiles to recall the experience of Abraham and Sarah for evidence of God's action in the lives of persons, they must have been comforted by what they saw. There was Sarah, advanced in years and suffering the stigma of barrenness with no hope of escape. God's promise of a son seemed so ludicrous that she responded by laughing. But the promise was more than just empty words. Isaac, the son born later to Abraham and Sarah, represented the fulfillment of the promise God gave to Abraham in Genesis 12. In recalling these ancestors, the exiles saw two ordinary people who, as a result of God's intervention in their lives, became founders of a nation, just as God had promised they would. Since God could be counted on to fulfill promises

made to their ancestors, surely the exiles could trust God to remain steadfast to them in their time of crisis.

Like the Israelites in Isaiah's day, we too have ancestors in the faith whose experiences with God give us hope for our own futures. In addition to biblical figures, we also have a long line of spiritual forebears, some of whose stories have been handed down through Christian history. We can look back on the legacy of these giants of the faith and see God's steadfastness. As in the case of Abraham and Sarah, we see ordinary persons who accomplish extraordinary missions because God was faithful in fulfilling promises. John Wesley, the founder of United Methodism, was such a person. He experienced doubts about his relationship with God and questioned the value of his ministry. Yet he persevered. In a worship experience, he felt his heart "strangely warmed" and knew the assurance of God's comforting, saving presence in his life. Through the work and faith of persons such as Wesley, we find guidance for our own faith journeys. Their experiences with God assure us that God will be faithful to us, no matter what our circumstances may be.

We also find hope in God's steadfastness as we remember spiritual ancestors whose influence may have touched us in a personal way on a regular basis. I have a friend who is having problems with the church. She is struggling to find meaning in the worship services, and she is struggling to find people who are seeking answers to the same questions she is asking. For a long time she did not attend church at all. When she finally decided to go back, she found herself crying when the old hymns were sung. As she heard the well-known tunes and sang the familiar lyrics, she was overcome with memories of her mother, standing next to her in church, week after week. Her mother was an ancestor in the faith, whose positive influence my friend continued to feel years later.

God's Promise of Comfort

Recall that in last week's lesson we discovered three ways to experience the comfort of God's presence: through forgiveness, through the removing of obstacles that stand in our way, and through the words and actions of others. In today's passage we see yet another way that God provides comfort in times of crisis.

Reread Isaiah 51:3 and try to put its message in your own words. One way to paraphrase the message of verse 3 in today's language is to say, "This too shall pass." Or, we might say "Things will get better." Here the experience of God's comfort is clear and direct: God says, "Do not fear, I will change things for you, and I will do it soon. Things will become so much better for you that you will feel as if you are in paradise."

When we are in the midst of a crisis or a challenging situation, one approach we sometimes use is to imagine ourselves on the other side of it. This is what the prophet is encouraging the Israelites to do here. He says to them, "Just think, once we return home our circumstances will be so much better we will think we are in the Garden of Eden compared to the way our lives are now."

I am not a runner—I never was a runner. But for many years I tried to be, for reasons I probably could not explain. Once I ran a 10K race, just to say I had done it. That was important to me. My children could not understand my motivations.

Why not run to win the race? Why run only because you want to be able to say you did it? Of course they did not understand that winning the race was never in the realm of possibility. Finishing the race was questionable.

In that race I finished last. Dead last. In fact, I ran the whole race about ten feet ahead of the police car that was assigned to bring up the rear. Every time I turned a corner the police officer would yell to the person standing there something like, "OK, that's it." That was demoralizing, but still I kept running. In fact, the whole race was agony for me. The only way I managed to cross the finish line was to imagine myself crossing the finish line. And that is what I did the entire second half of the race. I pictured myself standing there with my new T-shirt on, saying to my friends, "Well, we made it."

In a small way, I was doing what Second Isaiah was trying to get his audience to do. I was imagining myself through a tough situation. From about mile five I was thinking that I would be in paradise if I could just cross the finish line.

The Permanence of God in the Midst of Change

In two ways in this passage the prophet proclaims the message that God's presence is permanent. It is the one thing that we can count on in the midst of chaos. First, he contrasts God's promise of salvation (something we can count on) with the temporality or transitory nature of earthly things: "the earth will wear out like a garment, and those who live on it will die like gnats; but my salvation will be forever" (Isaiah 51:6). Second, the prophet expands on this contrast by drawing a vivid picture of what will happen to those who do not see themselves as recipients of God's promise of deliverance: "For the moth will eat them up like a garment, and the worm will eat them like wool" (Isaiah 51:8). So God is saying: (1) be comforted because my promise will stand when everything else seems temporary; and (2) those who do not believe in me will themselves become transitory.

God is permanent in the midst of change. Some years ago my husband served a two-point charge in Spring Hill, Tennessee. These two churches were separated by about three miles; they were on either side of a long stretch of pasture that would eventually become the site of the new Saturn plant. But back in the early 1980s, no one had heard of Saturn. In many ways Spring Hill was an example of the idyllic, small-town existence of which we often speak with nostalgia. The "downtown" had a post office, a small grocery store, a hardware store, and a diner. People liked and trusted each other. Life was peaceful.

When the people of Spring Hill discovered that Saturn was moving in, many were worried that the new plant would bring big-city problems as well as economic growth to the area. They worried about the quality of life in their small town. Recently my husband got a call from someone in one of these churches. A woman had died and her family wanted to honor her request that my husband sing at her funeral. He made the trip reluctantly in a way, afraid that what he would find would be very different from what he left ten years ago. And things were different there, at least on the surface. There is more traffic now; there is a new elementary school; the little churches he served have more members. But in many ways, life is still the same. People are still nice to one another and to visitors. The churches still use the same liturgy. The same people still have breakfast together each day in the diner. Permanence exists in the midst of change.

SHARING THE SCRIPTURE

PREPARING TO TEACH

Try to spend a few minutes each day reading Isaiah 51:1-8. Immerse yourself in the experience of the exiles and in the idea of God's comfort for those who are discouraged. As you begin to prepare yourself to teach the lesson, read the "Understanding the Scripture" section on Isaiah 51 first.

Spend some time thinking about persons who were influential in the formation of your faith. You might want to prepare a story or anecdote about someone who helped form your faith, in case you need to spark discussion.

Have you ever imagined yourself through a tough situation by seeing yourself on the other side of it? Think about that question. Try to do that this week and see what happens. You may want to relate your experience to the class.

During the week ahead, look around you for evidence of God's permanence in the midst of chaos. Have paper and pencils available.

LEADING THE CLASS

Introduction

Today's main question asks: **Is God steadfast in times of crisis and despair?** In other words, will God continue to love us and be faithful to promises to us, no matter what? Emphasize that these questions are always appropriate ones, and that the answer is always yes.

Choose a volunteer to read aloud Psalm 63:1-4. Point out that the psalmist is, in effect, answering today's question. Yes, God's steadfast love is always there for us. In fact, God's love is better than life itself.

Review last week's lesson by reminding the class who Second Isaiah is, when he wrote, and the situation of the Israelites as captives in Babylon. The review may be brief if most class members were present for the first lesson in the unit. In order for the class to appreciate the power of the prophet's message of God's steadfastness and certain salvation, everyone must understand the hopeless and discouraging circumstances that the Israelites faced daily.

Now have someone read aloud Isaiah 51:1-8. Ask class members to reflect silently on today's topic for a few moments, considering how they would have felt if they had heard these words in the midst of their despair.

God's Past Actions Bring Hope to Present Situations

Ask the class: **Why do you believe Isaiah called upon the exiles to remember their spiritual ancestors, Abraham and Sarah?** Help members recognize that because God has faithfully fulfilled promises in the past, we can know with assurance that God will continue to be steadfast in the present.

Personalize this concept by asking volunteers to recount a time when the memory of God's gracious action in the past helped them to trust God to be with them (or someone they know) in a difficult situation. Times of vulnerability or loss, such as illness, loss of a job, death of a loved one, or a major life decision often prompt us to remember what God has done for us in the past.

Encourage the class to think about their own spiritual ancestors by asking: **(1) Who is your favorite Bible character? (2) How do you see this person's life as a model of how God can act in your own life?** Spend a few minutes discussing their answers.

Now ask the class to consider persons who were influential in the formation of their faith. Perhaps someone would be willing to share an anecdote that shows how this person's influence remained with them, even in times of trial or crisis. You

may want to use the story of my struggling friend, found in the "Interpreting the Scripture" section.

God's Promise of Comfort

Ask the class to reread Isaiah 51:3. What is the prophet saying here? Read or retell the commentary information concerning Isaiah 51:3 in the "Understanding the Scripture" portion.

If possible, distribute paper and pencils. Ask class members to consider a difficult situation they are facing right now, either personally, at work, within the congregation, or as a concerned citizen of the world. Instruct them to describe the situation in a sentence or two. Then ask them to write a description of what the situation would be like and how they would feel if this wilderness experience could be transformed into Eden. Perhaps a few persons will volunteer to share their ideas, but do not press for comments on these personal insights.

As an alternative, use the story of the runner in the "God's Promise of Comfort" section as an example of how we can imagine ourselves on the other side of a difficult situation.

Close this section by pointing out God's promise that deliverance is near and will come about swiftly, as noted in Isaiah 51:5. We are to heed God's teaching and justice (verse 4), but it is God—not us—who not only has the power to bring salvation but promises to do so soon.

The Permanence of God in the Midst of Change

Spend a few moments brainstorming answers to these questions:
(1) **What do you believe is the most important change you have seen in your lifetime?**
(2) **Did you expect to ever see such a change?**
(3) **How has this change affected you?** Record answers on a chalkboard or newsprint.

Continue the discussion with ideas such as: Sometimes we are thrilled by changes. Perhaps the birth of a child or grandchild, a move to a new home, retirement, or the successful completion of a project brings you great joy. Other changes, such as the death of a loved one or loss of a job, cause great pain. Whatever happens and however we respond to it, we know that change is a part of life. Only God's steadfast presence and promise of salvation is permanent. Encourage members to share personal stories of how God's presence upheld them in the midst of change.

Invite a class member to read aloud the key verse Isaiah 51:6. Ask the class: **What images does the prophet use to contrast God's steadfast salvation and deliverance?** Or, you may choose to read aloud the information on verse 6 in the "Understanding the Scripture" portion.

Write the following question so that everyone can see it: How does the knowledge of the permanence of God in the midst of change bring hope to you, even in the most difficult circumstances? Ask class members to discuss their answers with a partner or small group. If time permits, ask a few persons to share their ideas.

HELPING CLASS MEMBERS ACT

Challenge class members to bring the prophet's comfort and encouragement to persons who are in difficult situations. One way to do this is to ask students to tell stories of how God has worked in their own lives, not as a means of giving advice but as a word of witness to God's steadfast love.

A second way is to ask students to help persons who are discouraged remember a time in their own lives when God has brought them through stormy waters, giving them hope that God will do so again.

Another way is to challenge class members to listen to a friend in need and encourage that person to imagine how life will be when the crisis he or she is experiencing has passed.

PLANNING FOR NEXT SUNDAY

As we approach Christmas, we are moving from despair to joy. Ask the class members to spend a few minutes each day reading Isaiah 9:1-7, a familiar passage that is often quoted at this time of the year. The main question in next week's lesson will have to do with how we experience hope in the midst of the turmoil and chaos of our world.

FOR THOSE WHO DESPAIR

PREVIEWING THE LESSON

Lesson Scripture: Isaiah 9:1-7
Background Scripture: Isaiah 9:1-7
Key Verse: Isaiah 9:6

Focus of the lesson:
Isaiah's prophecy regarding a child who will be born to bring the light of God's presence to the people

Main question(s) of the lesson.
(1) Where can we look for a sign of hope, a sign of God's presence with us in the midst of despair?

This lesson will enable adult learners to:
(1) encounter a well-known prophecy concerning the coming messiah who will reign on David's throne with peace, justice, and righteousness
(2) appreciate the impact this prophecy would have had on persons in exile
(3) respond by taking actions as prophets of hope in the midst of situations of despair known to them.

Today's lesson may be outlined as follows:
(1) Introduction
(2) Moving from Darkness to Light
(3) Finding Hope in Despair

FOCUSING ON THE MAIN QUESTION

The psalmist says, "I lift up my eyes to the hills—from where will my help come?" And then the psalmist goes on to answer his own question: his help comes from God, who made the heavens and the earth. Clearly for the author of Psalm 121, God is the source of hope in times of despair.

Try to draw a mental picture of the psalmist looking up at the mountain range spread before him and waiting patiently for a sign of God's presence with him.

Waiting is an appropriate posture for us, especially during this season of Advent. At this time in the rhythm of the church year we wait for the birth of the Christ child, who is a symbol of hope for us. He is Immanuel, God with us, a sign of God's presence. He is the light of the world, according to the Gospel of John.

Like the psalmist, we often ask the main question of today's study: **Where can we look for a sign of hope, a sign of God's**

presence with us in the midst of despair? We despair because our bodies do not do what we want them to do. We despair because our minds are cluttered with worries and cannot focus on what is really important to us. We despair because our loved ones are suffering and we feel powerless to help them. We despair because we feel overwhelmed by the crushing problems of our troubled world. We despair because our spirits seem far from God at times.

The people with whom Isaiah of Jerusalem lived and worked were in despair as well. They looked for a sign of God's presence with them, a sign of hope in the face of the threat of Assyrian domination. Into this situation of despair God sent Isaiah, a prophet whose task it was to proclaim hope to the chosen people. When we despair, where can we find our hope? Who are the prophets among us today, the ones God has sent to lead us from darkness into a brighter future?

READING THE SCRIPTURE

NRSV
Isaiah 9:1-7

1 But there will be no gloom for those who were in anguish. In the former time he brought into contempt the land of Zebulun and the land of Naphtali, but in the latter time he will make glorious the way of the sea, the land beyond the Jordan, Galilee of the nations.
²The people who walked in
> darkness
> have seen a great light;
> those who lived in a land of deep
> darkness—
> on them light has shined.
³You have multiplied the nation,
> you have increased its joy;
> they rejoice before you
> as with joy at the harvest,
> as people exult when dividing
> plunder.
⁴For the yoke of their burden,
> and the bar across their
> shoulders,
> the rod of their oppressor,
> you have broken as on the day
> of Midian.
⁵For all the boots of the tramping
> warriors
> and all the garments rolled in
> blood
> shall be burned as fuel for the
> fire.

NIV
Isaiah 9:1-7

1 Nevertheless, there will be no more gloom for those who were in distress. In the past he humbled the land of Zebulun and the land of Naphtali, but in the future he will honor Galilee of the Gentiles, by the way of the sea, along the Jordan—

²The people walking in darkness
> have seen a great light;
> on those living in the land of the shadow of
> death
> a light has dawned.

³You have enlarged the nation
> and increased their joy;
> they rejoice before you
> as people rejoice at the harvest,
> as men rejoice
> when dividing the plunder.
⁴For as in the day of Midian's defeat,
> you have shattered
> the yoke that burdens them,
> the bar across their shoulders,
> the rod of their oppressor.

⁵Every warrior's boot used in battle
> and every garment rolled in blood
> will be destined for burning,
> will be fuel for the fire.

Key Verse

⁶For a child has been born for us,
    a son given to us;
    authority rests upon his
        shoulders;
    and he is named
Wonderful Counselor, Mighty
        God,
    Everlasting Father, Prince of
        Peace.
⁷His authority shall grow
    continually,
    and there shall be endless
    peace
for the throne of David and his
    kingdom.
    He will establish and uphold it
with justice and with
    righteousness
    from this time onward and
    forevermore.
The zeal of the LORD of hosts
    will do this.

⁶For to us a child is born,
    to us a son is given,
    and the government will be on his
        shoulders.
And he will be called
    Wonderful Counselor, Mighty God,
    Everlasting Father, Prince of Peace.
⁷Of the increase of his government and peace
    there will be no end.
He will reign on David's throne
    and over his kingdom,
establishing and upholding it
    with justice and righteousness
    from that time on and forever.
The zeal of the LORD Almighty
    will accomplish this.

UNDERSTANDING THE SCRIPTURE

The prophecies that appear in chapters 1–39 of Isaiah are the words of the prophet we often call First Isaiah, or Isaiah of Jerusalem. First Isaiah lived and worked in Judah, known as the Southern Kingdom, from about 742 B.C.E. until 701 B.C.E. During this period, Israel, known as the Northern Kingdom, was threatened by the Assyrians and finally conquered in 722 B.C.E. The audience to whom First Isaiah addressed his prophecies lived with the constant fear that the same fate would befall them as well. The prophet calls for social justice and faith in time of despair. He preaches that the Holy God of Israel reigns over history and will be victorious.

Isaiah 9:1. In the first verse of the passage we can see an indication of the movement from despair to joy, from judgment to promise. The prophet draws a sharp contrast between those who were in anguish in the former time and those in the latter time who will walk in glory.

Isaiah describes the lands of two tribes that were included in the former Northern Kingdom: Zebulun and Naphtali. These territories near the Sea of Galilee were "brought into contempt" by the Assyrians who conquered them under the leadership of King Tiglath-pileser III (745–27 B.C.E. and Shalmaneser V (727–722 B.C.E. The "way of the sea" refers to the route that stretched between Damascus in the north and the Mediterranean Sea. The Assyrians used this road when making their way toward Judah. In Isaiah's time this was a road to fear since it was the path of the conquering enemy. To make the transition between the doom and gloom of chapter 8 and the promise of chapter 9, Isaiah pictures an era when this road will be glorious.

Isaiah 9:2-7. This passage has been traditionally called an oracle of promise concerning the messianic king. Its content is similar to that of Isaiah 11:1-9, and both passages are commonly read and studied during Advent because of the promises they contain of the future messiah. In fact, Matthew quoted this prophecy, asserting that it had been fulfilled in the person and ministry of Jesus (Matthew 4:15-16).

Originally these verses were probably an oracle celebrating the accession of a king to his throne (perhaps King Hezekiah, who was king in Judah during the time of Isaiah). Now, however, this passage proclaims the people's movement from despair to rejoicing due to the coming of a messianic king. As such, it is especially meaningful for us as it describes a Messiah we can recognize in Jesus Christ.

The content of this oracle is divided into three parts: (1) the transformation of darkness into light (Isaiah 9:2-3); (2) three reasons for rejoicing (Isaiah 9:4-6); and (3) the promise of a kingly rule (Isaiah 9:7).

Isaiah 9:2-3. Isaiah addresses God directly: "You have multiplied the nation." The prophet offers praise to God because of the joy the people are experiencing when they anticipate future deliverance. By using the contrast between darkness and light to describe the movement from despair to hope, the prophet is saying that deliverance out of their current situation (the Assyrian crisis) will be like the sunrise after a long, dark night.

When people walk in darkness they can see nothing in front of them; they are walking blindly. They are anxious and afraid, afraid for their physical well-being and afraid that God will abandon them. But the prophet affirms that light will come from God.

In verse 3 Isaiah paints a vivid picture of a large group of people gathered together to rejoice in their deliverance. The atmosphere is one of joy and thanksgiving as these people celebrate their freedom by praising God as the One responsible for their liberation.

Isaiah 9:4-6. These verses list three reasons for the prophet's audience to rejoice: overthrowing the oppressor ("the rod of their oppressor you have broken"); removing the symbols of war (the boots and the garments of the enemy will "be burned as fuel for the fire"); and the coming of the divinely endowed king to rule in an era of peace.

The prophet compares the overthrow of the oppressor (Assyria) to what happened "on the day of Midian." To understand this allusion you might want to read Judges 7:15-25, which describes Gideon's defeat of the Midianites in the face of what seemed to be insurmountable odds.

Authority (verse 6) is a symbol of power. The fact that authority rests upon the shoulders of this king means that he will not be defeated by enemies that threaten him and his kingdom.

In verse 6 the prophet uses four images to describe this messianic king. *Wonderful Counselor* refers to his integrity in the political sphere. Throughout their history the Israelites had certainly been ruled by a number of kings whose motivations and actions were questionable. In contrast, this king the prophet is describing will rule with integrity. *Mighty God* is another way to refer to the power of this king, whose power is divine, not human. *Everlasting Father* refers to the continual love and care of this king for his subjects. *Prince of Peace* proclaims this king as a conduit of peace and prosperity to a troubled nation. Peace as the Hebrews spoke of this notion was more than just the absence of conflict; it was a sense of overall well-being.

Isaiah 9:7. This verse serves as a kind of summary of the lasting effects of this promised messianic king's rule. The prophet makes the point that any kingdom destined to endure the test of time must be characterized by justice and righteousness.

INTERPRETING THE SCRIPTURE

Moving from Darkness to Light

Today's passage from Isaiah 9:1-7 contains a number of phrases that are memorable because they have become an integral part of our Advent and Christmas tradition. One vivid image comes from verse 2:

> The people walking in darkness
>   have seen a great light;
> on those living in the land of the shadow
>   of death
> a light has dawned.

These words may be so familiar to us that we no longer connect with their meaning. In today's lesson we will "reconnect" with this image of moving from the darkness into the light.

The movement from darkness into light is an image commonly used to picture the movement from despair to hope. Most everyone has experienced how much easier it is to see clearly in the light than in the darkness. Sometimes the ability to see comes about gradually. I walk most every day in a large room in the basement of the building where I work. Many people think it is a strange place to exercise because it is so dark. When they smile and shake their heads at what I am doing I sometimes try to explain that the room is not as dark as it seems to be at first. What other people do not realize is that after a few minutes I can see very clearly where I am going. My eyes just need to adjust to the darkness, and then the small slivers of light that come from adjacent rooms are more visible to me. As I walk, my way becomes gradually clearer. Soon, I am not "just walking down there in the dark."

Sometimes, however, the movement from darkness to light is immediate. Not far from where I live there is an amusement park with a roller coaster that is housed inside a building. The main attraction of this ride is that it is even more frightening than a regular roller coaster because those who ride it are in the dark and have no idea what to expect next. Against my better judgment I rode this roller coaster. At the very end of the ride, the cars emerge from the darkness of the inside of the building into a lighted area at the bottom. I looked behind me and saw the route the ride had taken. I saw the many twists and turns of the track and the structure that holds up the track. In the light, the roller coaster looked precarious, and I experienced my anxiety all over again. Viewing the structure in the light, I vowed never to ride it again.

For the prophet Isaiah, coming out of the darkness and into the light was a way to illustrate the movement from despair to hope. But moving from the darkness into the light is not always an easy task. Often we would rather remain in the dark because moving into the light brings clarity about the reality of our situation. It requires that we take hold of the darkness and put it aside. And this is not easy.

Moving through the darkness into the light is one way to describe the experience of a woman named Etty Hillesum. Etty was a Dutch Jew who was in her late twenties during the early 1940s. She was living in Amsterdam at the time when it fell to the Germans in 1940. She was later transported, along with her family and many of her friends, to a camp in Poland and finally to Auschwitz, where she died in 1943.

Etty Hillesum's story is captured in a volume entitled *An Interrupted Life*, which is a compilation of her diaries and other information about her life supplied by the editor of the volume. While in Amsterdam Etty lived not far from a young woman named Anne Frank. Although the two apparently did not know each other, their writings touch similar chords within their readers and shine the same beacon of hope in the midst of despair.

Etty's diaries radiate her spirituality. In the book the reader is taken by the hand and guided on Etty's spiritual journey as, in an effort to find meaning and purpose in the midst of the darkness that surrounded her, she discovers the light of God's continual presence with her. By the end of her journey she realizes that all of life is a dialogue with God. She wrote: "My life has become an uninterrupted dialogue with You, oh God, one great dialogue." In the midst of the chaos and despair that surrounded her, Etty wrote of her firm conviction that God was inside her and that prayer surrounded her like a protective wall.

However, Etty's spirituality was not just an inner reality; it radiated from her into the hearts and lives of those around her. The next section will touch on how she was able to use her discoveries about God to bring hope to others who were in despair. Like the biblical Esther, who did what was in her power to do to save her people and for whom Etty was named, Etty did not retreat into the darkness. Rather, she used her strength to bring the light of God into the lives of others.

Finding Hope in Despair

Sometimes despair descends upon us like a cloud, and we find it difficult to move out of the darkness. Often hope is hard to come by. We, like the psalmist, look upward and wonder where our hope is. God seems far away. As I write this lesson there is a family in the city where I live that is mourning the death of a fourteen-year-old boy. He was on a church hayride and somehow fell out of the wagon, and the tractor ran over him and killed him. This tragedy seems too close to home for me, since this boy was a student at the same school as one of my boys. They shared some classes together. For the last three days I have been wondering how the parents will be able to cope. How can a parent make sense out of something like this? My thoughts are with them as they struggle to move out of darkness toward the hope of a brighter future.

Sometimes it helps to have someone to show us the way—a kind of prophet who can help us envision the path we are to take. You will recall from our first two lessons that Second Isaiah fulfilled that role for the exiles. He drew for them vivid pictures of what the journey would be like and how God would help them succeed in returning to Judah. In today's passage, Isaiah of Jerusalem is performing that same function for his audience. In the midst of chaos and despair, he is helping the people see a brighter future. He is a prophet of hope.

Etty Hillesum was a prophet of hope for those she encountered during her days in the camps. As she drew closer and closer to God on her spiritual journey, she committed herself fully to using the strength of God's love to help others. This conviction was surely on her mind and in her heart as she tended the sick children in the camp and helped people pack for their last journey to Auschwitz. She wrote:

"This much I know: you have to forget your own worries for the sake of others, for the sake of those whom you love. All the strength and love and faith in God which one possesses, and which have grown so miraculously in me of late, must be there for everyone who chances to cross one's path and who needs it."

Etty's last written words were, "We should be willing to act as a balm for all wounds." She hoped to be able to use her craft—her words—toward this end. "And I shall wield this slender fountain pen as if it were a hammer and my words will have to be so many hammer-strokes with which to beat out the story of our fate," she wrote.

When I read Etty's diaries I am keenly aware that she did not fully realize the profound influence her words and actions had on those she encountered. Nor did she know, of course, how long lasting her influence would be. She was, indeed, a prophet of hope. She was a person who lived her faith. She stood her spiritual ground at a time when it was easy to go into hiding, both literally and symbolically. She encourages us—she inspires us—to always have hope in the midst of despair.

SHARING THE SCRIPTURE

PREPARING TO TEACH

The image with which today's passage opens, the movement from darkness into light, will be relatively easy to treat in a class discussion. The contrast between darkness and light is a common theme in music, literature, scripture, and our everyday experience. As you move through the week ahead and prepare to lead the class next Sunday, pay attention to the image of darkness and light. Where does it emerge in your experiences this week? Do you see allusions to this image as you read the paper or watch TV? The more you pay attention, the more the image will permeate your consciousness.

Practice the discipline of waiting. Pay attention to your thoughts and posture during times this week when you have to wait for something—whether it be children, a phone call, a line at the grocery store. Try to make your waiting times peaceful rather than impatient.

Think of examples of prophets of hope in our time. These may be people you know personally, or they may be public figures. Compile a set of newspaper clippings, magazine articles, or books that show examples of prophets of hope. Or prepare to tell a story of someone you know.

Spend some time reading and rereading the passage from Isaiah 9:1-7 and the material in this lesson under the heading "Understanding the Scripture." In addition, familiarize yourself with the material that illuminates the scripture passage found under "Interpreting the Scripture."

Since today's passage comes from an earlier portion of the book of Isaiah than the one we have studied previously, it will be especially important for you to explain the different historical circumstances that gave rise to the words of Isaiah of Jerusalem. The information directly under the heading "Understanding the Scripture" will prepare you to do this.

LEADING THE CLASS

Introduction

One way to introduce the main question for today is to paraphrase or read aloud the information under the heading "Focusing on the Main Question." The psalmist's heartfelt question, "from where will my help come?" is certainly a question everyone can understand.

Read aloud the main question: **Where can we look for a sign of hope, a sign of God's presence with us in the midst of despair?** Ask class members to meditate on this question. Perhaps a few adults would be willing to share illustrations of how they perceived God's presence during a difficult period.

Tell the class members that during the last two lessons we have been considering the promise of God's presence in times of despair, and that today's lesson begins the movement from despair to hope.

Have the class read responsively, Isaiah 9:1-7. Divide into two groups, perhaps having those whose birthdays are from January 1 through June 30 reading the odd-numbered verses, and the rest of the group reading the even-numbered verses.

Moving from Darkness to Light

Help the class work through the topic of moving from darkness into light by taking the following six steps.
(1) Open the discussion by asking for examples of commonly-used phrases that reflect the contrast between darkness and light. You may want to record these on newsprint or a chalkboard. Make two columns: on top of the left-hand column write "Phrase," and on top of the right-hand column write the word "Meaning." As an example to start the class members

thinking about this task, under the first column heading write "seeing the light," and under the second column heading write "understanding." Then ask them to call out other phrases as they think of them. (Others might include "the light of the world" or "being in the dark.") The meaning of these phrases can be suggested by anyone in the class.

(2) After you have recorded a number of these examples, have someone read aloud verse 2 of Isaiah 9. Ask whether anyone can paraphrase what the prophet is saying here.

· (3) Move the discussion into the area of experience. Now that we have a general idea of what the image means, how do we experience the movement from darkness to light? To turn their thinking in this direction, tell the class members about my experience walking in the darkened auditorium. Or, you may have an experience of your own to relate. Use personal experiences to spark their imaginations, and ask whether anyone in the class has a similar experience to share.

(4) Read aloud to the class the story of Etty Hillesum (the part that appears under the heading "Moving from Darkness to Light"). Ask the class members to reflect aloud on how this woman might have helped to move the people she encountered from darkness into light.

(5) Now consider the deeper experiences in our lives that reflect the movement from darkness into light. Here the examples, like the story of Etty Hillesum, will be on a deeper level than visiting an amusement park or walking in a dark auditorium. The most common illustration of moving from darkness into light is probably living through the grief process after a loss. But there are many other kinds of stories as well: recovering from an addiction or an illness, for example. Class members may

be reluctant to share experiences that are this personal. To handle this problem, offer a story from your own experience or ask the group members to think of persons they know or have heard about.

(6) Conclude the discussion by rereading verse 2 from today's passage. Remind the group of the prophet's continuing assurance of the presence of God in the movement from darkness into light.

Finding Hope in Despair

The second topic for discussion in today's lesson has to do with the role of the prophet as one who helps bring persons from darkness to light, from despair to hope. A prophet is one who helps those in despair to visualize a brighter future. Remind the class members of last week's discussion about visualizing ourselves on the other side of a tough situation. We cannot always do that by ourselves, and the prophets among us are those who have the insight and the ability to help us in that task.

As an example of a prophet who fulfilled this role in relation to those she encountered, read to the group the additional material about Etty Hillesum under the heading "Finding Hope in Despair" in the "Interpreting the Scripture" section. Lead the class in a general discussion about (1) how Etty went about helping people look toward a brighter future and (2) individuals they know personally or have heard or read about who fulfill this same role for us.

Now have someone read Isaiah 9:6-7. Using the material on these verses under the heading "Understanding the Scripture," help class members understand what the prophet is saying. Explain the meanings of the four descriptive images the prophet uses in verse 6: Wonderful Counselor, Mighty God, Everlasting Father, and Prince of Peace. Emphasize that Isaiah's role as a prophet is to help his people visualize a brighter future, and he does so by pointing to a future messianic king who will also fulfill that role.

Invite class members to reflect on the life and ministry of Jesus, whom we see as the fulfillment of Isaiah's prophecy. Ask: **How does Jesus Christ help move us from darkness into light?**

HELPING CLASS MEMBERS ACT

Often when I tell persons or groups the story of Etty Hillesum, I generate an interest in her life and in her writings. In my church school class we spent a few Sundays reading *An Interrupted Life* and talking about it together. Today's lesson may generate that kind of interest. If so, be prepared to plan how your group might learn more about Etty's story. The book was compiled and edited by J. G. Gaarlandt and published in English in 1983 by Pantheon Books, a division of Random House.

Despair is close to all of us. Situations abound in which people desperately need the good news of God's presence. In a few moments of quiet reflection at the end of the session, ask the class members to think about the situations they know of in which a message of hope is needed. Encourage them to consider these questions:

(1) **Who do they know who is in the darkness of despair?**

(2) **How can they help these persons move from darkness into light?**

(3) **What action can they take to be prophets of hope?**

PLANNING FOR NEXT SUNDAY

Remind the group members that next Sunday's class will be held on Christmas Eve day. Mention the Background Scripture: Isaiah 11:1-9 and Luke 2:1-20. Encourage the adults in your group to read these familiar passages sometime during the week ahead. Ask them to try to read with new eyes, and to remember one insight from each of the two passages that is anew to them with this reading.

FOR THOSE WHO SEEK PEACE

PREVIEWING THE LESSON

Lesson Scripture: Isaiah 11:1-6; Luke 2:10-14
Background Scripture: Isaiah 11:1-9; Luke 2:1-20
Key Verse: Isaiah 11:6

Focus of the lesson:
the reign of righteousness and peace that the promised messiah would usher in

Main question(s) of the lesson:
(1) What do God's people want their leaders to be and do?
(2) Given this kind of leadership, how would we "visualize world peace"?

This lesson will enable adult learners to:
(1) understand the qualities of leadership the messiah would exhibit in order to bring about an era of peace for all creation
(2) imagine what a reign of peace would be like
(3) respond by trying to bring peace to a troubled situation.

Today's lesson may be outlined as follows:
(1) Introduction
(2) Qualities of Leadership
(3) Expectations of Leadership
(4) A Reign of Peace

FOCUSING ON THE MAIN QUESTION

"Visualize world peace," the bumper sticker admonishes. That is just what Isaiah does in today's scripture passage: he visualizes for us what an ideal world would look like if the ideal king were to rule over it. Visualizing world peace seems an appropriate task on this day when we prepare to celebrate the coming of the Prince of Peace.

For Isaiah, the ideal world is ruled by the ideal, messianic king. Before visualizing the ideal, peaceful society, the prophet describes what this king would be like, and what he would do. The prophet knows we cannot have a peaceful society unless we have good leadership.

As Christians, we believe Jesus fulfills Isaiah's prophecy. He is the ideal ruler, the messianic king whose birth is announced to shepherds by an angel. In him, we see the kind of leader, foretold by Isaiah, whom God has promised to bring peace to all creation.

Today's lesson will focus on these questions: **What do God's people want their leaders to be and do? Given this kind of leadership, how would we "visualize world peace"?**

READING THE SCRIPTURE

NRSV
Isaiah 11:1-6
1 A shoot shall come out from
    the stump of Jesse,
     and a branch shall grow out of
      his roots.
²The spirit of the LORD shall rest
    on him,
     the spirit of wisdom and
      understanding,
     the spirit of counsel and might,
     the spirit of knowledge and the
      fear of the LORD.
³His delight shall be in the fear of
    the LORD.

He shall not judge by what his
    eyes see,
     or decide by what his ears
      hear;
⁴but with righteousness he shall
    judge the poor,
     and decide with equity for the
      meek of the earth;
   he shall strike the earth with the
     rod of his mouth,
     and with the breath of his lips
      he shall kill the wicked.
⁵Righteousness shall be the belt
    around his waist,
     and faithfulness the belt
     around his loins.

Key Verse
⁶The wolf shall live with the
    lamb,
   the leopard shall lie down with
     the kid,
   the calf and the lion and the
     fatling together,
   and a little child shall lead
     them.

Luke 2:10-14
¹⁰But the angel said to them, "Do not be afraid; for see—I am bringing you good news of great joy for all the people: ¹¹to

NIV
Isaiah 11:1-6
1 A shoot will come up from the stump of
    Jesse;
     from his roots a Branch will bear fruit.

²The Spirit of the LORD will rest on him—
    the Spirit of wisdom and of understanding,
    the Spirit of counsel and of power,
    the Spirit of knowledge and of the fear of the
     LORD—

³and he will delight in the fear of the LORD.

He will not judge by what he sees with his
    eyes,
    or decide by what he hears with his ears;

⁴but with righteousness he will judge the
    needy,
    with justice he will give decisions for the
     poor of the earth.
He will strike the earth with the rod of his
    mouth;
    with the breath of his lips he will slay the
     wicked.
⁵Righteousness will be his belt
    and faithfulness the sash around his waist.

Key Verse
⁶The wolf will live with the lamb,
    the leopard will lie down with the goat,
  the calf and the lion and the yearling
     together;
    and a little child will lead them.

Luke 2:10-14
¹⁰But the angel said to them, "Do not be afraid. I bring you good news of great joy that will be for all the people. ¹¹Today in

you is born this day in the city of David a Savior, who is the Messiah, the Lord. [12]This will be a sign for you: you will find a child wrapped in bands of cloth and lying in a manger." [13]And suddenly there was with the angel a multitude of the heavenly host, praising God and saying,

[14]"Glory to God in the highest
    heaven,
and on earth peace among
    those whom he favors!"

the town of David a Savior has been born to you; he is Christ the Lord. [12]This will be a sign to you: You will find a baby wrapped in cloths and lying in a manger."

[13]Suddenly a great company of the heavenly host appeared with the angel, praising God and saying,

[14]"Glory to God in the highest,
    and on earth peace to men on whom
        his favor rests."

UNDERSTANDING THE SCRIPTURE

Isaiah 11:1-9 comes from the same section of Isaiah as did last week's passage, and is similar in content to that passage (Isaiah 9:1-7). Both oracles originate from the collection of Isaiah of Jerusalem, a prophet who lived and worked in Judah (the Southern Kingdom) during the years of the Assyrian crisis. Isaiah prophesied between 742 B.C.E. and 701 B.C.E.

Like last week's passage, this oracle in chapter 11 portrays the characteristics of the ideal, messianic king. The hoped-for messiah is described here as one whose task it will be to bring about future salvation. This oracle probably had its origin in a ceremony that celebrated the accession of a king to the throne; this may have been King Hezekiah, who came to the throne in Judah during the time of Isaiah. Only later was the oracle seen to portray a future, messianic king. This was an appropriate interpretation, since each king in Judah who was a descendant of the Davidic dynasty was considered to be divinely anointed; he was a symbol of God and the hope that God would eventually restore the chosen people to their former status.

This passage is divided into three parts: (1) the anointing of the king (Isaiah 11:1-3a); (2) the characteristics of the reign of this king (Isaiah 11:3b-5); and (3) a description of the era of peace that will result from the reign of this messianic king (Isaiah 11:6-9).

Isaiah 11:1-3a. The prophet speaks of the future messiah in terms of a branch that will "come out from the stump of Jesse." Jesse was the father of King David (see 1 Samuel 16). By speaking of the messianic king in this way, Isaiah is making the point that the future king will come from the line of David; he will be divinely anointed. Just as King David came from obscure and humble origins, so will this future messiah.

In Isaiah 11:2 the prophet describes the messiah as a person who will carry within him the spirit of God. As a result of the divine spirit, the messiah will have six spiritual gifts that will enable him to fulfill his mission: wisdom, understanding, counsel, might, knowledge, and fear of the Lord (obedience).

Isaiah 11:3b-5. These verses discuss in more detail how the messiah will reign, by showing how his wisdom will be reflected in his actions. This ideal king will rule in righteousness; that is, he will make good, sound judgments about the people for whom he is responsible. He will be the champion of the poor and the downtrodden. He will be able to deal with evildoers by his very words.

Wisdom, sound judgment, and righteousness are characteristics that the people of Israel valued in their kings. The writer of Second Kings, for example, describes King Hezekiah as a king who "did what was right in the sight of the LORD" (18:3). That the king described in today's passage will continue to rule with justice and righteousness will be guaranteed by the continual presence of God's spirit with him. According to verse 5, faithfulness will be as close as an undergarment to this king.

Isaiah 11:6-9. Here the prophet speaks of this future king's rule in terms of paradise revisited: peace will rule on the earth once more as it did in the days of the Garden of Eden. Wild beasts who are instinctively enemies will live together in harmony. When the leopard lies down with the kid, it acts as though it were one of the flock.

In Isaiah 11:8 the prophet alludes to the enmity between the serpent and human beings that was established in the Garden of Eden. In this peaceful, idyllic future, human beings will no longer be at odds with the serpent. Their relationship will be such that little children, who cannot protect themselves against danger, will not need to be afraid of serpents.

Isaiah 11:9 is a partial quotation of Isaiah 65:25, which is an oracle of promise related to the vision of a new Jerusalem. "My holy mountain" refers to the temple in Jerusalem.

Luke 2:1-20. This is the familiar story of the birth of Jesus, told in a different version in Matthew 1:18–2:23. Writing his account as a historian would, Luke's narrative is striking in its simplicity. The story is divided into two main parts: the birth itself (verses 1-7) and the announcement of the angel to the shepherds (verses 8-20).

Luke 2:1-7. Luke spends the first five verses in this section explaining how Jesus came to be born in Bethlehem instead of in Nazareth, the home of his parents. Augustus Caesar, who reigned over the Roman Empire from 27 B.C.E. until 14 C.E., instituted a census that required citizens to register in the city of their birth. Joseph returned to his native home, Bethlehem. Mary, his pregnant wife, accompanied him. The birth of Jesus in Bethlehem rather than Nazareth brings to reality what is prophesied by Micah in 5:2: "But you, O Bethlehem of Ephrathah, who are one of the little clans of Judah, from you shall come forth for me one who is to rule in Israel, whose origin is from of old, from ancient days."

Luke says that Caesar's decree required "that all the world should be registered." We need to see "all the world" as Luke's way of saying "the entire Roman Empire," not literally the whole world. This census is not mentioned in any secular histories that record the events of this era, so all the information we have about it is contained in these verses in Luke.

Quirinius is mentioned as the "governor" of Syria, which in this case is a military term for a specially commissioned representative of Augustus Caesar.

In both the English and the Greek, the actual birth of Jesus is described in a single sentence: Mary gave birth to the child, wrapped him in cloths, and placed him in a feeding trough. All this took place in a stable because the local inn would have been full, due to the influx of people who needed to register for the census. Luke mentions Jesus as the "firstborn son" of Mary and later speaks of Jesus' siblings (see Luke 8:19). According to Catholic tradition, which reveres the image of Mary as a virgin who bears only Jesus, the word "firstborn" is a legal term and does not imply that other children were later born to Mary.

Wrapping a baby in cloths was a cultural custom at the time of Jesus; this was done to keep babies' bodies straight and ensure that they will grow properly.

Luke 2:8-20. It would not be unusual for shepherds to watch over their flocks during the night hours, since herds moved about constantly in search of new sources of food. When confronted by an angel in the middle of the night, these shepherds were naturally frightened, as were Zechariah and Mary when they had similar encounters with angels who had divine messages to share. As with Zechariah and Mary, the angel first attempts to relieve the listeners' fear before delivering the message.

The angel promises "good news of great joy" that will come to "all the people." That this promise is for everyone indicates the universality of Luke's audience; throughout his gospel he insists that the good news is intended not just for certain people but for everyone. Yet there is also a particularity about the message: the savior is born on this day and he is born to you. The coming of Jesus into the world is for everyone and for each one.

The angel describes Jesus in a threefold manner: he is Savior, Messiah, and Lord.

The refrain that is sung by the heavenly host (angels) is often called the "Gloria in Excelsis," which is the Latin for the first line of the anthem: "Glory to God in the highest." The variant reading for the second line that often appears in the notes of English versions (in the NRSV the variant reads "peace, good will among people") is due to the lack of one letter in some of the Greek versions. That one letter changes the meaning of the second half of the refrain.

Responding to the extraordinary pronouncement of the angel, the shepherds decide to go see for themselves. What they see amazes them, and their amazement becomes infectious when they tell others. Mary, however, was not surprised by any of this, since she had previously been visited by an angel (see Luke 1:26-38).

INTERPRETING THE SCRIPTURE

Qualities of Leadership

What do we expect our leaders to be? What qualities of leadership do we look for in those who are responsible for our welfare? In today's passage the prophet Isaiah answers this question on behalf of the people of Judah. In verses 2 and 3 the following characteristics are listed:

- "The spirit of the LORD shall rest on him." He will wear God's spirit like a garment; it will pervade his personality.
- He will have "the spirit of wisdom and understanding." What do we mean when we say someone we know has wisdom? Wisdom is a certain depth of knowledge that wise persons use as they operate in every area of their lives. It is a combination of common sense, good judgment, knowledge, and logic. Understanding is related to wisdom; perhaps as the prophet uses it here it

refers to qualities of the intellect, such as discernment and comprehension.
- He will have "the spirit of counsel and might." These terms refer more to the practical side of leadership. Isaiah is telling us that the ideal king will know how to both give good advice and receive the advice that others have to offer. Furthermore, he will have the power necessary to enforce the decisions he makes.
- The spirit of knowledge and the fear of the LORD" will also be with this king. The prophet does not mean just any kind of knowledge here; he is talking about knowledge of God. For Isaiah, the ideal leader will both have an intimate relationship with God and will place a high value on obedience to God. He will both know what God wants him to do and he will do just that.

What kind of picture does the prophet paint for us? What kind of a leader is this ideal messianic king? This person will have the wisdom he needs and will also be able to use it. He will be able to follow up on his decisions. He will operate constantly in the context of what God wants for the people he serves.

The prophet announces that this leader will emerge from the stump of Jesse, who is King David's father (Isaiah 11:1). As Luke recounts the Christmas story, he portrays Jesus as the promised messianic king. The angels' message of great joy is that a child, born in David's city, is Savior, Messiah, and Lord (Luke 2:11). The long-expected era of God's righteousness and peace is about to become a reality as this child grows and embodies the characteristics of leadership foretold by Isaiah. The angels' response to the news of this leader's birth is one of praise and adoration, for in him God's promise for a transformed world will be fulfilled.

In the birth of Jesus, we experience God's kingdom as both present and yet to come. The work of continuing transformation is entrusted to the church. We too need leaders who exhibit, at least to some degree, the spiritual characteristics of the messianic king. The General Council on Ministries of The United Methodist Church recently conducted a survey of United Methodist laity on the values and skills they most admired in their pastors. Regardless of age, gender, level of education, location, or size of congregation, the respondents agreed on three basic characteristics that were most highly valued in a pastor. They want their pastors to be caring, cooperative, and honest. In other words, what matters most is a kind of personal integrity that results in a caring attitude toward others and an honesty in dealing with the people they serve. These traits do relate, in part, to the leadership qualities of the messianic king.

Expectations of Leadership

Now that we have considered the kind of leader valued by the Israelites and the modern church, let us turn to the question of what God's people want these leaders to do. What expectations do we have of our leaders? Isaiah lists several of these in verses 3b-5 of today's passage.

- "With righteousness he shall judge the poor" and he will "decide with equity for the meek of the earth." This ideal king will take special care to ensure that the poor and the marginalized receive the equal treatment they deserve. In this ideal scenario, there will be a leveling out of justice so that no one receives special treatment because of status.

- "He shall strike the earth with the rod of his mouth" and "with the breath of his lips he shall kill the wicked." The words of this king will be powerful. They will function like those of the prophet: words are not just words; they make things happen. Just as the prophet can initiate events by proclaiming them, the king's words have a power that is greater than the words themselves.

- He will be clothed with righteousness and faithfulness at all times. These qualities will guide his decision making.

What kind of leader is Isaiah portraying here? What skills does this ideal king have? He has good judgment that he uses impartially. He is careful about what he says because his words have power. He makes decisions in the context of his faith in God.

In the recent survey of United Methodist laity, respondents were also asked about the skills they valued most highly in their pastors. Three skills rose to the top of the list: (1) preaching, (2) management and administration, and (3) pastoral care. These skills were consistently valued more highly than biblical knowledge, community involvement, communication skills, and so forth. Perhaps your class will want to discuss how these skills compare to those lifted up by the prophet as essential skills of an ideal king. Some suggestions are given in the section entitled "Leading the Class."

A Reign of Peace

In Isaiah 11:6-9, the prophet paints a picture of what society would look like if it were ruled by this ideal messianic king. If we were to have a leader with the characteristics and skills identified in the first part of the passage, what would life be like? What would a reign of peace look like?

A study of the meanings of peace may help us to envision such a reign. Peace as it is used in the Old Testament is a more general term than it usually is for us. Peace is more than just the absence of war; it is a kind of wholeness and sense of well-being. Here are some of the aspects of peace that are reflected in the Old Testament.

- the peace that results from the absence of enemies (see 1 Chronicles 22:18; Solomon's name derives from the Hebrew word for peace—shalom)
- the peace that comes from being protected by God (see Judges 18:6)

- the peace that characterizes the good life (see Psalm 4:8)
- the peace that is associated with posterity or one's future (see Psalm 37:37)
- the peace that comes at the time of death (see Genesis 15:15)
- the peace associated with economic prosperity (see Psalm 147:14)
- the peace that can be found in the natural world (see Ezekiel 34:25)
- the peace that comes with political security (see Isaiah 32:18)
- the peace that can be described as the absence of war (see Judges 21:13)
- the peace that comes after surrender to God (see Isaiah 27:5)
- the peace that comes from God (see Isaiah 45:7, especially King James Version)

These are just a few different nuances of the concept of peace as it appears in the Old Testament. Because the concept is so large and so complex, it is difficult to describe in a few words. Perhaps that is why the prophet found it necessary and useful to help his audience visualize it rather than merely describing it.

SHARING THE SCRIPTURE

PREPARING TO TEACH

Your preparation time will probably be at a premium this week, since it is the week before Christmas. Try to find some quiet time in the midst of all the hustle and bustle of the season.

In order to set the context for this week's scripture passages, read through the material under the heading "Understanding the Scripture," as well as the two background scriptures for the week: Isaiah 11:1-9 and Luke 2:1-20. You might want to read the Luke passages aloud to friends or family members at least once during the week.

Spend some time thinking about the

kinds of leaders you encounter this week, either those you know personally at church or at work, or those who are visible in current world events. Pay attention to their characteristics and to how they respond to the various situations they confront.

Also spend some time visualizing world peace. What does it look like to you? We know what it looks like to the prophet Isaiah—the leopard lying down with the kid is a vivid and powerful image. What is your own personal image of world peace?

To prepare for the group discussion of peace, you might want to spend some time looking up the scripture passages listed under the heading "A Reign of Peace."

LEADING THE CLASS

Introduction

Ask whether anyone has seen the bumper sticker that says "Visualize World Peace." Encourage students to recall other slogans about peace (such as, "If You Want Peace, Work for Justice") or songs and poems that discuss the concept of peace. Ask them to think about what message each slogan, song, or poem is communicating about peace.

Encourage the group to suggest various definitions of peace. Stress that there are no right or wrong answers here because the concept of peace is so complex. You may want to write these definitions on a chalkboard or newsprint so that class members can refer to them later. To get the group thinking about various ways to define peace, you may want to mention several possible contexts such as personal, communal, or global.

Choose a volunteer to read aloud the familiar passage from Luke's Christmas story. Here Luke announces the birth of a child whom he describes as Savior, Messiah, and Lord. Born in the city of David, Jesus is seen by Luke as the heir of David's throne. As the group listens to the reading, ask them to consider these questions:

(1) What kind of leader will this baby be?
(2) What will he do?
(3) What will characterize his reign?

Although Luke does not address these questions, the prophet Isaiah's description of a future, ideal king helps us to envision the person and work of this long awaited Messiah, the Prince of Peace.

Conclude the introduction by pointing out today's main question: **What do God's people want their leaders to be and do? Given this kind of leadership, how would we "visualize world peace"?**

Qualities of Leadership

Begin this discussion by having someone read aloud verses 1-3*a* from Isaiah 11 (ending with "fear of the LORD"). Use the material that discusses these verses under the heading "Understanding the Scripture" to explain words or phrases that are not clear and to set the passage in its proper context. Ask for volunteers to paraphrase these verses by describing what kind of leader this is. Be sure to focus the discussion on what the leader is rather than on what the leader does (this will come next). You may want to record these ideas on a chalkboard or newsprint. Ask whether anyone knows a leader like this, and who that leader might be.

Mention the most valued qualities of pastoral leaders (caring, cooperation, honesty) listed in the survey of United Methodist laity. Ask whether class members agree with the respondents, or whether they would suggest other characteristics that they believe are more important. You may want to record their answers on a chalkboard or newsprint.

Expectations of Leadership

Repeat the same process you used in the previous section. Have someone read verses 3*b*-5 aloud (beginning with "He shall not judge"). Use the material from "Understanding the Scripture" to explain anything that seems unclear. Ask the question, **What kind of leader is this?** Here the focus is on what the leader does. **Do the class members know anyone (or know of anyone) who does these things well?** Share the insights from the United Methodist survey if you determine that the class members would be interested. Have them list other skills in addition to, or instead of, the answers given by the survey respondents.

A Reign of Peace

Begin this section by acknowledging that peace is a difficult concept to grasp because of its complexity. Have someone read aloud Isaiah 11:6-9, and emphasize that this passage is the prophet's attempt to visualize world peace. Now make the concept specific by asking the question, **What would happen if we had a Department of Peace rather than a Department of Defense?** You can facilitate this discussion in one of two ways:

- If possible, divide the class members into groups of four or five persons. Direct each small group to create this new Department of Peace. As they work, ask them to answer the following questions: What would be the work of the department? What would its responsibilities be? What kinds of leaders should be employed? What would the organizational chart look like? Set a time limit, after which you ask the small groups to share their work with the larger group.
- Ask various members of the class to look up the scripture passages listed under "A Reign of Peace" in "Interpreting the Scripture." You may want to write this list on newsprint ahead of time, or you may prefer to give the references aloud. After each verse is read aloud, ask the class to reflect on what it says about what peace is. Then spend a few minutes in silence in which class members visualize their own image of world peace. Ask them to share these visions with the group if they are willing.

HELPING CLASS MEMBERS ACT

Class members can ponder several questions this week. The discussion about the qualities and expectations of leaders may heighten their awareness of different leadership styles, both in themselves and in the people who lead them. Ask them to consider how they can pattern themselves after the example of the messianic leader. Challenge them to take at least one step in that direction this week.

If you have asked the students to draw their own visual images of world peace, encourage them to act within their own families or circle of friends to make these images reality. Challenge class members to assume leadership in bringing about peace in troubled situations they encounter.

Close with a prayer that the peace of the Christ child will permeate their hearts and minds as they celebrate the Christmas season.

PLANNING FOR NEXT SUNDAY

Next week we will move ahead a hundred years or so and look at the prophecy of Third Isaiah, whose words are found in chapters 56–66. The topic will be good news. Ask the class members to be especially aware of what good news comes their way during the week ahead.

FOR THOSE WHO PROCLAIM GOOD NEWS

PREVIEWING THE LESSON

Lesson Scripture: Isaiah 60:1-4; 61:1-4
Background Scripture: Isaiah 60–61
Key Verse: Isaiah 61:1

Focus of the lesson:
the prophet's proclamation of God's good news

Main question(s) of the lesson:
(1) What good news do we need to hear?
(2) What good news do we have to proclaim?

This lesson will enable adult learners to:
(1) grasp the prophet's message of freedom and hope to the oppressed
(2) consider the good news that they need to hear
(3) respond by sharing God's good news with someone else.

Today's lesson may be outlined as follows:
(1) Introduction
(2) Proclaiming the Good News
(3) Freedom from Bondage
(4) Returning Home

FOCUSING ON THE MAIN QUESTION

Each of us likes to tell others good news. Conveying bad news is another matter; we often joke about not shooting the messenger when we approach someone else with some bad news. But sharing good news is one of life's pleasures. I smile when I think of the look on the face of our younger son when he has something good to tell us. He can hardly wait to get the words out of his mouth. He looks like he will burst if we don't sit down immediately and give him our full attention.

Like Second Isaiah before him, Third Isaiah (the name given to the author of Isaiah 56–66) had good news to proclaim to the chosen people. His sense of excitement and urgency was heightened by the fact that God had anointed him to proclaim this good news. Last week we were reminded of the "good news of great joy" of Jesus' birth as it was proclaimed to the shepherds by the heavenly host. In earlier lessons we read of the good news proclaimed to the exiles by Second Isaiah: they were about to be released from captivity and God would lead them home to Jerusalem.

Hearing these biblical witnesses to the good news causes us to think about our own good news. The questions before us today are: **What good news do we need to hear? What good news do we have to proclaim?**

READING THE SCRIPTURE

NRSV
Isaiah 60:1-4
1 Arise, shine; for your light has come,
  and the glory of the LORD has risen upon you.
2 For darkness shall cover the earth,
  and thick darkness the peoples;
  but the LORD will arise upon you,
    and his glory will appear over you.
3 Nations shall come to your light,
  and kings to the brightness of your dawn.

4 Lift up your eyes and look around;
  they all gather together, they come to you;
  your sons shall come from far away,
  and your daughters shall be carried on their nurses' arms.

Isaiah 61:1-4
1 The spirit of the Lord GOD is upon me,
  because the LORD has anointed me;
  he has sent me to bring good news to the oppressed,
  to bind up the brokenhearted,
  to proclaim liberty to the captives,
  and release to the prisoners;

NIV
Isaiah 60:1-4
1 "Arise, shine, for your light has come,
  and the glory of the LORD rises upon you.

2 See, darkness covers the earth
  and thick darkness is over the peoples,
  but the LORD rises upon you
  and his glory appears over you.

3 Nations will come to your light,
  and kings to the brightness of your dawn.

4 "Lift up your eyes and look about you:
  All assemble and come to you;
  your sons come from afar,
  and your daughters are carried on the arm."

Isaiah 61:1-4
1 The Spirit of the Sovereign LORD is on me,
  because the LORD has anointed me
  to preach good news to the poor.
He has sent me to bind up the brokenhearted,
  to proclaim freedom for the captives
  and release for the prisoners,

Key
Verse

²to proclaim the year of the
    Lord's favor,
  and the day of vengeance of
    our God;
  to comfort all who mourn;
³to provide for those who mourn
    in Zion—
  to give them a garland instead
    of ashes,
  the oil of gladness instead of
    mourning,
  the mantle of praise instead of
    a faint spirit.
  They will be called oaks of
    righteousness,
  the planting of the LORD, to
    display his glory.
⁴They shall build up the ancient
    ruins,
  they shall raise up the former
    devastations;
  they shall repair the ruined
    cities,
  the devastations of many
    generations.

²to proclaim the year of the LORD's favor
    and the day of vengeance of our God,
  to comfort all who mourn,

³and provide for those who grieve in Zion—
  to bestow on them a crown of beauty
    instead of ashes,
  the oil of gladness
    instead of mourning,
  and a garment of praise
    instead of a spirit of despair.
  They will be called oaks of righteousness,
    a planting of the LORD
    for the display of his splendor.

⁴They will rebuild the ancient ruins
    and restore the places long devastated;
  they will renew the ruined cities
    that have been devastated for generations.

UNDERSTANDING THE SCRIPTURE

Isaiah 60–61. Thus far in this series of lessons we have mainly been studying scripture passages that come from the book of Isaiah. During the first two weeks, the passages came from Second Isaiah, prophet of the exile. This prophet's words are found in Isaiah 40–55. The next two weeks the texts were from the first portion of the book of Isaiah, attributed to Isaiah of Jerusalem (chapters 1–39). Our passage for this week comes from a section of Isaiah that we usually call Third Isaiah (chapters 56–66).

The prophecies found in this third section of Isaiah are probably the responsibility of a prophet who was a disciple of Second Isaiah and who lived and worked in Jerusalem after the return from the exile in Babylon. At times in chapters 56–66 the words, images, and concepts used by this third Isaiah are very similar to those of Second Isaiah; this similarity is due largely to the fact that Third Isaiah was attempting to both draw on and expand the message of Second Isaiah. Both prophets focused much of their work on the image of restored Jerusalem: for Second Isaiah it was a future goal and for Third Isaiah it was a present reality.

The words and message of Isaiah 60–61 would have been inspirational to their original audience and can be for us as well. The prophet speaks eloquently about his vision of restored Jerusalem and its people living in the glow of God's glory.

This passage is divided into six parts: (1) the prophet's call to the audience (Isaiah 60:1-3); (2) the prophet's proclamation to persons who were already in Jerusalem (Isaiah 60:4-9); (3) the promise of a new era of salvation (Isaiah 60:10-16); (4) the contrast between Jerusalem's past and its future (Isaiah 60:17-22); (5) information about the prophet known as Third Isaiah (Isaiah 61:1-3); and (6) changes in the city of Jerusalem and its people (Isaiah 61:4-11).

Isaiah 60:1-3. Notice how this prophet is fond of using imperatives to get the attention of his audience: "Arise, shine; for your light has come." This style is reminiscent of Second Isaiah, who began his work with the command to "Comfort, O comfort my people" (Isaiah 40:1). Notice the contrast between light and darkness that permeates these verses. This contrast was also used in Isaiah 9 to distinguish between past despair and future hope.

Isaiah 61:4-9. In order to understand the original context of this prophecy, we must recognize that the exiles' return from Babylon and the restoration of Jerusalem were not overnight events. Even after the edict of the Persian King Cyrus in 538 B.C.E. that allowed the exiles to return home, not all Israelites chose to do so because they were settled in Babylon. Those who did return did so in smaller groups over an extended period of time. For many years there were at the same time people who had already returned to Jerusalem and were in the process of rebuilding the city and those who were still on the way back. These verses are addressed to the people inside Jerusalem. They are to wake up and look around them to see that the light of God has come. As Zion's sons and daughters return, they bring the wealth of other nations with them.

For the prophet, several foreign nations represented sources of the wealth that was to be brought to Jerusalem via caravan and ship to rebuild the city. Midian was to the south of Judah, just east of the Red Sea. Ephah refers to Arab tribes east of the Gulf of Aqaba. Sheba was to the south of Midian. Kedar was located in northern Arabia.

Nebaioth refers to an Arab tribe. Tarshish may have been in what is now southern Spain.

The end of verse 9 repeats a kind of refrain, that the restoration of the city is both because of and for the purpose of God's glory.

Isaiah 60:10-16. Here the prophet promises a new era of salvation for the chosen people, and describes in detail what the situation will be like in the city once it is rebuilt and restored. The walls will be rebuilt; the gates will always be open; wealth and prosperity will abound. The cypress, the plane, and the pine that will be used to rebuild the temple in Jerusalem (verse 13) will come from Lebanon, just as the wood Solomon used to build the first temple did (1 Kings 5:6). As in verse 9, the prophet concludes this section by reminding his audience of the ultimate goal of the return of the exiles and restoration of the city: that God may be glorified.

Isaiah 60:17-22. In these verses the prophet draws a sharp contrast between the former and the future Jerusalem. This contrast involves not only what is visible but also what is intangible. Gold, silver, bronze, and iron will replace what has been bronze, iron, wood, and stone. Salvation and praise will supplant violence, devastation, and destruction. God's light will guide the inhabitants of the city. Righteousness will characterize the motivations and behaviors of the people in the city.

Isaiah 61:1-3. This section provides us with more information than any other about the writer many scholars call Third Isaiah. The prophet describes his anointing by God to preach good news; that is, he has been given special authority to speak in the name of God. Jesus quotes parts of this passage in Luke 4:18-19 when he is describing his mission and ministry.

Isaiah 61:4-11. These verses elaborate on how circumstances will change in the restored Jerusalem. Again the prophet focuses not only on changes in outward appearances (repairing the ruins) but also on the inner changes that will take place in the hearts of the people, who "shall be called priests of the LORD" and "named ministers of our God" (verse 6).

Isaiah 61:7 echoes the words of Second Isaiah in 40:2. The people have suffered double for all their sins, and now the restoration will be a double portion. Isaiah 61:9 reasserts the reason for the glorious restoration: that all people may know what God has accomplished on behalf of the chosen people. Another echo of an earlier passage in Isaiah occurs in verse 11, which describes the population growth in the restored city in terms of shoots coming forth from the earth (Isaiah 11:1).

INTERPRETING THE SCRIPTURE

Proclaiming the Good News

The proclamation of good news pervades both the Old and New Testaments. In last week's lesson, we read Luke's account of the angel announcing good news to the shepherds about the birth of a babe in Bethlehem. Recall the comforting news that Second Isaiah preached consistently: comfort is found in God's continual presence during times of crisis and despair. In Isaiah 40:9 the prophet speaks of Jerusalem (Zion) as a "herald of good tidings"; or, if the variant reading is used, he speaks of good tidings that are to be proclaimed to the people of Jerusalem. In the often-quoted passage found in 52:7, Second Isaiah speaks of the feet of the messenger "who brings good news," the good news of the long-awaited release from captivity.

Third Isaiah speaks of his anointing by God as a messenger to bring good news to the oppressed. Here we can see a strong connection with the words and message of Second Isaiah, of whom Third Isaiah was probably a disciple. In today's lesson, Third Isaiah proclaims the good news of release from bondage *and* the restoration of Jerusalem (Isaiah 60–61).

During the next few weeks, we will be studying the mission and message of the suffering servant, an integral part of the message of Second Isaiah and alluded to here by Third Isaiah. What is the good news that God anoints this prophet to preach? It is the good news that the exiles will be freed from bondage and returning home.

Freedom from Bondage

Release from captivity is a concept that most adults can understand. Who among us did not watch with great excitement the events surrounding the release of long-held hostage Terry Anderson? We held our breath, hoping that nothing would get in the way of his release. We waited in anticipation to hear what he had to say about his bondage, his present feelings, and his hopes for the future.

Most of us have only experienced this kind of release from captivity vicariously since we have never physically been held hostage. But we have our own times of exile, or our own prisons from which God can release us. And that is how we can connect directly with this passage from Isaiah. For example, I know a woman with young children who is a single parent. She and her children live in a tiny apartment, and she drives a beat-up old car that does not start most of the time. People who perceive her circumstances but do not know her may feel sorry for this woman. But she is not a person to pity. She is happy. I understand her happiness because I know about the abusive situation that imprisoned her for several long years. Now she is free. Although she continues to need help in meeting her material needs, she is free.

What are our prisons? Some of the most talented, creative people I know are imprisoned by self-doubt. They are terrified to stand in front of a group of people and make a presentation. I have seen wonderful things happen when people like this are released from their fears and can overcome this kind of anxiety. A friend I have known for many years is a minister who at one time was terrified to step into the pulpit—not because of stage fright but because he was not certain that he had something valuable to say. Over the years, little by little, he was released from his fear by the affirmations of those who heard him preach. Now he preaches with confidence. Preaching will probably never be easy for him, but it is easier than it used to be. The good news of release from captivity became real in his professional life.

Returning Home

The prophet also proclaims the good news of returning home. Recall Second Isaiah's image of the way being prepared for the exiles to return to Jerusalem (Isaiah 40:3-4). Whereas Second Isaiah spoke to the exiles who were themselves about to return home, Third Isaiah speaks to those who live in the city, who have already returned home, proclaiming to them that the rest of the inhabitants are about to return as well. He says:

> Lift up your eyes and look
> 　　around;
> they all gather together, they
> 　　come to you;
> your sons shall come from far
> 　　away,
> and your daughters shall be
> 　　carried on their nurses'
> 　　arms (Isaiah 60:4).

This is a vivid picture of a homecoming.

Homecoming is a common image in the Bible. Sometimes the Scripture speaks of a homecoming to a particular place, such as Jerusalem in the book of Isaiah. Sometimes the homecoming is to a particular person—Joseph and his family, for instance. Although Joseph did not literally come home to his family (actually, his family came to him in Egypt after many years), the reunion scene among these family members is like a homecoming. Genesis tells us that when Joseph and his father were reunited after so many years, Joseph "wept on [Jacob's] neck a good while" (Genesis 46:29). The good news of this homecoming, in which families are reunited, is the kind of which the prophet speaks in Isaiah 61.

In the familiar parable of the prodigal son (Luke 15:11-32), the son comes home to both a place and a person: he comes back to his home and to his father. After leaving home and squandering his portion of the inheritance, he eventually comes to the point when he decides it is time to return home. Of course, Jesus' parable is about more than just a son running out of money and being welcomed back into the fold by his father. It is a message about God and God's children. In his book *Heartfelt: Finding Our Way Back to God*, Gerrit Dawson tells it this way:

> Sometimes, without even knowing it, we get ourselves on a road away from ourselves and God. We may not even know how far away we are until the money runs out and our stomachs growl with hunger. . . . At first we may not be able to describe home; we simply know we are not there. We may not know in those waking moments what being ourselves is supposed to be; but we feel sure that we have not been living in harmony with our innermost design. We may not have a description for what connecting with God could be like; we realize, however, that we are a long way from such a connection. Our need yanks us awake, we discover how far we are from home, and we begin to search for a way to get back.

In Jesus' story, the father who lets the son go clearly represents God. Somehow, then, God is intimately connected with all that makes up home. The father in the story is the source of blessing; his house is the place where life is in balance. On his land is to be found the work that satisfies and generates an abundant harvest.

The younger son left that home, pillaging part of its wealth, to live in his own way. He not only physically left home but tried to leave behind the person God created him to be. When we seek to escape who we most truly are, we leave God. God is not alien to us; God is within the inmost part of us, for we are created in the image of God. If we would be at peace and at home with ourselves, we will have to be at home with God.

When the exiles return home to Jerusalem, they are returning to their temple, their rituals, their liturgy, their religious tradition. They are returning to their God. They are going home. That is the good news the prophet of chapters 60–61 is proclaiming.

We know from reading much of the post-exilic literature in the Bible that the return and restoration were not as glorious as the prophets and people pictured that it would be. Certainly, as in any homecom-

ing, there were disappointments. How often does it happen that when we are away from home we pine for our familiar circumstances and for those we love. When we are in this kind of mood we tend to idealize our home situation; when we return we see the same old places with the same old repairs needing to be done. We find the same people behaving in the same ways.

Recently I attended a high school reunion in a distant state. I had not seen any of these people for many years, and I had not been back to the town I grew up in for a long time. I had mixed emotions during and immediately after this homecoming experience. The people who did not move away were, in many ways, just like I remembered them. I was both filled with nostalgia for the place and the people and overwhelmed with gratitude that I had chosen to move away.

The prophet's good news proclaims a freedom from bondage and a glorious return home. When you read through Isaiah 60–61, you will continually be reminded of what, in the prophet's mind, stands firmly behind this good news: the constant presence of God.

SHARING THE SCRIPTURE

PREPARING TO TEACH

Prepare to teach this lesson by reading the background scripture found in Isaiah 60–61. This is a particularly long passage, so you may want to read it in sections as listed under the heading "Understanding the Scripture." Also read the material under the heading "Interpreting the Scripture" to see how the main question and the topics for this week's discussion grow out of the background scripture passage.

Spend some time this week thinking about the concept of good news. How have you experienced good news lately? When and where have you heard good news?

When have you communicated good news to someone else? What was the news? Prepare to share your thoughts with the class during the discussion time next Sunday.

Read the following passages that speak of good news: Isaiah 40:9; 52:7; and Luke 2:10-11. As a teacher, you are a messenger with good news to share with your class. What good news is God calling you to proclaim? How can you share it most effectively with your students?

Give some thought ahead of time to this week's discussion topics: freedom from bondage and returning home. How have you experienced release and homecoming? Are there stories you can be prepared to share with the class?

LEADING THE CLASS

Introduction

Begin the class session by asking the class members first, what good news they have heard lately and second, what good news they may have proclaimed to someone else. Have someone read aloud Isaiah 61:1-3. Spend a few minutes listing the good news that is proclaimed in that passage. If you wish, record the list on a chalkboard or newsprint. Then tell the class members that this lesson will focus on two kinds of good news proclaimed by the prophet in today's scripture passage: the good news of release from captivity and the good news of returning home.

As we consider the good news, we will ask ourselves today's main questions: **What good news do we need to hear? What good news do we have to proclaim?**

Proclaiming the Good News

Begin the discussion by sharing with the class the material under the subheading "Proclaiming the Good News," found in "Interpreting the Scripture." Ask them to think of instances when others have said to them something like, "I have good news and bad news," or when they have used this tactic themselves.

Talk for a minute about the idea that good news is easier to communicate than bad news. Lead the class in a discussion of why it is difficult to communicate bad news to someone else and why telling good news is relatively easy.

Have someone read aloud the following scripture passages: Luke 2:10-11 (which was part of last week's lesson); Isaiah 40:9 (which we studied on December 3); Isaiah 52:7 and Isaiah 61:1-3 (which is part of the focus for today's lesson). Ask for paraphrases of each of these passages in order to help class members see how the concept of good news is used in each case.

To close the discussion of this topic, spend a few minutes in silence. Ask the class members to think of some good news that they need to communicate to someone else in the week ahead. Challenge them to think especially about how they can share the good news of God's salvation with others.

Freedom from Bondage

Perhaps someone in your class either knows a former hostage or knows someone who does. If so, ask that person to speak from experience about the release of that hostage from captivity.

Then move the discussion to a more personal level. Read or retell the two examples found in "Interpreting the Scripture" under the subtitle "Freedom from Bondage": the example of the single mother freeing herself from an abusive situation and that of the minister who overcame his fear of preaching. Have the class members spend some silent time thinking about the prisons they experience. These may be prisons created by economic or personal circumstances, as in the case of the single mother. Or they may be psychological prisons we find ourselves entrapped in, such as the fear that hindered the minister. Other prisons may be caused by stereotypes due to our age, gender, race, occupation, and so on. Or we may feel confined to physical prisons caused by illness or injury. If your class is comfortable sharing on a personal level, ask them to offer their own examples of prisons they are or have been in and how they were (or might be) released from these prisons. Or, ask them to share stories of people they know or have heard or read about. If the class is large, these discussions may take place with a partner or in small groups.

Close this discussion with a silent time or a brief prayer, asking God's help as we work to move beyond the prisons that hold us.

Returning Home

Open the discussion of this topic by asking: **Has anyone been to a class reunion or a family reunion recently. What feelings did these events evoke?** On the chalkboard or on newsprint, make a list of the feelings that are mentioned in the discussion.

Refer to the material under this heading in "Interpreting the Scripture" that relates to the story of Joseph and the parable of the prodigal son. Use this material to illustrate the fact that homecoming is a biblical concept as well as a contemporary idea. Then have someone read aloud Isaiah 60:4-7.

If your class is large enough, divide the group into two subgroups: (1) the group of exiles that is returning home to Jerusalem from Babylon and (2) the group of inhabitants of Jerusalem that is awaiting the return of the group of exiles. Give each subgroup two sentence fragments to complete:

We are excited because _____.

We are anxious because _____.

Give the group a time limit in which to come up with as many answers as they can to these two sentence stems. After the groups have finished their work, have them share their results with the whole class. As they make their reports, record the feelings on chalkboard or newsprint. Pay special attention to feelings that are shared in common.

Summarize the entire lesson by asking one member to read aloud Isaiah 61:1-4 and another person to read aloud Jesus' words in Luke 4:16-19. Note that as followers of Jesus, we too are called to proclaim good news. Discuss these questions:

(1) **Who are the kinds of persons to whom we are called to proclaim good news?**

(2) **In what ways are some persons oppressed or held captive?**

(3) **What words of encouragement can we, as individuals and collectively as the church, offer to captive persons?**

(4) **What good news can we share about returning home to God?**

HELPING CLASS MEMBERS ACT

Class members can act on what they have learned in today's lesson by becoming more conscious hearers and proclaimers of good news. Ask the class members to tell someone some good news during the week ahead, whether it be the Good News of Jesus Christ or some other good news that they know someone else needs to hear.

The class members spent some time thinking about their individual prisons. You might ask them to take one step out of whatever prison they found themselves in. Or, ask them to help someone else take a step he or she needs to take.

The concept of coming home, especially as it is reflected in the parable of the prodigal son, most importantly involves our coming home to God. Ask the class members to spend some time during the week ahead evaluating their relationship with God. Are they far from God? Do they, like the younger son in the parable, need to come home to God? Encourage them to ask for God's help in their homecoming journey.

PLANNING FOR NEXT SUNDAY

Next week we will move back into the words and message of Second Isaiah. We will begin a four-week unit on the suffering servant, in which we will examine the servant's call, his mission, his endurance in the face of despair, and his victory. Begin thinking about the idea of servanthood and how this concept is used today. A careful reading of Isaiah 42:1-9 may spark your imagination.

CALLED TO SERVE

PREVIEWING THE LESSON

Lesson Scripture: Isaiah 42:1-9
Background Scripture: Isaiah 42:1-9
Key Verse: Isaiah 42:1

Focus of the lesson:
God's call of the suffering servant

Main question(s) of the lesson:
(1) What does it mean to be called to serve God?

This lesson will enable adult learners to:
(1) be aware of the servant's call to serve all persons, especially the weak and helpless
(2) recognize that they too are called to serve God in some way
(3) respond by moving in the direction they believe God is calling them.

Today's lesson may be outlined as follows:
(1) Introduction
(2) We Are All Called to Serve
(3) Answering the Call
(4) Former Things and New Things

FOCUSING ON THE MAIN QUESTION

A hymn written in recent years asks the question, "Is it I, Lord?" Am I the one you are calling? Implicit in this question are two related questions; "Didn't you mean to call someone else?" and "Why me, Lord?" These questions are at the heart of the background scripture for this week's lesson. And there is not a person I know who has not asked them from time to time. They are universal questions.

A young boy goes to church camp and while there feels a tug from God in the direction of the ministry. Years later he acts on this early hint of his calling by enrolling in seminary. A woman who has just recently retired visits a friend of the family who has been placed in a nursing home. While there she experiences a desire to do something about the loneliness she sees all around her. She talks with her pastor about starting a church visitation program in the local nursing homes. Inspired by a program he hears about from one of his friends, a man organizes a monthly men's breakfast at his church. These men raise enough money to support a program to feed, house, and clothe the street people in their city. A young woman boards a bus bound for Nashville, not having a job ahead of her but knowing she wants a career in religious publishing.

These people all heard the call of God to serve in some way or another, and they all heeded that call. The ways God calls us are many and various, and the kinds of service to which we are called are too numerous to mention. But in each of these cases the call required a response. The question, "Is it I, Lord," is the beginning of the response to the call.

This week we will examine the call God issues to the unknown figure in Second Isaiah who we often call the suffering servant. From that starting point we will go on to examine the calls we each experience and the issues that these calls raise for us. Today's lesson raises the question: **What does it mean to be called to serve God?**

?

READING THE SCRIPTURE

NRSV
Isaiah 42:1-9

Key
Verse

1 Here is my servant, whom I
    uphold,
    my chosen, in whom my soul
      delights;
I have put my spirit upon him;
    he will bring forth justice to
      the nations.
²He will not cry or lift up his
    voice,
    or make it heard in the street;
³a bruised reed he will not break,
    and a dimly burning wick he
      will not quench;
    he will faithfully bring forth
      justice.
⁴He will not grow faint or be
    crushed
    until he has established justice
      in the earth;
    and the coastlands wait for his
      teaching.

⁵Thus says God, the Lᴏʀᴅ,
    who created the heavens and
      stretched them out,
    who spread out the earth and
      what comes from it,
    who gives breath to the people
      upon it
    and spirit to those who walk in
      it:
⁶I am the Lᴏʀᴅ, I have called
    you in righteousness,

NIV
Isaiah 42:1-9

K
Ve

1 "Here is my servant, whom I uphold,
    my chosen one in whom I delight;
I will put my Spirit on him
    and he will bring justice to the nations.

²He will not shout or cry out,
    or raise his voice in the streets.

³A bruised reed he will not break,
    and a smoldering wick he will not
      snuff out.
    In faithfulness he will bring forth justice;

⁴ he will not falter or be discouraged
    till he establishes justice on earth.
    In his law the islands will put their hope."

⁵This is what God the Lᴏʀᴅ says—
    he who created the heavens and stretched
      them out,
    who spread out the earth and all that
      comes out of it,
    who gives breath to its people,
    and life to those who walk on it:

⁶"I, the Lᴏʀᴅ, have called you in
      righteousness;

I have taken you by the hand
　　and kept you;
I have given you as a covenant
　　to the people,
　a light to the nations,
7　to open the eyes that are
　　blind,
　to bring out the prisoners from
　　the dungeon,
　from the prison those who sit
　　in darkness.
8I am the LORD, that is my name;
　my glory I give to no other,
　nor my praise to idols.
9See, the former things have
　　come to pass,
　and new things I now
　　declare;
　before they spring forth,
　　I tell you of them.

I will take hold of your hand.
I will keep you and will make you
　　to be a covenant for the people
　　and a light for the Gentiles,

7to open eyes that are blind,
　　to free captives from prison
　　and to release from the dungeon those
　　who sit in darkness.

8"I am the LORD; that is my name!
　I will not give my glory to another
　or my praise to idols.
9See, the former things have taken place,
　　and new things I declare;
　before they spring into being
　　I announce them to you."

UNDERSTANDING THE SCRIPTURE

This passage is divided into two parts: (1) the first servant song (Isaiah 42:1-4); and (2) a proclamation about God as creator and redeemer (Isaiah 42:5-9). We will examine each of these two parts in turn.

Isaiah 42:1-4. This is the first of four servant songs found in the prophecies of Second Isaiah. The other three servant songs are: 49:1-6; 50:4-11; and 52:13–53:12. We will be studying these other three servant songs in the next three weeks.

Biblical scholars through the centuries have written pages and pages of commentary pondering the identity of this suffering servant. Who was the prophet talking about? Who served as the model for this servant figure? Was it the nation of Israel? Was it the prophet himself? Was it King Cyrus of Persia, the liberator of the Babylonian captives? Was it some other important figure of the day whose identity has not survived the centuries? Although we can speculate, we will never know for certain who this servant was. The most important issue is not the identity of the servant but rather the message that the prophet is proclaiming to us through the life and work of the servant.

In these verses the prophet uses a style that is compact and measured; the words communicate efficiently and each word is important. Note the repetition of the word "not"—it is used or implied seven times in just these four verses. The prophet apparently is more intent on telling us who or what the servant is not than on revealing the identity of the servant. Notice also the repetition of the word "justice" (used three times). This concept is important, for the work of the servant is to bring justice to the people.

Isaiah 42:1. Many commentators have noted that the language of this verse is similar to the call of some of the Old Testament prophets. We picture God speaking to an unidentified group of people, getting their attention, and encouraging them to witness the call of this servant. "Here he is—this is the one whom I have called—pay attention to him." We learn in this verse that God has "upheld" (taken hold of) the servant, chosen him for a particular purpose, and endowed him with God's spirit so that he might accomplish his mission of bringing justice to the nations. Justice will be established when God's teaching (Torah) is known and obeyed. The reference to "the nations" indicates that Second Isaiah sees God not just as the God of Israel but as the God of everyone.

Isaiah 42:2-3. The servant will not accomplish his task with a flourish. Instead, he will go about his work of bringing God's justice in a quiet, unassuming way. The bruised reed and the dimly burning wick are images the prophet uses to demonstrate the extraordinariness of both the servant himself and the gentle ways in which he will accomplish his task.

Isaiah 42:4. This verse indicates the ultimate goal of the servant's work: he will bring God's teaching to everyone and restore justice. In doing so the servant will work not only quietly, but also patiently. He will not give up easily. The words "be crushed" are the only hint in this passage of the suffering element we often associate with the servant, which will be more evident in the other three songs.

Isaiah 42:5-9. This hymn-like passage celebrates God as both creator of the world and as author of salvation for all the people. God is still speaking to an unknown person here, who could be the servant.

Isaiah 42:5. This verse is a good example of the creation imagery that permeates the message of Second Isaiah. The prophet is speaking here of both past and present—note the change in tense in verse 5 from "created the heavens" to "gives breath." The message is that the same God who created the earth continues to create in us all the time. Heaven and earth are used to mean something like "absolutely everything."

Isaiah 42:6. "I am the LORD" is a phrase used often by this prophet, who is singling out God from among all the gods of surrounding nations. The same God who created the earth and established a covenant with the chosen people will now use this servant as a covenant to the people, or an instrument of salvation. The phrase "light to the nations" reminds us of the messianic king in Isaiah 9:2 who will lead the people from the darkness into the light.

Isaiah 42:7. In this verse the prophet develops further the idea of a light to the nations, indicating that the servant will liberate those who are blind and imprisoned. God is working through the servant for the good of others.

Isaiah 42:8. Here the prophet restates the reason for the servant's call: that God may be known apart from all other gods. God's name signifies God's identity.

Isaiah 42:9. The oracle concludes by contrasting the way things were previously to the way things will be as a result of the servant's work. Because the servant will persevere despite the odds he will face, God's activity will be evident in history.

INTERPRETING THE SCRIPTURE

We Are All Called to Serve

We are all called to serve in one way or another. Although we may think of a call as something that comes only to those who serve in the ordained ministry, the concepts of call and servanthood are much broader than that. God has created each person with gifts and talents that are to be used to serve God. Often we serve God by caring for other persons. The specific kinds of service we perform will vary, but God issues the call to serve to everyone. The question is not, "Will I be called?" but "How will I respond?"

The chorus of a song in *The United Methodist Hymnal* (page 593) reminds us of God's call and our response:

Here I am, Lord.
Is it I, Lord?
I have heard you calling in the night.
I will go, Lord, if you lead me.
I will hold your people in my heart.

There is a universality about these words that impresses me each time I hear the song. I read an article recently about *The United Methodist Hymnal*, published in 1989. The writer was analyzing the results of research that had been done among users of this new hymnal. The object of the research was to discover, among other things, how people felt about the changes in the hymnal, differences between this hymnal and its predecessor. Some new hymns had been added and some old ones had been dropped. There was much debate and discussion at the time the decisions were being made. How did people feel about the new hymns now that they had had a chance to use the new hymnal for a while?

One statistic that caught my attention was the fact that one of the three favorite new hymns was "Here I Am, Lord." Apparently many people have enjoyed the words and music to this song, which was written in 1981 by Dan Schutte. I was especially interested in this statistic because of a recent experience I had had with the hymn.

At a retreat some months ago, I attended a worship service focused on the theme of call. The preacher for the day delivered an inspiring sermon in which he examined his own call in light of some important events in his life, and encouraged us to do the same. We were all moved both by the intensity of his witness and by the opportunity to examine our own lives in light of what we per-

ceived God was calling us to do. At the close of the service we stood and sang the hymn "Here I Am, Lord." What a powerful way to conclude such a service! I will never forget looking around the room at my friends and colleagues and feeling the presence of God with all of us as we struggled with this difficult, intensely personal question. What is God calling me to do? Can we answer, "Here I am, Lord"?

Being called is a common experience, or at least it can be when we pay attention to what God is telling us. That is why the hymn speaks to us so profoundly. The Bible contains many stories of people being called by God and how they responded to that call. Remember Moses, who encountered God in the midst of the desert. God caught his attention through a bush that was burning brightly but was not being consumed. After some initial hesitation about his lack of skills as an orator, Moses accepts the challenge God sets before him and goes on to do great things. He responds affirmatively after he becomes convinced that God will remain with him. Martin Luther is reported to have said, "had Moses waited until he understood how Israel could elude Pharaoh's armies, they might have been in Egypt still." When he felt assured of God's abiding presence, Moses was not afraid to answer God's call and undertake his mission.

Do you remember the story of the young Samuel, who was sleeping soundly when the voice of God called him? Wakened from a deep sleep, he mistook God's voice for the voice of the priest, Eli. First Samuel 3 tells the story of how Samuel, once he recognized the voice as the call of God, dedicated himself to God's service. He spent the remainder of his life in response to God's call.

And then there was Second Isaiah, whose call we read and studied during the first lesson of this unit (Isaiah 40:6-8). God called this prophet to proclaim to the exiles in Babylon that it was time to return home. When he heard God's call, Second Isaiah answered by saying, in effect, "Here I am, Lord." The rest of his prophecies have been preserved for us as a visible reminder that he did, indeed, respond to the call of God in his life. "Here I am, Lord," is the response God expects from the servant who is called in today's passage. It is the response God wants from us as well.

Answering the Call

What happens when we do answer God's call? How shall we behave? What shall we do? Second Isaiah gives us a clue in 42:2, 4 when he describes how the suffering servant is to go about accomplishing the work God has given him: "He will not cry or lift up his voice . . . He will not grow faint or be crushed." In other words, the servant will do his work quietly and patiently, without drawing attention to himself. There will be no recognition, no awards, no fanfare. Just the servant, silently and patiently persevering in work that must have often seemed overwhelming. Can you imagine working under those conditions? We may find it difficult to do the Lord's work when no one acknowledges or seems to appreciate the contribution we are making.

Examples abound of people who serve in this unassuming way. A Catholic priest organizes and administers a program to feed and house the homeless in our city. A woman in a small, rural community fulfills her calling by moving from place to place, caring for the elderly in their homes. A woman with a career and children donates her lunch hour on a regular basis to answer the prayer line at The Upper Room.

What do all these people have in common? First, they are all God's servants. Second, their work is not publicly recognized or, if it is, they try to avoid the attention that such acknowledgment gives them. Third, they persevere in their work

even though they encounter barriers. These obstacles do not ultimately get in the way of servants doing the work that God has called them to do. Finally, the most important thing that these persons have in common is that they are making a difference. They will probably not reshape the entire world, but in small, important ways they are changing the lives of those whom they are called to serve.

Former Things and New Things

See, the former things have
come to pass,
and new things I now
declare;
before they spring forth,
I tell you of them.

What is the prophet saying here in Isaiah 42:9? God is still addressing the servant, explaining the task that God is giving him. But what are the former things and the new things? The message here is that after the servant is called, things will change. When we answer the call we do not know where God will lead us. The world will not look the same from this moment on. Everything will be different. The servant will move from the known into the unknown, and only God knows what will happen.

Doesn't it feel that way sometimes when God calls us to a new place in our lives? God calls, we answer, and nothing is the same. In the next chapter of Isaiah, the prophet proclaims that God is "about to do a new thing," and that our task is to perceive it (43:19). Likely we have all had times when we thought God was doing a new thing, was leading us in a certain direction and we wondered if God was doing the right thing. Or we questioned whether we were really understanding what God was telling us. Maybe something was missing in the translation. When has this happened to you? Looking back, can you see that God was declaring a new thing for you?

Many of us are struggling with some kind of call in our lives. We feel that God is taking us into the unknown. Some of us are making relationship choices, or we are struggling to understand and live with the ones we have already made. The prophet's message is that God proclaims new things through experiences like that.

One way Second Isaiah helps us visualize the contrast between former things and new things is by using an image his predecessor, Isaiah of Jerusalem, used: moving from darkness into light. God's mission for the servant involves bringing out "prisoners from the dungeon, from the prison those who sit in darkness" (Isaiah 42:7). Those who live in the prison of darkness are blinded by despair. But the prophet is proclaiming that God is not limited by what we can see. We may not know the way, but God is not limited by our blindness. God can see what we cannot see and, if we answer the call to serve, will guide us into the light of the new things God has in store for us.

For all that Second Isaiah tells us about the call of the servant, he really does not describe the task very specifically. Bringing justice to the nations probably did not give the servant much of a sense of direction. And we can probably identify with his confusion when we stop to think about our own call, about what God is asking us to do. But we can be assured of God's presence with us, as the servant was.

SHARING THE SCRIPTURE

PREPARING TO TEACH

To prepare for this week's lesson, you might want to meditate on the hymn, "Here I Am, Lord," which is found on page 593 of *The United Methodist Hymnal*. As you focus on the words of this powerful hymn, pray that God will lead you into a deeper understanding of your own call and empower you to respond.

Spend some time thinking about your own call(s) from God. Calls may be so momentous that they require a change of lifestyle or career, or they may involve something more simple. Think about the various calls you have received during your life and how you have responded to them. Prayerfully consider what God may be calling you to do at this time in your life.

You may want to make an appointment to speak with an ordained pastor, diaconal minister, missionary, Christian educator, church musician, or someone else you know who has been called by God to professional ministry within the church. Ask this person to tell you about the call from God and how it felt to respond to that call.

Request permission to recount this person's story if it seems appropriate to do so during the lesson.

Read Isaiah 42:1-9; also read the material under the heading "Understanding the Scripture." Since this week's lesson introduces the topic of the suffering servant for the first time, you might want to look at a commentary or other book that discusses the suffering servant. You might also want to reread the stories of the call of Moses in Exodus 3; the call of Samuel in 1 Samuel 3; and the call of Second Isaiah in Isaiah 40:6-8.

LEADING THE CLASS

Introduction

If possible, sing the hymn "Here I Am, Lord," accompanied either by a piano or tape. If you cannot arrange to sing the hymn, perhaps you can distribute hymnals or write the words on newsprint so that the class can read this moving hymn in unison as an opening for the session.

Read aloud (or ask someone else to read aloud) the information under "Focusing on the Main Question." This material will introduce the concept of call. Ask the main question: **What does it mean to be called to serve God?** You may want to invite class members to respond to this question, or you may prefer to have them meditate silently for a few moments.

We Are All Called to Serve

Ask whether anyone has heard of the suffering servant; if so, ask what class members know about this figure. Tell them that you will be looking at the call and mission of the servant today and during the weeks ahead.

Write on a chalkboard or newsprint the following four passages, which are the four servant songs: Isaiah 42:1-4; 49:1-6; 50:4-9; and 52:13–53:12. Use the information supplied under "Understanding the Scripture" to tell class members about the mystery surrounding the identity of the suffering servant. Emphasize that the message is more important than is the identity of this person. Now ask someone to read aloud verses 1-4 of Isaiah 42.

To develop and discuss the idea that we are all called to serve, begin by leading a general discussion on the subject of being called. To do this, you may want to ask questions such as: **(1) How do you define the word call? (2) What examples can you give of biblical figures being called by God?**

Mention the calls of Moses, Samuel, and Second Isaiah, and read excerpts from these passages if time allows. Talk with the class members about the similarities and differences among these calls.

Move the discussion to a more personal level by asking: **Have you or anyone else you know ever been called by God?** If so, briefly share the story of that call. If class members seem reluctant to respond, you may want to share information about the person you interviewed, or an acc ount of a call you received. Try to help the class see that God calls each of us, though few

persons will likely receive calls as dramatic as those of the prophets. If students are still having difficulty envisioning themselves as persons who are called by God, you may want to ask if anyone has ever felt led to teach a Sunday school class, or visit a homebound neighbor, or give respite care. These few examples may help the class realize that God calls us to engage in acts of justice, mercy, compassion, and the teaching of God's ways to others.

Answering the Call

Some persons hear God's call but choose to ignore it; others, such as the suffering servant, respond to the call in a modest way. These servants persevere despite obstacles and a lack of recognition for their work. Ask class members to think of persons they know in the church or community who have been called to serve God and who fulfill that call in a quiet, unassuming way. If you need to spark discussion, use the examples under the subheading "Answering the Call" in "Interpreting the Scripture." See if the class can identify any common elements in the work and attitude of these persons. You may want to list these ideas on a chalkboard or newsprint.

Former Things and New Things

Now have someone read aloud or paraphrase the information under the subheading "Former Things and New Things." This material elaborates on the idea that answering God's call is not always easy; sometimes a response takes us into places we have never been and may make us feel uncomfortable going.

Ask class members to think of a time when they have felt that God called them into a situation where they were unsure of themselves. Ask whether they responded with something like, "Why me, Lord?" On a piece of paper, have them write the following words:

Before I went into this situation I felt
_____.

After I went through this situation I felt
_____.

After class members have had enough time to complete these sentences, invite several volunteers to share their responses with the rest of the class.

HELPING CLASS MEMBERS ACT

Part of being called by God and answering that call involves just paying attention to the messages God is giving us. Class members can respond to today's lesson by paying special attention to God's messages during the week ahead.

Encourage the class members to pray for themselves and each other that they may discern the call of God in their lives at this time. Challenge students to take at least one step in the direction they think God is calling them. Emphasize that the first step is the most important one.

Remind the class that you spent some time thinking about persons you know who go about their servant work in a quiet and unassuming way. Reiterate that this attitude is not always easy to maintain since we live in a culture that craves recognition for the work we accomplish. Ask class members to think of one person they can privately express appreciation to for the work he or she is doing.

PLANNING FOR NEXT SUNDAY

The scripture passage for next week is the second servant song, found in Second Isaiah: 49:1-6. Ask class members to read the passage at least once before the class meets again. The topic of next week's lesson is the mission of the servant. To prepare for the session, teacher and students can spend some time thinking about the subject of mission and what it means for them in their daily lives.

SENT ON MISSION

PREVIEWING THE LESSON

Lesson Scripture: Isaiah 49:1-6
Background Scripture: Isaiah 49:1-6
Key Verse: Isaiah 49:6

Focus of the lesson:
the mission of the servant to proclaim salvation to all persons

Main question(s) of the lesson:
(1) What does it mean to be on a mission for God?

This lesson will enable adult learners to:
(1) appreciate the mission of the suffering servant
(2) discern their own mission in life
(3) respond by examining their own call to mission and their response to that call.

Today's lesson may be outlined as follows:
(1) Introduction
(2) Called from the Womb
(3) A Prophet Without Honor
(4) A Light to the Nations

FOCUSING ON THE MAIN QUESTION

Have you ever tried in vain to get someone's attention when that person was focused on a task or an idea? Maybe that person seemed to "have a one track mind" or "be wearing blinders." Perhaps you have responded to someone who wanted to speak with you by saying, "Don't bother me right now, I'm on a mission." When we find ourselves truly on a mission we often cannot be distracted by other persons or events that we encounter.

I have a friend who moved from a small town to Nashville with his family some years ago in order to attend seminary. He was well established in a lucrative profession, his wife had a career, and his children were happily entrenched among friends and extended family. Somewhere along the line my friend began to hear the voice of God speaking to him, calling him to the ministry. It took several years and some encouragement from his wife before he answered God's call. Since he has been in Nashville he has encountered several situations that could have distracted him. After his father died, my friend felt an obligation to care for his mother. His children began to experience the drawbacks of living in a bigger city. The family income was decreased. But my friend has remained focused on fulfilling his mission. He is finishing his divinity degree, serving a small church in a nearby county, and wondering what God has in store for him.

Today we will look at the second in a series of four servant songs in the book of Isaiah. We call the mysterious figure that is portrayed in these songs the "suffering servant" for a good reason. As we will see in next week's lesson, this servant of God does suffer in the service of God. He knows firsthand that answering God's call is not always easy. But the suffering servant is indeed "a man with a mission." His clear sense of mission will both support him through the tough times and keep him focused on his task when people and events threaten to distract him.

What does it mean to be on a mission for God? We will try to answer that main question today as we will enter into a dialogue between the servant and God in which the servant comes to three conclusions: (1) God has called him before he was even born, and that kind of call cannot be ignored; (2) his words will not always be well received; and (3) with God's help, his mission is to be a light to the nations.

READING THE SCRIPTURE

NRSV
Isaiah 49:1-6
1 Listen to me, O coastlands,
    pay attention, you peoples
        from far away!
The LORD called me before I
        was born,
    while I was in my mother's
        womb he named me.
2 He made my mouth like a sharp
        sword,
    in the shadow of his hand he
        hid me;
he made me a polished arrow,
    in his quiver he hid me away.
3 And he said to me, "You are my
        servant,
    Israel, in whom I will be
        glorified."
4 But I said, "I have labored in
        vain,
    I have spent my strength for
        nothing and vanity;
    yet surely my cause is with the
        LORD,
    and my reward with my God."

5 And now the LORD says,

NIV
Isaiah 49:1-6
1 Listen to me, you islands;
    hear this, you distant nations:
    Before I was born the LORD called me;
    from my birth he has made mention of my
        name.
2 He made my mouth like a sharpened sword,
    in the shadow of his hand he hid me;
    he made me into a polished arrow
    and concealed me in his quiver.

3 He said to me, "You are my servant,
    Israel, in whom I will display my
        splendor."

4 But I said, "I have labored to no purpose;
    I have spent my strength in vain and for
        nothing.
    Yet what is due me is in the LORD's
        hand,
    and my reward is with my God."

5 And now the LORD says—

who formed me in the womb
to be his servant,
to bring Jacob back to him,
and that Israel might be
gathered to him,
for I am honored in the sight of
the LORD,
and my God has become my
strength—

⁶he says,
"It is too light a thing that you
should be my servant
to raise up the tribes of Jacob
and to restore the survivors of
Israel;
I will give you as a light to the
nations,
that my salvation may reach to
the end of the earth."

he who formed me in the womb to be his
servant
to bring Jacob back to him
and gather Israel to himself,
for I am honored in the eyes of the LORD
and my God has been my strength—

⁶he says:
"It is too small a thing for you to be my
servant
to restore the tribes of Jacob
and bring back those of Israel I have kept.
I will also make you a light for the Gentiles,
that you may bring my salvation to
the ends of the earth."

Key Verse

UNDERSTANDING THE SCRIPTURE

Today's passage from Isaiah is often called the second servant song, since it is the second in a series of four in the book of Isaiah. This song is divided into three parts: (1) the call of the servant (Isaiah 49:1-3); (2) the servant's initial hesitation (Isaiah 49:4); and (3) the task given to the servant (Isaiah 49:5-6).

Isaiah 49:1-3. Here the speaker is the servant himself, and the audience is the "peoples from far away," or those from other nations. The servant summons these people to gather around and listen in on a dialogue between God and the servant. This summons is a good example of what is called *parallelism* in the Hebrew language. Commonly used by the prophets and poets of the Old Testament, parallelism is a way of adding extra emphasis to what is being said. This particular example is *synonymous parallelism*, in which the first and second lines say the same thing. "Listen to me" parallels "pay attention," and "coastlands" parallels "peoples from far away."

Like the prophet Jeremiah, this servant is convinced that God called him—sent him on a mission—even before he was born (see Jeremiah 1:5.) This conviction certainly must have added authority to his sense of calling and helped to carry him through the times of trial that he had to endure.

In verse 2 we read that, like the prophets, the servant realizes that his mission has to do with words. His mouth will be "like a sharp sword"; what he has to say will not always be well received. Nevertheless, he will be God's instrument ("polished arrow"). As such, his words have the power to pierce those who hear him. God may choose to hide the servant, possibly to protect him. The purpose of the servant's mission is stated in verse 3: that God may be glorified through the people.

Isaiah 49:4. Here we see the servant's initial response to God's call. The servant has doubts because it seems like his work thus far has been in vain. He seems dejected over his lack of success. In this verse especially, we get the feeling that we are reading an excerpt from the spiritual journal of this servant. We can imagine him dialoguing with God about his call: "What do you want me to do, God? Please make it clear. So far it doesn't seem that I am making any difference in what I am trying to do. Yet I know that you are with me. Please help me make sense of my mission."

Isaiah 49:5-6. In these verses God responds to the servant's plea for guidance. All of verse 5 describes what God has done in regard to the servant. As stated in the first servant song (Isaiah 42:6) and reiterated in chapter 49 verse 6, the servant will bring light to the nations that are living in the darkness. The wording of this verse also indicates that the servant is to restore Israel as well. In sum, God wants salvation to "reach to the end of the earth," and the servant is the one who is to undertake this mission.

A word about the identity of the servant: Earlier in this series of lessons on the servant songs we discussed briefly the question of the identity of the servant.

Was the servant the people of Israel? Or was this servant an unknown figure who was popular and influential at the time of Second Isaiah? Or was the servant the prophet himself? In this particular song, the identity of the servant seems most closely associated with the prophet himself. We perceive the similarities between the call of the servant and that of the prophets, especially Jeremiah. We realize that the mission of the servant has to do with words. We see the personal nature of the dialogue in this section. All these factors point to the identity of the servant as Second Isaiah himself. On the other hand, the servant is called Israel in verse 3. Some commentators suggest that "Israel" is a later addition to verse 3, and argue on that basis that this song proves that the servant is the prophet. Again, we must accept the fact that the writer of these servant songs evidently intended that the identity of the servant remain hidden. Who the servant is seems irrelevant in light of the importance of the servant's mission.

INTERPRETING THE SCRIPTURE

Called from the Womb

"The LORD called me before I was born, while I was in my mother's womb he named me" (Isaiah 49:1b). The conviction that we have been called by God for a mission even before our birth gives a powerful kind of authority to our sense of calling and a real energy to our work. After all, who can say no to this kind of call? Like the psalmist who seems to ask, "How can I avoid you, O God?" we have a certain sense of inevitability about answering a call of God that comes to us so clearly and forcefully. Like the prophets and the servant, we just cannot seem to say no. And like these people before us, we keep on saying yes to the call even when we

encounter obstacles that appear insurmountable. Second Isaiah's servant of the Lord is a good model for us as we wrestle and struggle with the tasks that God gives us to do.

Dietrich Bonhoeffer was a Lutheran pastor who lived in Germany during World War II. Out of a conviction that Hitler was a force who had to be defeated, Bonhoeffer joined the resistance movement and was later executed in a concentration camp at the age of 39. Before his death he was able to make a substantial contribution to twentieth-century theology through his many writings.

Throughout the latter years of his life, most of which were spent in a concentration camp, Bonhoeffer contemplated and wrote about his calling to join the resistance movement and what that calling ultimately meant for him. He was constantly aware of the possibility that he would have to give his life for the cause he was fighting for. In *Letters and Papers from Prison*, he wrote about the idea of calling: "We [Germans] have looked upwards, not in servile fear, but in free trust, seeing in our tasks a call, and in our call a vocation."

Toward the end of his life he wrote to a friend:

> Please don't ever get anxious or worried about me, but don't forget to pray for me—I'm sure you don't! I am so sure of God's guiding hand that I hope I shall always be kept in that certainty. You must never doubt that I am travelling with gratitude and cheerfulness along the road where I am being led. My past life is brim-full of God's goodness, and my sins are covered by the forgiving love of Christ crucified. I am most thankful for the people I have met, and I only hope that they never have to grieve about me, but that they, too, will always be certain of, and thankful for, God's mercy and forgiveness.

Like the suffering servant in Isaiah 49, Bonhoeffer was secure in his conviction that God was calling him on his mission to suffer for the cause of freedom. Like the servant, he was convinced that God was present with him through the struggle, and would remain with him always. The servant says, "I am honored in the sight of the LORD, and my God has become my strength" (Isaiah 49:5); Bonhoeffer expressed his profound faith and gratitude for God's mercy even in the face of his own suffering and death.

When God calls, we may wonder whether we are indeed fit for the task. But like Dietrich Bonhoeffer and the suffering servant of Isaiah 49, we perceive that we are on a mission that was given to us by God. That sense of mission and of God's continual presence with us as we become "a person on a mission" will help keep us on track.

A Prophet Without Honor

"He made my mouth like a sharp sword, in the shadow of his hand he hid me; he made me a polished arrow, in his quiver he hid me away" (Isaiah 49:2). With these words the servant gives us a hint of what is to come: even when God first called him to his mission he was aware of the fact that his words would not be well received. His mouth would be like a sharp sword that utters words that cut like a knife. Here we see again the similarity between the servant's mission and a prophet's task: the servant's mission will have to do with words, and those words will pierce the hearts of his audience. Jeremiah also had this realization: "Is not my word like fire, says the LORD, and like a hammer that breaks a rock in pieces?" (Jeremiah 23:29).

Jesus alluded to the difficulty in proclaiming the prophetic message when he warned the people in Nazareth that, "Prophets are not without honor except in their own country and in their own house" (Matthew 13:57). Like servants of the Lord, true prophets must expect to encounter resistance to their ministry and their message, especially in their home territory.

I recently ate lunch with a friend, an ordained minister in a mainline church, who told me the story of her call and how she responded to it. She was raised in a denomination that was, during the time this woman was a young adult, struggling with the issue of ordaining women to the ministry. She received her initial call from God to the ministry when she was nine years old. For the next ten years or so, the people in her local church and in her community supported her in every way they could; during this time she regularly spoke to them about her call to "full-time Christian service." After graduating from college she went on to seminary and graduated three years later. Looking back on this time, she realizes now that the people "back home" were generally under the impression that she would eventually become a missionary.

After graduating from seminary, my friend went back to her local congregation and, according to the polity of the denomination, asked this local church to ordain her into the ministry. At that time the pastor told her that if she had indeed received a call to the ministry it must have been from the devil, not from God, since the Bible teaches that women cannot be ordained.

Like the suffering servant, my friend initially thought all her work had been in vain. She asked for a meeting of the board to discuss the issue, and this request was denied by the pastor. She called people on the board—her friends—one by one and asked them whether they could authenticate her call. They did authenticate her call, one by one. But they would not do so as a group. My friend was a prophet without honor in her own country, a minister without a means of ministry.

Firm in her conviction that God had called her to the ministry and would remain with her in her journey, my friend transferred her membership to a different denomination and became an ordained minister. We can see a close parallel between my friend's long and arduous journey and the mission of the servant. Both were firm in their belief that God had indeed called them at a very early age. Both encountered obstacles that might have caused others to give up the task. Both had messages that were not well received. Both, however, had a strong sense of mission. And both were secure in God's presence with them as they pursued that mission in the face of overwhelming obstacles.

A Light to the Nations

Many commentators have pondered the meaning of this enigmatic phrase: "a light to the nations." What is the prophet talking about? What would a mission to bring a light to the nations involve? What would the servant be doing? How would his work affect others? All these questions are worth pondering even though there are no clear answers.

It seems clear that the servant's mission involves seeing himself as a kind of tool, an instrument that God uses to bring about good for others in the world. Can we envision ourselves as such an instrument? Can we see our mission as one that brings God's light into the world for the good of others?

If we look around us, we can see examples of people bringing God's light into the world. For instance, our local paper has a weekly feature entitled "Volunteer of the Week." Each Sunday this column highlights the work of one person in the community whose mission is to help others. These are not stars we read about every day; rather, they are ordinary people who work quietly and efficiently, usually without recognition. I would guess that if these persons were asked they would speak of their volunteer work as a kind of mission. What about the persons who work with AIDS patients, bringing light into the lives of those who suffer? Or the high school teachers who works extra hours to tutor students? Or the people who volunteer in homeless shelters or soup kitchens? Or those who visit shut-ins regularly? All these people are bringing light into the world. With God's help, they are on a mission.

In the early 1800s, Ann Hasseltine Judson and her childhood friend, Harriet Newell, were the first two women from the United States to be sent overseas as missionaries. These two women, along with their husbands, went to India but were soon deported because of opposition to Christian mission efforts. The Newells intended to work in the Isle of France, but Harriet died soon after their arrival, having birthed a premature child who died at sea. The Judsons went first to the Isle of France and then to Burma. Neither their initial lack of success in winning converts, nor her husband's imprisonment as a suspected spy, nor a serious illness dampened the Judson's enthusiasm for their work. These servants of the Lord persevered in spite of adversity to bring a light to the nations.

SHARING THE SCRIPTURE

PREPARING TO TEACH

Try to take a few minutes each day this week to study the scripture passage (Isaiah 49:1-6). Read it slowly and prayerfully, allowing its message to permeate your thinking. Spend some time thinking about the idea of mission. When was the last time you considered yourself to be "on a mission"? How would you describe people who are on a mission?

Read the commentary material provided in the section entitled "Understanding the Scripture"; this material will provide the background necessary to understand the scripture passage.

If you have access to Dietrich Bonhoeffer's *Letters and Papers from Prison*, skim through this volume to get the flavor of his writing.

As you read the section entitled "A Prophet Without Honor," make mental lists of prophets without honor whom you know personally and those you have read about. Spend some time thinking about persons you know who bring light into the world and into the lives of others. Make a mental list, or clip newspaper or magazines articles that show examples you can share with the class.

Read the material provided above about the first two women missionaries to serve on foreign soil. Prepare to present this material to the class.

If you plan to do the first activity under "A Light to the Nations," collect commentaries and bring them to class. Your public library, church library, and pastor are good sources for such material.

If there are members of your congregation who have previously served as missionaries, consider contacting one or more of these persons and requesting that they come and speak with the class about their own personal sense of mission.

LEADING THE CLASS

Introduction

One way to introduce the class members to the concept of mission is to bring a stack of newspapers and news magazines into the classroom. Begin the session by handing each class member one or more publications and asking them to scan them for stories or examples of people who have a mission and are acting on that calling. Allow time for the class members to scan the reading material; then ask them to share what they have found with the rest of the class. If your class is large, consider doing this activity in small groups. At the end of the allotted time, ask one person from each group to report on what the group has discovered.

Conclude this activity by telling the class that the main question for today has to do with mission: **What does it mean to be on a mission for God?** Then have the class spend a few minutes in silence considering this question in general and their own sense of mission in particular. (You might want to read the story regarding the seminary student under the heading "Focusing on the Main Question" to get their thinking started.) After a few minutes, ask volunteers to share their thoughts with the group. Or, if your group is large, divide the class members into groups of two or three and ask them to share their experiences with each other.

Since today's scripture lesson includes only six verses, you might want to begin this main portion of the lesson by sharing the information from the "Understanding the Scripture" portion. If you choose to do this, precede each section by reading (or having someone read) the scripture verses that are being discussed.

Called from the Womb

Read aloud Isaiah 49:1. Then share the bibliographical information about Dietrich Bonhoeffer that is provided in this lesson. Following this, read the two quotations from *Letters and Papers from Prison*. These quotes help us see how he felt about his calling in light of the suffering he had endured and knew he would continue to endure. Ask class members to suggest answers Bonhoeffer might have given to the question, "What is my mission?"

Invite class members to share their own sense of calling. Some persons may believe that they were born to fulfill a certain mission.

A Prophet Without Honor

Read aloud verse 2 of Isaiah 49, and then read Jeremiah 23:29. Explain to the class members that the message here is that the words of the servant (or the prophet) will not be well received by those who hear it. As an example of the difficulties one might encounter, read or retell the story about the woman minister, or share another situation that illustrates the same point. After the story is completed, ask whether anyone has a similar story to tell about a person without honor in his or her own territory. These may be people the class members know personally or famous people we all know about. As the stories are shared ask whether God's presence provided encouragement during times of trial. Note that God's presence is an important element of the servant's story.

A Light to the Nations

To help the students explore the meaning of the servant's mission (to be a light to the nations), bring a variety of commentaries on Isaiah to class. If the class is large enough, divide it into small groups. Students in a smaller class may do this work individually. Give each group or individual a commentary and have them look up the phrase "to be a light to the nations" found in Isaiah 49:6. After a few minutes, have the groups report to the larger group. Then have the whole class work together on a paraphrase (restating in their own words) of this phrase that makes sense to everyone.

If you have contacted a missionary to come and speak with the class, this is the most appropriate time in the session to have this person speak. Make sure the speaker focuses not only on his or her experiences while serving as a missionary, but also on the idea of mission in general. You might give this person a list of questions to consider in preparation, such as the following. You will probably think of other questions to add to this list.

(1) How did you experience God's call to be a missionary?
(2) In what ways do you think of your work as a response to God's call?
(3) What obstacles did you encounter in your work? Did these obstacles cause you to question your mission?
(4) Did God's presence encourage and affirm you in your work?

Share the brief stories of the women missionaries that are told in this section under "Interpreting the Scripture." This will be especially useful if you do not have anyone in your congregation who has been a missionary. Or, perhaps the class members know stories about missionaries that they can share with the rest of the class. As you help the class discuss the work of the missionary, remind the group as often as you can of any parallels you see between the work of the missionary and the work of the suffering servant in Isaiah.

Close this discussion by bringing the idea of mission closer to home. Make the point that mission is not always in a foreign country. People like Dietrich Bonhoeffer and the Volunteer of the Week, workers with AIDS patients and volunteers in homeless shelters are all working in response to a mission, a calling from God. Ask the class to think silently about what mission they might take on—or are already engaged in—within their own community.

HELPING CLASS MEMBERS ACT

During the week ahead, encourage members to consider any or all of the following questions that arise from this lesson. You may want to write them on newsprint or a chalkboard ahead of time so the class can copy them, or prepare a handout that the students can take home:

(1) How am I a person with a mission?

(2) What obstacles do I encounter as I seek to follow God's call?

(3) How do I work to overcome these obstacles?

(4) In my attempts to follow God's call, what role models do I know or did I read or hear about this week?

(5) What sharp words is God calling me to proclaim?

(6) How do I receive the sharp words delivered to me by others?

(7) What light do I have to bring to others? How can God help me do this?

Discuss with the class the possibility of supporting a missionary or a project (such as a soup kitchen) that clearly fulfills a mission for God.

PLANNING FOR NEXT SUNDAY

To prepare for next week's study of the third of the four servant songs, ask the class to read Isaiah 51:1-11 in advance. Tell students the topic for next week is endurance—the servant shows us a model for endurance through hardship. Ask them to note times during the week ahead when they feel challenged to endure.

STRENGTHENED TO ENDURE

PREVIEWING THE LESSON

Lesson Scripture: Isaiah 50:4-11
Background Scripture: Isaiah 50:1-11
Key Verse: Isaiah 50:7

Focus of the lesson:
the steadfast endurance of the servant even in difficult circumstances

Main question(s) of the lesson:
(1) Can we endure all the trials and tribulations that come our way, no matter what?

This lesson will enable adult learners to:
(1) learn about the third song of the suffering servant
(2) discern ways to feel strengthened, especially through prayer and other means of listening for God's voice
(3) respond by practicing prayers that strengthen them to endure.

Today's lesson may be outlined as follows:
(1) Introduction
(2) Enduring in Difficult Situations
(3) Amazing Grace
(4) Helping Others Endure
(5) Listening for God's Voice

FOCUSING ON THE MAIN QUESTION

Have we ever felt so weighted down by burdens or overwhelmed by circumstances that we sigh, "I just cannot go on like this any longer"? We may want to persevere but lack the energy and motivation to do so. Today's lesson, which focuses on the third servant song, has an important word for us when we are wearied by life's demands and injustices. Isaiah speaks to us about the strength God gives us to endure. Isaiah calls us to reflect on this question: **Can we endure all the trials and tribulations that come our way, no matter what?** Our answer is the same as that of the suffering servant portrayed in these songs: Yes, with the help of God.

In Psalm 27:1

> The LORD is my light and my
> salvation;
> whom shall I fear?
> The LORD is the stronghold of
> my life;
> of whom shall I be afraid?"

The implied answer for the psalmist—and for us—is that we need not fear whatever befalls us because God is always available to uphold us. How does God's help come to us? It comes through prayer and regular communion with God. It also comes to us through the presence of others in our lives who support and sustain us through the difficult times. We learn from the example of the suffering servant and by our own experience that God's amazing grace fortifies us to endure even the most humiliating, agonizing situations.

READING THE SCRIPTURE

NRSV

Isaiah 50:4-11

⁴The Lord GOD has given me
    the tongue of a teacher,
  that I may know how to sustain
    the weary with a word.
  Morning by morning he
    wakens—
  wakens my ear
  to listen as those who are
    taught.
⁵The Lord GOD has opened my
    ear,
  and I was not rebellious,
  I did not turn backward.
⁶I gave my back to those who
    struck me,
  and my cheeks to those who
    pulled out the beard;
  I did not hide my face
    from insult and spitting.

Key Verse

⁷The Lord GOD helps me;
  therefore I have not been
    disgraced;
  therefore I have set my face like
    flint,
  and I know that I shall not be
    put to shame;
⁸ he who vindicates me is near.
  Who will contend with me?
  Let us stand up together.
  Who are my adversaries?
  Let them confront me.
⁹It is the Lord GOD who helps
    me;
  who will declare me guilty?
  All of them will wear out like a
    garment;
  the moth will eat them
    up.

NIV

Isaiah 50:4-11

⁴The Sovereign LORD has given me an
    instructed tongue,
  to know the word that sustains the weary.
  He wakens me morning by morning,
    wakens my ear to listen like one being
    taught.

⁵The Sovereign LORD has opened my ears,
  and I have not been rebellious;
  I have not drawn back.

⁶I offered my back to those who beat me,
  my cheeks to those who pulled out
    my beard;
  I did not hide my face
    from mocking and spitting.

⁷Because the Sovereign LORD helps me,
  I will not be disgraced.
  Therefore have I set my face like flint,
    and I know I will not be put to shame.

⁸He who vindicates me is near.
  Who then will bring charges against me?
  Let us face each other!
  Who is my accuser?
  Let him confront me!
⁹It is the Sovereign LORD who helps me.
  Who is he that will condemn me?
  They will all wear out like a garment;
  the moths will eat them up.

¹⁰Who among you fears the LORD
    and obeys the voice of his
      servant,
  who walks in darkness
    and has no light,
  yet trusts in the name of the
      LORD
  and relies upon his God?
¹¹But all of you are kindlers of
      fire,
  lighters of firebrands.
  Walk in the flame of your fire,
    and among the brands that you
      have kindled!
  This is what you shall have from
      my hand:
  you shall lie down in torment.

¹⁰Who among you fears the LORD
    and obeys the word of his servant?
  Let him who walks in the dark,
    who has no light,
  trust in the name of the LORD
    and rely on his God.

¹¹But now, all you who light fires
    and provide yourselves with flaming
      torches,
  go, walk in the light of your fires
    and of the torches you have set ablaze.
  This is what you shall receive from my hand:
    You will lie down in torment.

UNDERSTANDING THE SCRIPTURE

Today's passage is divided into two parts: (1) the third servant song (Isaiah 50:4-11); and (2) an introduction to the song (Isaiah 50:1-3).

Isaiah 50:1-3. These verses speak of issues such as unfaithfulness to the covenant, judgment, and punishment. The point the prophet is making here is that Israel is not forsaken by God, nor are the people being sold into slavery. Rather, Israel is being justly punished by God for the unfaithfulness of the people to the covenant.

The background to these verses is found in the legal system of ancient Israel. We can imagine Israel as the plaintiff, accusing God of forsaking the covenant. The response of God (who is the defendant in the proceedings) comes at the end of verse 1: I had to punish Israel because of its transgressions. At least one commentator has remarked that there has been a separation between God and the people of Israel, but there has been no divorce.

In verse 1 God asks, "Where is your mother's bill of divorce?" According to Deuteronomy 24:1-4, a woman was allowed to remarry only if her husband provided her with a bill of divorce. In the case as presented by Isaiah there is no bill of divorce, since there was no divorce. That proves that God has not forsaken the covenant people.

According to verse 2, when God appeared to the people, whether through prophets or through the natural world, no one responded. The image of clothing the heavens with blackness in verse 3 probably refers to an eclipse of the sun.

Isaiah 50:4-6. These verses form the opening portion of the servant song itself. As in the previous song, we see many similarities between the call and mission of the servant and that of the prophet. For example, the servant is taught by God what to say and do in much the same way as was Jeremiah (see Jeremiah 1:4-10). The servant has the sense of God's presence with him continually as he sustains the weary exiles. These exiles are so exhausted, having been captives for at least fifty years by now, that they must actually be awakened before the word is proclaimed to them.

"Morning by morning" God awakens the servant's senses and makes him receptive both to the message God has for him and to what other people are asking of him. God tells the servant not only what to say, but also when to say it.

According to verses 5-6, the servant was obedient to God but the people did not respond appropriately. Not only that, they also treated the servant shamefully—striking him, insulting him, spitting on him, and pulling out the hairs of his beard. Pulling out hair was so insulting and degrading that it could be seen as an invitation to war; recall the incident in Second Samuel when the Ammonite king, Hanun, shaved off the beards of David's servants in an attempt to humiliate both servants and master (see 2 Samuel 10:4-5). In spite of everything done to him, however, the servant does not respond by becoming rebellious and shirking his duty. "I did not turn backward," he says in verse 5.

Isaiah 50:7-9. The prophet returns to legal terminology, expressing his firm conviction that God will vindicate him. Notice the repetition of the interrogative "Who" in verses 8-9, which gives added force to the message. In verse 7 we read of the servant's conviction that God is the one who stands with him in his suffering and expects him to accept it. The image the servant uses—setting his face like flint—symbolizes his firm conviction that God is and will remain on his side. This conviction is proven by the silence of the servant's opponents.

Isaiah 50:10-11. These verses conclude the poem by speaking of the true light from God as it contrasts with the light created by humanity. The prophet's words are reminiscent of a passage in Isaiah that spoke of the people who walked in darkness (see Isaiah 9:2).

INTERPRETING THE SCRIPTURE

Enduring in Difficult Situations

Can we endure the trials and tribulations that life hands us? Yes, we can, with God's help. Today's lesson will help class members understand how we, like the servant, can live with the constant sense of God's presence. Once we begin to do that, we will find it much easier to listen for the voice of God amid all the noise and confusion in our lives. And when we can hear God's voice we will be assured of God's presence. We will also be attuned to the needs of others so that we can help them find that same assurance.

In today's reading, the prophet paints a picture of a servant of the Lord who is in constant communication with God. "Morning by morning" God awakens the ear of the servant so that he might listen to what God and others have to say to him on that day. What is actually going on here? We are looking in on the morning prayer of the servant of the Lord. The servant reminds me of the psalmist who wrote Psalm 63, which appears here as adapted for singing in *The Upper Room Worshipbook*:

In the morning I will sing glad songs of praise to you.
　　You are my God, I long for you from early in the morning.
　　My whole being desires you like a dry, worn, waterless land,
　　My soul thirsts for you.

What the psalmist and the servant are talking about is a kind of constant living with God, a constant awareness that God is present with us in every breath we take. In Isaiah 42:5, the prophet speaks of God as the one who gives us our every breath. God is surely present with us all the time. This is the kind of relationship the servant has with God.

How can we live each moment of our lives with the awareness that God is always present with us? How can we remain constantly aware that God gives us our every breath? One way we can do this is through developing and using what some call the "breath prayer." In his book *The Breath of Life*, Ron DelBene calls the breath prayer a way to have on our lips what is always in our heart. It is a way to remain constantly aware of God's presence with us. One of the earliest and perhaps most well known breath prayers was the prayer "Lord Jesus Christ, have mercy on me a sinner." But that is not the only breath prayer; actually, there are as many breath prayers as there are people to pray them.

Each one of us can create his or her own breath prayer by following a few simple steps.

(1) First, spend a few minutes thinking about what you call God when you pray. What feels most comfortable? Do you pray to God the creator? God the sustainer? A loving God? Some people pray to a more personal God, such as God the father or God the loving parent. Or, some prefer to pray to the Holy Spirit or to Jesus. Or to the living Christ. Many forms of address are available; each person should use what feels most comfortable. When you have decided on your own personal form of address, move on to the second step in the process.

(2) If God (or the Holy Spirit, or Jesus) were to ask you, "What is your deepest desire?" how would you answer? What do you want from God? Do you want God to take your hand as you travel through life? Do you want God to sustain you through your trials? Do you want a sense of God's peace in your heart at all times? Do you want reconciliation? Love? Justice? What is your deepest longing? Spend a few moments in silence reflecting on this question. Now you are ready for the next step.

(3) When you have come to a conclusion about what your deepest desire is, write a sentence that combines your own personal address for God with your deepest longing. For instance, you might come up with something like these examples: Lord Jesus, take my hand; O God my creator, let me feel your peace; Holy Spirit, sustain me always; or let me know your love, O God.

The order of the elements is not important, as long as the elements are there. Six to eight syllables is the optimum length for your breath prayer. Play around with the words until you have created a sentence that feels comfortable and sounds good to your ears. Once you have created your breath prayer, begin to practice saying it over and over. Say the first half of the prayer as you breathe in, and the second half as you exhale. Say it so many times that it begins to feel like breathing.

Experiment with your breath prayer by saying it several times, each time with an emphasis on a different word. Pay attention to how the meaning of the prayer changes as the emphasis changes. You might want to choose the emphasis that seems most meaningful to you to be your permanent breath prayer.

Once you have established and internalized your breath prayer, begin to think of how you might use it in your everyday life. It helps to establish certain times when you can use it. For example, I have the kind of job where I am interrupted many, many times throughout the day. I try to use my breath prayer every time the phone rings or when I see someone coming to knock on my door. If my door is closed and someone knocks on it, I try to remember to say my breath prayer before saying "Come in." Other people use their breath prayer each time they look at their watch, each time they stop at a traffic light, each time they encounter a different patient or client. When Ron DelBene talks to groups about the breath prayer, he usually passes out strips of very small circle stickers to place at strategic points so that participants will encounter them regularly. For instance, you might place a circle sticker on your mirror, your watch, your daily calendar, your computer, any place at which you will encounter the sticker and allow it to remind you of your breath prayer.

There are endless ways to use this prayer. And when you begin to use it more and more, it becomes more and more significant for you. Try it and see how you like it. Perhaps it will help you feel the kind of closeness to God that the suffering servant had.

Amazing Grace

John Newton has written about enduring hardships in one of the verses of the beloved hymn, "Amazing Grace":

> Through many dangers, toils, and snares,
> I have already come;
> 'tis grace hath brought me safe thus far,
> and grace will lead me home.

Not long ago I found myself in a situation where I felt as though I were navigating through some perilous and stressful waters. During that period I took much comfort in the words of Newton. Soon after this time of trial ended I was worshiping in a small community of people I know well. One of the hymns was "Amazing Grace," and I sang that verse about the dangers, toils, and snares with joy in my heart and a smile on my face. My spirits were lifted even higher when I looked around the room and saw others smiling at me because they knew what I was thinking.

In the previous servant song we saw a hint of the hardship that must have been endured by the servant. "I have labored in vain, I have spent my strength for nothing and vanity" (Isaiah 49:4). In the song we are studying today however, the writer becomes more specific about these hardships. He leaves no doubt in our minds that physical and mental hardships are involved in servanthood at times. There will indeed be dangers, toils, and snares to overcome. The behavior of the servant, who is in constant communication with God throughout his hardships, can be a model for us. Because of his relationship with God, he will endure them.

Helping Others Endure

According to Isaiah 50:4, the close relationship between God and servant benefits not only the servant but also those he serves. He says, "The Lord GOD has given me the tongue of a teacher, that I may know how to sustain the weary with a word." Those who are weary are the exiles. Convinced that God had divorced them, they had lost hope by this time that they would ever be able to return home.

The servant's words prompt us to ask ourselves how we sustain others during their times of trial. How are we supported by others? I remember some time ago when I was going through a difficult time in my life. A friend called one day and said that she knew things were kind of rough for me and that she had read a book recently that she thought would help. Later that day the book appeared at my back door. And she was right—that book was just what I needed at that particular time.

Sometimes we sustain others during their difficult times by just being there. When persons are seriously ill, our presence with them in their suffering may be all they need. These are times when words not only are not sufficient; they are really unnecessary. Sometimes we help others endure by doing small acts of kindness for them. Actually, these acts may seem small to us—making a dinner, transporting children, adding someone's grocery list to ours—but to others they are significant. They help others endure.

Listening for God's Voice

Since the servant is so closely connected to God, he is constantly listening for the voice of God. "Morning by morning" God awakens him to hear a new message. We often lament that the world is so noisy— our lives are so cluttered and so busy— there is so much confusion that we have difficulty hearing the word of God to us. However, if we listen for God's voice, as the servant did, we will know what to do, when to do it, and who needs our help.

In her Advent book *The Vigil*, Wendy Wright speaks of the tendency we all have to let the world drown out the voice of God, and how that voice spoke to her in an unexpected moment. She says, "most of our moments are cluttered with concerns and busyness that tend to bury our hearts' longings." She goes on to tell a story that clearly illustrates the fact that the voice of God is there, and we can hear it if we just stop and listen.

Her story took place on a weekday during Advent in Boston some years ago. At that time, she was the mother of two young children and a third was on the way. She found herself with no food in the house and no husband at home at the moment to care for the children. So she loaded them in the car and drove through the snow and traffic to the grocery store. The heat and the smells inside the store made her sick and uncomfortable, and the children were tired and cranky. One of the children had tried to eat the grocery list, and the words on the paper were obscured. In the midst of all this confusion, noise, and discomfort, though, something happened.

I had just entered the canned vegetable section and was trying to make out the handwriting on the wet shredded paper I had taken from her, and I had just reached my hand out to pick up a can of generic tomato paste, when I was suddenly stopped.

Joy to the world, the Lord is come! The percussive upbeat of the first notes of the carol bored a hole into my awareness as the supermarket Muzak was suddenly switched on.

Let earth receive her King! I stood there transfixed, with the tomato paste in my hand.

Let every heart prepare him room. The floodgates of my heart were flung open and a vast and spacious wonderment filled me.

God's voice spoke clearly to that author that day, and God's voice can speak clearly to us, too. We just need to take time to listen to the voice that will strengthen us to endure.

SHARING THE SCRIPTURE

PREPARING TO TEACH

Read and internalize Psalm 27:1, which relates to the main question for this week. You might want to use this verse in your prayer time as a way of focusing your thoughts on God and God's constant presence with you as you move through this week and as you prepare to teach this lesson.

Read the third servant song in Isaiah 50:1-11 repeatedly until you have the feeling that you understand its message.

Read the background commentary material provided under the heading "Understanding the Scripture." Decide how and when you will present this material to the class members.

Ask yourself the main question of this lesson: **Can I endure all the trials and tribulations that come my way, no matter what?** Be honest with yourself when you try to answer this question.

Read the section entitled "Enduring in Difficult Situations." If you do not already have a breath prayer that you use on a regular basis, go through the steps listed to create one for yourself. Be prepared to share it with the class members if you decide to take the class through these steps. Use your newly created breath prayer during the week ahead so that you can talk about the experience with the class on Sunday.

Find a copy of the hymn "Amazing Grace," or make certain there are hymnals in the classroom that contain this hymn.

Make a special effort to listen for God's voice above the noise and confusion in your life this week. Pay special attention to what small things you do for others and what things others do for you.

LEADING THE CLASS

Introduction

Begin the session by asking class members: **What kinds of fears do you face?** List their ideas on a chalkboard or newsprint. Possible answers include: death of a spouse, loss of a job, serious illness, alienation within the family, violence, accident, or war. If the class is large, divide into groups so that everyone will have an opportunity to participate.

Point out that all persons have fears because we all face trials of some sort. Announce today's main question: **Can we endure all the trials and tribulations that come our way, no matter what?** Provide a few moments of silence for class members to think about this question and their response.

Move to an introduction of the scripture lesson by noting that the servant described by Isaiah surely faced many fears. Choose a volunteer to read aloud the background scripture, Isaiah 50:1-11. Ask: **What fears might the servant have faced?** Answers may include: physical abuse, humiliation, ostracism.

Help the group to study the servant song (Isaiah 50:4-11) and its opening (Isaiah 50:1-3) by sharing information provided under the "Understanding the Scripture" portion. Conclude the introduc-

tion to the lesson by noting that although the servant faced real fears and difficult circumstances God strengthened him so that he could endure. God will likewise strengthen us.

Enduring in Difficult Situations

Introduce to the class the idea of the breath prayer. Ask whether anyone has ever heard of the breath prayer or has used one. If so, ask whether anyone would be willing to share his or her experience with the breath prayer. If not, use the information provided in the "Interpreting the Scripture" segment under the category "Enduring in Difficult Situations" to explain the concept to the class.

If time allows, take the class through the three steps listed previously, so that each class member has an opportunity to create a breath prayer. Suggest that each person establish a time or times at which he or she can use the prayer on a regular basis. Tell the class members that you will check with them next week about their progress related to the breath prayer. If the class wishes to do so, they could share their prayers with one another.

Amazing Grace

Have someone lead the class in singing several verses of "Amazing Grace"; be sure to include the verse about dangers, toils, and snares. Ask whether anyone has had a special experience with that song or attaches special meaning to it. If no one responds, you may want to share my story.

Helping Others Endure

How can we sustain the weary? That is the subject of this portion of the lesson. Each person in the class knows at least one person who needs to be sustained. During a few moments of silence, ask the class members to focus on situations they know about where they could offer their help.

After the silent time ask class members to relate situations they know about, if they feel such information may be shared publicly. The class may want to decide together on a group project to help a person or family in need. Or, you might want to spend this time talking about the progress the class has made in an ongoing caring project.

Listening for God's Voice

Begin this portion of the lesson by reading the material under the heading "Listening for God's Voice." The class may want to discuss Wendy Wright's story; various class members may have had similar experiences they want to share with the rest of the group.

Continue the discussion by asking these questions: **What clutters your life?** and **What is the noise in your life?** Give class members a few minutes to think about this question; they may want to jot down ideas as they occur. Then ask for volunteers to suggest thoughts. Record them on a chalkboard or newsprint if you like.

Taking the time to listen is not as easy as it sounds. Brainstorm with the class members about strategies for finding the time to listen to God and to other persons.

HELPING CLASS MEMBERS ACT

Encourage the class members to make a covenant to take thirty minutes sometime during the week ahead to pay attention to what God is saying. Ask them to consider how God's words give them strength to endure a difficult or annoying situation.

Ask the class members to work on their breath prayers during this week. Perhaps they could use the breath prayer as a beginning for their thirty-minute listening time. Slow, steady breathing can help us focus and center ourselves at the beginning of our prayer time.

If the class discussed beginning or continuing a class project to help someone or a family in need, make sure some concrete steps are taken during this coming week. You may need to assign volunteers to particular tasks.

PLANNING FOR NEXT SUNDAY

Next week we will be studying the fourth and final servant song. Since these songs have a message both individually and taken as a whole, you might want to encourage the class members to read all four servant songs in preparation for next week. They are found in Isaiah 42:1-4; 49:1-6; 50:4-11; and 52:13–53:12. The topic for next week is "Victory Through Suffering"; ask class members to pay special attention during the week ahead to different kinds of suffering they encounter or read about.

VICTORY THROUGH SUFFERING

PREVIEWING THE LESSON

Lesson Scripture: Isaiah 53:1-6, 10-11
Background Scripture: Isaiah 52:13–53:12
Key Verse: Isaiah 53:11

Focus of the lesson:
the servant's victory as recorded in the fourth servant song

Main question(s) of the lesson:
(1) Can we, like the servant, find victory in the midst of suffering?

This lesson will enable adult learners to:
(1) comprehend that success in God's kingdom is often marked by the rejection, sorrow, and suffering experienced by the servant
(2) identify with both the suffering and the victory of the servant
(3) respond by serving others.

Today's lesson may be outlined as follows:
(1) Introduction
(2) Appearance versus Reality
(3) The Suffering of the Servant
(4) Victory Through Suffering

FOCUSING ON THE MAIN QUESTION

In the most well-known of all the Psalms, the psalmist proclaims to God: "Even though I walk through the darkest valley, I fear no evil; for you are with me; your rod and your staff—they comfort me" (Psalm 23:4). We know this psalm so well that we may not stop to think about what it really means. What the psalmist is saying is basically this: "I feel so close to you, God, that no matter what happens to me I can still be assured of your presence in my life. Even if I have to endure the worst possible circumstances, I can bear them with your help."

By now we know something of the mind and heart of Second Isaiah's servant of the Lord. Can't you imagine this suffering servant uttering these same words?

We know that he had a close relationship with God, a kind of communion that carried him through his times of trial and adversity. So he could say, with the psalmist, The LORD is my shepherd, I shall not want . . . (Psalm 23:1).

Can we make that affirmation for ourselves? Our lives are filled with valleys. We have to watch those we love suffer with illness. We see violence all around us. Friends and colleagues endure pain and suffering. We ourselves encounter physical and mental anguish, and we may despair. **Can we, like the servant, find victory in the midst of suffering?** That is our question for today.

READING THE SCRIPTURE

NRSV
Isaiah 53:1-6
1 Who has believed what we
    have heard?
  And to whom has the arm of
    the LORD been revealed?
2For he grew up before him like a
    young plant,
  and like a root out of dry
    ground;
  he had no form or majesty that
    we should look at him,
  nothing in his appearance that
    we should desire him.
3He was despised and rejected by
    others;
  a man of suffering and
    acquainted with infirmity;
  and as one from whom others
    hide their faces
  he was despised, and we held
    him of no account.

4Surely he has borne our
    infirmities
  and carried our diseases;
  yet we accounted him stricken,
    struck down by God, and
    afflicted.
5But he was wounded for our
    transgressions,
  crushed for our iniquities;
  upon him was the punishment
    that made us whole,
  and by his bruises we are
    healed.

NIV
Isaiah 53:1-6
1 Who has believed our message
  and to whom has the arm of the LORD
    been revealed?

2He grew up before him like a tender shoot,
  and like a root out of dry ground.
  He had no beauty or majesty to attract us to
    him,
  nothing in his appearance that we should
    desire him.

3He was despised and rejected by men,
  a man of sorrows, and familiar with
    suffering.
  Like one from whom men hide their faces
    he was despised, and we esteemed
    him not.

4Surely he took up our infirmities
  and carried our sorrows,
  yet we considered him stricken by God,
    smitten by him, and afflicted.

5But he was pierced for our transgressions,
  he was crushed for our iniquities;
  the punishment that brought us peace
    was upon him,
  and by his wounds we are healed.

⁶All we like sheep have gone
      astray;
  we have all turned to our own
      way,
  and the LORD has laid on him
      the iniquity of us all.

Isaiah 53:10-11
¹⁰Yet it was the will of the LORD
      to crush him with pain.
  When you make his life an
      offering for sin,
  he shall see his offspring, and
      shall prolong his days;
  through him the will of the LORD
      shall prosper.
¹¹Out of his anguish he shall see
      light;
  he shall find satisfaction through
      his knowledge.
  The righteous one, my
      servant, shall make many
      righteous,
  and he shall bear their iniquities.

Key Verse

⁶We all, like sheep, have gone astray,
  each of us has turned to his own way;
  and the LORD has laid on him
    the iniquity of us all.

Isaiah 53:10-11
¹⁰Yet it was the LORD's will to crush him and
  cause him to suffer,
  and though the LORD makes his life a
    guilt offering,
  he will see his offspring and prolong his
    days,
  and the will of the LORD will prosper
    in his hand.
¹¹After the suffering of his soul,
  he will see the light life and be satisfied;
  by his knowledge my righteous servant
    will justify many,
  and he will bear their iniquities.

Key Verse

UNDERSTANDING THE SCRIPTURE

Today's passage is the fourth and final in a series of servant songs found in the book of Isaiah. This song describes both the humiliation and the exaltation of the servant, and so creates a fitting climax to the songs as a group. The power of the passage is especially apparent when the song is read aloud. Similarly, the brevity of the phrases and the repetition of key words give the song a kind of cadence that can be best appreciated when it is read out loud.

The passage is divided into three parts: (1) an introduction in which God speaks about the servant (Isaiah 52:13-15); (2) a report about the servant from the perspective of others (Isaiah 53:1-9); and (3) some concluding words about the servant spoken by God in the first person (Isaiah 53:10-12). Thus, this final song both begins and concludes with a word from God.

Isaiah 52:13-15. In these verses we read both of God's intention to exalt the disfigured servant and of the reaction of amazement on the part of the rulers of the world. God's speech is introduced with the words "See, my servant," a parallel to the introduction of the first servant song (Isaiah 42:1). Recall that the main message of the first servant song has to do with the calling of the servant by God; in this final song we see the culmination of that call and mission.

In the previous song (Isaiah 50:4-11) we saw the close communion between God and the servant that sustained him through his suffering. In Isaiah 52:13-15 we see that same communion from God's perspective. God calls the suffering servant, "My servant" and promises him future exaltation and prosperity.

Verses 14 and 15 draw a sharp contrast

between the disfigurement of the servant—his marred physical appearance was almost inhuman—and the exalted status that God had in store for him. Two groups of people will be astonished and amazed by the servant: those who encounter him will be astonished by his appearance, and rulers of nations will be amazed that someone who looks like this will be the one chosen by God for service and vicarious suffering on behalf of others.

At the end of verse 15 the prophet indicates that the mission of the servant is something entirely unique; nothing like this has ever happened before. In fact, these words are quoted by the apostle Paul to describe the newness and uniqueness of the gospel message (see Romans 15:21).

Isaiah 53:1-3. In these verses the speaker changes from God to a group of unidentified people who offer a collective testimony about the servant. In their testimony, these people chronicle the life history of the servant and assess his current situation. Their report begins with two rhetorical questions, the assumed answer to which is "no one." No one has believed what has been said about the servant, and no one has understood what God was doing. The images of a young plant and a root out of the dry ground are reminiscent of the messianic predictions of Isaiah 11:1, where the future messiah is described as a shoot from the stump of Jesse.

Verse 2 speaks of the servant's physical appearance. In verse 3 the subject moves to his humiliation, his total rejection by the community. This kind of rejection was especially painful in ancient Israel because individuals gained a large portion of their identity in the context of community. The words here are reminiscent of Job's situation, which was just as traumatic (see Job 19:13-19). Reading these verses we have the impression that the servant did not just endure a kind of temporary suffering that came on suddenly and then went away.

Rather, these words and phrases describe a lifetime of affliction—the servant was "a man of suffering."

Isaiah 53:4-6. Here the speakers interrupt their report about the servant to offer a kind of confession. They proclaim their conviction that the servant has borne their infirmities and carried their diseases. How did they know that this was the purpose of the servant's suffering? How did they come to this astonishing conclusion? At least one commentator has remarked that the answer to that question is as elusive as the identity of the servant. We are not told how these people came to this insight; they just did, and in verse 4 they proclaim it to all who can hear. Because of the servant's suffering on behalf of others, the people of God are restored to a right relationship with God.

Isaiah 53:7-9. In these verses the speakers continue their report about the servant, which was interrupted by their confession in Isaiah 53:4-6. Here the focus is on the fact that, unlike Jeremiah and many of the psalmists, the servant suffered in silence. He is likened to a lamb being sent to be slaughtered; this allusion is the background for John the Baptist's announcement of Jesus as the lamb of God (see John 1:29). In verses 8 and 9 the speakers tell of the servant's suffering, death ("he was cut off from the land of the living"), and burial. The language reminds us of a portion of the Apostles' Creed: "He was crucified, dead, and buried." Continuing the theme of humiliation, the servant was buried with evildoers. We see examples of the two most common forms of suffering that are mentioned in the psalms of individual lament: violence and illness. The difference is that whereas the lament psalms are sung in the first person, others are lamenting the fate of the servant in this passage.

Isaiah 53:10-12. Here we see the intervention of God into the servant's situation to bring about the exaltation that God promised in Isaiah 52:13-15. As in those earlier verses, the speaker is God, who promises that the servant "shall see his offspring, and shall prolong his days." Scholars have argued for centuries about whether or not these words refer to a physical resurrection or a restoration of the servant's honor and reputation after his death.

This fourth servant song becomes linked to Jesus in the New Testament. According to the book of Acts, Isaiah 53:7-8 is quoted by Philip during his now famous encounter with the Ethiopian eunuch (Acts 8:32-33). The Ethiopian was perhaps a converted Jew who was one of the first converts to Christianity. This is the first time in the recorded history of the early church that Isaiah 53 is quoted as an Old Testament prediction concerning Jesus as the expected Messiah. Apparently the eunuch was reading the Old Testament aloud and was overheard by Philip. When Philip asked him if he understood what he was reading and his answer was essentially no, Philip seized the opportunity to witness to this man about the good news of Jesus. Following Philip's testimony, the eunuch's response was a request to be baptized in a nearby stream.

Ever since this encounter between Philip and the Ethiopian eunuch, the Christian church has looked upon this passage in Isaiah as a description of the suffering, death, and resurrection of Jesus. As with the messianic predictions in Isaiah that we studied earlier in this quarter (in chapters 9 and 11), we cannot read today's passage without thinking of the parallels between the life history of this suffering servant and that of Jesus Christ.

INTERPRETING THE SCRIPTURE

Appearance versus Reality

Today's passage serves to stretch our imagination in several ways. Perhaps most importantly, the prophet is challenging us to think about the distinction between appearances and reality. What was most astonishing about the servant of the Lord and his mission was that people did not expect someone who looked as the servant did to accomplish the things God had commissioned him to do. After all, he just did not look like someone who could perform great things. The prophet tells us that many people were astonished at his marred appearance (Isaiah 52:14). We, as well as the prophet's audience, are challenged to look behind and beyond what appears to be in order to see what is real.

The distinction between appearance and reality was made clear to me recently. I read an account, told by a director of a homeless shelter in the heart of a city, about his efforts to secure funding. His task was to present a proposal to a group of potential sponsors. Since the members of this group were economically and socially advantaged, the director wondered if they would act favorably on his request for funding. The initial interview supported the director's stereotypes about this group. He left the meeting assuming they would not consider the shelter as one of their projects. He was very surprised to be invited to a second interview. During this meeting his stereotypes began to dissolve. Not long after that second meeting he received word that the shelter would indeed receive the $50,000 he had requested. Within two years the sponsors had built a large facility that houses sixteen women and nine families. In addition to their financial support, members of this well-to-do group were staffing day care, educational events, life skills workshops, and other programs.

Like the people who witnessed the suffering of the servant, the shelter director had difficulty believing that this privileged group would be willing to help homeless persons. Who would have thought that they could—and would—accomplish what they did? The shelter director discovered the distinction between appearance and reality, and what can happen when we move beyond appearance to perceive reality.

The Suffering of the Servant

Isaiah 53:1-9 describes the suffering of the servant as other persons witness it. The servant experiences rejection as other persons turn away from him because of his battered appearance. They neither respect him nor treat him with dignity. Imagine his loneliness and isolation even in the midst of a crowd.

The behavior of the people is especially ironic because the servant is suffering on their behalf. He bears their diseases and sins as the servant of God. He does not rail against his pain but suffers silently so that the people may be restored to God. The people recognize, though we are not told how they know, that the servant was taken away "by a perversion of justice" (Isaiah 53:8). Although he is not guilty of either violence or deceit, he is put to death and buried with the wicked. He has indeed born the burden of God's judgment upon the people, all of whom have strayed from God as sheep wander away from the fold.

In this song, Isaiah concentrates on the physical suffering of the servant. The idea of physical disfigurement is especially real to me as I write this lesson. Yesterday I fell on the pavement outside our front door and smashed my face. My disfigurement will be only temporary, for the stitches will guard against future scarring. Right now, however, that future prospect is hard to keep in mind when I look in the mirror. My eye is swollen shut and is surrounded by skin that is a glorious shade halfway

between red and purple. When I gaze at people through my one good eye I realize how I must look to others. As I vow to myself to encounter as few people as possible for the next few days, I have a clue as to how God's servant must have felt.

Victory Through Suffering

Many commentators on the servant songs mention that this fourth song brings the group of four to a resounding conclusion. For it is here, especially in 52:13 and 53:10-12, that we discover that there will be victory in the suffering that the servant must endure. God will exalt the servant, and his suffering will ultimately bring blessing to many people. We have a natural tendency to want to see the good in the bad, to want to see that suffering was, after all, for a good cause. That is what we see in this fourth song—the servant's victory through his suffering.

Recently the concept of victory through suffering was demonstrated to me in a powerful and meaningful way. About a month ago I had an opportunity to visit the memorial site that now exists at Dachau, one of the concentration camps used during the reign of Hitler. Dachau is now a suburb of Munich, our point of departure from a European trip. We had heard that the German government intended to tear down this camp, and thought that the chance to see it should not be missed, even though the experience might turn out to be a painful one.

In retrospect the hour we spent at Dachau was time well spent. No one is there to lead tourists around and explain the various parts of the camp; visitors are left to their own solitude and can look at their own pace. No one makes eye contact with anyone else; all are free to think their own thoughts and process the information in solitude. As we entered the camp I came upon a large plaque that proclaimed, in four languages, "Never Again." Something about that plaque and its message haunted me and, as we left the camp, I stood in front of it for a long time, just looking and thinking.

It was raining the day we visited Dachau, and the wind whipped the rain onto our legs and feet so that we were very uncomfortable during the visit. As we were leaving we remarked that the rain seemed fitting somehow. As we turned onto the main street that now stretches in front of the camp, my friend said, "Look over there." I looked off to the field on my left and saw the most beautiful rainbow I have ever seen in my life. Actually, it was not one rainbow, but two. The inside rainbow was visible all the way from one side to the other, and it proceeded through all the colors on the spectrum twice. The colors were so vivid that the rainbow almost looked neon. And then outside of the first arc was a second arc that disappeared in the clouds part way up. Just the bottom ends of this second one were visible. It was breathtaking.

We stopped the car and sat and looked for a few minutes. My mind went to the story of Noah and the rainbow, and all of a sudden I remembered God's promise in Genesis 9:11: I will never again destroy the earth by flood. Never again! There was my own visible symbol of God's "never again," a kind of confirmation of the message on the plaque that had captivated me so thoroughly.

To draw a lesson from a visit to a concentration camp seems almost too superficial, for someone like me will never fully understand what happened there. But the idea of "never again" helps us to begin to come to terms with all of it. It is for me a hint of victory through suffering.

SHARING THE SCRIPTURE

PREPARING TO TEACH

As you read Isaiah 52:13–53:12, try to imagine yourself (1) as God looking beyond the physical appearance of the servant to his victory; (2) as persons who recognize that the servant is suffering for them; and (3) as the servant himself who trusts God completely even in the midst of incredible pain and loneliness.

Go over the material under the heading "Understanding the Scripture" and decide how you will present it to the class this week. Familiarize yourself with the story of Philip and the Ethiopian eunuch in Acts 8:26-40.

Decide whether or not you want to use the appearance-altering activity described under the Introduction section. If you decide to use this activity, gather three or four hats or other apparel to use during the session.

Work diligently on your own breath prayer this week. (See last week's discussion of this practice.) Keep a journal or notes on your progress, and be prepared to share your experiences with the group this coming Sunday.

Read the section entitled "Victory Through Suffering" under "Interpreting the Scripture." Perhaps you can think of a similar example from your own experience that illustrates this idea. Or, perhaps a story in a magazine or the newspaper will appear during this coming week. Be on the lookout for something that illustrates the point of victory through suffering to share with the group; or, be prepared to retell the rainbow story in your own words.

LEADING THE CLASS

Introduction

As class members arrive this week, give three or four persons funny-looking hats or other articles of clothing that will attract attention. Be creative—the more outrageous the better. Ask them to wear whatever you give them but do not tell them why, and ask them not to talk to anyone else about what they are wearing.

If you introduced the idea of the breath prayer during last week's session, check on the progress class members have made during the previous week. Share your own thoughts first, to get the discussion started. Note that the constant communication with God strengthens our own close relationship with God, just as it strengthened the servant's relationship with God.

Turn to this week's lesson by asking for volunteers to read the fourth servant song in its entirety. Select one person to read Isaiah 52:13-15, another to read Isaiah 53:1-9, and a third to read Isaiah 53:10-12. Before the readers begin, instruct the class members to focus on the images they see in their minds as the scripture is read. Allow a few moments for them to meditate on the servant and his suffering.

Conclude the introduction by noting that all of these images portray a man who has indeed suffered but who is victorious because he is God's chosen servant. God has willed that "he shall be exalted and lifted up" (Isaiah 52:13). The servant's example prompts us to ask: **Can we, like the servant, find victory in the midst of suffering?**

Appearance versus Reality

Ask the class to look carefully at Isaiah 52:13-15 in their Bibles. Point out the surprise felt by the kings and the people when they see God's servant. They are astonished because they do not expect someone who looks like the servant to accomplish what he does. In short, they have stereotyped him and based their expectations of him on his appearance.

Perhaps we too have stereotyped images of persons who serve the Lord. We too may be surprised when we look beyond appearances to see the reality of a person or situation. To illustrate this point, retell the story of the homeless shelter in your own words, or choose a volunteer to read it aloud to the class. Ask class members to reflect on times in their lives when they have had insights into their own stereotypes. Relate their answers to the stereotypical responses of many persons to the servant, found in Isaiah 52:13-15.

Encourage class members who are wearing silly articles of clothing you distributed to reflect on what it feels like to be conspicuous. Do they feel different? Do they feel ridiculed or rejected? Ask the other group members whether it is more difficult to relate to these people because they look so different. Remind the group of the distinction between appearance and reality that is so important in the life of the servant. Despite his appearance, God will exalt him and lift him up.

The Suffering of the Servant

Direct the class's attention to Isaiah 53:1-9. If members do not have Bibles handy, reread this passage aloud. Discuss the following questions:

(1) **How would you describe the servant's physical appearance?** (Answers may include: marred, disfigured, wounded, bruised.)

(2) **What is the purpose of the servant's suffering?** (He bore the people's illnesses and sins so that they might be restored to a healthy, whole relationship with God.)

(3) **How does the servant respond to the task that God has given to him?** (He chooses to be obedient and meekly accepts physical pain, unjust accusation, and death.)

Read aloud or retell the story of Philip and the Ethiopian eunuch, found in Acts 8:26-40. Point out the quote from Isaiah 53:7-8, found in Acts 8:32-33. Refer to the information at the end of the "Understanding the Scripture" section to help the class understand the importance of this quotation, which links Jesus to Isaiah's description of the servant.

Ask the class: **(1) In what ways do you perceive Jesus to be the suffering servant? (2) In what ways do we as the church continue to go astray and, therefore, continue to need the suffering servant?**

Victory Through Suffering

Choose a volunteer to reread Isaiah 53:10-12. Discuss how God rewards the servant for his suffering. These rewards include: offspring, longevity, enabling God's will to be done, enlightenment, satisfaction, making other persons righteous before God, and blessings for himself and the people. If time permits, compare and contrast God's rewards with socially expected rewards for a job well done, such as fame, wealth, power, or status.

Retell the story of the rainbow in the midst of a concentration camp, found under this heading in "Interpreting the Scripture," or relate your own illustration to reinforce the idea of victory through suffering. One or more class members may have stories to tell of persons who have been victorious in the midst of suffering.

HELPING CLASS MEMBERS ACT

Ask the class: **Are there persons who you pay no attention to because of their appearance or some other superficial trait?** Challenge students to make an effort to get to know one of these persons so that you can move beyond outward appearances to discover who this person really is. Encourage them to give thanks for the image of God that they see in this person.

The servant suffered on behalf of other persons. We seldom physically suffer, but we are often called upon to act on behalf of someone else. Our action may cost us time and/or money. The need for action may come at an inconvenient time. Challenge the class to be aware of opportunities to serve other persons, especially those who cannot or would not be likely to return their kindness.

Try to spend time this week reading about some modern servants, such as Martin Luther King Jr. or Mother Teresa, who suffer on behalf of others. Or, if there is someone in your church or community who is well known for selfless service, encourage students to talk with this person to gain an understanding of why this person serves, how she or he handles the criticism and/or rejection that servants often experience, and what this servant perceives to be the rewards for service.

PLANNING FOR NEXT SUNDAY

Next week we will move from our study of the suffering servant to a new unit entitled "God's Love for All People." During the next four weeks we will be looking at the evidence of God's love in the Scripture and all around us. We will begin with Jonah and then move to Ruth. Suggest to the group members that they spend some time during this week reading the book of Jonah. It is a short book with profound insights about God and God's relationship with us.

RUNNING FROM GOD

PREVIEWING THE LESSON

Lesson Scripture: Jonah 1:1-4, 10-15, 17; 2:1, 10
Background Scripture: Jonah 1–2
Key Verse: Jonah 1:3

Focus of the lesson:
Jonah's flight from God

Main question(s) of the lesson:
(1) Is there nowhere I can hide?

This lesson will enable adult learners to:
(1) follow Jonah's attempt to flee from God's call upon his life and God's response to Jonah's efforts
(2) recognize that they cannot hide from God
(3) respond by facing a task that confronts them, rather than hiding from it.

Today's lesson may be outlined as follows:
(1) Introduction
(2) Hiding from God
(3) Fearing for Our Lives
(4) A Psalm of Thanksgiving

FOCUSING ON THE MAIN QUESTION

How often have we asked ourselves in frustration, "Is there nowhere I can hide?" We feel pulled in so many directions. Our lives are literally out of control. Everywhere we turn there are people wanting something from us: a sales report, a decision, a minute of our time, a favor, a comforting word.

In the midst of all this confusion and turmoil, God wants something from us too. God is there waiting, waiting for us to come out of hiding. Jonah experienced this firsthand. God seemed to come to him from out of nowhere and make great demands on him. Jonah's response may have been something like, **"Is there nowhere I can hide?"** In our study of the first portion of Jonah in this session, we will see that the answer to today's main question is no. We can run from God, as Jonah did at first, but like Jonah, we cannot hide.

FEBRUARY 4

READING THE SCRIPTURE

NRSV

Jonah 1:1-4

1 Now the word of the LORD came to Jonah son of Amittai, saying, [2]"Go at once to Nineveh, that great city, and cry out against it; for their wickedness has come up before me." [3]But Jonah set out to flee to Tarshish from the presence of the LORD. He went down to Joppa and found a ship going to Tarshish; so he paid his fare and went on board, to go with them to Tarshish, away from the presence of the LORD.

[4]But the LORD hurled a great wind upon the sea, and such a mighty storm came upon the sea that the ship threatened to break up.

Jonah 1:10-15

[10]Then the men were even more afraid, and said to him, "What is this that you have done!" For the men knew that he was fleeing from the presence of the LORD, because he had told them so.

[11]Then they said to him, "What shall we do to you, that the sea may quiet down for us?" For the sea was growing more and more tempestuous. [12]He said to them, "Pick me up and throw me into the sea; then the sea will quiet down for you; for I know it is because of me that this great storm has come upon you." [13]Nevertheless the men rowed hard to bring the ship back to land, but they could not, for the sea grew more and more stormy against them. [14]Then they cried out to the LORD, "Please, O LORD, we pray, do not let us perish on account of this man's life. Do not make us guilty of innocent blood; for you, O LORD, have done as it pleased you." [15]So they picked Jonah up and threw him into the sea; and the sea ceased from its raging.

Jonah 1:17

17 But the LORD provided a large fish to swallow up Jonah; and Jonah was in the belly of the fish three days and three nights.

NIV

Jonah 1:1-4

1 The word of the LORD came to Jonah son of Amittai: [2]"Go to the great city of Nineveh and preach against it, because its wickedness has come up before me."

[3]But Jonah ran away from the LORD and headed for Tarshish. He went down to Joppa, where he found a ship bound for that port. After paying the fare, he went aboard and sailed for Tarshish to flee from the LORD.

[4]Then the LORD sent a great wind on the sea, and such a violent storm arose that the ship threatened to break up.

Jonah 1:10-15

[10]This terrified them and they asked, "What have you done?" (They knew he was running away from the LORD, because he had already told them so.)

[11]The sea was getting rougher and rougher. So they asked him, "What should we do to you to make the sea calm down for us?"

[12]"Pick me up and throw me into the sea," he replied, "and it will become calm. I know that it is my fault that this great storm has come upon you."

[13]Instead, the men did their best to row back to land. But they could not, for the sea grew even wilder than before. [14]Then they cried to the LORD, "O LORD, please do not let us die for taking this man's life. Do not hold us accountable for killing an innocent man, for you, O LORD, have done as you pleased." [15]Then they took Jonah and threw him overboard, and the raging sea grew calm.

Jonah 1:17

[17]But the LORD provided a great fish to swallow Jonah, and Jonah was inside the fish three days and three nights.

Key
Verse

Ke
Ver

Jonah 2:1

1 Then Jonah prayed to the LORD his God from the belly of the fish.

Jonah 2:10

10 Then the LORD spoke to the fish, and it spewed Jonah out upon the dry land.

Jonah 2:1

1 From inside the fish Jonah prayed to the LORD his God.

Jonah 2:10

10And the LORD commanded the fish, and it vomited Jonah onto dry land.

UNDERSTANDING THE SCRIPTURE

In general, the scripture for this week reads less like prophecy and more like a prose narrative about a prophet—Jonah—and his experiences. The prophet Jonah does not fit our stereotypical picture of an Old Testament prophet—attuned to God and following God's commands as closely as possible. Rather, Jonah comes across as reluctant, even unwilling (at first, anyway) to answer God's call.

Jonah was a prophet from Galilee who was an advisor to Jeroboam II, king in Israel (the Northern Kingdom) from 786 until about 746 B.C.E. He is mentioned elsewhere in the Old Testament only in 2 Kings 14:25. In the book of Jonah, his story is told by a later prophet. Some scholars date the book to the period after the exile (sixth century B.C.E. or later), while others believe it was written during the exile.

Today's passage is divided into three parts: (1) Jonah refuses God's call (Jonah 1:1-3); (2) Jonah is punished for his reluctance (Jonah 1:4-16); and (3) Jonah is rescued (Jonah 1:17–2:10).

Jonah 1:1-3. The book opens with a word of the Lord coming to Jonah, just as the word of God came to many other Old Testament prophets. If you read through the superscriptions (opening verses) of most of the prophetic books you will see similar introductions to what we have here in Jonah 1:1. Jonah is identified as the "son of Amittai," the only biographical information that is given about him. This notation associates this reluctant prophet with the figure in the Second Kings narrative (14:25).

God commands Jonah to go to Nineveh, the capital city of the Assyrian empire, and prophesy about the wickedness that was rampant there. Nineveh did not enjoy a good reputation among the Old Testament prophets; for example, it is the "city of bloodshed" referred to by Nahum in chapter 3 of his prophecy (see verse 1). Jonah's response to God's call, as recorded in Jonah 1:3, was to literally turn and run in the other direction. Tarshish has not been positively located, but it may have been a city in the southern part of Spain.

Jonah 1:4-16. This section begins with the word "but," indicating that God did not intend for Jonah to have the final word in this situation. God, the Creator, caused a great storm so that Jonah's ship was tossed about on the waves. As the hapless mariners were frantically trying to pray to their gods and lighten the ship's load, Jonah was in the hold fast asleep. The ship's captain awakened Jonah and urged him to call on his God.

The casting of lots, as seen in verse 7, was a common way of determining guilt in ancient Israel. (See 1 Samuel 14:40-42 for another example). When the lot fell to Jonah, everyone in the ship became suddenly interested in him—his occupation, his hometown, his ethnic background. The more he told them, the greater their fear.

These sailors showed a remarkable understanding of Jonah's predicament. After exacting a confession from him, they set about trying to straighten out the situation. Jonah himself provided the answer to their dilemma by calmly suggesting that they throw him overboard. Reluctantly they did so, after praying to the God of Israel that they not be declared guilty of shedding innocent blood. Many commentators have noted the irony in the story's conclusion: Jonah, who was unwilling to prophesy on God's behalf in Nineveh, becomes an unwitting evangelist to a group of sailors who come to believe in God as a result of Jonah's reluctance to answer God's call.

Jonah 1:17. In the original Hebrew text, verse 17 of chapter 1 is verse 1 of chapter 2. This arrangement makes logical sense, since this verse seems to introduce the next chapter in Jonah's story. In just this single verse Jonah's situation changes dramatically: he is now not drowning in the sea but safe and protected inside a large fish, which God provides for him just in the nick of time. According to this verse, Jonah remained inside this fish for three days and three nights, until the fish spewed him out (see 2:10). Three days and three nights is the narrator's way of describing a significant amount of time.

Jonah 2. If we put ourselves in the place of Jonah, what happens now is a bit of a surprise. Being inside the belly of a fish, Jonah's logical response at this point would probably have been to cry out to God for help. After all, he was far from rescued, at least by our standards. However, Jonah's response is to offer a psalm of thanksgiving for God's deliverance. The psalm is divided into three stanzas, verses 2-4, verses 5-7, and verses 8-9.

Jonah 2:2-4. Speaking directly to God, Jonah the psalmist acknowledges that God has indeed released him from Sheol, from certain death. Sheol is the Hebrew word for the land of shadows, where people go after they die. In anguish, Jonah laments that he has been cut off from life, from everything that is familiar, and from God.

Jonah 2:5-7. Here Jonah looks backward and relives what happened to him in a poignant retelling of the events. Again he refers to his almost certain death, this time by speaking of "the Pit," another name for Sheol. Still speaking directly to God, Jonah describes a last-minute prayer, as he turns to God in desperation when his situation looked absolutely hopeless: "My prayer came to you, into your holy temple."

Jonah 2:8-10. Here Jonah turns to the subject of idolatry. He draws a sharp contrast between the kind of help idols can give and the help that God gave to him in his time of need. At the conclusion of the psalm Jonah has come full circle: the reluctant prophet who hid from God's call has now come into God's presence as an act of faith. God's response is to cause the fish to spew Jonah out (verse 10), and his rescue is complete.

INTERPRETING THE SCRIPTURE

Hiding from God

Hiding. We have all done it on occasion. For one reason or another, we run from our responsibilities or we run from a task we are called upon to do. Our scripture passage for today says, " 'Go at once to Nineveh, that great city, and cry out against it; for their wickedness has come up before me.' But Jonah set out to flee to Tarshish from the presence of the LORD" (Jonah 1:2-3). We have no indication of what was going on in the mind of this unwilling prophet. Why did he run in the opposite direction? Why did he want to hide?

Was he involved in some special project that he wanted to be sure and finish? Did he have friends and loved ones who were counting on him? Was he an introvert who didn't like to be around a lot of people? Was he lazy? Or sick? Or apathetic? Did he just pretend he did not hear God's voice calling to him? What reasons do we give for avoiding God's voice?

A friend of mine received a call to the ministry when he was a teenager. At that time he was active in his local church youth group. He was one of those rare teens who spent most of his free time at the church. It seemed only natural to everyone who knew him when he announced his plans to attend seminary after college. And he did attend seminary, serving various churches during his seminary years. After seminary he started on the upward ladder, but somewhere along the line something had happened. He was not aware of it at the time, and still cannot pinpoint the moment at which the road he was following became twisted. But it did. And he began to question his call. He began to hide from God. He left the ministry in anger and frustration. He avoided his former minister friends. He avoided church altogether. He avoided God.

After several years, things began to change. He cannot tell you why or how. But little by little he began to talk about what had happened. He renewed his acquaintances. He re-established his church connections. He came out of hiding. He found God. Or God perhaps found him.

We often say to one another in jest, "You can run but you cannot hide." Jonah knew this after his harrowing experience in the belly of the fish. And my friend knows this now.

Fearing for Our Lives

Jonah's story is not all about hiding from God, being rescued, and being thankful. It is also about fear; the fear of Jonah when he realized that he was being punished, and the fear of the sailors when they thought they would perish in the storm.

This fear is eloquently expressed in a poem entitled "Jonah," which was written in a Nazi death camp by the Lutheran pastor, Dietrich Bonhoeffer, in the fall of 1944. Bonhoeffer must have identified with Jonah and the sailors aboard the tempest-tossed ship. The imprisoned pastor, who was executed several months after penning this poem, expresses the terror of the sailors who cry aloud in fear and seek signs from their gods to know who has brought them to the brink of certain disaster.

Surely anyone who has been a prisoner of war or a hostage can identify with the terror Jonah and the sailors must have felt. Other persons who have been aboard foundering ships or caught in a house fire or trapped in a barrage of gunfire must have experienced the gripping fear that Jonah knew. The rush of adrenaline is familiar to anyone who has narrowly avoided an accident.

In truth, we need not be in dramatic circumstances to understand how Jonah and the sailors must have felt. We have all had times when we have literally feared for our lives. I remember one time when I was about eight years old. I was swimming in the pool of some friends of the family at night. All of a sudden I began to feel an electric current coming from the water. I panicked and tried to get out of the pool. I put my hands on the concrete around the edge of the pool, and there the current was even stronger. So I had the feeling that I could not get out. I started screaming and was immediately (although help did not seem to be immediate at the time!) pulled out of the water. I was later told that the underwater light was giving off a "mild" current to indicate that it was time to replace the light with a new one. I did not realize that all I had to do was swim away from the light to escape the current. The main thing I remember from that experience was the terror I felt when I thought I could not escape. That is why I cringe when I read

Jonah's words: "The waters closed in over me; the deep surrounded me; weeds were wrapped around my head" (Jonah 2:5). I know just how he felt.

A Psalm of Thanksgiving

We may be a bit surprised that Jonah's response when he found himself in the belly of a large fish in the middle of the ocean was to offer a psalm of thanksgiving. Perhaps he did offer a poignant plea for help, which was left out somehow in the final compilation of the book. Perhaps Jonah was so assured of God's deliverance that he did not feel the need to ask God for it. That is real faith! Or perhaps he considered his situation in the belly of the fish to be such an improvement over swimming alone in the sea that he was overcome with gratitude. Jonah was moved to offer a psalm of thanksgiving patterned after the personal psalms of thanksgiving that we find in the Psalter.

There are many examples of psalms of thanksgiving in the Psalter: 18, 21, 30, 32, 34, 40, 92, 103, 116, and 138. We can think of these psalms of thanksgiving as prayers to God offered by a person after having been rescued from what seemed like a hopeless situation. Typically, these thanksgiving psalms have four main parts: (1) an opening statement offering praise to God; (2) a retelling of the experience in order to explain why God is to be praised; (3) a description of the turning point in the experience in which God's intervention is evident; and (4) a follow-up statement concerning what the psalmist considers the future to hold in view of the experience.

Let us take a look at Jonah's psalm of thanksgiving to see whether it contains any or all of these four parts.

(1) The opening statement offering praise to God is found in verse 2: "I called to the LORD out of my distress, and he answered me; out of the belly of Sheol I cried, and you heard my voice." That statement introduces the psalm by summing up the prophet's experience in a phrase or two.

(2) A retelling of the experience occurs in verses 3 through 5. In vivid and gripping language the prophet tells of his being cast into the sea, being buffeted to and fro by the waves, and being pulled downward into the ocean depths so far that the weeds wrapped themselves around his head.

(3) A description of the turning point when God's intervention is evident is found in verses 6 and 7. The prophet describes himself as turning to God at just the last moment, just "as my life was ebbing away." He was reassured by the thought that his last-minute prayer did indeed reach God. God would intervene in his situation, and he knew it.

(4) A statement about what the future holds is in verses 8-9 where Jonah elaborates on what he will now do as a result of his near-death experience: he will sacrifice to God with the "voice of thanksgiving." He will be forever grateful for God's intervention. He will, finally, answer God's call.

Interestingly, the conclusion we reach from reading most of the Psalter's individual thanksgiving psalms is that God is present in all situations. There is nowhere that we can hide from God. God is everywhere, lurking behind the scenes waiting to be called upon. That is the same conclusion that Jonah reaches, and it holds true for us as well.

SHARING THE SCRIPTURE

PREPARING TO TEACH

Begin your preparation time by reading the first and second chapters of the book of Jonah, as well as the material under the heading "Understanding the Scripture." Decide how you want to present the commentary material to the class.

In preparation for the "Introduction," decide whether you want to reproduce the list of tasks on a sheet to be copied or on newsprint that can be seen by everyone. If you decide on newsprint, make sure you have enough index cards for class members to use when they prioritize these items. Provide pencils.

For the activity section "Hiding from God," decide whether you want to have the class members do the role-play activity or the sentence completion.

Recall an incident in your own life when you have been very afraid. Prepare to tell the class about it to open the discussion of fearing for our lives.

Familiarize yourself with the various parts of the standard psalm of thanksgiving and how to recognize them. You may want to write a psalm of your own ahead of time.

LEADING THE CLASS

Introduction

Below is a list of various tasks to which any one of us might be called at some time in our lives. Make certain this list is available to the class members, either on chalkboard/newsprint, or on a photocopied sheet that you prepare ahead of time.

- ☐ heading the annual financial campaign for the church
- ☐ agreeing to teach an adult Sunday school class for a period of one year
- ☐ co-teaching a children's class for an indefinite period of time
- ☐ being liturgist in worship next Sunday
- ☐ going on a two-week mission trip to Mexico
- ☐ preparing food for the homeless shelter, once a week for a month
- ☐ visiting a nursing home patient weekly for a year
- ☐ staffing the prayer hotline once a week for one hour
- ☐ being an usher once a month for a year
- ☐ doing the children's sermon once a quarter
- ☐ staffing the nursery during worship once a month
- ☐ serving on the Christian Education committee
- ☐ being a spiritual friend on a six-month trial basis
- ☐ joining a covenant group that meets weekly
- ☐ leading a Wednesday night Bible study for adults during Lent
- ☐ taking dinner once this week to a church family in trouble
- ☐ visiting a prisoner on death row on a weekly basis

These tasks involve varying degrees of risk and personal investment. They are all tasks from which we may have a tendency to hide, but they are all tasks we could easily be called on by God to perform. Ask the class members to rank them in order of their willingness to follow through. If you provide photocopied sheets, students can number the items in the boxes at the left. If you copy this list onto newsprint, then provide note cards on which they can write the items and then arrange them in the appropriate order. Note cards will probably work best, since class members will have space on which to make notes.

Introduce the main question by asking class members to think about their priorities. Have them arrange the listed items in the order that reflects their willingness to perform the tasks, beginning with the task they would be most willing to perform and concluding with the least appealing task. Then ask them to turn to the person next to them and talk about the process of decision making. **(1) How hard was this task? (2) How difficult is it to juggle priorities and accept responsibilities?**

If your group is relatively small, draw the class members together and have them compare where various items were placed on their lists. (If the class is large, do this in smaller groups.) Lead the class in a discussion of similarities and differences among their lists. Then remind the class that these are all tasks that we can hide from for various reasons. Point out that the topic of today's lesson concerns hiding from God, and that we will be studying the story of Jonah, probably the most famous biblical figure who hid from God. Like Jonah, we may ask the main question for our lesson: **Is there nowhere I can hide?**

Hiding from God

If your class members enjoy doing role-play activities, this portion of the lesson provides a good opportunity. The text does not elaborate on why Jonah turned and ran to Tarshish when God summoned him to Nineveh. Explore what his thoughts and reasons may have been by dividing the group into pairs. Have each pair create a dialogue between Jonah and God in which God calls, Jonah objects, and God responds. If you wish, you can assign various categories of objection to the different groups so that the dialogues come out differently (for example, family responsibilities, vocational reasons, or personal reasons). When the groups are ready, have each one do its role-play for the whole class.

If your students don't like to do role-plays, you might want to open up this topic in another way. For instance, ask the class members to finish the following sentence in the way that seems most natural to them: "I can't do that, I'm too _____." (examples: too introverted, too busy, too tall, too afraid) Then tell the group that any or all of these reasons may have stopped Jonah from answering God's call and may hold us back as well. Ask:

(1) Are we guilty of using excuses to hide from God?

(2) What has caused us to set aside our excuses and respond to God?

(3) In what ways do you see yourself like Jonah?

Fearing for Our Lives

Ask the class: **"When have you been afraid for your life or the life of a loved one?"**

Then ask: **What words, phrases, or images would you use to describe how you felt?** You may want to list these ideas on a chalkboard or newsprint. Answers may include: terror stricken, pounding heart, sweaty palms, feeling like I couldn't breathe, and experiencing bad dreams.

Then move to the issue of fear in the scripture passage for today. Ask class members to read the first chapter of Jonah and name the various allusions to fear in the passage. Why were these people afraid?

A Psalm of Thanksgiving

For this portion of the lesson, have someone read aloud Jonah's psalm of thanksgiving found in Jonah 2:2-9. Help the class to identify each of these four parts of a thanksgiving psalm in Jonah's psalm. Use the information in "Understanding the Scripture" and in the "Interpreting the Scripture" section entitled "A Psalm of Thanksgiving" to enable students to understand what has happened and why Jonah is giving thanks.

After the class members have a good understanding of the parts of a thanksgiving psalm, have them write one of their own. Point out that we often find it much easier to call upon God in times of trial and stress than during times of thanksgiving. Begin by asking students to think of a recent time when they were overcome by a feeling of gratitude for something. Suggest that they make that time the focus of their thanksgiving, being sure to incorporate the four parts into their psalm. When class members have finished their psalms, ask for volunteers to read the psalms aloud. Suggest that they make these psalms a part of their prayer time during the week ahead.

HELPING CLASS MEMBERS ACT

Class members can act on what they have learned today by doing any or all of these things during the week ahead:

(1) making a promise (to themselves or to others) that they will not hide from the next task with which they are confronted;
(2) taking a step to help someone they know face his or her fear;
(3) using their psalm of thanksgiving on a regular basis.

PLANNING FOR NEXT SUNDAY

Next week we will conclude the story of Jonah. Suggest to the class members that they read the final two chapters of Jonah to prepare for the lesson. The topic is the mercy of God, and how it operates to provide us with second chances.

EXTENDING MERCY

PREVIEWING THE LESSON

Lesson Scripture: Jonah 3:1-5, 10; 4:1-5, 11
Background Scripture: Jonah 3–4
Key Verse: Jonah 4:2

Focus of the lesson:
the mercy that God extends to all persons

Main question(s) of the lesson:
(1) Is it right for us to be angry?
(2) Do we really believe that God's mercy is all-encompassing, that it extends to everyone, even our enemies?

This lesson will enable adult learners to:
(1) examine Jonah's prophecy against the Ninevites, their repentance, and God's merciful response to them
(2) develop their own understandings of God's mercy
(3) respond by finding ways to show mercy to their own enemies.

Today's lesson may be outlined as follows:
(1) Introduction
(2) Second Chances
(3) Changing God's Mind
(4) Loving Our Enemies
(5) God's Mercy

FOCUSING ON THE MAIN QUESTION

In a dialogue we will be reading between Jonah and God, God asks Jonah the same question twice: "Is it right for you to be angry?" (Jonah 4:4 and 4:9). In Jonah's case the answer is no. In God's eyes, it was not right for Jonah to be angry. The remainder of the dialogue in chapter 4 is God's attempt to explain why Jonah's anger was inappropriate.

Why was Jonah angry? The text tells us that he was angry because he knew that God, in God's mercy and grace, would save the people of Nineveh, who were Jonah's mortal enemies. He knew in his heart that God's mercy extended to all people, and that made him angry.

Our question this week is twofold: **First, is it right for us to be angry? And second, do we really believe that God's mercy is all-encompassing, that it extends to everyone, even our enemies?**

READING THE SCRIPTURE

NRSV
Jonah 3:1-5

1 The word of the LORD came to Jonah a second time, saying, 2"Get up, go to Nineveh, that great city, and proclaim to it the message that I tell you." 3So Jonah set out and went to Nineveh, according to the word of the LORD. Now Nineveh was an exceedingly large city, a three days' walk across. 4Jonah began to go into the city, going a day's walk. And he cried out, "Forty days more, and Nineveh shall be overthrown!" 5And the people of Nineveh believed God; they proclaimed a fast, and everyone, great and small, put on sackcloth.

Jonah 3:10

10 When God saw what they did, how they turned from their evil ways, God changed his mind about the calamity that he had said he would bring upon them; and he did not do it.

Jonah 4:1-5

1 But this was very displeasing to Jonah, and he became angry. 2He prayed to the LORD and said, "O LORD! Is not this what I said while I was still in my own country? That is why I fled to Tarshish at the beginning; for I knew that you are a gracious God and merciful, slow to anger, and abounding in steadfast love, and ready to relent from punishing. 3And now, O LORD, please take my life from me, for it is better for me to die than to live." 4And the LORD said, "Is it right for you to be angry?" 5Then Jonah went out of the city and sat down east of the city, and made a booth for himself there. He sat under it in the shade, waiting to see what would become of the city.

Jonah 4:11

11 "And should I not be concerned about Nineveh, that great city, in which

NIV
Jonah 3:1-5

1 Then the word of the LORD came to Jonah a second time: 2"Go to the great city of Nineveh and proclaim to it the message I give you."

3Jonah obeyed the word of the LORD and went to Nineveh. Now Nineveh was a very important city—a visit required three days. 4On the first day, Jonah started into the city. He proclaimed: "Forty more days and Nineveh will be overturned." 5The Ninevites believed God. They declared a fast, and all of them, from the greatest to the least, put on sackcloth.

Jonah 3:10

10When God saw what they did and how they turned from their evil ways, he had compassion and did not bring upon them the destruction he had threatened.

Jonah 4:1-5

1 But Jonah was greatly displeased and became angry. 2He prayed to the LORD, "O LORD, is this not what I said when I was still at home? That is why I was so quick to flee to Tarshish. I knew that you are a gracious and compassionate God, slow to anger and abounding in love, a God who relents from sending calamity. 3Now, O LORD, take away my life, for it is better for me to die than to live."

4But the LORD replied, "Have you any right to be angry?"

5Jonah went out and sat down at a place east of the city. There he made himself a shelter, sat in its shade and waited to see what would happen to the city.

Jonah 4:11

11"But Nineveh has more than a hundred and twenty thousand people who

Key Verse

FEBRUARY 11

223

there are more than a hundred and twenty thousand persons who do not know their right hand from their left, and also many animals?"

cannot tell their right hand from their left, and many cattle as well. Should I not be concerned about that great city?"

UNDERSTANDING THE SCRIPTURE

Jonah 3 and 4 describe the prophet's second call to prophesy; this time the results are very different. The passage is divided into three parts: (1) Jonah obeys God's command (Jonah 3:1-4); (2) Nineveh repents (Jonah 3:5-10); and (3) a dialogue between God and Jonah (Jonah 4:1-11).

Jonah 3:1-4. The second time God calls Jonah the message is only slightly different: "Get up, go to Nineveh, that great city, and proclaim to it the message that I tell you." This time, however, Jonah's response is entirely different. Instead of heading in the opposite direction, Jonah "set out and went to Nineveh," the capital of the Assyrian empire. Nineveh is described as a city that was very large, making Jonah's task all the more overwhelming. The prophet's message is that after a forty-day grace period Nineveh will be overthrown.

Jonah 3:5-10. Here we read of an almost miraculous response—an immediate repentance on the part of the people of Nineveh, who "believed God." Fasting, putting on sackcloth, and sitting in ashes are all visible signs of repentance. The king gives authenticity to his decree by practicing these rituals himself. According to verses 8-9, even the animals are to participate in the great fast. This is the author's way of pointing out that the repentance of Nineveh would have a far-reaching effect. The "violence that is in their hands" is also discussed by the prophet Nahum (see chapter 3), who gives more details about the corruption that was rampant in the city.

Jonah 3:9 introduces a note of realism: perhaps these acts of repentance will

change God's mind, but perhaps they will not. "Who knows?" asks the king. Only God knows. We do not have to wait long for God's answer, however. In verse 10 we see God's change of mind and the reversal of fortune for Nineveh. A similar dynamic takes place in Amos 7:1-6, where the prophet intercedes to change God's mind about the fate of the chosen people.

Jonah 4:1-11. Here is a complicated dialogue between prophet and God. In the opening verse we are surprised in a way similar to what took place in chapter 2, where Jonah responded to being trapped inside the fish not by praying for release but by offering a psalm of thanksgiving. Here, we are again surprised by Jonah's response. Rather than rejoicing over the reprieve God has given the city and its inhabitants, Jonah's response is a very intense anger. The prophet knew, even before he left home, that the merciful God would turn aside from the punishment he intended. Jonah could not find it in his heart to rejoice over the good fortune of his enemies. In fact, Jonah is so outraged that God has acted mercifully that he wants to die.

God's question in verse 4 is rhetorical; of course it is not right for Jonah to be angry. In his anger he sits inside a booth outside the city to sulk. Just as God had previously provided a fish to protect Jonah, now God provides a bush, possibly a bean plant, to shield Jonah's head from the harsh rays of the noonday sun.

But God gives and God takes away. The following morning God sends a worm to destroy the bush, so that the hot wind and sun would render the prophet defenseless later in the day. For the second time Jonah asks for death to come to him. He is miserable. God's response to his request is to continue the dialogue. Whereas Jonah did not answer God's question the first time, now he does. Is it right to be angry? "Yes," says Jonah.

The dialogue ends in verses 10-11, with God having the last word: whereas Jonah seems to be concerned with things like worms and hot sun and his own welfare, God is concerned for every creature under the sun. Nineveh is full of people who are spiritually confused, who "do not know their right hand from their left." God cares intensely about them.

INTERPRETING THE SCRIPTURE

Second Chances

Recall the events of last week's lesson: God called Jonah, Jonah responded by running the other way, he was punished and subsequently rescued by God, and responded by offering a psalm of thanksgiving. Jonah's story could well have ended there, for that is a fitting conclusion to a story of transgression and forgiveness. But the story does not end there—God gives Jonah a second chance. What Jonah does with that second chance is the subject of today's story.

This time Jonah's response is very different. He does not turn and run in the other direction; rather, he goes immediately to Nineveh. There is no hesitation. As was the case the first time God called Jonah, we do not know what Jonah was thinking as he responded to God's second call. Did he say to himself something like, "I better go this time or I will end up in the water again"? Perhaps he reminisced about a time while he was inside the great fish and he prayed for a second chance, which had now been given to him. Maybe he did not want to disappoint God this time. Whatever his reasons, Jonah goes immediately to Nineveh. While there his mission is successful, in that his words do not fall on deaf ears. He does get the attention of the Ninevites—not just the city's leaders but all the inhabitants. They respond by taking his warnings to heart—just what a prophet would hope for.

Second chances are difficult to come by, especially when we depend on the forgiveness and generosity of others. Yet we often ask for second chances as we try to learn what we can from life's experiences.

- After an unhappy marriage and divorce, we vow to "do it right" the second time.
- We hurt someone deeply, and when we realize what we have done we ask to be forgiven so that we might make a fresh start in the relationship.
- We do a halfway job on a particular project at work, and when confronted by our supervisor we ask for the chance to redo it before it becomes part of the permanent file.
- We go off on a long trip without taking the time to replace the spare tire, and we vow that if we can just return home without a flat tire we will never again do something that stupid.

Often when we realize that we are getting a second chance we vow to make the best of it. I wonder whether Jonah made such a vow. As we will see, his earlier mishaps helped to change his behavior, but his attitude still left something to be desired.

Changing God's Mind

Can anyone really change God's mind? Yes, such a change is possible, as seen in Amos 7:1-6. Not once, but twice the prophet Amos intercedes for his people, asking for a change of God's mind. First, God shows Amos a swarm of locusts that are devouring the harvest, which Amos rightly interprets as a symbol of the impending destruction of Israel. "Please, God, don't do this" is his response. And the prophet tells us that God "relented concerning this" and decided not to punish Israel because of Amos's intercession. Again Amos received a vision from God of impending doom in the form of a fire that was devouring the land. After a similar intercession by Amos, God relented. There would be no punishment.

In today's passage we see the king of Nineveh pondering the issue of whether God might have a change of heart concerning the fate of the city. "Who knows? God may relent and change his mind; he may turn from his fierce anger, so that we do not perish" (Jonah 3:9). It almost seems like this king thought that it was possible to change God's mind. But the king of Nineveh was also a realist. He knew there were no guarantees.

We follow in Amos's footsteps every time we intercede in prayer for others. We may not stop to think about the fact that what we are doing is trying to change God's mind; we are just trying to help make a bad situation better. There are times, however, when bad situations are not going to get better, no matter what anyone does. Like Nineveh's king, we need to (1) do what we can and (2) be realistic about the outcome.

Loving Our Enemies

Again we are surprised at Jonah's response when God acts. Rather than rejoicing when the city to which he prophesied is spared, he becomes angry with God for saving the city and its inhabitants from destruction. Why was Jonah so angry? Why couldn't he celebrate the deliverance of these people? In short, Jonah could not celebrate because he considered these people to be his enemies. He could not love his enemies.

At a retreat I attended recently one of the topics was prayer—various kinds of prayer for various kinds of people. When the speaker began to talk about praying for our enemies people began to sit up and pay attention. You could just feel the energy level increase among those of us who were listening to the lecture. Later that evening a small group of us were discussing how we felt about the day's presentations. When we got to the question of unresolved issues the first issue to surface was that of praying for our enemies. Some of us were not convinced. How can we do this and really mean it? Isn't it hypocritical to pray for our enemies if we are not sure we really mean what we say? Often we do not want the best for them. How do we deal with that in our praying?

Several suggestions were made. Perhaps we could pray that the relationship be reconciled or restored. Or we might pray for wisdom to understand the situation better as a first step toward reconciliation. Someone suggested that we pray for the ability to pray for enemies and that such a prayer would be enough for a start. Another person said she tried to visualize her enemies while praying without using words. That guards against saying something she does not really mean.

All these suggestions were good ones. We each had a genuine interest in trying to pray for our enemies. Even though we came to no definite conclusions, talking about the issue helped us because we all have problems in this area. The question for each of us is, can we really love our enemies in a way that Jonah could not? Can we rejoice in their good fortune?

God's Mercy

"There's a wideness in God's mercy," the hymn proclaims, "like the wideness of the sea." For Jonah, God's mercy has a downside. It was God's mercy that caused Jonah's enemies to survive God's wrath.

And what may have bothered Jonah the most was his own part in making God's mercy evident. If it had not been for his response to God's call, his prophetic warning to the inhabitants of Nineveh, his enemies would have gotten what they deserved.

In frustration and anger, Jonah lashed out at God: "I knew that you are a gracious God and merciful, slow to anger, and abounding in steadfast love, and ready to relent from punishing" (Jonah 4:2). Now at last we understand the reason Jonah turned and ran the first time God called him: he knew even then that God, in God's mercy, would spare the hated Assyrians, and he did not want to participate in the reversal of fortune of his enemies.

Jonah's small-mindedness is a sharp contrast to God's all-encompassing love and mercy. What is mercy? What is God's mercy? It is something we ask for continuously. We often conclude each of our intercessory prayers with the phrase "Lord, have mercy." But what does God's mercy really mean for us?

Two other words are commonly used in connection with the mercy of God: steadfast love and lovingkindness. These words refer to the same general idea: the compassionate attitude that God has toward humankind. In fact, the Hebrew word for mercy comes from the same root word that means "womb"; God's mercy toward us is the same kind of feeling that a mother has for her unborn child. God is predisposed to deal kindly with us. Jonah knew that, and we need to hear that message as well.

Aspects of God's mercy are listed in a prayer by Kenneth Phifer entitled "I Seek Mercy." A portion of that prayer from *A Book of Uncommon Faith* is quoted here:

Be my vision
   that I may see what is truly good in life.
Be my courage
   that I may faithfully pursue it.
Be my fortress
   in the hour of temptation,
   a house of defense to save me from
      myself.
Be my light
   when the day is dark
   and I know not which way to turn.
Be my strength
   when I am weak
   and my spirit is troubled and distressed.
Be my assurance
   when those I love are taken from my
      sight
   and you alone can uphold and comfort
      me.
Be my hope
   when my own hopes fail
   and, but for you, I should give way to
      despair.
Be at all times my help and my salvation.
Until at length by your great mercy,
I win the victory over sin and death
   and come to everlasting life
   through Jesus Christ our Lord. Amen.

SHARING THE SCRIPTURE

PREPARING TO TEACH

When have you been angry lately? Do some kinds of situations make you especially angry? Does your anger tend to focus more on people or on situations? Spend some time thinking about your anger, in general, as well as specific instances recently when you have been angry at someone or something.

Read Jonah 3–4 and the commentary information provided under the heading "Understanding the Scripture." Decide how you want to present this latter material to the class.

Read Amos 7 and familiarize yourself

with the story there; you will need to retell it for the section entitled "Changing God's Mind."

Think for a while about your enemies. We all have them. Are they the same people you identified when you were remembering your recent anger?

Read the prayer by Kenneth Phifer about God's mercy.

If you decide to have the class sing the hymn "There's a Wideness in God's Mercy," (page 121 of *The United Methodist Hymnal*), make sure you have enough hymnals handy.

Before class, write the sentence completion exercise on newsprint for the section entitled "Loving Our Enemies." Be sure to have on hand enough index cards or sheets of paper and pencils for each person in the class.

Collect the references you will need for the word study on mercy under the heading "God's Mercy." These include a Bible dictionary, concordance, Bible translation, commentary on Jonah, and articles or books that include the term "mercy." Also have newsprint and markers available.

LEADING THE CLASS

Introduction

One issue that will be raised in today's lesson is the anger of Jonah—toward God, toward the people of Nineveh, and probably toward himself. Begin today's session by asking class members to think about the last time they were angry for a sustained period of time. Note that anger is a universal phenomenon. Today's session will help us to address the question that God called Jonah to consider: **Is it right for you to be angry?**

The second part of today's main question has to do with whether we really believe that the mercy of God extends to everyone, including our enemies. Jonah did not believe that, unfortunately, and that was the source of his anger toward God. Intro-

duce the idea of God's mercy by having the class sing the first verse of the hymn "There's a Wideness in God's Mercy." If your hymnals do not include this song, select another hymn dealing with mercy. Discuss with the class the second part of the main question: **Do we really believe that God's mercy is all-encompassing, that it extends to everyone, even our enemies?** Perhaps some class members will share anecdotes related to this question.

Second Chances

Begin this discussion by reading aloud the first two paragraphs under this section in "Interpreting the Scripture." This material introduces the topic by describing God's second call of Jonah as the prophet's second chance. Then ask the class members to think of a time in their own lives when they perceived God to be offering them a second chance. To start their thinking you may want to read aloud the list of examples that is provided following the material you just read aloud. Suggestions by class members will augment this list and help others think of even more examples from their own experience. Close the discussion by reminding the group that the way in which Jonah responds to his second chance is determined by his attitude as well as his behavior.

Changing God's Mind

Work through the first six verses of Amos 7 by having them read aloud and sharing the commentary information on them provided in "Changing God's Mind" under "Interpreting the Scripture." In a few moments of silence, ask class members to think about persons or situations they would like to change. Then lead the class in a brief time of intercessory prayer. Ask for intercessions in each of the following areas in turn: friends and loved ones, the church, the community, and the world. Instruct those who offer intercessions to close each intercession with the words: "In peace let us pray to the Lord." Each time that phrase is uttered, the group will respond "Lord, have mercy." At the close of this prayer time, say a few words about the power of intercessory prayer, both for the ones prayed for and for the community who is doing the praying.

Loving Our Enemies

Introduce the concept of loving our enemies by asking a class member to read aloud Matthew 5:43-48; this is Jesus' famous admonition to love our enemies. Now raise the question, "Who are our enemies?" Without mentioning specific people, have the class members list various categories of enemies. Record this list on a chalkboard or newsprint. After this list is complete, reread verses 43 and 44 of Matthew 5, stating that these are the people Jesus intended that we love.

To help class members make this issue even more specific to their own experience, distribute note cards and pencils. Write these sentence stems on a chalkboard or newsprint:

- Today, my worst enemy is (name of person).
- I am angry with this person because he or she (what this person has done).
- My prayer for (person's name) is that he or she (what you hope person will do). Before class members begin to work individually, assure them that they will not be asked to share their completed sentences aloud.

When everyone has finished, ask the group members to share their feelings about this exercise, though not the specifics of how they completed the sentences. Whenever appropriate in the course of the discussion, point out similarities between the experience of the class members and that of Jonah. At the end of the discussion, encourage students to place these cards in a safe place where they can refer to them during the week ahead.

God's Mercy

If time allows, help the group engage in a word study of the term "mercy," especially as it is used in the Old Testament prophetic books. Have on hand some or all of the following resources for this exercise: (1) a Bible dictionary; (2) a concordance; (3) various translations of the Bible, as many as you can locate; (4) a commentary on Jonah or the minor prophets; and (5) articles or books on theological terms that include the term mercy.

If your class is large, divide the group into smaller subgroups for this work. Provide newsprint for the groups to use when recording the information and insights they find. Give each group (or individual, if the class is small) one of the resources listed above. Each group or person will complete one of the following assignments:

(1) **Bible dictionary group** — Ask them to look up *mercy, steadfast love,* and *loving-kindness* and report on what they find. Have them pay special attention to the material they read about these concepts in the Old Testament, especially in the prophetic books.

(2) **Concordance group** — Have them look up *mercy, steadfast love,* and *loving-kindness* in the concordance. Ask them to pay special attention to where most of the passages are located that contain these words. If time allows, have them begin to look up some of these passages and paraphrase them to illustrate the meaning of the words as they are used in the passages.

(3) **Bible translations group** — Ask them to look up the following passages, and take note of the differences among translations. How do the various translations change the meaning of the word mercy (*or steadfast love, or loving-kindness*)? How do the different translations give different meanings to these passages: Jonah 4:2; Daniel 9:9; Ezekiel 39:25; Jeremiah 31:20; and Habakkuk 3:2?

(4) Commentary group — Give them copies of the commentaries you have collected, and ask them to look up passages listed above. Have them make special notations about what the commentators have to say about the meaning of God's mercy in these passages.

(5) Book and/or article group — The task for this group is the same as that for the commentary group.

Set a time limit to work on this task. Then, ask each person or group to share what they have learned with the whole group. Tape the newsprint up on the walls for easy reference. Lead the class in a summary of whatever new insights have been gained from this word study. You might want to share the material in the section entitled "God's Mercy" under the heading "Interpreting the Scripture."

HELPING CLASS MEMBERS ACT

Challenge class members to find ways to love and show mercy to an enemy. Encourage them to read daily the prayer they wrote during this session and perceive this enemy to be surrounded with the mercy that God extends.

Ask class members to be aware of times this week when God is giving them a second chance to act on a call to action that they had failed to answer. How was their response to the second chance different from that of the first call?

Read aloud the prayer by Kenneth Phifer to end the session. Invite class members to develop their own list of characteristics of God's mercy this week.

PLANNING FOR NEXT SUNDAY

During the next two weeks, we will continue with the theme of God's love for all people by studying the book of Ruth. Ask class members to read Ruth 1, which focuses on Ruth's loyalty, and give some thought to issues and experiences related to loyalty.

REMAINING LOYAL

PREVIEWING THE LESSON

Lesson Scripture: Ruth 1:1-8, 16-18
Background Scripture: Ruth 1
Key Verse: Ruth 1:16

Focus of the lesson:
Ruth's loyalty to her mother-in-law, Naomi

Main question(s) of the lesson:
(1) Where are our loyalties?
(2) How do we make decisions when our loyalties are in conflict?

This lesson will enable adult learners to:
(1) value Ruth as a role model of loyalty
(2) empathize with the changes that Ruth, Orpah, and Naomi experienced
(3) respond by evaluating their own loyalties.

Today's lesson may be outlined as follows:
(1) Introduction
(2) Introducing the Book of Ruth
(3) Focus on Naomi: Her Bitterness at the Loss of Her Family
(4) Focus on Orpah: Her Decision
(5) Focus on Ruth: Her Loyalty
(6) Focus on Ruth: Her Move

FOCUSING ON THE MAIN QUESTION

The focus of today's lesson is on loyalty: the loyalty Ruth had for her widowed mother-in-law, Naomi. Ruth's loyalty evidenced itself when she decided to remain with Naomi after the death of her husband and two sons, one of whom had been Ruth's husband. Although Ruth was under no obligation to stay and could have returned to her home country of Moab, she chose to remain with Naomi.

We encounter the issue of loyalty every day in many ways. Sometimes loyalty to a cause, ideal, or person forces us to examine and reorder our priorities. We may be faced with tough ethical decisions that make us question where our loyalties are. We occasionally read or hear about examples of family loyalty that warm our hearts and help us maintain our faith in human nature. On the other hand, sometimes we see attitudes and behaviors in others that cause us to question their values. "Where is that person's loyalty?" we ask, shaking our heads. The question of loyalty seems to be constantly before us.

Most of us can recall the troubled times of Watergate and the eventual resignation of Richard Nixon. During that era we were constantly bombarded with rhetoric about loyalty. Many of the people who surrounded Nixon while he was in the White House were confronted daily with the question of where their loyalty was. Should they be loyal to their president, their leader, their boss? Should they keep quiet about what was happening and so

protect the man they served? Or should they be loyal to their country, to the values on which it rests? Should they tell the truth even though it would jeopardize the presidency?

Most of us will not have to face decisions like that, fortunately. But we all make decisions on a daily basis that reflect where our loyalties are. As we read the story of Ruth we see an example of loyalty that can be a model for all of us. Ruth had a choice to make and she opted for loyalty to Naomi. **Where are our loyalties? How do we make decisions when our loyalties are in conflict? These are our questions for today's lesson.**

READING THE SCRIPTURE

NRSV
Ruth 1:1-8

1 In the days when the judges ruled, there was a famine in the land, and a certain man of Bethlehem in Judah went to live in the country of Moab, he and his wife and two sons. ²The name of the man was Elimelech and the name of his wife Naomi, and the names of his two sons were Mahlon and Chilion; they were Ephrathites from Bethlehem in Judah. They went into the country of Moab and remained there. ³But Elimelech, the husband of Naomi, died, and she was left with her two sons. ⁴These took Moabite wives; the name of the one was Orpah and the name of the other Ruth. When they had lived there about ten years, ⁵both Mahlon and Chilion also died, so that the woman was left without her two sons and her husband.

6 Then she started to return with her daughters-in-law from the country of Moab, for she had heard in the country of Moab that the LORD had considered his people and given them food. ⁷So she set out from the place where she had been living, she and her two daughters-in-law, and they went on their way to go back to

NIV
Ruth 1:1-8

1 In the days when the judges ruled, there was a famine in the land, and a man from Bethlehem in Judah, together with his wife and two sons, went to live for a while in the country of Moab. ²The man's name was Elimelech, his wife's name Naomi, and the names of his two sons were Mahlon and Kilion. They were Ephrathites from Bethlehem, Judah. And they went to Moab and lived there.

³Now Elimelech, Naomi's husband, died, and she was left with her two sons. ⁴They married Moabite women, one named Orpah and the other Ruth. After they had lived there about ten years, ⁵both Mahlon and Kilion also died, and Naomi was left without her two sons and her husband.

⁶When she heard in Moab that the LORD had come to the aid of his people by providing food for them, Naomi and her daughters-in-law prepared to return home from there. ⁷With her two daughters-in-law she left the place where she had been living and set out on the road that would take them back to the land of Judah.

the land of Judah. ⁸But Naomi said to her two daughters-in-law, "Go back each of you to your mother's house. May the LORD deal kindly with you, as you have dealt with the dead and with me."

Ruth 1:16-18

¹⁶But Ruth said,
    "Do not press me to leave you
        or to turn back from following
            you!
Where you go, I will go;
    Where you lodge, I will lodge;
your people shall be my people,
    and your God my God.
¹⁷Where you die, I will die—
    there will I be buried.
May the LORD do thus and so to
        me,
    and more as well,
    if even death parts me from
        you!"
¹⁸When Naomi saw that she was determined to go with her, she said no more to her.

8 Then Naomi said to her two daughters-in-law, "Go back, each of you, to your mother's home. May the LORD show kindness to you, as you have shown to your dead and to me."

Ruth 1:16-18

¹⁶But Ruth replied, "Don't urge me to leave you or to turn back from you. Where you go I will go, and where you stay I will stay. Your people will be my people and your God my God. ¹⁷Where you die I will die, and there I will be buried. May the LORD deal with me, be it ever so severely, if anything but death separates you and me." ¹⁸When Naomi realized that Ruth was determined to go with her, she stopped urging her.

Key
Verse

UNDERSTANDING THE SCRIPTURE

This chapter introduces the story of Ruth, a woman from Moab who became involved with an Israelite family through marriage. In this first chapter of Ruth the two main characters are Ruth and Naomi, her Israelite mother-in-law. The third character we will encounter is Orpah, the other daughter-in-law of Naomi.

The story begins with the author setting the scene, introducing the characters, and giving us a hint of the problems that will develop. By the end of chapter 1 we see Ruth making the first of several major decisions that will affect her life.

Chapter 1 is divided into four parts: (1) an introduction (Ruth 1:1-5); (2) Orpah returns home (Ruth 1:6-14); (3) Ruth decides to stay with Naomi (Ruth 1:15-18); and (4) Naomi's bitterness (Ruth 1:19-22).

Ruth 1:1-5. The story takes place during the time of the judges (between 1200 and 1000 B.C.E.) though the book may have been written much later. The famine that was present in Israel during that time caused a hardship for many families who were trying to live off the land, including the family of a man named Elimelech. The story tells us that Elimelech lived in Bethlehem, just south of Jerusalem, with his wife Naomi and their two sons, Mahlon and Chilion. The storyteller mentions in passing that the members of this family were Ephrathites; that is, they lived in Ephrathah, which was a suburb of Bethlehem.

A famine forced this family to move to Moab, a territory located about fifty miles south of Israel, just east of the Dead Sea.

While living in Moab each of the two sons married a Moabite woman. This now-extended family was thrown into confusion and grief when Elimelech died, leaving Naomi behind to be cared for by her sons and their wives, Ruth and Orpah. The family continued to live in Moab until the two sons died, leaving the three widows bereft. We can imagine that Naomi was especially grief-stricken at that point, since she had lost both husband and children and was still living in a foreign country.

Ruth 1:6-14. Hearing that the famine had ended in Israel, Naomi decided to return home from Moab, taking her two daughters-in-law with her. The narrator tells us that they actually "set out" from Moab. But after a short time Naomi stopped and gently suggested that Ruth and Orpah return to their own families in Moab, rather than making the journey back to Israel and remaining with her. Naomi's close relationship with God is evident in her speech to her daughters-in-law: she asked God's favor on them as they journeyed back to Moab and made new lives for themselves by remarrying.

When they refused to leave at first, Naomi raised a question that may seem rather curious to us: "Do I still have sons in my womb that they may become your husbands?" she asks in verse 11. Her reference is to the law of levirate marriage, which required one of a dead man's brothers to marry and care for his dead brother's wife (see Deuteronomy 25:5-10). If Naomi had had any other sons, they would have been required to marry Ruth and Orpah. Naomi reminded her daughters-in-law that she was too old to bear any more sons who would eventually marry them; they had no hope of future security in Naomi's family.

In her grief Naomi's bitterness emerged when she lamented that her fate was worse than theirs. They had hopes of a future family; she was too old. Her logical conclusion was that "the hand of the LORD has turned against me" (verse 13).

With Orpah's kiss (verse 14) we realize that she has decided to return to Moab. Ruth, however, will stay with Naomi.

Ruth 1:15-18. Here we have Ruth's now famous answer to Naomi's request that she return to Moab. Because Ruth invoked the name of God in her vow to stay with Naomi, the discussion is over. Naomi knew that further argument was not appropriate because such a vow simply cannot be broken.

Ruth 1:19-22. We saw the first hint of Naomi's bitterness when she was talking with Ruth and Orpah, trying to convince them to leave her and return to Moab. Now the narrator elaborates on Naomi's bitterness by recording the change of her name. When Ruth and Naomi returned to Bethlehem, the town came alive with the news that Naomi was back. "Could this really be Naomi?" the townspeople asked. "No," she answered. "I'm changing my name to Mara, which means bitterness." Naomi's new name is a sharp contrast to her old name, since Naomi means "my pleasure" or "my pleasant one" in Hebrew. During her sojourn in Moab, Naomi has turned from pleasantness to bitterness. In her explanation Naomi reiterated her conviction that God had caused her suffering.

The narrator concludes chapter 1 by putting the story in context: the women returned at the time of the barley harvest (late April). This detail will become important later in the story.

INTERPRETING THE SCRIPTURE

Introducing the Book of Ruth

When we think of the book of Ruth we think of a story that illustrates the value of strong family ties and familial loyalty. This is a skillfully told short story, a mini-novel that is permeated throughout with the reality and the wonder of God's love. Who wrote the book of Ruth? We have no clue to the authorship of this book. This is unfortunate because our narrator is a wonderful storyteller. The writing style is concise and easy to understand; the characters are well-developed; the plot builds in suspense toward an eventual climax; the characters "live happily ever after."

When was the book of Ruth written? Our narrator places the story itself during the time of the judges, but the actual writing of the story probably took place at a later time. Most commentators place the writing of the story during the post-exilic period for two main reasons: (1) the language, vocabulary, and content of the writing suggest a relatively late date; and (2) the preoccupation with the relationship between Israelites (Naomi) and foreigners (Ruth) reflects the cultural situation during the post-exilic period, when persons were concerned about the influence of foreigners on the culture and the religious practices of Israel.

In English Bibles, the book of Ruth is located just before First Samuel; in this location it interrupts the flow of the historical narrative found in the books of Joshua through Second Chronicles. What is a short story doing here in the middle of this historical material? Presumably, the collectors placed it after the book of Judges because its opening words (Ruth 1:1) place it in the time of the judges.

We call this story the book of Ruth, and our tendency is to think of Ruth as the only character in the story. But chapter 1 introduces three women to us, and each has an important role to play in the story. In our lesson today we will focus in turn on each of these three women and the issue(s) she faced and resolved in the story.

Focus on Naomi: Her Bitterness at the Loss of Her Family

Each of us has experienced the heartache of loss. We know how lonely it feels to lose a loved one. Think of Naomi's grief, for she lost everyone in her family. She was past middle age by the time this story begins, so we can be fairly certain she has already lost her parents by now. The narrator does not mention any brothers or sisters. And even if she had them, she had spent more than ten years in another country and so had surely lost touch with them somewhere along the way. The move to Moab also meant a loss of valuable friendships that were available to her in Bethlehem. So when her husband and sons died, she was bereft.

Avery Brooke, an author and former publisher, writes of the feelings that overwhelmed her after the death of her husband in an article in *Weavings: A Journal of Christian Spiritual Life*:

> Where was God in all this? I tried to pray. I needed prayer. During my publishing years, I had had little time for prayer—although it was somehow bound into the work. Now I had plenty of time, and I found prayer almost impossible. My feelings were still numbed—including feelings about God. God was just an intellectual concept. . . . I would call on God to help me hold it [a wall of darkness] back, but I found myself alone.
>
> It was in this state of mind that I was trying to make decisions.

At times like these we naturally turn to God with our questions, just as Avery Brooke and Naomi did. In looking back on these times, we find that God was not absent; God was closer to us than ever.

Focus on Orpah: Her Decision

Orpah has the supporting role in this story; most people who know the story do not even remember her name. Like Ruth, Orpah originally came from the country of Moab. She took a risk and married a foreigner, an Israelite. When we meet her in the story, she is childless and about to become a widow at a young age.

When her husband died, Orpah was thrust into the same position as Ruth. If Naomi had had other sons, they would have been required by the levirate law (see Deuteronomy 25:5-10) to marry and take care of her financially. However, there were no other sons, so Orpah had two options. In her grief, she had to decide whether to (1) stay with Ruth and Naomi, her present family, or (2) return to her family of origin.

Apparently, Orpah initially decided that her best option would be to travel to Bethlehem with Naomi and Ruth, for Ruth 1:7 says they "went on their way to go back to the land of Judah." We can imagine the wise Naomi stopping in the middle of the road and saying to her daughters-in-law something like, "Look, are you sure you really want to do this? You don't have to stick around on my account. I really don't have much to offer you. I won't be upset if you decide to turn around right now and go home. Don't worry about me—really. I can take care of myself. You have your whole life ahead of you."

Orpah's response to Naomi was a kiss, indicating her intention to do just as Naomi suggested. Orpah turned and headed back to Moab for a fresh start in her life. Unfortunately, we lose track of her at this point and are not told how her life turned out and whether her decision was ultimately a good one. But on the surface it certainly seemed to make sense.

Focus on Ruth: Her Loyalty

The loyalty that Ruth had for Naomi has become the focal point of the story. It is the one element that most people recall when they think of the story of Ruth. Ruth's response to Naomi, "whither thou goest," (Ruth 1:16, KJV) is quoted at weddings and by others who want to give a good example of the concept of loyalty.

But what is loyalty, exactly? A dictionary may define it as allegiance to a person, cause, or an idea. We cannot merely be loyal; we must be loyal to something. Those things that demand our allegiance are part of the concept of loyalty. What are those things for us? Looking at them will help us understand our loyalties, our priorities, our values, and the resulting decisions we make.

Ruth's understanding of loyalty prompted her to remain with her mother-in-law, even though that decision meant that she would be a stranger in a land whose culture and customs were different from those in her native Moab. Furthermore, Ruth was apparently forfeiting her chance to remarry and have children when she decided to stand by Naomi. Although loyalties are often based on an intellectual commitment to an ideal, Ruth's loyalty is clearly based on a loving relationship with her mother-in-law. Caring for this elderly widow was more important to Ruth than starting her own life anew.

Focus on Ruth: Her Move

Ruth's loyalty resulted in a major upheaval in her life: having just recently lost her husband, she packed her belongings and moved to another country. True, Moab was not that far from Israel by today's standards. Fifty miles was in the next county; but for Ruth, it was two or three days' walking distance and far removed in its political and religious ways. Even the god of Moab was a different god than the God of Israel. In saying yes to Israel, Ruth was saying yes to Israel's God.

In our mobile society, the idea of moving is both commonplace and constantly traumatic to us. Many of us moved around a lot when we were young. I did, and when people ask me where I am from I always have a difficult time answering the question. How I answer depends on the context in which the question is asked. I think many of us face this dilemma; the other day I overheard someone ask someone else, "Where are you from?" and the person answered, "Oh, all over." As a society, we are relatively used to the idea of moving around, but that does not make our moves any less traumatic.

As I write this lesson we are making plans to put our house on the market in anticipation of a move to another state.

When people ask me what is going on, my response is usually something like, "Well, I have taken a new position." When my children are asked the same question, however, they usually say something like, "We have to move to Cleveland." For them the move will be traumatic, I know.

For Ruth the move was all the more traumatic because her only link to her new circumstances was one person: Naomi. Everything else was strange and different. Yet her loyalty to her beloved mother-in-law enabled Ruth to set aside her own concerns about the future and prospects of remarriage in order to stand faithfully by Naomi.

SHARING THE SCRIPTURE

PREPARING TO TEACH

To prepare for this week's session, read Ruth 1. Also read Deuteronomy 25:5-10, which gives the background for the concept of levirate marriage.

Think of an example from your own experience that illustrates conflicting loyalties. Be prepared to share that experience with the class during this week's session.

Write the words WHO, WHAT, WHERE, WHEN, AND WHY on a chalkboard or newsprint before class begins.

Locate one or two persons who would be willing to talk about their feelings related to the death of a spouse. Or be prepared to read or retell Avery Brooke's description of her feelings after the death of her husband, as found in "Interpreting the Scripture" under the heading "Focus on Naomi: Her Bitterness at the Loss of Her Family."

If you wish, print the scenarios provided in this section under "Focus on Ruth: Her Loyalty" on note cards for use by individuals during the session.

LEADING THE CLASS

Introduction

To open today's session, ask: **What does it mean to have conflicting loyalties?** Encourage students to suggest ideas or to define the phrase. Invite class members to suggest examples.

Ask the class what they know or remember about the story of Ruth. If no one brings up the issue of loyalty, remind the class that that is the main topic of the story. Ruth's story prompts us to ask two main questions: **Where are our loyalties?** and **How do we make decisions when our loyalties are in conflict?**

Introducing the Book of Ruth

In just the first four verses of chapter 1, the narrator provides us with the who, the what, the where, the when, and the why of the story. Write the words WHO, WHAT, WHERE, WHEN, AND WHY in a single column on a chalkboard or newsprint. Ask the class members to read these verses in

Ruth 1:1-4 and fill in the blanks. Then write their answers in the spaces next to these words. WHO (Ruth, Naomi, Orpah, Elimelech, Mahlon, and Chilion); WHAT (move to Moab, deaths in the family); WHERE (Bethlehem and Moab); WHEN (the time of the judges); and WHY (famine). You may wish to add information found under this heading in the "Interpreting the Scripture" portion to provide further background on the Book of Ruth.

Focus on Naomi: Her Bitterness at the Loss of Her Family

Naomi's feelings of loss are universal; most of us can identify with the kind of trauma she had to endure.

If you invited someone in advance to speak with the class about a grief experience; ask that person (1) to share his or her feelings; (2) to comment on Naomi's transformation from sweetness to bitterness; and (3) to address the question, Where was God in my experience? As an alternative, read or retell Avery Brooke's story and ask the class to respond to the three points above as they think this widow might.

Focus on Orpah: Her Decision

After giving the group a little background on the character of Orpah, have them brainstorm possible reasons for her decision to stay behind. Possibilities include: she may have been close to her family of origin; she may have known a man in Moab that she thought she might eventually marry; she wanted to forget her loss and begin life anew.

Emphasize that although we often tend to look at Ruth as the heroine of this story, Orpah's decision made logical sense and was probably a good decision to make in light of her circumstances. It was a decision born out of a realistic assessment of her situation.

Focus on Ruth: Her Loyalty

Write each of the following scenarios on an index card. Add or substitute other situations that also involve conflicting loyalties.
(1) Employees of a corporation discover that funds are being used illegally by top management. They are aware that whoever tries to expose this misuse of funds will run the risk of losing his or her job.
(2) A father has committed himself to attend eight different sessions of a spiritual retreat. He discovers that one of the sessions takes place during the time one of his children will participate in the city-wide spelling bee.
(3) A child becomes disruptive at school and is suspended for three days. The parents conclude that the punishment does not fit the crime.
(4) A supervisor observes behavior in an employee that is grounds for dismissal, but hesitates to act because the employee's personal life is unstable at the moment.
(5) Someone is engaged in a potentially self-destructive habit. A best friend finds out.

Pass out the cards to different individuals (or teams if the class is large) and have them describe the scenarios to the class. In a general discussion, ask the class members to identify the conflicting loyalties that are present in each of these scenarios. Record their answers on a chalkboard or newsprint. Once the loyalties have been identified, encourage individual class members (or teams) to struggle to reach an appropriate decision in each of these cases. Persons may make different, equally valid decisions that are based upon different criteria for determining loyalty. Suggest that the teams consider the pros and cons of each decision. What are the risks, rewards, and consequences of each possible choice? To conclude this activity, have the participants share their thinking with the whole group.

Focus on Ruth: Her Move   HELPING CLASS MEMBERS ACT

To help class members get in touch with their feelings related to moving, ask various people to share their own experiences. Encourage persons to answer questions such as:

(1) Why did you make this move?

(2) Did you choose to move or did you feel the move was thrust upon you by a change in employment, the death of a family member, the inability to live alone, or some other reason?

(3) How did you feel about being uprooted?

(4) How do you feel God led and supported you in this time of transition? Stress that all these feelings may have been shared by Ruth, Orpah, and Naomi as they moved from Moab to Bethlehem.

Challenge class members to examine the criteria they use to determine where their loyalties are and, if need be, reevaluate their priorities.

Encourage students to help someone who is grieving this week by being there for that person. They may be able to provide a service (such as transportation), or offer a gift (such as food or a memento of the deceased), or listen attentively to the mourner's feelings and recollections of the loved one.

Ask class members if they happen to know anyone who is moving from one town to another. If so, encourage them to try to assist this person or family during their time of transition.

PLANNING FOR NEXT SUNDAY

Next Sunday's lesson continues and concludes the story of Ruth. Tell class members to pay special attention to the kindness of Boaz toward Ruth and Naomi as they read chapters 2 through

4. Also ask students to be sensitive to acts of kindness done on their behalf or that they might do for others during the coming week.

SHOWING KINDNESS

PREVIEWING THE LESSON

Lesson Scripture: Ruth 2:1, 8-12; 4:13-17
Background Scripture: Ruth 2–4
Key Verse: Ruth 2:20

Focus of the lesson:
the kindness of Boaz

Main question(s) of the lesson:
(1) How does kindness affect the doers and recipients of loving deeds?

This lesson will enable adult learners to:
(1) understand how the kindness of Boaz, a kinsman of Naomi's husband, profoundly affected Ruth and Naomi
(2) appreciate the power of kindness to change lives
(3) respond by performing acts of kindness for someone else.

Today's lesson may be outlined as follows:
(1) Introduction
(2) The Providence of God
(3) The Kindness of Boaz

FOCUSING ON THE MAIN QUESTION

We all appreciate acts of kindness, especially when they are unexpected and done without any obligation of return. As recipients of such acts, we are thrilled to open a card remembering our birthday, or hear words of praise for a job well done, or receive unsolicited help with a task, or be told how a new outfit or hairstyle becomes us. As doers of acts of kindness, we find ourselves brightening someone else's day by doing a small good deed or offering an encouraging word. The person toward whom we show kindness may respond with a smile, a thank you, or a comment like, "You've made my day."

In today's lesson we will examine the kindness of Boaz toward Ruth and Naomi. As a near kinsman of Naomi's deceased husband, Elimelech, Boaz was helpful and supportive in his dealings with these two widows. More than that, he went far beyond legal obligations to ensure that Ruth was treated with justice and kindness. Boaz not only treated her this way but also showed great consideration to his hired reapers. Boaz did act with kindness that did not forsake either the living or the dead.

As we see the story of Ruth, Naomi, and Boaz develop, we will want to consider these questions: How does Boaz show kindness? How does his kindness affect the lives of Ruth and Naomi? How is the hand of God present in the events of this story, which may at times seem coincidental, so that Naomi and Ruth are ultimately protected? These questions undergird our main question: How does kindness affect the doers and recipients of loving deeds?

READING THE SCRIPTURE

NRSV

Ruth 2:1

1 Now Naomi had a kinsman on her husband's side, a prominent rich man, of the family of Elimelech, whose name was Boaz.

Ruth 2:8-12

8 Then Boaz said to Ruth, "Now listen, my daughter, do not go to glean in another field or leave this one, but keep close to my young women. 9Keep your eyes on the field that is being reaped, and follow behind them. I have ordered the young men not to bother you. If you get thirsty, go to the vessels and drink from what the young men have drawn." 10Then she fell prostrate, with her face to the ground, and said to him, "Why have I found favor in your sight, that you should take notice of me, when I am a foreigner?" 11But Boaz answered her, "All that you have done for your mother-in-law since the death of your husband has been fully told me, and how you left your father and mother and your native land and came to a people that you did not know before. 12May the LORD reward you for your deeds, and may you have a full reward from the LORD, the God of Israel, under whose wings you have come for refuge!"

Ruth 2:20

20 Then Naomi said to her daughter-in-law, "Blessed be he by the LORD, whose kindness has not forsaken the living or the dead!" Naomi also said to her, "The man is a relative of ours, one of our nearest kin."

NIV

Ruth 2:1

1 Now Naomi had a relative on her husband's side, from the clan of Elimelech, a man of standing, whose name was Boaz.

Ruth 2:8-12

8So Boaz said to Ruth, "My daughter, listen to me. Don't go and glean in another field and don't go away from here. Stay here with my servant girls. 9Watch the field where the men are harvesting, and follow along after the girls. I have told the men not to touch you. And whenever you are thirsty, go and get a drink from the water jars the men have filled."

10At this, she bowed down with her face to the ground. She exclaimed, "Why have I found such favor in your eyes that you notice me—a foreigner?"

11Boaz replied, "I've been told all about what you have done for your mother-in-law since the death of your husband— how you left your father and mother and your homeland and came to live with a people you did not know before. 12May the LORD repay you for what you have done. May you be richly rewarded by the LORD, the God of Israel, under whose wings you have come to take refuge."

Ruth 2:20

20"The LORD bless him!" Naomi said to her daughter-in-law. "The Lord has not stopped showing his kindness to the living and the dead." She added, "That man is our close relative; he is one of our kinsman-redeemers."

Ruth 4:13-17

13 So Boaz took Ruth and she became his wife. When they came together, the LORD made her conceive, and she bore a son. ¹⁴Then the women said to Naomi, "Blessed be the LORD, who has not left you this day without next-of-kin; and may his name be renowned in Israel! ¹⁵He shall be to you a restorer of life and a nourisher of your old age; for your daughter-in-law who loves you, who is more to you than seven sons, has borne him." ¹⁶Then Naomi took the child and laid him in her bosom, and became his nurse. ¹⁷The women of the neighborhood gave him a name, saying, "A son has been born to Naomi." They named him Obed; he became the father of Jesse, the father of David.

Ruth 4:13-17

¹³So Boaz took Ruth and she became his wife. Then he went to her, and the LORD enabled her to conceive, and she gave birth to a son. ¹⁴The women said to Naomi: "Praise be to the LORD, who this day has not left you without a kinsman-redeemer. May he become famous throughout Israel! ¹⁵He will renew your life and sustain you in your old age. For your daughter-in-law, who loves you and who is better to you than seven sons, has given him birth."

¹⁶Then Naomi took the child, laid him in her lap and cared for him. 17 The women living there said, "Naomi has a son." And they named him Obed. He was the father of Jesse, the father of David.

UNDERSTANDING THE SCRIPTURE

In these chapters we read of the relationship that develops between Ruth and Boaz, a relative of Naomi, after the women return from Moab to Bethlehem. This section of Ruth is divided into five parts: (1) introduction of Boaz (Ruth 2:1-7); (2) Ruth gleans in the fields (Ruth 2:8-23); (3) Naomi gives advice, which Ruth follows (Ruth 3:1-18); (4) the marriage of Ruth and Boaz (Ruth 4:1-12); and (5) conclusion (4:13-22).

Ruth 2:1-7. In these verses we encounter Boaz, a rich, prominent landowner who was actually an in-law of Naomi, a relative of her husband Elimelech.

In verses 2 and 7 the reader is reminded of Ruth's status as a foreigner: she is usually called "Ruth the Moabite" rather than just "Ruth."

In Deuteronomy 24:19-22 and elsewhere in the Old Testament legal material, we find laws that make provisions for poor persons who could not afford to buy food. The laws concerning gleaning state that when harvesting a field, reapers are required to leave enough extra grain so that those who wish to do so can come later and gather it to take home. This gleaned grain is free. Since Ruth and Naomi are poor, Ruth's decision to glean is understandable. Because of their economic insecurity, Ruth was looking for "someone in whose sight I may find favor," that is, someone who would take care of her (Ruth 2:2).

It seems curious that at this point Naomi does not instruct Ruth to go to the field of Boaz. However, Ruth does end up in his field by chance, and it also just so happens that Boaz comes to his field at the same time. His salutation to the workers indicates that he is a good and kind man, traits that will be borne out as the story unfolds.

Ruth 2:8-23. Boaz's first words to Ruth address her as "my daughter," signifying both the age difference between them and his parental concern. In order to assure her safety Boaz instructs Ruth to stay with his young women so that she would not be left alone. He even thinks to provide drinking water for her from the containers in the field. In fact, Boaz seems to think of everything, and Ruth responds to him with deep gratitude.

Gleaning among the standing sheaves (verse 15) is a special favor for Ruth; normally the gleaning is done only among the sheaves that have been cut down and are lying on the ground. After a day's work Ruth has gathered about an ephah of grain—probably at least a bushel.

When Ruth returns to town that night, her good fortune occasions a discussion with Naomi about Boaz. Naomi tells Ruth that Boaz is a relative of Elimelech. Naomi sees the hand of God at work in the situation.

Ruth 3:1-18. In this chapter the focus moves from grain to marriage. The chapter opens with Naomi's instructions to Ruth about how to attract the attention of Boaz. Naomi's plan turns out to be a good one, since events proceed just as she had planned.

When Boaz is contentedly full of food and drink, Ruth approaches him as he lies on the threshing floor. Uncovering his feet may be a euphemism for sexual activity, since in Hebrew feet can be an oblique reference to genitals. If so, the storyteller is doing a good job of providing subtle overtones without stating the obvious. Ruth reminds Boaz that he is her next of kin. This is a reference to the law of levirate marriage, which requires the brother of a dead man to marry the widow in order to provide her offspring and financial security (see Deuteronomy 25:5-10). Though Boaz is not Ruth's brother-in-law, he is a near kinsman of Naomi's deceased husband.

Boaz sees only one problem in Ruth and Naomi's plan: there is another relative who is closer to Elimelech than Boaz is. According to the law, the closest relative has a right of first refusal and might choose to marry Ruth. It is clear that Boaz wishes to marry Ruth and will find a way to do so. Naomi evidently feels the same way, according to verse 18.

Ruth 4:1-12. Here we read of another seeming coincidence: the next morning Boaz goes to the city gate (where most business is transacted), and soon after he arrives the unnamed next of kin just happens to pass by. Boaz secures ten elders, who could interpret the law in cases where there was a dispute, and tells his story. The mention of the parcel of land is a new element in the story; perhaps Boaz had discussed this with Naomi previously. This man is interested in buying Naomi's land until Boaz points out to him that the sale would also include Ruth. Apparently this man does not think it would be financially feasible to care for another woman and her family. Boaz completes the transaction in the presence of witnesses. Tamar, whose story is told in Genesis 38, is mentioned in Ruth 4:12 because she was in a situation similar to that of Ruth.

Ruth 4:13-22. Here the story concludes with everyone involved living "happily ever after." Even Naomi's friends recognize the hand of God in all the events that take place. The son that Ruth bears, Naomi's first grandson, becomes the grandfather of King David, and so is mentioned in the genealogies of Jesus (Matthew 1:5 and Luke 3:32).

INTERPRETING THE SCRIPTURE

The Providence of God

Many commentators on the book of Ruth have raised the question of whether the book is a series of coincidences or demonstrates that the hand of God is behind the scenes, helping to bring about the kind of ending Naomi had in mind all along. The characters in the story certainly seemed to think that God was at work in the events that were taking place. They call upon God or give credit to God at most of the strategic points in the story.

(1) Naomi decided to return to Bethlehem from Moab because she heard that God had brought an end to the famine (Ruth 1:6).

(2) Ruth perceived the choice to travel to Bethlehem with Naomi as a choice in favor of Israel's God (Ruth 1:16).

(3) Naomi perceived the deaths of her husband and sons to be a fate sent to her by God (Ruth 1:20-21).

(4) Boaz greeted the workers in his field with a request for God's presence with them as they worked (Ruth 2:4).

(5) Boaz asked for God's protection for Ruth as she gleaned grain in the field (Ruth 2:12).

(6) When Ruth returned to Naomi with a bushel of grain, Naomi attributed Ruth's good fortune to the kindness of God (Ruth 2:20).

(7) Boaz perceived Ruth's presence on the threshing floor as a sign of Ruth's loyalty to Naomi and to Israel's God (Ruth 3:10).

(8) The witnesses to the transaction between Boaz and the next of kin asked God's blessing on the union of Boaz and Ruth (Ruth 4:11-12).

(9) According to the narrator, it was God who caused Ruth to conceive, and it was God who was to be praised when her son was born (Ruth 4:13-14).

Except for the last incident mentioned, the characters, rather than narrator, consistently mention the name of God. That raises the question of whether or not the narrator intended that God's activity behind the scenes be apparent, be only hinted at, or be an idea only in the minds of the characters and not be the intention of the narrator. What is God's role in this story? Is God actively at work here or is this story just a combination of coincidences? Consider the following events in the story.

(1) Naomi and her family were in a foreign country at the time when her sons were of marriageable age, so they married foreign women.

(2) The famine in Israel came to an end when Naomi had lost her husband and sons and needed a place to go.

(3) Ruth decided to remain with Naomi.

(4) Ruth ended up gleaning in the field of Boaz, her mother-in-law's relative.

(5) Boaz showed up at the field when Ruth was there. Somehow he knew who she was and what she had done for Naomi.

(6) The next of kin came strolling by the city gate at just the time Boaz needed to talk with him.

(7) The next of kin was not interested in buying Naomi's land when he discovered that Ruth was included in the deal.

In *To Taste and See*, Thomas W. Mann ponders the question of the ambiguity of God's role in human events: "Nowhere are those ambiguities and uncertainties more apparent than in the story of Ruth, and nowhere does the presence and activity of God seem more opaque, rather than transparent." Later, he concludes:

Human struggle itself is divine activity. What an equation! "Responsible human beings act as God to one another." What an incredible simile! I do not pretend, of course, that these are the only answers to that most human of aspirations—the search for the presence of God. But I do know this: that presence is most often (I am tempted to say always) found embedded in the utterly commonplace ambiguities and uncertainties of life, not in transparent "crystal clear" flashes of revelation.

The Kindness of Boaz

Probably the one thing most people remember about Boaz is his kindness. In a culture where women were largely thought of as property, and where widowed, childless women were often ignored, Boaz stands out as a person who did what he did out of respect for Ruth. When he is first introduced to us, we see Boaz as a respecter of others. He greets the workers in his field by saying: "The Lord be with you." Their response indicates that they respect him as well: "The Lord bless you" (Ruth 2:4). How many times in our corporate culture do we see a supervisor come into a room of workers and say something like "The Lord be with you"? I doubt that any of us has witnessed such a thing!

In *The Different Drum*, M. Scott Peck tells a story of what can happen when people treat each other with kindness and respect. There was a monastery that at one time was full and prospering but had recently become run down. Many monks had left, and now the monastery had dwindled to four aging monks and their abbot.

In the woods nearby was a hermitage that was occasionally visited by a wise old rabbi. One day the abbot thought it might be a good idea to approach this rabbi to see whether he had any advice on how the abbot might revive the monastery and encourage more monks to come and live there. Although the rabbi lamented the fact that he had no advice for the abbot, he did leave the old monk with something to think about: "The Messiah is one of you."

When he returned to the monastery the abbot reported to the other monks what the rabbi had said. No one could figure out what the rabbi had meant, but the monks spent many hours thinking about the possibility that the Messiah might actually be one of them. They pondered and talked among themselves about the various messiah-like characteristics of each of the five inhabitants of the monastery. And gradually, as a result of these discussions, the monks began to treat one another as though each one of them might be the Messiah. They began to treat each other with great respect.

Peck concludes the story this way:

> Because the forest in which it was situated was beautiful, it so happened that people still occasionally came to visit the monastery to picnic on its tiny lawn, to wander along some of its paths, even now and then to go into the dilapidated chapel to meditate. As they did so, without even being conscious of it, they sensed this aura of extraordinary respect that now began to surround the five old monks and seemed to radiate out from them and permeate the atmosphere of the place. There was something strangely attractive, even compelling, about it. Hardly knowing why, they began to come back to the monastery more frequently to picnic, to play, to pray. They began to bring their friends to show them this special place. And their friends brought friends.
>
> Then it happened that some of the younger men who came to visit the monastery started to talk more and more with the old monks. After a while one asked if he could join them. Then another. And another. So within a few years the monastery had once again become a thriving order and, thanks to the rabbi's gift, a vibrant center of light and spirituality in the realm.

Peck's story illustrates the importance of kindness and respect for others. The narrator of Ruth tells us about the following acts of kindness that Boaz performed:

(1) He greeted his workers politely, rather than focusing on how much work they had or had not accomplished (Ruth 3:4).
(2) He provided Ruth with extra security while gleaning in the fields (Ruth 2:8-9a).
(3) He provided her with food and drink to sustain her while she was working (Ruth 2:9b).
(4) He allowed her to glean grain among the standing sheaves, and even instructed his workers to pull grain off the sheaves to help her (Ruth 2:15-16).
(5) He made certain they both left the threshing floor before it was light so that they would not be recognized and her reputation called into question (Ruth 3:14).

(6) He made certain that Ruth did not return to Naomi empty-handed (Ruth 3:15).

(7) He followed Israelite law and tradition in arranging for marriage to Ruth (Ruth 4:1-10).

Of course, we do not find ourselves in positions like Boaz. Sheaves and grain and next-of-kin marriages are not part of our world. But we can, and do, perform acts of kindness when opportunities present themselves; acts such as these:

- A friend of mine makes it a point to send everyone she knows a birthday card, even if she rarely sees these persons throughout the year.
- Another friend ministers to others through food. She is usually the first to show up at someone's door with a casserole or dessert when help is needed.
- My mother has a list of people she visits in the nursing home down the road. She does this visiting on a regular basis and encourages others in her church to do the same.
- A church member types the bulletin every Friday afternoon.
- A neighbor mows the lawn of an elderly woman who lives nearby. In return, this woman watches his home during the day when no one is home.

Have you ever had a secret pal? Have you ever been one? There is an elaborate system of secret pals at the office where I work. Although I am not a part of this phenomenon, I constantly marvel at the kinds of things that are done by and for secret pals. They remember each other's birthdays, wedding anniversaries, and work-related anniversaries. They give each other gifts on Christmas, Easter, even Halloween. They send cards to each other when there is an illness or an accident. They serve as constant reminders to one another that there is at least one other person in the world who is thinking about them all the time. Once a year they have a big party and reveal who was whose secret pal during the past year. They then exchange names to use during the year ahead.

Some people involved in spirituality and spiritual formation speak of acts of kindness as a spiritual discipline. A spiritual discipline is an act of obedience to God that is performed without the thought or expectation of receiving something in return. We do not expect God to reward us in some way for doing our spiritual disciplines on a regular basis. Rather, we do these disciplines with no expectations, no string attached. If we do them long enough, they become part of us—they transform us.

What are these acts of obedience? Each person who writes on the topic of spirituality will provide a slightly different list of spiritual disciplines. Most of these lists would include elements such as prayer, worship, and spiritual reading. These disciplines enhance our inner, spiritual life. But there are outer-directed disciplines as well, and performing acts of kindness falls into this category.

Perhaps the discipline of performing acts of kindness could be added to our own individual lists of spiritual disciplines, if it is not there already. If we were to perceive kindness as a spiritual discipline we would go about our daily rhythms in constant awareness of the needs of others. It would mean that we would be attuned to the small things we might do to make others' lives easier or more pleasant. Acts of kindness—a word of encouragement, an affirmation of a job well done, a greeting card, a ride to the doctor's office—can make a big difference. All they require is a little time and an attention to opportunities that present themselves.

SHARING THE SCRIPTURE

PREPARING TO TEACH

Review Ruth 1 and read the rest of the book. Spend enough time on the text so that you can retell the story in your own words. Read and become familiar with the material given under the heading "Understanding the Scripture." Decide whether you will present this material yourself or ask someone else to present it.

Spend some time thinking about the question of whether you see God's hand behind the events of the story, or whether you think the story is a series of coincidences.

Become familiar with the story of the monks in the monastery, found under the subheading "The Kindness of Boaz" in "Interpreting the Scripture."

In preparation for the discussion of acts of kindness, sometime early in the week, send cards in the mail to class members or call them on the phone.

Think about each of your class members in turn. What qualities do you see in each of them that reflect the qualities of the messiah? Have paper and pencils on hand.

LEADING THE CLASS

Introduction

To help class members begin to think about kindness—the kindness that is shown to them and that which they show toward others—ask: **(1) Has anyone been the recipient of an act of kindness this week? (2) How do you feel when someone does something nice for you?** If you have sent cards or made phone calls this week, a class member might mention your kindness.

After several examples of kindness have been shared, turn the discussion to Boaz's kindness and point out our questions for the day:

(1) How does Boaz show kindness?
(2) How does his kindness affect the lives of Ruth and Naomi?
(3) How is the hand of God present in the events of this story, which may at times seem coincidental, so that Naomi and Ruth are ultimately protected?

Summarize these questions by asking today's main question: **How does kindness affect the doers and recipients of loving deeds?**

Share the commentary information given in the section entitled "Understanding the Scripture." During the class session, make certain that the basic story line is understood by the class members. Have someone look up the gospel passages mentioned at the end of this section and read them aloud to the rest of the class.

The Providence of God

Ask class members to locate passages in all four chapters of the story where God (or the Lord, or the Almighty) is mentioned. Answers include Ruth 1:6, 8, 9, 13, 16, 17, 20, 21; Ruth 2:4, 12, 20; Ruth 3:10, 13; Ruth 4:11, 12, 13, 14. Many of these references are listed under "The Providence of God" in the section entitled "Interpreting the Scripture." Have students make notes about where these passages are found and the details of who is speaking and what the characters say. Have them compare notes in the whole group.

Now have the class follow the same procedure for the events that happen in the story that some persons may label coincidences. Many of these are listed in "Interpreting the Scripture," but class members may find others. Encourage their creativity and imagination. Again, make sure this information is shared in the group as a whole.

Now read the two quotes from Thomas W. Mann. Lead the class in a discussion of two questions: **(1) Is the story of Ruth a story of coincidences, or does the narrator intend us to see the activity of God throughout? (2) Consider Mann's idea of finding God in the commonplace? Is this easy or difficult to do? Is seeing the hand of God in events always easier to do in retrospect or while the events are occurring?**

The Kindness of Boaz

Begin this portion of the lesson by mentioning the kindness of Boaz as a point readers usually remember from the story of Ruth. Either ask the class for examples of Boaz's kindness that they can remember or read the list found under "The Kindness of Boaz" in "Interpreting the Scripture." You may want to consider how these kind acts were received and appreciated.

Then retell (or ask someone to read aloud) the story of the monks in the monastery. After making certain that class members understand the relationship between respect for others and the kindness shown to them (these go hand-in-hand in both stories), lead the class in a discussion of the monastery story. You might ask some or all of the following

questions to start the discussion and/or keep it going:

(1) What role does the rabbi play in the story?

(2) What did he mean when he said that the messiah was one of them?

(3) Why did the monks begin to treat one another with respect?

(4) What did they learn from this experience?

(5) What was different about the monastery after the monks' view of one another changed?

(6) What is the message for us in this story?

If you have the time and if members of your class know one another well, ask class members the qualities of the messiah they see in one another.

HELPING CLASS MEMBERS ACT

Challenge class members to be aware of signs of the providence of God in their own lives this week. As they recognize them, ask them to offer a prayer of thanksgiving.

Ask class members to brainstorm acts of kindness that they can perform for other persons and/or that they appreciate having performed for them. Encourage each person to choose at least one act of kindness to perform during the week.

PLANNING FOR NEXT SUNDAY

With this week's lesson we come to the end of this unit on God's love for all people. The first lesson for the next unit, which focuses on Jesus' teachings, will be on the parable of the sower, found in Matthew 13:1-23.

Please turn now to the Quarterly Evaluation form on pages 487-88. Complete this form for the Second Quarter.

THIRD QUARTER

MARCH 3 — MAY 26, 1996

Our study for the spring quarter is entitled *Teachings of Jesus*. This three-unit study is especially exciting because it draws upon familiar parables, the Sermon on the Mount, and other key teachings that Jesus set forth to help us understand what life in the kingdom of God is all about.

Our first unit, *Teachings About* the *Kingdom* of *Heaven*, looks at parables from Matthew and Luke over the course of five sessions. All of these parables focus on the nature of the kingdom of God. The lesson for March 3, "Hearing and Understanding the Word," looks at the parable of the sower as it is recorded in Matthew 13:1-9 and 18-23. We will examine this parable from the point of view of our tasks as sowers—evangelists of the words—as well as from the perspective of how we receive the word of God in our own lives. Our second lesson, "Unlimited Forgiveness," studies Matthew 18:21-35. In this parable of the unforgiving servant, we learn that God's forgiveness is an act of grace that knows no bounds. On March 17, we will study the parable of the vineyard workers, found in Matthew 20:1-16. This parable clearly shows that, by our human standards, God's will and grace are upside down, for the last do become the first. Our fourth lesson is based on the familiar parable of the ten talents in Matthew 25:14-30. This parable calls us to achieve our potential; we all have a vital role to play in God's kingdom, whether we are given one talent or five. This unit concludes on March 31 with a study of the parable of the great feast as recorded in Luke 14:15-24. Here we learn that God's kingdom is open to all who will come; indeed, the host sends his servant to compel persons to come into the banquet hall and partake of the feast.

Unit 2, *Teachings About God*, includes four lessons from Luke and John that focus on the nature of God and Christ. "The Living Lord!," which will be taught on Easter, recounts the beloved story of the walk to Emmaus as told in Luke 24:13-27. God's compassion for the lost is clearly seen in "The Loving God," based on the familiar parables of the lost sheep and the lost coin in Luke 15:1-10. On April 21, we will consider the image of Jesus as the Good Shepherd, as revealed in John 10:1-18. This unit closes with another familiar image of Jesus, that of the Vine, as described in John 15:1-17.

Unit 3, *Teachings About Living*, includes four lessons from Matthew that show us how to live as Christians. On May 5 we will study the Beatitudes, which teach us how to find true happiness. Next, we will look at Matthew 5:38-48 to learn how to love our enemies. "Trusting God for Our Daily Needs," based on Matthew 6:19-21 and 24-34, continues our study of the Sermon on the Mount, teaching us that we are to strive first for God's kingdom. This unit closes with an in-depth look at Jesus' teachings on prayer, as recorded in Matthew 6:5-15.

MEET OUR WRITER

DR. PAT McGEACHY

Dr. Pat McGeachy retired in 1994 after forty years of ministry. He most recently served at Downtown Presbyterian Church in Nashville, Tennessee. He is the author of many books, including *The Gospel According to Andy Capp* and *Help, Lord!*, a book on prayer. Pat is perhaps best known for his Psalm paraphrases, having set all 151 Psalms (yes, there is a Psalm 151) to familiar folk tunes and spirituals. Pat and Alice, who have three grown children, live on a forest farm called "Songwood," where he does writing, woodworking, cartooning, nature watching, and what he calls "three-chord" picking. He has been writing for *The International Lesson Annual* for the past ten years.

HEARING AND
UNDERSTANDING THE WORD

PREVIEWING THE LESSON

Lesson Scripture: Matthew 13:1-9, 18-23
Background Scripture: Matthew 13:1-23
Key Verse: Matthew 13:23

Focus of the lesson:
Jesus' teaching through the parable of the sower that his followers are to be both sowers of seed of the word and receptive to that seed in their own lives

Main question(s) of the lesson:
(1) What is our task as sowers of the seed?
(2) How receptive are we to the seed that is sown in our own lives?

This lesson will enable adult learners to:
(1) discern the meaning of this parable and its interpretation as recorded in Matthew
(2) consider their own response to the Word in terms of a type of soil
(3) respond by being faithful sowers of the Word.

Today's lesson may be outlined as follows:
(1) Introduction
(2) The Task of the Sower (Matthew 13:1-9)
(3) The Receptivity of the Hearers (Matthew 13:18-23)

FOCUSING ON THE MAIN QUESTION

I'm not much of a farmer, but I know a little about dirt. For one thing, it isn't dirty. It feels clean and rich as it runs through your fingers, and it smells heavenly. It's good to get your hands in it. Soil comes in all sorts: acid and alkaline, clay and loam, shallow and deep. And it's wonderfully fertile. No wonder Jesus chose different types of soil to illustrate varieties of believers!

The word human comes from the same root as *humus*, the dark, organic material in soils, produced by the decomposition of vegetable or animal matter, which is so essential to growth. The root meaning of both words is earth. We are indeed, as Paul said, "of the earth, earthy" (1 Corinthians 15:47, KJV).

In the parable of the sower, found in

Matthew 13:1-9, Jesus identifies four soils, which are: (1) the solidly packed soil of the path; (2) the thin layer of shallow soil that covers the rocks; (3) the weed and thorn infested soil that chokes out other plants; and (4) the good soil that yields an abundant harvest. The sower is called to scatter seeds over all of these soils, even though they will not be equally fertile.

In the interpretation of the parable, found in Matthew 13:18-23, the emphasis is on the receptivity of those who hear the Word. Some hear the Word but do not understand it. Others hear it and respond with joy, but their roots are so shallow that when hard times come, their faith dies. Still other persons hear the word, but their commitments are so divided that the cares of the world choke off the Word. Finally, there are persons who hear the Word and respond so faithfully that it produces an abundant harvest in their lives.

As we look at this week's scripture lesson from these two angles our main questions are: **What is our task as sowers of the seed? and How receptive are we to the seed that is sown in our own lives?**

READING THE SCRIPTURE

NRSV
Matthew 13:1-9

1 That same day Jesus went out of the house and sat beside the sea. 2Such great crowds gathered around him that he got into a boat and sat there, while the whole crowd stood on the beach. 3And he told them many things in parables, saying: "Listen! A sower went out to sow. 4And as he sowed, some seeds fell on the path, and the birds came and ate them up. 5Other seeds fell on rocky ground, where they did not have much soil, and they sprang up quickly, since they had no depth of soil. 6But when the sun rose, they were scorched; and since they had no root, they withered away. 7Other seeds fell among thorns, and the thorns grew up and choked them. 8Other seeds fell on good soil and brought forth grain, some a hundredfold, some sixty, some thirty. 9Let anyone with ears listen!"

Matthew 13:18-23

18 "Hear then the parable of the sower. 19When anyone hears the word of the kingdom and does not understand it, the evil one comes and snatches away what is sown in the heart; this is what was sown on the path. 20As for what was sown on

NIV
Matthew 13:1-9

1 That same day Jesus went out of the house and sat by the lake. 2Such large crowds gathered around him that he got into a boat and sat in it, while all the people stood on the shore. 3Then he told them many things in parables, saying: "A farmer went out to sow his seed. 4As he was scattering the seed, some fell along the path, and the birds came and ate it up. 5Some fell on rocky places, where it did not have much soil. It sprang up quickly, because the soil was shallow. 6But when the sun came up, the plants were scorched, and they withered because they had no root. 7Other seed fell among thorns, which grew up and choked the plants. 8Still other seed fell on good soil, where it produced a crop—a hundred, sixty or thirty times what was sown. 9He who has ears, let him hear."

Matthew 13:18-23

18"Listen then to what the parable of the sower means: 19When anyone hears the message about the kingdom and does not understand it, the evil one comes and snatches away what was sown in his heart. This is the seed sown along the path. 20The one who rocky ground, this is the one who hears the word and immediately receives it with joy; [21]yet such a person has no root, but endures only for a while, and when trouble or persecution arises on account of the word, that person immediately falls away. [22]As for what was sown among thorns, this is the one who hears the word, but the cares of the world and the lure of wealth choke the word, and it yields nothing. [23]But as for what was sown on good soil, this is the one who hears the word and understands it, who indeed bears fruit and yields, in one case a hundredfold, in another sixty, and in another thirty."

received the seed that fell on rocky places is the man who hears the word and at once receives it with joy. [21]But since he has no root, he lasts only a short time. When trouble or persecution comes because of the word, he quickly falls away. [22]The one who received the seed that fell among the thorns is the man who hears the word, but the worries of this life and the deceitfulness of wealth choke it, making it unfruitful. [23]But the one who received the seed that fell on good soil is the man who hears the word and understands it. He produces a crop, yielding a hundred, sixty or thirty times what was sown."

Key Verse

UNDERSTANDING THE SCRIPTURE

Matthew 13:1-2. The house may have been that of Simon and Andrew at Capernaum, and the sea is, of course, Galilee, the freshwater lake where most of the Gospel sea stories take place.

Matthew 13:3. Parable is an important word. Its roots are *para* (alongside of, as in "parallel") and *ballo* (to throw, as in "ball"). Thus it means "to throw beside" or "to make a simile." It is Jesus' favorite method of teaching, especially in the Synoptic Gospels: Matthew, Mark, and Luke. He uses everyday objects, such as soil, and common experiences, such as tending sheep, to teach his listeners complex ideas, usually concerning the kingdom of God. There are also a few parables in the Old Testament, such as 2 Samuel 12:1-4 and, some say, the book of Jonah.

Jesus often teaches in parables in response to a question or situation. In the parable of the sower, however, he speaks without prompting by calling for his audience to listen. The sower to which Jesus referred did his task differently than we would today. It was the custom, before modern agriculture, to scatter the seed broadly across the ground, and then to plow, so that not all of the seed would end

up buried. The Word goes out, indiscriminately to many ears.

Matthew 13:4. The path was unplowed ground, tramped solid by many feet; the seed there would be completely exposed as a feast for the birds.

Matthew 13:5-6. The reference here is not to ground with rocks lying about, but to ground in which the rock layer is only a few inches below the surface. In such shallow soil the cedar trees prosper, but the land is not very good for planting, for there is little room for the roots to go down. This lack of soil, coupled with the sun's scorching heat, would cause the sprouts to wither and die.

Matthew 13:7. Weeds and thorns encroach on the edges of the field from the unplowed land next to it. Such unwanted plants spread naturally and quickly to take it over. Although the soil is deep enough for the sower's seeds, they are soon choked by the weeds.

Matthew 13:8. *The Interpreter's Bible* tells us that in the United States, where the average yield for the country is fifteen to twenty bushels per acre, twentyfold to thirtyfold would be average, and a good crop might return forty times the sowing or more. A hundredfold would be a marvelous crop! In Palestine, before modern irrigation, the average yield would be even less. Jesus may be using hyperbole here, but he surely promises miraculous results.

Matthew 13:9. This command to let those who have ears listen is a characteristic formula with Jesus (see Matthew 11:15, 13:43; Mark 8:18; Luke 9:44, 14:35). It may have been a common saying in those days. Jesus uses it to drive home his point. He wants his listeners to think about what he has said and relate his point to their own lives.

Matthew 13:10-17. In this scripture passage, which is not included in our printed passage, Jesus answers his disciples' question about his reason for teaching in parables. The meaning of this passage is disputed, though Matthew's version seems to be less harsh than Mark's. Jesus does not seem to be saying that he is teaching in a way that is intentionally unintelligible. Rather, persons are not comprehending what he has to say.

Matthew 13:18-23. Matthew presents Jesus' explanation of the parable. Usually, Jesus leaves his stories uninterpreted, as though, like the scattered seed itself, the parables will be understood or not, depending upon the receptivity of the soil, that is, the people who hear them. Another way to say this is that Jesus trusts God to see that the Word is heard (or not, verse 17). Scholars raise questions about the explanation in these verses because of its allegorical nature. In an allegory, each element of the story has a specific meaning; such is not the case with a parable, which can be interpreted in a variety of ways. Jesus generally taught in parables, not allegories. Confusion arises because the allegorical meanings assigned to each of the elements in the story—the one who hears, the word, the evil one, and the seed—are inconsistent. The allegorical interpretation may have been the way the early church interpreted this parable.

Matthew 13:19. This soil is solid or dense, like persons who simply do not understand the Word. Before it has time to sink in, the birds (the evil one) have snatched it away.

Matthew 13:20-21. Some persons hear the word and respond with joy, but their commitment is shallow. When trouble or persecution comes, they doubt and fall away.

Matthew 13:22. Other persons are so caught up in worrying about security and pleasure that the word is choked off and cannot bear any fruit.

Matthew 13:23. The good soil is the fertile ground of those persons who spend their lives in bearing a rich harvest of fruit; they die to self, and are reborn to eternal life (see John 12:24 and 1 Corinthians 15:36).

INTERPRETING THE SCRIPTURE

Introduction

There are two ways to look at this parable, both supported by scripture passages. The first way, which is seen in Matthew 13:1-9, emphasizes the work of the sower who spreads the word of God far and wide. The sower is called to continue spreading seed, knowing full well that not all of it will take root and grow to maturity because it falls on different kinds of soils. The second way, seen in Matthew 13:18-23, focuses on the reception of the Word among those who hear it. This allegorical interpretation is more difficult to deal with because the meaning of the seed shifts from being the word of God in verse 19 to being the hearer in verses 20, 22, and 23. Note that this allegorical interpretation was likely added later to the original story.

Where do you put the emphasis as you interpret this story? On the spreading of the Word, or on its reception? Let's look at it from both sides.

The Task of the Sower

There was never a time when the soil, which can be understood as the people of the world, was more in need of the good news than today. Even the remotest villages have at least one transistor radio, if not a television set, enabling religious pronouncements of all sorts to be scattered throughout the earth. The good news from what used to be the Soviet Union is that the faith of many people has managed to survive the attempt of official communism to stamp out the worship of God. But in spite of these hopeful signs, the spread of the gospel is not keeping up with the growth of the population. Although there are more Christians on earth than ever before, there are also more non-Christians than ever before. Jesus' instructions to his disciples are more relevant than ever: "The harvest is plentiful, but the laborers are few; therefore ask the Lord of the harvest to send out laborers into his harvest" (Luke 10:2). We have a job to do.

Looking at our parable from the point of view of the one who is scattering the seed, our job is simply to "broad-cast" the message. I use that word literally, meaning "to scatter widely," not in the sense that it is used to mean radio and television. The best evangelism takes place in the daily encounters of human beings face to face with each other. It is in such "I-Thou" relationships that the seed is truly sown. I like what D. T. Niles said: "Evangelism . . . is one beggar telling another beggar where to get food." We are not to think of ourselves as looking down on others, calling them to come up where we are. Rather, we are to share what we have seen, and heard, and felt (see 1 John 1:1-4) with others, so that they too may see, and hear, and feel.

We might think of the sower's work in terms of this three-part definition:

- Evangelism is the word proclaimed (Romans 10:17).
- Evangelism is the word enacted by good deeds (Matthew 10:42).
- Evangelism is the word incarnate in the lifestyle of Christians (Matthew 5:16; Acts 2:43-47; Ephesians 4:11-16).

We are to speak, and do, and live in such a way that the seed, which is the word of God, may be scattered far and wide, almost indiscriminately. We are to sow it among the rocks and thorns, as well as where the soil appears to be most fertile. Ours is a "whosoever will come" (Mark 8:34, KJV) gospel. We are not to make judgments; our job is not to put out other candles, but to let our light shine (Matthew 5:16).

Furthermore, we are not to worry about the consequences of our seed scattering. Of course we care very much what happens to others, but their destiny is not in our hands. "Salvation belongs to our God" (Revelation 7:10), and the Spirit of God will bring about the fruit, wherever and whenever God chooses. We are to scatter the seed in hope, witnessing to everyone whom we encounter with equal generosity. The message of the parable from this perspective is basically that we should sow with assurance that our work is not in vain, even when the seed we scatter seems unfruitful.

The Receptivity of the Hearers

Now let's look at this parable from the other angle, which focuses on how persons receive the message. Four types of hearers are described in the interpretation of this parable, found in Matthew 13:18-23.

1. **Persons who hear without understanding**—Jesus indicates in Matthew 13:19 that "the evil one" will snatch away

what is sown in the heart (that is, the seed) of the person who "hears the word of the kingdom and does not understand it." A portion of a scripture passage that is not included in our printed text, Matthew 13:14-15, may shed light on what is intended here. These verses are a quotation from Isaiah 6:9-10. This prophecy can be interpreted as a description of a situation that exists, not necessarily as one that either God or the prophet intends. In other words, according to some commentators, God is not preventing the people from turning to him in order to be saved. Instead, the people have figuratively "shut their eyes" and their ears. Thus, while they may receive the message through their senses, they do not comprehend it.

Perhaps we too have heard the words as they are spoken, but we do not really think about them or let them sink in. Our minds may wander as we listen to a sermon, a Sunday school lesson, or a word of witness. Similarly, we may glance over a Bible passage and recognize the meaning of each word but fail to put the words together to form a comprehensible unit. In each of these cases, we hear or read the words, but they do not penetrate into our minds and hearts. It's as if they went in one ear and out the other or right over our heads. They have no meaning for us, so we forget them as soon as we hear or read them.

2. **Persons who respond without commitment**—the comparisons shift in Matthew 13:20. Here the person is compared to "what was sown," that is, the seed. The people referred to in Matthew 13:20-21 hear the word and initially respond to it with joy. This joy only lasts as long as the seed can sprout in a thin layer of soil, however. When its roots touch the impenetrable rock of trouble or persecution that lies just below the soil, the seed shrivels and dies. The roots of faith are shallow and easily destroyed.

Surely we have all known persons who are fair-weather Christians. As long as things are going well in their lives, they seem content with their relationship to God. Yet, when serious illness, the death of a loved one, or other crisis strikes, they become angry and suddenly want nothing more to do with God. Unfortunately, the roots of their faith have not gone deeply enough to prevent such a turn from faith.

3. **Persons who respond with divided commitment**—in Matthew 13:22, we again see that the seed that is "sown among thorns," is what is being compared to the person, rather than the soil of the thorny ground. Let's set aside this inconsistency, though, and look at the spiritual problem identified here: divided commitment.

How hard it is to be a faithful Christian in today's world! It has always been hard, of course, but it seems especially so in the days of instant news, jet travel, and intermingling societies. Single-minded commitment to God is difficult when our daily calendars and secular cultures pull us in different directions. We must not let the noises of this world cause us to deviate from the narrow path of justice and mercy to which we are called. In verse 22, Jesus names two specific things that will be especially tempting: "the cares of the world and the lure of wealth." What keeps us from a vital faith is often not the more obviously tempting sins (passion, appetite, lust, and anger) but the daily grind. It is the details of making a living, worrying over paying the bills, or wishing we were rich that choke off our unreserved commitment to God.

4. **Persons who understand and make a commitment**—in Matthew 13:23, our key verse, the person is again seen in comparison to what was sown (that is, the seed), rather than the ground. Persons who understand the word of the kingdom and make a serious commitment to it yield an extremely fruitful harvest.

This is the task to which we are called as Christians. We are to be open and receptive to receiving God's word and allow it to come to fruition within our lives. God will give the increase in our lives if we allow God to do so.

SHARING THE SCRIPTURE

PREPARING TO TEACH

This week's lesson is challenging to teach because, as we have already seen, the biblical text itself is difficult. Elements of the story change their meanings. Be sure that you read and study the parable carefully this week, preferably from several Bible translations. Students are likely to ask a question such as: Is the seed to be understood as (a) the Word of God or (b) the person who hears it? The answer is (a) if you are discussing the parable itself in Matthew 13:1-9 and also the interpretation in Matthew 23:19. However, in verses 20-23 the answer changes to (b).

Another helpful way to become more familiar with this parable is to study Matthew's account in relation to Mark and Luke's telling of it. The parable of the sower is one of only a few that are contained in all three of the Synoptic Gospels, Matthew, Mark, and Luke. (John does not record the parables). In addition to the story from Matthew, read Mark 4:1-20 and Luke 8:4-15. The slight differences among the three give us hints about Matthew's particular purpose. He had Mark as his source, and follows Mark's basic outline, but he includes this parable in a whole collection of Jesus' stories about the Kingdom, those who accept it, and those who reject it. If you have the time, read one of the commentaries on all three of the Gospel accounts.

Write in your spiritual journal about how you see yourself as being receptive to the word of God.

Think about how you can be a sower of the Word. You have an excellent opportunity to do this as a teacher. What other avenues are open to you? The three-part definition of evangelism may spark ideas.

Be guided by the scripture lesson itself in your teaching this week. Try to listen and understand, to dig deep, and to avoid being distracted by the world. Let the fertile soil of your own imagination respond to the Bible and bear fruit with fresh ways to make the points you are trying to teach.

If you plan to use soil samples to introduce the main question, be sure to collect them during the week.

If you want to have the class illustrate the story, have paper and pencils handy.

LEADING THE CLASS

Introduction

Note that during this quarter, we will be studying a number of parables. You may want to begin this session by asking the class to define *parable*. You will find a definition under Matthew 13:3 in the "Understanding the Scripture" portion. Point out that parables rely on elements that are familiar to their hearers to teach a lesson.

Set out soil samples if possible. Depending on the size of the class, allow at least a few persons to touch and smell some good friable (dry enough that you can dip your hand in it and let it run through your fingers) soil. Do the same for other soil types that may be available in your area, such as sand, clay, or soil that is filled with stones.

Ask the class: **Which of these soils would more likely produce a good harvest? Why?**

Point out that Jesus uses the common element of soil to tell a parable. Mention the four types of soil that Jesus discusses:
- the solidly packed soil of the path
- the thin layer of shallow soil that covers the rocks;
- the weed and thorn infested soil that chokes out other plants and
- the good soil that yields an abundant harvest.

Ask our main questions for today:

(1) What is our task as sowers of the seed?

(2) How receptive are we to the Word of God in our own lives?

The Task of the Sower

Read aloud Matthew 13:1-9. If your class enjoys creative activities, you might want to try having them illustrate the Bible story. All you need is plain paper and a pencil for each person. As the story is read aloud, each student draws what he or she hears. The progression of the story is thereby captured, just as a cartoon strip may be drawn in boxes. This kind of activity helps students to recognize how concrete and simple Jesus' story is. Assure students that artistic ability is not necessary.

Discuss these questions:

(1) How is the Word spread in our day?

(2) In what ways are we as Christians called to scatter the Word?

(3) What does this story say to persons who are sowing the seed of God's Word and feeling discouraged over the results they are seeing?

If your class prefers a lecture format, use the ideas under "Understanding the Scripture" and "Interpreting the Scripture" to develop your talk.

The Receptivity of the Hearers

Ask a student to read aloud Matthew 13:18-23.

Discuss the meaning of this story by asking these questions, using information under "Understanding the Scripture" and "Interpreting the Scripture" to supplement students' answers.

(1) How are each of the four hearers described?

(2) What reasons can you think of that a person would hear but not understand the Word?

(3) What are some of the circumstances that can cause persons whose roots are shallow to turn away from God? (Students may want to share some anecdotes here. If so, ask them to keep their stories short so as to give everyone a chance to speak.)

(4) What pressures do many persons you know face? How do these pressures or distractions affect one's Christian discipleship?

(5) What does the extremely generous yield of the seed in the fertile ground say to us about possibilities for our own lives?

Provide a few moments for class members to reflect silently on these questions or to write brief journal entries:

(1) How faithful am I to the task of sewing the seeds of God's Word?

(2) Which of the four soil types best describes my own receptivity to God's Word?

(3) If I recognize that I'm not the rich, fertile spiritual soil that receives and understands God's Word, what changes do I need to make in my life?

HELPING CLASS MEMBERS ACT

Ask class members to think during the week about the ways in which they can bear fruit. A partial list might be started in class by looking at the threefold definition of evangelism suggested in "Interpreting the Scripture." Help students list several examples of how to: (1) proclaim the word, (2) do the word, and (3) live the word.

If you brought soil samples to class, ask a few volunteers to plant seeds in each type of soil. If possible, place the containers (which may be large paper cups or inexpensive flower pots) in an area of the church where children can watch what happens. Put a Bible opened to the parable, or a sign about the parable, next to the containers so that children will be able to understand the purpose of these soil containers.

Challenge students to recognize the wide influence they have by trying to keep a count of the number of persons with whom they interact in the week ahead. Remind them that, like the sower, they may be scattering seeds in all directions. Ask them to consider the impact of this influence and to take stock of the kind of word and witness they are spreading.

PLANNING FOR NEXT SUNDAY

Next week's lesson is on forgiveness, as shown in the parable of the unforgiving servant. Ask class members to read Matthew 18:21-35. Also ask them to think about two things: (1) something that they wish forgiveness for, and (2) something that they need to forgive in another. Assure them that you are not going to ask them to confess their sins in class, but that the lesson will be more real for them if they are thinking about something concrete as they prepare the lesson.

UNLIMITED FORGIVENESS

PREVIEWING THE LESSON

Lesson Scripture: Matthew 18:21-35
Background Scripture: Matthew 18:21-35
Key Verse: Luke 6:37

Focus of the lesson:
Jesus' teaching on the unconditionality and boundlessness of forgiveness

Main question(s) of the lesson:
(1) Can we offer unlimited forgiveness to all persons?

This lesson will enable adult learners to:
(1) comprehend Jesus' expectations regarding forgiveness
(2) consider their own willingness to offer unlimited forgiveness to others
(3) respond by forgiving someone who has wronged them.

Today's lesson may be outlined as follows:
(1) Introduction
(2) Perfect Forgiveness (Matthew 18:21-22)
(3) God's Generosity (Matthew 18:23-27)
(4) Our Ingratitude (Matthew 18:28-35)

FOCUSING ON THE MAIN QUESTION

Where do you draw the line? It has been proposed that, if you knew the answer to that question, you would know the answer to all ethical questions. Everybody knows, "Don't kill," but what if someone is attacking your family? Everybody knows, "Don't labor on the Sabbath," but what if you are a physician who gets an emergency call? Everybody knows, "Don't steal," but what if your family has no food?

Most of us in the Western world have been taught for centuries to celebrate the "middle ground." We inherited the idea

from Aristotle, who developed the concept of "the golden mean." In most decision making, this is good advice. However, there are times when it is disastrous. For example, what if you applied this principal to driving down a two-lane highway? Those who are in the middle of the road would be run over by traffic from both directions! You'd better know whether it is the custom in your society to keep your car all the way to the left or the right.

Jesus teaches that forgiveness is such an "all the way" decision. His followers are to go the whole way with it. Probably one of the first verses you memorized as a child in Sunday school was Ephesians 4:32: "And be ye kind one to another" (KJV). But how far does that kindness go? The rest of the verse says, "tenderhearted, forgiving one another, even as God for Christ's sake hath forgiven you." And how far did Christ go? All the way to the cross, saying, "Father, forgive them; for they do not know what they are doing" (Luke 23:34). We are to forgive unconditionally. That awesome expectation prompts us to ask today's main question: **Can we offer unlimited forgiveness to all persons?** Certainly with us such perfection is impossible, but with the help of God, all things are possible (Mark 10:27).

READING THE SCRIPTURE

NRSV
Matthew 18:21-35

21 Then Peter came and said to him, "Lord, if another member of the church sins against me, how often should I forgive? As many as seven times?" 22Jesus said to him, "Not seven times, but, I tell you, seventy-seven times.

23 "For this reason the kingdom of heaven may be compared to a king who wished to settle accounts with his slaves. 24When he began the reckoning, one who owed him ten thousand talents was brought to him; 25and, as he could not pay, his lord ordered him to be sold, together with his wife and children and all his possessions, and payment to be made. 26So the slave fell on his knees before him, saying, 'Have patience with me, and I will pay you everything.' 27And out of pity for him, the lord of that slave released him and forgave him the debt. 28But that same slave, as he went out, came upon one of his fellow slaves who owed him a hundred denarii; and seizing him by the throat, he said, 'Pay what you owe.' 29Then his fellow slave fell down and pleaded with him, 'Have patience with me, and I will pay you.' 30But he refused; then he went and threw him into prison until he would pay the debt. 31When his fellow slaves saw what had happened, they were greatly distressed, and they went and reported to their lord all that had taken place. 32Then his lord summoned him and said to him, 'You wicked

NIV
Matthew 18:21-35

21Then Peter came to Jesus and asked, "Lord, how many times shall I forgive my brother when he sins against me? Up to seven times?"

22Jesus answered, "I tell you, not seven times, but seventy-seven times.

23"Therefore, the kingdom of heaven is like a king who wanted to settle accounts with his servants. 24As he began the settlement, a man who owed him ten thousand talents was brought to him. 25Since he was not able to pay, the master ordered that he and his wife and his children and all that he had be sold to repay the debt.

26"The servant fell on his knees before him. 'Be patient with me,' he begged, 'and I will pay back everything.' 27The servant's master took pity on him, canceled the debt and let him go.

28"But when that servant went out, he found one of his fellow servants who owed him a hundred denarii. He grabbed him and began to choke him. 'Pay back what you owe me!' he demanded.

29"His fellow servant fell to his knees and begged him, 'Be patient with me, and I will pay you back.'

30"But he refused. Instead, he went off and had the man thrown into prison until he could pay the debt. 31When the other servants saw what had happened, they were greatly distressed and went and told their master everything that had happened.

32"Then the master called the servant in.

slave! I forgave you all that debt because you pleaded with me. [33]Should you not have had mercy on your fellow slave, as I had mercy on you?' [34]And in anger his lord handed him over to be tortured until he would pay his entire debt. [35]So my heavenly Father will also do to every one of you, if you do not forgive your brother or sister from your heart."

'You wicked servant,' he said, 'I canceled all that debt of yours because you begged me to. [33]Shouldn't you have had mercy on your fellow servant just as I had on you?' [34]In anger his master turned him over to the jailers to be tortured, until he should pay back all he owed.

[35]"This is how my heavenly Father will treat each of you unless you forgive your brother from your heart."

Key Verse

Luke 6:37

37 "Do not judge, and you will not be judged; do not condemn, and you will not be condemned. Forgive, and you will be forgiven;

Luke 6:37

[37]"Do not judge, and you will not be judged. Do not condemn, and you will not be condemned. Forgive, and you will be forgiven.

K‹ Ve

UNDERSTANDING THE SCRIPTURE

Matthew 18:21-22. Peter's question reminds us of a cry of vengeance found in Genesis 4:24: "If Cain is avenged seven-fold, truly Lamech seventy-seven fold." In Genesis the statement concerns infinite blood revenge, whereas in Matthew the discussion focuses on forgiveness. According to Jesus, seven instances of forgiveness are insufficient. He calls for "seventy-seven times" or "seventy times seven" (KJV). This number is not meant to be taken literally but means that we are to offer forgiveness "to infinity."

Matthew 18:23. As was his custom, Jesus illustrates his point with a parable. This parable, set in a kingdom, features a king and his slaves. The setting and characters seem particularly appropriate to illustrate a point about the kingdom of God. More specifically, the focus of this parable is on the nature or character of God.

Matthew 18:24. Ten thousand talents was a huge amount of money. The value of coins was originally based on their intrinsic worth: that is, coins were worth more or less according to their weight or purity. A talent of gold was worth about 25 gold shekels. A shekel was about an

ounce and a half, so a talent was about 37.5 ounces of gold. If we multiply on that basis (using the value of gold as listed on Wall Street on the day of this writing, about $375 an ounce),which would put the value of one talent at around $14,000. So the debt that the slave owed was $140 million! Another way to figure the debt comes out close to the same amount. A denarius (see verse 28; KJV says "pence" or penny) was a silver coin that was the usual day's wage for a laborer (see Matthew 20:1-16). If we figure that on the basis of today's minimum wage (at this writing about $32 a day), a laborer might earn a little over $8,000 per year. Now a talent was worth more than fifteen years of such wages, or more than $120,000, which means the slave owed the king $120 million! The actual figure is not important, however. Jesus uses an incredibly large sum of money to illustrate the point that the slave would never be able to repay the debt.

Matthew 18:25. According to Leviticus 25:39 and 2 Kings 4:1, Mosaic law provided for the selling of persons to satisfy debt.

Matthew 18:26-27. The slave begged for

mercy, promising to pay. Note that, although the slave only asked for more time, the king mercifully forgave the whole debt. God is willing to do more than we ask or think (Luke 11:13).

Matthew 18:28. By the above figuring, we should say that the slave's fellow worker owed him $3,200 far less than the first slave owed the king. In contrast to the king who had the debtor "brought to him" in verse 24, the forgiven slave grabs his fellow slave "by the throat" and demands payment.

Matthew 18:29. The second slave responds in the same way that the first slave had responded to the king. Both fell down and pleaded for patience (more time) on the part of the one to whom the money was owed.

Matthew 18:30 and 34. Debtors' prisons were still in use in our great-grandparents' day, though torture was not considered a proper punishment among the Romans or the Jews in Jesus' day. However, Jesus may have been telling a story about an Eastern sheik, who might well have used it to try to make the slave admit whether he had any hidden money.

Matthew 18:31. Thus far, there have been two scenes in the parable: (1) the king and the forgiven debtor, and (2) the forgiven debtor and the slave who owes him money. This verse shows a third scene: the fellow slaves reporting to the king how the forgiven debtor had treated one of his peers.

Matthew 18:32-33. The point of the parable is made apparent: the king had forgiven the first slave, absolving him of a debt he could never begin to repay; therefore, that slave should have had mercy on his peer as well.

Matthew 18:34-35. Punishment was meted out to the one who refused to forgive as he had been forgiven. The parable teaches that we are to imitate God's mercy by forgiving others. We remember how much God has forgiven us and recognize that what others owe us is a paltry sum by comparison.

Luke 6:37. This verse, taken from Luke's Sermon on the Plain (similar to the Sermon on the Mount in Matthew), teaches that we are to forgive others. In doing so, we will be forgiven. Although this verse is not from the parable of the unforgiving servant, it is our key verse because it sums up the parable's message.

INTERPRETING THE SCRIPTURE

Anger

Forgiveness is a difficult concept for many of us. Just last week I was trying to comfort a woman whose mother had died. The mother had been a very abusive person to her children (physically and sexually), and, quite naturally, the daughter was having trouble with her grief work. At some point in our conversation she said, "I can never forgive her for what she did to me." How do you respond to that? Of course, right on the heels of the funeral is not an appropriate time to give pious advice. (Is there ever such a time?) It is more important to let the grieving person express her anger, which is certainly understandable, even appropriate. But, as the days pass, I can confidently predict that, if she does not learn to deal with her anger toward her mother, and eventually turn loose of it, she is in for trouble. Such anger can simmer within in us, like a boiling pot, until it blows off the lid.

The Bible recognizes the importance of appropriate anger, but warns us against harboring it (see for example Psalm 4:4 and Ephesians 4:26). To "take it to bed with you," that is, to nurture it and even enjoy it, can, in the long run be destructive. Therefore, we are told, "do not let the sun go down on your anger" (Ephesians 4:26).

MARCH 10

Jesus' Example

Jesus certainly provides a role model for us of one who is able to set aside his anger and offer forgiveness. The picture of Jesus, hanging in agony on the cross, and, at the same time, forgiving his enemies, is a haunting one. I can identify with his cry of loneliness ("My God, my God why have you forsaken me?" Matthew 27:46), and even with his act of turning it all over to God ("Father, into your hands I commend my spirit" Luke 23:46). I can express agony, and I can even, sometimes, express trust. But often I find it terribly difficult—even impossible—to forgive those who are harming me. I wonder how can we live up to our role model when he offers unlimited forgiveness to those who are in the very act of executing him?

The picture of Christian martyrs praying for those who are piling the kindling for burning around them makes me say, "I must be less than a Christian." And this becomes even more problematical when tormentors keep at it, over and over and over. Surely you have to draw the line somewhere, I rationalize.

No, Jesus won't let us off the hook. "If a bully knocks you down, get up and let him hit you again. If anyone sues you for your sweater, give him your shirt, too. If a hated Roman soldier forces you to carry his pack for a mile, go the second mile. If anybody asks you for anything, give it to him, even if you know he will be back tomorrow, asking again. If anybody wants to borrow from you, don't refuse her." That's how Matthew 5:39-42 sounds to me. Is Jesus telling me that I am supposed to be a doormat and just let people walk all over me? If so, that seems like such an injustice that I want to cry out, "It's not fair!" I want to say, "I hope they get what they have coming!" Or, as the law of retaliation put it, "eye for eye, tooth for tooth" (Leviticus 24:20).

But is that law really unfair? I'm told that the eye for eye rule was instituted to make things fair. Before then, the punishment often did not fit the crime; that is, a person might have a hand cut off, or worse, simply for stealing a crust of bread in hunger. What if we all learned to treat each other fairly? Life would surely be better.

But what if God really were fair? Am I so sure that the scales would balance in my favor? As a matter of fact, we had better be grateful that God is not fair, but, in Christ, has gone more than the second mile. God's own cheek was turned to us at Calvary. Jesus said to us, in effect, "Though you slay me, I will still love you." How could anyone love like that?

Do What You Can Do

Just as I did not want to burden my grieving friend with her need to forgive, I must also forgive myself for not always being perfect. The thing is, if I don't learn to forgive others, I will never learn to forgive myself. Deep down, I know that I deserve God's punishment. If I am honest, I must pray like David (Psalm 51:1, 3-4):

> Have mercy on me, O God . . .
> For I know my transgressions,
>   and my sin is ever before me.
> Against you, you alone, have I
>   sinned,
>   and done what is evil in your
>   sight,
> so that you are justified in your
>   sentence
>   and blameless when you pass
>   judgment.

When I can come to realize the depths of God's forgiveness to me, then, and only then, will I begin to move toward real forgiveness of others. God is willing and able to forgive me. Yet, often I choose not to forgive others of their comparatively minor offenses against me. God is patient and merciful with me, and God expects me to treat others this way as well. This truth is the point of Jesus' message to us in the parable of the unforgiving servant.

If I choose not to forgive, however, I am confronted by the awful truth of Matthew 18:34-35: I will be tortured until I pay my entire debt—a sum that is so astronomical that it can never be repaid. What can this mean? God certainly takes no delight in torturing us, for God is not vindictive. As I understand this verse, God knows what we cannot seem to understand: if we harbor hatred in our hearts, refusing to forgive others, we will torture ourselves with it. The young woman who cannot yet forgive her mother will carry the scars of her child abuse to her grave if she does not forgive and learn to turn it loose. Her anger and unwillingness to forgive may cause her even to abuse her own children. As long as this woman or any of us demand our "just desserts" from God, that is exactly what we will get, and if we are honest, that is more than we can bear.

The Inexorable Justice of God

At the risk of being misunderstood, let me try a parable of my own. I do not want you to think that God's judgment is automatic and impersonal, like electricity. It is not, for God is loving and caring, like a parent. For the sake of argument, imagine that resentment (the refusal to forgive) is like a wire carrying a thousand volts of electricity. God says to me, "Don't take hold of that wire! It will kill you!" If I grab it, it will kill me, just as God said. However, it is not as though God were sitting up in heaven like a vindictive police officer or judge, or even a capricious petty king, thinking, "Ha, ha! If he picks up that wire, I'm going to zap him!" No, God is rather like one who runs between me and the wire, and even grabs it and absorbs the deadly voltage. God longs for me to be safe and happy. But if I insist on cherishing my anger, enjoying my resentment, and refusing to be a forgiving person, that harbored hatred will zap me for certain. As the young woman who cannot forgive her mother illustrates, many of us find it hard to let go of a hot wire. Perhaps we find it even more difficult to turn loose of our self-justification.

Where do you draw the line? When it comes to forgiveness, there is no line. The mercy of God knows no limits. Nor should yours or mine.

SHARING THE SCRIPTURE

PREPARING TO TEACH

If you plan to use the suggested activity under "Leading the Class," review the Bible verses in advance. Numerous examples exist of biblical uses of the number seven, so you may want to check a concordance and jot down other possible responses.

Consider how you will use the information and examples from "Interpreting the Scripture" to help the class deal with the issues that underlie today's parable.

If you plan to use a hymn of forgiveness, select one and have hymnals on hand.

LEADING THE CLASS

Introduction

Introduce this lesson by leading a brief discussion on the number seven. Ask the following questions. If the class is large, you may want to divide up into smaller groups so that more people will have a chance to participate.

(1) **How many common uses of seven can you think of?** (examples include: deadly sins, hills of Rome, seas, wonders of the world, lucky roll of the

?

dice, seventh son of a seventh son, seventh heaven).

(2) **How is the number seven used in the Bible?** (examples include: the seven sections, each with seven subsections of the book of Revelation; seven churches mentioned in Revelation 2–3; seven deacons selected in Acts 6:1-6; seven days of creation in Genesis 1; Sabbath of the land every seven years in Leviticus 25:2-7; seven good years and seven lean years in the Pharaoh's dream interpreted by Joseph in Genesis 41:1-36; sevenfold vengeance to come upon anyone who would kill Cain in Genesis 4:15; sevenfold punishment for sins in Leviticus 26:18; Pentecost (meaning fiftieth) comes from the forty-nine days, the "week of weeks" (seven times seven), which follows Passover; and Jubilee year after forty-nine years in Leviticus 25:8-55).

(3) **What does the number seven symbolize in the Bible?** (perfection or completeness; and seventy-seven means ultraperfect).

Observe that our parable for today, the unforgiving servant, is told by Jesus in response to Peter's question about how often someone should be forgiven. Peter suggests seven times. Jesus answers "Not seven times, but, I tell you, seventy-seven times" (Matthew 18:22). Note that Jesus' point is that we are to offer unlimited forgiveness to others, just as God offers unlimited forgiveness to us.

As we consider this parable, we will want to challenge the class by asking today's question: **Can we offer unlimited forgiveness to all persons?**

Perfect Forgiveness

Select someone to read aloud Matthew 18:21-22.

Pick up on the theme of the number seven as symbolic of perfection or completion by reading aloud Matthew 5:48, a verse from the Sermon on the Mount that disturbs many Christians: "Be perfect, therefore, as your heavenly Father is perfect." Note that the word for "perfect" (*teleos*) has the root meaning of "completion." We could translate Jesus' words as "You must be completed."

Ask the class: **How can we possibly achieve perfect forgiveness like God's, not seven times, not even seventy-seven times, but an infinite number of times?** Class members are likely to answer that we cannot do this. Of course, they are right. Read aloud Jesus' words from Matthew 19:26: "For mortals it is impossible, but for God all things are possible." Note that this teaching comes at the end of the story about the Rich Young Man, who was unable to sell all that he had to follow Jesus. It is impossible for us to achieve perfection, but the grace of God can make us perfect.

God's Generosity

Choose a volunteer to read Matthew 18:23-27.

You may want to use the information for Matthew 18:24 under "Understanding the Scripture" to give the class an idea of the amount of money involved.

Try to help the class enter into the first slave's situation by asking class members if they have ever experienced great indebtedness or worried about how they would pay their bills. A few students may be willing to share brief anecdotes.

Then ask the class:

(1) **Suppose someone were to come to your door today and say that every debt you owed had been forgiven. You no longer owe anyone anything. How would you feel?**

(2) **What would be your attitude toward the person who forgave the debt?**

(3) **How might you describe the character of the person who was willing to set aside all your debt?**

Follow the previous discussion with some scripture references that show us that God's grace knows no limitations.

Choose a student to read as many of the passages as you want to use. The question following each reading is: **What does this passage tell us about God's gracious nature?** Ideas to augment the discussion (or to use in a lecture) are suggested.

(1) **Psalm 100**, especially verse 5. We are to make that joyful noise not simply because it is fun to shout, but because "the LORD is good; his steadfast love endures forever, and his faithfulness to all generations." "Steadfast love" is the Hebrew word *chesed*, which the King James Version translates, "mercy." It is very close to the New Testament word "grace."

(2) **Hosea 11:1-9**. These verses describe how God's compassion endures, despite Israel's ingratitude. God offers the forgiveness of a loving parent.

(3) **Luke 15:11-32**, especially verses 11-24. The familiar parable of the prodigal son could more properly be called the parable of the waiting father. Here we see how the father's love extends to a beloved child who has ignored his father for years, turned aside from everything that his father had taught him, and squandered his father's wealth. Yet, his father joyously welcomed home his son. Similarly, God graciously loves, forgives, and welcomes home all who have roamed from God.

Read or retell this familiar anecdote to the class: A song popular some years back called "Tie a Yellow Ribbon 'Round the Old Oak Tree" told a story of great forgiveness. But it is a much older story than that. I first heard it as a child from an evangelist who told it like this: A mother received a letter from her long lost son who had been in prison. It read, in part, "I will take the train that runs behind the house, and if it is OK for me to come home, hang something white on the clothes line. If I don't see anything white, I will go on past, and you won't have to bother with me again, but if I see something white I will know that you have forgiven me." Of course he stares in agony out the window as the train approaches his house, and what does he see but every sheet and shirt in the house, covering not only the clothes line, but the barn and the house and the back fence. Her forgiveness knows no bounds.

After telling this story, ask the class to think quietly for a few moments about these questions:

(1) **Who in my life needs to see a backyard full of white clothes or yellow ribbons decking a tree as signs of my forgiveness?**

(2) **How can I let this person know that he or she is forgiven?**

(3) **In whose backyard do I yearn to see signs of forgiveness for something I have done?**

(4) **Is there any way that I can let this person know how much his or her forgiveness would mean to me?**

Our Ingratitude

Direct the class's attention to Matthew 18:28-35.

Ask class members:

(1) **How did you feel about the first servant's treatment of the second servant?**

(2) **How did you feel about the first servant being punished at the end of the story?**

(3) **How would you summarize Jesus' teaching on forgiveness in this parable?** (To receive, I must give. To receive forgiveness, I must give forgiveness.)

Note how this forgiveness is not only healing to the other person but liberates the one who forgives as well. You may want to refer to "Interpreting the Scripture," pulling together ideas concerning how our anger eats at us unless we learn to let go of it. The example of the grieving woman who could not forgive her mother may be helpful. My parable under "The Inexorable Justice of God" may also be useful in this regard.

Conclude this segment by asking the class to read in unison today's key verse, Luke 6:37.

If possible in your setting, you may want to close with a hymn that concerns forgiveness. "Freely, Freely," found on page 389 of *The United Methodist Hymnal,* is very appropriate.

HELPING CLASS MEMBERS ACT

Challenge class members to offer forgiveness this week to someone who they believe has wronged them. Have the students notice how this action strengthens their relationship with God.

Encourage class members to be aware of the persons who make them angry, such as discourteous drivers, unhelpful store clerks, a gruff boss, or a demanding spouse. As the students feel themselves becoming angry, ask them to remember Jesus' parable and forgive the other person, whether for the first time or the zillionth time.

Suggest that class members write their own parables this week, using ideas and images about forgiveness that they would find especially helpful. If you have not already used the parable I shared, you may want to do so now as an example of how we can take that which is familiar to us, such as electricity, and use it to tell a story with a spiritual truth.

PLANNING FOR NEXT SUNDAY

Tell the class that next week's lesson will continue the theme of trying to see others through God's eyes. We will be considering our view of the world and its justice as we study the parable of the vineyard workers. Most of us, from the time we are children, have a pretty good idea about justice. We learned in kindergarten about sharing, about taking turns, about being kind. But did we really learn all we need to know about life in kindergarten? What happens to the child who grows up with ideals of fairness and then confronts the real world? Ask class members to consider this question during the week: "Is life fair?" Direct them to read the Background Scripture in Matthew 19:27–20:16, focusing especially on the parable in Matthew 20:1-16.

THE FIRST WILL BE LAST

PREVIEWING THE LESSON

Lesson Scripture: Matthew 20:1-16
Background Scripture: Matthew 19:27–20:16
Key Verse: Matthew 20:16

Focus of the lesson:
Jesus' teachings about God's concept of fairness

Main question(s) of the lesson:
(1) Could it be that we have to put on special spiritual glasses to see the world as it really is?
(2) If so, what does that upside down world really look like?

This lesson will enable adult learners to:
(1) explore the radical challenge of the message of the parable of the vineyard workers to society's concept of fairness
(2) experience a greater understanding of how God's fairness is different from what humans normally define as fairness
(3) respond by helping to meet the needs of someone else.

This lesson may be outlined as follows:
(1) Introduction
(2) Our View of Reality Is Inverted (Matthew 19:27-30)
(3) Is Life Fair? (Matthew 20:1-14)
(4) God Is Incredibly Generous (Matthew 20:15-16)

FOCUSING ON THE MAIN QUESTION

Scientists tell us that the image of what we see is refracted by the lens of the eye and appears upside down on the retina. Somehow the brain, or the optic nerve, manages to invert this image, so that it appears to us to be right side up. I don't think the scientists know how the brain does that, but things do look right side up to me. Experiments have been conducted in which people were given special glasses to wear that inverted everything. Amazingly, after a few days, the subjects of this experiment grew accustomed to seeing things from a different perspective and everything seemed right side up to them. They could even do such things as ride on motorcycles. Then, when the subjects took their special glasses off, the "normal" frame of reference seemed upside down! Apparently we can see the world as we have been taught to expect to see it.

Many things that Jesus taught seem upside down to our way of looking at life. "Blessed are those who mourn," or "the last will be first" are two teachings that challenge our traditional way of viewing the world. Indeed, Jesus' followers were accused of inverting the world (see Acts 17:6). But could it be that we are the ones who are upside down? We pretend that things are the way we want them to be, and we think we are fooling God into believing that things are right side up (see Isaiah 29:16).

In this lesson we will be taking a close look at a fundamental principle of Jesus' teaching: the first will be last. We read such a teaching and think that Jesus seems to have gotten things reversed. Is it not far more likely that our view of reality has somehow become distorted? We say, "Fair is fair." But this week's parable seems to be saying that "Unfair is fair." **Could it be that we have to put on special spiritual glasses to see the world as it really is? If so, what does that upside down world really look like?** Jesus offers us a new way of looking at the world, not through rose-colored but through truth-colored glasses.

READING THE SCRIPTURE

NRSV
Matthew 20:1-16

1 "For the kingdom of heaven is like a landowner who went out early in the morning to hire laborers for his vineyard. 2After agreeing with the laborers for the usual daily wage, he sent them into his vineyard. 3When he went out about nine o'clock, he saw others standing idle in the marketplace; 4and he said to them, 'You also go into the vineyard, and I will pay you whatever is right.' So they went. 5When he went out again about noon and about three o'clock, he did the same. 6And about five o'clock he went out and found others standing around; and he said to them, 'Why are you standing here idle all day?' 7They said to him, 'Because no one has hired us.' He said to them, 'You also go into the vineyard.' 8When evening came, the owner of the vineyard said to his manager, 'Call the laborers and give them their pay, beginning with the last and then going to the first.' 9When those hired about five o'clock came, each of them received the usual daily wage. 10Now when the first came, they thought

NIV
Matthew 20:1-16

1 "For the kingdom of heaven is like a landowner who went out early in the morning to hire men to work in his vineyard. 2He agreed to pay them a denarius for the day and sent them into his vineyard.

3"About the third hour he went out and saw others standing in the marketplace doing nothing. 4He told them, 'You also go and work in my vineyard, and I will pay you whatever is right.' 5So they went.

"He went out again about the sixth hour and the ninth hour and did the same thing. 6About the eleventh hour he went out and found still others standing around. He asked them, 'Why have you been standing here all day long doing nothing?'

7" 'Because no one has hired us,' they answered. "He said to them, 'You also go and work in my vineyard.'

8"When evening came, the owner of the vineyard said to his foreman, 'Call the workers and pay them their wages, beginning with the last ones hired and going on to the first.'

9"The workers who were hired about the eleventh hour came and each received a they would receive more; but each of them also received the usual daily wage. [11]And when they received it, they grumbled against the landowner, [12]saying, 'These last worked only one hour, and you have made them equal to us who have borne the burden of the day and the scorching heat.' [13]But he replied to one of them, 'Friend, I am doing you no wrong; did you not agree with me for the usual daily wage? [14]Take what belongs to you and go; I choose to give to this last the same as I give to you. [15]Am I not allowed to do what I choose with what belongs to me? Or are you envious because I am generous?' [16]So the last will be first, and the first will be last."

denarius. [10]So when those came who were hired first, they expected to receive more. But each one of them also received a denarius. [11]When they received it, they began to grumble against the landowner. [12]'These men who were hired last worked only one hour,' they said, 'and you have made them equal to us who have borne the burden of the work and the heat of the day.'

[13]"But he answered one of them, 'Friend, I am not being unfair to you. Didn't you agree to work for a denarius? [14]Take your pay and go. I want to give the man who was hired last the same as I gave you. [15]Don't I have the right to do what I want with my own money? Or are you envious because I am generous?'

[16]"So the last will be first, and the first will be last."

Key Verse

UNDERSTANDING THE SCRIPTURE

Matthew 19:27-28. After hearing Jesus' discussion with the rich young man (verses 16-22), Peter (verse 27) asks what reward those who have given up everything for Jesus' sake can expect to receive. Peter's question was misguided. Jesus could have rebuked him as he did James and John (Matthew 20:22), but he accepts it as understandable and tells the disciples they can expect to share in his victory in heaven (see Revelation 7:4-8). The "renewal of all things" literally means, "rebirth" or "re-creation" (see Isaiah 65:17; 66:22; Revelation 21:1-5; Galatians 6:15; Romans 8:18-25; and 2 Corinthians 5:17.)

Matthew 19:29. The disciples will also be part of the new family of God, which will take the place of those whom they have had to give up in order to follow Jesus. Jesus also promises that those who have followed him will enter the kingdom of God.

Matthew 19:30. In the Kingdom, there will be wonderful surprises! Roles and fortunes will be reversed. The story of the rich man sometimes known as Dives and Lazarus (Luke 16:19-31, especially verse 25) contains a reference to such a heavenly role reversal. Luke 1:52-53 and 13:28-30 contain a similar idea of reversal. It is a common notion that earthly injustices will be set right in heaven. Jesus' promise also applies to life here on earth, where those who truly trust God, and follow Jesus without reservation, will find their trust justified.

Matthew 20:1-16. Picking up on his surprising statement in 19:30, Jesus tells a story to illustrate how the first will be last.

Matthew 20:1. Jesus clearly states that the purpose of this parable is to teach his listeners about the kingdom of heaven. The vineyard is often understood as a symbol for Israel, as seen in Isaiah 5.

Matthew 20:2. A fair day's wage for a laborer was a denarius; see the discussion about money under Matthew 18:24, 28 in last week's lesson. Note that the temporary laborers had agreed to work for the usual wage.

Matthew 20:3-7. The marketplace (*agora*) was the normal place where the labor pool gathered for possible employment. The normal Hebrew day was measured from sunrise until the appearance of the first stars, as the NRSV makes clear. Counting from 6 A.M. The third hour was 9 A.M. The sixth hour was noon; the ninth hour was 3 P.M.; the eleventh hour was 5 P.M. We still use the expression eleventh hour to mean "last chance."

Matthew 20:8-9. The last to be hired were the first to be paid. These persons received a full day's wages (that is, a denarius).

Matthew 20:10-12. Aware that the workers who had labored the least amount of time had received a full wage, the other workers' expectations were raised. They looked for more money but did not receive it. The grumbling of those who had worked all day is certainly understandable in human terms.

Matthew 20:13-15. The story is not about fairness as we define that term; it's about God's generosity and justice. God promises everyone, even prodigals, the right to a living wage. God points out that those who began early in the morning received what they had been promised. No one was cheated.

Matthew 20:16. Jesus repeats the surprising truth of 19:30: "So the last will be first, and the first will be last." God does not look at justice in the same way the world does. God generously offers mercy to all persons.

INTERPRETING THE SCRIPTURE

Jesus' Upside Down World

"So the last will be first, and the first will be last," our key verse for this week, is one way of stating the key to life, the basic principle that underlies all of Jesus' message, and indeed, his own life and example. From the point of view of the world, everything about Jesus is upside down. Consider:

The Creator of the universe turns out to be a baby.
Not only that, he is a poor peasant baby, born in a barn.
The Lord of all declares himself to be a servant.
The King of kings comes to town riding on a lowly donkey.
The only innocent person who ever lived is cruelly executed.
Death is overcome by the Lord of Life.

There are dozens of ways in which Jesus drives this point home in his teachings and actions. For those who have not understood the principle of an inverted world order, his words make no sense at all; but for those who have understood, Jesus' point comes through with wonderful clarity. Let's look at some of these teachings.

First of all, the inverted order is seen in today's key verse itself that is found twice in today's lesson (Matthew 19:30 and 20:16), though the order is different. In chapter 19, the "first" are listed first, whereas in chapter 20 the "last" are listed first. This arrangement may serve to bracket Jesus' teaching. The same reference is made in other places (Mark 10:31 and Luke 13:30).

A similar teaching on inverted order is found elsewhere: "All who exalt themselves will be humbled, and all who humble themselves will be exalted" (Matthew 23:12; see also Luke 14:11; 18:14; and 1 Peter 5:6). The idea of reversal is stated, perhaps even more strongly, in these words: "For to all those who have, more will be given, and they will have an abundance; but from those who have nothing, even what they have will be taken away (Matthew 25:29; Mark 4:25; and Luke 8:18).

The same basic principle of reversal underlies dozens of other important sayings of our Lord. His sayings about cross-bearing and self-denial (Matthew 16:24; Luke 9:23; Mark 8:34) are followed by the formula that teaches that to seek life is to lose it and to lose life is to find it.

Jesus' assertion that his message (like those hard-to-open pill bottles) can only be understood by children (Matthew 11:25; Luke 10:21) also inverts the usual world order. Many other times Jesus uses the children to illustrate what he means (Matthew 18:1-5; 19:13-15; Mark 9:33-37; 10:13-16; Luke 9:46-48; 18:15-17).

And as if all that weren't enough, Jesus has a number of sermons that teach an inverted order: the poor are better off than the rich (Matthew 19:16-26; Mark 10:17-27; Luke 18:18-27); the tax collectors and prostitutes are better off than the chief priests and the elders (Matthew 21:31), and Sodom is more perceptive than Jerusalem (Matthew 11:24). This seemingly upside down world finds its most familiar expression in the Beatitudes (Matthew 5:1-12 and Luke 6:20-26), which we will look at in detail when we get to lesson 10.

But we're not through yet! There is a whole collection of stories and events, all of which make this same point: our way of looking at things is upside down. Here are some of them:

- The Pharisee and the publican (Luke 18:9-14). Here the churchgoer is condemned for his pride and the sinner is declared justified.
- The good Samaritan (Luke 10:30-37). The hero is not one of the good guys, but a despised foreigner.
- Mary and Martha (Luke 10:38-42). The busy, productive homemaker is rebuffed, while her sister is commended for sitting and listening to Jesus' teaching.
- Our parable for today, the laborers in the vineyard, falls in this category. Those employees who worked hard all day in the hot sun were no more greatly rewarded than those who had worked only one hour.

The Servant of the Lord

Jesus not only taught about an inverted world order where roles are reversed and the last are the first, but he also lived a life that modeled such a reversal. He was proclaimed "the Beloved" of the Lord at his baptism (Matthew 3:17; Mark 1:11; and Luke 3:22). Yet "the Beloved" son lived as a suffering servant (Isaiah 42:1-4; 49:1-6; 50:4-11; 52:13–53:12). Satan tried to lure him to follow the way of security and self-service (Matthew 4:1-11; Mark 1:12-13; Luke 4:1-13), but he overcame the temptation and chose the route of vulnerability and servanthood. He announced his intention to fulfill the role of the servant at the beginning of his ministry (Luke 4:16-21), and demonstrated it throughout his life (Matthew 12:15-21). When he performed miracles, he asked people not to tell (Matthew 8:4; 9:30; 16:20; Mark 7:36; Luke 5:14, and others), lest people follow him purely for his miracles (John 6:26). And ultimately he gave his life utterly, suffering the ignominy of the cross.

All along the way his disciples missed the point (Matthew 16:22-23), and even after his resurrection they were still expecting him to bring in an earthly kingdom with power and pomp (Acts 1:6). Because he didn't, Judas betrayed him and Peter denied him. He was truly "despised and rejected." Yet, through his servanthood, Jesus was able to turn the world upside down. We who are his disciples are called to follow his lead.

The World Cannot Understand

Today we still find it difficult to believe that God's way does not conform to the way we expect the world to be. God's ideas of justice, fairness, and success are upside down when compared to what our society teaches us. In my first pastorate, I worked extra hard to prepare my young people for confirmation, but, when they were being examined, one of them was asked, "Are you a sinner?" "No sir!" she replied, although I had tried to teach her that that was the wrong answer. I know why she got it wrong. All of her life she had been taught, if a grown-up asks you, "Have you been a bad girl?" you must answer, "No." This is Santa Claus theology, not the Christian faith. Santa Claus rewards the good little boys and girls, but the miracle of Christ is that he died for sinners (John 3:17; Romans 5:8; and 1 John 4:10). We are raised on the theology of the world, which thinks that if your nose is shiny and bright, all the reindeer will love you. But the incredible truth of our faith is the opposite of that. To join the clubs of the world you have to have all the right credentials; to join the family of God you have to be meek and lowly of heart, and come with empty hands (Ephesians 2:8-9).

We are saved by God's generous grace, not by our own doing. God is out from early in the morning until late in the day inviting persons to come into the vineyard. It doesn't matter whether we come early or late. That's difficult for us to understand because we've been taught to look at life upside down. We've been told that fairness means being rewarded on the basis of what we deserve. We must somehow invert our spiritual vision, so as to see that, in the mystery of God, the last will be first, and the first will be last. Through God's generosity, all persons will have an opportunity to come into the vineyard and receive the bounty that God wants to bestow on each one.

SHARING THE SCRIPTURE

PREPARING TO TEACH

Today's parable is a difficult one to deal with because it goes against the grain of fairness as our society teaches this concept. We have such a powerful world view and work ethic, which has been handed down over generations, that to break through and understand Jesus' teachings that the first will be last requires a radical breakthrough, a kind of spiritual "Aha" experience. As you study the scripture passages and lesson for this week, try to get in touch with your own understandings about Jesus' teachings. Can you view it as God's gracious justice and generosity? You may want to write an entry in your spiritual journal about your own attitude.

For the "Introduction" segment, either prepare to tell my version of *The Princess Bride* (or your own version), or clip news articles concerning unfair situations that will be used for a discussion.

Decide how you will present the scripture passage information under "Our View of Reality Is Inverted."

LEADING THE CLASS

Introduction

If your class enjoys stories, you may want to begin the lesson by telling my version of the story called *The Princess Bride.* William Goldman abridged this tale by S. Morgenstern in the book and movie by that name. My version, which is not exactly how the book tells the story, is as follows:

The princess had been captured by the Black Pirate. The hero pursued them, trying to rescue her. At every point he encountered impossible difficulties: giant rats, an unclimbable cliff, and a super swordsman. The Black Pirate and the captive princess were always far ahead of the hero. Finally, in frustration, he went into the tent of a guru, and, pounding his fist on the table, cried, "It's not fair!" "It's not supposed to be," said the guru. The young man looked at him in astonishment. "It's not?" he cried. "I always thought it was." And, in great relief, he leaped up, continued his quest, and rescued the princess.

Another way to introduce the main question is to bring in a few news clippings of situations that seem unfair. Let the class as a whole (or groups if the class is large) discuss why the situation seems unfair. They may have some ideas of their own for righting what appears to be an injustice.

Whichever method you choose, point out that whenever we think life is supposed to be fair, we are always second guessing ourselves. If good things happen, we take the credit, and if bad things happen, we ask, "What have I done wrong?" But all this is useless (see the story of Job; or John 9:1-3; or Matthew 5:45; or Luke 13:1-5). God's standards of justice and fairness seem to be upside down from our point of view. In fact, our parable this week seems to be saying that "unfair is fair." Indicate that our main questions for today's lesson are: **Could it be that we have to put on special spiritual glasses to see the world as it really is? If so, what does that upside down world really look like?**

Our View of Reality Is Inverted

Help set the stage for the parable of the vineyard workers by discussing the background scripture for Matthew 19:27-30. Read aloud the background scripture (which is not printed). Point out that verse 30 is the same as Matthew 20:16, our key verse, except that in Matthew 19:30 the "first" are listed first, whereas in Matthew 20:16 the "last" are listed first.

Use the information and scripture passages in the section "Jesus' Upside Down World" under "Interpreting the Scripture" in one of three ways:

(1) If your class members are knowledgeable Bible students, ask them to name some instances where roles or situations were reversed, or where the worldview that Jesus taught and lived seemed totally opposite of the worldview that society espoused.

(2) If your class members enjoy discussion but are not as well versed in the Bible, list the scriptures in this section under "Interpreting the Scripture" on a chalkboard or newsprint. Depending on the size of the class, either work together or in small teams to look up the selected passages and consider how they show a worldview that is opposite of what we would normally expect.

(3) If your class prefers a lecture, use the information in this section to create a lecture that will help the students perceive the difference between society's worldview and Jesus' upside down worldview.

Is Life Fair?

Ask the class to think of situations (either general or specific) that seem unfair. List these ideas on a chalkboard or newsprint. As each example is being discussed, ask the class to come up with a principle that we have been taught that would explain why we think this situation is unfair. Here are several ideas that you can use for discussion starters if necessary:

(1) A drunk driver hit the car of your best friends, killing the husband and one of their grandchildren and leaving the wife permanently disabled. The drunk walked away with a few bruises. (Principle we've been taught: The good should not suffer, but the bad should be punished.)

(2) You've been employed by a company for many years and have worked your way up the ranks. You just learned that a young adult fresh out of school has been hired at the same salary you make. (Principle we've been taught: People who have been in a job longer have more experience and should be better rewarded financially than a newcomer.)

After a few minutes, turn the discussion to the biblical parable, noting that it, too, seems to present a situation that from our society's point of view seems to be very unfair.

Choose a volunteer to read aloud Matthew 20:1-16. If you have some students who enjoy pantomime, ask one to act as the landowner, one to act as the manager, and a group to be the laborers. Let them mime the action while another student reads the story aloud.

Challenge the class to look at this story from several different perspectives. Read each character's description and then discuss the parable from each character's point of view. Encourage the students to put themselves in each character's position as much as possible.

Character 1: You are the head of the local labor union. Word has reached you that employees of a certain vineyard owner all received a day's wage for their work. This news does not strike you as remarkable, until you learn that some persons had labored in the scorching Palestinian sun all day, while others reported for work just before closing. You are on your way to see this owner, and you're planning what you want to say.

Character 2: You are a day laborer who was delighted to get work early in the morning. You needed that denarius so that your family would have food on the table tonight. You worked hard, hoping that the owner would pay as promised. For some strange reason, the owner instructed his manager to pay those workers who came later in day before you were paid. You realize that these latecomers are each receiving the silver denarius coin. Your hopes are rising, assuming that you will get a bonus, but no, you only get one coin. So much for the equal pay for equal work ideal.

Sum up this section by noting that these two characters are looking at the situation from the "right side up" point of view that our society has taught us.

God Is Incredibly Generous

Now turn the discussion to two other characters in the story who will have a different perspective.

Character 3: You are also a day laborer, but you got to the marketplace a little late today. Your child was ill, and you hated to leave, but you knew that without work there would be no food on the table tonight. You stood around with the other unemployed folks, hoping against hope that someone would hire you. You really needed the money. When a vineyard owner offered you work late in the day you were thrilled. When wages were distributed, you thought there had been some mistake. You had been paid for a full day's work. No, the amount is correct, the manager reassured you. You couldn't believe your good fortune. This vineyard owner seems too good to be true.

Character 4: You are the owner of the vineyard. You want to be fair to your employees, and you are. After all, you paid the ones who came early exactly what you agreed to pay. You certainly didn't cheat them. You chose to be generous to those workers who, for whatever reason, had not been hired to work anywhere. You wonder what all the fuss is about. You sure would like to know why some of the very people that you hired and kept your contract with are so upset about your generosity to others.

Ask the class:

(1) **How would you feel if you were the person who came late and still received a full day's wage?**

?

(2) Can you give any examples of this extraordinary gratitude for God's generous mercy, perhaps from testimonies or stories you have heard of persons whose lives have been particularly ungodly until they came late into the vineyard and met Christ?

(3) Are the earlybirds who grumble that they only got the denarius they bargained for like the older brother in the parable of the prodigal son (Luke 15:25-32). If so, what does this attitude say about what we believe we "deserve" from God?

(4) Based on this parable, how would you describe God's nature?

(5) Are you comforted by the promises of an upside down world order—at least one that is upside down from the way we know it—that exists within the kingdom of God? Explain your answer.

HELPING CLASS MEMBERS ACT

In the parable of the vineyard workers, God is making sure that the needs of all persons are being met. Challenge students to find at least one person this week who, for whatever reason, has never felt invited into God's kingdom through the church. Offer a word of witness and/or invite this person to worship with you next Sunday.

Encourage students who know an unemployed person to pray for that person this week and, if possible, to offer some tangible assistance.

PLANNING FOR NEXT SUNDAY

Next week's lesson is entitled "Achieving Your Potential." Direct your class to read the parable of the talents, found in Matthew 25:14-30. Ask them to think of at least one talent they have. Since many people believe they have no talents, assure them that each person does indeed have at least one God-given talent.

ACHIEVING YOUR POTENTIAL

PREVIEWING THE LESSON

Lesson Scripture: Matthew 25:14-30
Background Scripture: Matthew 25:14-30
Key Verse: Matthew 25:29

Focus of the lesson:
Jesus' teaching on the use of the talents and financial resources God has entrusted to each person

Main question(s) of the lesson:
(1) Are we willing to risk using the gifts that God has entrusted to us, or will we bury them in the ground where they will be fruitless?

This lesson will enable adult learners to:
(1) understand that they are God's stewards and, as such, must take risks to act on God's behalf
(2) identify their own God-given resources
(3) respond by examining their use of their own talents and material resources.

Today's lesson may be outlined as follows:
(1) Introduction
(2) We All Have Talents (Matthew 25:14-18)
(3) What Does God Expect of Us? (Matthew 25:19-30)

FOCUSING ON THE MAIN QUESTION

Often as we celebrate a birthday, we look back over our lives and assess our accomplishments. For some of us, such an exercise brings great satisfaction. We think about what we have done and feel good about ourselves. We believe that we have developed our natural abilities and used them wisely. To reach this point, we have worked hard, taken risks, and likely met failures along the way, but we continued to strive to achieve our potential. We have learned to live life to the fullest by making the best use of what we have.

In contrast, others of us will argue that our talents are so meager that they really aren't worth developing. Perhaps we are afraid to try to fulfill our God-given potential, preferring the safety of a sure—though bland—existence to the work and risk involved in reaching for the brass ring on the carousel of life. We may sing in the choir, but since we don't sound like an opera diva we won't risk singing a solo. Or we may play a sport, but we don't practice much because we know we'll never be as good as our favorite major league player. The trouble is that our gifts are fruitless if we don't use them. And to use them involves risk. We can't learn to ice-skate without falling down, and we can't learn to love without risking heartbreak. But it is worth a few falls to go gliding up a frozen stream, and it is worth a heartbreak to find a friend.

Even more tragically, another group of us concludes that we have no talents at all. We may deliberately choose to bury the talents we do have because we feel that they are not the extraordinary physical or mental gifts of a superstar. Or we may have never received affirmation from anyone who told us the talents they perceived in us, so our talents lie buried as unrecognized treasures.

Jesus has a word for us about learning to be good stewards of the talents God has entrusted to us. It makes no difference whether we are given five talents or only one. God expects us to use what we have according to our ability. The main question this week is this: **Are we willing to risk using the gifts that God has entrusted to us, or will we bury them in the ground where they will lie fruitless?**

MARCH 24

READING THE SCRIPTURE

NRSV
Matthew 25:14-30

14 "For it is as if a man, going on a journey, summoned his slaves and entrusted his property to them; [15]to one he gave five talents, to another two, to another one, to each according to his ability. Then he went away. [16]The one who had received the five talents went off at once and traded with them, and made five more talents. [17]In the same way, the one who had the two talents made two more talents. [18]But the one who had received the one talent went off and dug a hole in the ground and hid his master's money. [19]After a long time the master of those slaves came and settled accounts with them. [20]Then the one who had received the five talents came forward, bringing five more talents, saying, 'Master, you handed over to me five talents; see, I have made five more talents.' [21]His master said to him, 'Well done, good and trustworthy slave; you have been trustworthy in a few things, I will put you in charge of many things; enter into the joy of your master.' [22]And the one with the two talents also came forward, saying, 'Master, you handed over to me two talents; see, I have made two more talents.'

NIV
Matthew 25:14-30

[14]"Again, it will be like a man going on a journey, who called his servants and entrusted his property to them. [15]To one he gave five talents of money, to another two talents, and to another one talent, each according to his ability. Then he went on his journey. [16]The man who had received the five talents went at once and put his money to work and gained five more. [17]So also, the one with the two talents gained two more. [18]But the man who had received the one talent went off, dug a hole in the ground and hid his master's money.

[19]"After a long time the master of those servants returned and settled accounts with them. [20]The man who had received the five talents brought the other five. 'Master,' he said, 'you entrusted me with five talents. See, I have gained five more.'

[21]"His master replied, 'Well done, good and faithful servant! You have been faithful with a few things; I will put you in charge of many things. Come and share your master's happiness!'

[22]"The man with the two talents also came. 'Master,' he said, 'you entrusted me with two talents; see, I have gained two more.'

²³His master said to him, 'Well done, good and trustworthy slave; you have been trustworthy in a few things, I will put you in charge of many things; enter into the joy of your master.' ²⁴Then the one who had received the one talent also came forward, saying, 'Master, I knew that you were a harsh man, reaping where you did not sow, and gathering where you did not scatter seed; ²⁵so I was afraid, and I went and hid your talent in the ground. Here you have what is yours.' ²⁶But his master replied, 'You wicked and lazy slave! You knew, did you, that I reap where I did not sow, and gather where I did not scatter? ²⁷Then you ought to have invested my money with the bankers, and on my return I would have received what was my own with interest. ²⁸So take the talent from him, and give it to the one with the ten talents. ²⁹For to all those who have, more will be given, and they will have an abundance; but from those who have nothing, even what they have will be taken away. ³⁰As for this worthless slave, throw him into the outer darkness, where there will be weeping and gnashing of teeth.' "

Key Verse

²³"His master replied, 'Well done, good and faithful servant! You have been faithful with a few things; I will put you in charge of many things. Come and share your master's happiness!' ²⁴"Then the man who had received the one talent came. 'Master,' he said, 'I knew that you are a hard man, harvesting where you have not sown and gathering where you have not scattered seed. ²⁵So I was afraid and went out and hid your talent in the ground. See, here is what belongs to you.' ²⁶"His master replied, 'You wicked, lazy servant! So you knew that I harvest where I have not sown and gather where I have not scattered seed? ²⁷Well then, you should have put my money on deposit with the bankers, so that when I returned I would have received it back with interest. ²⁸" 'Take the talent from him and give it to the one who has the ten talents. ²⁹For everyone who has will be given more, and he will have an abundance. Whoever does not have, even what he has will be taken from him. ³⁰And throw that worthless servant outside, into the darkness, where there will be weeping and gnashing of teeth.' "

K Ve

UNDERSTANDING THE SCRIPTURE

Matthew 25:14-30. In Matthew's arrangement of Jesus' teachings, the parable of the ten talents is grouped with several other stories about the coming of Jesus in triumph. It comes between a parable about preparation (oil for lamps, Matthew 25:1-11) and a story about the great judgment (the sheep and the goats, Matthew 25:31-46).

Matthew 25:14. The journey on which the master goes may be intended to represent Jesus' ascension into heaven. If so, this parable teaches us about how we are to live in the time between Jesus' ascension and his return to judge the earth. In Jesus' day, slaves were often allowed to conduct their own business affairs, even

keep shop, teach school, or otherwise order their own lives. Note, however, that the money (talents) is not given to the slaves, but "entrusted . . . to them." Slaves served as stewards or managers of a household, tending the master's affairs and ensuring that everyone in that household was properly cared for.

Matthew 25:15. We have already discussed the monetary value of the talent (see lesson 2, Matthew 18:24). It represents a great deal of money, even a fortune. The word *talent* came into the English language through the Latin translation of the word used in Jesus' parable. In English, the word means "gifts of skill and natural ability." Jesus' story makes this connection between money and skill in verse 15 when he notes that each slave was given talents "according to his ability." Consequently, when we read this parable, we consider its meaning from the twofold perspective of money and ability.

Matthew 25:16-17. The slaves who had received the five talents and two talents, respectively, took risks to increase their master's holdings. Although the scripture records that both slaves were able to double the money entrusted to them, they also could have lost money in the trading process. The word translated "made" here actually means "gained" and can be understood in a religious context as gaining or winning converts.

Matthew 25:18. In those days, it was not unusual for people to hide their money in the ground for use later. (See Matthew 13:44. It is in such caches, long forgotten, that archaeologists have been able to find examples of ancient coins.) The point Jesus is making here is that the third slave took no risks with the money. He sought to preserve what belonged to the master but did not do anything to try to increase his holdings. Whereas the other two slaves had to continue to oversee the accounts, the third slave apparently assumed no further responsibility once the money was buried.

Matthew 25:19. This verse points to the last judgment when accounts will be settled. The time of the master's return is deliberately vague. No one knows when the master will arrive.

Matthew 25:20-23. When the householder returns, the judgment of how the slaves have overseen that which was entrusted to them begins. "Well done," is a wonderful word to hear from the master.

Those who put their talents to use enter into the joy of their Lord. One of the lessons of this story is that it is not from our ability, but from our faithful diligence that we can expect reward. The "joy" of the master refers here to the kingdom of God, which the two faithful slaves are invited to enter.

Matthew 25:24-25. The third slave excused his inaction on the basis of his fear of the master. He did return what belonged to the master, but no more. We are not excused from duty simply because our talents are few. This one-talent slave did not recognize the master's grace, which accepts the sincere efforts of our very limited resources, but judged the master by his own selfish standards.

Matthew 25:26-27. Berating the one-talent slave for his failure to do anything, the master describes him as both "lazy" and "wicked." Even if the slave were not willing to actively manage the money entrusted to him, the owner expected him to put it in the bank where it would at least earn interest.

Matthew 25:28-29. While it may seem unfair to us that the poor one-talent slave must give his wealth to the one who had ten talents, he was reaping the reward of his own inaction. Of both physical and spiritual things we can say: if you use your faculties, they will develop and increase; if you do not use them, eventually you will lose them.

Matthew 25:30. Apocalyptic imagery—"outer darkness" and "weeping and gnashing of teeth"—is used to described the punishment facing the slave who chose not to manage the talent entrusted to him.

INTERPRETING THE SCRIPTURE

Life Is a Risky Business

Here we go again! Just as in last week's lesson, we are up against Jesus' view of the world that is so different from ours that he appears to be thinking backwards. Matthew 25:29 sums it up: "For to all those who have, more will be given, and they will have an abundance; but from those who have nothing, even what they have will be taken away." How can a just God permit what appears to us to be such an inequity? Yet God appears not only to permit such inequity, but to support it!

We are not, in spite of what the Declaration of Independence says, created equal in respect to our talents. In a way, that doesn't seem fair either. But it's what makes life interesting. C. S. Lewis wrote in *God in the Dock*: "I cannot conceive how one would get through the boredom of a world in which you never met anyone more clever, or more beautiful, or stronger than yourself. The very crowds who go after the football celebrities and film-stars know better than to desire that kind of equality!" Because all people are created unequal—short and tall, progressive and conservative—the world is a rich and fascinating place. The gene pool of the universe is enormous!

Life is difficult. In the beginning we are all utterly helpless. We have to spend our formative years learning to stand up for ourselves, becoming independent of our parents, and launching out into life. Then we have to learn how to be interdependent, cooperating with others, competing with them and their talents, and coping with an increasingly complex world. Just about the time we begin to develop some skill at that, we find that we are becoming increasingly dependent, and have to learn how to turn loose of our hard-won individuality. Life is tough, and, as we learned last week, often unfair.

In such a world, unless we learn to risk, we are in for trouble. We have to ask questions, in spite of our fear of looking foolish, in order to learn. We have to try new activities, in spite of our fear of looking clumsy, in order to develop our physical and mental skills. And we have to venture out, with both our skills and our means, in order to earn a living. Not to risk is to die. But risking is scary. R. D. Laing, a British psychiatrist, suggested in *The Politics of Experience* that perhaps the schizophrenics are the only realists among us; the rest of us, if we were as wise as they, would invent imaginary worlds where we can manage things and survive. He was only partly kidding; life is frightening, and it is a wonder that more of us do not flee from it.

Burying Your Talent

Years ago, when I was doing clinical training in a large mental hospital, I encountered a young man whose psychosis had rendered him completely catatonic; he had withdrawn from the world altogether. Though in his twenties, he sat all day, curled in a fetal position, having to be bottle-fed and diapered, making no response whatever to the stimuli of the world around him. But some of the less disturbed patients on his ward, together with one of the orderlies, decided to try to get through to him. It happened that there was a patients' band which played (though not very well) for hospital dances. They picked up their catatonic friend, chair and all, and carried him each afternoon to band practice. There they sat him down by the big bass drum, stuck the drumstick in his hand, and left him sitting throughout the practice. For weeks this went on, with no response. But then, one afternoon, only God could say why, he hauled off and hit the drum! It wasn't in time with the music, but it was the first sign of awareness of the outside world that he had displayed since being hospitalized. The bandleader nodded encouragingly to him and went on with the practice. The next day, he hit the drum a few more times. Finally he began to play more or less in rhythm, and eventually to talk. Today, I understand, he has left the hospital and resumed the struggle of living.

I call that a miracle! Until his friends cared enough for him to help him make the move, he had allowed his fears to prevent him from living at all. He was buried within himself. Ralph Waldo Emerson spoke of the "terror of life," and we have all experienced it. But terror can be seen in two different ways. It makes life frightening, but it also makes life exhilarating! (Otherwise, why the popularity of roller coasters, sky diving, and bungee jumping?) In the lesson for today, Jesus calls us to the same miracle: to dig our talent out of the ground and put it to work. Only then will life begin to have the joy and the zest that we were meant to know (see John 10:10*b* and Philippians 4:4-7).

Taking the Risk

God is certainly a risk taker. What more risky business could you imagine than creating the universe and turning it loose in the charge of us human beings? Now that I have become a grandfather, I have become more and more conscious of the truth that God has taken the most important job in the world (raising children) and placed it in the hands of amateurs. What a risk!

Imagine the risk God took in sending the only Son into the world and expecting him to turn the world upside down! How risky of Jesus to turn the job over to twelve apostles, not the brightest and most powerful individuals but ignorant fishermen and tax collectors! The church in our own day continues to engage in the battle against the powerful forces of darkness in the world. How can we, with no more power than we have, ever hope to convince the mighty—those powerful leaders with political savvy and technical skill—that they need to turn around and come to Christ? We are a shaky institution in a risky world, sheep in the midst of wolves. Indeed, as I am told Origen said around two hundred years after Christ, the church is like Noah's ark, and if it weren't for the storm outside, he didn't think he could stand the smell.

But here we are, in a leaky boat, in a sea of conflicting theories and demonic powers (Ephesians 4:14 and 6:12). What are we to do? We are to take the risk and live! We are to dare to dream and to follow Jesus, the Pioneer of our faith, who set out boldly on an impossible quest, and won the day (see Hebrews 12:1-2). Life is a risky business, but the risk of withdrawing from life is greater than the risk of living. We have each been given gifts (Romans 12:6-8; 1 Corinthians 12:4-13; and Ephesians 4:11-13) greater than we know, and we believe that the One who gave them to us wants us to use them.

Our scripture lesson for today clearly challenges us to take such risks for the sake of the kingdom of God. This stewardship parable calls us to look at how we use both the natural abilities and financial resources that God has entrusted to us. The servant who was given just one talent to oversee claimed that he hid the talent in the ground because he was afraid of the master. In other words, he blamed someone else for his own failure to take a risk and act. The servant assumed that the master would be satisfied just to get back the one talent. Such was not the case. The master was so angry that the talent was completely ignored—not even deposited into the bank to accrue interest—that he took it away from the "worthless slave."

In contrast to the laziness of the one-talent slave, the other two servants spent the time needed to invest their talents in profitable ways. The story tells us that they were both able to double the talents they had been given. We are not told, however, how often they gambled and lost and had to try even harder. These slaves persevered despite the risks and the considerable time that this oversight must have required. They had to be ready to give an account at any time because the master had not indicated when he would be returning. When he did come back and find that they had used the talents wisely, he affirmed the servants for their good

work and rewarded them by entrusting even more of the household's assets to them.

Our lesson calls us to do some serious soul-searching: Are we willing to take risks in order to use the natural abilities and financial resources that God has entrusted to us? Or are we like the one-talent servant who, fearing failure, assumes that what he has is so meager that he need not nurture it and watch it multiply?

SHARING THE SCRIPTURE

PREPARING TO TEACH

As you prepare yourself to teach this week, think about what this parable means to you. It is a stewardship parable calling us to use whatever gifts have been entrusted to us as wisely as possible until the master returns. The original meaning of the story concerned financial resources. How are you using the money and other material goods that God has put in your care? Will the master return and commend you on what you have done with those resources? The story also relates to the use of our natural gifts and abilities. What talents do you have? How are you using them? Do you expect God to commend you for the risks you have taken to use these talents? You may want to record your thoughts in your spiritual journal.

One of the most difficult challenges you will face in teaching this week's lesson is that of getting class members to admit that they have talents. Strange as it seems, most of us find it easier to list our faults than to number our strengths. Ideas are given under the "We All Have Talents" segment to help class members identify and affirm their talents.

Another challenge you will face is in helping persons understand the theology that underlies this parable, for it is upside down compared to our society's under-

standings. Note that the man who leaves on the journey owns the resources. The servants or slaves (the word is the same in Greek) are to act as trustees or managers. They have not been given the money outright. Similarly, we are the trustees of the resources we have. They belong to God because everything belongs to God (Psalm 24:1). This parable demonstrates that we are accountable unto God for the way we use our tangible resources (money, material goods) and our personal assets (talents and skills).

Have slips of paper or note cards and pencils available for the activity under "We All Have Talents."

LEADING THE CLASS

Introduction

If your class enjoys discussion, begin by asking a few persons to share anecdotes of trying to learn a new skill. These stories may be recent or date back to childhood. Ask persons to share with the class or in small groups how they felt about: (1) taking the risks involved in appearing foolish before others; (2) the possibility of failure and; (3) later affirmation for a job well done once they mastered the skill. You may want to tell a story from your own experience to begin.

Or you may want to use this one from my experience of learning to dive: I climbed onto the high diving board, thinking I was ready to take the plunge. In spite of the fact that it takes no athletic skill at all to fall off a diving board, I couldn't do it! Actually, I did something even more difficult: I went back down the ladder to the jeering of my peers. I learned from this experience that it's sometimes easier to risk than not to risk. I thought of the fellow who was praised for his bravery in swimming in a river full of crocodiles. He set aside their praise saying, "You didn't see all those lions and tigers in the jungle on the other side."

If your class prefers a lecture format, read or retell the story of the catatonic drummer found under the section "Burying Your Talent."

Conclude this segment by announcing the main question: **Are we willing to risk using the gifts that God has entrusted to us, or will we bury them in the ground where they will lie fruitless?** Be sure to note that there are two points here: (1) We all have gifts, and (2) God expects us to use them.

We All Have Talents

Read or ask a student to read Matthew 25:14-18 aloud.

Make certain that the class understands that this parable can be interpreted from the perspective of our use of money and our use of natural abilities. Note that the three servants in the parable were all given talents.

Point out that we all have talents, though sometimes we fail to see or acknowledge them because we are not superstars. In God's eyes, the person in the back row of the choir who may not read music at all but who is willing to sing unto the Lord is using his or her talent just as wisely as the concert hall star. Also note that not all talents result in a tangible product, such as a work of art or a song or a sermon. Some

persons have a talent for making others smile, or for comforting those who are hurting, or for settling disputes.

Ask class members to each think of at least one talent they possess and to write that on a slip of paper or note card. Collect these anonymous slips of paper. Then engage in a litany of thanksgiving for gifts. Ask several students to read these slips in turn. As each talent is read, the class responds "Praise the Lord!" or "The Lord's name be praised."

If your class is small and well acquainted with one another, go around the room and mention each person's name. As an individual's name is called, other class members may respond with words such as, "I give thanks to you, O God, for (*students name*) talent of. . . ." This method can be very affirming to students as long as each person is recognized. Be prepared yourself to give a response for each student, especially if no one else says anything.

If your class does not like to participate aloud, and if you know the students well enough, you could list students' talents and read them aloud. You could attach names to the talents or be more generic, noting that you have observed these talents in class members. The second option may be better if the class is very large because if you do mention names you will have to include everyone to avoid hurt feelings.

Summarize this portion of the lesson by noting that we all have talents and that these talents are not given to us by God as gifts to keep but are entrusted to us so that we might use them on God's behalf.

What Does God Expect of Us?

Ask a volunteer to read Matthew 25:19-30.

Direct the students to look carefully at the parable and answer these questions, either as an entire class or in small groups. If the class prefers a lecture, you may want to use this information to help students understand the story:

? **(1) Do you think the master was fair in entrusting different amounts of money to each servant? Why or why not?** (Probably he was fair by our standards. Verse 15 tells us that the distribution was made according to the ability of each servant.)

(2) Do you think the master was fair in returning unannounced to settle accounts? (Yes. If the servants were carefully tending the resources, it should not make any difference when the master returns.)

(3) The first servant returned with ten talents and the second with four talents. How did the master respond to each of these servants? What does this response say to us? (Despite a large difference in the bottom line, the master responded exactly the same way. He affirmed and rewarded both servants. This response helps us to understand that we are not expected to use talents we don't have, but we are to make the best use of what we are given.)

(4) The third servant comes before the master bringing the one talent he had been given. He had, after all, returned it intact. Why is the master so angry? (This servant had taken no risks whatsoever. Furthermore, he spent no time nurturing that which the master had entrusted to him. He just buried it in the ground and forgot it. The master deemed such irresponsible behavior a punishable offense.)

After conducting this discussion, ask class members to summarize what they believe God expects of us in terms of using whatever talents (financial resources or natural abilities) God has entrusted to us. You may want to list their answers on a chalkboard or newsprint. Be sure to include these ideas: (1) we all have talents; (2) God expects us to achieve our potential with whatever we have been given; (3) we need to be constantly using our talents for we do not know when we will be called to account; (4) while different people have been entrusted with different kinds and amounts of talent, God does not hold us accountable for what we have not been given, only how we have used what we have; and (5) the use of our talents builds up the kingdom of God.

HELPING CLASS MEMBERS ACT

Challenge class members to use at least one of their talents in service to God this week.

Invite students to think of a talent that they have wanted to develop but for whatever reason have failed to do so. For example, perhaps they enjoy music and have wanted to learn to play the piano but have been afraid to risk failure by taking lessons. Encourage them to take a step this week in beginning to nurture that talent.

Encourage class members to take a look at their finances, perhaps by reviewing their check book and credit card statements. Have them ask themselves: Would God commend me for the way I use these resources? If not, what changes do I need to make?

PLANNING FOR NEXT SUNDAY

Next Sunday's lesson will focus on Luke 14:15-24, the parable of the great feast. This story includes the remarkable instruction: "compel people to come in." Ask the class to read the background scripture, Luke 14:1-24, and to consider these questions: God is giving a great party. Have you been invited? Will you go, or do you have an excuse? If you don't go, who might go in your stead?

A COMPELLING INVITATION

PREVIEWING THE LESSON

Lesson Scripture: Luke 14:15-24
Background Scripture: Luke 14:1-24
Key Verse: Luke 14:23

Focus of the lesson:
Jesus' teaching about the responses to the invitation to the heavenly banquet

Main question(s) of the lesson:
(1) Are you invited?
(2) Will you go?
(3) Who else will be there?

This lesson will enable adult learners to:
(1) encounter persons' responses to the invitation to enter into the kingdom of God
(2) consider their own responses to the invitation
(3) respond by providing a "banquet" for persons who would not likely be invited to a banquet.

Today's lesson may be outlined as follows:
(1) Introduction
(2) Dinner with a Pharisee (Luke 14:1-14)
(3) The Invitation and the Excuses (Luke 14:15-20)
(4) Compelling Others to Come In (Luke 14:21-24)

FOCUSING ON THE MAIN QUESTION

Movies and television may be wonderful stuff, but I feel sorry for anyone who doesn't remember the days when the entertainment had to come to you. When word began to spread that the circus was coming to my town, we children began to dream. We could hardly wait to see the tiny little car from which fifty clowns (or so it seemed) would emerge. We could almost taste those wonderful boxes of Crackerjacks with prizes inside them. There would be a house that caught on fire, and a fire truck driven by monkeys would come and put it out. There would be an elephant. I cannot tell you how badly I wanted to go! But I had been misbehaving, and my parents thought I had better not. I was crushed. However, after a while, they talked it over and decided they were being unfair. "The circus doesn't come every year," they said.

"Let's let him go." But I had developed a case of something called "the sulks," and had gone off to nurse my sorrows in a neighbor's barn, so they couldn't find me.

That sad tale is not a perfect illustration of the invitation in Jesus' banquet story, but it does make one valid point: I didn't get to go to the circus, not because I wasn't invited, but because I was too preoccupied with my own agenda. If God wants to give me heaven, but, like Milton's Satan, I would rather "reign in Hell, than serve in Heav'n," I won't get there.

The invitation is universal: "Whosoever will come after me, let him deny himself, and take up his cross, and follow me" (Mark 8:34, KJV). But few manage to get in that narrow gate. **Are you invited? Will you go? Who else will be there?** These are our main questions for today's lesson.

READING THE SCRIPTURE

NRSV
Luke 14:15-24

15 One of the dinner guests, on hearing this, said to him, "Blessed is anyone who will eat bread in the kingdom of God!" [16]Then Jesus said to him, "Someone gave a great dinner and invited many. [17]At the time for the dinner he sent his slave to say to those who had been invited, 'Come; for everything is ready now.' [18]But they all alike began to make excuses. The first said to him, 'I have bought a piece of land, and I must go out and see it; please accept my regrets.' [19]Another said, 'I have bought five yoke of oxen, and I am going to try them out; please accept my regrets.' [20]Another said, 'I have just been married, and therefore I cannot come.' [21]So the slave returned and reported this to his master. Then the owner of the house became angry and said to his slave, 'Go out at once into the streets and lanes of the town and bring in the poor, the crippled, the blind, and the lame.' [22]And the slave said, 'Sir, what you ordered has been done, and there is still room.'" [23]Then the master said to the slave, 'Go out into the roads and lanes, and compel people to come in, so that my house may be filled. [24]For I tell you, none of those who were invited will taste my dinner.'"

Key Verse

NIV
Luke 14:15-24

[15]When one of those at the table with him heard this, he said to Jesus, "Blessed is the man who will eat at the feast in the kingdom of God."

[16]Jesus replied: "A certain man was preparing a great banquet and invited many guests. [17]At the time of the banquet he sent his servant to tell those who had been invited, 'Come, for everything is now ready.'

[18]"But they all alike began to make excuses. The first said, 'I have just bought a field, and I must go and see it. Please excuse me.'

[19]"Another said, 'I have just bought five yoke of oxen, and I'm on my way to try them out. Please excuse me.'

[20]"Still another said, 'I just got married, so I can't come.'

[21]"The servant came back and reported this to his master. Then the owner of the house became angry and ordered his servant, 'Go out quickly into the streets and alleys of the town and bring in the poor, the crippled, the blind and the lame.'

[22]" 'Sir,' the servant said, 'what you ordered has been done, but there is still room.'

[23]"Then the master told his servant, 'Go out to the roads and country lanes and make them come in, so that my house will be full. [24]I tell you, not one of those men who were invited will get a taste of my banquet.'"

Key Verse

UNDERSTANDING THE SCRIPTURE

Luke 14:1. Jesus is on his way to dinner on the sabbath at the home of a Pharisee. The text notes that the Pharisees were watching Jesus closely, a point that Luke may have made to show that these religious leaders wanted to trap Jesus. This dinner provides the context for his parable on the great feast.

Luke 14:2. Dropsy (Greek *hydrops*) means "water in the joints." The modern term for it is "edema," a swelling. This word occurs only in Luke, who, as a physician, often used medical terms.

Luke 14:3-6. Jesus asks the lawyers and Pharisees, who are the experts in Jewish law, about the propriety of healing on the sabbath. No one responds to his question. Jesus does heal the man and then explains his action. Rabbinical tradition said that "an ox or an ass, a son or a daughter, a man-servant or a maid-servant" could be pulled out of a well on the sabbath. Even a lost or fallen animal is to be helped (Deuteronomy 22:1-4). Note that some manuscripts use the word "child" in verse 5, whereas others use the word "donkey." The legal experts could not rebut Jesus' argument.

Luke 14:7. Now Jesus has arrived at the home of the Pharisee who is hosting the dinner. When he sees how people are putting themselves forward to select the best seats, he tells a parable about a wedding banquet.

Luke 14:8-11. Jesus' teaching in this parable regards humility. The same idea is expressed in Proverbs 25:6-7. The place of honor at a Palestinian feast would have been the center grouping of three groups. It would not have been uncommon for a distinguished guest to arrive late. The statement in verse 11 is a fundamental principle of Jesus' teaching that is also seen in Luke 18:14 and Matthew 23:12. It deals with the reversal of roles that will come about in the kingdom of God.

Luke 14:12-14. Note that Luke speaks directly to his host in verse 12 concerning his guest list. Jesus makes it clear that persons who cannot repay such hospitality are to be invited. The people he lists are those who would not be invited into the temple. This teaching is peculiar to Luke, whose Gospel is particularly sensitive to the poor, minorities, women, and outcasts such as Samaritans. Jesus does not mean that we should never have our friends over for supper, only that we need not expect any reward in heaven from this; it is its own reward (see Luke 6:32-36). But a heavenly blessing is reserved for those who are hospitable to those who cannot return the invitation (see Hebrews 13:2).

Luke 14:15. A guest at the Pharisee's dinner party makes a remark about a meal in the kingdom of God. The guest's comment may have been triggered by the mention of the Resurrection in verse 14. Isaiah 25:6 records a prophecy concerning a feast in the age to come. The rabbis taught that the Messianic Era would be ushered in by a great feast to which the patriarchs, prophets, and heroes would come, but from which the Gentiles would be excluded.

Luke 14:16-17. Jesus uses the guest's comment as the context for a parable. Customarily, persons would have received two invitations to a dinner party. In response to the first one, guests would indicate their intention to attend. A second invitation was issued when the meal was ready. Guests who indicated that they would attend and then failed to show up when the second invitation was given were considered very rude.

Luke 14:18-20. As is often the case with oral stories, three examples are given. The excuses offered are certainly not legitimate emergencies (though marriage did exempt a man from military service for one year according to Deuteronomy 24:5). The invitation to enter into the kingdom of God is therefore rejected by persons who are making the everyday business of life their top priority.

Luke 14:21-22. The host of the party becomes angry and directs his slave to invite persons who were not on the original guest list. Note that this generic list—the poor, the crippled, the blind, and the lame—is the same list (though in different order) that Jesus had commended to his Pharisee host in verse 13. These persons may be understood as Jews who would not have been able to participate in the established religious practices.

Luke 14:23. The slave reports that the master's order has been executed, but room is still available. The reference to "roads and lanes" may be understood to mean that the slave is to invite Gentiles. "Compel" can also be translated as "urge."

Luke 14:24. Here Jesus switches to the first person, and uses the plural "you." He is clearly speaking to his audience at the banquet. Jesus is the host of the dinner; he will preside over the eschatological feast. We need to hear his warning to the Pharisees as a warning to us as well, lest we have our priorities confused and fail to respond to his gracious invitation.

INTERPRETING THE SCRIPTURE

God's Banquet

The call to come into the kingdom of God, as it appears in today's parable, is issued as an invitation to a meal. The sharing of a meal together is not only a customary act of hospitality and friendship in our own times but a familiar biblical theme. Abraham invited the three men who appeared to him by the oaks of Mamre to have a meal (Genesis 18:1-8). The Passover seder is a central meal in Jewish tradition (Exodus 12). God acted as the host of the Hebrew people by feeding them manna in the wilderness (Exodus 16). Jesus acted as the host at the feeding of the multitude, the only miracle recorded in all four Gospels. He is again the host at the Passover meal during which the Lord's Supper is instituted (Matthew 26:17-29; Mark 14:12-25; Luke 22:7-38; and John 13:1-38). After his resurrection, Jesus eats with his disciples (Luke 24:30; 42-43; and John 21:12-14). The church continues the tradition of gathering to break bread together (Acts 2:42, 46).

This natural act of eating with friends takes on the symbolic meaning of a heavenly banquet. In addition to the parable in Luke 14:15-24, we find references to heavenly feasts in Matthew 22:1-14; 25:10; Luke 12:35-38; Revelation 19:9; and Isaiah 25:6-10. The church, particularly as it gathers around the table to celebrate the Lord's Supper, provides us with a foretaste of the promised heavenly banquet.

God invites all of us to come and share in the heavenly banquet. Invitations have gone out and continue to be issued. Some persons respond with joy to such an invitation. Ideally, children who are born into Christian families are baptized in the church and nurtured by a loving family, a warm church, and a helpful society. Such persons grow up happy and well adjusted, never having known what it means to be apart from Christ. They know they have an invitation to the banquet and make their preparations for this big event their first priority. In my experience, however, that kind of person is extremely rare.

Refusing the Invitation

More often, persons misplace or forget about their invitations, at least for a time.

Even those who grow up with the tenderest nurturing usually rebel and have to be brought back to the fold. I doubt if the "prodigal" really intended to be a bad person when he asked for his inheritance (Luke 15:12). He surely did not say, "Dad, let me have what's coming to me so I can go waste it in riotous living." More than likely he thought, "I've got to get out of this suffocating environment and find the real me. I have to taste life and amount to something!" But when he did indeed come to himself (Luke 15:17), he had to come back, embarrassed and chagrined. Even if children don't rebel against their parents, some fire-breathing preacher may scare them into thinking they aren't really saved, or a secular philosophy will lead them astray, or the sensual world will tempt them into its byways, and they will have to undergo a dramatic turnaround (that is what conversion means) in order to get back. Many persons insist on going out "on their own," failing to see that, as one poet/theologian once said, "The one principle of hell is 'I am my own!'"

Other persons, like Paul before his Damascus road experience, dismiss the invitation. In fact, they are not even headed in the direction of the banquet hall. They are so sure that what they are doing is right, that they are not easily convinced to make a change. Paul accepted the invitation only after he had been knocked down in the road, blinded, and utterly humbled by the risen Christ. Then he was able to do a complete "one-eighty," for such a total change of direction is what conversion is all about. Many of us, like Paul, have to be "compelled" to come.

Let me share two other conversion experiences of persons who were "compelled" to come. One is that of C. S. Lewis, the British atheist who became an "apostle to the skeptics." In his autobiography, *Surprised by Joy*, Lewis describes his conversion in the very language of our parable for this week:

You must picture me alone in that room in Magdalen, night after night, feeling, whenever my mind lifted even for a second from my work, the steady, unrelenting approach of Him whom I so earnestly desired not to meet. That which I greatly feared had at last come upon me. In the Trinity Term of 1929 I gave in, and admitted that God was God, and knelt and prayed: perhaps, that night, the most dejected and reluctant convert in all England. I did not see then what is now the most shining and obvious thing; the Divine humility which will accept a convert even on such terms. The Prodigal Son at least walked home on his own feet. But who can duly adore that Love which will open the high gates to a prodigal who is brought in kicking, struggling, resentful, and darting his eyes in every direction for a chance of escape? The words *compelle intrare,* compel them to come in, have been so abused by wicked men that we shudder at them; but, properly understood, they plumb the depth of the Divine mercy. The hardness of God is kinder than the softness of men, and His compulsion is our liberation.

The other conversion experience was my own call to the ministry. Unlike Lewis, I grew up in the church; indeed I am a fifth-generation clergyman on my father's side (with two more on my mother's side). I was burdened under a heavy pyramid of religious ancestors, the point of which seemed to come right down on the top of my head. I tried as hard as possible to get away from God. Though I never became a theoretical atheist (those are very rare), I was certainly a practicing atheist, that is, one who lived as far apart from God as possible (there are a lot of those around). I tried to get into medicine, law, architecture, writing, cartooning, music, radio, teaching, and a good many other careers that would remove me further from the church. Yet, here I am, a professional Christian pastor for more than forty years.

What happened to change me? I do not know. I once asked my father, a hard-nosed Calvinist, "How do you know when you are called into the ministry?" "Try as hard as you can to get into something else," he counseled, "and if you still end up in the ministry you will know you were called." Of course he was being facetious, but in many ways that was right. God would not let me do anything else. One day, as distinctly as if it were a voice (though it was not), I heard God say, "The only place you will be able to practice all those talents is in the church; what do you think I gave them to you for? Don't think of that pyramid as pointing down on top of your head; turn it over, and stand on it as a foundation." And so I went, kicking and screaming. I have never liked clergy, and I hate being one; I truly believe that what the world needs is not more professional Christians but more Christian pro-fessionals (such as Christian teachers or doctors). I wish I could be a layman. But here I am, and though I don't like it, I am glad I'm doing it.

We have all kinds of reasons as to why we don't plan to come to the banquet. Some of us accept the invitation only to find that we have what appears at the time to be a more pressing commitment. Business, family relationships, recreation, and other interests push our interest in the heavenly banquet to the bottom of our list of priorities. God wants us to be present—and will urge us to come. But only we can make the final decision. God is inviting us to dinner. The invitation was issued to us through Jesus Christ. What will your response be?

SHARING THE SCRIPTURE

PREPARING TO TEACH

Read Luke 14:1-24 and think about it before you consult the commentaries or my suggestions. You may also want to check some of the scripture references concerning biblical meals, as discussed under the "God's Banquet" section of "Interpreting the Scripture."

Think about the invitation God has issued to you. How have you responded? Was your response immediate, or did you have to be compelled to come? You may want to write about your response in your spiritual journal.

Decide whether you will suggest the idea of a covered dish supper that will include persons who would not normally attend such a function (homeless individuals or families, mobile residents of a nearby nursing home, clients who live in a home for the mentally handicapped, and so on). If so, think how you may want to do this activity.

If you plan to use a closing hymn, have hymnals available. The suggested hymn, "Come, Sinners, to the Gospel Feast," is based on today's parable. It is found in *The United Methodist Hymnal* on pages 339 and 616.

LEADING THE CLASS

Introduction

Ask class members to discuss this question: **What are the requirements for membership in the** (*use the name of an organization—or perhaps several organizations—in your community to which at least some of the class members belong*)? Include any ongoing commitments you must fulfill to remain a member in good standing. You may want to list their answers on a chalkboard or newsprint.

Then ask: **What are the requirements for admission into our congregation?** Again, include any ongoing commitments you must fulfill to remain a member in good standing. Be sure that the class notes any unwritten expectations, such as a weekly contribution or certain dress code.

Finally ask: **What are the requirements for admission into the kingdom of God?** The answer can be summed up in words such as these: If you acknowledge yourself to be a sinner and trust in Jesus Christ as your Savior, you have the only admission ticket you need.

Introduce today's main question by stating that we will be discussing the parable of the great feast, as recorded in Luke 14:15-24. That parable calls us to ask: **Are we invited to the banquet? The answer to that question is a resounding yes! Will we attend? God urges us to come, but we must make the decision for ourselves. Who else will be there? The answer to this question may surprise us?**

Dinner with a Pharisee

Luke 14:1-12 is not included in the printed portion of your scripture lesson. However, this background information may be very helpful in setting forth the context of Jesus' parable. Help the class to see how this actual dinner that Jesus attends at the home of a Pharisee provides the setting for yet another statement of the amazing upside down theology of Christ's Gospel: All who exalt themselves will be humbled, and those who humble themselves will be exalted.

Note that Jesus was being closely watched (verse 1) by some members of the religious establishment, and that he deliberately allowed them to catch him in an act of mercy. Also point out that Jesus gives some directions for social behavior that Miss Manners would surely approve of in our day: don't seek a seat of honor (Luke 14:7-10), and don't give a dinner to impress people in the hope that your invitation will be reciprocated (Luke 14:11-14).

The information found under "Understanding the Scripture" will help you present this background material.

The Invitation and the Excuses

Choose someone to read aloud Luke 14:15-20.

Use the information under "Understanding the Scripture" to familiarize the class with the custom of issuing two invitations.

Have the class look at this situation from the perspective of the guests. Discuss the following questions or include this kind of information in a lecture.

(1) **The guests had been invited to a posh party. What kinds of excuses did they give for their failure to attend? Do you think these excuses are reasonable? Why or why not?**

(2) **What does the failure of the guests to attend after they have already accepted the invitation say about their priorities?**

(3) **If you had been invited, what would your response have been? What excuses might you have used?**

Now ask the class to consider this situation from the perspective of the host.

(1) **What kinds of preparations would a host have to make in order to throw a great dinner to which many persons were invited?** (Class members may want to think of this dinner in terms of a major celebration, such as a wedding reception, anniversary party, or retirement banquet.) You may want to list their ideas on a chalkboard or newsprint.

(2) **If you had been the host, how would you have felt as you anticipated such a party?**

(3) **If you had been the host, how would you have felt when your servant returned to say that many of your invited guests had declined the invitation at the last minute?**

Close this segment by asking the class to think about this party in terms of a heavenly banquet to which God has invited us. Discuss these questions:

(1) **Why might some persons not truly believe that they are invited to attend the banquet?** (Note that many Christians really do not believe that they are invited because they have been taught from birth to believe that God's invitation is the same as earthly invitations: If you are worthy, you may come. Help class members see that they are all on the guest list.)

(2) **We have seen the three excuses given by the guests in the story. What excuses have you heard people give?** (You may want to make this question very concrete by asking: What keeps Christians from regular participation in the life of the church?)

(3) **Why don't modern believers live out their Christianity with more commitment?**

Compelling Others to Come In

Read aloud Luke 14:21-24.

Help class members identify the persons involved. The guests who were initially invited had likely been part of the religious establishment. The guests who were brought in from the nearby streets—"the poor, the crippled, the blind, and the lame"—would have been Jewish persons who because of their physical or economic condition would not have participated in the religious life at the temple. Note that these were the same persons Jesus told his Pharisee host should have been included in the guest list for the party to which Jesus was invited. The persons in the "roads" would have been the Gentiles.

Ask the class: **Do you think the host's attempt to fill up the table was appropriate? Why or why not?**

Note that the word translated as "compel" can also be translated as "urge." For many persons, the word compel is very strong, especially given the fact that we have the free will to accept or reject God's invitation, though of course God truly wants us to attend.

Ask the class: **Does Jesus really compel people to come in?** If you have time you may want to read Mark 1:16-20 and ask: What charisma did Jesus possess that caused those whom he invited to drop everything and follow him?

Discuss this idea with the class, either as a whole or in teams:

(1) **Is there a message in today's parable for us concerning evangelism?**

(2) **To whom should we be taking the invitation of the gospel?**

(3) **How can we do that?**

You may want to close the session by singing a hymn of invitation, such as "Come, Sinners, to the Gospel Feast."

HELPING CLASS MEMBERS ACT

Challenge class members to take one step to deepen their own commitment to Christ this week. This commitment may take the form of a regular spiritual discipline, such as prayer or Bible study, that some individuals may have found excuses to avoid. Or it may take the form of service to someone else.

Encourage students to act as the servant in this week's parable by extending the invitation to the banquet to someone else. Challenge each one to invite a guest to Sunday school next week.

The class may want to plan a party, perhaps a covered dish supper. If there is a nursing home, shelter, or other social services type agency near the church, try to include on your guest list those persons who would not normally attend such a function. Some class members may need to be available to provide transportation.

Encourage class members to call on several homebound members of the church and their caretakers, especially those who formerly attended this class. Have the students remind those whom they visit that they are invited into the kingdom of God. These persons may need to hear that message, particularly if their physical condi- tions have prevented them from worshiping with the church for an extended period of time.

PLANNING FOR NEXT SUNDAY

Next week is Easter Sunday. Suggest that your class prepare for the lesson by thinking of a time in their lives when they have experienced the living Lord. You might give them each a card with "Emmaus Walk" written on one side. On the other you could write: When have you been especially aware that Jesus was walking with you? Ask students to recall specific instances and write about them in their spiritual journals. Also ask them to be prepared to share one experience with the rest of the class next Sunday. Encourage them to read Luke 24:1-36, especially verses 13-27.

THE LIVING LORD!

PREVIEWING THE LESSON

Lesson Scripture: Luke 24:13-27
Background Scripture: Luke 24:1-36
Key Verse: Luke 24:27

Focus of the lesson:
the encounter with the living Lord on the road to Emmaus

Main question(s) of the lesson:
(1) Is Jesus really alive and in our midst?
(2) If our answer is no, could it be that Jesus is here, but that we do not recognize him?
(3) If our answer is yes, do we believe that Jesus is walking right beside us?

This lesson will enable adult learners to:
(1) appreciate the life-changing effect the Emmaus road experience had on the disciples
(2) participate in the excitement of Cleopas and his companion as they recognized that the living Lord had journeyed with them
(3) respond by recognizing the importance of the Scripture in their own lives and sharing it with others.

Today's lesson may be outlined as follows:
(1) Introduction
(2) The Unrecognized Christ (Luke 24:13-17)
(3) The Witness (Luke 24:18-24)
(4) The Christ Revealed (Luke 24:25-27)

FOCUSING ON THE MAIN QUESTION

I have a friend who is an artist in wood. He was born in the Appalachian Mountains in 1915 and has spent his life carving the stories of the New Testament out of various hardwoods. All of his characters are depicted in turn-of-the-century mountain dress. I once asked him why, if he were not going to use the dress of Bible times, he did not carve his figures wearing contemporary clothing. "Because," he said, "what's in style today is a fad, but the old mountaineer style belongs to a period of history." He has attempted to carve the life of Christ in the midst of scenes from his own boyhood.

My friend has done one carving called "Emmaus Walk." I wish I could show you this image that is carved in a very hard, blonde, South American wood. There are two men hiking down a mountain slope, one with a feed sack over his shoulder, the other carrying a basket of apples. An old hound is walking beside them. They are passing by a mountain laurel bush, which is in bloom. Behind them comes Jesus, dressed in an old circuit rider's three-quarter length coat. One of the men has just heard a footfall and is starting to turn. From there on we know the story. These two will not recognize Jesus on the road, not even when he explains the Scriptures, but only later in the day in the breaking of the bread.

My friend has not only caught a glimpse of the living Lord but has been able to recreate him in a three-dimensional image that enables others to see him too. **Is Jesus really alive and in our midst?** If our answer is "no," could it be that Jesus is here, but that our eyes, like those of the disciples on the road to Emmaus, have been "kept from recognizing him"? **If we do believe that Jesus is alive, are we living our lives as if he is walking right beside us on the road to Emmaus or Dallas or Nashville or wherever we call home?** These are the questions we will consider during this week's lesson.

READING THE SCRIPTURE

NRSV
Luke 24:13-27

13 Now on that same day two of them were going to a village called Emmaus, about seven miles from Jerusalem, [14]and talking with each other about all these things that had happened. [15]While they were talking and discussing, Jesus himself came near and went with them, [16]but their eyes were kept from recognizing him. [17]And he said to them, "What are you discussing with each other while you walk along?" They stood still, looking sad. [18]Then one of them, whose name was Cleopas, answered him, "Are you the only stranger in Jerusalem who does not know the things that have taken place there in these days?" [19]He asked them, "What things?" They replied, "The things about Jesus of Nazareth, who was a prophet mighty in deed and word before God and all the people, [20]and how our chief priests and leaders handed him over to be condemned to death and crucified him. [21]But we had hoped that he was the one to redeem Israel. Yes, and besides all this, it is now the third day since these things took place. [22]Moreover, some women of

NIV
Luke 24:13-27

[13]Now that same day two of them were going to a village called Emmaus, about seven miles from Jerusalem. [14]They were talking with each other about everything that had happened. [15]As they talked and discussed these things with each other, Jesus himself came up and walked along with them; [16]but they were kept from recognizing him.

[17]He asked them, "What are you discussing together as you walk along?"

They stood still, their faces downcast. [18]One of them, named Cleopas, asked him, "Are you only a visitor to Jerusalem and do not know the things that have happened there in these days?"

[19]"What things?" he asked.

"About Jesus of Nazareth," they replied. "He was a prophet, powerful in word and deed before God and all the people. [20]The chief priests and our rulers handed him over to be sentenced to death, and they crucified him; [21]but we had hoped that he was the one who was going to redeem Israel. And what is more, it is the third day since all this took place. [22]In our group astounded us. They were at the tomb early this morning, ²³and when they did not find his body there, they came back and told us that they had indeed seen a vision of angels who said that he was alive. ²⁴Some of those who were with us went to the tomb and found it just as the women had said; but they did not see him." ²⁵Then he said to them, "Oh, how foolish you are, and how slow of heart to believe all that the prophets have declared! ²⁶Was it not necessary that the Messiah should suffer these things and then enter into his glory?" ²⁷Then beginning with Moses and all the prophets, he interpreted to them the things about himself in all the scriptures.

addition, some of our women amazed us. They went to the tomb early this morning ²³but didn't find his body. They came and told us that they had seen a vision of angels, who said he was alive. ²⁴Then some of our companions went to the tomb and found it just as the women had said, but him they did not see."

²⁵He said to them, "How foolish you are, and how slow of heart to believe all that the prophets have spoken! ²⁶Did not the Christ have to suffer these things and then enter his glory?" ²⁷And beginning with Moses and all the Prophets, he explained to them what was said in all the Scriptures concerning himself.

Key Verse

Key Ve

UNDERSTANDING THE SCRIPTURE

Luke 24:1-7. The best news in all of history is recorded in these verses! Luke 23 ends with the grieving women preparing spices for Jesus' burial, and then interrupting their work for the sabbath rest. They go "on the first day of the week," which would have been Sunday. When they arrive, night is turning to day, darkness is giving way to light. The women are startled by "two men in dazzling clothes," which may be compared to the "two men in white robes" who appear at the time of Jesus' ascension in Acts 1:10. The question of the two men, "Why do you look for the living among the dead?" is perhaps a mild rebuke, for Jesus is not to be found in a graveyard. These two men remind the women of Jesus' prophetic words about his death and resurrection.

Luke 24:8-12. The women who are named in verse 10 act as evangelists, telling the good news to the eleven male apostles. According to verse 11, the apostles thought the women were making the story up. Verse 12, which concerns Peter's visit to the tomb, is omitted from some ancient manuscripts.

Luke 24:13-14. These verses describe the walk to Emmaus. There seems to be an allusion to this same event in Mark 16:12-13. This walk occurs on what we now call Easter Sunday. The persons in this story are seven miles outside Jerusalem. Although scholars disagree as to exactly where they would have been, four villages are considered possibilities. The two walkers seemed to live together (see verse 29); possibly they were husband and wife. No mention is made of the reason for their trip to Emmaus, or exactly what they were discussing.

Luke 24:15-17. Jesus joins the two. They know that someone is with them, though they do not perceive that their new companion is their resurrected Lord. Apparently these two dejected persons have been spiritually blinded, perhaps for some purpose that is not explained here. There are several other recorded instances of people not recognizing the risen Christ (see John 20:14; 21:4; and Acts 9:5). Could his resurrected body have been materially different (see Mark 16:12)?

Luke 24:18. One of the two disciples

was named Cleopas. Apparently the events surrounding the crucifixion and resurrection of Jesus were big news, since the two believe that even a visitor to Jerusalem should have heard of it.

Luke 24:19-20. This is a little sermon very much like the apostolic preaching in the book of Acts (see Peter's message in Acts 2:22-23). It is not the Jewish people or the Romans who are accused of crucifying Jesus, but the religious leaders.

Luke 24:21-24. Cleopas expresses the disappointment that all the disciples must have felt; they had indeed hoped that Jesus was the one who would restore Israel. He gives Jesus the full story, noting the women's story. This point seems ironic in view of the fact that the two walkers do not recognize Jesus.

Luke 24:25-26. Jesus begins to reveal himself, calling his two companions foolish for not believing the message of the prophets. He reminds them that what has happened is in accord with the prophecies regarding the suffering messiah.

Luke 24:27. This verse, which speaks of Jesus' teaching ministry to these two disciples, raises questions for us: Why did the two not recognize Jesus when they obviously were excited by his preaching (verse 32)? What purpose could Jesus have had in keeping his identity secret?

Luke 24:28-29. Jesus lets the two disciples take the initiative leading to further revelation of himself. Putting up strangers for the night was a common act of hospitality.

Luke 24:30. Notice the four action verbs: took, blessed, broke, and gave. They are to be found also at the feeding of the multitude (Matthew 14:19; 15:36; Mark 6:41; 8:6; Luke 9:16) and at the Last Supper (Matthew 26:26; Mark 14:22; Luke 22:19; 1 Corinthians 11:23-26). Such repetition is an indication of their importance, and we will need to look at this, especially in the light of verse 35. These verbs are central acts, both in Holy Communion and in life itself. Furthermore, in Luke 22:16, 18 (describing the Lord's Supper) Jesus said that he would not eat or drink with his disciples again until the coming of the Kingdom. His action of eating with them indicates that the Kingdom has indeed come.

Luke 24:31-32. As a result of this fourfold action (taking, blessing, breaking, and giving), the two disciples recognize Jesus. When they do, he disappears from sight. In retrospect, they recall how excited they were by his teaching.

Luke 24:33-36. The two disciples return immediately to Jerusalem to report what has happened.

INTERPRETING THE SCRIPTURE

On the Road to Emmaus

Imagine yourself on the road to Emmaus, walking with Cleopas and his unnamed companion. The three of you are down, really down. You had been devoted followers of this man Jesus, the one you had expected to restore Israel. But now he's dead, and so are your hopes for the salvation you had anticipated—or so you think.

A stranger seemingly arrives from nowhere and joins your party. He notices your sadness and asks what's wrong. You can't believe such a question! Where has this fellow been? All of Jerusalem seems to be talking about Jesus' death. To be polite, you tell him how your own religious leaders condemned him to crucifixion. You even explain that something mysterious seems to be going on, for women who were also disciples of this man Jesus had visited his tomb. His body was gone! Incredibly, angels appeared unto them and said that Jesus was alive.

Suddenly, this stranger is calling you to task for your failure to heed the prophets. He teaches you great spiritual truths about the Messiah, going all the way back to the books attributed by tradition to Moses, Genesis through Deuteronomy.

He prepares to depart but you urge him to stay. Not until he breaks bread at your table, though, do you realize that this man, whose teaching excited you is Jesus. You have seen the Lord. He is alive!

Hurriedly, you set off to walk the seven miles to Jerusalem. You can hardly wait to tell the eleven and the others who are with them. When you arrive, you learn that Simon Peter has also seen the Lord. Excitement seems to fill every square inch of the room. There can be no mistake: The Lord is risen indeed!

We may find it difficult to imagine that such an experience or conversation could have ever taken place. For many of us, Bible characters walked with their feet not quite touching the ground. We tend to think of them as unreal folk, living in "Bible times," who said "thee" and "thou" to one another, and were constantly having "religious experiences." Yet, that is not the case. They had real conversations, mourned the loss of a loved one, were disappointed that their plans had not materialized as they had hoped they would, developed blisters on their feet, had trouble discerning the meaning of events, and could be spiritually short-sighted—just like us. Such insight gives us hope: if these disciples could meet the living Lord, so can we.

A Personal Journey to Emmaus

Our meetings can take place anywhere. Here are two Emmaus experiences from my own life that I offer as a witness to the powerful presence of God. God is with us even when we are not expecting God to be there. God is also present even when we think we do not want God to be with us.

The first took place at a New Year's Eve watch night service. It was the custom for members of our church to spend the last hour of the old year in prayer. There were often parties that night, but many people slipped away from them to greet the New Year in a more sober way. (There was usually somebody attending church in a tuxedo or evening dress.) On this particular night, I was one of the persons responsible for preparing the service. We had a candle on the Lord's Table, with a brazier in front of it, and the worshipers were invited, one at a time, to come to the Table with a slip of paper. On these papers they had written some goal they had in life, such as a character flaw they would like to correct, or an end they would like to achieve. Each parishioner would burn the paper in the flame and drop the ashes in the brazier, offering them to God, not as New Year's resolutions, but as acts of prayer in the sense of casting our burdens on the Lord.

One of my jobs, along with some other college students, was to prepare and read appropriate scripture verses while the people came forward. I had worked hard on my choice of verses because I was personally very conscious of the passing of time and struggling with my own career decision. As a rebellious youth, I felt somehow that God was far from me, not really interested in me and my problems. I was having thoughts like these: "What could the death of a man nearly two thousand years ago have to do with my life today? Do I really want to go to a heaven where people sit around bored, playing the harp all the time?" (Such questions seem silly to me now, but I was serious in asking them.)

As it happened, in my search for scripture passages, I discovered Psalm 90. This psalm struck me as particularly appropriate for a New Year's Eve service. It speaks about the transitory nature and apparent futility of human life, compared to God's eternity. I was particularly attracted to verse 4: "For a thousand years in your sight are like yesterday when it is past, or like a watch in the night."

As I read those words, I felt a loving Presence surrounding me. In the deepest places of my heart, I heard the Presence say something like this: "My child, you are thinking human thoughts, not the thoughts of God. Do you think I am limited to time as you are limited? I am the One who was, and is, and is to come. I did not merely live two thousand years ago; I am the same, yesterday, and today, and forever. I am the Author of your story, and not limited as a character in my book. I am with you today. And do you think that in my heaven eternity is endless boredom; no, it is endless delight. When my trumpet sounds, time shall be no more, and you will understand something of my greatness." My understanding of life has not been the same since I began to think on those things. I like to think it has been an ever increasing discovery of the magnitude of God. I hope it never ceases to expand.

The other experience took place not too long ago, when my wife was undergoing neurosurgery. I had no certainty that she would survive the operation, or that, if she lived, she would be able to function normally. I don't mean this to be a suspense story, so I will tell you in advance that she is fine today; if you did not know her as well as I do, you would never guess that she had once had a stroke. I was in the surgery waiting area, surrounded by well-meaning friends and family, but they weren't helping much; there isn't really anything anybody can say at such a time, but I was grateful that they were there. However, there was another Presence. It suddenly came over me at a level too deep for words, assuring me that everything was going to be all right (see Romans 8:26). I still did not know if my wife would live or die; I only knew that whatever happened, all would be well. So deep was that certainty, that I cannot put it into words without giving the impression that I didn't care what happened next, but somehow I knew that "God's in His heaven—/All's right with the world!"

My own experiences with God cause me to answer our main question with a resounding yes! Jesus is alive and in our midst. I believe this to be true, and the longer I live, the more firmly I believe that the Author of our story can dip into its pages at any point and be a part of our lives. God lives in eternity, and therefore has infinite "time" to spend with each one of us. Indeed, God is always walking with us, keeping our hearts beating, and guiding our steps. Sometimes, though, like the two Emmaus disciples, we are unaware of that Presence. We're not living as if the risen Lord is walking beside us as we journey along our own road to Emmaus.

SHARING THE SCRIPTURE

PREPARING TO TEACH

During this Holy Week, spend as much time as possible preparing your heart for the celebration of the Resurrection. Consider how you would have felt had you been Cleopas and his companion. Imagine the sorrow over losing your friend, the disappointment at what you perceive to be a failed promise, and the feelings of confusion you must have experienced. Then think about how it must have felt to have seen and talked with the risen Lord on the road to Emmaus. When have you walked with him on your own Emmaus road? You may want to record your thoughts in your spiritual journal.

If you can use a tape or CD player in your teaching area, you may want to secure a copy of Handel's *Messiah*. The

"Hallelujah" chorus could be a grand finale for today's class, or you may prefer a more meditative selection, "I Know That My Redeemer Liveth."

Be sure to read all of the background scripture and material in this lesson. The experience on the Emmaus road is only recorded in Luke. You may want to check Mark 16:12-13, which alludes to this experience. Note the difference between Mark 16:13 and Luke 24:34.

As you prepare your lesson, be sure to focus on the Emmaus road experience itself, which is recorded in our printed scripture found in Luke 24:13-27. A suggestion is provided for including the Easter story, which is included in today's background scripture. Write questions for "The Witness" activity on a chalkboard or newsprint.

Decide whether you will tell your own story for "The Christ Revealed" segment of the lesson or whether you will read or retell one of mine found under "A Personal Journey to Emmaus" under "Interpreting the Scripture."

LEADING THE CLASS

Introduction

If you will be using music from Handel's *Messiah* to close the class, have the tape or CD player set up before class. Play other selections from the Easter portion as background music while the class is gathering in order to set the atmosphere for this glorious day.

Begin today's session by reading Luke's account of the Easter story, found in Luke 24:1-12. Before you begin to read, ask class members to close their eyes and try to visualize the scene. Tell them to concentrate on what they might have seen, heard, smelled, tasted, or touched. Also ask them to think about the emotions they would have experienced. After reading, spend a few moments discussing their responses.

Point out to the class that while the first Easter morning can never again be experienced, all Christians have opportunities to discover the presence of the living Lord in their own lives. Introduce today's main questions: **Is Jesus really alive and in our midst? If our answer is no, could it be that Jesus is here, but that we do not recognize him? If our answer is yes, do we believe that Jesus is walking right beside us?**

The Unrecognized Christ

Direct students' attention to Luke 24:13-17. Ask each one to read this passage silently.

Now read aloud the first two paragraphs entitled "On the Road to Emmaus" under "Interpreting the Scripture." Discuss these questions, reminding students that they are traveling with Cleopas and his companion:

(1) **How are you feeling?** (Students will likely mention grief, disappointment, and confusion. Help them also see that the disciples may have also been angry that this man Jesus did not redeem Israel. They may have felt duped that they had spent their time following someone who seems to be an impostor. They also might have been afraid that they too might be rounded up and crucified.)

(2) **What questions are you asking?** (Some questions may be objective, regarding the events and their meaning. Others may focus on a sense of guilt: What could I have done to prevent this tragedy? Still others may focus on the future: What will we do now that Jesus is dead?)

Note that in verse 15, Jesus comes and joins the walkers but no one recognizes him. We have no solid evidence as to why this is so. Spend a few moments asking the class to suggest reasons why they think Jesus would have been unrecognized. The information on Luke 24:15-17 found under "Understanding the Scripture" may be helpful. If time permits, point out other accounts of the risen Lord not being recognized.

The Witness

Have a volunteer read aloud Luke 24:18-24.

Ask the class to list all the information that Cleopas gave to Jesus. Record these answers on a chalkboard or newsprint. You may want to compare Cleopas' witness to that of Peter in Acts 2:22-24. If your class does not enjoy discussion, be sure to include the following in a lecture:

- Jesus was a prophet.
- Jesus acted and spoke powerfully before God and the people.
- The religious leaders (not the Jewish people as a whole) were responsible for turning Jesus over to the Roman authorities to be crucified.
- Jesus' followers had reason to believe that he would set Israel free.
- The crucifixion took place three days ago.
- Some women had visited Jesus' tomb and they did not see his body. A vision of angels told them that Jesus was alive.
- The report of the empty tomb was verified by some other members of the group.

Point out that the word "apostle" means "one who is sent" in Greek. Apostles of Christ are sent with the message of his resurrection. Surely Cleopas and his companion are apostles in this sense, though they are not officially part of the twelve.

Note that these verses show Cleopas and his companion openly telling the story of Jesus to a stranger. Surely such candor could have been dangerous. Ask class members to talk with a partner or small team about these questions that you may want to write on a chalkboard or newsprint in advance:

(1) Are we willing to tell the good news of Jesus to strangers?
(2) If not, why do we lack the enthusiasm to run to tell others? Do we take the good news for granted, or have we forgotten how exciting it is?
(3) Do we hesitate because we think others may be skeptical of a supernatural story, or do we not believe in the resurrection ourselves?
(4) In what ways do other persons see Christ in us?

The Christ Revealed

Choose a student to read Luke 24:25-27 in which Christ reveals his identity.

Tell a story from your own life about such a time when Christ was present, but you did not perceive who he was. Or, you may want to read or retell one or both of my stories, found under the heading "A Personal Journey to Emmaus" under "Interpreting the Scripture."

Now use the following meditation exercise to encourage students to consider the presence of Christ in their own lives, a presence that is sometimes unrecognized. Direct them to sit comfortably with their eyes closed in a meditative mood as you read the following statements. Be sure to pause for a few moments to allow time for reflection.

(1) Think of a time when you felt especially close to Christ. Picture the place where you were, trying to remember the sights and sounds and smells of the this place . . . . (pause)
(2) Think about why you felt Christ's presence so strongly. Perhaps you were facing an operation or mourning the loss of a loved one or celebrating the birth of a child. Try to recapture the emotions of the moment . . . . (pause)
(3) Think about how you experienced Christ. Did that presence manifest itself as some special feeling within your own body, or as a voice within your

heart, or through the words or actions of someone else? Try to recall how you knew that God was especially with you at that moment . . . . (pause)

(4) Think about Christ's living presence in your own life on this Easter morning. Imagine yourself talking with him. Think about what you would want to say and offer those words to Christ . . . . (pause)

To celebrate the presence of Christ in our lives, you may want to play the "Hallelujah" chorus from Handel's *Messiah* if it is appropriate to do so in your teaching area. If you want to keep a more meditative mood, play "I Know That My Redeemer Liveth."

HELPING CLASS MEMBERS ACT

Encourage the class to note the importance of the Scriptures in Luke 24:27. Encourage them to consider this week the importance of the Scriptures in their own lives. Ask them:

(1) **Do they find the Scriptures exciting?**
(2) **Do they feel they really know the Bible well?**
(3) **Do they read the Bible regularly?**
(4) **Do they study the Bible on their own as well as with the class?**
(5) **Do they share their love of the Scriptures with someone else?**

If the answer to any of these questions is no, challenge class members to take whatever steps are necessary to correct the situation.

Ask class members to think about persons with whom they need to share the good news of Christ's living presence. Challenge them to talk with at least one person this week.

Remind students that other persons see Jesus in us. Ask them to be especially mindful this week of the picture that others are getting. Are they finding someone who is willing to reach out to the stranger or one of the least of these? If students feel that other persons are getting a distorted view of Jesus through them, challenge them to begin to make whatever changes necessary so that, with God's help, they can conform more nearly to the image of Christ.

PLANNING FOR NEXT SUNDAY

Next week we will be discussing the nature of God. Tell the class to read the lesson in Luke 15:1-10, which includes two familiar stories, the lost sheep and the lost coin. Ask students to come prepared to answer these questions: What image comes to my mind when I think of God? How do I emotionally experience that image? In other words, do I find it frightening, loving, stern, forgiving, or what?

THE LOVING GOD

PREVIEWING THE LESSON

Lesson Scripture: Luke 15:1-10
Background Scripture: Luke 15:1-10
Key Verse: Luke 15:10

Focus of the lesson:
the joy that God experiences when the lost are found and sinners repent

Main question(s) of the lesson:
(1) What is God really like?

This lesson will enable adult learners to:
(1) perceive the diligence with which God seeks all persons
(2) experience the joy of God's love in their own lives
(3) respond by sharing God's love with someone else.

Today's lesson may be outlined as follows:
(1) Introduction
(2) Criticism of His Company (Luke 15:1-2)
(3) The Searching Shepherd (Luke 15:3-7)
(4) The Heedful Homemaker (Luke 15:8-10)

FOCUSING ON THE MAIN QUESTION

Once long ago a grackle flew into the badminton net in our backyard and became hopelessly entangled. When I tried to rescue him he fought so hard that it was difficult to keep from injuring him. This past winter, just before the first frost, when my wife brought in the plants from the front porch, a wren who had nested in one of them woke up to find himself trapped inside our house. It took me nearly fifteen minutes to catch him, during which time he flew at himself in the mirror a dozen times and bloodied his head

badly. I pleaded in soft tones, as though he could understand me, "Please relax little bird, I only mean you well." When I finally trapped him in a sheet, carried him out the garage door, and released him, he flew back into the house and I had to start all over again!

Just so does God pursue us—lost sheep, lost coins, lost children, and sparrows that fall—and just so do we flee from God in terror, thrashing about in a vain attempt to escape. We flee from the very things that make for our own peace.

Many of us, as children, learned to fear the God that we felt was being described to us by our parents, or the church, or the society we grew up in. As soon as we became old enough to manage our own affairs, we avoided God, like a lost sheep, or a trapped bird, fleeing from our only source of love and joy and peace.

What is God really like? That is our main question for today. Is God out to get us, as the terrified birds believed I was out to get them? Or does God seek us to deliver us from the snare of the fowler (Psalm 91:3)? In the stories from Luke that we will discuss today, Jesus makes it clear to us that if we, like Jonah, are running away from God, we ought to let God catch us. Within the fold of God we will find incomparable peace and joy. All of heaven will rejoice that we have come in, lost no more but safely snuggled in the loving arms of the Good Shepherd.

READING THE SCRIPTURE

NRSV

Luke 15:1-10

1 Now all the tax collectors and sinners were coming near to listen to him. ²And the Pharisees and the scribes were grumbling and saying, "This fellow welcomes sinners and eats with them."

3 So he told them this parable: ⁴"Which one of you, having a hundred sheep and losing one of them, does not leave the ninety-nine in the wilderness and go after the one that is lost until he finds it? ⁵When he has found it, he lays it on his shoulders and rejoices. ⁶And when he comes home, he calls together his friends and neighbors, saying to them, 'Rejoice with me, for I have found my sheep that was lost.' ⁷Just so, I tell you, there will be more joy in heaven over one sinner who repents than over ninety-nine righteous persons who need no repentance.

8 "Or what woman having ten silver coins, if she loses one of them, does not light a lamp, sweep the house, and search carefully until she finds it? ⁹When she has found it, she calls together her friends and neighbors, saying, 'Rejoice with me, for I have found the coin that I had lost.' ¹⁰Just so, I tell you, there is joy in the presence of the angels of God over one sinner who repents."

Key Verse

NIV

Luke 15:1-10

1 Now the tax collectors and "sinners" were all gathering around to hear him. ²But the Pharisees and the teachers of the law muttered, "This man welcomes sinners and eats with them."

³Then Jesus told them this parable: ⁴"Suppose one of you has a hundred sheep and loses one of them. Does he not leave the ninety-nine in the open country and go after the lost sheep until he finds it? ⁵And when he finds it, he joyfully puts it on his shoulders ⁶and goes home. Then he calls his friends and neighbors together and says, 'Rejoice with me; I have found my lost sheep.' ⁷I tell you that in the same way there will be more rejoicing in heaven over one sinner who repents than over ninety-nine righteous persons who do not need to repent.

⁸"Or suppose a woman has ten silver coins and loses one. Does she not light a lamp, sweep the house and search carefully until she finds it? ⁹And when she finds it, she calls her friends and neighbors together and says, 'Rejoice with me; I have found my lost coin.' ¹⁰In the same way, I tell you, there is rejoicing in the presence of the angels of God over one sinner who repents."

Key Verse

UNDERSTANDING THE SCRIPTURE

Luke 15:1-2. The Pharisees and scribes complain that Jesus associates with the wrong kind of folks. The four groups mentioned in these two verses may be described as follows:

Pharisees: The strictest of the Jewish parties (see Acts 26:5), the Pharisees carefully observed Jewish laws and rituals. Although the New Testament paints this group as being legalistic and hypocritical, modern research is challenging that portrait. One of their conflicts with Jesus is that he fellowships around the table with persons who are not ritually observant Jews.

Scribes: Copiers, and hence students, of the Law and other holy texts, the scribes were respected for their biblical knowledge.

Tax collectors: Considered as traitors who cheated their fellow Jews on behalf of the Romans and for the sake of lining their own pockets, tax collectors were excluded from the Jewish congregation.

Sinners: The word translated "sinners" has its roots in archery, meaning "to miss the mark." Obviously immoral persons, such as prostitutes, were sinners, but so too were persons who did not observe Jewish law. Sinners were also excluded from temple worship.

In response to the complaints from the Pharisees and the scribes, Jesus tells three stories in Luke 15. The parables of the sheep, coin, and lost son all concern the joy of finding that which was lost. For the early church, all three of these stories would have been a word of comfort to sinners in general, but particularly to the Gentiles, who would feel cut off from the house of Israel. Both the parable of the sheep and the coin contain a reference to joy in heaven (verses 7 and 10), which is the evangelist's way of telling us that God is one who truly cares about sinners and is

filled with joy whenever one repents. The heavenly celebration is as natural as the earthly party of friends and neighbors.

Luke 15:3. Jesus responds to his critics by telling the parable of the lost sheep. A similar parable is recorded in Matthew 18:12-14.

Luke 15:4. Although the image of the shepherd may be foreign to most modern Christians, it was well known in Jesus' day. In fact, shepherds are still seen in the Palestinian countryside. (For other images of God or Jesus as shepherd, see Psalm 23; John 10:1-18; Ezekiel 34:11-31; Jeremiah 23:1-4; and Zechariah 11:4-17.) A hundred sheep would be a rather large flock in Jesus' time, but not so large that the loss of one could be overlooked. The wilderness was a place of danger where wild animals could attack not only the sheep but also the shepherd. To venture into the wilderness in search of a stray could cost the shepherd his life. From an objective point of view, the shepherd acts foolishly by taking such a risk and by leaving behind the other sheep to search for one.

Luke 15:5. The picture of the shepherd carrying the sheep on his shoulders is linked to God's comforting presence (see Isaiah 40:11). Such an image shows the shepherd as tender and caring.

Luke 15:6. The shepherd is so overjoyed that he calls his friends to have a celebration. Note that the shepherd took the initiative to find the sheep ("I have found my sheep"); the animal did not just wander back home.

Luke 15:7. Numbers are not important here. The conversion of one sinner is cause for greater joy in heaven than the knowledge of ninety-nine other persons who are righteous. Of course the Pharisees and scribes needed to repent but, unlike the more obvious sinners, they did not know it.

Luke 15:8-10. In the parable of the lost coin God is depicted as a woman. (For other female images for God, see Isaiah 66:13; Psalm 131:2; and Matthew 23:37). This parable teaches the same lesson as the previous one, though the one who does the seeking is a female. Here an inanimate object is lost indoors.

Luke 15:8. The *drachma* was a Greek coin, worth about the same as the Roman denarius, about a day's pay for a laborer. (See our previous discussions about coinage, lesson 2, Matthew 18:24.) By today's standards it would have been worth over thirty dollars, a considerable sum for anyone to lose, but especially a peasant woman who may have been patiently saving for many months. Palestinian houses had few windows, so a lamp would surely be necessary for a thorough search. The act of sweeping indicates the intensity of God's longing for those who are lost.

Luke 15:9-10. Note the similarity between these verses and verses 6 and 7. The theme of joy and community celebration is important in both of these parables.

INTERPRETING THE SCRIPTURE

This week's lesson carries us into somewhat the same territory as lesson 5, the parable of the banquet guests who were "compelled" to come in. In our two parables for today, the lost sheep and the lost coin, God is depicted as one who searches with utmost diligence to find that which has been lost, and he rejoices when the lost is found. We will look first at this image of God from the point of view of the lost soul itself. Then we will consider how God joyfully searches for those who are lost.

The Hound of Heaven

One of the great classics of Victorian poetry is Francis Thompson's "The Hound of Heaven." By today's literary standards it is wordy and overblown, but it still has the capacity to move us with its vision of God pursuing the fleeing soul. In the spirit of Psalm 139:7-12 and the story of Jonah, it describes the human desire to run away from our very source of life and hope. As adolescents sometimes rebel against the family that nurtures and sustains them, so we rebel against God and think that if we could only "get away from the dogma" or

"avoid the straight-jacket of religion" we would be truly free and happy. Here are a few lines (of more than 180), from the beginning and end of this well-known poem:

I fled Him, down the nights and down the days;
  I fled Him, down the arches of the years;
I fled Him, down the labyrinthine ways
  Of my own mind; and in the midst of tears
I hid from Him. . . .
From those strong Feet that followed,
          followed after.
      But with unhurrying chase,
      And unperturbèd pace,
  Deliberate speed, majestic instancy,
      They beat—and a Voice beat
      More instant than the Feet—
"All things betray thee, who betrayest Me."
. . . .
      Halts by me that footfall:
      Is my gloom, after all,
  Shade of His hand, outstretched
          caressingly?
      "Ah, fondest, blindest, weakest,
      I am He whom thou seekest!
Thou dravest love from thee, who dravest Me."

Be we prodigal or elder brother (Luke 15:11-32), Mary or Martha (Luke 10:38-42), tax collector or Pharisee (Luke 18:9-14), we all are chased by the Hound. Sinners run away from God, who is the source of forgiveness, and the "righteous" run after God, only to be caught and convicted of pride.

Fleeing From God

God would not need to pursue us if we stayed within the fold. What is it that makes us flee from God? What causes us to believe that we will be better off in the wilderness?

The answer lies in the heart of our humanity, and we can trace it all the way back to the garden of Eden, where Adam was warned not to eat of the tree of the knowledge of good and evil (Genesis 2:15-17). The serpent tempted Eve by promising her that if she ate, she would know the difference between good and evil and be like God (Genesis 3:5). Whether we are a "terrible two" or a "troublesome teen" or a searching "thirtysomething," we all want to be our own god. We want to control our own destiny, to "do our own thing." Unlike the Little Engine in the classic story, who believed in salvation by huffing and puffing (like Jonathan L. Seagull and the Big Bad Wolf), I want to tell you the story about the little engine that *couldn't*. "I hate to be stuck here on these rails. Over those hills are all sorts of interesting places where I cannot go, because I am limited to this narrow path. I believe I will take out across the fields." So he did, and, of course, immediately his drivers became mired in the mud so that he could not move at all! His attempt to be free had led him to complete slavery. But when the wrecking crews had put him back on the tracks, he discovered true freedom, for there is an infinite variety of switches in God's railway, and no end to possible journeys.

The desire to be in charge of ourselves is perfectly natural from the human point of view. Indeed, the ability to make our own decisions and take responsibility for our actions is a sign of maturity. Yet, we must surrender to God in order to find perfect freedom. Here again we see how the upside down view of the world brings us into a harmonious relationship with God. When we put our whole selves at the disposal of God, we are free to venture into all the universe. In contrast, when we adhere to the principle that, "I am my own," we are confined by our own limited vision. The best thing to do, if you want to be truly free, is to be obedient to the Word, and let the Truth enfold you (John 8:31-32), or set your sails, and let the Wind fill them (John 3:8).

The Joyful Searcher

Is God really like a hound? Yes, insofar as a hound is one who stubbornly keeps on the scent and will not give up the chase. But the images of God in our two parables are even better. Imagine the shepherd, hot and tired from a day of following his sheep over all sorts of terrain. He is ready to call it day, settling his flock where they will spend the night. Ninety-seven, ninety-eight, ninety-nine. Where's the other sheep? he wonders. He counts again, but still comes up one short. The shepherd takes off into the wilderness, risking his own life to find this one lost sheep. If he waits until morning, it may be too late. Many wild animals would be thrilled to find a lamb chop dinner just waiting to be snatched. So the shepherd goes out and, like the hound, searches and searches until he finds this one sheep that is so valuable to him that he is willing to risk everything for it. He is overjoyed, just as you or I would be to find a lost pet. In fact, he is so happy that he throws a party for his friends. This news is too good to keep to himself. He must share it with others.

Now consider the second image, the diligent homemaker who searches for the lost coin. Here God is depicted as a woman, to whom the coin is as precious as the sheep to the shepherd. She scours the house from top to bottom, continuing her search until she finds that which was lost! And then, like the shepherd, she throws a party for her friends. She searches diligently, and she rejoices greatly!

I can picture the woman in the parable bustling around the house, putting up decorations, preparing refreshments, and sending out her children with the invitations. I can imagine the joyful chatter as the guests celebrate with one another over her good news. The picture in my mind is friends at a baby or bridal shower, telling old tales, maybe singing old favorites, and congratulating their neighbor on her good fortune. But the joy depicted by this party is nothing compared to the celebration that takes place in heaven whenever a prodigal comes home. They say that around the throne of God, the angels never cease to sing (Revelation 4:8). I don't know about you, but I'm looking forward with great anticipation to that choir. And I can't wait to see the kind of celebration that God throws for the beloved ones.

SHARING THE SCRIPTURE

PREPARING TO TEACH

Although Luke 15:1-10 is the complete scripture for today's lesson, I would suggest that you read all of chapter 15. Together, the parables of the lost sheep, the lost coin, and the prodigal son (also known as the waiting father) teach us that God lovingly seeks the lost and rejoices when they are found.

Consult a Bible dictionary to learn more about the types of persons discussed under "Understanding the Scripture": tax collectors, sinners, Pharisees, and scribes. Use this information to help set the context for the two parables of today's lesson.

If you plan to use "The Hound of Heaven," you may want to locate the entire poem. You will likely find it an anthology that includes English poetry of the Victorian (late 1800s) era.

To prepare yourself spiritually to teach this lesson, think about how you feel—really feel—about the fact that God does seek out not only the "respectable" people but those who are on the fringes of society.

According to these parables, those who are in the wilderness of life or have rolled between the cracks in the floor, are the very ones who God so lovingly seeks out. You may want to record your feelings in your spiritual journal.

If you want to have a picture of the Good Shepherd available, locate one during the week.

If you plan to ask class members to write their own parable, have paper and pencils on hand. If you want to have a "party," arrange for refreshments.

LEADING THE CLASS

Introduction

Remind the students that last week you asked them to prepare for this class by thinking about how they imagined God. Our main question for this week is: **What is God really like?**

Spend a few moments making a list of characteristics or attributes of God. Also ask the class to tell you how they emotionally perceive God. Is God loving, frightening, forgiving, tender, like a Santa Claus in the sky, or what?

At this point, you may want to read the excerpt from the poem "The Hound of Heaven" found under the "Interpreting the Scripture" portion. Point out that one image we have of God is as one who pursues us, seeking the lost until we are found.

Close this segment by telling the students that we will focus today on the image of the loving God who does seek us, as seen in two parables in Luke 15.

Criticism of His Company

Direct the class's attention to Luke 15:1-2.

Note the four groups mentioned: the tax collectors, sinners, Pharisees, and scribes. Ask the class: **What do you know about each of these groups?** Supplement their knowledge with information from "Understanding the Scripture" and any research you did.

Ask the class: **What seems to be the issue that scribes and Pharisees are raising?** (Jesus is eating with persons who do not follow the law of Moses.) If you have time, you may want to check several other citations concerning practices and table fellowship with persons whom the religious persons would find "unacceptable," such as: Matthew 9:10; Mark 2:15; Luke 11:38; and Luke 14:12.

Point out to the class that such concerns about table fellowship still exist within the church. Read the following anecdote to the class: I knew a congregation that had a meal at the church every Wednesday. At first, homeless people occasionally came and were fed leftovers. Little by little the number of the poor increased, and, as they did, the number of "paying customers" decreased, until there was only a small group of faithful table servers left, and a crowd of diners who smelled something between a saloon and a rest room. The pastor came in for considerable criticism, and eventually the meal was moved to another location some distance from the church.

Ask these questions:

(1) **Who were the scribes and Pharisees or the tax collectors and sinners in this situation?**
(2) **What would Jesus have done?**
(3) **Why do respectable Christians so often seem to turn aside from those persons who look or act differently from what we would expect?**
(4) **What are we called to do in order to represent the loving God to a lost world that is both physically and spiritually hungry?**

The Searching Shepherd

If you can find a picture illustrating the Good Shepherd, position it where everyone can see it as you read the parable from Luke 15:3-7.

Help the class to understand the risks the shepherd was taking by sharing information from "Understanding the Scripture" and any other research you have done.

Invite students to share their own stories, either with the class as whole or in small groups, of times when they lost something of value. Ask them to recount:

• **what was lost**
• **how they sought to find the lost item**
• **how they felt when the lost item was found.**

If you have access to some old hymnbooks, you may want to try to locate a song that was a favorite for men's quartets around the turn of the century entitled "The Ninety and Nine" by Ira Sankey. Perhaps you could arrange for a group to sing this, or you may want to read it aloud.

The Heedful Homemaker

Note that only Luke records this parable. Have someone read it aloud from Luke 15:8-10.

Students who think of God only in male terms may need some help in understanding that God is neither male nor female but encompasses traits that we associate with masculinity and femininity (see Genesis 1:27).

Point out that Jesus is teaching the same thing in this parable as he did in the previous one. Ask the class: **Why do you think Jesus told essentially the same parable twice?** (Answers will vary, but an important point is that Jesus wants as many different kinds of people as possible to hear this good news. Although we will not be studying the rest of Luke 15, the parable of the waiting father or prodigal son gives the same message a third time.)

Note that in both of today's parables there is a great sense of joy when the lost is found by the one who has been diligently seeking. C. S. Lewis once wrote, "Joy is the serious business of Heaven." You may want to speculate about the celebrations in heaven as a lost soul is found and is restored unto God. You may also want to think about the joy in heaven as loved ones are reunited in eternal life.

If the class enjoys creative activities, provide an opportunity for them to write their own parable of the one who diligently searches for something that is lost and rejoices when it is found. Remind class members that what they are doing here is exactly what Jesus did: sharing a message in words and images that are familiar to listeners. Some class members may want to target their parable to a specific individual (perhaps a friend or family member) and so will use an image that is dear to that person. Here are some ideas to spark imagination: a lost pet, a lost car, a lost piece of jewelry with great sentimental value, or a lost wallet. Provide paper and pencils for this activity. If time permits, invite a few volunteers to read what they have written.

If possible in your classroom setting, a fun way to conclude today's lesson would be to serve some light party refreshments, such as pastries. This act of celebration and eating together (especially if you do not normally do so) may help students remember the joy in heaven when a sinner repents.

HELPING CLASS MEMBERS ACT

If class members have written parables, encourage them to share the story with someone who needs to hear that God loves them and is diligently searching for them. Ask the students to invite these persons to attend Sunday school next week with them.

Suggest that students take a hard look at how they individually and collectively as a church treat persons who are the "tax collectors and sinners" in our day. Challenge them to think of at least one way to let such persons know that God loves them and that they are truly welcome in the fellowship of your church.

Challenge class members to think of how God views them. Too often we think of ourselves as the scribes and Pharisees—the good church folks. Suggest that students examine their own hearts this week and see what sin they need to repent of so that they might experience the joy of a fuller relationship with God.

PLANNING FOR NEXT SUNDAY

Remind the class that next week we will continue today's theme by dealing in depth with the image of the Good Shepherd as associated with Jesus. If there are any persons in your class who have firsthand knowledge of sheep or shepherding, you might ask them to be prepared to share some information with the group to give them a sense of what the image really means. Encourage class members who have access to Bible dictionaries or other references to look up "shepherd." Ask the entire class to read John 10:1-30, focusing especially on verses 1-18.

THE GOOD SHEPHERD

PREVIEWING THE LESSON

Lesson Scripture: John 10:1-18
Background Scripture: John 10:1-30
Key Verse: John 10:11

Focus of the lesson:
the characteristics of the Good Shepherd as seen in Jesus

Main question(s) of the lesson:
(1) What is God like?

This lesson will enable adult learners to:
(1) explore the image of the Good Shepherd
(2) relate to Jesus as the Good Shepherd of their own lives
(3) respond by acting as a shepherd for someone who is struggling.

Today's lesson may be outlined as follows:
(1) Introduction
(2) The Shepherd Who Knows Me (John 10:1-6)
(3) The Shepherd Who Intercedes for Me (John 10:7-10)
(4) The Shepherd Who Lays Down His Life for Me (John 10:11-18)

FOCUSING ON THE MAIN QUESTION

This week's lesson continues to address the question: **What is God like?** In today's scripture lesson from John 10, Jesus identifies himself as the Good Shepherd. He is the one who will risk all, even his life, for the sake of his sheep. He will guard and guide them, for he knows each one by name. He lovingly cares for his sheep. This image, which was so real and meaningful to Jesus' Palestinian audiences, surely describes what God is like. For many modern Christians, this image still holds tender associations that strengthen their relationship with God.

Unfortunately, the shepherd image does not speak to everyone—especially those of us who live in urban or suburban areas where the closest they get to sheep is a wool rug. Carl Burke, in his book *God Is for Real, Man!*, describes how the juveniles in the Erie County Jail in Buffalo had difficulty with some of the Bible images. These city kids had never seen a sheep, let alone a shepherd! Once, when a young man asked "Chaplain, what is God like?" he replied without much thought, "Like your father." The youngster retorted that if God was like his father, he didn't want to have anything to do with God. So Burke began his quest of helping his charges look for images they could identify with. They eventually translated Psalm 23:1 by comparing the Lord to their probation officers. This comparison reflects a positive feeling about the correctional system in Buffalo among the chaplain's young charges. They perceive the probation officer to be someone who cares for them, looks for them, and tries to keep them out of trouble.

If you were not allowed to use the word "shepherd," how would you translate Psalm 23:1? I asked this question of a group of Christians once and was surprised at the different answers. They said everything from school teacher to scout master. But by far the most common answer was, "The Lord is like my mother."

When you think of God, what image comes to your mind? Willie Keith, in *The Caine Mutiny*, thought of a kind of cosmic "jack-in-the-box," who jumped out and frightened him. Other images are even less personal: a light, a force, a Presence. Francis Thompson pictured God as a bloodhound.

John's Gospel says (1:18) that no one has ever seen God, but that Jesus Christ has made God known. Thus, our images of Jesus help us to know God. Today we will focus on the image of the shepherd to better understand the nature of God.

READING THE SCRIPTURE

NRSV
John 10:1-18

1 "Very truly, I tell you, anyone who does not enter the sheepfold by the gate but climbs in by another way is a thief and a bandit. 2The one who enters by the gate is the shepherd of the sheep. 3The gatekeeper opens the gate for him, and the sheep hear his voice. He calls his own sheep by name and leads them out. 4When he has brought out all his own, he goes ahead of them, and the sheep follow him because they know his voice. 5They will not follow a stranger, but they will run from him because they do not know the voice of strangers." 6Jesus used this figure of speech with them, but they did not understand what he was saying to them.

7 So again Jesus said to them, "Very truly, I tell you, I am the gate for the sheep. 8All who came before me are thieves and bandits; but the sheep did not listen to them. 9I am the gate. Whoever enters by me will be saved, and will come in and go out and find pasture. 10The thief comes only to steal and kill and destroy. I came that they may have life, and have it abundantly.

NIV
John 10:1-18

1 "I tell you the truth, the man who does not enter the sheep pen by the gate, but climbs in by some other way, is a thief and a robber. 2The man who enters by the gate is the shepherd of his sheep. 3The watchman opens the gate for him, and the sheep listen to his voice. He calls his own sheep by name and leads them out. 4When he has brought out all his own, he goes on ahead of them, and his sheep follow him because they know his voice. 5But they will never follow a stranger; in fact, they will run away from him because they do not recognize a stranger's voice." 6Jesus used this figure of speech, but they did not understand what he was telling them.

7Therefore Jesus said again, "I tell you the truth, I am the gate for the sheep. 8All who ever came before me were thieves and robbers, but the sheep did not listen to them. 9I am the gate; whoever enters through me will be saved. He will come in and go out, and find pasture. 10The thief comes only to steal and kill and destroy; I have come that they may have life, and have it to the full.

11 "I am the good shepherd. The good shepherd lays down his life for the sheep. ¹²The hired hand, who is not the shepherd and does not own the sheep, sees the wolf coming and leaves the sheep and runs away—and the wolf snatches them and scatters them. ¹³The hired hand runs away because a hired hand does not care for the sheep. ¹⁴I am the good shepherd. I know my own and my own know me, ¹⁵just as the Father knows me and I know the Father. And I lay down my life for the sheep. ¹⁶I have other sheep that do not belong to this fold. I must bring them also, and they will listen to my voice. So there will be one flock, one shepherd. ¹⁷For this reason the Father loves me, because I lay down my life in order to take it up again. ¹⁸No one takes it from me, but I lay it down of my own accord. I have power to lay it down, and I have power to take it up again. I have received this command from my Father."

¹¹"I am the good shepherd. The good shepherd lays down his life for the sheep. ¹²The hired hand is not the shepherd who owns the sheep. So when he sees the wolf coming, he abandons the sheep and runs away. Then the wolf attacks the flock and scatters it. ¹³The man runs away because he is a hired hand and cares nothing for the sheep.

¹⁴"I am the good shepherd; I know my sheep and my sheep know me—¹⁵just as the Father knows me and I know the Father—and I lay down my life for the sheep. ¹⁶I have other sheep that are not of this sheep pen. I must bring them also. They too will listen to my voice, and there shall be one flock and one shepherd. ¹⁷The reason my Father loves me is that I lay down my life—only to take it up again. ¹⁸No one takes it from me, but I lay it down of my own accord. I have authority to lay it down and authority to take it up again. This command I received from my Father."

UNDERSTANDING THE SCRIPTURE

John 10:1-30. Jesus did not originate the shepherd image in the Bible. It is found in many places in the Old Testament, such as Psalm 23; 2 Samuel 5:2; Ezekiel 34:11-31; Isaiah 40:11; Jeremiah 23:1-4; and Zechariah 11:4-17. As recorded in John 10, Jesus uses this image immediately after the Pharisees expel the blind man (9:34). By their action, these religious leaders demonstrate that they are not very good pastors (shepherds). They are like the false shepherds in Ezekiel 34:1-10, with whom God, the true Shepherd, is contrasted. This week's verses contain not only a description of Jesus' role but also provide a good model for all Christians.

John 10:1-2. Jesus begins by making a sharp contrast between the shepherd, who enters the sheep pen by the gate to care for the flock, and the thieves and bandits, who climb into the pen illicitly in order to steal or harm the sheep.

John 10:3. Permanent Palestinian sheepfolds were stone enclosures with one gate in which several flocks might be guarded at night by one person. Sometimes temporary folds were constructed from thorns. Wild animals, such as wolves, bears, or lions, could endanger the flock (see Genesis 31:39; 1 Samuel 17:34; and Matthew 10:16). In the morning the shepherds would come and call out their sheep, who would recognize the voice of their true owner.

John 10:4-5. The true leader must be out in front, showing the way, but not so far from the sheep that they cannot take comfort from the shepherd's familiar voice. The sheep will not follow a stranger.

John 10:6. Although Jesus was clearly speaking to the Pharisees, they did not discern that he was talking about them.

John 10:7. "I am the gate." The shepherd may have literally used his own body to guard the entrance to the sheepfold. The gate of the Lord through which the righteous will enter is an image found in Psalm 118:20.

John 10:8. "All who came before me" surely refers to any messianic pretenders or revolutionaries who through their own ambitions would lead their flocks astray.

John 10:9. Under Christ's shepherding, the Christian has freedom to come and go in security. The "gate" image is mentioned a second time.

John 10:10. In contrast to the thief who comes to harm or steal the sheep, Jesus comes offering abundant life.

John 10:11. "I am the Good Shepherd," belongs to a whole class of Jesus' sayings, found especially in John's Gospel, which are his affirmations about himself. He said: "I am . . . the Bread of Life (6:48); the Light of the World (8:12); the Gate (10:9); the Resurrection and the Life (11:25); the Way, the Truth, and the Life (14:6); the True Vine (15:1); the Root . . . of David; and the bright Morning Star (Revelation 22:16)." In all of these images there may be an echo of God's own I AM (Exodus 3:14; see also John 8:58). The good shepherd will risk his very life for the sheep, a likely reference to Jesus' passion. The Greek word translated here as "good" carries the idea of noble or ideal.

John 10:12-13. The hired hand, though paid for his labor, will not risk himself to save the sheep.

John 10:14-15. Here Jesus compares the relationship that he has with his sheep to the relationship he has with the Father. Again he makes an allusion to his passion.

John 10:16. Jew and Gentile will be united as one flock.

John 10:17-18. Christ's death was not God's punishment, or Satan's victory, but Jesus' free decision.

John 10:19-21. As was the case in John 7:20, Jesus is again accused of being possessed by a demon, though the Jews are divided as to whether or not this is the case.

John 10:22-30. Jesus reiterates his oneness with the Father. His teaching, and the dispute concerning him, occur at the time of the festival of Dedication (Hanukkah), which marked a purification of the temple by Judas Maccabeus after it had been defiled by pagan gods.

In conclusion, note that true to Jesus' basic principle (see Matthew 20:28), the shepherd is not at all concerned for his own glory, but for the good of the sheep. Indeed, in a supreme example of this reversal of roles, the shepherd himself turns out to be a Lamb (see Revelation 7:17).

INTERPRETING THE SCRIPTURE

The Image of the Shepherd

The image of the Good Shepherd has been a favorite one since the earliest days of Christianity. It is frequently found in sculpture or paintings in the catacombs of ancient Rome, and was often placed on gems or seals. This image is depicted in many stained-glass windows and often seen on religious greeting cards. Sometimes sheep are at Jesus' feet, looking up to him with gratitude as he carries one of their number on his shoulders.

The image of the shepherd as one who cares for God's flock goes back much further than the New Testament. There is a rabbinical tradition that Moses, while tending the flocks of his father-in-law, Jethro, went after a lost kid that had gone astray and carried it home on his shoulders. God is said to have been pleased, and announced: "Since you have shown pity in bringing home this sheep, you will be the shepherd of my flock Israel for the rest of your life."

The image of the Good Shepherd is

especially pleasing to Christians because it deals not only with God's broad love for the world (John 3:16-17), but also with Jesus' personal concern for each individual. No wonder the Twenty-third Psalm is such a favorite.

I wrote a setting of that beloved psalm to be sung to the tune of "In the Garden." I once mentioned that I didn't care for that particular song because it seemed to me that it had an inadequate theology. A woman said, "But it's my favorite hymn!" I tried to argue with her that it spoke of God's love for me, but neglected my responsibility for love of neighbor. "It's got a vertical theology," I said, "about 'Me and Jesus,' but it excludes the horizontal. In fact, it says that the joys we share, none other has ever known." But she wouldn't let me off the hook. "How do you feel about the Twenty-third Psalm?" she asked. "That says that God leads me by the green pastures, and fixes a table for me in the presence of everybody else." And of course, she had a point. We cannot reach out to others with the love of God if we have not experienced it for ourselves. So, defeated, I went home and put the psalm to that old tune:

O Lord, you're my Shepherd and Guide,
what more could I ask to fulfill?
For I'm led to sleep where the grass is deep,
and to drink beside the waters still.
I'm restored in soul, and my life's made whole;
for your Name, I walk in the right.
And I fear no foe, even though we go
through the valley of darkest night.

O Lord, you're my Shepherd and Guide,
and your rod and your staff are my comfort.
In the midst of my dread is your table spread,
and my head, your healing oil anoints.
And your cup is bestowed till it's overflowed,
and your goodness and mercy you give,
So that all of my days I will sing your praise,
And forever in your house I shall live.

Jesus as Shepherd

Jesus draws on this familiar image of the shepherd in John 10 to describe himself

and his relationship with the people. As we see Jesus, we also come to know God. An understanding of how Jesus perceives himself to be a shepherd will help us to know more fully what God is like. In John 10:2-4 Jesus uses a variety of verbs to describe his work as a shepherd: enters, calls, leads, brought out, and goes ahead. Let's take a closer look at each of these words.

First, Jesus "enters by the gate." In other words, he comes to the place where the sheep are. He does not expect them to find him, but keeps them gathered together in a safe place. Once inside the sheep pen, Jesus calls his sheep by their names. Note that he knows who they are, and they recognize his voice. Next, Jesus leads them out. While the sheep might be much safer within the confines of their pen, they will starve to death if they do not go out into the pasture to graze. After they have all come out of the pen, Jesus does not just turn them loose, but goes ahead, leading them in the direction of food and water. The sheep follow their shepherd because they can recognize his voice.

Such a description helps us to understand how Jesus is our shepherd. Of course, as with any figure of speech, we cannot overextend its meaning. Christians need not be unduly docile. However, through prayer, mediation, worship, Bible study, and interaction within the community of faith, we can hear the shepherd's comforting voice and discern where the shepherd would have us go.

Jesus continues on in John 10 to contrast himself to persons who pretend to be shepherds but are really thieves. He speaks out against them, intending the religious leaders who are listening to perceive their own inadequate shepherding in his story. Yet, they do not (John 10:6). As teachers and possibly ordained pastors we need to heed Jesus' words of warning carefully as we consider how we are to be shepherds of God's flock.

Shepherds of Each Other

The Good Shepherd does call us to give of ourselves to others (John 15:12-14). The image of God as shepherd is reflected in our shepherding of each other. As we study this lesson, we should not identify ourselves only with the sheep; we must see ourselves as shepherds. We sometimes call our ordained ministers, "pastors," which means, of course, "shepherds." The word "pasture" comes from the same root. Not only are professional pastors called to shepherd the flock, but all Christians are called to minister to others in the same loving manner in which Christ ministers to us (see Ephesians 4:32).

Of course, we can either be good shepherds, truly following Jesus' example, or we can be the bad shepherds, the thief or hired hand who are not unreservedly committed to the sheep. The Old Testament has some particularly harsh things to say about bad shepherds in Jeremiah 23:1-4 and 25:34-38; Ezekiel 34; and Zechariah 10–11.

Jesus' description of the Good Shepherd provides those of us who teach with some important guidelines for relating to our students. Here are some examples:

(1) The teacher needs to know each class member by name (John 10:3-4). Good teaching does not take place in a vacuum. The more you can know about your students, the more effectively you can teach. Good classroom discussion is essential to the learning process because it helps you to know your "sheep" better and them to know everyone else. If your class is particularly large, use name tags, or appoint "under-shepherds," or find some other means to make sure everyone feels a part of the group. At the very least, when there are discussion questions, divide the students into groups of two to four, and let them share together before reporting to the class as a whole.

(2) The teacher is the gatekeeper (John 10:7). Teaching is not a matter of pouring knowledge into other people's heads; it is, rather, an opening of doors or gates through which they may walk.

(3) The teacher needs to set an example in his or her personal life (John 10:8). A good teacher will act out in word and deed the spirit of the lesson that is being taught.

(4) The teacher should lay down his or her life (John 10:11). You will not likely be called to do this literally, but a good teacher is willing to risk, to take some pedagogical chances, such as getting into controversial areas if the scripture lesson calls for it, or sharing personal uncertainties. Moreover, the time spent in preparing the lesson is a gift of a portion of the teacher's life, valuable hours offered up for others. Good teachers put their whole selves into the task.

SHARING THE SCRIPTURE

PREPARING TO TEACH

Several references to shepherd have already been given, but if you have the time you may conduct your own research into the Bible's use of the shepherd image.

One good way of coming at this is to look up, in an unabridged concordance, all of the Bible's references to sheep, shepherds, sheepfold, and lambs. Some of them will be simply about sheep, but many will be teachings about God's relationship to Israel, or Christ's relationship to us. Perhaps the greatest such verse is Isaiah 53:6:

All we like sheep have gone astray;
    we have all turned to our own way,
and the LORD has laid on [the Servant]
    the iniquity of us all.

Use the information under "Shepherds of Each Other" in the "Interpreting the Scripture" portion to consider how you as the group leader functions as a shepherd. What changes could you make to become more like the Good Shepherd?

LEADING THE CLASS

Introduction

Open the class by mentioning our main question for this week: **What is God like?**

Have the class begin to answer this question by thinking of as many images for God as they can. List these ideas on a chalkboard or newsprint so that you can refer back to them at the end of the session. Now ask the class to identify those images that are most meaningful to them. Spend a few moments talking about why students feel the way they do.

Focus on the image of the shepherd. Ask the class to suggest characteristics of the shepherd that make this image helpful in understanding what God is like. If you or a student in your class has firsthand knowledge of shepherding, this would be an appropriate time to share information on the work of the shepherd.

Here is an alternative way of introducing the main question if your class enjoys games. Have them pretend to be sheep and see if you (or someone appointed as shepherd) can herd them into a fold made up of a circle of chairs with an opening in it. If your people act like real sheep they will stray in all directions and rarely go where you want them. If you know their names you will find it easier to control them. And if you have a couple of "sheep dogs" to assist you, that might help. It has been suggested that, in

the Twenty-third Psalm there are two "sheep dogs" named "Goodness" and "Mercy" (verse 6)!

The Shepherd Who Knows Me

Direct the class's attention to John 10:1-6.

Note the verbs Jesus uses to describe the Good Shepherd in these verses: *enters, calls, leads, brought out,* and *goes ahead.* These verbs are discussed in the section "Jesus as Shepherd" under "Interpreting the Scripture."

Help the class talk about the personal relationship between God and each of us. Here are some possible questions:

(1) **Do you think God cares about your personal problems? Why or why not?**
(2) **Which of the following words best describe Jesus as he relates to you: Shepherd, Master, Teacher, Friend, Savior, Comforter, Redeemer?** (Of course they all may apply at different times, but which one stands out?)
(3) **How do you react to the following descriptions of the way God may relate to you?**
    (a) God is a mighty force for good, but I don't think of God as a person with whom I can talk to about my personal problems.
    (b) Often, when I pray, it seems that my prayers just bounce off the ceiling and come back to me.
    (c) Nobody seems to be listening.
    (d) I don't know how to talk to God.

Point out that this passage also tells us something about the sheep. One of the major qualities must be trust, for the sheep do follow the shepherd when they hear his voice. Ask the class:

(1) **Although we are not created to follow blindly, we are to trust God. In what ways do we show our trust?**
(2) **In what circumstances do we lack trust?**

The Shepherd Who Intercedes for Me

Read aloud John 10:7-10.

Point out that in verse 9, Jesus offers us a door to salvation. The meaning of this ancient word is related to the word *salve*, a healing ointment. Ask the class: **How does entering the gate that is Jesus (in 14:6 he calls himself "the way")** make our lives whole? Note that the Hebrew word, *shalom*, which we often translate as peace, refers to this sense of health and wholeness.

Divide class members into teams and ask each team to make a list of as many characteristics of a healthy, whole life—a life of salvation—that they can think of. At a designated time, ask each group to share their ideas. You may want to list them on a chalkboard or newsprint, noting the number of different ideas as well as ones that were often repeated. If the class is too small for group work, do this activity together.

Note that people often feel very much alone, especially those who live alone far away from family, or those who have been newly separated from their loved ones by death or divorce. Ask the class: **(1) In what sense does the Good Shepherd relieve this sense of being lost? (2) How can we intercede for one another, as the shepherd does, to ease this loneliness?**

The Shepherd Who Lays Down His Life for Me

Choose a volunteer to read aloud John 10:11-18.

Point out that Jesus provides more for us than nurture. He gives us his very life. The shepherd image implies that one might die fighting wolves for another. Ask the class: **What other images can you think of that relate to giving one's life for another?** (Possible answers include a rescue in which the rescuer is killed; undergoing an operation to provide a transplant for someone who is dying; an act of heroism).

Note that different people understand Jesus' giving of his life for us in different ways. Below are listed some theories of atonement. Lead the class in a discussion that will help them to consider how the Good Shepherd gave his life.

(1) Conflict: Jesus does battle with Satan for us.
(2) Substitution: Jesus receives the punishment meant for us.
(3) Example: Jesus, by dying, shows us how to give our lives.
(4) Moral Influence: Jesus' death empowers us to give up our lives.

Ask: **(1) Could all of these be true? (2) What would your theory of atonement be?**

Before the class concludes, go back to the list that you brainstormed to open the class. Look at the descriptions that students suggested for the image of a shepherd. Give them an opportunity to add other characteristics that may have occurred to them during the lesson.

One of the loveliest passages in the Bible is the "Great Shepherd" benediction at the end of the letter to the Hebrews (13:20-21), which you might wish to use as a closing prayer with your class.

HELPING CLASS MEMBERS ACT

Suggest that the class members identify one person whom they know is struggling with his or her faith. Challenge them to act as a shepherd to this person, offering whatever care and resources are necessary to move toward God.

Encourage students to think of a problem or need they have and invite them to pray that the Good Shepherd will help them find ways to address this problem. Remind them that the Good Shepherd does care for us and wants to keep us from all harm. Invite everyone to read Psalm 23 at least once during the coming week and consider how they perceive Jesus to be the shepherd of their lives.

APRIL 21

PLANNING FOR NEXT SUNDAY

Next Sunday we will be looking at still another image for Jesus, that of the Vine. It has to do with connections. How are we (or should we be) connected to Jesus? How should we be connected to one another? What connections already exist? What connections should we strive for? Ask students to read John 15:1-17 in preparation for the class.

THE TRUE VINE

PREVIEWING THE LESSON

Lesson Scripture: John 15:1-17
Background Scripture: John 15:1-17
Key Verse: John 15:5

Focus of the lesson:
the vital relationship between Jesus and his followers as seen in the image of the vine and branches

Main question(s) of the lesson:
(1) How are we connected to Christ?
(2) What sustains our relationship between ourselves and him, and between ourselves and other members of the community of faith?

This lesson will enable adult learners to:
(1) become aware of the intimate connectedness that believers have with Jesus
(2) experience the joy of the connectedness in their personal relationship with Jesus
(3) respond by reaching out to someone who does not feel connected to Jesus and the church.

Today's lesson may be outlined as follows:
(1) Introduction
(2) The Connection (John 15:1-6)
(3) The Joy of the Connection (John 15:7-11)
(4) The Fruit of the Connection (John 15:12-17)

FOCUSING ON THE MAIN QUESTION

Antaeus, a giant and a mighty wrestler in Greek mythology, was said to be one of the sons of Gaia, Mother Earth. As long as he kept one foot on the ground, he was invincible. If he were thrown down, he would spring up again, having regained his power by touching the earth from which he drew his strength. According to legend, he forced all who passed by to wrestle with him to the death. So many had died that Antaeus had almost completed roofing a temple with the skulls of his victims. But Hercules, having completed his twelve labors, figured out the secret of Antaeus' connection to the earth, and slew him by holding him off the ground until his strength was depleted, and then strangling him.

Despite its brutal elements, this ancient

myth illustrates the basic human need for connectedness. One cannot possess power who is not connected to the ultimate source of power. An Anglican bishop once said, "No one possesses authority who is not under authority." A military force is bound to fail in its mission if it does not have connections with supply lines. Electrical service is interrupted when a power line is knocked down by a tree. Space travelers may find themselves out of touch with "ground control" due to some interference or problem across such a vast distance. Such technological marvels make us admire the travelers of old who did not have convenient electrical outlets in which to plug in their wagons, yet they were connected

with one another as they sat around their campfires.

What are your connections? In John 15:1-17, Jesus draws upon the Old Testament image of the vine to show how we are connected to him and to each other. We are cared for by God the vinegrower or husbandman who tends the plants, nurturing the fruitful branches and pruning the barren ones. Those persons who obey God's commands bear the fruit of love. Jesus said, "Apart from me you can do nothing" (John 15:5). **How, then, are we connected to Christ? What sustains our relationship between ourselves and him, and between ourselves and other members of the community of faith?** These are our main questions for today's lesson.

READING THE SCRIPTURE

NRSV
John 15:1-17

1 "I am the true vine, and my Father is the vinegrower. [2]He removes every branch in me that bears no fruit. Every branch that bears fruit he prunes to make it bear more fruit. [3]You have already been cleansed by the word that I have spoken to you. [4]Abide in me as I abide in you. Just as the branch cannot bear fruit by itself unless it abides in the vine, neither can you unless you abide in me. [5]I am the vine, you are the branches. Those who abide in me and I in them bear much fruit, because apart from me you can do nothing. [6]Whoever does not abide in me is thrown away like a branch and withers; such branches are gathered, thrown into the fire, and burned. [7]If you abide in me, and my words abide in you, ask for whatever you wish, and it will be done for you. [8]My Father is glorified by this, that you bear much fruit and become my disciples. [9]As the Father has loved me, so I have loved you; abide in my love. [10]If you keep my commandments, you will abide in my love, just as I have

NIV
John 15:1-17

1 "I am the true vine, and my Father is the gardener. [2]He cuts off every branch in me that bears no fruit, while every branch that does bear fruit he prunes so that it will be even more fruitful. [3]You are already clean because of the word I have spoken to you. [4]Remain in me, and I will remain in you. No branch can bear fruit by itself; it must remain in the vine. Neither can you bear fruit unless you remain in me.

[5]"I am the vine; you are the branches. If a man remains in me and I in him, he will bear much fruit; apart from me you can do nothing. [6]If anyone does not remain in me, he is like a branch that is thrown away and withers; such branches are picked up, thrown into the fire and burned. [7]If you remain in me and my words remain in you, ask whatever you wish, and it will be given you. [8]This is to my Father's glory, that you bear much fruit, showing yourselves to be my disciples.

[9]"As the Father has loved me, so have I

Key
Verse

kept my Father's commandments and abide in his love. [11]I have said these things to you so that my joy may be in you, and that your joy may be complete.

12 "This is my commandment, that you love one another as I have loved you. [13]No one has greater love than this, to lay down one's life for one's friends. [14]You are my friends if you do what I command you. [15]I do not call you servants any longer, because the servant does not know what the master is doing; but I have called you friends, because I have made known to you everything that I have heard from my Father. [16]You did not choose me but I chose you. And I appointed you to go and bear fruit, fruit that will last, so that the Father will give you whatever you ask him in my name. [17]I am giving you these commands so that you may love one another."

loved you. Now remain in my love. [10]If you obey my commands, you will remain in my love, just as I have obeyed my Father's commands and remain in his love. [11]I have told you this so that my joy may be in you and that your joy may be complete. [12]My command is this: Love each other as I have loved you. [13]Greater love has no one than this, that he lay down his life for his friends. [14]You are my friends if you do what I command. [15]I no longer call you servants, because a servant does not know his master's business. Instead, I have called you friends, for everything that I learned from my Father I have made known to you. [16]You did not choose me, but I chose you and appointed you to go and bear fruit— fruit that will last. Then the Father will give you whatever you ask in my name. [17]This is my command: Love each other."

UNDERSTANDING THE SCRIPTURE

John 15:1-17. Like the image of the Good Shepherd, the image of the vine comes from the Hebrew Scriptures. The prophets used the vine to symbolize Israel (see Psalm 80:8-15; Isaiah 5:1-7; Jeremiah 2:21; and Hosea 10:1.) Jesus also used this image in Matthew 21:33-41. This use of the image of the vine in chapter 15 is the closest that John comes to including a parable of Jesus in his gospel.

John includes this story as a part of the upper room discourses, which took place after the Lord's Supper and the footwashing in chapter 13. Jesus uses the image of the vine to describe the organic unity of the church. It is a symbol of the connectional nature of the church, and of the need of the individual to be connected to the church in order to bear fruit. Paul later uses the image of the body in a similar way (see 1 Corinthians 12:12-27; Romans 12:5; Ephesians 4:4-16; and elsewhere).

John 15:1. "My Father is the vine-grower." The Greek word is *georgos*, from

the root meaning "the earth." It's the root from which we get our words "geography" and "geology." The King James version (see also Matthew 21:33, Luke 20:29, and Mark 12:1) translates this word "husbandman" which literally means "house-bound-man." In those days both men and women were rooted to their homes and came to be called "house-bound-man" and "house-wife." Perhaps the simplest way to translate it is the English word "farmer."

John 15:2-3. There is a wordplay here between "prune" and "cleanse," which in the Greek are the same word. Verse 3 seems to offer reassurance to Jesus' companions in the upper room that they are not in danger of such pruning.

John 15:4-5. "Abide" comes from the Greek root *meno*, meaning "to stay," which is the origin of such words as "remain," "mansion," and "permanent." Notice that the act is mutual; Christ and the believer abide in each other.

John 15:6-7. The consequences of not abiding in the vine are dreadful, not because God wills our destruction, but because the unconnected vine (like the unused talent) is doomed to wither and die. In contrast, the one that does abide will be cared for.

John 15:8. The work of the disciples is to bear fruit. This action will glorify the Father. Soon, the disciples will be Jesus' representatives in the world for he will no longer be with them.

John 15:9. Love is seen here as a mutual relationship between God the Father and Jesus, and Jesus and the disciples. God is the source of this love. Both Jesus and his disciples are expected to keep the Father's commands.

John 15:10. The words "commandment" or "command" occur nine times in all of the upper room conversations. The early church was so aware of this emphasis that the Thursday of the Last Supper came to be called "Maundy Thursday," from the Latin word *mandatum*. In John's writings the word commandment is associated with the word love, as in John 13:34. In other words, abiding in Christ is not simply a mystical union, but always has ethical dimensions. To be connected to Christ, the vine, is to be connected with the other branches, too.

John 15:11. A relationship with Jesus brings joy.

John 15:12. This verse sets forth a clear statement of our purpose in being part of the vine: we are not only to draw nourishment for ourselves, but to nourish each other. We abide in Christ both for his joy and ours (verse 11) and in order that we may bear fruit (verse 12), which means love for one another (verse 17).

John 15:13. The supreme example of love for a friend is to lay down one's life. Once again we touch the heart of Jesus' teaching: to lose life is to find it; to die for another is the ultimate fulfillment of Christ's orders, and the perfect embodiment of Christ's own example.

John 15:14-15. Fellowship with Jesus is the condition for receiving revelations from God. Only Jesus' friends hear everything that he has heard from the Father.

John 15:16-17. Jesus takes the initiative in choosing his followers. They are selected for the purpose of bearing fruit. The result of obeying the commandments is that the disciples will love one another.

INTERPRETING THE SCRIPTURE

The Community of Belonging

In 1970, I spent several weeks on a mission station in what was then called the Congo, now Zaire. The station was located far up in the headwaters of the great river (the setting for Joseph Conrad's *Heart of Darkness*), in cannibal country. Cannibalism had been outlawed by the government, but it was still being practiced in secret by some groups, and I was, to say the least, uneasy. Three of us spent one night in a village, many kilometers from the nearest paved road, sleeping in grass huts (they really do keep off the rain). After dark, the entire village gathered around a central fire circle to watch a filmstrip about the life of Christ, shown on a projector attached to the battery of our Land Rover. In the light of that lamp, I was very conscious of the hundreds of eyes that surrounded us. Was their look one of friendliness, curiosity, or hostility? I could not tell.

But then something happened that changed my whole mood. Hymnbooks were passed around, and everyone began to sing in wonderful harmony all the old nineteenth-century gospel songs that the missionaries had taught them: "What a Friend We Have in Jesus" and

"Come, Thou Fount of Every Blessing." I knew no Tshiluba, but since the missionaries had translated the hymns phonetically, I was able to sing along, delighting in the familiar tunes and knowing the meaning of the words that I had sung since childhood. It was no longer a question of "us versus them." Instead I felt a great bonding warmth. We were connected, across cultural, racial, and continental barriers, to each other, through the common convictions about which we were singing. It was an evening I shall never forget.

I have since experienced the same thing in my own country, and I suspect you have, too. Whenever you worship in an unfamiliar denomination, you feel a little foolish, perhaps, and out of place, hoping you don't do or say the wrong thing. But then something happens to express your commonality. You say the Apostles' Creed, or you sing "Amazing Grace," or you pass the peace with handshakes or hugs. After that there is a sense of community, a feeling that "these are my people."

Such "connectedness" is absolutely essential to the survival of the Christian. I can describe what this connectedness means to me in another way: I spent three years as a traveling evangelist, doing celebrations and worship renewal in churches and on college campuses. It was a great time, and I had some joyful, intense experiences. But then I would move on to another place, and then to another, developing in each place only a superficial sense of community. I didn't get to live with my successes, and I didn't have to live with my mistakes. I was happy, but there was something I couldn't quite define that was missing. Then my family and I became connected with a small rural congregation. I continued my travels, but there was always a place to come home to. I called it my "community of belonging." I know now that I had a deep need to be abiding in the Vine.

The Pain of Community

Anyone who has been married knows that the closer you get to someone else, the more suffering becomes likely. Remember the old song, "You Always Hurt the One You Love"? A philosopher once said that the human race is like porcupines huddling together in winter. You have to stay close enough to keep warm, but far enough apart so that you don't stab each other to death. All close relationships are like that, especially in the church.

To abide in the vine is to subject yourself to pruning (John 15:2), for dwelling in community is hard work. It means learning to give up something of one's self in order to become interdependent with Christ and Christ's community. Abiding in the vine is painful. We sometimes wish it were otherwise, but those who try to experience love without hurt are doomed to failure. Naive brides and grooms sometimes think that because two people love each other they will automatically "live happily ever after." But this is folly. Marriage means discipline and hard work, and if you try to build community without it, you will soon become disappointed. At this point, the naive begin to say things like, "The love has gone from our marriage; perhaps we weren't meant for each other." Then they separate and go on looking for the impossible magic of a Hollywood romance, which never comes.

Poor souls! They were right on the verge of discovering what true love is all about. They were ready to move from eros and friendship to agape. In an oversimplified translation, of C. S. Lewis's lines from *The Four Loves* you might say: "from companionship to passion to divine charity." Those who are willing to make the effort to abide, ultimately discover the true joys of marriage. As is true of all democratic communities, you have to work to make them work. Freedom demands responsibility, and vigilance is the price of liberty. These maxims are especially true of the Christian life. For those who are willing to pay the cost of discipleship, the rewards are beyond measure.

The Joy of Community

"I have said these things to you," said Jesus, "so that my joy may be in you, and that your joy may be complete" (John 15:11). We are accustomed to thinking of Jesus as "a man of sorrows, and acquainted with grief." Quite so, but that is only part of the picture, and not even half of it. You might as well say that having children means labor pains and heartbreak. It does, but the joys make all the pain worthwhile. At the risk of sounding flippant, let me suggest that Jesus had more fun than anyone else who ever lived. Sure he had no place to lay his head, but then every place he stopped was his home. Certainly he had problems with his disciples, but they were his friends (John 15:14) and he loved them. Of course he knew pain and sorrow, but his joy was greater than that of anyone I know. And he had a wonderful sense of humor.

In next week's lesson we will look at the secret of Jesus' joy, the peace that is not of this world, which comes from utter surrender to and trust in God. But for this week, let us simply point out that Jesus goes immediately from saying "my joy may be in you" to saying that the greatest thing you can do is lay down your life for your friends. The world cannot see this, but those who have come to know what it means to abide in the Vine have been set free from fear and pain and given an everlasting peace, so that no matter what adventures life may bring, even in the darkest jungle, there will be gladness.

SHARING THE SCRIPTURE

PREPARING TO TEACH

Read the scripture passage and all of the material in this lesson. It may be a difficult lesson to teach because the idea of community—of being the branches of the vine—requires us to move back and forth between polar opposites: joy and suffering; fruitfulness and barrenness; togetherness and isolation; reward and discipline.

Consider your own understanding of connectedness to Christ and to other persons. How do you experience that connectedness? How does it enrich you? You may want to write about connectedness in your spiritual journal this week.

Have paper and pencils on hand for the activity under "Introduction."

LEADING THE CLASS

Introduction

Distribute paper and pencils. Announce that our lesson for today, which is on John 15:1-17, calls us to consider our connectedness to God through Christ, as well as our connectedness to one another through him.

Now direct class members to draw a tree or vine on the paper you have given. Assure students that artistic ability is not necessary. Ask them to label the branches with the names of persons or groups to which they feel connected. One large limb, for example, could be the name of your church, with smaller branches showing names of individual members or church groups to which the student feels connected. Another large branch may be for each student's family, while a third one may represent connections with work.

After a few minutes, ask the class members to talk informally about their connections. See if they can answer these questions: **(1) Why do you feel connected to these persons or groups? (2) Sap sustains the branches of a tree. What sustains your relationships?** (Note that answers will vary from one relationship to another. What sustains a work relationship is probably different from that which nourishes a friendship.)

As an alternative activity for classes that prefer a lecture format, read or retell my experience of feeling a connection with worshipers in Zaire, found under "The Community of Belonging," which is the first section under "Interpreting the Scripture."

Whichever activity you choose, conclude the introduction by announcing today's main questions: **How are we connected to Christ? What sustains our relationship between ourselves and him and between ourselves and other members of the community of faith?**

The Connection

Direct the class's attention to John 15:1-6.

Spend some time considering the painful words in these verses: "prunes" (verse 2); "thrown away" (verse 6); "withers" (verse 6); and "burned" (verse 6). Ask the class these questions:

(1) What do these negative images tell us about the need to be connected to the vine?

(2) What do these images tell us about the need to bear fruit?

(3) How do you perceive the relationship between connection to the vine and fruit-bearing? (You may want to argue that fruit-bearing occurs naturally when one is receiving the life sustaining nourishment of the vine.)

Turn the discussion to our understanding of connection within the life of the church. If you did the suggested activity for in the "Introduction," you may have already talked about connections within the congregation. If not, encourage your class to talk about their own sense of belonging, and to give examples of it.

Push this idea of church connectedness further by asking: **In addition to our friendships and group memberships, how do we experience connectedness within the church?** Here are some possible answers:

(1) Participation in the Sacrament of Baptism affirms connectedness. Infants do not understand the meaning of the mystery, but, like all of us, they are a part of the family and the church into which they have been born. Indeed, one of the meanings of baptism, from long tradition, is our "engrafting into Christ."

(2) Participation in the Eucharist or sacrament of the Lord's Supper affirms our connectedness. This is a communal act. Note that when Paul says in 1 Corinthians 11:29 that we bring judgment on ourselves if we eat and drink without "discerning the body," he is not speaking of understanding the mystery of Christ's presence in the bread, but of our recognizing the community that is Christ's body (1 Corinthians 12:27).

(3) Decision making requires connectedness. For example, in the church that I serve it is against the rules to let anyone vote by proxy in a meeting. The idea is that only in the fellowship can we experience the spirit of our connectedness, and thus vote with mutual understanding. Among the Quakers, it is the custom to make decisions only after everyone has come to a "sense of the meeting."

(4) Many activities within the church affirm connectedness. For example, we experience corporate worship, group

study, fellowship activities, and opportunities for singing together.

(5) Some churches have organizational structures that encourage or enhance connection, not only within one congregation but across the denomination. The United Methodist Church, for example, refers to itself as a "connectional church."

The Joy of the Connection

Read aloud John 15:7-11. Instruct class members to pay particular attention to the joys suggested by these verses.

Then ask: **What are the joys mentioned here?** List these on a chalkboard or newsprint. The class list (or your lecture notes) should include the following:

- the joy of knowing that our prayers will be answered (verse 7)
- the joy of bearing fruit (verse 8)
- the joy of knowing God's love (verse 9)
- the joy of right living and abiding in that love (verse 10)
- the joy of Jesus that is in us, making our own joy complete (verse 11).

There is a delightful acronym that you might enjoy sharing with your class, because it is related to the idea of community. The word JOY spells out Jesus, Others, and You:

J: Trust Jesus.
O: Trust Others.
Y: Trust Yourself.

Ask the class: **(1) How does the joy of connection contrast with life lived in isolation? (2) How do you think your own life would be different if you did not have the connection with Jesus and with the others who are also branches of the vine?**

Close this segment by reminding the class that abiding in the Vine brings joy, but not the superficial or fleeting joy that the world offers. It is the deep, abiding joy, that comes with knowing whose you are, and hence, who you are. We will be dealing in detail with the secrets of discovering this joy in next week's lesson on the Beatitudes.

The Fruit of the Connection

Choose a volunteer to read aloud John 15:12-17.

Point out the repetition of the word "command" or "commandment" as discussed in John 15:10 under "Understanding the Scripture."

Note that, like a grape vine, the vine to which Jesus refers is not simply planted for decoration or as an end unto itself. Instead, abiding in the Vine enables us to bear the fruit of love. Encourage the class to think of acts or expressions of love. List these ideas on a chalkboard or newsprint. (You may want to take a look at the fruit of the Spirit, found in Galatians 5:22-26. Note that love is the first on the list, and the others are expressions of a loving person.)

Point out that in John 15:13, Jesus says that the greatest fruit, that is, the greatest expression of love, is the giving up of one's life. Note that there are, of course, dramatic ways in which we can give up our lives for others, by literally dying for them, but rarely are we called upon in times of peace to do this. We thank God that we live in an age when physical martyrdom for the faith is rare. It does occur in our day in other parts of the world, and class members may have some examples of such supreme love.

Ask the class: **In what ways can we give our lives in love for others?** Answers may include examples of common acts such as: the gift of our money, our time, our prayers, our energy, our compassion, our support, or our willingness to invest ourselves for a cause greater than ourselves. Note that there is great reward in such giving (Mark 8:34-36).

Finally, help the class to consider what it means to be chosen by Jesus (John 15:16). One way to do this would be to remind students of the verbs used in Luke 24:28-32 when Jesus revealed himself to Cleopas and his companion on the Emmaus road and in the breaking of bread. Those verbs were *take, bless, break,* and *give.* Here's how they can apply to us:

We have been taken (chosen) by Christ.

We have been blessed by Christ.

We have been broken by Christ. (This saying is hard, but it means that we have learned to lose our lives for his sake, to lay them down.)

We have been given by Christ. (We are sent as apostles to bear the message of God's love to others.)

HELPING CLASS MEMBERS ACT

Ask students to think of their connectedness so that when they encounter one another they will remember: this person with whom I am associated is a part of Christ, and so am I. I will act as though that were true, in trust, in love, and in self-giving.

Challenge each student to find a way to bear fruit this week by doing one loving act, especially for someone who may be isolated (physically or emotionally) and not feel connected to Christ through the church.

Encourage students to take some time this week to think of ways in which their relationship with Christ—individually and collectively through the church—provides them with a solid foundation on which to build their lives. Have them think about what difference this relationship makes in the way they live. Suggest that students who keep a spiritual journal may want to write their thoughts in their journals.

PLANNING FOR NEXT SUNDAY

Next week's lesson, on the Beatitudes, is about finding true happiness. Ask the class to complete the definition, "Happiness is _____," and bring their answers next Sunday. Ask them to be sure to read Matthew 5:1-12. If they have time, they may also want to read Luke 6:20-26. We will not discuss Luke's version, but students may want to read it in order to do their own comparison.

FINDING TRUE HAPPINESS

PREVIEWING THE LESSON

Lesson Scripture: Matthew 5:1-12
Background Scripture: Matthew 5:1-12
Key Verse: Matthew 5:12

Focus of the lesson:
Jesus' teachings on happiness as found in the Beatitudes

Main question(s) of the lesson:
(1) What does Jesus teach about happiness?

This lesson will enable adult learners to:
(1) compare and contrast Jesus' teachings on happiness with society's teachings
(2) explore their own definitions of happiness
(3) respond by acting on at least one of the Beatitudes.

Today's lesson may be outlined as follows:
(1) Introduction
(2) Overview of the Beatitudes (Matthew 5:1-12)
(3) Individual Beatitudes (Matthew 5:1-12)

FOCUSING ON THE MAIN QUESTION

The American Declaration of Independence says that "the pursuit of happiness" is one of our inalienable rights. But what is happiness? And how do you pursue it?

There have been songs ("Happiness is . . .") and books (*Happiness Is a Warm Puppy*) written to try to define it. An old Yiddish proverb implies that it is no big deal: "Happiness is when you don't have a broken leg." Benjamin Franklin defined it as produced "not so much by great pieces of good fortune that seldom happen, as by little advantages that occur every day." And here's a very secular definition by Jean-Jacques Rousseau: "a good bank account, a good cook, and a good digestion."

There are a number of places in the Bible that might be called "secrets of happiness." One of the best known is Psalm 1, which begins, "Happy are those who do not follow the advice of the wicked, or take the path that sinners tread, or sit in the seat of scoffers." In Proverbs 14:21 we read: "Those who despise their neighbors are sinners, but happy are those who are kind to the poor." Jesus' words to his Pharisee host in Luke 14:13-14, which we studied several weeks ago, also teach us how to be happy: "But when you give a banquet, invite the poor, the crippled, the lame, and the blind. And you will be blessed, because they cannot repay you, for you will be repaid at the resurrection of the righteous." These are but three examples. You can find many more by looking in a good concordance under the words "happy" and "blessed," which have similar meanings.

Although teachings regarding happiness permeate the Bible, nowhere is the subject dealt with in more detail, or with a more astonishing conclusion, than in what we call the Beatitudes, which are the opening verses of the Sermon on the Mount. Here we have the heart of Jesus' teaching, a view entirely upside down to that of the world. Here again we encounter a basic principle of Jesus' worldview: To lose life is to find it. Our main question, then, is: **What does Jesus teach about happiness?** Those of us schooled in the world's understanding of happiness are sure to be surprised.

READING THE SCRIPTURE

NRSV
Matthew 5:1-12

1 When Jesus saw the crowds, he went up the mountain; and after he sat down, his disciples came to him. 2 Then he began to speak, and taught them, saying:

3 "Blessed are the poor in spirit, for theirs is the kingdom of heaven.

4 "Blessed are those who mourn, for they will be comforted.

5 "Blessed are the meek, for they will inherit the earth.

6 "Blessed are those who hunger and thirst for righteousness, for they will be filled.

7 "Blessed are the merciful, for they will receive mercy.

8 "Blessed are the pure in heart, for they will see God.

9 "Blessed are the peacemakers, for they will be called children of God.

10 "Blessed are those who are persecuted for righteousness' sake, for theirs is the kingdom of heaven.

11 "Blessed are you when people revile you and persecute you and utter all kinds of evil against you falsely on my account. 12 Rejoice and be glad, for your reward is great in heaven, for in the same way they persecuted the prophets who were before you."

NIV
Matthew 5:1-12

1 Now when he saw the crowds, he went up on a mountainside and sat down. His disciples came to him, 2 and he began to teach them, saying:

3 "Blessed are the poor in spirit,
    for theirs is the kingdom of heaven.
4 Blessed are those who mourn,
    for they will be comforted.
5 Blessed are the meek,
    for they will inherit the earth.
6 Blessed are those who hunger and thirst for righteousness,
    for they will be filled.
7 Blessed are the merciful,
    for they will be shown mercy.
8 Blessed are the pure in heart,
    for they will see God.
9 Blessed are the peacemakers,
    for they will be called sons of God.
10 Blessed are those who are persecuted
    because of righteousness,
    for theirs is the kingdom of heaven.

11 "Blessed are you when people insult you, persecute you and falsely say all kinds of evil against you because of me. 12 Rejoice and be glad, because great is your reward in heaven, for in the same way they persecuted the prophets who were before you."

Key
Verse

UNDERSTANDING THE SCRIPTURE

Matthew 5:1-12. This portion of scripture is commonly known as the Beatitudes. The word "blessed" is not easy to define. The English word (which means the opposite of "cursed"; see Deuteronomy 27:11–28:6) probably comes from an old root meaning "to hallow with blood," and is somewhat akin to "sanctify." The Latin word *beatitudo* is sometimes translated "blessed" and sometimes "happy." And the Greek word *makarios*, which Matthew uses here, can also be translated either way. The NRSV is probably right to translate it "blessed," because "happy" sometimes has a frivolous meaning, but the word really encompasses both ideas. It includes temporal happiness, but in the New Testament it is particularly associated with salvation (Romans 4:6-9). To get the full meaning, we probably ought to say, "holy and happy," or maybe "eternally happy." In any event, "blessedness" means "true happiness," as opposed to the temporary happiness that the world offers.

For some other New Testament uses of the word, check Matthew 16:17; Luke 1:48; 6:20-26; Acts 20:35; and Revelation 14:13.

Matthew 5:1-2. These verses set the stage for Jesus' teachings, which we have come to call the Sermon on the Mount. Luke 6:20-26 also records the Beatitudes in his Sermon on the Plain. Matthew's setting may derive from his efforts to show Jesus as the successor to Moses, who went to the mountain to receive the Ten Commandments. Matthew and Luke both set forth a variety of Jesus' ethical teachings. Likely these teachings did not occur within the context of one session but were collected and presented as a unified whole.

Matthew 5:3. "Poor in spirit" means the opposite of pride. Luke's version (6:20, 24) is not spiritualized, but refers to actual poverty.

Matthew 5:4. Compare this verse with Luke 6:21*b*, 25*b*. God will strengthen and console those who mourn.

Matthew 5:5. "Meek" does not mean "smarmy" or "milquetoast." It has a kind of heroic quality that refers to self-control (see Numbers 12:3 KJV and Psalm 37:11). With reference to animals, meek means much the same as "tame" or "gentle."

Matthew 5:6. Matthew spiritualizes this beatitude as (compared to Luke 6:21*a*, 25*a*). It is important to realize that Jesus did not say, "Blessed are the righteous" because no one could meet that condition (Romans 3:10). Instead, he referred to those who long, or hunger and thirst, for righteousness.

Matthew 5:7. The merciful are those who show kindness to the unfortunate. See also Matthew 17:15, in which the father of an epileptic boy cries to Jesus, "Kyrie eleison" ("Lord have mercy").

Matthew 5:8. "Pure in heart" means purity of both body and mind. See Psalm 24:4.

Matthew 5:9. "Shalom" means more than the absence of hostility, though it certainly includes that. Shalom is the purpose of Christ's coming (Luke 2:14), and means the reconciliation of all things (2 Corinthians 5:19). We make peace most powerfully when we love our enemies (Matthew 5:44-48) and so approach the perfection of God's children. See also Psalm 34:14.

Matthew 5:10-11. We can be persecuted for standing up for the right. Usually we do not get to choose those things on which we take our stand; they come to us unexpectedly, as in verse 11. Especially in Matthew's day, people were persecuted for professing faith in Jesus. There are still places in the world where this profession is a capital offense.

Matthew 5:12. God does not keep books (remember the parable of the laborers in Matthew 20:1-16) but rewards with extravagant generosity.

INTERPRETING THE SCRIPTURE

Jesus Versus the World

I have been looking forward all this quarter to Lesson Ten because it is the best expression of the secret of Jesus' teaching. We have said more than once that Jesus seems to view life from an upside down perspective because the reasoning of the world is so completely opposite of his. Nowhere is this more apparent than in the Beatitudes. The sharp contrast between Jesus' secrets of happiness and what the world calls happy can clearly be seen by listing these polar opposites together. There are nine Beatitudes (or eight, if you think the last two are essentially the same). I have listed them here in simplified form, with the world's beatitudes following.

(1) Jesus: Happy are the poor in spirit.
World: Happy are the rich.
(2) Jesus: Happy are those who mourn.
World: Happy are the cheerful.
(3) Jesus: Happy are the meek.
World: Happy are the assertive.
(4) Jesus: Happy are those who hunger and thirst.
World: Happy are the well fed.
(5) Jesus: Happy are the merciful.
World: Happy are those who are tough on sin.
(6) Jesus: Happy are the pure in heart.
World: Happy are those who indulge the sins of the world.
(7) Jesus: Happy are the peacemakers.
World: Happy are those who are well armed.
(8) Jesus: Happy are the persecuted.
World: Happy are those who avoid suffering.
(9) Jesus: Happy are you when people revile you.
World: Happy are you when people speak well of you.

Freedom from Pain

This division between Jesus and the world is powerfully stated in his final words to the disciples in the upper room (John 14:27): "my peace I give to you. I do not give to you as the world gives." By peace, the world means the absence of conflict. But Jesus calls us to conflict, to a cross.

At the outbreak of World War II, President Roosevelt, in an attempt to unify America behind the war effort, spoke of what he called "The Four Freedoms: Freedom of Speech, Freedom of Religion, Freedom from Fear, and Freedom from Want." He commissioned Norman Rockwell to paint these freedoms for posters, so that people could see what we were fighting for. Before making them public, he called in a number of community leaders to get their reaction to his plans. Most of them thought the idea was excellent, and heartily applauded the Four Freedoms. But, I was told, a minister at the back of the room was heard to say, "Nero had them all." "What was that?" asked the president, not understanding, and the minister repeated his words, but still no one understood.

The minister was right. Nero could say anything he wanted to, but Jesus and his followers were forbidden to preach. Nero made himself a god, but Jesus and his followers were put to death for their religious beliefs. Nero, as emperor, need fear no one, but Jesus' followers had to hide in catacombs. Nero had a retinue of servants ready to bring him food and drink, but Jesus and his followers had to pick corn as they passed through someone else's fields.

True happiness is not dependent on creature comforts and the absence of war, but on something far deeper, the peace that passes understanding (see Philippians

4:7 and Romans 5:1). Peace without pain may be impossible; it is probably an escape. Carl Gustav Jung, I am told, defined neurosis as the avoidance of necessary pain. But Jesus calls us to embrace the pain of life, to take up our cross, and find our true happiness.

Dancing for Joy

Our key verse says: "Rejoice and be glad, for your reward is great in heaven." But this does not mean that all happiness is reserved for the "sweet bye and bye." Many Christians can testify that deep happiness is available here and now for those who are willing to put Jesus' teaching to the test by living as he lived. How can we express our joy? One way is through music and dance. My dance to the Beatitudes, sung to the tune of "We Are Climbing Jacob's Ladder," may help imprint the happiness to which Jesus calls us on your class members. Here is the first verse with the simple gestures:

Happy (*On this word, throw your hands into the air and give a hop or leap.*) are the poor in spirit. (*As you sing this, simply open your hands in a gesture of emptiness. Do these motions three times to fit the repetition in "We Are Climbing Jacob's Ladder," and after the third time, sing*):

They shall reign in heaven! (*As you sing these words, make a crown or a halo over your head with your hands.*)

All the other verses start with the same leap, and use the following words and gestures:

Happy are those who mourn. (*Cover your face with your hands.*)

They shall be consoled. (*Give yourself a hug.*)

Happy are those who're meek. (*Stand with your thumbs out, like the Fonz on "Happy Days."*)

They shall win the earth. (*Include the world in a sweeping gesture.*)

Happy are those who hunger (*Rub your stomach.*) and thirst (*Pretend to drink.*) for righteousness.

For they shall be filled. (*Make a filling gesture with your hands as if your cup is full and running over.*)

Happy are the merciful. (*Make an offering gesture with both hands.*)

Mercy shall be theirs. (*Turn the gesture back on yourself.*)

Happy are the pure in heart. (*Put your hand over your heart.*)

For they shall see God. (*With your hand shielding your eyes, look around at each other.*)

Happy are the peacemakers. (*Join hands with each other.*)

They shall be God's children. (*Skip like kids.*)

Happy are the persecuted. (*Act like you have been hit in the stomach.*)

They shall reign in heaven. (*Make another crown.*)

Happy are you, when folk revile you. (*Cover your ears.*)

Great is your reward. (*Take hold of a huge, imaginary bag containing a whole lot of something you have always wanted and be seated, putting your reward down on the floor beside your seat.*)

Whenever I have done this with my congregation, I give them extra credit for getting their feet off the ground. Be sure you offer some words of affirmation, especially if you have class members who are reluctant to do such an activity.

SHARING THE SCRIPTURE

PREPARING TO TEACH

Be sure to take plenty of time this week to read and study the Beatitudes. Although short in length, these nine sayings contain profound teachings that could literally turn the world upside down, just as Jesus intended, if we understood and acted upon them. Try to meditate on at least one of the Beatitudes each day.

If you have time to supplement your preparation, read Luke's version of the Beatitudes, found in Luke 6:20-26. Note how Luke includes both blessings and woes. Note also how Luke's version is less spiritualized than Matthew's. For example, in Luke, the poor are contrasted with the rich; they are not poor only in spirit. Likewise, the hungry are physically malnourished, not hungering for righteousness.

The Beatitudes mark the beginning of the Sermon on the Mount. If you have time this week, read all of this sermon, which is found in chapters 5–7 of Matthew. This sermon is likely a collection of Jesus' teachings, rather than material that was shared with the crowd during one event.

If you plan to do the contrast between the world's beatitudes and those of Jesus, decide how you will present this material. Will you include it in a lecture? Will you write Jesus' teachings on one side of a chalkboard or newsprint and ask the class to fill in the other side? Will you write what I have presented under "Jesus Versus the World" in the "Interpreting the Scripture" section and encourage the class to respond to it?

If you plan to use the dance under "Dancing for Joy" in the "Interpreting the Scripture" section, decide how you will cue the class to do the gestures. You may write the directions and post them where everyone can see them or just lead the dance and ask the class to follow you. Some students will probably want to make up their own gestures. Practice the dance during the week, or contact someone to lead this activity for you.

LEADING THE CLASS

Introduction

Begin the class by writing Happiness is . . . on a chalkboard or newsprint. Ask class members to fill in the blank. If the class is large you may want to do this activity in small groups. If the class prefers a lecture format, you will find some ideas to include under the "Focusing on the Main Question" segment.

Note today's main question: **What does Jesus teach about happiness?** Spend a few moments defining "happy" and "blessed" as these words are used in the Bible. You will find information to help you do this at the opening of the "Understanding the Scripture" portion. You may want to supplement these ideas with other verses concerning happiness that are quoted under "Focusing on the Main Question."

Conclude this portion of the lesson by briefly introducing the Sermon on the Mount. Here are some important points that you will want to include:

- This sermon was probably not preached in exactly this way by Jesus, but is Matthew's collection of Jesus' teaching.
- The sermon takes its popular name from the setting named in verse 1.
- Neither John nor Mark include such a sermon.
- Luke's version of the Beatitudes (Luke 6:20-26) is found in a much briefer collection (Luke 6:17-49), which is sometimes called the "Sermon on the Plain."
- One other difference between the two accounts is that Luke describes Jesus as standing, while Matthew says he preached sitting down.

- Although it is easier to have eye contact with people on a level place if you are standing, persons who taught in the synagogue were generally seated (see Luke 4:20).

Overview of the Beatitudes

One way to give an overview of the Beatitudes would be to do a class litany based on them. Have someone read them, pausing after each one for about twenty seconds of meditation, and then use the following versicle:

Leader: Lord have mercy upon us.
People: And incline our hearts so to live.

Another option would be to compare and contrast the Beatitudes that Jesus teaches to the prescriptions for happiness that our society offers. My ideas are found under "Jesus Versus the World" in the "Interpreting the Scripture" section. See the "Preparing to Teach" segment for ideas on how you can present this information. However you choose to do this activity, conclude by asking: **What might it cost us, especially in terms of social acceptance, to live by these high ideals of Christian discipleship?**

If your class enjoys creative activities, a third option would be to do the dance suggested under "Dancing for Joy." Suggestions for this activity are found under the "Preparing to Teach" section.

Individual Beatitudes

- "Blessed are the poor in spirit, for theirs is the kingdom of heaven."

(1) **How would you describe the "poor in spirit"?** (resigned, hopeless, desperate, oppressed)

(2) **What implications does this Beatitude have for those persons who are not oppressed?**

- "Blessed are those who mourn, for they will be comforted."

(3) **What kinds of losses do we experience in this life?** (death, broken relationships, physical illness and deterioration, loss of community)

(4) **How would you describe a person who does not mourn?** (Scrooge would be a good example: one who does not care about anything or anyone except himself.)

(5) **What form will God's comfort take?**

- "Blessed are the meek, for they will inherit the earth."

(6) Note that the word *meek* always gives us trouble. Ask your class to respond to C. S. Lewis's definition of a humble person, found in *Mere Christianity*:
he will not be a sort of greasy, smarmy person, who is always telling you that, of course, he is nobody. Probably all you will think about him is that he seemed a cheerful, intelligent chap who took a real interest in what *you* said to *him*. If you do dislike him it will be because you feel a little envious of anyone who seems to enjoy life so easily. He will not be thinking about humility: he will not be thinking about himself at all.

(7) **What does it mean to "inherit the earth"?** (This idea does not refer to owning, but to participating in the process of growth and community.)

- "Blessed are those who hunger and thirst for righteousness, for they will be filled."

(8) **Have you ever been really thirsty? Do you long for God that much? If so, does this Beatitude give you hope?**

(9) **What other Bible references to spiritual hunger and thirst can you recall?** (See Psalm 42:1-2; 63:1; Luke 4:2-4; and John 6:35.)

- "Blessed are the merciful, for they will receive mercy."

(10) **What kinds of behaviors and attitudes are unmerciful?** (bitterness, envy, grudges, unwillingness to forgive, vengeance)

(11) **How is Jesus' teaching an antidote to such attitudes and behaviors?** (He talks about and enacts forgiveness, the canceling of debts, reconciliation, and non-retaliation.)

(12) **Do you think of yourself as in need of mercy? Why or why not?**

• "Blessed are the pure in heart, for they will see God."

(13) **How do you define purity? Do you believe purity of heart is really possible?** (see Psalm 24:1-6 and James 1:27.)

(14) **What does it mean to see God?** (This idea certainly has eternal dimensions, but we can experience God in the midst of our day-to-day lives when our hearts are pure.)

• "Blessed are the peacemakers, for they will be called the children of God."

(15) **Share with the class my references to peace under the section called "Freedom from Pain" under "Interpreting the Scripture."** How do you define peace?

(16) **How does one make peace? Is there a difference between a pacifist and a peace lover?**

(17) **It has been suggested that there are three ways to deal with conflict: flee it, fight it, or face it. Which is most likely to make peace?**

• "Blessed are those who are persecuted for righteousness' sake, for theirs is the kingdom of heaven."

(18) **What is the difference between martyrdom and "a martyr complex"?**

(19) **What sort of faith must a person have to be able to "turn the other cheek," to accept undeserved cruelty from others?**

(20) **How do you respond to the charge that Jesus is just being unrealistic here?**

• "Blessed are you when people revile you and persecute you and utter all kinds of evil against you falsely on my account. Rejoice and be glad, for your reward is great in heaven. . . ."

(21) **Notice that this Beatitude refers to persecution for Jesus' sake, not simply because we have made enemies on our own. What are some ways in which we may cause other persons to dislike or persecute us because of our religious beliefs?**

(22) **How do you feel when persons speak ill of you?**

(23) **Isn't it human nature to want to conform to behaviors and attitudes that will make a good impression on others and cause them to like us? If so, how can we override these tendencies so as to be willing to speak out and act for Christ, regardless of the cost?**

You may want to close the class by doing one of the activities under "Overview of the Beatitudes" that you did not do earlier in the session.

HELPING CLASS MEMBERS ACT

Remind class members that Jesus has told us that these attitudes, which seem strange and unreal from our society's perspective, are the source of our happiness. Challenge the students to select at least one Beatitude that they will intentionally try to put into practice in the coming week.

Ask the class to search their own hearts this week to see if there is someone to whom they need to extend mercy. If so, ask them to offer a word of forgiveness, or set aside a grudge, or let go of bitterness, or whatever else they need to do.

Encourage students to find at least one situation during the week in which they can serve as peacemakers. That situation may be one in which they need to make peace within themselves.

Challenge students to think about their willingness to undergo persecution—or at least have to deal with enemies—because of their faith in Christ. Are they facing such persecution now because of their unwillingness to engage in behaviors that they find unchristian?

PLANNING FOR NEXT SUNDAY

Next week we will talk about loving our enemies. Have the students ask themselves, "Who are my enemies? Can I really love them?" Also ask them to read Matthew 5:38-48 and Luke 10:25-37 as background scripture. We will focus on the verses from Matthew in class.

LOVING THE UNLOVABLE

PREVIEWING THE LESSON

Lesson Scripture: Matthew 5:38-48
Background Scripture: Matthew 5:38-48; Luke 10:25-37
Key Verse: Matthew 5:44

Focus of the lesson:
Jesus' challenge to love one's enemies

Main question(s) of the lesson:
(1) How far are we to go in trying to love the unlovable, the enemy?

This lesson will enable adult learners to:
(1) evaluate Jesus' teaching that calls for love of enemies rather than revenge
(2) perceive Jesus' teaching to be a guide for their lives
(3) respond by living in peace and love with all persons during the coming week.

Today's lesson may be outlined as follows:
(1) Introduction
(2) Going the Second Mile (Matthew 5:38-41)
(3) Boundless Generosity (Matthew 5:42)
(4) Loving as God Loves (Matthew 5:43-48)

FOCUSING ON THE MAIN QUESTION

Again Jesus defies our common sense. A little boy once drew a picture for his preschool teacher. It was a typical child's drawing, except for the background. His house and tree were shown against a landscape that consisted of the page divided, from top to bottom, into thirds: blue sky, blank paper, and green grass. "Very good," said the teacher, "but you should color the sky blue all the way down to the ground. Look out of the window, and you will see that is the way it is." "I know it looks like the sky touches the earth," he argued, "but I've been out there, and it doesn't!"

It's hard to argue with the logic of the obvious. No wonder it took the human race so long to get used to the notion that the earth goes around the sun. It just looks like the sun goes around us. We now know otherwise, but we still talk of sunrise and sunset. It's hard to change the way we perceive the world. But Jesus would have us look at the world not as "you have heard that it was said," but as "I say to you." And he said things that upset our common sense. Our common sense says: Don't fall for con artists. Jesus said: "Give to everyone who begs from you, and do not refuse anyone who wants to borrow from you." Does he really mean that? We want to say: "Be practical, Jesus. You don't mean that literally, do you?" But there are his words, stark and real. Yet we think that if we act on his teaching, we won't have a dime left because we've all become such soft touches! I work in the inner city, where there are panhandlers on every corner. Most of them have a drinking problem, and I think that a lot of them are professional cheats. Must I give them whatever they ask? **How far are we to go in trying to love the unlovable, the enemy?** This is the question that today's lesson compels us to consider as we continue our study of the Sermon on the Mount.

READING THE SCRIPTURE

NRSV
Matthew 5:38-48

38 "You have heard that it was said, 'An eye for an eye and a tooth for a tooth.' 39But I say to you, Do not resist an evildoer. But if anyone strikes you on the right cheek, turn the other also; 40and if anyone wants to sue you and take your coat, give your cloak as well; 41and if anyone forces you to go one mile, go also the second mile. 42Give to everyone who begs from you, and do not refuse anyone who wants to borrow from you.

43 "You have heard that it was said, 'You shall love your neighbor and hate your enemy.' 44But I say to you, Love your enemies and pray for those who persecute you, 45so that you may be children of your Father in heaven; for he makes his sun rise on the evil and on the good, and sends rain on the righteous and on the unrighteous. 46For if you love those who love you, what reward do you have? Do not even the tax collectors do the same? 47And if you greet only your brothers and sisters, what more are you doing than others? Do not even the Gentiles do the same? 48Be perfect, therefore, as your heavenly Father is perfect."

NIV
Matthew 5:38-48

38"You have heard that it was said, 'Eye for eye, and tooth for tooth.' 39But I tell you, Do not resist an evil person. If someone strikes you on the right cheek, turn to him the other also. 40And if someone wants to sue you and take your tunic, let him have your cloak as well. 41If someone forces you to go one mile, go with him two miles. 42Give to the one who asks you, and do not turn away from the one who wants to borrow from you.

43"You have heard that it was said, 'Love your neighbor and hate your enemy.' 44But I tell you: Love your enemies and pray for those who persecute you, 45that you may be sons of your Father in heaven. He causes his sun to rise on the evil and the good, and sends rain on the righteous and the unrighteous. 46If you love those who love you, what reward will you get? Are not even the tax collectors doing that? 47And if you greet only your brothers, what are you doing more than others? Do not even pagans do that? 48Be perfect, therefore, as your heavenly Father is perfect."

Key Verse

Ke Ver

UNDERSTANDING THE SCRIPTURE

Matthew 5:38-48. This portion of the Sermon on the Mount helps us to understand how we are to relate to our enemies and others we consider unlovable. Jesus' proposals are a radical departure from commonly accepted behavior. The segment we will study today is divided into three sections: verses 38-41, verse 42, and verses 43-48.

Matthew 5:38. Jesus begins the first section of this teaching by quoting the law regarding retaliation and compensation for damages, known as *lex talionis* (see Exodus 21:23-25; Leviticus 24:19-21; and Deuteronomy 19:21). The idea of an "eye for eye" may sound harsh, but the purpose of this law was to prohibit punishment that was far out of proportion to the crime. When it was originally adopted, this law provided a moral advancement over other ancient societies.

Matthew 5:39. Jesus' radical teaching is that we are not to retaliate at all. Instead, we are to avoid violence. No amount of injury done to us excuses destructive behavior on our part (see Proverbs 24:29). Our passive resistance (turning the other cheek), rather than physical confrontation, can cause the enemy to change his or her mind. Jesus is not teaching us to ignore or be resigned to evil but to overcome it in a loving way.

Matthew 5:40. A second example of a loving response to an evil act concerns giving one's cloak (a heavy garment that protected one from the weather) as well as one's coat (an inner tunic). Palestinian peasants would use their outer garment as a blanket, so it was doubly important (see Exodus 22:26-27).

Matthew 5:41. A third example of a loving response involves the practice of forcing civilians to go with soldiers or kings to carry their parcels. The word "forces" is the same one Matthew used to record that Simon of Cyrene was compelled to carry

our Lord's cross (Matthew 27:32). Civilians were generally required to go one mile; to go the extra mile would stun the hated Roman enemy.

Matthew 5:42. The final example of a loving response does not relate to evil as much as it shows us how to be kind and loving to all persons. Most commentators hedge on this statement of extreme generosity. Yet, Jesus is clearly calling for unlimited expressions of love.

Matthew 5:43. This verse begins a section on loving one's enemies. Jewish law said that "you shall love your neighbor as yourself" (Leviticus 19:18). Nowhere does the law teach that we should hate our enemies. However, there are numerous examples, especially in the Psalms, that such an attitude exists (see for example Psalm 3:7; 109; and 139:21).

Matthew 5:44. The Greek word translated here as "love" is *agape*. This is the type of love Jesus displayed when he forgave his enemies from the cross (Luke 23:34) and that Paul describes in 1 Corinthians 13. One way of showing this love is to pray for those who persecute us.

Matthew 5:45. To become "children" (or "sons") of God means that our lives are patterned after the nature of God. God loves all people, as evidenced by the fact that the sun rises and the rain falls on everyone, regardless of their relationship with or attitude toward God. For us to live in accordance with the nature of God requires a reversal of the way we normally respond to those whom we perceive to be enemies.

Matthew 5:46. If we love those who love us, they will return that love; our reward is simply more love from them. Jesus uses the tax collector, a person whom most of Jesus' audience would think lacked moral character, as an example of one who would return love.

Matthew 5:47. In the Near East, a greeting was a prayer. The reference to Gentiles provides a clue that this gospel is addressed to Jewish Christians.

Matthew 5:48. The word translated "perfect" has at its root *telos*, "end." Hence it means "completed" or "matured" or "finished" (see John 19:30). For us to fulfill all righteousness we must go all the way to the end. We are to be perfect in love.

Luke 10:25-37. The parable of the good Samaritan, found only in Luke, is included in today's background scripture reading as an example of the kind of love that Jesus is speaking of in the Sermon on the Mount. This parable is complex, but the main point for our lesson today is that everyone is our neighbor. In other words, all people are to be shown God's love, even those whom we have been taught to think of as enemies. Furthermore, the person in the story who showed love—the Samaritan—is the one who followed God's law to love one's neighbor.

INTERPRETING THE SCRIPTURE

Going Beyond the Law of Eye for Eye

In Matthew 5:38-42, Jesus teaches us how we are to respond to those persons whose ill treatment of us seems to warrant retaliation. He begins this teaching by quoting from the law concerning retaliation that was adopted in the days of Moses (see Exodus 21:23-25; Leviticus 24:19-21; and Deuteronomy 19:21). We may smugly recoil in horror at such words as "eye for eye," insisting that we as Christians should forgive. And of course, we are called to do that. Yet we need to understand that the "eye for eye" law was a giant step beyond the punishment that other ancient peoples meted out. A simple act of injustice could lead to wholesale killing of one's enemies. The Mosaic law circumscribed the retaliation so that the punishment more nearly fit the crime.

Jesus radically moves beyond this idea by insisting that we forgo the retaliation completely. Instead of returning evil for evil, no matter how measured it may be, we are called to return good for evil. This incredible idea rubs our humanity the wrong way. We really want to throttle someone who hurts us or our loved ones. We like the satisfaction of making sure that our enemies get what's coming to them. Perhaps that's why we cling so tenaciously to an ineffective prison system and capital punishment. No, says Jesus, return evil behavior with a gracious, loving act. Such behavior is in keeping with the nature of God.

Jesus gives some concrete examples as to how we are to resist evil in such a way that it will make the perpetrators sit up and take notice. Our reactions will stun them. If someone hits us, we are not to hit back but offer the other cheek. Of course, this teaching does not call persons who are in abusive situations to continue to remain there, but it does set forth the principle of nonviolence. In the second example, if we are sued we are to give not only the lesser item that was requested (the inner coat) but the heavier, more valuable cloak that served double duty as clothing and a blanket. Thirdly, when the hated Roman soldiers force us to carry their baggage for one mile, which they could do whenever they chose, we are to go with them for two miles. This teaching must have sounded especially nettlesome to Jesus' listeners, for the Jews certainly did not want to be labeled as Roman collaborators. Jesus was not making a political point here, but was calling his followers to do the unexpected as an act of love.

Giving to All Who Ask

Jesus closes the portion of his teaching concerning nonviolence with a more general statement about giving to all who beg and lending to all who want to borrow. This teaching confronts me on a daily basis. I work in an inner-city church, where there is a constant stream of poor people, some not very pleasant to look upon or smell. I have a modest discretionary fund with which to help such folk, but there is far more need than there is money. This very morning I was approached by an HIV positive man needing bus fare, a prostitute who wanted her telephone turned back on, two men needing prescriptions filled, and more than fifty who said they were hungry. For years I was tormented with the question, "How do you decide who is worthy of your gifts, that is, the so-called 'deserving poor'?"

To my astonishment, I found help for my dilemma in the writings of Calvin, the sixteenth-century spokesman for the Reformation, who is famous for his stern theology and infamous "Calvinist work ethic." Listen to his startling words from *Institutes of the Christian Religion*, Book III, Chapter VII, "A Summary of the Christian Life. Of Self Denial" (italics mine):

Therefore, whoever be the man that is presented to you as needing your assistance, *you have no ground for declining to give it* to him. Say he is a stranger. The Lord has given him a mark which ought to be familiar to you: for which reason he forbids you to despise your own flesh (Galatians vi. 10). Say he is mean and of no consideration. The Lord points him out as one whom he has distinguished by the lustre of his own image (Isaiah lviii. 7). Say that you are bound to him by no ties of duty. The Lord has substituted him as it were in to his own place, that in him you may recognise the many great obligations under which the Lord has laid you to himself. Say that he is unworthy of your least exertion on his account; but the image of God, by which he is recommended

to you, is worthy of yourself and all your exertions. But if he not only merits no good, but has provoked you by injury and mischief, still this is no good reason why you should not embrace him in love, and visit him with offices of love. Everyone should rather consider that, however great he is, he owes himself to his neighbors, and that the only limit to his beneficence is the failure of his means.

At first glance Calvin's words terrified me, and made me realize that Jesus had said very much the same thing: "Give to everyone who begs from you, and do not refuse anyone who wants to borrow from you" (Matthew 5:42). Moreover, our Lord went on to say that this applies not simply to your friends, but to your foes (Matthew 5:44). To put the matter in simple English, the answer to my question has nothing to do with the "worth" of the recipient or whether I consider this person a friend or foe, but with whether or not I have any money!

Loving Our Enemies

I don't have to like my enemies, but I do have to love them. I don't have to approve of them, but I do have to accept them. I don't have to pretend they are nice when they are not, but I must be nice, even when they are not. These ideas may strike us as strange, but Jesus is again teaching us to view the world from the radical, upside down perspective of God.

Loving my neighbor is difficult enough. Although nowhere in the Bible can we find an injunction to hate our enemies, we see examples of persons—especially psalmists—calling God to avenge them. I suspect if we are honest, we have shared the psalmists' feelings at times. Jesus says, however, that we are to love our enemies and pray for them. Sounds impossible, doesn't it? Well, it is, at least from the human perspective. Jesus is telling us that such behavior reflects the nature of God, who makes sure that everyone—the good and the evil alike—have the benefit of the sun and the rain. To reflect such love is truly to be a child of God. Lest someone miss the point, Jesus goes on to say that loving those who love us is not enough. Even the hated tax collectors who extort money from their own Jewish colleagues will love those who love them. And just greeting our friends isn't enough, either. No, we are called to be perfect just as God is perfect.

When Jesus speaks of being perfect, he doesn't mean that we can throw away our erasers. He's talking here about completeness, spiritual maturity, wholeness. To pattern ourselves after the nature of God means that we need not contemplate revenge when we've been wronged. Our loving response will undo our enemy. We should not worry about how to hang on to what is ours but be willing to give even more than what is requested. We need not be stingy with our time and energy but, instead, stand ready to "go the extra mile." We are to love our neighbor, of course, but to be like God we must love the unlovable person who always seems to be under our skin. That person, too, is our neighbor.

In another place (Luke 10:25-37), Jesus teaches a parable that demonstrates the kind of selfless love for the enemy and the unlovable that he speaks about in the Sermon on the Mount. In this parable of the good Samaritan, we see good "church" folk—a priest and a Levite—pass by a seriously injured man who is lying in a ditch. They're on their way to worship, so they don't want to defile themselves by touching something ritually unclean, even if that "something" does happen to be a hurting human. No, they pass by on the other side of the road so as not to come too close. Along comes a Samaritan, a bitter enemy of the Jews. He not only stops to render first aid, but hoists the man onto his donkey, takes him to the local motel, pays the tab, and promises to pick up any additional charges. What an incredible response of love and compassion! In essence, Jesus is saying that there is no one outside the circle of our love. Friends and enemies are all loved by God. We are called to love them all as well.

SHARING THE SCRIPTURE

PREPARING TO TEACH

Today's lesson again calls us to think and act from Jesus' upside down view of the world. He teaches us not only to avoid revenge but also to act with lovingkindness to those who have wronged us. As you read the scripture and lesson material for this week, reflect on the changes you would need to make in your own life to live as Jesus calls you to live. You may want to write your thoughts in your spiritual journal.

Decide which activities you want to use and how you will present them.

For your own enrichment you may want to read Dietrich Bonhoeffer's classic exposition of the Sermon on the Mount as recorded in his widely available book *The Cost of Discipleship*. A Lutheran pastor, Bonhoeffer died as a martyr who resisted Hitler.

LEADING THE CLASS

Introduction

Today's main question is: **How far are we to go in trying to love the unlovable, the enemy?**

To introduce that question, have the class consider one or more of the following case studies to determine: **(1) How would most of us respond to such a situation? (2) How does Jesus call us to respond?**

You may want to work together, or divide into teams if the class is large. If you divide the class, spend a few moments reporting to the entire group.

Case 1

A homeless man comes to your church during a fellowship lunch and asks if he can have some leftovers. You seat him and graciously serve him. He returns next week when you are again having lunch, this time with two friends. Word soon spreads among the homeless population in your area that food is available here, causing no slight amount of upset among some members of the congregation as more and more people crowd in on what was once a church members only event. What can you do?

(This case is based on a true story, so let me share what happened in case you want to tell the class. The church leaders decided that they must feed the hungry but could not feed the entire city. So they decided what their limits were, and they began giving out tickets to the first fifty hungry who came. The others, regrettably, they had to turn away. But a wonderful thing happened. One person's "No" became someone else's "Yes." Today there are as many as seven churches in that city serving the hungry at noon, every day of the week. The church has been having that midweek meal for the poor for nearly twenty years, and, though it has never put it in the church budget, it has been operating in the black for all those years. "Why?" some people have asked. I think it is because they are doing what Jesus told them to.)

Case 2

As you are leaving a shopping mall you are accosted by a man who points a gun at you, steals your wallet or purse, and then drives off in your car. How do you respond?

Case 3

Someone you thought was a friend has been making false accusations against you resulting in your arrest for child abuse. You are innocent, but your reputation is badly tarnished and you've spent a fortune in lawyer's fees. How do you respond to this person?

Going the Second Mile

Choose someone to read Matthew 5:38-41.

Use the material from "Understanding the Scripture" and the "Interpreting the Scripture" subsection entitled "Going Beyond the Law of Eye for Eye" to provide background information for a class discussion or lecture.

Verse 38: The law of retaliation

Be sure to note that although this law originally meant to ensure that the punishment would fit the crime, Jesus teaches us to go beyond vengeance. Some people, including some Christians, still think "eye for eye" is a pretty good rule. Ask the class:

(1) **Why do you think vengeance is important to so many people, even though Jesus clearly speaks against it?**

(2) **In what situations, if any, do you personally support this law?**

(3) **How do we see this law at work in our criminal justice system?**

(4) **If we were to be faithful to Jesus' teaching, what changes would we make in our lives?**

(5) **What changes would we work to enact in the life of our community and nation?**

(6) **What forces prevent us from making these personal or social changes?**

Verse 39: Nonviolence
Ask the class:

(1) **How does this verse relate to the teachings and actions of Mahatma Gandhi (who studied Jesus' teachings) and to Dr. Martin Luther King Jr. (who studied Jesus and Gandhi)?**

? **(2)** **Is Jesus simply calling for a nonviolent response here, a passive resistance, or is what he is teaching more proactive?** If so, how? (Note that Jesus calls for a positive response. Turning the other cheek is an astonishing response that has the potential to win over the enemy.)

? **(3)** **What might Jesus have to say about assertiveness training and its place, if any, in the Christian life?**

Verse 40: Giving more than is asked

Note that Christians were taught not to sue one another at all (see 1 Corinthians 6:1-8). However, Jesus teaches that if his followers were hauled into court, they were to go beyond settling on whatever was requested

? and give something of greater value. **(1) How does this teaching fit into our society, which is far more prone to lawsuits than Jesus could have imagined? (2) If a Christian is in a situation where he or she could bring suit against another, what should determine whether the suit is filed?**

Verse 41: Going the second mile

? Ask the class: **(1) When we say that someone went the "extra mile," what are we saying about that person's actions? (2) Jesus notes that such actions are to be the norm not the exception. What are some ways that we can go the extra mile for other persons, especially those who are strangers or persons we intensely dislike?**

Boundless Generosity

Read aloud Matthew 5:42.

? Ask the class: **How far should our generosity go?** Likely you will get responses such as I shared in the "Giving to All Who Ask" section under "Interpreting the Scripture." You may want to use these ideas if you are preparing a lecture. Follow up such points with the reading from John Calvin in the same section. Ask the class to respond to his ideas.

Depending upon your class's position on this matter of generosity, you may want to add these points to the discussion: If we are really to help people in need, we must do more than hand out money. We need to identify with them as human beings (1 Corinthians 9:19-22; Hebrews 13:3; and Romans 12:15), to become "incarnate" among them (John 1:14), to assist them in finding the help they need (Luke 10:34-35), and to proclaim the good news to them through acts of love (James 2:14-16). There is no end to our responsibility to our fellow human beings because there is no end to God's merciful care for us.

Loving As God Loves

Choose a student to read aloud Matthew 5:43-48.

Be sure to note two important points as you give background information: First, there is no biblical teaching that says we are to hate our enemies. Second, we love the enemy or otherwise unlovable person for a purpose: "so that [we] may be children of [our] Father in heaven."

Ask the class:

(1) What do these teachings of Jesus say to us about the nature of God? ?

(2) What does he mean when he tells us to be perfect like God?

(3) How can we achieve such an impossible goal?

(4) While it may appear that we are responding in a loving way for the benefit of the other person (and indeed that is true), we are also reaping benefits. What benefits do you see here? (Point out that we become spiritually mature and complete as we pattern ourselves after the nature of God. This completeness makes us whole, healthy, well-integrated beings who are at peace with God, with one another, and with ourselves.)

You may want to close this segment by taking a brief look at the parable of the good Samaritan. Ask the class: **How does this parable demonstrate Jesus' teachings?** You may want to supplement their answers by using material under the "Loving Our Enemies" section of "Interpreting the Scripture."

HELPING CLASS MEMBERS ACT

Suggest that the class consider this question: What would happen if I treated every single person I met as my friend? Or, to put it another way, what if I treated every-

one as someone who has been reconciled to God and me through Jesus Christ (2 Corinthians 5:16-21)? Challenge class members to try living this way for a week and see what happens.

Some students may be interested in reading more about the teachings and practice of Gandhi and Dr. Martin Luther King Jr. If so, urge them to consider as they read how these twentieth-century giants have interpreted and acted upon Jesus' teaching.

PLANNING FOR NEXT SUNDAY

Next week's lesson is about priorities. Ask the class to prepare by writing on a note card: The three most important things in my life are 1._____, 2._____, and 3._____. Ask them to read Matthew 6:19-21; 24-34; and Luke 12:13-21. Our class will focus on the scriptures from Matthew.

TRUSTING GOD FOR DAILY NEEDS

PREVIEWING THE LESSON

Lesson Scripture: Matthew 6:19-21, 24-34
Background Scripture: Matthew 6:19-21, 24-34; Luke 12:13-21
Key Verse: Matthew 6:33

Focus of the lesson:
the priority of the kingdom of God in the lives of believers

Main question(s) of the lesson:
(1) Do we dare to believe Jesus' claim that we can trust God to meet our needs?

This lesson will enable adult learners to:
(1) understand Jesus' teaching regarding total dependence upon God
(2) develop a greater level of trust in God's ability and willingness to meet daily needs
(3) respond by examining and, if need be, changing their own priorities.

Today's lesson may be outlined as follows:
(1) Introduction
(2) You Can't Take It with You (Matthew 6:19-21)
(3) Trust God for Your Needs (Matthew 6:24-32)
(4) Seek God's Kingdom First (Matthew 6:33-34)

FOCUSING ON THE MAIN QUESTION

In the Beatitudes, we heard Jesus say that the poor are happy. How much did we believe it? At the moment I write this lesson, all my bills are paid and I have a couple of hundred dollars in my pocket. Of course there are the house payments, and the car payments, and the quarterly income taxes, and a big insurance premium due next month, but, for the moment, I'm solvent and can afford groceries. Right after Christ-mas, I wasn't able to cover quite all the bills and had to charge some stuff on my credit card. And there was almost no cash in my billfold for about two weeks. Now tell me, why do I feel so much better this month than I did in January? Could it be that I am putting my trust in the wrong place?

Benjamin Franklin said, "One who multiplies riches multiplies Cares." Most of us have been overheard to say, "Well, I know that, but I'd like to take the chance." Just as it seems that the earth is flat, it also seems that money is dependable. When Jesus starts talking about God taking care of the lilies of the field and the birds of the air, he sounds like a dreamer. What does he know of the hard realities of life?

He knew the hard facts better than we do. "Foxes have holes," he said, "and birds of the air have nests; but the Son of Man has nowhere to lay his head" (Matthew 8:20). He faced reality more honestly than anyone else who has ever lived. Tempted in every form, he knew without a doubt that he could trust God. Jesus calls us to do the same, to put our trust in God—not cash (mammon)—to meet our daily needs. He seems to be asking us to step out, like Indiana Jones, into the unknown, on an invisible walkway. **Do we dare to believe Jesus' claim that we can trust God to meet our needs?** This is the main question that confronts us today.

READING THE SCRIPTURE

NRSV
Matthew 6:19-21

19 "Do not store up for yourselves treasures on earth, where moth and rust consume and where thieves break in and steal; 20but store up for yourselves treasures in heaven, where neither moth nor rust consumes and where thieves do not break in and steal. 21For where your treasure is, there your heart will be also.

Matthew 6:24-34

24 "No one can serve two masters; for a slave will either hate the one and love the other, or be devoted to the one and despise the other. You cannot serve God and wealth.

25 "Therefore I tell you, do not worry about your life, what you will eat or what you will drink, or about your body, what you will wear. Is not life more than food, and the body more than clothing? 26Look at the birds of the air; they neither sow nor reap nor gather into barns, and yet your heavenly Father feeds them. Are you not of more value than they? 27And can any of you by worrying add a single hour to your span of life? 28And why do you worry about clothing? Consider the lilies of the field, how they grow; they neither toil nor spin, 29yet I tell you, even Solomon in all his glory was not clothed like one of these.

NIV
Matthew 6:19-21

19"Do not store up for yourselves treasures on earth, where moth and rust destroy, and where thieves break in and steal. 20But store up for yourselves treasures in heaven, where moth and rust do not destroy, and where thieves do not break in and steal. 21For where your treasure is, there your heart will be also.

Matthew 6:24-34

24"No one can serve two masters. Either he will hate the one and love the other, or he will be devoted to the one and despise the other. You cannot serve both God and Money.

25"Therefore I tell you, do not worry about your life, what you will eat or drink; or about your body, what you will wear. Is not life more important than food, and the body more important than clothes? 26Look at the birds of the air; they do not sow or reap or store away in barns, and yet your heavenly Father feeds them. Are you not much more valuable than they? 27Who of you by worrying can add a single hour to his life?

28"And why do you worry about clothes? See how the lilies of the field grow. They do not labor or spin. 29Yet I tell you that not even Solomon in all his

MAY 19

³⁰But if God so clothes the grass of the field, which is alive today and tomorrow is thrown into the oven, will he not much more clothe you—you of little faith? ³¹Therefore do not worry, saying, 'What will we eat?' or 'What will we drink?' or 'What will we wear?' ³²For it is the Gentiles who strive for all these things; and indeed your heavenly Father knows that you need all these things. ³³But strive first for the kingdom of God and his righteousness, and all these things will be given to you as well.

34 "So do not worry about tomorrow, for tomorrow will bring worries of its own. Today's trouble is enough for today.

splendor was dressed like one of these. ³⁰If that is how God clothes the grass of the field, which is here today and tomorrow is thrown into the fire, will he not much more clothe you, O you of little faith? ³¹So do not worry, saying, 'What shall we eat?' or 'What shall we drink?' or 'What shall we wear?' ³²For the pagans run after all these things, and your heavenly Father knows that you need them. ³³But seek first his kingdom and his righteousness, and all these things will be given to you as well. ³⁴Therefore do not worry about tomorrow, for tomorrow will worry about itself. Each day has enough trouble of its own.

UNDERSTANDING THE SCRIPTURE

The portion of the Sermon on the Mount that we will be studying today concerns learning how to trust God with our whole heart.

Matthew 6:19-21. The adobe-like walls of a first-century house could be easily attacked by a robber with a pick and shovel. Valuables made of cloth are vulnerable to mothholes, while those made of metal can rust. Earthly treasure refers not only to material wealth, but also to all those fleeting human rewards with which the world seduces us, such as popularity, power, and ease. In contrast to these perishable earthly goods, Jesus calls us to store up treasures before God where they are not subject to theft or deterioration. Our heart and treasure are indeed found together. We care for and think about that which is most important to us.

Matthew 6:24. The NRSV reads "wealth" where the King James Version has "mammon." *Mammon* is literally what the Greek says; it is an Aramaic word for "riches," and was simply transliterated, first to Greek, and then to English, and has been thought by some to be the name for a pagan god. The

word means, "cash." But money can surely be worshiped to our peril (1 Timothy 6:10). Just as a master would not allow his servants to work for him and for another master, Jesus says we cannot divide our loyalties.

Matthew 6:25-34. Jesus' basic teaching in these verses is that we are not to worry about material things. Preoccupation with daily responsibilities can derail our spiritual lives (Matthew 13:22). Jesus is not saying that we should pay no attention to practical matters. He often argued for prudence (see Matthew 10:16; 25:27; and Luke 14:28-32). The important point is that we are to get our priorities straight: God's kingdom comes first (see especially Matthew 6:33).

Matthew 6:25. Note how this verse and verse 34, which are similar, bracket the material in between. The word translated here as "worry" means to be absorbed by or preoccupied.

Matthew 6:26. God the creator cares for the birds of the air who neither plant nor harvest their food. The implication here is that we can trust God to care for us as well.

Matthew 6:27. Preoccupation with the details of life will not add any more time to our lives or, as some translations suggest, height to our stature.

Matthew 6:28-29. The lilies, like the birds, are cared for by God the creator. They do not "toil," which may be a reference to the work men did. Nor did they "spin," which likely referred to a woman's task. Despite the fact that they neither work nor have a long life, God clothes them. King Solomon's wealth was enormous. The queen of Sheba, who was wealthy in her own right, was overwhelmed by Solomon's riches, including the clothing of his servants (1 Kings 10:5).

Matthew 6:30. Compare this verse with Psalm 90:5-6 and Isaiah 40:6-8. Jesus has called his listeners' attention to the way in which God lovingly cares for creation. When we are preoccupied with daily concerns, we are not trusting God to take care of us and, therefore, are of "little faith."

Matthew 6:31. Jesus says that we are not to worry over the basic necessities, that is, what we will eat, drink, or wear.

Matthew 6:32. The Gentiles—people who are not part of the Jewish community of faith—are preoccupied with meeting their basic needs. God's people, though, should know that God is aware of what they need.

Matthew 6:33. The key verse is the crux of this passage. Jesus is not speaking here as if there were two things to seek, the kingdom of God and God's righteousness. The two are inseparable. If our priorities are in order, then we need not worry about how we will get the basic necessities.

Matthew 6:34. "Today's trouble is enough for today." This is a fine example of Jesus' humor. It may have been a common proverb in his day.

Luke 12:13-15. In response to someone in the crowd who wants Jesus to settle a dispute regarding an inheritance, Jesus warns against greed and says that "life does not consist in the abundance of possessions" (verse 15).

Luke 12:16-21. The question about inheritance provided the setting for the parable of the rich fool. This story fits in beautifully with our lesson because it is a supreme example of one who puts his trust in cash rather than God. (Compare Luke 12:21 with Matthew 6:21 and 33.) The rich landowner in this story was well prepared to live a hedonistic life ("relax, eat, drink, be merry," verse 19), but he was not prepared to die. His earthly treasures would belong to someone else, but he apparently had taken no thought for storing up heavenly treasures.

INTERPRETING THE SCRIPTURE

The Beatitudes of Mammon

One of the best ways of analyzing the priorities of a people is to read their advertisements. From long experience, Madison Avenue has learned what they think is most likely to make us happy. If we look carefully at how they go about trying to make us buy things, we get strong clues as to what they think motivates us.

This morning I noticed a magazine ad trying to entice readers to take a course so as to improve their lives. The woman, whose scantily clad husband is shown embracing her (you can often find that sort of motivation in contemporary ads), lamented about how frustrating her job was. She found it difficult to go to work every day. Her frustrations spilled over into her personal life, creating problems at home. She and her husband would argue, often about money. Then they discovered an educational opportunity that would enable them to change careers. They took advantage of that opportunity and within a few months their whole lives were changed. Not only did they have new jobs that they both liked, but they also had money to buy whatever they wanted. They even took a fabulous vacation.

Now maybe taking a course can change your life; there is no question that education and training are good things. The point is, what does this ad say about our priorities? What do the ad writers think will inspire us to purchase their products? The answer is clear: money (with a little sex thrown in). The woman in that ad has goals in life for happiness, and they all boil down to this: Blessed are the well-to-do.

Money, of itself, is not an evil. Indeed, in the parable of the talents (see Lesson 4), Jesus advises us to use it for good. It is the love of money that is the root of evil (1 Timothy 6:10). To restate Jesus' warning: You cannot have two gods; you must choose between God and cash. We can't worship and strive after both. Money is a means, not an end; the kingdom of God is both the means and end!

Idolatry

Because we do not worship statues, we moderns sometimes fool ourselves into thinking that we are not idolaters. But the false gods and their temples are all around us. Our idolatry is more subtle, but just as real as that of the ancient world (see Paul's description of Athens in Acts 17:22-23). My inner-city church, which at one time was the tallest building in our city, is now dwarfed by the towers of banks and insurance companies. We can easily be deceived because many of the things we are in danger of worshiping are good things; sex and appetite, for example were declared good in Genesis 1:28-31. The problem comes when we give them our first allegiance. We can enjoy money and the things it can buy, but we are not to worship it. If we seek God first, then other blessings will be added (Matthew 6:33).

The false gods (I prefer to call them "the lesser gods") are very subtle. They seem to promise happiness. The following dialogue is heard quite often:

"How are you doing?"

"Oh, fine. There's nothing wrong with me that a hundred thousand dollars wouldn't cure."

We think, "If only I had someone to love me. . . . If only I had some peace and quiet . . . . If only I could have a drink. . . ." The false gods pretend to offer salvation, but they cannot save. All the money in the world cannot make a person whole. And what is worse, although these false gods do not have the power to save, they do have the power to destroy. How many people do you know who have been literally brought to their doom by lust for prestige, property, or pleasure?

The lesser gods may have their place, but that place is always secondary. We must get our priorities straight. As C. S. Lewis wrote, "When God arrives (and only then) the half-gods can remain." Money, put to the service of God, can become a wonderful thing. Sexuality, when it is pure, (that is, offered to God as a sacrament), can produce the greatest of joys. It is not an accident that the Bible uses sexuality as a metaphor for the kingdom (see Jeremiah 31:32; Ephesians 5:25; Mark 2:19-20; Revelation 19:7; 21:2; and many other places.) Even the lesser gods of prestige and power have their place, but only when they are put at the disposal of the One to whom power alone belongs.

As an adolescent, I remember saying to my mother, "I wish I had more friends." She answered, "The way to have friends is to be a friend." I did not understand then what she meant, but, slowly, through the years I have learned that she was right. As long as I sought friendship as a means to my own pleasure, I was merely using people. But, insofar as I have learned to love people, I have found that I have hundreds of friends. Here again is the familiar principle that we have come to recognize as the heart of Jesus' message: to lose is to save; to achieve happiness, I must give it away.

Priorities

You may remember the Texas shoe magnate who kept a sign on his desk which read: GOD FIRST, FAMILY SECOND, SHOES THIRD. We should all have such a sign posted in the back of our minds at all times. And it should read, in one form or another: "But strive first for the kingdom of God, and his righteousness, and all these things will be given to you as well" (Matthew 6:33).

Our lesson this week urges us to decide what really matters. This search is a struggle that is repeated in the life of each person. The wisdom book called Ecclesiastes describes such a search. The author tried all manner of the world's blessings, seeking to find happiness in life: wisdom (Ecclesiastes 1:17), pleasure (2:1), and power (2:9), and concluded that "all was vanity and a chasing after wind" (2:11). Finally he came to the conclusion that there is nothing to do but "fear God, and keep his commandments" (12:13). He was on the right track. As a Christian, I cannot help but believe that Jesus represents the answer to Ecclesiastes' life-long quest. One of the last Old Testament books to be written, Ecclesiastes bemoans that "there is nothing new under the sun" (1:9), and yet Jesus proclaims, "I am making all things new" (Revelation 21:5; see also 2 Corinthians 5:17). When we can learn this secret, all the old longings find their answer, our priorities fall into place, and life makes sense at last. We know that we can indeed trust God to care for us.

SHARING THE SCRIPTURE

PREPARING TO TEACH

In keeping with the spirit of our Teacher, as we plan this lesson, we must get our own priorities straight. At the end of last week's lesson, I suggested that we ask students to list their priorities. What did you list for yours? Do you sense that you need to make any changes in these, or are you and God both satisfied with them?

When we trust God to meet our needs, we simplify our lives. We learn that we can live without things that we thought we needed. Richard J. Foster's book *Freedom of Simplicity* (San Francisco Harper-Collins, 1981) is very helpful in teaching us how we can do this. You may want to read this excellent book.

Depending on how you choose to do the "Introduction," you may need newsprint and markers.

If you plan to use the hymn, "Seek Ye First," (or another hymn that relates to seeking God's kingdom) have hymnals available.

If you plan to do the written paraphrase activity under "Seek God's Kingdom First," have note cards or paper and pencils available.

LEADING THE CLASS

Introduction

Begin the class by asking students to discuss the three priorities they were asked to select during the week. As an option, if most students arrive before the designated opening time, have three sheets of newsprint posted and labeled Priority 1, Priority 2, Priority 3, respectively. As students enter the room, have them write their priorities on these sheets using markers. If this plan is not feasible in your setting, have them share their priorities with the entire class or in smaller groups. Record their answers yourself on a chalkboard or newsprint divided into three columns. Tabulate numbers in each category. For example, seven students may have rated their families as priority one, while ten said that their jobs were most important. Have the class note any trends. Ask them: **(1) Do you think the priorities we have listed are in keeping with Jesus' teaching? If not, why do you suppose that we have made other choices? (2) What do our priorities say about where we have placed our trust?**

Conclude this segment by reading aloud Matthew 6:24. Say something such as: It is hard to trust a Jesus whom we cannot see in the flesh, rather than a bank account, whose balance we can see, or a purse of gold that we can actually handle. We may want to trust God, but we hedge our bets by trusting money as well. But our lesson for today calls us to trust God as instinctively as the birds and the flowers. Can we learn to do that? **Do we dare to believe Jesus' claim that we can trust God to meet our needs?** This is our main question for today.

You Can't Take It with You

Direct the class's attention to Matthew 6:19-21.

You may want to use one or both of these old anecdotes to stimulate the class's thinking on where their treasure really is. Suggested discussion questions follow each one.

Anecdote 1: A rich man loved his Mercedes, and left instruction that he be buried in it. When the car was lowered into its huge grave, with the corpse sitting stiffly in the driver's seat, one of the grave-diggers remarked, "Man, that's really living!"

Ask the class:

(1) Is that really living?

(2) Why do we feel so much better when we have money in our pocket?

(3) We can also ask that question from another perspective: Why do rich people seem to have so many worries?

(4) Is it better to be rich or to be poor? (The answer of course is that one is neither better nor worse than the other. The point of life is not determined either by the presence of money or the lack of it.)

(5) What are some examples of true riches?

(6) If money is not the "other master" who tempts you away from God, what (or who) is your "master"?

Anecdote 2: A wealthy man had died. Curious to know the extent of his fortune, a friend asked, "How much did he leave?" The bereaved family member wryly replied, "All of it."

Ask the class: **(1) What does the incontestable fact that we can't take it with us say to us about what our priorities should be? (2) Does storing up treasures in heaven mean that we have to live as ascetics, not caring about the things of this world, or does Jesus mean something else here? If so, what?** (Note that Jesus is talking about priorities and preoccupations. We can enjoy what we have so long as we treat it lightly rather than let our possessions, power, prestige, or whatever wedge itself between us and God.)

You may want to conclude this segment by making reference to the parable in Luke concerning the wealthy landowner who died (Luke 12:13-21). The point of that story and these anecdotes is very similar. Be sure to briefly retell the parable since all students will not likely have read this background scripture.

Trust God for Your Needs

Select a volunteer to read Matthew 6:25-34 aloud.

Ask the class to look carefully at verse 25. Note that the King James Version translates it as "Take no thought...." A better translation is "Do not be anxious" (RSV) or "Do not worry" (NRSV). But all three of these are negatives. In its positive form, we would say, "Trust God."

Now ask the class for a definition: **What does trust mean?** Supplement their answers with the following information: Trust is closely related to faith; indeed the two words are almost synonymous. It is unfortunate that the English word "faith" is not used in the verb form as well as the noun, so that we must say "have faith," which does not carry the idea of commitment that we really need here. "Belief" is another synonym, and it does have the verb form "believe," which is a help. But belief is often seen merely as "acceptance of a creed." It is that, of course, but in the New Testament it means more. (Remember the story of the man who was asked, "Do you believe I can push this wheelbarrow across this tightrope." He said yes, but he wouldn't get in it.) To believe, or to have faith, means to trust: to risk one's life on the thing or person in whom we believe.

Point out that trust in God generally calls us to simplify our lives, to live as simply as the birds of the air and the lilies of the field. You may want to share this story with the class: A friend of mine, who is a nun, has taken vows of poverty and simplicity. Once she was invited to spend the night with a middle-class family, and in her bedroom was a television set. She enjoyed watching an interesting program. Afterwards she was hungry, so she went down into the kitchen to raid the refrigerator. There she encountered another member of the family, who had watched the same program in his room, and they had an interesting discussion about it. One by one, all the family came into the kitchen for a snack, and they discovered that they had all been watching the same program. My friend was astonished. "How many television sets do you have?" she wondered aloud. They counted seven. As the sister said afterwards, "If they had had seven refrigerators we would never have had the good fellowship and discussion that took place in the kitchen." Prompt the class to respond to this story by asking:

(1) How do the things of this world interfere with our relationships with one another? (2) How do they interfere with our relationship with God?

End this segment by noting that most people in our society are like the middle-class family, not the nun, in the story above. Ask the class: **(1) How can we help people who feel that material things are necessary for their happiness learn to forget all that and live like the birds of the air and the lilies of the field? (2) What changes do we need to make in our own lives to trust God more fully?**

Seek God's Kingdom First

Read in unison today's key verse, Matthew 6:33. If you have access to hymnbooks that include the song, "Seek Ye First," you may want to sing instead of reading the verse. This hymn is on page 405 of *The United Methodist Hymnal.*

Ask the class members to restate Matthew 6:33 in their own words. Distribute note cards or paper and pencils. Allow time for reflection and writing. Then talk about their paraphrases. Ask them to keep what they have written and refer to it during the week ahead.

Now ask class members to design their own wallet cards on the back of their note card or paper with their paraphrase of Matthew 6:33. On this card, they will list two to four concrete actions that they can take to put God first in their lives. Talk with the class about ways in which they can put God first in their day-to-day lives. Help them move beyond the usual answers—go to church, sing in the choir, read the Bible, and pray—all of which are important. Have them look at Micah 6:8; James 1:27; and other scriptures they can think of to discern ways to seek God's kingdom. Help them remember that creative activities (writing a poem) and appreciating God's creation (smelling the flowers) are also ways that we can put God first.

HELPING CLASS MEMBERS ACT

Remind students that we often say that our priorities are in order, but the way we spend our time, talent, and money is not consistent with our list. Challenge students to keep track of their time for an entire day. One way to do this is to jot down at regular intervals (every fifteen to twenty minutes) who they are with and what they are doing. Then they are to compare this log with their priorities. They may be surprised to discover what their real priorities are.

Challenge students to take at least one step this week to simplify their lives. Here are some ideas: (1) go through closets and give away serviceable clothing that you are no longer wearing; (2) consolidate bills insofar as possible so that you have a good handle on how you are spending your money; (3) perform at least one act of justice this week so that some other person may catch a glimpse of the kingdom of God, and (4) brown bag your lunch and contribute the money you saved to a missions project.

Invite the class to read chapters 1 and 2 of Ecclesiastes this week to discover what Qoheleth (the Preacher) learned about the futility of seeking things on earth that do not satisfy our longings for God.

PLANNING FOR NEXT SUNDAY

Next week's lesson is about prayer. Ask students to read Matthew 6:5-15; 7:7-14; and Luke 11:1-13 as background scripture. Our lesson will focus on Matthew 6:5-15. Encourage students to write their own prayers. Invite anyone who is willing to bring a short prayer to class next week that they would be willing to read (or have read) aloud.

LORD, TEACH US TO PRAY

PREVIEWING THE LESSON

Lesson Scripture: Matthew 6:5-15
Background Scripture: Matthew 6:5-15; 7:7-14; Luke 11:1-13
Key Verse: Matthew 6:6

Focus of the lesson:
Jesus' teachings about the method and content of prayer

Main question(s) of the lesson:
(1) How does one pray?

This lesson will enable adult learners to:
(1) encounter the Lord's Prayer as a model for their own prayers
(2) appreciate prayer as a vital means of communication with God
(3) respond by establishing or enhancing regular prayer habits in their own lives.

Today's lesson can be outlined as follows:
(1) Introduction
(2) Jesus' Directions for Prayer (Matthew 6:5-8)
(3) The Lord's Prayer (Matthew 6:9-13)
(4) Forgiveness (Matthew 6:14-15)

FOCUSING ON THE MAIN QUESTION

When I was a seminarian, I was leading a preaching mission in a rural church, and I called upon one of the old-time members to lead us in prayer. I was young then, and had not learned to be careful about embarrassing people by calling on them without warning. As it turned out, I discovered later, this particular person had never prayed in public before. But he was too proud and embarrassed to say so, so he got up and bravely began. It was, in fact, a pretty good prayer. But it went on and on and on. He was racking his brain, he told

me afterwards, to remember how you ended a prayer. He could not think of the phrase, "through Jesus Christ our Lord," or, "in your holy Name we pray," or any of the stock phrases most public pray-ers use. But finally he could think of nothing else to pray about, so, in desperation, he concluded, "Yours truly. Amen."

That is not a bad ending for a prayer. But I tell this story because it reminds me that most of us do not know how to pray. Praying is an art. Not a "fine" art, usually, like painting or sculpture, which may be limited to the specially gifted few, but a humble art, like conversation or folksinging. It belongs to all of us. And Jesus has some art lessons for us. Our earnest desire is that of the disciples: "Lord, teach us to pray." Let us see what lessons we can learn as we examine the prayer that Jesus taught his followers to pray. In last week's lesson, we learned to put our trust where our true treasure is; this week we need to learn to put our words there, too. This then is the main question with which our quarter's study of the teaching of Jesus comes to an end: **How does one pray?**

READING THE SCRIPTURE

NRSV
Matthew 6:5-15

5 "And whenever you pray, do not be like the hypocrites; for they love to stand and pray in the synagogues and at the street corners, so that they may be seen by others. Truly I tell you, they have received their reward. 6But whenever you pray, go into your room and shut the door and pray to your Father who is in secret; and your Father who sees in secret will reward you.

7 "When you are praying, do not heap up empty phrases as the Gentiles do; for they think that they will be heard because of their many words. 8Do not be like them, for your Father knows what you need before you ask him.

9   "Pray then in this way:
    Our Father in heaven,
        hallowed be your name.
10   Your kingdom come.
        Your will be done,
            on earth as it is in heaven.
11   Give us this day our daily
            bread.
12   And forgive us our debts,
            as we also have forgiven our
            debtors.
13   And do not bring us to the
            time of trial,
            but rescue us from the evil
            one.

14For if you forgive others their trespasses, your heavenly Father will also forgive you; 15but if you do not forgive others, neither will your Father forgive your trespasses.

NIV
Matthew 6:5-15

5"But when you pray, do not be like the hypocrites, for they love to pray standing in the synagogues and on the street corners to be seen by men. I tell you the truth, they have received their reward in full. 6But when you pray, go into your room, close the door and pray to your Father, who is unseen. Then your Father, who sees what is done in secret, will reward you. 7And when you pray, do not keep on babbling like pagans, for they think they will be heard because of their many words. 8Do not be like them, for your Father knows what you need before you ask him.

9"This, then, is how you should pray:

    " 'Our Father in heaven,
    hallowed be your name,
10your kingdom come,
        your will be done
            on earth as it is in heaven.
11Give us today our daily bread.

12Forgive us our debts,
        as we also have forgiven our debtors.

13And lead us not into temptation,
        but deliver us from the evil one. '

14For if you forgive men when they sin against you, your heavenly Father will also forgive you. 15But if you do not forgive men their sins, your Father will not forgive your sins.

Key Verse

UNDERSTANDING THE SCRIPTURE

Matthew 6:5-15. Jesus' teaching on prayer comes between two other ways in which we are tempted to take pride in our piety: almsgiving (Matthew 6:2-4) and fasting (Matthew 6:16-18).

Matthew 6:5. Jesus is speaking against acts of piety that are performed to impress other persons. Hypocritical persons who pray ostentatiously have already received their reward in the praise that others give them. Standing was the common attitude for prayer among the Jews (see Luke 18:11, 13), just as kneeling is for some of us today. It does not matter, of course, what our posture is, so long as it is reverent. In the Middle Ages, when royalty came into the room, those present would kneel; today, when a prominent person enters, we stand. Either position is intended to show respect.

Matthew 6:6. "Go into your room" is Jesus' way of saying that praying is to be a private matter. This is not an attack on public worship; it was clearly Jesus' pattern to take part in the synagogue (Luke 4:16), and a practice of the early church as well (Acts 2:46).

Matthew 6:7. According to Jesus, it was not just the hypocrites who prayed improperly, but also the heathen (Gentiles) who made use of magical texts, in attempts to manipulate the gods. There is no formula that can make our prayers effective.

Matthew 6:8. Jesus tells us not to be like either the hypocrites or the heathen. We must neither impress anyone nor give a lengthy recitation to God, for God knows what we need.

Matthew 6:9. "Our Father" was a frequent address to God in Jewish prayer. Jesus probably used the familiar Aramaic, "Abba." This address reflects a childlike trust, which can be related to our previous discussion on trusting God to meet our needs. "Hallowed be your name" is also a very Jewish expression. The name of God has always been a powerful symbol for Jews (Exodus 20:7), who do not even speak it, but substitute Adonai, "Lord," for it wherever it occurs. Indeed so do we, spelling it with four capital letters, LORD, to correspond with the four-letter Hebrew name for God, YHWH.

Matthew 6:10. "Your kingdom come" and "your will be done" are parallel phrases, saying essentially the same thing: Where God's will is done, the reign of God is present.

Matthew 6:11. "Daily bread" means everything that we need (like that which the flowers and the birds receive in Matthew 6:26-29). It may be a reference to the daily manna in the wilderness (Exodus 16:1-36).

Matthew 6:12. "Debts" is a Jewish word for "sins" (see Matthew 18:23-35, the parable of the dishonest steward). Note that God forgives us as we forgive others. Although God's mercy far surpasses ours (see Matthew 20:1-6), we are called to imitate the nature of God by forgiving in the way that God forgives.

Matthew 6:13. The request that we not be led into temptation is probably an apocalyptic reference that means: "Do not let us fall to temptation during the end-time persecution." "For thine is the kingdom and the power, and the glory, forever. Amen" (KJV) was added by the church as early as the first century, and is certainly appropriate, but was not a part of Jesus' original form of the prayer. Because this phrase was a later addition, it is not included in the NRSV, the NIV, or other recent translations.

Matthew 6:14-15. Jesus reiterates the reciprocal nature of forgiveness as seen in verse 12. There is a cause and effect relationship between our willingness to forgive others and God's willingness to forgive us.

Matthew 7:7-11. Although God's name is not mentioned, it is clear that God is the one who will respond to our prayers. God's willingness and ability to respond is far greater than that of earthly parents who want to provide good gifts for their children.

Matthew 7:12. The "Golden Rule" is found in many ancient writings, but in this positive form is unique to Jesus.

Matthew 7:13-14. The two gates, one wide and one narrow, lead to death and life, respectively. Jesus sounds an uncharacteristically pessimistic note in saying that few persons will find the way that leads to life.

Luke 11:1. Jesus teaches the disciples to pray in response to their request. Distinctive forms of prayer marked different religious communities, as implied in the reference here to John teaching his disciples to pray.

Luke 11:2-4. Note that Luke's version of the Lord's Prayer is shorter than Matthew's. Recall that Luke is writing for a Gentile audience that did not have the same religious background as Matthew's readers.

Luke 11:5-8. The parable of the midnight friend drives home the importance of our perseverance in prayer.

Luke 11:9-13. These words are also found in Matthew 7:7-11.

INTERPRETING THE SCRIPTURE

The Discipline of Prayer

Some of us have the notion that prayer ought to "come naturally," like breathing. Perhaps it ought to, but it doesn't. Like marriage, it has to be worked at. Jesus' teaching in the scripture lesson for this week raises many questions that we will never entirely settle, but which we must constantly be struggling with. For instance, in Matthew 6:6 Jesus seems to be saying that all prayer should be like a spontaneous, private conversation with God. Yet Jesus himself worshiped and taught in the temple, surely participating in corporate prayer. In thousands of churches every Lord's Day, the Lord's Prayer is either prayed in unison or read.

The fact that most of us have memorized the Lord's Prayer raises another concern. Some Christians think that a prayer that is written down and then recited inhibits the work of Spirit, and that we should "just pray from the heart." But others think that, if we do not learn "proper" prayers, our undisciplined minds will concentrate on our own ends and neglect that which should be included in our prayers.

Who is right? Both, I think. We do need to pray freely and from the heart, but we also need the discipline of praying great prayers from the Bible and church tradition.

I think the best pray-er I ever heard was an uneducated preacher who could not read, but he had been steeped in the language of the King James Version from childhood. Though he prayed spontaneously, the great phrases rolled out with meaning. I can hear him now, crying, "Vouchsafe to us, O Lord, of thy tender mercies. . . . " He was not reciting those words, he was praying them. We should learn the rules of the game, practice the scales, sketch the bowls of fruit and, when we have mastered their art, become broken field runners, playing by ear and painting in the abstract. The Lord's Prayer can serve as a both a traditional prayer and as a model for all other prayers.

Praying to Whom?

Prayer is an important means of communication and communion between ourselves and God. It is a critical component in our spiritual lives. Thus, prayers should be prayed to God. How often, though, have we heard prayers that seem to be addressed to God, but are really aimed at somebody else? Whenever the liturgist says, "O Lord, you know that . . ." the congregation had better brace itself for a mini-sermon disguised as a prayer. It may be for the purpose of trying to impress people, as in the following prayer that I heard a preacher deliver: "O Lord, we have gathered here this day, by many different modes of transportation. Some of us have cloven the skies in airplanes, some have ridden in trains or buses, some have crossed the seas in ships, some have driven in private limousines, and some of us have walked. . . ."

I've forgotten just what the point of all that was, since surely neither God nor we needed to be reminded of the different modes of available transportation. It must have been for rhetoric's sake alone.

But some prayers, like the following, which was offered by a very religious acquaintance of mine, are clearly designed to persuade: "Our Father, help Pat to decide how to respond to the church that is calling him. And, help him to decide according to the rules laid down by our good friend, Dr. So and So, in his book about knowing the will of God, which are, One. . . ." And she proceeded to enumerate the chapter headings of the book. Maybe the Lord appreciated the book review, being thereby delivered from having to read it, but the truth is, she was not praying to God at all; she was praying to me.

Honesty

We do not pray to impress God, or other people, or to change God's mind, or to explain things to God, as though there were some things God does not know (see Matthew 6:8). Having ruled out these other reasons, we come to what may be the central purpose of prayer: discovering who we are. If we really want God to help us know who we are, we should pray with utter honesty. You would think that praying to God would be the most honest thing we do, but I wonder if it isn't often the most dishonest? I know that ever since I was a child there has been a piece of me that wants to "make a good impression" on God. I think I learned early on that you can fool grown-ups if you wash behind the ears, get a hair cut, and speak politely; it doesn't matter so much what you are, but what kind of impression you make. But you can't fool God, who searches all hearts (Romans 8:27); you can only fool yourself. So, if you are, let us say, in a hospital waiting room while a friend is undergoing radical surgery, it might be better not to pray, "Lord, if it is your will, let my friend live." (Of course if that is what you really mean, say it, but Jesus is the only person I know who was honest enough to say, "Not my will, but yours, be done.") It would be better to say what you really mean, such as, "God, please let my friend live!" Prayer can and does change things, but it is usually you and I who are changed as we pour out our hearts to God.

Answers to Prayer

The story of the midnight friend (Luke 11:5-8; it is found only in Luke) teaches us an important lesson about God's desire to answer our prayers. We may paraphrase this whimsical parable like this: "If you would give a friend a loaf of bread just because he's driving you crazy in the middle of the night, how much more would God answer your needs if you keep on asking! Surely you are no more generous than God!"

Somebody has suggested that God answers prayer in only two ways: "Yes" and "You've got to be kidding!" I think this means that God answers not the prayers of our lips, but the deepest prayers of our hearts (Romans 8:26). In the beautiful three-part saying, "Ask, Search,

Knock" (Matthew 7:7-8; note that the word ASK is an acronym for it), Jesus promises us that God will answer, but the answers may not necessarily be what we are expecting. For instance, to paraphrase verses 9-11 with a slight twist: "Is there anyone among you, who, if your child asks for stones to eat, will not give bread? Or if a child asks for a snake to eat, will not feed the child fish? If you then, as sorry as you are, know what your child really needs, how much more will your Father in heaven give us the things that we really need when we ask for things that are not good for us!"

In keeping with this understanding, sometimes we must recognize that God answers our prayers by not answering, because that is the best for us. I am finally beginning to learn that when I pray, over and over, and passionately, "Lord, tell me what to do in this situation," and no answer comes, that is the Lord saying to me, "My child, you need to stand on your own feet. I trust you to make up your own mind." And I am given the courage to do it. At what is, for me, the turning point of history, God left Jesus on his own, hanging on the cross. In his pain Jesus cried, "My God, my God, why have you forsaken me?" (Matthew 27:46; Mark 15:34.) What greater compliment could Jesus' Father have given him than to trust him on his own with the destiny of the world in his hands? God's non-answers may be painful indeed, but it is in those awesome silences that our faith finds its full maturity.

SHARING THE SCRIPTURE

PREPARING TO TEACH

Begin at the heart of the lesson itself by praying for God's guidance. Then read all the background scripture with an open mind and consult commentaries if you have the time.

If you choose to do the dance to the Lord's Prayer, decide whether you will have the class sing and how you will cue them as to the motions.

If you plan to teach the GRACE model prayer, decide how you will present the information. You may want to make up a handout for distribution.

LEADING THE CLASS

Introduction

In Lesson 10, I suggested a dance to the Beatitudes. If that one worked for you, this one on the Lord's Prayer may work even better because it is easier to do. You can simply speak the prayer as you go through the movements, or you can sing it. If you use Albert Hay Malotte's familiar tune, be sure to start it low enough (about D) so that the ending isn't too high. This version of the prayer was developed by the English Language Liturgical Consultation in 1987. I have added my own gesture.

(1) Our Father
(Open your hands in a gesture to include those on either side of you.)
(2) In heaven,
(Lift your hands high.)
(3) Hallowed be your name,
(Bow with your hands folded as in prayer.)
(4) Your kingdom come,
(Join hands with your neighbors.)
(5) Your will be done, on earth as in heaven.
(On the word heaven, lift your neighbors' hands high.)
(6) Give us today our daily bread.
(Make your hands into a cup.)
(7) Forgive us our sins
(Bow in penitence; hands crossed.)
(8) As we forgive those who sin against us.

(Repeat first gesture.)

(9) Save us from the time of trial,

(Grab your fingertips and pull.)

And deliver us from evil.

(Release fingertips joyfully.)

(10) For the kingdom,

(Spread hands widely.)

The power,

(Make fists and feel your muscle.)

And the glory are yours

(Raise your hands again.)

Now and for ever. Amen.

(Reach for the sky.)

If your class cannot move about—or prefers not to—introduce the main question by reading or retelling this anecdote: I have a friend who says, "the Lord's Prayer is my favorite part of the church service." When pressed as to why, he says, "Because it is familiar, I learned it at my mother's knee, we have it in common with all other Christians, and it's simple enough so that I understand it. At least while I am saying it, I know what I am doing."

Then ask the class: **(1) Do you really think that you understand this profound prayer? (2) As you say it aloud with the congregation (if such is the practice in your church), do you really feel and believe what is says, or do you sometimes just recite it, in a kind of monotonous monotone?**

However you choose to begin, be certain that the class knows that our question for today is this: **How does one pray?**

Jesus' Directions for Prayer

Read aloud Matthew 6:5-8. Use information from the "Understanding the Scripture" section, along with other material you have gleaned from commentaries to explain Jesus' points here.

Then ask the class to consider the following questions as they relate to prayer in their own lives in a different day and time from that which Jesus experienced:

(1) Jesus calls us to pray in private. What do you perceive to be the place of prayer in the midst of a worship service, Sunday school class, or other gathering?

(2) If all prayer is to be in private, what should be the role of the worship leader?

(3) Should we say grace in a restaurant? (I have a private way of saying grace in a restaurant. I quietly lift my fork to a vertical position, pointing at God, to say, "I'm grateful." What is your practice?)

The Lord's Prayer

If you did not use the dance or otherwise pray the Lord's Prayer in class this morning, do so now. If possible, ask everyone to read the prayer from the same translation as it appears in Matthew 6:9-13.

Note that Jesus' disciples could ask him questions about prayer, as they did in Luke 11:1. If your class enjoys thought-provoking activities, challenge them to make a list of questions they would like to ask Jesus about prayer. List these questions on a chalkboard or newsprint. Then, as you study the Lord's Prayer in depth, see how many of these questions can be answered.

It would take more than one lesson to do justice to this, the greatest of prayers. The numbers correspond to those given under "Introduction."

(1) We approach God as we would a loving parent, along with others.

(2) We approach God with humility.

(3) We pray for the ability to glorify God in word and deed.

(4) We pray for evil to be destroyed, and good to triumph.

(5) We pray for the humility to submit like angels to God's will.

(6) We pray for a fair portion of the blessings of life.

(7) We repent and ask forgiveness.

(8) Without forgiveness, we can't accept God's grace toward us.

(9) We pray to be seldom tempted, and for strength when we are.

(10) We conclude by giving God the glory.

Use this outline to carefully examine each part of the scripture. Information from "Understanding the Scripture" will help you. Be sure to note that the concluding doxology (number 10 above) was a later addition, which is why it does not appear in newer Bible translations (that tend to use the oldest manuscripts) but is retained in the King James Version. The questions that will guide you as you step through each part of the Lord's Prayer outline are:

(1) **What does this phrase mean?**
(2) **What am I called to do?**
(3) **What kind of relationship does this phrase assume that I have with God and/or with other persons?**

Call for a few volunteers to share the prayers that they wrote during the week, as suggested last Sunday. If students are uncomfortable about praying aloud, note that many persons feel uneasy about praying in front of a group. If time permits, you may want to read or retell the story in the first paragraph under "Focusing on the Main Question." You may also want to share this little formula that I use when asked on the spur of the moment to lead in prayer. The acronym, GRACE, is easy to remember. Write this information on a chalkboard or newsprint, or prepare handouts in advance.

G Give God Glory. Mention something you are glad about.
R Repent. Confess something you are sorry about.
A Announce Our Absolution. Thank God for our forgiveness.
C Consider God's Call. Ask for God's will for our lives.
E Enlist in God's Enterprise. "Here I am, send me."

Provide a few moments for class members to reflect in silence, praying a prayer that follows this GRACE model.

Forgiveness

Select a volunteer to read Matthew 6:14-15.

Ask the class: **Why do you think Jesus chose to highlight forgiveness when it was already mentioned in Matthew 6:12?** (Answers will vary, but make sure that class members recognize that forgiveness is essential for healing broken relationships, whether they are between ourselves and God or ourselves and other persons.)

If you have time, ask class members to do a brief Bible study on forgiveness. Either work together as an entire group, or divide into teams. If you choose to work in teams or with partners, be sure to ask each group to report to the entire class. Here are several references that make the same point as Matthew 6:14-15: Matthew 18:35; Mark 11:25-26; Ephesians 4:32; and Colossians 3:13. Summarize students' findings by noting that the biblical teaching is clear: Persons who forgive will receive forgiveness, but those who refuse to forgive will not be forgiven by God.

HELPING CLASS MEMBERS ACT

Encourage your class members to establish regular prayer habits and, for at least part of their prayer time, to use some of the great church prayers as a guide. Most hymnals provide excellent prayer resources.

If your class brainstormed questions that they would like to ask Jesus about prayer, encourage students to research questions that could not be answered today. Obviously, some questions will remain unanswered because they are unknowable, but a commentary, Bible dictionary, or other resources may provide the answers to many questions.

Invite students to make up their own prayers based on the GRACE model we learned in class.

Challenge students to think of someone they need to forgive and to contact that individual this week to seek forgiveness and, if possible, make amends.

PLANNING FOR NEXT SUNDAY

I have enjoyed being with you this quarter. Next week you will begin a study on the Letter of James. A good assignment for the week would be to read the whole book at least once (it has only five chapters) to get a feel for it. The first lesson in the summer quarter, "The Challenge of Hard Times," will focus on James 1.

Please turn to the Quarterly Evaluation form on pages 487-88. Complete this form for the Third Quarter.

FOURTH QUARTER

JUNE 2—AUGUST 25, 1996

During the summer quarter, we will look intently at two books that seem to be quite different yet share much in common. James, a letter written to the early Christian church, and the beloved book of Psalms each offers practical wisdom for daily living. Whereas James is a prose work that sounds more like a sermon than a letter, the Psalms sing to us in some of the most sublime poetry known to humanity. Despite their dissimilarities, both books tell us much about how to live the godly life. The counsel of James provides words that we need to hear in order to show our faith to a world that desperately needs to know the love of God. The Psalms give voice to some of our deepest longings, touching the secret places of our hearts and souls in language that soars to the height of heaven and plumbs the depths of human existence.

Unit 1, entitled *A Practical Religion*, includes five sessions on the letter of James. The purpose of this unit is to help adult learners discover how they are called to put their faith into action—to be doers of the word. Each lesson challenges class members to respond to the issues of living that this short letter addresses: (1) faith and faithfulness, (2) faith and relationships, (3) faith and action, (4) faith and wisdom, and (5) faith and righteousness. As you study James, students may be particularly interested in noting the parallels between this epistle, the wisdom literature of the Old Testament, and Jesus' teachings as recorded in Matthew 5–7, the Sermon on the Mount.

For the rest of the summer, the class will study a central theme of the Psalms: the presence of God in our lives. The Psalms repeatedly demonstrate that God is both present in the world and purposefully involved in our lives. Such good news inspires joyous celebration among the people of God.

During July, a four-session unit entitled *Praising God* will focus on four aspects of God's presence with us, which elicit our praise: (1) God creates and sustains us (Psalm 104), (2) God acts mightily on our behalf (Psalm 105), (3) God delivers us from trouble (Psalm 34), and (4) God knows us intimately and cares for us (Psalm 139).

Our unit for August, entitled "Responding to God," looks at four other beloved psalms that help us, to appreciate how we, like our spiritual ancestors, may respond to the presence of God. When we are aware that God is with us, we experience a deep and abiding trust in God (Psalm 40). We are also anxious to keep God's laws for we value God's Word (Psalm 119). God's presence may remind us of our sin and cause us to repent, confess, and seek forgiveness (Psalm 51). Finally, we feel led to worship God and to witness to others in God's name (Psalm 96).

MEET OUR WRITER

DR. ELLSWORTH KALAS

Ellsworth Kalas was a United Methodist pastor for thirty-eight years in Watertown, Green Bay, and Madison, Wisconsin, and Church of the Saviour in Cleveland, Ohio. Retirement has meant increased activity. In 1988 he became an associate in evangelism with the World Methodist Council, and then in 1993 he was appointed the first Beeson Senior Pastor in Residence in the Beeson Center for Preaching, Asbury Theological Seminary, Wilmore, Kentucky. His daughter, Taddy, is an associate professor of French at Augustana College in Rock Island, Illinois, and his son, David, is a United Methodist minister in Virginia.

Ellsworth first read the Bible from Genesis to Revelation as an eleven year old, and his continuing passion is to see others become engrossed in Bible study. Some of his books include *365 Days from Genesis Through Revelation, Parables from the Backside*, and *If Experience Is Such a Good Teacher, Why Do I Keep Repeating the Course?*, all published by Abingdon Press.

THE CHALLENGE OF HARD TIMES

PREVIEWING THE LESSON

Lesson Scripture: James 1:2-4, 12-15, 19-27
Background Scripture: James 1
Key Verses: James 1:3-4

Focus of the lesson:
the opportunities difficult situations provide for maturing in faith

Main question(s) of the lesson:
(1) How can we meet the challenge of hard times so as to grow toward spiritual maturity?

This lesson will enable adult learners to:
(1) grasp that trials bring about spiritual growth and are to be expected
(2) perceive trials in their own lives in a positive light
(3) respond by becoming doers of the Word, especially for persons facing hard times.

Today's lesson may be outlined as follows:
(1) Introduction
(2) Christians Can Expect to Experience Trials (James 1:2-4)
(3) Those Who Resist Temptation Will Receive the Crown of Life (James 1:12-15)
(4) True Worship Is Rooted in Action (James 1:19-27)

FOCUSING ON THE MAIN QUESTION

Most football coaches believe in the power of motivation. Some of them cover the locker room walls and bulletin boards with inspirational messages to keep the adrenaline flowing. One of the favorites with athletes of all ages declares: "When the going gets tough, the tough get going."

James might well have written that. The people to whom he was addressing his letter were going through hard times. The letter covers a host of topics, but it begins with advice for people who are facing trials. Everything that follows is in some sense related to that theme. In his letter, James instructs people how to live with such effectiveness and quality that they will be able to survive hard times.

The writer never becomes specific about the nature of his readers' trials. He seems deliberately to remain general, using the term "trials of any kind" (James 1:2). One reason for his generality is that his letter was to be circulated widely among the churches, rather than addressed to a single congregation with particular problems. Another possible reason James chose to avoid specifics may have been that he wanted his readers to apply his counsel to the whole business of life, perhaps ranging all the way from a passing irritation to the threat of martyrdom.

For our sakes, it's good that he handled the subject this way. If he had talked about a specific problem, some of us might have concluded that his words mean little for this late twentieth century. But what he has to say is timeless. Just as are hard times! The particular circumstances of hard times change from day to day, but hard times themselves are a continuing possibility. They're part of the normal business of life.

It's halftime, and the believers seem to be losing. James gathers them around him in his locker room and assures them that they're going to win. They're fortunate, he says, to be having such a hard time, because it's in this process that they will become "mature and complete" (James 1:4). Winners, as we might say. James's letter spurs us to ask: **How can we meet the challenge of hard times so as to grow toward spiritual maturity?**

READING THE SCRIPTURE

NRSV
James 1:2-4

2 My brothers and sisters, whenever you face trials of any kind, consider it nothing but joy, ³because you know that the testing of your faith produces endurance; ⁴and let endurance have its full effect, so that you may be mature and complete, lacking in nothing.

James 1:12-15

12 Blessed is anyone who endures temptation. Such a one has stood the test and will receive the crown of life that the Lord has promised to those who love him. ¹³No one, when tempted, should say, "I am being tempted by God"; for God cannot be tempted by evil and he himself tempts no one. ¹⁴But one is tempted by one's own desire, being lured and enticed by it; ¹⁵then, when that desire has conceived, it gives birth to sin, and that sin, when it is fully grown, gives birth to death.

NIV
James 1:2-4

²Consider it pure joy, my brothers, whenever you face trials of many kinds, ³because you know that the testing of your faith develops perseverance. ⁴Perseverance must finish its work so that you may be mature and complete, not lacking anything.

James 1:12-15

¹²Blessed is the man who perseveres under trial, because when he has stood the test, he will receive the crown of life that God has promised to those who love him.

¹³When tempted, no one should say, "God is tempting me." For God cannot be tempted by evil, nor does he tempt anyone; ¹⁴but each one is tempted when, by his own evil desire, he is dragged away and enticed. ¹⁵Then, after desire has conceived, it gives birth to sin; and sin, when it is full-grown, gives birth to death.

Key Verses

James 1:19-27

19 You must understand this, my beloved: let everyone be quick to listen, slow to speak, slow to anger; 20for your anger does not produce God's righteousness. 21Therefore rid yourselves of all sordidness and rank growth of wickedness, and welcome with meekness the implanted word that has the power to save your souls.

22 But be doers of the word, and not merely hearers who deceive themselves. 23For if any are hearers of the word and not doers, they are like those who look at themselves in a mirror; 24for they look at themselves and, on going away, immediately forget what they were like. 25But those who look into the perfect law, the law of liberty, and persevere, being not hearers who forget but doers who act—they will be blessed in their doing.

26 If any think they are religious, and do not bridle their tongues but deceive their hearts, their religion is worthless. 27Religion that is pure and undefiled before God, the Father, is this: to care for orphans and widows in their distress, and to keep oneself unstained by the world.

James 1:19-27

19My dear brothers, take note of this: Everyone should be quick to listen, slow to speak and slow to become angry, 20for man's anger does not bring about the righteous life that God desires. 21Therefore, get rid of all moral filth and the evil that is so prevalent and humbly accept the word planted in you, which can save you.

22Do not merely listen to the word, and so deceive yourselves. Do what it says. 23Anyone who listens to the word but does not do what it says is like a man who looks at his face in a mirror 24and, after looking at himself, goes away and immediately forgets what he looks like. 25But the man who looks intently into the perfect law that gives freedom, and continues to do this, not forgetting what he has heard, but doing it—he will be blessed in what he does.

26If anyone considers himself religious and yet does not keep a tight rein on his tongue, he deceives himself and his religion is worthless. 27Religion that God our Father accepts as pure and faultless is this: to look after orphans and widows in their distress and to keep oneself from being polluted by the world.

UNDERSTANDING THE SCRIPTURE

James 1:1. The identity of this author, known as "James, a servant of God and the Lord Jesus Christ," is unknown. The letter has been attributed to James, the brother of Jesus, and the leader of the Jerusalem church (see Acts 15:13); James, the son of Zebedee; or an unknown person who wrote or edited teachings of Jesus' brother, James. The "twelve tribes in the Dispersion" are not the twelve tribes of Israel; ten of those tribes ceased to exist shortly after 722 B.C.E. when the northern tribes were taken captive by the Assyrians. The church is sometimes referred to as "the new Israel." Hence, by using the reference to the twelve tribes the writer may be linking Christians,

especially Jewish Christian readers, with the heritage of the Hebrew Scriptures.

James 1:2. The word *trials* can also be translated "temptations," as it is in the King James Version. Anything that tests the mettle of a person's faith can be understood as a trial. James calls the reader to rejoice in trials because these challenges have the potential to increase one's faith.

James 1:3-4. The goal of the Christian life is always maturity. The most vivid picture of initiation into the faith, the new birth, suggests immediately that growth is expected, since birth is not an end in itself, but a first step toward maturity. James teaches that trials are a means of growing toward spiritual maturity.

James 1:5-8. This epistle is linked to the Wisdom literature of the Old Testament. Wisdom is a gift that God freely gives to persons whose lives are single-mindedly focused on God. (This passage will be treated in greater detail in Lesson 4.)

James 1:9-11. James speaks of reversals—the poor will be raised up and the rich brought low. To make his point in verses 10-11, James uses images from Isaiah 40:6-7.

James 1:12. In the first-century world the crown was a mark of royalty, but it was also worn for festive occasions, such as weddings, and was awarded as a symbol of victory in athletic events. "Crown" became a favorite figure of speech for New Testament writers, appearing in several epistles and in the book of Revelation.

James 1:13-16. Whereas some persons apparently were blaming God for their temptations, James teaches that persons must accept responsibility for their own sins. God cannot be tempted, nor does God cause humans to be tempted.

James 1:17-18. God the creator ("Father of lights") gives good gifts. Unlike the heavenly bodies that turn and create shadows, God is unchanging. By the "word of truth" God created us. We are compared to the "first fruits" of the harvest, which were offered to God (see Leviticus 23:10 and Deuteronomy 18:4).

James 1:19-20. Except for its explicit Christian references, this letter could easily fit in the Hebrew Scriptures. It is marked by the kind of down-to-earth, straight-forward instruction that is typical of Jewish Wisdom literature. The three admonitions concerning our behavior—"quick to listen, slow to speak, slow to anger"—are necessary because of the righteousness of God.

James 1:21. James uses the language of a gardener when he urges us to root out the "rank growth of wickedness," and replace it with "the implanted word" of the gospel. Life abhors a vacuum, so unless we find a substitute for life's "rank growth," there will eventually be something far worse. Jesus gives us the same insight in another way (Matthew 12:43-45).

James 1:22-25. James is a practical counselor who has little sympathy for theoretical religion. When we hear God's word we must act upon it. James likens the person who hears but does not act to one who looked in the mirror, saw something that needed to be changed, and then walked away without taking any action. Persons who act, rather than walk away and forget, will be blessed. The "doers of the word" look into the mirror of the "perfect law" (see Psalm 19:7), which James understands to be the Mosaic law as interpreted by Jesus. Through this "law of liberty" the believer gains freedom.

James 1:26-27. In these verses James measures genuine religion by three simple but demanding tests—the use of the tongue, our care for those in need, and our freedom from worldly corruption.

INTERPRETING THE SCRIPTURE

Christians Can Expect to Experience Trials

Our generation may be the first to assume that life should be easy. The political programs of the past fifty years have been developed to protect the population from the worst of the economic cycles and to assure some measure of security in life's later years. Medical science has gone far toward reducing pain. Any number of social agencies have come into existence to sustain us through life's various misfortunes.

It isn't surprising therefore that people expect their religion, too, to be nothing but pleasantness. We are a people who shop for churches the way we look for an automobile, wondering where we can get the best deal. James wouldn't understand such an outlook, nor would any other of the New Testament writers. They expected to suffer for their faith. A person didn't come into the church in the first century without contemplating that he or she might pay for this decision with life itself, or at the least, with persecution. When a first-century proclaimer asked, "Will you give your life to Christ?" it was a physical question as well as a spiritual one.

James's letter, however, is no sad song. The people were going to face trials; that was a given. But when that happens, James says, they are to "consider it nothing but joy" (James 1:2). I have always loved the story a pastor tells of his saintly aunt. Whatever happened to her, she unfailingly responded, "This is going to do me a world of good." She would have qualified for James's honor roll.

James wants us to know that his position is logical. He has a progressive equation: testing produces endurance, and if endurance is given full opportunity for development, the eventual product will be people who are "mature and complete, lacking in nothing" (James 1:4). The trials are not an end in themselves. Instead, they will produce qualities of character that will eventually lead to spiritual maturity.

When my daughter was just over three years old, she suffered a ruptured appendix. The pediatrician had missed the diagnosis because of her age, so by the time emergency surgery was performed, it was almost too late. One day when the eventual outcome was still uncertain, a brother pastor stopped to see me at her bedside. "Ellsworth," he said, "I would give almost anything to get what you will gain from this experience. But I would pay anything to avoid going through it." He was right on both counts. Hard times cause a person to gain mightily in spiritual maturity, but

they aren't the course we would choose to follow.

Those Who Resist Temptation Will Receive the Crown of Life

Temptation is a particular form of trial. We don't usually think of it that way, perhaps because temptation doesn't frighten us as much as it should. These trials and temptations are opportunities for testing our mettle as Christian believers. Those who endure temptation will receive "the crown of life" (James 1:12). To first-century readers, the crown evoked images not only of royal power but of joyous occasions on which wreaths of flowers were worn or athletic competitions where crowns were awarded to the winners. If James were writing in our day he might say, "Resist temptation and you'll get your World Series ring." James's readers had seen victors crowned; now such a celebration was being promised to them.

Apparently some early Christians who were failing the test sought to blame someone else—even God. Evidently they were inclined to excuse their misconduct on the ground that God had sent temptation their way. James insists that his readers face this temptation and its outcome honestly. He makes clear that our temptations don't come from God; they're homegrown: "One is tempted by one's own desire" (James 1:14).

What James does not go on to say is that these desires, in their earliest stages, seem so harmless, even good. That's the problem. If temptation came to us fully developed—as a murder, or as adultery with all its attendant pain, or as embezzlement with imprisonment—it would hold no charm. But adultery begins with a longing for love, and what could be more legitimate than that? And embezzlement begins with family needs, or perhaps with ambition to get ahead, and these are praiseworthy drives in our society. Most murders occur within the circle of family or friends, which means that their original setting was probably one of love or affection, but few emotions are so volatile as love scorned or abused. Even that most pharisaical sin, self-righteousness, begins as a highly desirable goal: a hunger for righteous living. That's why sin is so difficult to handle; it starts in such good ground that we're likely not to see its peril until it is full grown. Then it's too late!

True Worship Is Rooted in Action

In James 1:19-27 the writer helps us to understand how believers can truly worship God. We show forth our faith not just by agreeing with certain doctrines but by living as persons who act on the Word of God. As we overcome temptations and grow toward spiritual maturity, God's righteousness is more and more evidenced in our lives.

A major obstacle to mature growth is the way we use our tongue. The book of Proverbs includes numerous verses that deal in one way or another with the use of the tongue. Since James's epistle stands within the Wisdom tradition of Proverbs, we shouldn't be surprised that he touches on this theme several times within his short letter.

We are first urged to be "quick to listen, slow to speak" (James 1:19). Properly observed, that advice alone would save us from all manner of sin and pain. Someone once said of a great linguist that he could be silent in seven different languages. Most of us find it easy to talk too much in one! Sometimes I wish I had thought of a clever put-down during a conversation; as the years go by, I'm becoming increasingly thankful that I'm not usually that quick. Even with my slowness, I have words enough to repent of.

James is not very broad-minded about the tongue. Religion that doesn't bridle the tongue is "worthless," he says in verse 26.

If you've been hurt by someone's gossip or sharpness of speech, you'll probably agree. Most of us can think of someone who has done much good but who nevertheless is remembered negatively because of something he or she said. Words are so powerful. No wonder we sometimes say, after an unfortunate slip, "I could have just bitten my tongue!"

James's definition of religion is utterly practical: it is a life that cares for orphans and widows and is "unstained by the world" (James 1:27). His measure is entirely at the level of conduct. I don't think he takes this position because he considered beliefs unimportant, but rather that he expected beliefs to manifest themselves in deeds. James clearly states his position in verse 22: "But be doers of the word, and not merely hearers who deceive themselves." Believers who act will be blessed (James 1:25).

James was especially concerned that religious persons act to help the helpless. Personally, I think he expected "hands-on" expression, not just gifts or committee action. This concept is hard for most of us because we so easily isolate ourselves from the neediest persons in our society. In James's world, widows and orphans were extremely vulnerable because they had no economic means of caring for themselves.

I'm not sure how to define "unstained by the world" (James 1:27). In my youth, that meant avoiding some specific types of "worldly amusements" and undesirable habits. The intention was right, but the specifics were sometimes too simple and legalistic. I'm very certain that the "world" stains us today in ways we hardly realize. Ours is such a dominantly secular society that Christians may hardly realize that their thinking is shaped almost entirely by a secular ethic. In such a society, we have to struggle very hard to keep tuned to the eternal and worship only God.

SHARING THE SCRIPTURE

PREPARING TO TEACH

Our lesson from the Epistle of James should be especially enjoyable to teach because it deals with such day-to-day, down-to-earth matters. These practical matters open the door to free discussion. You will want to plan carefully so as to keep the discussion focused on meeting the challenge of hard times.

Read all the material above and James 1. You may also want to consult other commentaries.

Check some of the references to the tongue in Proverbs, such as 6:17; 10:31; 12:18-19; and 15:2, 4. You want to use these references to demonstrate to the class how James is similar to Proverbs. Look up "tongue" in a concordance for additional references in Proverbs.

Think about your own understanding of trials and temptations. Be aware of trials you may face this week. How do you respond to them? Can you sense, as James teaches, that these tests of your Christian character are enabling you to grow toward greater spiritual maturity? If you keep a spiritual journal, record the trials you faced and your responses to them this week.

Consider what the phrase "doers of the word" (James 1:22) means to you. Look at how Jesus used similar words and ideas in Matthew 7:24-27. How do you perceive a "doer" to be different from one who hears the word but does not act upon it? During the week, be alert for situations in which you can be a "doer of the word."

Have paper and pencils on hand if you want students to write answers to the final activity under "Those Who Resist Temptation Will Receive the Crown of Life."

LEADING THE CLASS

Introduction

You may want to open the class by referring to the locker room slogan, "When the going gets tough, the tough get going." Briefly discuss with the class how this slogan may relate to the Christian life. Note that, contrary to some popular theology that seems to guarantee success and personal happiness, Christianity does not exempt us from life's trials and temptations. Times will be tough! But our Christianity provides us with resources to "get going" and deal with our trials. Not only can we survive these trials, but we should experience them joyfully because they afford us unique opportunities to grow as Christians.

Tell the class that we are beginning a five-week unit on the Epistle of James, a letter that was written for early Jewish Christians who faced hard times and daily tests, just as we do. Today's lesson, based on the first chapter of James, will help us to address the question: **How can we meet the challenge of hard times so as to grow toward spiritual maturity?**

Christians Can Expect to Experience Trials

Select a volunteer to read aloud James 1:2-4.

Ask class members to describe what they mean by "trials" or "hard times." You may want to record their answers on a chalkboard or newsprint. Answers may include: periods of economic depression, unemployment, physical separation from family and friends, alienation, sickness, or bereavement. So that the description is broad enough to cover the passage under discussion, add if necessary the point that James's letter includes the idea of temptation, and probably also persecution—trials that most of us have never had to face.

Note that James tells us in verse 2 that we are to consider "trials of any kind" to be nothing but joy. This testing of our faith enables us to endure and grow toward spiritual maturity. Encourage class members to give examples of such trials in their own lives that (at least in retrospect) they can see as means to spiritual growth. You may want to use the story of my daughter's illness, found under "Interpreting the Scripture," or an example from your own life to start the discussion.

Those Who Resist Temptation Will Receive the Crown of Life

Choose a volunteer to read James 1:12-15.

Use the information under this heading "Interpreting the Scripture" and also verse 12 under "Understanding the Scripture" to help the class understand the image of the crown of life. Note that the crown is given to those persons who endure the testing of their character.

Discuss these questions based on James 1:13-15:

(1) **What reasons were James's original readers giving for their failure to stand against temptation?** (Some Christians apparently tried to avoid responsibility for their own behavior by blaming God for sending temptations their way.)

(2) **How does James refute their excuses?** (He says that God cannot be tempted; neither does God tempt anyone.)

(3) **What kinds of excuses do Christians today make for their failure to withstand temptation?** (Our generation often takes refuge in secular excuses. We look to both the physical and the social sciences and develop a kind of pseudo-science of human conduct, blaming what we do on our genes, our heredity, environmental influences, and even on the stars.)

Ask each class member to reflect silently on a temptation that she or he has recently faced as you read the following prayer. If you prefer, distribute paper and pencils and let the class write their thoughts so that they can refer back to them during their private devotions this week. Be sure to pause long enough for students to collect their thoughts and bring their concerns silently or in writing before God. No one but you is to speak aloud.

- "Loving God, you know that I have recently faced a trial or temptation that involved . . . (*pause for students to describe the trial*).
- When this happened, I wanted to blame . . . (*pause for students to name themselves, another person, or God*).
- I coped with this trial by . . . (*pause for students to describe what they did*).
- As a result of this trial, I feel that I have grown spiritually because . . . (*pause for students to describe new spiritual understandings*).

I give you praise and thanks, O God, for this opportunity to grow spiritually and for your abiding presence in my life. Amen."

True Worship Is Rooted in Action

Read aloud James 1:19-27.

Note that verse 26 and part of verse 19 refer to the use of the tongue. You may want to point out that James is a book of wisdom, like the book of Proverbs, for it helps us to know how to conduct ourselves ethically and morally in relation to God and other persons. This would be an appropriate time to cite examples of the use of the tongue found in Proverbs, as listed in the "Preparing to Teach" section.

Focus on the famous command in James 1:22: "But be doers of the word, and not merely hearers who deceive themselves." Point out that Jesus used similar words in Matthew 7:24-27, a portion of the Sermon on the Mount. Note that for James true worship of God resulted in action. It was not merely listening to words about religion or agreeing to certain doctrines of faith.

In 1:27, James defines pure religion as one that cares for widows and orphans.

Ask class members: **If James were writing his letter today, who are the groups of people he might name as being vulnerable and unable to care for themselves?** Answers may include: homeless persons, refugees, single parents with few economic resources, poor persons, persons with AIDS, victims of abuse, the frail elderly, neglected children.

Invite the class to brainstorm ideas as to how they as a group or as individuals might care for such persons. Ideas may include: assisting at a shelter for the homeless or soup kitchen, serving Meals on Wheels, making monetary contributions to a shelter for battered women, acting as a grandparent for a child who needs attention, or calling to check on an elderly or sick neighbor.

HELPING CLASS MEMBERS ACT

Ask class members to consider times of personal trial that have, in the long run, enabled them to grow spiritually. Encourage them to thank God during their devotional time for these opportunities. Challenge class members who are in the midst of such trials to ask God to be able to endure the situation and experience it with joy.

Ask each student to select and implement at least one idea for action from the list brainstormed by the class. If you did not use the brainstorming activity, challenge each person to find a way to be a doer of the word in the coming week. Help class members recognize that even small acts of kindness, such as a card, visit, or gift of food, are usually appreciated.

PLANNING FOR NEXT SUNDAY

Ask class members to prepare for next Sunday's lesson by reading James 2:1-13 and 4:11-12. In this lesson James challenges us to treat all persons with love, no matter what their position in life. As you read the scripture lesson, note how James gives a specific example of partiality. Urge the class to be equally specific by asking themselves if there are people who are shut out of their fellowship because they make them feel uncomfortable or even unwanted.

LOVE IMPARTIALLY

PREVIEWING THE LESSON

Lesson Scripture: James 2:1-13; 4:11-12
Background Scripture: James 2:1-13; 4:11-12
Key Verse: James 2:8

Focus of the lesson:
God's expectation that persons love one another impartially

Main question(s) of the lesson:
(1) How can I love my neighbor impartially?

This lesson will enable adult learners to:
(1) recognize that favoritism is a sin
(2) confront their own biases for or against particular groups of people
(3) respond by speaking out against discrimination.

Today's lesson may be outlined as follows:
(1) Introduction
(2) The Challenge of Loving Impartially (James 2:1-4)
(3) The Poor Have Special Standing (James 2:5-7)
(4) The Law Is All of One Piece (James 2:8-11)
(5) Judging Is Not Our Business (James 2:12-13; 4:11-12).

FOCUSING ON THE MAIN QUESTION

We usually think of the early church as our model. We imagine that in those days the church was young and pure. But such was not the case. Constant vigilance was necessary to keep the church faithful to its calling. An example of such vigilance is recounted in the story of Ananias and Sapphira (see Acts 5:1-11). Problems and conflicts often arose then, just as they do today. I sometimes think the Epistles would never have been written if it weren't for the assorted sins and problems of the earliest congregations.

The scripture passage that we will study this week from the Epistle of James deals with a particularly regrettable situation. Young as the church was, people were already becoming class conscious. Members of Christian congregations were showing partiality to those who were richer and who wore better clothes. James is dismayed by this situation, especially since rich persons often oppressed the poor by failing to pay their wages or by hauling them into court.

We find this kind of favoritism toward the rich hard to imagine, not only in light of what Jesus said about being a servant to all, but also because of the many places in the Hebrew Scriptures where we are told of God's love and concern for the poor. Paul was preaching that all human distinctions were lost in Christ; in him, Paul said, there is neither Jew nor Greek, slave nor free, male nor female (see Galatians 3:28). I'm sure this message was not singular to Paul; it was no doubt commonly taught through the early church. Yet partiality was rearing its ungodly head.

Try as we will, most of us find it hard to be utterly impartial. We're more comfortable with some people than with others. We relate more easily to those who have a similar lifestyle or who like the same things. Before we know it, we are shutting others out, or at the least, making them uncomfortable. James has a word for the likes of us. His epistle prompts us to ask: How can I love my neighbor impartially?

READING THE SCRIPTURE

NRSV
James 2:1-13

1 My brothers and sisters, do you with your acts of favoritism really believe in our glorious Lord Jesus Christ? 2For if a person with gold rings and in fine clothes comes into your assembly, and if a poor person in dirty clothes also comes in, 3and if you take notice of the one wearing the fine clothes and say, "Have a seat here, please," while to the one who is poor you say, "Stand there," or, "Sit at my feet," 4have you not made distinctions among yourselves, and become judges with evil thoughts? 5Listen, my beloved brothers and sisters. Has not God chosen the poor in the world to be rich in faith and to be heirs of the kingdom that he has promised to those who love him? 6But you have dishonored the poor. Is it not the rich who oppress you? Is it not they who drag you into court? 7Is it not they who blaspheme the excellent name that was invoked over you?

8 You do well if you really fulfill the royal law according to the scripture, "You shall love your neighbor as yourself." 9But if you show partiality, you commit sin and are convicted by the law as transgressors. 10For whoever keeps the whole law but fails in one point has become accountable for all of it. 11For the one who said, "You shall not commit adultery," also said, "You shall not murder." Now if you do not commit adul-

NIV
James 2:1-13

1 My brothers, as believers in our glorious Lord Jesus Christ, don't show favoritism. 2Suppose a man comes into your meeting wearing a gold ring and fine clothes, and a poor man in shabby clothes also comes in. 3If you show special attention to the man wearing fine clothes and say, "Here's a good seat for you," but say to the poor man, "You stand there" or "Sit on the floor by my feet," 4have you not discriminated among yourselves and become judges with evil thoughts?

5Listen, my dear brothers: Has not God chosen those who are poor in the eyes of the world to be rich in faith and to inherit the kingdom he promised those who love him? 6But you have insulted the poor. Is it not the rich who are exploiting you? Are they not the ones who are dragging you into court? 7Are they not the ones who are slandering the noble name of him to whom you belong?

8If you really keep the royal law found in Scripture, "Love your neighbor as yourself," you are doing right. 9But if you show favoritism, you sin and are convicted by the law as lawbreakers. 10For whoever keeps the whole law and yet stumbles at just one point is guilty of breaking all of it. 11For he who said, "Do not commit adultery," also said, "Do not murder." If you do not commit adultery but do commit

Key Verse

**Ke
Ver**

tery but if you murder, you have become a transgressor of the law. ¹²So speak and so act as those who are to be judged by the law of liberty. ¹³For judgment will be without mercy to anyone who has shown no mercy; mercy triumphs over judgment.

murder, you have become a lawbreaker. ¹²Speak and act as those who are going to be judged by the law that gives freedom, ¹³because judgment without mercy will be shown to anyone who has not been merciful. Mercy triumphs over judgment!

James 4:11-12

11 Do not speak evil against one another, brothers and sisters. Whoever speaks evil against another or judges another, speaks evil against the law and judges the law; but if you judge the law, you are not a doer of the law but a judge. ¹²There is one lawgiver and judge who is able to save and to destroy. So who, then, are you to judge your neighbor?

James 4:11-12

¹¹Brothers, do not slander one another. Anyone who speaks against his brother or judges him speaks against the law and judges it. When you judge the law, you are not keeping it, but sitting in judgment on it. ¹²There is only one Lawgiver and Judge, the one who is able to save and destroy. But you—who are you to judge your neighbor?

UNDERSTANDING THE SCRIPTURE

James 2:1-13. This entire section uses a technique, known as *diatribe*, which was common among certain Greek philosophers. A speaker would pretend to engage in a dialogue with someone else. The speaker would raise rhetorical questions that were not intended to be answered but were asked only to emphasize the speaker's point. Verse 5 is an example of such a rhetorical question.

James 2:1. This verse sets forth an important principle of Christian conduct: as believers in the glory of the Lord Jesus Christ, Christians are forbidden to show partiality.

James 2:2-4. James offers an example of partiality being shown within the church ("assembly," which literally means "synagogue"). Although neither visitor seems to be known to the congregation, the rich one is favored over the poor on the basis of appearance alone. Christians who engage in such biased behavior act as "judges with evil thoughts."

James 2:5-7. To discriminate against the poor runs counter to God's own special care of the poor. The early Christians,

many of whom were poor, were often oppressed by the rich who dragged them into court and disdained their religion.

James 2:8. The key verse, which includes a quote from Leviticus 19:18, summarizes the law of God. Jesus quotes this second great commandment in Matthew 22:39. If we love our neighbor as ourselves, we cannot favor one person over another.

James 2:9-11. The law was seen as a seamless garment. To break any part of it was to break all of the law. Persons who show partiality are breaking God's law concerning love of neighbor and, therefore, are guilty of sin.

James 2:12-13. James urges Christians to act according to the "law of liberty." He is not speaking here of legalistic prescriptions but of freely choosing to obey God's law (see James 1:25). Those who show mercy to others will receive it themselves.

James 4:11-12. James returns to one of his favorite subjects, the use (and misuse) of the tongue, especially within the Christian congregation (see James 1:26 and 3:2-10). The Greek word which is used, *katala-*

leo, means to speak against, to speak evil of, or to slander. To utter slanderous words not only judges a brother or sister but also judges the law referred to in James 2:8. James reminds us that when we pass judgment, we are out of our territory; only God, who is the source of the law, is in a position to judge. To speak harshly of another is a most presumptuous sin; we are acting as if we are God.

INTERPRETING THE SCRIPTURE

The Challenge of Loving Impartially

I find it easier to rail against partiality than to be consistently impartial in my treatment of others. I succeed only to the degree that I put myself in the other person's shoes. But that's difficult because I haven't experienced every other person's experiences. For instance, I can usually be understanding of the poor because I knew poverty in my childhood. But I am sometimes quick to judge young persons who were raised with economic and social advantages. From the vantage point of my experience, they have everything going for them, so there's no excuse for them to fail. Without God's help, I can never manage to be truly unbiased. How can I love my neighbor impartially? I can achieve that high goal only if I look at the human race as God does, through the eyes of compassionate love.

The Poor Have Special Standing

Most of the early believers were poor. The poor were likely conscious of their need, while the well-to-do were keenly aware of what they would have to give up if they accepted Christ. But a few rich persons did follow Jesus, and as the Christian community began to grow, others joined the fellowship. When I look at the picture James draws for us, I imagine a very wealthy person visiting the community of believers. The people are awestruck by the presence of such a prominent person in their humble meeting place. They want to make a good impression, so they push aside a poor person in "dirty clothes" (James 2:2) in order to give the wealthy visitor a prime seat.

We may recoil from the bias of this scene, but I wonder if our modern churches are truly different from the ones James addresses. In forty years of associating with clergy, I've heard many pastors tell about the new bank president or school superintendent who has joined the church, but I haven't heard many tell about the family on public assistance they've brought into church membership. We may need to hear James's message of impartial love for all persons today just as much as his readers in the first-century church did.

If we favor the rich, we're not looking at things the way God does. James is quite pointed in his analysis: God has "chosen the poor in the world to be rich in faith" (James 2:5). Does this mean that God plays favorites? Specifically, is God for the poor and against the rich? In a measure, yes, in that God is on the side of those who need help; that message is declared repeatedly in both the Old and New Testaments.

James is not arguing that poverty itself is a virtue; we may be poor as a result of wrong or sinful conduct as surely as we may get rich by dishonesty or other sinful means. In James's day, though, people were usually poor because they had been oppressed by rich, powerful rulers or military leaders. Consequently, poverty was usually the result of an unjust social arrangement. According to the world's values, favoritism and exploitation were acceptable standards of conduct. Such standards, however, were clearly unacceptable for God's people.

The wealthy may seem to have everything going for them. But wealth has special perils; and what is worse, those perils are hidden beneath such attractive and distracting exteriors that we're likely to be dull to the dangers. Wealth tends to give us a false sense of self-sufficiency. The poor person facing a crisis is likely to turn immediately to God, simply because there's nowhere else to go. But the well-to-do are familiar with the power structures of life, ranging all the way from medical specialists to financial counselors to political leaders. In the minds of some wealthy persons, God is a pleasant additional factor, but only in a complementary way, or perhaps as a last resort. The well-to-do are often conditioned to look elsewhere first—to rely on themselves and their resources—except in those instances where they have had a profound religious experience.

As James sees the situation, the "poor in the world" are more likely to be "rich in faith" (James 2:5). Now we even have a measure of scientific proof of James's observation. Over the years, Dr. George Gallup, Jr. has made a continuing study of the religious life of America, trying to determine who are the truly committed believers in this country. He has at last come up with what might be called a profile of a saint—the people whose walk with God and whose daily conduct is truly outstanding. He concludes that such persons are found in every walk of life, at every economic and educational level, and among all ethnic and racial groups. But he has also discovered that the "saints" are more likely to be found in some situations than others. Among his findings is the fact that the percentage of godly persons is roughly one and a half times as high among those making under $25,000 a year than among those with more. When an apostolic writer in the first century and a premier researcher in the twentieth century come up with essentially the same

conclusion, we ought to stop and think, especially if we are among those who are relatively comfortable economically.

The Law Is All of One Piece

Both Jesus (see Matthew 5:19) and Paul (see Galatians 3:10) make the same point as James is making in 2:8-11: the Law is all of one piece. If we break one commandment, we are guilty of all. At first this strikes us as extreme, until we realize that law always operates on this principle. The person who robs a convenience store is classified as a criminal; he may argue that he hasn't committed any murder or rape or assault, but the courts will still send him to jail because he has broken the law. As a matter of fact, he has kept most of the laws, but that one violation makes him a criminal.

This principle is all the more true as regards the law of God because the law of God gives us the will of God. To violate the law is to violate God's will and thus to be guilty of sin. The writer is not suggesting that all sins are of equal seriousness or severity in their effect on others, but all are equally violations of God's purpose.

James tells us in 2:8 that if we keep the royal law, that is, if we love our neighbor as ourselves, then we are keeping God's law. If, however, we break this law by showing favoritism, we are guilty of breaking the whole law.

Judging Is Not Our Business

In James 2:12-13 and 4:11-12, James also has penetrating words for us about judging others. We ourselves will be judged by the law of love, found in Leviticus 19:15-18, which concludes with the words quoted in James 2:8: "You shall love your neighbor as yourself." James warns us that when we speak evil against one another we speak evil against the law and judge the law (James 4:11). Love of neighbor faces no greater test than in the exercise of the tongue. When we judge and slander others, we do indeed show partiality and, in doing so, break the law of love. Few of us ever serve as judge or jury in the courts of law, but all of us pass judgment in the daily court of social conversation; and without a doubt, far more persons are condemned in this way than in any legal court. The insidious danger of this "social court" is that presumed evidence is rarely tested, and the person "on trial" almost never has a chance to defend himself or herself; usually, in fact, the person isn't even present to hear the charges. Many individuals who might be reasonably kind to an unappealing person for civility's sake will let their true feelings be known in a private conversation.

These teachings of James regarding our tendency to judge others by our speech are especially important for church members to hear. Passing judgment on others is a sin to which "good people" are especially susceptible. We care about goodness; it's an issue to us, so we think about it and talk about it. A person who is unapologetically dishonest or sexually promiscuous isn't likely to speak judgmentally about others who do these things because such a person doesn't think of these behaviors as issues. But those who seek to be honest and sexually moral are sensitive to such matters. Since Christians are conscious of moral breaches and troubled by them, we

are, ironically, more likely to pass judgment on those who fall short.

James is not implying that we should lose our sense of right and wrong; nor should we take the wimpish attitude that "Of course I wouldn't do such a thing, but it's all right for them, if that's the way they feel." The Christian faith contends that some patterns of conduct are wrong, and to say otherwise is not to be broadminded but simply superficial or unknowing.

The issue, as James makes clear, is that we are not the ultimate judges; only God holds that role. The apostle Paul puts the matter sharply: "Who are you to pass judgment on servants of another? It is before their own lord that they stand or fall" (Romans 14:4). In other words, only God has a right to pass judgment because only God has all the data in hand. When we usurp God's position as judge, we become a judge not only of that other person but of God's law as well. We may not intrude on God's domain. Instead of judging each other, we should look on one another with great compassion and mercy, knowing that we too are capable of falling. And we should never, under any circumstances, consider ourselves superior to any other person. It is at this point that the passing of judgment becomes most perilous to the soul.

SHARING THE SCRIPTURE

PREPARING TO TEACH

As you read the background scripture and the material in this lesson, focus on the main question: How can I love my neighbor impartially? Prayerfully ask God to help you identify situations in your own life in which you are showing partiality to other persons. Seek God's guidance in overcoming this sinful behavior.

Be especially sensitive this week for

opportunities in which you can show love to someone, especially a person in difficult life circumstances who may need to know that God loves everyone.

Gather newspaper or magazine articles that show persons being treated with partiality. Examples of such situations may include: homeless persons being barred from city streets; older workers being discriminated against during a plant layoff; persons of a particular nationality, religious group, or ethnic group being unfairly treated because of their origins or beliefs; poor persons being denied medical care in a hospital emergency room. Be prepared to read, have someone else read, or retell one or more of these stories in order to introduce the main question.

Secure paper and pencils for the final activity, unless your students usually carry notebooks to class.

LEADING THE CLASS

Introduction

Begin the lesson with one or more news articles that illustrate persons being treated with partiality. Read or share these with the class. If you have enough articles, divide the class into small teams and direct each team to consider one article in order to answer this question: **What would God have to say about the treatment of the individual or group highlighted in this article?** Discuss their answers for a few moments.

Conclude the discussion by reading aloud (in unison, if possible) the key verse, which is James 2:8. Indicate that the focus of today's lesson is on learning to love impartially. Our goal for the class period will be to answer the question: **How can I love my neighbor impartially?**

The Challenge of Loving Impartially

Select a volunteer to read James 2:1-4.

Ask the class: **What point is James trying to make?** Refer as needed to the information in the "Understanding the Scripture" section. Point out that James's example of discrimination takes place within the church assembly. Though God does not show partiality, the congregation acted in a way that is contrary to the loving, inclusive nature of God.

Bring the discussion closer to home by encouraging the class to examine the practices of your own church and Sunday school class. Look carefully at church practices so as not to overlook behaviors or attitudes that have been part of the church's practices for so long that members hardly recognize their own biased actions. Discuss questions such as:

(1) **Are we guilty of showing favoritism in any ways? If so, how?**

(2) **Do we work as hard to bring a family on public assistance into our membership as we do the new school superintendent or bank officer? If not, what changes do we need to make?**

(3) **Do we sometimes shut some of our members out of church social activities by thoughtlessly making them too "pricey"? How can we ensure a balance of activities so that all persons can be included?**

(4) **When new members join the church, are they encouraged to hold offices immediately, or must they wait years before they can have a voice in the decision-making process? How can we help new persons become involved in decision making?**

(5) **Are there other ways in which our actions send the message " 'Stand there,' or, 'Sit at my feet' " (James 2:3) to members or visitors? If so, what are they? How can we change?**

Close this segment of the lesson by asking the class to suggest ways that your church and class could make all visitors feel more welcome. Also consider how you can get new members actively involved in the life of the church as quickly as possible. You may want to list ideas on a chalkboard or newsprint.

The Poor Have Special Standing

The Hebrew law said, "you shall not be partial to the poor or defer to the great" (see Leviticus 19:15), but James 2:5-7 tells us that God has given special consideration to the poor. Read this passage from James aloud.

Ask: **How in our society (or community) do we insult the poor or make them feel as if they are somehow not equal to everyone else?** Answers will vary, depending upon the community, but here are some possibilities: we grow impatient or feel superior in a grocery checkout line as the customer ahead of us pays with food stamps; we fight against the building of low-income housing in our area; we vote not to set up a soup kitchen or homeless shelter in our church; we stereotype persons who need public assistance.

Conclude this segment by asking: **How do you think God wants us to treat the poor?** Consider this question from two perspectives. First, how should we relate to poor persons as individuals? Second, what might we as Christians be called to do in order to change an unjust social structure?

The Law Is All of One Piece

Ask a volunteer to read James 2:8-11 aloud.

Read or retell the paragraphs in this section, as found under "Interpreting the Scripture." Note that Jesus also quoted Leviticus 19:18 (see Matthew 22:39).

Ask the class: **How will we be able to keep all of God's law if we learn to treat all persons equally?** The discussion may focus on the fact that we would not commit crimes against others (such as murder, adultery, or theft) if we truly respected them and considered them as equals in the sight of God.

Judging Is Not Our Business

Direct the class's attention to James 2:12-13.

Invite class members to close their eyes and meditate silently as you read the following script. Pause for a few moments between each sentence so as to give students a chance to collect their thoughts.
- Think of a time when you were hurt by gossip or unkind words . . . .

- Remember what was said that upset you or damaged a relationship . . . .
- Picture the person or persons who said these hurtful things . . . .
- In your imagination tell these persons how you felt about their judgment of you . . . .
- Silently offer forgiveness and words of God's loving mercy to those persons . . . .

Without breaking the meditative mood, challenge class members to remember a time in which their unbridled tongue spoke evil or gossiped against someone else. You may want to read James 4:11-12 aloud. Remind the class that in taking such action they put themselves in the place of God, for God is the only one able to give the law and judge by it. Distribute slips of paper and pencils. Encourage class members to write a note to the person they have hurt, acknowledging their action and seeking forgiveness.

Close this segment with a brief prayer, asking God to forgive us when we have hurt others and to strengthen us that we might be able to truly love our neighbors impartially, just as God compassionately loves all persons.

HELPING CLASS MEMBERS ACT

Ask students to phone, write a note, or take some other concrete step to make a church visitor or new member feel welcome in the life and program of their church and its various organizations. If there are new members in your church, perhaps one or more class members would be willing to extend a specific invitation to them to join this Sunday school class.

Encourage the group members to seek forgiveness from the person about whom you had gossiped. Send a copy of the note written in class, or contact the person and offer forgiveness for your behavior.

Challenge the class to write a letter to an elected official or newspaper editor to protest a discriminatory law or practice in your own community or state. Emphasize that as Christians they oppose such action.

Ask the class to consider organizing members of your own congregation and neighboring churches to protest a discriminatory law or practice. Peaceful expressions by religious coalitions are often highly effective in promoting changes.

Invite the group to consider some need of poor persons in your community that the church could address, such as homelessness. Ask each person to jot down some ideas for action that the church could take, and pass these ideas to the appropriate committee for consideration.

PLANNING FOR NEXT SUNDAY

The point of next Sunday's lesson is to make religion practical by learning to live faithfully. Ask your class to study James 2:14-26 and 5:7-20. Challenge them to list at least five specific ways that they can put their faith into action.

LIVING FAITHFULLY

FOCUSING ON THE MAIN QUESTION

We evaluate institutions and individuals on the basis of whether they fulfill what they promise to do. We judge a factory by its product and a school by its graduates; the attractiveness of the building and grounds may distract us for a time, but we want eventually to know if the institution is doing what it is supposed to do. We look at a baseball player's batting and fielding percentages, or his win-loss record if he is a pitcher or a manager. We ask whether a sales representative is developing his or her territory.

So too with the church and with individual believers. The average person doesn't pay as much attention to our doctrinal statement as to the way we live our lives and the kind of people we are. Indeed, our profession of faith may seem hollow if people discover that our actions are not consistent with our words.

In recent years, various studies of public morals have caused Christians some real discomfort. Church members don't seem that much better than the population at large on such practical matters as cheating on income taxes or integrity in business. We're startled to find professing Christians guilty of spousal abuse or mistreatment of children. True, the statistics show that Christians aren't quite as bad as the general population, but neither are the figures good enough to make us feel that we're the kind of people we ought to be. James dealt with the same sort of issue in the first century. A high standard of conduct had been held by the church, but the members weren't necessarily living up to it. So the apostle cried out, **"What good is it, my brothers and sisters, if you say you have faith in God, but do not have works?"** (James 2:14). What good, indeed! James's question to his readers is our question as well.

READING THE SCRIPTURE

NRSV
James 2:14-26

14 What good is it, my brothers and sisters, if you say you have faith but do not have works? Can faith save you? [15]If a brother or sister is naked and lacks daily food, [16]and one of you says to them, "Go in peace; keep warm and eat your fill," and yet you do not supply their bodily needs, what is the good of that? [17]So faith by itself, if it has no works, is dead.

18 But someone will say, "You have faith and I have works." Show me your faith apart from your works, and I by my works will show you my faith. [19]You believe that God is one; you do well. Even the demons believe—and shudder. [20]Do you want to be shown, you senseless person, that faith apart from works is barren? [21]Was not our ancestor Abraham justified by works when he offered his son Isaac on the altar? [22]You see that faith was active along with his works, and faith was brought to completion by the works. [23]Thus the scripture was fulfilled that says, "Abraham believed God, and it was reckoned to him as righteousness," and he was called the friend of God. [24]You see that a person is justified by works and not by faith alone. [25]Likewise, was not Rahab the prostitute also justified by works when she welcomed the messengers and sent them out by another road? [26]For just as the body without the spirit is dead, so faith without works is also dead.

NIV
James 2:14-26

[14]What good is it, my brothers, if a man claims to have faith but has no deeds? Can such faith save him? [15]Suppose a brother or sister is without clothes and daily food. [16]If one of you says to him, "Go, I wish you well; keep warm and well fed," but does nothing about his physical needs, what good is it? [17]In the same way, faith by itself, if it is not accompanied by action, is dead.

[18]But someone will say, "You have faith; I have deeds."

Show me your faith without deeds, and I will show you my faith by what I do. [19]You believe that there is one God. Good! Even the demons believe that—and shudder.

[20]You foolish man, do you want evidence that faith without deeds is useless? [21]Was not our ancestor Abraham considered righteous for what he did when he offered his son Isaac on the altar? [22]You see that his faith and his actions were working together, and his faith was made complete by what he did. [23]And the scripture was fulfilled that says, "Abraham believed God, and it was credited to him as righteousness," and he was called God's friend. [24]You see that a person is justified by what he does and not by faith alone.

[25]In the same way, was not even Rahab the prostitute considered righteous for what she did when she gave lodging to the spies and sent them off in a different direction? [26]As the body without the spirit is dead, so faith without deeds is dead.

Key
Verse

389

James 5:13-16

13 Are any among you suffering? They should pray. Are any cheerful? They should sing songs of praise. ¹⁴Are any among you sick? They should call for the elders of the church and have them pray over them, anointing them with oil in the name of the Lord. ¹⁵The prayer of faith will save the sick, and the Lord will raise them up; and anyone who has committed sins will be forgiven. ¹⁶Therefore confess your sins to one another, and pray for one another, so that you may be healed. The prayer of the righteous is powerful and effective.

James 5:13-16

¹³Is any one of you in trouble? He should pray. Is anyone happy? Let him sing songs of praise. ¹⁴Is any one of you sick? He should call the elders of the church to pray over him and anoint him with oil in the name of the Lord. ¹⁵And the prayer offered in faith will make the sick person well; the Lord will raise him up. If he has sinned, he will be forgiven. ¹⁶Therefore confess your sins to each other and pray for each other so that you may be healed. The prayer of a righteous man is powerful and effective.

UNDERSTANDING THE SCRIPTURE

We're often reminded that Martin Luther, with his emphasis on faith, didn't like this letter, referring to it as an "epistle full of straw." Preferring Paul's focus on faith alone, Luther was so opposed to the Epistle of James that he argued against including it in the Bible. But I don't think James's letter and the teachings of Paul are really in contradiction. Each is trying to deal with a potential heresy, and in doing so, each states his point so strongly that it may seem at times that he is overstating it. Paul feared that people would rely on their good works as their means of salvation, so he argued vigorously in both Galatians and Romans on the side of faith. James, on the other hand, is dealing with people who aren't living up to their profession, so he reminds them—emphatically!—that the only real proof of faith is in the works we do. Martin Luther said that good works do not make a person good, but a good person does good works. I think that is precisely the point James wants to make.

James 2:14-26. If there were a name for James's theology it would have to be "Common Sense Theology" or "Practical Theology." He doesn't have much use for theory unless it is lived out in action. When persons say they have faith but do not act on it, James believes their faith is of no value. In fact, it's dead! The works of a faithful person are not self-serving but make a positive impact on the lives of other persons, especially those in need.

James 2:14-17. Anyone can claim to have faith, but verbal agreement with a particular belief or doctrine is not sufficient. A vital faith shows itself in action that is in keeping with God's will. Works are the lively factor that keep faith from dying. James reiterates this point in 2:26, today's key verse.

James 2:18-19. The writer anticipates that some Christians may argue that faith and works are distinct gifts, with some of us possessing one and some possessing the other. Not so. The two, he insists, are one and inseparable. Likewise, God is one. Even the demons know that truth about God.

James 2:20-24. Some commentators feel that James uses Abraham as an example of works to refute Paul's use of him as an example of faith (Galatians 3:6-9). It's interesting that James and Paul quote the same verse from Genesis (15:6) to make what might seem to be contrary points. Paul emphasizes Abraham's absolute trust in God. But James wants us simply to understand that "faith was brought to completion by the works" (James 2:22). Abraham's faith was not based on mere words but showed itself in action when he took his son Isaac to be sacrificed at God's command. James has no argument with faith as such, but he speaks against faith that is all talk and no action.

James 2:25. James uses Rahab, the Jericho prostitute who protected the Hebrew spies (Joshua 2:1-21), as a second example of one's faith being shown through works. The writer of Hebrews includes Rahab, along with Abraham, in his dramatic listing of faith heroes and heroines (Hebrews 11:31) who were justified (made right) by God.

James 2:26. James concludes the argument that began in verse 20 by using an analogy. Just as the body and spirit are a unified whole—the body is dead without the spirit—so too faith and works are one.

James 5:7-11. James exhorts his readers to be patient as they wait for the coming of the Lord. They are not to complain about one another. Instead, they are to endure, even in suffering, just as Job did.

James 5:12. This verse is similar to Jesus' teaching in the Sermon on the Mount, found in Matthew 5:33-37. Persons swore oaths to indicate they were telling the truth. James follows Jesus' teaching in expecting Christians to tell the truth at all times. If one is always truthful, there is no need for an oath.

James 5:13-20. The writer applies his "living faithfully" theme to some of the most practical issues of daily life in the Christian community. He argues that we should act on our faith in all situations—whether we're happy, in pain, or physically ill. Most of this section, as detailed below, relates to the ministry of prayer in various situations.

James 5:14-16. The Roman Catholic Church uses these verses as a basis for its sacrament of anointing someone who is near death. Many Protestant bodies refer to verse 14 for their method of praying for the sick. James makes an important tie between confession of sin and the ensuing sense of forgiveness with the healing of the body, though this statement should not be construed to mean that persons are ill because they have sinned.

James 5:17-18. Just as he used Abraham and Rahab as Old Testament figures to demonstrate his point about faith and works, James uses the prophet Elijah as an example of one who prayed effectively. The story of Elijah praying first for drought and then for rain is found in 1 Kings 17:1 and 1 Kings 18:1.

James 5:19-20. James closes his epistle with a call to Christians to lead those who have wandered back to the path of righteousness. To speak the word of God in truth is an action that fulfills the law of love because it offers forgiveness from a multitude of sins and saves the one who has strayed from death.

INTERPRETING THE SCRIPTURE

Living Up to Our Profession

Perhaps no higher compliment is paid to a Christian than the simple phrase, "She (or he) really lives up to her faith." That sentence is a tacit admission that it isn't easy to be a practicing Christian! We have set a high standard for ourselves when we confess that we are followers of Jesus Christ, and often others seem to know that even better than we do. People sometimes hesitate to call themselves Christians because they doubt that they can live up to such a standard. We should remember, however, that we are made Christians, not by the excellence of our lives but by the grace of God in Jesus Christ. The issue, therefore, is to accept the name with both pride and humility, then seek to live up to it by our faithful actions.

But living as a Christian disciple takes some doing. As someone quipped, "The problem is that it is so daily." If our Christianity were to be judged by an entrance exam or even by a series of semester exams, we could brace ourselves for the occasions. Unfortunately, ours is a life made up of almost endless pop quizzes, unannounced and often imposed upon us at the most unlikely times and places. Some years ago, when Cleveland, Ohio was passing through a particularly difficult series of crises, people began wearing sweatshirts with the name of the city and this simple message printed in large letters: "You have to be tough." Christians might well adopt the same motto. This way of life is not for the faint of heart.

That challenge is what makes the Christian journey so exciting, however. One of my favorite college professors used to remind us of Browning's line from the poem "Andrea del Sarto": "Ah, but a man's reach should exceed his grasp, Or what's a heaven for?" Our Christian faith always keeps us reaching, striving to be more than we've been and perhaps more than we ever dreamed we might be. During a time of honest self-inquiry, we may be thrilled to discover that we're better than we used to be. We may not yet be all that we hope to be—or all that God wants us to be—but we're making progress. We're coming closer to the image of Jesus Christ. Our behaviors and attitudes are approaching the quality of our faith statement. The Christian life will never be easy, but God's presence inspires us to a reach that exceeds our grasp.

The Crucible of Faithful Living

Several years ago I was asked to give an inspirational lecture for an employee train-ing day at a large retirement and nursing facility. After much pondering, I asked for two statistics: the number of residents in the home and the number of employees. I added these two figures and added a representative number—three—for the average number of family members in the employees' homes, then titled my talk, "562 Secrets of Greatness." I was contending that our best chance to prove our greatness is found in the midst of the people with whom we work and live most intimately.

I think I would make the same case for saintliness. Our godliness is tested and demonstrated by the people with whom we are in contact, whether those contacts are frequent—as with family members or co-workers—or infrequent, like the driver we encounter in a traffic snarl. People provide the crucible of faithful living. It's no wonder that some well-meaning but misguided souls in the early centuries of the Christian faith decided to be hermits! They sensed rightly that the biggest impediment to godly living is people. I venture they may also have learned, however, that you don't really escape people by going into isolation; they follow us in our memories and imaginations.

If people are so often the practical testing ground of our faith, they are also the source of our grandest opportunity to live out our discipleship. Jesus taught that the second half of the great commandment is that we should love our neighbors as ourselves. Given that understanding, each person we meet offers us a God-given privilege. As we interact with other persons, we have opportunities to be servants of God's love.

These opportunities are especially great when we encounter persons in need. Too often, though, Christians find it easier to talk their religion than to live it with appropriate actions. James was distressed that believers were simply dismissing persons in need with a blessing instead of providing practical help (see James 2:15-

19). We too often offer a pious platitude when people need a concrete act. A young woman who was going through a very difficult experience said, after an older person embraced her, "I needed that. I needed to know that God has skin." It was a graphic way of saying that words are sometimes not enough.

Two Who Put Faith to Work

James is dealing with the immediate issue of compassionate works on behalf of the poor, but his underlying concern is the whole matter of faith and works. He makes his case in 2:20-26 with two examples from the Hebrew Scriptures: Abraham and Rahab. In one sense, his examples could hardly be more diverse. Abraham was the friend of God and the father of the Jewish people; and while at times he fell short of God's standards, he was as exemplary as we can expect a human being to be. Rahab, in contrast, was a harlot who belonged to a nation generally despised by Israel.

Both the patriarch and the prostitute proved their faith by their works. And each had to do so in life or death situations. Abraham's faith was shown in laying his son Isaac on the altar of sacrifice (where at the last moment God intervened), and Rahab protected the Israelite spies at extreme danger to her own life. Abraham and Rahab both acted on what they believed. If their faith had simply been a verbal assent to some doctrine about God without any action to back it up, faith would have been meaningless. It would have been, as James puts it, "dead."

Faith, Health, and Forgiveness

Christians have a faith that is for all seasons: in sickness and health, in times of suffering and joy. In 5:13-16 James lists two responses to different life situations in quick order, then enlarges on the third. Eugene Peterson's translation of the New Testament emphasizes the directness of James's no-nonsense approach: "Are you hurting? Pray. Do you feel great? Sing. Are you sick? Call the church leaders together to pray." It's as if James, a true doctor of the soul, were dispensing prescriptions; he's confident he has an answer for all the changing fortunes of life.

The emphasis on prayer for the sick is experiencing renewal in many branches of Christendom. I find churches of nearly every denomination are offering healing services at regular intervals. In many instances, they use the ritual that James recommends, anointing the person with oil, usually on the forehead. Those who come for prayer include not only the physically ill, but also those who are emotionally distraught or burdened with some profound concern. James seems to anticipate this tie between our physical and emotional and spiritual needs. He brings together physical and spiritual well-being in James 5:15: "The prayer of faith will save the sick . . . and anyone who has committed sins will be forgiven." The pains of the body are frequently related to the distress of the soul. A sense of divine forgiveness is sometimes the best medicine the body can receive.

SHARING THE SCRIPTURE

PREPARING TO TEACH

As you study the first passage, James 2:14-26, ask yourself if you have ever been guilty of giving a superficial "religious answer" to someone when you should have helped in a specific way. Recall the incident. What did you do? What else could you have done? James has in mind this sort of practical, applied Christianity.

As you read the second passage of background scripture, James 5:7-20, focus on the ways in which persons can perform acts of compassion for others. Think of at least one person you know who could benefit from prayer or some other act that you could do this week. Do whatever is in your power to do for that individual.

If you keep a spiritual journal, make a list of two columns. Label one side, "Actions" and the other side, "Faith." Under "Actions," list any deeds of compassion you performed recently. Under "Faith," write a few words about how or why your faith impelled you to perform each action. This exercise may help you begin to get a sense of the interrelationship between faith and action. They are, as James teaches, two sides of the same coin.

For the "Two Who Put Faith to Work" segment of the lesson, be prepared to tell the stories of Abraham and Rahab. To do this, read the information regarding James 2:20-25 under "Understanding the Scripture" and "Interpreting the Scripture." Also read excerpts from Abraham's story in Genesis 15:1-6 and Genesis 22:1-19, as well as Rahab's story in Joshua 2:1-21 and Joshua 6, especially verses 22-23.

If you plan to use a hymn for today's session, have hymnals available.

LEADING THE CLASS

Introduction

Read aloud today's main question, which is the first part of James 2:14: **"What good is it, my brothers and sisters, if you say you have faith in God, but do not have works?"**

Spend a few moments discussing this question: **How do you understand the relationship between faith and works?** Answers will vary. Allow students to debate their ideas for a limited time, but do not try to dissuade them from their viewpoints.

Living Up to Our Profession

Use the information under "Understanding the Scripture," as well as any other commentary information that you have, to help the class understand James's perspective on the relationship between faith and works. Help the class make this important distinction: James is not claiming that we are saved by our works. Instead, he is arguing that simply saying that we have faith is not enough. Faith in Jesus Christ shows itself in the lives of believers through their works.

Read aloud or retell the section entitled "Living Up to Our Profession" under the heading "Interpreting the Scripture." Ask the class to discuss the characteristics of a Christian who is living up to his or her profession of faith. Record ideas on a chalkboard or newsprint. If the class is large, you may want to divide into small teams for this discussion.

The Crucible of Faithful Living

Choose someone to read James 2:15-19 aloud.

Then ask the class to think silently for a few moments about the following questions. Either read them aloud and pause for the class to meditate or write them on a chalkboard or newsprint.
(1) **Can you remember a time when you told someone, "Go in peace," when you ought also to have done something for the person?**
(2) **How did you feel about this incident?**
(3) **If you had the chance to relive this incident, what would you do?**
Move to a class discussion by asking: **Can you think of instances where our church, or this class, has been guilty of such a lapse?** You may want to list the students' answers on a chalkboard or newsprint. If so, make two columns and list these answers on the left-hand side.

Now turn the discussion to a more positive direction. Ask: **What are some specific instances where individual Christians or churches (especially your own) have shown their love by means of food, clothing, or other specific acts of kindness and love?** List these answers on the right-hand side of your chalkboard or newsprint.

Try to close this segment with a positive comment, such as we are making progress in living out the faith we profess.

Two Who Put Faith to Work

Select a volunteer to read James 2:20-26.

Help the class to recall the stories of Abraham and Rahab. You may want to do this by asking class members to share what they know about these two persons. Add information as needed from your own study. Point out that the Epistle writer uses Genesis 15:6 as the basis for James 2:23.

Invite class members to tell several stories of persons they know who have lived out their faith by their actions. These may be well-known figures, such as Mother Teresa or Martin Luther King Jr., or they may be individuals whom class members know personally.

Faith, Health, and Forgiveness

Choose a volunteer to read aloud James 5:13-16.

Ask your class if they have a favorite song they enjoy singing or hearing when they're feeling "up." If a song mentioned is well known to the group, you may want to sing a verse or two at this time. Or, if your class closes with a hymn, plan to use one of these suggestions to conclude the class.

Ask if any class members have been to services where the sick were anointed and prayed for, as James describes. If this kind of a ministry is not practiced in your own church, invite someone who has attended such a service to describe it.

Point out that James ties together physical healing and the forgiveness of sins

(James 5:15-16). Ask: **What connection do you see between a sense of forgiveness and physical health?** Handle this discussion with care. Although medical science is more aware of the link between the body and our emotions (including guilt), sickness is not to be understood as a punishment for sin. This issue may be an especially sensitive one if you have class members who have long-term or chronic illnesses.

Note that James urges us to confess our sins to one another (James 5:16). Ask:

(1) **Have you experienced anything like this in a small group to which you belong?**
(2) **What benefits can you see in such a practice?**
(3) **What barriers inhibit people from confessing their sins to one another?**

Answers will vary but may include: pride, fear that confessed information will be used against them, lack of trust, or embarrassment about sinful behavior. If you are familiar with Wesley's class meetings, you may want to discuss how these small groups were accountable to each other for their spiritual well-being.

HELPING CLASS MEMBERS ACT

Challenge each class member to take one concrete action this week to show their faith by works. This action may involve personal service to an individual, volunteer work in the church or agency, or a monetary contribution.

Secure information on helping the poor through a denominational agency. One such group is UMCOR (United Methodist Committee on Relief). Choose a particular class project and take an offering to support it.

Encourage students to think of persons who have been special examples in your own life. If possible, contact at least one of them this week and tell this person how much his or her influence has touched your life. If the person is now deceased, consider making a memorial gift to the church.

Help the members to make a list of persons who are sick and covenant together as a class to pray for them this week. If your church does not have a prayer chain, consider starting one with class members.

If your own church does not hold healing services, ask class members to consider visiting a church where such services are held. Encourage them to share this experience with other class members and, if appropriate, discuss the possibility of holding such services with your own church's pastor.

PLANNING FOR NEXT SUNDAY

Next week's lesson deals with the subject of godly wisdom. Remind the class that the book of James is much like the Jewish Wisdom literature of Proverbs. Ask your students to read the background scriptures, James 1:5-8; 3:1-5a, and 3:13-18, to see how they resemble Proverbs. Encourage them to think of a definition of wisdom specifically from a Christian point of view. Also ask them to determine what differences there are, if any, between Christian wisdom and general secular wisdom.

LETTING WISDOM GUIDE

PREVIEWING THE LESSON

Lesson Scripture: James 1:5-8; 3:1-5*a*, 13-18
Background Scripture: James 1:5-8; 3:1-5*a*, 13-18
Key Verse: James 3:13

Focus of the lesson:
the wisdom God gives to guide persons in their faith journeys

Main question(s) of the lesson:
(1) How can God's wisdom guide me and show forth in my life?

This lesson will enable adult learners to:
(1) describe godly wisdom and contrast it to earthly wisdom
(2) show forth God's wisdom in their own lives through their works
(3) respond by exercising wisdom in their speech, just as a teacher is called to do.

Today's lesson may be outlined as follows:
(1) Introduction
(2) The Biblical Definition of Wisdom (James 1:5-8)
(3) Controlling the Power of the Tongue (James 3:1-5*a*)
(4) Two Kinds of Wisdom (James 3:13-18)

FOCUSING ON THE MAIN QUESTION

Wisdom isn't as sought after today as it was in some other generations. Knowledge and skill are highly prized, but the very word "wisdom" has almost gone out of our vocabulary. In former eras, the few persons who had access to advanced formal education were held in high esteem, and their opinions were earnestly sought. Now that thousands of students receive undergraduate or graduate degrees each year, knowledge is no longer perceived to be as mysterious as it once was. Many persons seek knowledge, but wisdom seems to be less prized.

Knowledge can be studied and learned, but wisdom is more than the sheer accumulation of data. Wisdom includes insights into life and the qualities of character to put that data to good use. While we have had an explosion of knowledge in our generation, not many would argue that we've had an explosion of wisdom. If anything, our knowledge itself seems to frighten or overwhelm us at times. What can we do with the wonders we have wrought? How can we control the marvels of nuclear power? Having found ways to extend life and to begin it with *in vitro* fertilization, who will help us decide where life's terminal point shall be, or how to control these new powers of conception? As we continue to invent new labor-saving devices and restructure our businesses to compete more effectively in the global marketplace, where will we create employment opportunities for those workers who are being replaced by machines or caught in a permanent "downsizing" layoff? And who will show us how to use our new leisure time, if the work week is cut back to thirty hours a week? In other words, where will we get the wisdom to direct and control our brave new world?

James, of course, knew nothing of our knowledge explosion. Our technological advances are likely beyond his wildest imaginings. Yet James knew that the source of wisdom was God—the same God who continues to be our source of wisdom. James's letter invites us to seek wisdom from God. It also calls us to ask: **How can God's wisdom guide me and show forth in my life?**

READING THE SCRIPTURE

NRSV

James 1:5-8

5 If any of you is lacking in wisdom, ask God, who gives to all generously and ungrudgingly, and it will be given you. 6But ask in faith, never doubting, for the one who doubts is like a wave of the sea, driven and tossed by the wind; 7, 8for the doubter, being double-minded and unstable in every way, must not expect to receive anything from the Lord.

James 3:1-5a

1 Not many of you should become teachers, my brothers and sisters, for you know that we who teach will be judged with greater strictness. 2For all of us make many mistakes. Anyone who makes no mistakes in speaking is perfect, able to keep the whole body in check with a bridle. 3If we put bits into the mouths of horses to make them obey us, we guide their whole bodies. 4Or look at ships: though they are so large that it takes strong winds to drive them, yet they are guided by a very small rudder wherever the will of the pilot directs. 5So also the tongue is a small member, yet it boasts of great exploits.

James 3:13-18

13 Who is wise and understanding among you? Show by your good life that your works are done with gentleness born of wisdom. 14But if you have bitter envy

NIV

James 1:5-8

5If any of you lacks wisdom, he should ask God, who gives generously to all without finding fault, and it will be given to him. 6But when he asks, he must believe and not doubt, because he who doubts is like a wave of the sea, blown and tossed by the wind. 7That man should not think he will receive anything from the Lord; 8he is a double-minded man, unstable in all he does.

James 3:1-5a

1 Not many of you should presume to be teachers, my brothers, because you know that we who teach will be judged more strictly. 2We all stumble in many ways. If anyone is never at fault in what he says, he is a perfect man, able to keep his whole body in check.

3When we put bits into the mouths of horses to make them obey us, we can turn the whole animal. 4Or take ships as an example. Although they are so large and are driven by strong winds, they are steered by a very small rudder wherever the pilot wants to go. 5Likewise the tongue is a small part of the body, but it makes great boasts.

James 3:13-18

13Who is wise and understanding among you? Let him show it by his good life, by deeds done in the humility that comes from wisdom. 14But if you harbor

Key Verse

Ke
Ver

and selfish ambition in your hearts, do not be boastful and false to the truth. ¹⁵Such wisdom does not come down from above, but is earthly, unspiritual, devilish. ¹⁶For where there is envy and selfish ambition, there will also be disorder and wickedness of every kind. ¹⁷But the wisdom from above is first pure, then peaceable, gentle, willing to yield, full of mercy and good fruits, without a trace of partiality or hypocrisy. ¹⁸And a harvest of righteousness is sown in peace for those who make peace.

bitter envy and selfish ambition in your hearts, do not boast about it or deny the truth. ¹⁵Such "wisdom" does not come down from heaven but is earthly, unspiritual, of the devil. ¹⁶For where you have envy and selfish ambition, there you find disorder and every evil practice.

¹⁷But the wisdom that comes from heaven is first of all pure; then peace-loving, considerate, submissive, full of mercy and good fruit, impartial and sincere. ¹⁸Peacemakers who sow in peace raise a harvest of righteousness.

UNDERSTANDING THE SCRIPTURE

James 1:5-8. The Epistle of James is often described as being in the tradition of the Wisdom literature of the Old Testament, particularly the book of Proverbs. Proverbs has much to say about wisdom, a word that is mentioned forty-nine times (NRSV). James introduces the theme of wisdom in verses 5-8.

James 1:5. Wisdom comes from God. Those persons who lack it should ask of God who will give it generously. Similar teachings are found in Proverbs: Proverbs 2:6 states that God is the source and giver of wisdom; Proverbs 4:5, 7 admonish persons to get wisdom.

James 1:6. Although James is often accused of pitting works against faith, this verse indicates the importance he gives to faith. When we seek wisdom, we must do so "in faith, never doubting."

James 1:7-8. We too often think of faith as a feeling or a sensation; James measures it by constancy and steadfastness. By contrast, the doubter is "double-minded." James uses an interesting Greek word (*dipsuchos*), which means literally a person with two souls or two minds (psyches). Such a person is trying to focus on God and on something else. The person who is not single-mindedly focused on God should not expect to receive anything from

God. Compare Jesus' teaching in Matthew 21:21-22 regarding praying in faith without doubting.

James 3:1. In the early church list of ministries, teachers ranked third only to apostles and prophets (1 Corinthians 12:28). The teaching office was held in extremely high regard; after all, Jesus himself was most often addressed as rabbi, or teacher. Anyone accepting such an important position must accept tremendous responsibilities. Those who teach "will be judged with greater strictness."

James 3:2. Now James zeroes in on a particular peril, the use of the tongue. Teachers are especially vulnerable to mistakes because the major instrument of their work is the tongue. The "perfect" person referred to here is one who is spiritually mature. This maturity is reflected in one's ability to keep the entire body, including the tongue, in check.

James 3:3-5. James compares the tongue to the bit in the mouth of the horse and to the rudder on a ship, noting that these relatively small items are of unparalleled power. So it is with the tongue.

James 3:13-17. In this passage James contrasts two kinds of wisdom. The wisdom that comes from God manifests itself in a good life and humble deeds. Here again James returns to his basic theme that one's character is shown in one's life and works. The wisdom that comes from God is "first pure, then peaceable, gentle, willing to yield, full of mercy and good fruits, without a trace of partiality or hypocrisy." In other words, wisdom reflects the characteristics of godliness. "Willing to yield" carries the idea of being teachable. This is an especially important quality in wisdom, for the peril of wisdom is that its possessor will come to think of himself or herself as beyond correction. Godly wisdom always has an element of humility. In contrast, there is a wisdom that is "earthly, unspiritual, devilish." This wisdom does not come from God but springs from "envy and selfish ambition."

James 3:18. This final verse seems more closely related to James 4:1, for the peacemaker acts in the midst of conflict. Righteousness is the harvest or fruit of peace. James 1:19 relates righteousness to one's behavior.

INTERPRETING THE SCRIPTURE

The Biblical Definition of Wisdom

Most of us know what we mean when we hear the word "wisdom," but we would have a hard time defining it. We would probably point to some person who has always seemed to us to be wise, and would let that identification settle for our definition.

The Jews were more certain. They revered wisdom greatly, and they saw it in highly practical, rather than in mystical, terms. To them, wisdom was something to be exercised at the workplace, the dinner table, or in family life; it was by no means best demonstrated in a classroom or a think tank. What we might define as native intelligence, or perhaps even with the slang term, "street smart," the Jews would have classified as wisdom. The Hebrew word *chakam* means wise in the sense of intelligent, skillful, artful, or cunning. Thus, the artisans who built the tabernacle (Exodus 36:8) are called wise hearted (KJV). The prophet Ezekiel used the same Hebrew word to describe the pilots and shipbuilders of Tyre, the port city (Ezekiel 27:8-9, KJV). The writer of Proverbs comes up with even more interesting examples when he praises such creatures as ants, badgers, locusts, and lizards for their wisdom (Proverbs 30:24-28). They know enough to survive and be effective within their realm of life, and that, in the Jewish mind, was wisdom. It's a much more practical point of view than we usually associate with the word.

The Jews were certain that true wisdom has its origins in God. It is not simply a matter of education or breeding. The God who endows earth's tiniest creatures with wisdom for survival will also bless humanity with wisdom to meet the challenges of our complex existence. So the writer of Proverbs says:

> Trust in the LORD with all your
> 　　heart,
> 　　and do not rely on your own
> 　　　　insight.
> In all your ways acknowledge
> 　　him [God]
> 　　and he will make straight your
> 　　　　paths.
> (Proverbs 3:5-6)

James echoes this outlook when he says that if we lack wisdom, we should ask God; we will find the Lord generous and ungrudging (James 1:5). James also makes clear that our request must be made with single-minded devotion to God. Persons who try to divide their loyalty and energies between God and something else are in James's word, double-minded. Such persons need not expect to receive God's good gift of wisdom.

Our need for God's wisdom is apparent. The issues in modern society have become so complex that we clearly need wisdom beyond our present store. It sometimes seem that our wondrous learning and achievements have turned in upon themselves, so that our brightest signs of progress become in the next turn our greatest perils. When Harry Emerson Fosdick wrote a poem/hymn for the dedication of New York's Riverside Church earlier in this century, he prayed for wisdom and courage "for the living of these days." The prayer has a startling relevance for our times.

Controlling the Power of the Tongue

The tongue is the nuclear energy of the soul. Used wisely, it can bless life; all of us can recall a kindly or helpful word timely spoken. But used wrongly, the tongue can destroy life almost beyond repair. All of us, unfortunately, know something about that, too.

The problem with the tongue is that it must be used. After some disastrous misstatement, we sometimes vow, "I don't think I'll ever speak again." Silence is no solution, though. To be silent can be as wrong a use of the tongue as to misspeak. The tongue is a power to be exercised; the problem is to exercise it rightly. And that is never easy.

We are especially in danger of misusing our tongues when we're in positions of power. James refers specifically to the role of teacher (James 3:1). Teaching is a special calling, but all of us fill this role at some time in our lives. Every parent is a teacher (the most basic of all!); so is a worker who tries to help a newcomer learn a job, or the student who tutors another student. When we are persons in authority, even briefly, we are especially in danger of using the tongue in hurtful ways.

James writes in chapter 3 verse 2 that the only persons who have perfect control over their tongues are those who are spiritually mature. The rest of us do make mistakes. The tongue seems so small to wreak so much damage. Yet James points out that by using a bit, a rider can control a horse. Likewise, the rudder is insignificant in size compared to the rest of the ship. But the captain can steer even a large vessel with precision by means of the rudder. James's lesson for us is that we must be aware of the tremendous potential of our tongues.

One seventeenth-century British cleric was probably as godly a person as ever lived. He was also, however, a man capable of sharp words. The very skills that made him an effective writer and speaker made him also a formidable opponent. When one of his foes died, the clergyman could not forgive himself for many of the things he had said. He lamented that every sour or cross word made him almost unreconcilable with himself. Similarly, a distinguished psychiatrist of our era, who has written with keen insight about the thinking and feeling of children, recalls with pain some of the hasty words he spoke to his own three sons as they were growing up. No one is exempt from misuse of the tongue.

Two Kinds of Wisdom

All of our human gifts are open to good use or to misuse. So it is with wisdom. James realizes that even believers may pervert the power of wisdom to harmful purposes, so he challenges us to a goodness that will bring works "done with gentleness born of wisdom" (James 3:13). Gentleness is by no means weakness; it is strength that is under control. Most important of all, those who possess true gentleness have themselves under control. They are not driven to show off their power; nor—in the language of James—are they under the control of "bitter envy and selfish ambition" (James 3:14).

So what is the difference between good and evil wisdom? Evil wisdom is "earthly, unspiritual, devilish" (James 3:15). It lacks commitment to the eternal, to the spiritual, and to the godly. It is the kind of wisdom that knows how to play the game. This wisdom may push to get ahead and succeed, though the success it brings is often short-lived and may hurt others. But for those who want success at any price, this kind of wisdom is attractive. Such ambitious wisdom is summed up in a phrase that is only occasionally spoken but quite often followed: "I'll get the other person before he or she gets me."

Heavenly wisdom is diametrically opposite. It is described by James in beautiful words: "first pure, then peaceable, gentle, willing to yield, full of mercy and good fruits, without a trace of partiality or hypocrisy" (James 3:17). No wonder that it brings a "harvest of righteousness" (James 3:18).

Such a godly view of wisdom runs counter to our customary secular outlook. Too many are inclined to agree with the old sports adage that "nice guys finish last." James believes otherwise, partly because he has a different definition of winning, and partly because he is looking for a different kind of final score. He understands that those who live by envy and selfish ambition lose even while they seem to be winning, whereas those who choose the way that is pure and peaceable cannot really lose. Such qualities are on the side of the universe, and in the end they must win. We need such wisdom to guide our living in these challenging days.

SHARING THE SCRIPTURE

PREPARING TO TEACH

Like all of the lessons in James, this one deals with wonderfully practical matters. After you have read the material in this lesson and the assigned scripture passages, with their emphasis on wisdom and the use of the tongue, look at the newspaper for a few minutes in light of these two issues. What examples of wisdom do you see in the news reports, the political and international scene, the comics, or the sports section? Find some examples that are "earthly, unspiritual, devilish" and some that are "pure and peaceable." Consider how the media, especially newspapers, magazines, or television news, are using the power of words.

Think about the following questions in light of your own understanding of wisdom. When have you used wisdom for good, and when for primarily selfish advantage? In what circumstances are you most likely to misuse the power of the tongue by saying sharp words? In what ways or situations are you likely to mis-

use the power of the tongue by being silent? You may want to write about one or more of these incidents in your spiritual journal.

James issues a special warning to teachers in 3:1. Spend some time this week thinking about how God might judge your words. Do you treat each student with respect, allowing him or her to voice an opinion or raise a question without feeling threatened or belittled? Are you able to refrain from making derogatory, judgmental, or hurtful remarks about persons or situations within the church or community? Are you able, according to James 3:13-18, to show forth your wisdom in peace, gentleness, mercy, and without hypocrisy? Pray about your answers that God may lead you into more perfect (that is, more spiritually mature) speech.

If you plan to do the written exercise under "Controlling the Power of the Tongue," be sure to have paper and pencils available.

If you choose to sing (or read in unison) "God of Grace and God of Glory" (page

577 in *The United Methodist Hymnal*) to close the session, have hymnals available.

LEADING THE CLASS

Introduction

State or write in a conspicuous place the main question for today's lesson: **How can God's wisdom guide me and show forth in my life?**

Ask class members if they have ever known a really wise person. If so, select two or three students to tell about these persons, and why they perceive them to be wise. Try to elicit from these speakers how they see wisdom guiding the life of the wise individual.

Then make a distinction between knowledge and wisdom. Let the class suggest several examples in our time where our increased knowledge has meant increased problems, so that we need wisdom more than ever in order to cope with our problems. Keep this discussion brief, taking care not to allow it to become a listing of problems and proposed solutions. You may want to use examples from the news articles you have perused this week. Or you may want to raise some of the questions listed in the second paragraph under "Focusing on the Main Question." The purpose here is to help adults recognize that an increase in knowledge does not necessarily lead to an increase in wisdom. Quite the contrary! The more we know the more we need to become aware of God's wisdom and allow that wisdom to guide our lives.

The Biblical Definition of Wisdom

After engaging the class in a discussion of their own experiences with people they perceive to be wise, talk about the very practical nature of biblical wisdom, using the examples of the artisans of Exodus, the shipbuilders of Tyre, and the wise little creatures in Proverbs found under this section in "Interpreting the Scripture." You may want to compare several Bible translations to clarify various nuances of wisdom, such as wise, skilled, artful, or cunning. Your class members likely will have identified persons with many of these same qualities. In fact, their definitions or descriptions of wisdom may be very much in keeping with practical, down-to-earth biblical understandings of wisdom.

Choose a volunteer to read aloud James 1:5-8.

Direct the class to recall some instances when they were "lacking in wisdom." Then raise these questions:

(1) **Did you ask God for wisdom in these situations?**

(2) **How did they perceive God giving you the wisdom you needed?**

(3) **How was the outcome of this situation influenced by God's gift of wisdom?**

Most of us need more opportunities to share such experiences, and to hear the experiences of others. In too many cases, we have no idea of the degree to which God is at work in the lives of our friends. Here is an opportunity for such expression and sharing.

Point out the importance of asking for wisdom with single-minded faith. Use the material under chapter 1 verses 7-8 in "Understanding the Scripture" to help the students understand what James means when he talks about being "double-minded and unstable" (James 1:8). Ask the class to give some examples of double-mindedness. Here are a few to spark discussion:

- a student prays for wisdom as he studies but then decides to hide notes so that he can cheat during a test
- praying for wisdom, a mother turns the problems of her married daughter over to God but continues to intervene in an attempt to straighten out the problems herself and

- a church leader prays for wisdom in resolving a church conflict but creates further hostility between the two warring factions.

Note that in each case the person appears to trust God but has a back-up plan in case God does not do what the petitioner had hoped.

Controlling the Power of the Tongue

Select a student to read aloud James 3:1-5a. End with "great exploits."

Ask for a show of hands of persons in the class who are teachers. Several who are professional educators may respond, but most class members will not see themselves as teachers. Help the class to recognize that we are all teachers. Encourage them to identify circumstances in which anyone may be cast in the role of the teacher. You may want to list answers on a chalkboard or newsprint. Answers may include: parents, Sunday school teachers, scout leaders, workers who assist new employees, students who tutor their peers, experienced mothers who advise new mothers. When class members see themselves as teachers, they will be able to apply James's words to themselves. James warns the teachers that they are in danger because their office allows them to use the tongue more freely than others and because their opinions are more often sought. When we act as teachers, we must take special responsibility for our actions.

Use the information for James 3:1-5a under "Understanding the Scripture" to clarify that the perfect person is the one who is spiritually mature. Such persons are in control of themselves, just as a bit controls a horse or a rudder controls a ship.

Ask class members to give suggestions or examples of how they attempt to control their tongue. You may want to do this activity in pairs or small teams. If you think persons may be reluctant to talk about this, distribute slips of papers and allow time for them to write a helpful hint. Collect these anonymous papers and read them aloud. Ideas for controlling the tongue include: 1) learning how to express anger in ways that do not destroy another person; 2) avoiding gossip; 3) speaking up when an individual or group is being maligned; and 4) recognizing times when we are apt to "mouth off" and seeking God's wisdom to control ourselves in those moments.

Two Kinds of Wisdom

Read aloud James 3:13-18.

Ask the class: **(1) What two kinds of wisdom do you see here? (2) What are the origins and characteristics of each?** Record their answers on a chalkboard or newsprint, divided in half. Label one column "Godly Wisdom" and the other "Earthly Wisdom."

Now ask the class for a few examples from their own experience, from history, or even from novels or movies of wisdom that could be described as "earthly, unspiritual, devilish."

Spend more time discussing examples of persons who exemplify wisdom that is "pure" or "peaceable" or "willing to yield." To avoid embarrassment, ask class members not to name these persons (unless they are famous or public figures) but simply to describe how this person lives out the godly wisdom that James describes. Point out how the behaviors of such persons help to make the world a better place.

Ask class members to reflect quietly on a particular circumstance in their lives where godly wisdom is needed, or on a setting or relationship where they find it especially hard to use the tongue well. Then join in a prayer, perhaps with hands clasped, for strength to fulfill these high goals. This prayer can be silent, or it can be led by you or by a volunteer.

You may want to close today's session by singing "God of Grace and God of

Glory," a well-known hymn by Harry Emerson Fosdick that asks God to grant us wisdom and courage as we seek to live faithfully in these days.

HELPING CLASS MEMBERS ACT

Challenge class members to be alert for opportunities to serve in the teaching role. Encourage them to recognize the special responsibilities that accompany this influential position and to guard their speech accordingly.

Invite each person to make a special effort to use the tongue wisely at least once each day this week. They may do this by trying to be a peacemaker in a dispute, by offering a word of encouragement to someone who needs to hear a kind word, by offering a word of praise, by answering a sharp word with a gentle reply, or by speaking a word of truth in a situation where it would be easier to remain silent.

Suggest that class members use concordances to locate Bible passages that refer to wisdom. Ask students to consider how these understandings differ from or are similar to our society's views or wisdom. Challenge them to act with biblical wisdom in a situation where secular wisdom would require a different kind of response.

PLANNING FOR NEXT SUNDAY

The ultimate battleground of life is the human soul. Ask your class members to read James 4:1-10 and to think about the ways in which sins first show themselves in the struggles of the mind. Then ask them to read James 4:13-17. Encourage them to try using the phrase, "if the Lord wishes" (James 4:15), when announcing plans for the day or for the future.

DOING RIGHT

PREVIEWING THE LESSON

Lesson Scripture: James 4:1-10, 13-17
Background Scripture: James 4:1-10, 13-17
Key Verse: James 4:17

Focus of the lesson:
God's expectation that persons do what is right

Main question(s) of the lesson:
(1) What keeps you from doing right?

This lesson will enable adult learners to:
(1) identify the reasons for human failure to do what is right before God
(2) move toward a more righteous personal relationship with God
(3) respond by evaluating their own shortcomings and taking action to overcome them.

Today's lesson may be outlined as follows:
(1) Introduction
(2) The Source of Our Conflicts (James 4:1-6)
(3) How to Deal with Our Conflicts (James 4:7-10)
(4) How to Avoid Future Conflicts (James 4:13-17)

FOCUSING ON THE MAIN QUESTION

We might easily think that James wrote the verses for this lesson after watching several days of American television. I find something comforting, in a negative sort of way, about his warnings, because they remind me that the problems we face are not new. Nowadays these problems are accentuated by the power of the ever-present media, but the basic issues have been with us since the human race began.

Conflicts and disputes, with cravings that consummate in murder, coveting, and violence, are common in our society. Our nightly news is a conglomerate of violence, much of it related to our human cravings for physical possessions, for sexual fulfillment, or for power. And ironically, between these reports on violence and destruction, we have commercials that are calculated to heighten our yearnings, so that we will want still more.

James is worried, too, because the people to whom he was writing were so set on getting the things they desired that they were oblivious to God and God's wishes for them. So James reminds us how brief and uncertain life can be, telling us that all our plans ought to be developed with the recognition that our lives are lived under the will of God. When he warns about the dangers into which our cravings are taking us, I want to say, "James, you should see how our generation has complicated the problem!" But at the same moment I marvel that these words from nineteen centuries ago are so relevant to life today. So if James made such a clear diagnosis of our human condition from so long past, perhaps his prescription is worth hearing, too. He may know just the medicine we need. James's letter challenges us to ask: **What keeps us from doing right?**

READING THE SCRIPTURE

NRSV
James 4:1-10

1 Those conflicts and disputes among you, where do they come from? Do they not come from your cravings that are at war within you? ²You want something and do not have it; so you commit murder. And you covet something and cannot obtain it; so you engage in disputes and conflicts. You do not have, because you do not ask. ³You ask and do not receive, because you ask wrongly, in order to spend what you get on your pleasures. ⁴Adulterers! Do you not know that friendship with the world is enmity with God? Therefore whoever wishes to be a friend of the world becomes an enemy of God. ⁵Or do you suppose that it is for nothing that the scripture says, "God yearns jealously for the spirit that he has made to dwell in us"? ⁶But he gives all the more grace; therefore it says,

"God opposes the proud,
    but gives grace to the
        humble."

⁷Submit yourselves therefore to God. Resist the devil, and he will flee from you. ⁸Draw near to God, and he will draw near to you. Cleanse your hands, you sinners, and purify your hearts, you double-minded. ⁹Lament and mourn and weep. Let your laughter be turned into mourning and your joy into dejection. ¹⁰Humble yourselves before the Lord, and he will exalt you.

NIV
James 4:1-10

1 What causes fights and quarrels among you? Don't they come from your desires that battle within you? ²You want something but don't get it. You kill and covet, but you cannot have what you want. You quarrel and fight. You do not have, because you do not ask God. ³When you ask, you do not receive, because you ask with wrong motives, that you may spend what you get on your pleasures.

⁴You adulterous people, don't you know that friendship with the world is hatred toward God? Anyone who chooses to be a friend of the world becomes an enemy of God. ⁵Or do you think Scripture says without reason that the spirit he caused to live in us envies intensely? ⁶But he gives us more grace. That is why Scripture says:

"God opposes the proud
    but gives grace to the humble."

⁷Submit yourselves, then, to God. Resist the devil, and he will flee from you. ⁸Come near to God and he will come near to you. Wash your hands, you sinners, and purify your hearts, you double-minded. ⁹Grieve, mourn and wail. Change your laughter to mourning and your joy to gloom. ¹⁰Humble yourselves before the Lord, and he will lift you up.

James 4:13-17

13 Come now, you who say, "Today or tomorrow we will go to such and such a town and spend a year there, doing business and making money." ¹⁴Yet you do not even know what tomorrow will bring. What is your life? For you are a mist that appears for a little while and then vanishes. ¹⁵Instead you ought to say, "If the Lord wishes, we will live and do this or that." ¹⁶As it is, you boast in your arrogance; all such boasting is evil. ¹⁷Anyone, then, who knows the right thing to do and fails to do it, commits sin.

Key Verse

James 4:13-17

¹³Now listen, you who say, "Today or tomorrow we will go to this or that city, spend a year there, carry on business and make money." ¹⁴Why, you do not even know what will happen tomorrow. What is your life? You are a mist that appears for a little while and then vanishes. ¹⁵Instead, you ought to say, "If it is the Lord's will, we will live and do this or that." ¹⁶As it is, you boast and brag. All such boasting is evil. ¹⁷Anyone, then, who knows the good he ought to do and doesn't do it, sins.

Ke Ver

UNDERSTANDING THE SCRIPTURE

James 4:1-10. In this passage James sets before us the conflict between our desires and the will of God. Throughout the Bible, God's relationship with his people is based on a covenant in which mutual fidelity is expected (see, for example, Exodus 19:5-6; Mark 14:24; and Hebrews 9:15). The form of verses 4-10 is a three-part covenantal form: 1) verses 4-5 sound warnings against persons who are unfaithful to the covenant; 2) verse 6 offers God's grace and blessings to those who submit to God's will; 3) verses 7-10 state obligations of those persons who are part of the covenant.

James 4:1. All of us agree that there is tremendous conflict in the world, but we usually look for the cause in society at large or in conflicts between nations or between races and ethnic groups. James wants us to understand that the root origins are within us. We have a war inside that manifests itself in many external conflicts.

James 4:2. Philo, the first century Jewish philosopher, believed that the commandment against coveting came as the last of the Ten Commandments because this was the culminating danger. From such desires all other evils are born.

James 4:3. James's words remind us of Jesus' teachings in Matthew 7:7, 11. James cites two reasons for our failure to receive from God. First, we fail to ask. Second, we ask for something that is not in keeping with God's will but is desired to fulfill our own passions. God will not grant such requests.

James 4:4. If our translation were true to the Greek, it would read "adulteresses." The feminine is used because the passage is of course not referring to physical adultery, but to a violation of our spiritual union with God. And since the church, like Israel before it, is pictured as God's bride, our spiritual infidelity classifies us as adulteresses. The metaphor of adultery is also used in the Old Testament to refer to persons who break God's covenant (see Hosea 3:1 and Ezekiel 16:38). When James and other New Testament writers refer to the world in a negative way, they are referring neither to nature nor to humanity, but to the corrupted or sinful spirit of the world that is antagonistic toward God. It is what Paul had in mind when he said that Demas had left the faith because he was "in love with this present world" (2 Timothy 4:10).

James 4:5-6. The "war within" (James 4:1) is not weighted on the side of evil.

James reassures us that "God yearns" for us, and that God has implanted in us a spirit that is inclined to God. Although God's jealousy is often noted (see, for example, Exodus 20:5 and Zechariah 8:2), no exact scripture reference can be found in known manuscripts for the quotation in verse 5. Verse 6 includes a quotation from Proverbs 3:34 as it appears in a Greek version, the Septuagint.

James 4:7-8. James's formula for success is simple and straightforward. If we resist the devil, he will flee, and if we will draw near to near God, God will draw near to us. But James is not saying, "simply believe." Drawing near to God means a change in actions ("Cleanse your hands") and in thoughts ("purify your hearts"). In fact, the psalmist says that clean hands and pure hearts are needed to approach God (Psalm 24:4). The ability to make these changes is given by God through grace to those persons who will humble themselves (James 4:6). The ones who need to make these changes are "sinners" and "double-minded" (see also James 1:8).

James 4:9-10. Joy is one of the characteristics of the Christian life and one of the fruits of the Spirit. But it is never a superficial joy; it is based on godly living. Apparently the believers had become complacent and self-satisfied, so James calls for the kind of mourning that comes from serious self-examination. Verse 10 hearkens back to verse 6 and can also be linked to Jesus' teaching on God's exaltation of the humble found in Matthew 23:12.

James 4:13. Here is further evidence of complacency: the believers are so engrossed in their secular pursuits that they take no thought of God's will or purposes. They arrogantly believe that they are truly in charge of their lives, seemingly forgetting that they live by God's mercy and grace. A similar idea is found in Proverbs 27:1.

James 4:14. When James says that our life is like a mist, it reminds one of Jesus' story of the rich man who felt so secure in his wealth, never realizing how brief his life was going to be (Luke 12:16-21).

James 4:15. A person might easily adopt the phrase, "God willing," as a kind of magic protection. James is recommending no such thing; he wants us to have an attitude that constantly remembers that God is ultimate.

James 4:16. Persons who boast about what they will do are arrogant because they fail to recognize that their lives are conditional.

James 4:17. The worldliness, arrogance, and other evil that James discusses in this chapter are all perceived as sin. As always, James is practical. A person who knows the right thing to do but then fails to do it is guilty of committing sin.

INTERPRETING THE SCRIPTURE

The Source of Our Conflicts

A popular catchphrase in religious circles says that Christians need to "walk the talk." I think James would have liked that. His recurring concern in this letter is for believers who talk good religion but walk in a manner that is not consistent with their profession.

It's a built-in problem, of course. Christianity calls us to such a high standard of living that we always fall somewhat short of its best expectations. Part of the glory of the Christian life is that it isn't easily packaged in a few clever rules, or a short (or even a long!) list of do's and don'ts. After we have done our best, Jesus said, we will still have to confess that we are "unprofitable servants" (Luke 17:10, KJV).

James wants us to know where our

problems begin, and how to emerge victorious. We're usually inclined to excuse ourselves on the basis of matters outside ourselves or beyond our control. James will have none of it. The conflicts, he says, come from within, from cravings that are at war within us. No wonder there are disputes without when there are such wars within! The issue can of course be oversimplified, but it's hard to find a misdeed that doesn't begin in the thought life.

The writer goes on to warn us that these unworthy thoughts can invade even our prayer lives. Having told us that we do not have because we do not ask, he continues to say that sometimes our asking is wrong in itself, because we want things simply for our own pleasure. If our prayers have no thought for the will of God or for the well-being of others, they are as evil as can be. James uses a strong word—adultery. Christians are supposed to be married to Christ, so when their affections are tied so closely to this earth, they are guilty of spiritual infidelity.

How different are we who profess Christ from the general secular society? The saints of every generation have called for simple living. They have warned against love of wealth and clamoring for more baubles. Our predecessors in the faith have found it difficult to hold to such standards, but the challenge in our day is probably more intense than at any previous time. Literally hundreds of times a day we are urged to buy, to experience, to get. Our nineteenth-century ancestors were solicited to buy only when a traveling peddler came by or when they went on an infrequent shopping tour. Now the peddlers approach us by newspaper, billboard, radio, and television— and almost everywhere else we look or listen! In a world like ours, it is very difficult to be satisfied with the "simple things in life." We need a greater conversion than ever.

How to Deal with Our Conflicts

I don't by any means think the cause is lost. To the contrary, I see more hope than in fully a generation. I think vast numbers of us have become more conscious of the danger of materialism and that we are examining our lifestyle far more seriously. I'm impressed by the popularity of the writings of Richard Foster, appealing for a simple life; I won't suggest that we are practicing all that he and others recommend, but I think we're developing a more sensitive conscience. I'm impressed, too, that when a respected business magazine tried to analyze the spirit of this closing decade of the twentieth century, it ran a collection of articles asking why we're feeling so bad when we have it so good. Secular society itself wonders what has gone wrong with our love of things.

James offers a typically practical bit of counsel: submit to God and resist the devil. If this seems overly simple, consider the power of our habits. Those who form the practice of resisting evil have a much easier time when confronted with temptation than do those who acquiesce to evil again and again. It is, indeed, as simple as that!

But it's also very difficult. Listen to the strong verbs James uses as he instructs us in this process of yielding and resisting: *cleanse, purify, lament, mourn, weep, humble.* See, too, the vigorous language he uses to describe us: *sinners* and *double-minded.* If we are to draw near to God, we must turn our laughter into mourning and our joy into dejection so as to humble ourselves before God. This kind of spiritual discipline is not for casual disciples (if there is such a thing!) or for half-hearted followers.

These strong mandates remind us that many of our troubles in living a victorious Christian life stem from our casual commitment. When we make our inner life a second or third (or lower!) matter of priority, is it any wonder that we aren't more happy and effective in our faith? James wants us to know that all the other issues of life result from what goes on in our inner being—and this is a matter of submitting ourselves to God and resisting the devil.

How to Avoid Future Conflicts

What about tomorrow? Counselors tell us we should learn to live our lives in "day-tight compartments," but most of us find that difficult to do. Naturally, we want to know some things about tomorrow, and reasonably, we want to do some planning. After all, it doesn't make good sense to march into the future without thought or aim. So how does the Christian look at tomorrow?

The Christian remembers that, as the old folk wisdom puts it, "Man proposes, but God disposes." It is both wise and proper to plan for the future, but all our plans should be under the purpose and will of God. So James insists that we should never say that tomorrow we will do this or that, but that our planning should always be with the conditional understanding, "If the Lord wishes" (James 4:15).

Half a century has gone by, but I still remember the summer day when I received a letter from a godly man who noted that he was planning to make a trip west later that month, "D.V." In my reply, I asked the meaning of "D.V." and learned that it was an abbreviation for *deo volente*, "God willing."

I don't often put those letters into my correspondence (though occasionally they find their way into my journal), but I try to make them the key factor in my planning. Mind you, a phrase like "the Lord willing" can become a kind of magic formula, and I'm surely not recommending that. Such words should never be spoken in mere rote. But their philosophy should by all means become part of our outlook on life. They are a conscious declaration of the lordship of Christ in our lives.

When we fail to acknowledge that our future is in the hands of God, we are acting arrogantly. Our boast is hollow. Indeed, it is evil. James has told us about the pitfalls of worldliness and what we must do (submit to God and resist the devil) in order to draw near to God. In other words, we now know the right thing to do (James 4:17). The choice is ours. We can live aright before God, or we can choose to commit sin. James again has shown us, in practical terms, how we can live faithfully before God in the midst of a sinful world.

SHARING THE SCRIPTURE

PREPARING TO TEACH

Some lessons are difficult to teach because they are theologically complex. This lesson begins that way, but true to James's usual style, it quickly slips into very practical matters. Remember that these practical issues of daily living are based upon the theological issues with which the chapter opens.

As you read James 4:1-10, consider James's point about the source of many problems: our "conflicts and disputes" come largely from our inner lives. Make a list of the "conflicts and disputes" (both personal and social) that seem to characterize your own life and the lives of your class members. How many of these conflicts can be attributed to our cravings within? You may want to pray for wisdom in recognizing and dealing with the inner attitudes that lead to conflicts.

Consider the statement in James 4:4 that "friendship with the world is enmity with God." What does "the world" mean to you? What do you think it means to your class members? Perhaps, like me, you remember when preachers talked often about "worldly pleasures." How does James's insight hold meaning for our times? In what ways is our world at enmity with God? You may want to record your thoughts in your spiritual journal.

Now consider the matter of "If the Lord wishes" (James 4:15). Be alert this week for instances when you either assumed that you could make your own plans, or when you clearly sought God's will as you planned. See if you can devise some internal signal to remind you when you have forgotten that God is truly in charge of your life.

List some decisions where the will of God should be a primary consideration. Be prepared to ask your class whether they ever think of the will of God in decision-making and planning and if so, to identify some instances. This exercise will itself help us to consider more seriously the lordship of Christ in our lives.

If you have time, you may want to read Richard Foster's *Celebration of Discipline* or *Freedom of Simplicity*. These books call us to live spiritually disciplined lives that include the practice of a more simplified lifestyle.

LEADING THE CLASS

Introduction

Remind your class at the outset that everyone wants to do right. This feeling is so strong that even people who are living wicked lives usually try to justify their conduct, simply because they want to feel that they're all right. Christians also sometimes say or do the wrong thing, in spite of their good intentions.

Since everyone wants to do right, why do we do wrong? Or, to phrase the question a different way: **What keeps us from doing right?** Spend a few minutes brainstorming answers to these questions with the entire group, recording their answers on a chalkboard or newsprint if you

choose. Or, you may want to ask pairs or small groups to discuss these questions if your class is large.

After this brief discussion, point out that James's letter calls us to ask these same questions. He will help us to arrive at an answer but, as always, James is not content that we simply gain an intellectual understanding. He challenges us to do what is right by telling us, in 4:17, that if we know what is right but fail to do it, we have committed sin.

The Source of Our Conflicts

Choose a volunteer to read James 4:1-6. Ask the class:

(1) What question does James raise for us in these verses? (Where do our conflicts come from?)

(2) How does James answer his own question? (They come from our own cravings.)

(3) Do you agree with James? Why or why not?

Explore these ideas in a brief discussion. Note that James's answer counters much of the popular philosophy of our time. We hear a great deal about the role of society in human misconduct, and also about the influence of our genes—matters that seem to be out of our control. If we take James seriously, we are compelled to look at ourselves as the center of responsibility.

Ask the class to identify some of the problems that are troubling our world. What part do inner cravings, such as greed, jealousy, lust, and coveting, play in both interpersonal conflicts and in larger community and international concerns?

Note that most of us will admit that we can never expect the whole world to be kind, loving, and unselfish. If that be so, how much difference will it make if individuals deal effectively with their cravings? Certainly they will feel better, but how much difference will it make in society as a whole? You may want to hold a brief debate on this question, with one group arguing that such action could make a huge difference, while another group counters that effective control of one's cravings will make little or no difference in a society that prizes friendship with the world.

How to Deal with Our Conflicts

Begin this segment by reading aloud James 4:7-10.

Note that James 4:7 contains two difficult words, though the difficulties are for quite different reasons. "Submit" is not an attractive word to most of us; our culture trains us to assert ourselves. Surely there's a place for the kind of healthy self-esteem that resists being submissive; Ask: **(1) What is the role of submission in life in both our learning experiences and in our relationship to God? (2) Is it not true that the very recognition that God is God implies submission on our part?** Discuss these questions with the class.

The other difficult word is "devil." Do not let your class get bogged down in a discussion about the reality or the nature of the devil, because to do so will prevent the lesson from proceeding any further. You may want simply to note that, whatever the personal beliefs regarding the devil, all of us recognize that there is evil in the world and that our main concern in this lesson is to deal with the evil rather than to discuss where it comes from. You might suggest that when James speaks of resisting the devil, he is of course urging us to resist temptation.

Then discuss the vigor and seriousness of James's counsel, noting the strong language he uses, as explained in the third paragraph of "How to Deal with Our Conflicts" section under "Interpreting the Scripture." This kind of earnest discipleship may not appeal to those who think of Christianity as primarily a way of solving their problems and providing comfort. It is, however, the kind of costly discipleship to which our Lord calls us.

How to Avoid Future Conflicts

Select a volunteer to read James 4:13-16.

Point out that James is telling us that tomorrow must be brought under God's domain, as well as today. Ask your class:
(1) **How many of you ever use the phrase, "God willing"?**
(2) **Who recognizes the abbreviation, D.V.? (This is the Latin phrase for *deo volente*.)**
(3) **How much of a role should God's will take in our planning?**
(Emphasize that the issue is not using this phrase each time we make some statement about the future, but rather, having a particular attitude toward God and our future. In other words, it is a matter of living in the spirit of "God willing," rather than using the words. But the words are a good reinforcement for our commitment; they serve to remind us that we belong to God, and that our tomorrows are committed to God.)

Summarize the lesson by asking everyone to read James 4:17, the key verse, in unison. Provide a few moments for the class to silently review the preceding week. You may want to write the following questions on a chalkboard or newsprint so that everyone can see them and meditate silently at their own pace.

- When did you know what God expected you to do and either failed to take any action or took action that was clearly not in keeping with God's will?
- Were these failures, which James labels sin, the result of your own inner cravings? Encourage each person to ask for God's forgiveness for past sins and God's grace to live in a close, faithful relationship to God.

HELPING CLASS MEMBERS ACT

Invite each person to think of one specific inner craving which, if brought under better control, would make life better for themselves and for someone else, too.

Then challenge them to concentrate on that matter this week.

Suggest that class members be aware of situations in which they did not act according to God's will this week. If such a lapse occurs, challenge class members to take action to rectify their error or inaction.

Encourage class members to identify a conflict or dispute within their families, workplace, or community. Challenge them to take at least one step to do right so as to lessen or resolve this problem.

Ask class members to sit down with their calendars this week. Likely, they will see many events and appointments scheduled months in advance. Encourage students to pray over their schedules, bringing before God each activity and seeking God's will about their participation in each one.

PLANNING FOR NEXT SUNDAY

Next Sunday we shift gears, as we move into the beloved book of Psalms for the next two months. The first unit will focus on psalms that praise God. Ask the class to read Psalm 104, paying particular attention to verses 24-34. Encourage students to think about how they celebrate the gift of life. They may also want to spend time this week reading psalms that are meaningful to them.

CELEBRATING THE GIFT OF LIFE

PREVIEWING THE LESSON

Lesson Scripture: Psalm 104:24-34
Background Scripture: Psalm 104
Key Verse: Psalm 104:24

Focus of the lesson:
praise to God, the creator and sustainer of life

Main question(s) of the lesson:
(1) How can we celebrate the gift of life God has created for us?

This lesson will enable adult learners to:
(1) understand our reasons and need to praise God
(2) experience the wonder of God's good creation
(3) respond by appreciating and giving thanks for God's creating and sustaining presence.

Today's lesson may be outlined as follows:
(1) Introduction
(2) The Wonder of Creation (Psalm 104:24-26)
(3) God's Provision for Creation (Psalm 104:27-30)
(4) A Song of Adoration (Psalm 104:31-34)

FOCUSING ON THE MAIN QUESTION

In the past twenty years, we have become increasingly conscious of the world of nature. Space exploration, on the one hand, has made the heavens seem far more accessible; when we look at the fabled "man in the moon" we remind ourselves that human beings have, indeed, walked on that moon. On the other hand, we've also become much more concerned about preserving the face of nature on our own planet. The media give us a running box score on the vanishing species, and we ask ourselves what we can do to save nature from the encroachments of civilization.

The biblical writers were conscious of the world of nature, too, but it was no new enthusiasm for them. They lived close to nature, and they knew how much they depended on it for survival. They couldn't have dreamed of a visit to the moon, nor did they worry about the extinction of species. But they looked at nature with an awe and a reverence that perhaps we should envy. For them, nature was a revelation of the glory and power of the Creator. To look at nature was to see the greatness of God.

Isaac Watts, the great eighteenth-century poet-preacher, felt the same way. He began a hymn of praise to God, the Creator of all nature, with these stirring words: "I sing the almighty power of God, that made the mountains rise, that spread the flowing seas abroad, and built the lofty skies." Watts, like hundreds of other writers before and after him, was continuing the spirit and message of the psalmists, who were so enraptured by the beauty of nature that they could express their feelings only by giving praise to God. They saw nature, in all its parts, as God's gift of life, of which we, too, are a part. We have abundant reason to celebrate this precious gift, though sometimes we fail to do so. As we study Psalm 104 today, we will want to ask ourselves: **How can we celebrate the gift of life that God has created for us?**

READING THE SCRIPTURE

Key Verse

NRSV
Psalm 104:24-34

24 O LORD, how manifold are your
works!
In wisdom you have made
them all;
the earth is full of your
creatures.
25 Yonder is the sea, great and
wide,
creeping things innumerable
are there,
living things both small and
great.
26 There go the ships,
and Leviathan that you formed
to sport in it.

27 These all look to you
to give them their food in due
season;
28 when you give to them, they
gather it up;
when you open your hand,
they are filled with good
things.
29 When you hide your face, they
are dismayed;
when you take away their
breath, they die
and return to their dust.
30 When you send forth your
spirit, they are created;

NIV
Psalm 104:24-34

24How many are your works, O LORD!
In wisdom you made them all;
the earth is full of your creatures.

25There is the sea, vast and spacious,
teeming with creatures beyond number—
living things both large and small.

26There the ships go to and fro,
and the leviathan, which you formed
to frolic there.

27These all look to you
to give them their food at the proper time.

28When you give it to them,
they gather it up;
when you open your hand,
they are satisfied with good things.

29When you hide your face,
they are terrified;
when you take away their breath,
they die and return to the dust.

30When you send your Spirit,
they are created,

and you renew the face of the
    ground.
[31] May the glory of the LORD
    endure forever;
may the LORD rejoice in his
    works—
[32] who looks on the earth and it
    trembles,
who touches the mountains
    and they smoke.
[33] I will sing to the LORD as long as
    I live;
I will sing praise to my God
    while I have being.
[34] May my meditation be pleasing
    to him,
for I rejoice in the LORD.

[31]May the glory of the LORD endure forever;
    may the LORD rejoice in his works.

[32]He looks at the earth, and it trembles;
    he touches the mountains, and they
    smoke.

[33]I will sing to the LORD all my life;
    I will sing praise to my God as long as
    I live.

[34]May my meditation be pleasing to him,
    as I rejoice in the LORD.

UNDERSTANDING THE SCRIPTURE

Psalm 104. This psalm, like Psalms 8, 19, and 29, takes as its theme the praise of God as the Lord of creation. Some scholars feel that Israel may have used these psalms as part of their New Year's festivals. The combination of awe and exuberance would make them especially desirable for such a purpose. In Psalm 104, the poet sees the glory of God in the whole realm of nature. Creatures both great and small inspire him and lift him to song.

Psalm 104:1. The psalm opens by calling the psalmist to praise God who is great.

Psalm 104:2-4. The psalmist speaks first of the creation of the heavens. God's dwelling is depicted as being built on waters.

Psalm 104:5-9. Next the creation of the earth in the midst of waters is described. God is portrayed as the one who tames the chaos, which is symbolized by water.

Psalm 104:10-18. God provides care for the creatures on earth by causing springs to gush forth. God also furnishes food for humans and different types of animals.

Psalm 104:19-23. By making the moon, the sun, and darkness, God was marking off the days and the season. Israel used the lunar calendar, so the moon measured the seasons. The sun set the limits on the day. The light of the sun and the darkness cued both animals and persons as to when to work and when to rest.

Psalm 104:24. The psalmist describes God's works as manifold, meaning that they have many forms or parts. The writer notes that all these denizens of nature belong to God for they have been created by God in God's wisdom.

Psalm 104:25. The Israelites were not a sea-going people; they left that to their neighbors, the people of Tyre. Nevertheless, the writer is filled with wonder at the inhabitants of the sea, including "creeping things innumerable."

Psalm 104:26. The term *Leviathan* is used at least three ways in the Scriptures: as a crocodile that personifies chaos (Job 41:1); as a dragon (Isaiah 27:1); and as a huge marine animal (here, and in Job 3:8). Leviathan was not understood as a real creature but as a mythological term to describe a mysterious sea animal that God had the power to tame. Usually dangerous and uncontrollable, Leviathan is portrayed in Psalm 104 as a domesticated animal playing in the water.

Psalm 104:27-28. Nature instinctively depends totally on God for sustenance. Jesus also deals with this theme in the Sermon on the Mount, describing God's care for the birds of the air and the lilies of the field (Matthew 6:26-30).

Psalm 104:29-30. The Hebrew language uses the same word for breath, wind, and spirit. These nuances enrich the meaning of the words "breath" in verse 29 and "spirit" in verse 30. The reference to creatures returning to the dust reminds us that Genesis 2:7 and 2:19 portray God making animals and human beings from the dust of the earth. The idea of humans returning to the dust at death is stated in Genesis 3:19.

Psalm 104:31-32. The psalmist concludes the poem by again praising God. He sees the power of God in the earthquake and the volcano, but rather than frightening him, these phenomena simply demonstrate the presence, power, and glory of God.

Psalm 104:33-34. The manifold wonders of nature inspire the psalmist to sing. But his song does not simply extol the created wonders of nature; it causes him to praise God, the creator, whom the poet will continue to praise as long as he lives. He prays that God will be pleased with the meditation that he offers.

Psalm 104:35. The psalmist asks that the wicked, the ones who have rebelled against the creator and his creation, be removed from the earth.

INTERPRETING THE SCRIPTURE

The Wonder of Creation

The poet William Blake said, "To some people a tree is something so incredibly beautiful that it brings tears to the eyes. To others it is just a green thing that stands in the way." The psalmist would take Blake's statement a step further, for the tree—and for that matter, all creation—not only brought tears to his eyes, but also worshipful praise to his lips. Everything about nature inspired him to adore God. Everywhere he turned, he saw God's wondrous gifts, and they were good. We might expect the psalmist to be terrified at the sight of the legendary sea monster, Leviathan, but instead he sees the creature as a playful thing; God has formed it to "sport" in the sea. The psalmist writes in a happy, almost ebullient mood that draws us into his words of praise. I can almost picture him gesturing with an expansive sweep of his arm as he says, "Yonder is the sea" (Psalm 104:25).

When we think of the wonder of creation, most of us think of the stars, or the ocean, or the desert, or the mountains. The very size and majesty of these elements put us in awe. The psalmist was also awed by the infinite variety—the "creeping things innumerable"—of God's creation. A theologian once asked J. B. S. Haldane, the eminent biochemist, what inference one might draw about the nature of God from a study of creation. Haldane answered, "An inordinate fondness for beetles." He was no doubt referring to the fact that science has identified more than 300,000 species of beetles. Such variety exists in some measure in nearly every phase of our created world, including even the stars. Cecil Alexander's lovely poem reminds us that "all creatures great and small . . . the Lord God made them all."

George Santayana taught philosophy at Harvard for over twenty years. The wide-ranging and original nature of his lectures held a whole generation of students in awe. On an April day in 1911, he was giving his last lecture at Harvard. Suddenly,

Santayana spied a forsythia blossoming in a patch of mud and snow. He stopped mid-sentence, picked up his hat, walking stick, and gloves. As he walked out the door, announced, "Gentlemen, I shall not be able to finish that sentence. I have just discovered that I have an appointment with April." This lesson calls us to have an appointment with the God of April—and the God of September and December, too!

To do so is to see nature through different eyes. Vast numbers of people appreciate nature, for a wide variety of reasons. The hiker, the trout fisherman, the spelunker, the botanist, the backyard gardener can each tell you how wonderful nature is, or at least extol the specific corner of nature that enchants him or her. But they may not have the expansive vision that characterizes Psalm 104. Many who love nature see it as an end in itself. To the psalmist, however, it is a revelation of the wonder of God's power and a reason for praising God.

We should remember, too, that this psalm was not written by an armchair enthusiast of nature. There is little natural romance in the rocky soil or the barren sand of the Middle East if you must scrape your living from it or contend with the wild beasts that roam the landscape. Yet the psalmist is inspired to raise heart and voice in adoration of God as he looks at the natural world that surrounds him.

God's Provision for Creation

God is not only the creator but the sustainer. God makes sure that all creatures have what they need to exist. The psalmist portrays the relationship between God and creatures in tender images. A more prosaic writer would imagine these creatures struggling for existence, but the psalmist sees them "look to you [God] / to give them their food in due season" (Psalm 104:27); when God opens the divine hand, nature is "filled with good things" (Psalm 104:28). It's as if all these creatures were waiting at some feeding center for God to provide. The country preacher said of his existence, "I am living from hand to mouth—God's hand to my mouth." The psalmist sees all nature in such a mode.

If it seems that the face of God is hidden, then nature is "dismayed" (Psalm 104:29). All creatures die whenever God takes away their breath. The psalmist knows that life is so surely from God that he feels that the end of life, too, is God's decision. Most of us would reason that the life and death of animals are a natural process. Perhaps the psalmist also thinks so, from a logical point of view. But he isn't writing a scientific dissertation here, and we shouldn't expect it to sound like one. He is a poet, a very devout one, and he is rejoicing in the power of God that he sees all around him as he surveys the world of nature.

A Song of Adoration

The psalmist writes in the same celebrative mood when he describes the earthquake and the volcano. These two events may well be the most terrifying of all the natural phenomena. All other disasters seem to give fair warning, so we can run from them, but the volcano comes with such relentless speed that there is little chance to escape, and the earthquake leaves no place to hide, since it claims the very ground itself.

But to the psalmist, they are simply other, very awesome examples of God's power. The earthquake, he says, comes as God looks at the earth, and the volcano when God touches the mountain. Again, he is speaking of course as a poet, and his language is beautiful in both its simplicity and its figures of speech.

In asserting that the psalmist writes as a poet and as a scientist, I don't intend to minimize his words. Not at all. I think of a sentence from one of the greatest scientific thinkers of all times, Albert Einstein. Having said that he wanted "to know how God created the world," he went on: "I am not interested in this or that phenomenon. I want to know his thoughts, the rest are details." That desire has more to do with poetry than with matters that can be submitted to scientific measure. There is much more to our universe than that which can be run through test tubes, just as there is more to us human beings than can be discerned by statistics.

In a special sense, the saint understands nature best of all because the saint sees nature through the eyes of faith. Not simply faith as to the way it was created, but faith in the quality of its purpose. For that reason, I am enchanted with what Julian of Norwich, who lived in England during the difficult times of the fourteenth century, said of creation. She said she saw "three properties" in creation: "the first is, that God made it. The second is, that God loveth it. The third is, that God keepeth it. But what beheld I therein? Verily, the Maker, the Keeper, the Lover."

Viewing nature through the eyes of faith does not explain the volcano or the earthquake, nor does it comprehend the workings of space. But it lifts our understanding to a higher level; it informs our data with faith and glory.

No wonder, then, that our writer says that he will "sing to the LORD" (Psalm 104:33) all of his life, and that he will praise God as long as he lives! If one feels that all of nature glorifies God, then surely we human beings ought to do so. Nature does so instinctively, but we do so by choice. We do so with far more reason than nature could ever have because we understand the glory and the potential of the life God has given us. If, as the psalmist reasons, nature celebrates life, then how much more should we?

Most scholars point out (and even most casual readers are likely to notice) that this psalm often reflects the Genesis story of creation. In his book *The Psalms*, Alexander Maclaren goes a step further. He notes that in its close the Psalm seems to come to the seventh day of creation, a sabbath of praise to God. As the ancient writer promises that he will sing to God all of his life and will praise God as long as he lives, it is as if he were entering the rest of the Sabbath day—a rest that will bless him all the days of his life.

When we look upon life, and all of creation, as instruments of God's love, and when we see the glory of God in everything from the innumerable creeping things of the sea to the earthquake, we have indeed entered a kind of sabbath. For with such an outlook on life and on our world, everything we touch partakes of glory.

SHARING THE SCRIPTURE

PREPARING TO TEACH

With today's lesson we begin a biblical book that is generally a favorite with most of our class. For many people, it is the only book in the Hebrew Scriptures to which they turn easily. Whereas James centers on practical counsel and admonition, the mood of the Psalms is one of prayer and worship expressed in exquisite poetry. Because these two books are so different, you may have to make adjustments in your teaching. It's easier to give advice than to inspire awe!

In preparation, look into the index of your hymnbook and make a list of hymns that are adaptations of psalms. See if you can locate a hymnal (perhaps from the Reformed tradition) that is made up entirely of metrical versions of the Psalms. Read some of these for your own inspiration. Choose one that you can read to the class or have them sing as an introduction to the study that will follow during these eight weeks. For example, two hymns based on Psalm 104 are in *The United Methodist Hymnal*: "O Worship the King" (page 73) and "Many and Great, O God" (page 148). Joseph Addison's hymn, "The Spacious Firmament on High," appears in many hymnbooks; it is a version of one of the other nature psalms, Psalm 19. If you plan to sing a psalm, be sure to have hymnals available.

Have paper and pencils available if you plan to ask students to write their own psalms.

During the week, either prepare to read Psalm 104 aloud yourself, or contact a student who is an expressive reader and ask him or her to be ready to read.

What is especially important in planning this lesson is to catch the spirit of worship that inspires the psalmist as he observes nature. See if you can feel something of the same mood as you think about some aspect of nature—flowers, trees, mountains, the sea, a lake—that especially appeals to you. You may want to write a psalm of your own that expresses your own feelings of praise and worship to God.

One word of caution may be in order as you prepare this lesson. Nature is much on peoples' minds these days, but not often in a way that focuses on God. We need to be careful lest this lesson slip into little more than a nature study. Our goal is much higher. Martin Luther said that "God writes the gospel not in the Bible alone, but on trees, and flowers and clouds and stars." That might be a good thought to keep in mind as you begin this lesson. Keep watch for the glory of God, and celebrate it! The mood of this lesson should be very upbeat.

LEADING THE CLASS

Introduction

Begin by asking your class what about nature especially inspires them. This is the kind of question that calls forth quick, popcorn answers.

Now ask if they can remember a time when God seemed very close because of an experience with nature. Invite a few persons to share their ideas with the whole class or in small groups.

Introduce Psalm 104 as a hymn of praise to God the Creator. Either read this psalm aloud yourself, or call on a student who has agreed in advance to read it aloud. Invite class members to close their eyes and picture the psalmist's description of God's creation as the psalm is read. Follow the reading by announcing today's main question: **How can we celebrate the gift of life that God has created for us?**

If you plan to sing a hymn of praise, this would be an appropriate time to do so.

The Wonder of Creation

Read or retell this section under "Interpreting the Scripture." Invite your class to share their own observations of the wonder of creation. You may want to ask them to answer these questions:

(1) **What scenes in nature cause you to praise God?**
(2) **What natural events prompt you to fear or stand in awe of God?**
(3) **In which natural setting do you feel especially close to God?**

Help the class to make a list of the kinds of activities, such as fishing or nature photography, they do while enjoying nature. List these activities on a chalkboard or newsprint. Some class members may realize that they share a common interest or hobby with others.

Encourage class members to think about the wonders of the human body, with its complex genetic code and brain that is far more complex than a computer. Remind them of the great powers the body has to restore itself after illness or injury. Then ask: **How might the knowledge that God creates, restores, and sustains our bodies influence persons in caring for this amazing gift?** Try to encourage negative answers (persons should stop smoking, lose weight) and positive answers (persons should eat nutritious food, engage in regular exercise).

God's Provision for Creation

Invite someone in the class who is familiar with agriculture or is a student of nature to offer some insights about the way we human beings have worked with nature to develop new or improved plant life or a hardier breed of livestock. Students may want to debate whether they believe such activity enhances or harms God's creation.

Ask students to consider the following questions. You may want to have the entire class address each one, or you may want to divide into groups and assign each group one or more questions. It would be helpful for group work if you write the questions on a chalkboard or newsprint.

(1) To what degree are we human beings the instruments of God's provision for creation?

(2) In what ways have we abused our powers? (For example, a veterinarian tells me we have been irresponsible in the degree to which certain breeds of pets have been specialized.)

(3) How has humanity affected the balance of nature, especially its fragile ecosystems?

(4) What has our urbanization done to plant and animal life? (For example, when I see a dead animal on a highway, I am reminded that wild creatures were never meant to cope with high speed vehicles.)

Conduct a class discussion on our responsibility as humans to be stewards of God's creation. Emphasize that we are trustees, not owners, for all creation was made by and belongs to God (see Psalm 24:1 and Exodus 19:5-6). Ask the class: **What can we do as church members and as individuals to care for God's creation so that we can pass on to future generations a healthier world than we inherited?** Try to generate as many ideas as

possible such as: recycling, purchasing recycled goods, conserving energy, composting, consolidating trips in the car, and using water-saving fixtures.

A Song of Adoration

The psalmist sings of the glory of the Lord as he ponders the wonders of creation. Ask the class whether they ever praise God for creation. Probably everyone does. Pet lovers, for example, probably thank God for a loyal dog or a cheerful bird. Nearly everyone sometimes pauses before a starlit sky, and most of us have thanked God for a day of extraordinary beauty. Provide some time for each person to write a psalm or a prayer of praise for one or more aspects of creation that are important to him or her. You may need to distribute paper and pencils. Assure class members that heartfelt praise, not their ability as poets, is the key element in completing this activity. Encourage several volunteers to read what they have written.

As a means of adoration, create a class litany. Ask students, as they feel led, to prayerfully say aloud a gift of nature for which they want to praise God. After each speaker, the class responds with an agreed upon phrase of thanksgiving. For example: (student) "For the beauty of the sunrise breaking through the darkness of night," (class) "We give you thanks, Creator God."

HELPING CLASS MEMBERS ACT

Urge class members to be attentive this week to the marvels of nature that surround them. You might even challenge them to make a list of elements of creation that impress them in the next several days. Things become more real when they are made specific.

If you have provided an opportunity for students to share their own interests in the natural world, encourage persons who have identified similar interests to make a date to get together and pursue that interest in the fellowship of Christian friends.

If you talked about the human body, encourage persons to take one step this week in caring for their bodies in ways that acknowledge them as gifts from God. For example, some persons may choose to begin an exercise program or a healthy eating program, while others will resolve to put aside a harmful habit such as smoking.

Encourage all members who are physically able to experience the outdoors this week, perhaps by taking a walk or by sitting on a porch and watching the sunset. As they do, invite them to offer a prayer of thanks and praise unto God.

PLANNING FOR NEXT SUNDAY

Next week we will talk about remembering our promises and commitments to God as we study God's dealings with the people of Israel as recalled in Psalm 105. Ask the class to think about promises they have personally made to God, and also of promises our nation has made in times of war and economic depression.

REMEMBER PROMISES AND COMMITMENTS

PREVIEWING THE LESSON

Lesson Scripture: Psalm 105:1-11, 43-45
Background Scripture: Psalm 105
Key Verse: Psalm 105:1

Focus of the lesson:
praise to God for promises fulfilled and continuing commitment to act on behalf of humanity

Main question(s) of the lesson:
(1) How do our remembrances of God's promises and mighty acts prompt us to praise God?

This lesson will enable adult learners to:
(1) recognize God as one who acts in human history
(2) find hope for the future by remembering God's mighty deeds in the past
(3) respond by praising God for faithful action.

Today's lesson may be outlined as follows:
(1) Introduction
(2) A Call to Praise (Psalm 105:1-4)
(3) A Call to Remember (Psalm 105:5-11)
(4) A Call to Joy (Psalm 43–45)

FOCUSING ON THE MAIN QUESTION

Memory is the stuff on which civilizations and cultures are built. Our elders want us to remember from whence we have come because knowledge of our past provides hope and direction for the future. We record and pass on this collective memory not only by means of written history but also through our songs, our symbols, our art, and our laws or statutes. We human beings have learned that our dearest values are safe only if we have a good memory, and that those values are in danger if we forget our traditions.

Such memories are as important to us as individuals as they are to nations or communities. An especially fine woman attributed her stability of character to a sentence she so often heard from her father: "Remember whose daughter you are." Those words summarized the principles of a way of life and a heritage.

The people of Israel were especially sensitive to their memories because their understanding of God was based more on the memory of God's deeds than on doctrinal statements. They were called again and again to remember the covenant God had made with their ancestors and to recall their many experiences of divine deliverance. The book of Psalms has a number of songs that help the people to remember who they are and how God has been actively present in their lives.

Israel's memories include both God's promises and their own human commit-

ments. The memory of what God had promised lifted their faith and sustained them through difficult experiences, while the memory of their own commitments would keep them faithful in times—especially prosperous times—when they might forsake the Lord God. Accurate memories can save us from both despair and arrogance. We will profit as we remember life's promises and its commitments.

Our focus for today's lesson, Psalm 105, presents the memory of God's dealings with the Israelites from the time of God's covenant with Abraham to fulfillment of that promise as they joyfully enter the land of Canaan. As we study this lesson, we will want to ask ourselves: **How do our remembrances of God's promises and mighty acts prompt us to praise God?**

READING THE SCRIPTURE

NRSV
Psalm 105:1-11
1 O give thanks to the LORD, call
        on his name,
        make known his deeds among
            the peoples.
2 Sing to him, sing praises to him;
    tell of all his wonderful works.
3 Glory in his holy name;
    . let the hearts of those who
        seek the LORD rejoice.
4 Seek the LORD and his strength;
    seek his presence continually.
5 Remember the wonderful works
        he has done,
    his miracles, and the
        judgments he uttered,
6 O offspring of his servant
        Abraham,
    children of Jacob, his chosen
        ones.

7 He is the LORD our God;
    his judgments are in all the
        earth.

NIV
Psalm 105:1-11
1 Give thanks to the LORD, call on his
        name;
        make known among the nations what
            he has done.
2 Sing to him, sing praise to him;
    tell of all his wonderful acts.
3 Glory in his holy name;
    let the hearts of those who seek the
        LORD rejoice.
4 Look to the LORD and his strength;
    seek his face always.
5 Remember the wonders he has done,
    his miracles, and the judgments he
        pronounced,

6 O descendants of Abraham his servant,
    O sons of Jacob, his chosen ones.

7 He is the LORD our God;
    his judgments are in all the earth.

Key
Verse

Key
Verse

⁸He is mindful of his covenant
    forever,
  of the word that he
    commanded, for a
    thousand generations,
⁹the covenant that he made with
    Abraham,
  his sworn promise to Isaac,
¹⁰which he confirmed to Jacob as
    a statute,
  to Israel as an everlasting
    covenant,
¹¹saying, "To you I will give the
    land of Canaan
  as your portion for an
    inheritance."

Psalm 105:43-45
⁴³So he brought his people out
    with joy,
  his chosen ones with singing.
⁴⁴He gave them the lands of the
    nations,
  and they took possession of
    the wealth of the peoples,
⁴⁵that they might keep his statutes
  and observe his laws.
    Praise the LORD!

⁸He remembers his covenant forever,
  the word he commanded, for a
    thousand generations,

⁹the covenant he made with Abraham,
  the oath he swore to Isaac.

¹⁰He confirmed it to Jacob as a decree,
  to Israel as an everlasting covenant:

¹¹"To you I will give the land of Canaan
  as the portion you will inherit."

Psalm 105:43-45
⁴³He brought out his people with rejoicing,
  his chosen ones with shouts of joy;

⁴⁴he gave them the lands of the nations,
  and they fell heir to what others had toiled
    for—

⁴⁵that they might keep his precepts
  and observe his laws.
    Praise the LORD.

UNDERSTANDING THE SCRIPTURE

Psalm 105. The celebrative mood of this psalm prompts some scholars to suggest that it may have been written especially for the Feast of Tabernacles or the Feast of Weeks. Some psalms talk to God and some talk of God; this is in the latter category. The writer is telling others of the goodness and greatness of God, obviously with the intention that they will join in the song. This psalm reviews Israel's history from Abraham to the Exodus and entry into Canaan, thereby emphasizing God's covenant promise and its fulfillment. Verses 1-15 of this psalm are quoted in 1 Chronicles 16:8-22 (along with portions of Psalm 96 and 106) as a hymn of thanksgiving.

Psalm 105:1-2. Note the emphasis on God's deeds. "Peoples" is often translated "nations," and refers particularly to Israel's neighbors who are followers of other gods. The psalm is calling the people to witness to the deeds of God to those who do not believe. This hymn also encourages Israel itself to sing praises to God.

Psalm 105:3. Here, as in verse 1, emphasis is given to the name of God. This emphasis reflects the ancient sense that a name embodies the personality of its owner, a reason for not taking the name of God in vain.

Psalm 105:4. The Israelites are called to seek both the presence and the strength of the Lord. The "face" of the Lord (see KJV and NIV) is another way of referring to God's presence.

Psalm 105:5. God is able to perform mighty acts. The "miracles" God performed for Israel became "judgments" on their enemies. We may be troubled by reports of the destruction of these enemies, but the Israelites saw such events as evidences of both justice and love. Justice demanded that evil be punished and that the perpetrators of evil be restrained.

Psalm 105:6. This verse clearly shows that the psalmist is calling the covenant people—those persons who are descendants of Abraham and Jacob—to remember, give thanks, and sing. This specificity adds to the power of their national memory.

Psalm 105:7. This verse reminds Israel of its relationship with God, who is their Lord.

Psalm 105:8-10. Covenant is one of the key words of the Scriptures. The theme begins with Noah, following the flood, and continues into our Christian tradition with the Sacrament of Communion, which is a "covenant meal." Here the psalmist is referring to the covenant that God made with their ancestor, Abraham. He is reassuring the people that God will always remember this covenant. For the psalmist, "everlasting" would refer to a historical measure of earthly time, not to eternity.

Psalm 105:11. God's covenant with Israel had several elements, but the issue that is on the psalmist's mind has to do with Israel's claim to Canaan, as their national "inheritance." Some scholars feel this psalm was written during the time of captivity in Babylon, in which case this claim to Canaan would be intended to restore their hope and their national pride. Even if the land was not in their possession at a given moment, they may be confident that it is still theirs because it was God who promised it to them.

Psalm 105:12-42. These verses, which are not included in our printed portion, cover Israel's history from the time of Jacob through their captivity in Egypt, their deliverance from slavery, and their travels in the wilderness en route to Canaan. While reminding the people of these events, the psalmist focuses on how God cared for the people every step of the way.

Psalm 105:43. Hebrew poetry is built on parallel lines and often also on synonymous words. In this verse, "people" and "chosen ones" and "joy" and "singing" are used to reinforce, by means of repetition, what the author wants to emphasize.

Psalm 105:44. Here again, "nations" refers to non-Jewish peoples. As the Israelites take possession of the land, they will also gain wealth, such as homes and gardens, which they had not toiled to create.

Psalm 105:45. In the final verse, the writer comes to the point of all this activity. Their remarkable history has been to a purpose, which is that they shall be faithful in keeping God's laws and statutes. They are to establish a new way of life in the land they have received. This is the moral responsibility of their covenant with God. The worshipers are to respond with the words "Praise the LORD!"

INTERPRETING THE SCRIPTURE

A Call to Praise

Promises and commitments are the two sides of the coin of relationship. If someone makes a promise to us, we are obligated in turn to offer our commitment. Israel was blessed by God's generous promises; now they are expected to respond with a commitment worthy of such kindness.

Psalm 105 is a covenant song. I think we could say that it is like a wedding song in which the parties recall the time of their courtship, the basis for their love, and the commitment that binds them together. Except, of course, that unlike a wedding, this is not a covenant between two equals. In mercy, God has reached out to Israel, even though Israel has little to offer in return. And so it is in all of our relationships with God. No wonder we speak of grace!

The first fifteen verses of this psalm appear in 1 Chronicles 16:8-22, on the occasion when the Ark of the Covenant was returned to Israel after its period with the Philistines. The chronicler reports that David committed the song to Asaph (his choir director) that day, as an expression of thanks to the Lord (1 Chronicles 16:7). The song of praise in 1 Chronicles 16 continues with Psalm 96:1-13 and Psalm 106:1, 47-48, but we do not know who edited these psalms into a composite hymn for this joyous occasion.

A Call to Remember

Psalm 105 is a wonderfully exuberant expression of thanksgiving to God, and an equally strong call to commitment. The key word is surely the opening word of verse 5: *remember*. Having called the people to give thanks, to sing, and to seek the Lord, the poet lets us know that we will find the reason for such a celebration if only we will remember the mighty acts that God has performed.

I return to my hometown, Sioux City, Iowa, anytime I can find an excuse to do so. I go to visit an older sister, but I know I would make the trip if she were not there, even though I have no other known friends in the area now. It is a nostalgic experience for me. I walk to a parking lot where once there was a Methodist church, and to another building, which was once a church and is now used for other purposes, because at those two places my faith was nurtured. I walk past school houses, libraries, and the homes in which

my family lived during the years I grew up. And all along the way, I remember. Some of the memories are lovely, and others are painful; but all of them bless me. I pause again and again to give thanks to God, sometimes within my soul and sometimes aloud. At each place I am reminded that God has been faithful to me; in some instances, I stop to repent because I recall that my faithfulness has sometimes fallen short. I sometimes refer to these trips to my hometown as sentimental journeys, but of course it is much more. It is a kind of pilgrimage; it is a remembering of promises and commitments.

On many communion tables you will find the carved message, "Do this in remembrance of me"—the words our Lord spoke at the first celebration of the sacrament with his disciples. I wonder how often, and to what degree, we "remember" during such a service. I think the intention of the service is twofold. The first remembering, of course, is directed to Jesus' sacrifice at Calvary. But we should go from there to remember God's faithfulness in our lives, and to recall our own spiritual pilgrimage. If we would do so, the service would be an occasion of both repentance and rejoicing. We would repent for our failures of commitment, but we would rejoice at the memory of God's promises and the faithfulness with which those promises have been fulfilled in our lives.

Psalm 105 reminds us that God is active in history. The Israelites were very sure of this. They were sure God was no mere spectator, but an active player in their story. This belief explains the very specific language that the psalmist uses. He names persons, places, events, and occasions. If the psalmist were a philosopher or a theologian, he might be content simply to talk in a detached way about God's involvement in human life. But Israel's experience is far too real for that. At each step of the journey, the writer sees God at work. As someone has said, what God does is the best revelation of what God is. The psalmist sees the hand of God in the unfolding events of Israel's history, and he is inspired to give thanks and to sing.

In *Christianity and History*, Herbert Butterfield, who was for many years a distinguished professor of modern history at Cambridge University in England, insisted that, "One of the most fundamental of the differences between people must be the question whether they believe in God or not; for on that depends their whole interpretation of the universe and of history— on that depends their answer to so many other questions." I would venture to say that many who believe in God have not, however, asked themselves whether God is involved in human history. Obviously it isn't an easy question. We rejoice in those instances where it seems God is clearly at work, but we confess that there are also many events where God seems to be absent. In this tension, of course, we're no different from many of the persons in the Old Testament. They, too, wondered from time to time, especially when their nation was in decline or when brutal leaders seemed to go unchecked.

But on the whole, they returned again and again to the conviction that God has not forsaken the world, and that because God cares, justice will eventually prevail. We may not see God's judgment as quickly as we would like, nor will it always be as sharply defined as we might wish. But in time, the hand of God will appear. Such was the faith of the psalmist, and I confess it is my faith, too.

A Call to Joy

I like the mood with which this psalm concludes. Looking back on the exodus of Israel from their centuries of Egyptian bondage, the poet tells us that God brought the people out with joy and with singing. We are the inheritors of a faith that sings. When Israel passed through the Red Sea, Miriam led them with a timbrel (Exodus 15:20-21), and when (in the 1 Chronicles version of our text of the day), they brought back the ark, David led the way with dancing. The great revivals of religion through the centuries—including those inspired by Francis of Assisi, Martin Luther, and the Wesleys, along with the holiness and Pentecostal movements of more modern times—have all been marked by song. If you examine these songs, you will find that most of them are recitals of the faithfulness of God. This is true whether it is Martin Luther singing "A Mighty Fortress Is Our God" or followers of Martin Luther King Jr., singing "We Shall Overcome." When we remember the promises and commitments, we sing.

And when we remember, we also conduct our lives in a new and better way. The psalmist knew why Israel had been delivered. It was not simply for their own comfort and pleasure, but so that they would keep God's statutes. As Alexander Maclaren put it, their office was to be "the world's evangelist." Their evangelism was to happen, at least in part, by their evident faithfulness to God's law—and beyond that, to their joyous singing of God's goodness.

SHARING THE SCRIPTURE

PREPARING TO TEACH

Today's lesson is another one that ought to be dominantly marked by a tone of rejoicing. Perhaps a teacher's most important preparation will be internal because it will be difficult to do this lesson justice unless you come at it in such a mood. Take time this week to rehearse the memory of the goodness of God in your own life. You may want to record some of these memories in a spiritual journal.

Try to spend some time prayerfully remembering your own nation's history. Do you see occasions when your nation seemed to suffer the judgment of God for its sins? Have there been times when God's blessing was clearly evident? What part has been played by national leaders in reminding the people of their responsibility to God? You may want to record these thoughts in your spiritual journal as well.

As you read and study Psalm 105, be aware of ways in which it applies to your own life and to the lives of your class members. You may want to ask yourself: "What do I know, personally, about God's promises? In what ways have I made specific commitments to God? How am I fulfilling those commitments?"

Since this psalm was meant to be sung by a congregation, and since it calls the people to rejoice and sing, think for a few minutes about songs of promise and commitment. Do you recall some hymn that has been especially effective in reminding you of either God's promises or your own commitments? I think of a great hymn of commitment, "A Charge to Keep I Have." Do you find any of this emphasis on promise and commitment in your nation's patriotic songs? Is God an issue in such music?

If you plan to use a hymn of praise during the session, be sure to have hymnals handy.

If you plan to have the class make time lines under "A Call to Remember," have paper and pencils on hand.

If you plan to use the guided imagery exercise under "A Call to Joy," try reading this through several times, allowing pauses for the students to call up images.

LEADING THE CLASS

Introduction

Read "Focusing on the Main Question" aloud or retell the information there in your own words. Ask the class: Do you think the case is overstated here? Is memory really that important to a nation? Is it that important to individuals? Allow students a few moments to debate this point.

Help the class focus on today's lesson by asking the main question: **How do our remembrances of God's promises and mighty acts prompt us to praise God?**

A Call to Praise

Choose a volunteer to read aloud Psalm 105:1-4. Note that these four verses are about as jubilant and upbeat as one could ask.

Point out that these four verses (along with verses 5-15) also appear in 1 Chronicles 16:8-22). The 1 Chronicles version is set in the context of a worshipful time of praise marked by the return of the Ark of the Covenant by the Philistines. The congregation was overjoyed and moved to sing. Discuss these questions with the class:

(1) **Under what circumstances are we moved by such a spirit of praise?**
(2) **Are our worship services marked by such gladness?**
(3) **If not, how can we, as the people of God, be more jubilant as we participate in worship?**

Note that the psalmist urges us to "tell of all his wonderful works" (Psalm 105:2). Invite the class to list some of the wonderful works of God. Perhaps a spirited sense of praise will emerge as class members share their ideas. You may want to record their answers on a chalkboard or newsprint, perhaps categorizing them as "God's wonderful works for me and my family," "God's wonderful works for the church," and "God's wonderful works for the world."

In response to this list of works, you may want to sing a hymn of praise that you selected during the week, or one that class members suggest.

A Call to Remember

Choose a student to read aloud Psalm 105:5-11. Point out that we are to remember because God remembers. The psalmist tells us that God "is mindful of his covenant forever" (Psalm 105:8). That isn't a way of measuring time, but of telling us that God's remembering is beyond measure.

Note that our human remembering certainly is not beyond measure. We must find ways to create and reinforce our memories. Ask the class to consider how we do this by answering the questions below. If you have enough students, divide the class into three groups and assign one of these questions to each. After an agreed upon time limit, ask each group to report their insights to the total class.

Group I: How do we create and reinforce personal and family memories?

Group II: How does the church help us to create and reinforce memories of our relationship with God and with the people of God? (Note that this group may want to give special attention to the sacraments of communion and baptism.)

Group III: How does our nation help us to create and reinforce memories of who we are as a people with our own culture, national heroes, and national history?

If your class enjoys activities, provide an opportunity for them to make individual time lines as a way of remembering their spiritual journeys to date, just as Israel remembered the important events in its history. Distribute paper and pencils. Ask students to draw a line across the width of the paper. Have them mark the year of their birth on the far left side and the current year on the far right. Then encourage them to make a line at points that mark an important spiritual event, such as a confirmation, conversion experience, an illness, or crisis through which God's presence was made vividly known. If time permits, several volunteers may want to highlight special moments in their lives when God seemed particularly persent to them. Conclude this activity by asking class members to refer to these time lines each day this week and, as they do, to give thanks for God's active presence in their lives.

A Call to Joy

Ask a volunteer to read Psalm 105:43-45. Try to imagine with your class the kind of joy that Israel must have felt as it left Egypt and slavery. Some students will recall the movie classic, *The Ten Commandments*, which provides a good visual image of this joy. Perhaps class members will find it easier to sense the joy that the Israelites felt as they left Egypt if they recall the end of World War II or the end of the Gulf War or some other historic occasion.

Point out that the Israelites are rejoicing because God has been faithful to the covenant made with Abraham. God not only made that promise but had both the love for Israel and the power to keep it. Use the following guided imagery exercise, or one you have developed, to help the class recall such an experience in their own lives. Prepare them for this activity by asking them to sit comfortably in silence with their eyes closed. They are to picture whatever comes to mind as you read. Be sure to pause at the . . . marks. Do not read the numbers. They are simply cues for you.

(1) Think back over your life to a time of great joy. Perhaps you were celebrating a marriage, a birth, a career-related event, a special spiritual experience, or some other significant event . . .

(2) Picture yourself at this time. How old were you? What were you wearing? . . .

(3) Picture the place where you experienced this great joy. Were you indoors, or outdoors? What did the place look like?

(4) Picture the people who were with you. Who were they? How did they share in your joy? . . .

(5) Picture God lovingly looking upon this scene. Were you aware of God's presence at the time? Give thanks to God now for the joy of that moment, just as if it were happening all over again . . .

Invite the class members to return to the present, carrying in their hearts the kind of intense joy and thanksgiving unto God that they felt at that special moment.

Note that in Psalm 105, God has kept the covenant by bringing the people into the promised land. They, too, had a responsibility. They were to keep God's statutes and laws. Ask the class:

(1) **What commitments do you think God expects us to keep in our day as individual Christians?**

(2) **What commitments do you think God expects us to keep as the church?**

(3) **How would you rate our progress in each of these areas?**

(4) **If we have fallen short of upholding our commitments, what changes do we need to make in our personal and corporate (that is, church) lives?**

HELPING CLASS MEMBERS ACT

Encourage class members to remember some of the "wonderful works" of God that they have experienced in their own lives, and in the life of their nation. One way to do this would be to spend some time this week with a photo album or scrapbook. As pictures or souvenirs bring an experience to mind, ask class members to give thanks to God.

Invite students to make God's deeds known and to sing God's praises this week to at least one stranger. Point out that this word of witness can be shared in ordinary places, like the barbershop or grocery store. A simple word of how God has brought joy into class members' lives may well open a door to a relationship with God for someone else.

Challenge class members to prepare themselves for the next service of Holy Communion by remembering "promises and commitments." To do so might bring a whole new quality to the experience. Perhaps the class could attend that service and sit as a group. Even if that arrangement is not possible, urge each member to attend the service.

PLANNING FOR NEXT SUNDAY

Next Sunday's lesson takes up a theme with which all of us have had some personal experience: trouble! But it shouldn't be a downbeat lesson, nor simply a recital of pain. We're going to learn how to handle trouble with faith.

Ask class members to read all of Psalm 34, and to think of the psalmist's testimony: while the righteous may have many afflictions, the Lord delivers them out of them all.

WHEN TROUBLE COMES

PREVIEWING THE LESSON

Lesson Scripture: Psalm 34:2-10, 18-22
Background Scripture: Psalm 34
Key Verse: Psalm 34:18

Focus of the lesson:
God's ability to deliver those in trouble and their praise to God for deliverance

Main question(s) of the lesson:
(1) What can we do when trouble comes?
(2) What can we expect God to do?

This lesson will enable adult learners to:
(1) examine personal and biblical witness to God's readiness to deliver those in trouble
(2) appreciate God's constant presence in times of distress
(3) respond by assisting someone confronted by adversity.

Today's lesson may be outlined as follows:
(1) Introduction
(2) A Call to Praise (Psalm 34:2-3)
(3) A Testimony from Experience (Psalm 34:4-10)
(4) Remembering God's Faithfulness (Psalm 34:18-22)

JULY 21

FOCUSING ON THE MAIN QUESTION

When I was seventeen years old, I was asked to preach for a youth meeting in my home church. "Youth" was defined differently in those days; the group included ages 12 to 35. But a great many others also came that evening to encourage a young man who felt called to the ministry.

I preached that evening from Psalm 34, particularly verse 19:

> Many are the afflictions of the
> righteous,

> but the LORD rescues them
> from them all.

So many times since then I have recalled that evening with embarrassment. Not simply for the quality of the sermon; I've preached others of uncertain quality since then! But I marvel at how presumptuous I was to use such a text. After all, I knew very little at the time of either afflictions or righteousness. Some of the middle-aged and older adults must have looked at the teenager that night and thought, "Some day he'll know something about affliction. But not just yet."

If they did, they were partly right, but they were also partly wrong. I don't think there is anyone, of any age, who doesn't know something about affliction. Mind you, the pains of a ten-year-old are quite different from those of an octogenarian; but so, too, are the capacity and experience for dealing with pain. The weight of life's burdens varies, but it is no less real.

After thirty-eight years as a parish pastor, and a lifetime of observing the human race, I know that trouble comes to everyone. I know, too, that some people who seem to the detached observer to be free of any disappointment are often ones whose private burden is almost unbearable. No lesson could be more to the point of universal human experience than this one. I'm grateful for a psalm that provides a way to tell the story.

As we delve into Psalm 34 and hear David's song of thanksgiving for deliverance, let us keep before us these questions: **What can we do when trouble comes? What can we expect God to do?**

READING THE SCRIPTURE

NRSV
Psalm 34:2-10
²My soul makes its boast in the
    LORD;
    let the humble hear and be
    glad.
³O magnify the LORD with me,
    and let us exalt his name
    together.

⁴I sought the LORD, and he
    answered me,
    and delivered me from all my
    fears.
⁵Look to him, and be radiant;
    so your faces shall never be
    ashamed.
⁶This poor soul cried, and was
    heard by the LORD,
    and was saved from every
    trouble.
⁷The angel of the LORD encamps
    around those who fear him,
    and delivers them.
⁸O taste and see that the LORD is
    good;
    happy are those who take
    refuge in him.
⁹O fear the LORD, you his holy
    ones,

NIV
Psalm 34:2-10
²My soul will boast in the LORD;
    let the afflicted hear and rejoice.

³Glorify the LORD with me;
    let us exalt his name together.

⁴I sought the LORD, and he answered me;
    he delivered me from all my fears.

⁵Those who look to him are radiant;
    their faces are never covered with shame.

⁶This poor man called, and the LORD
    heard him;
    he saved him out of all his troubles.

⁷The angel of the LORD encamps around those
    who fear him,
    and he delivers them.
⁸Taste and see that the LORD is good;
    blessed is the man who takes refuge
    in him.

⁹Fear the LORD, you his saints,
    for those who fear him lack nothing.

for those who fear him have
   no want.
¹⁰The young lions suffer want and
   hunger,
   but those who seek the LORD
      lack no good thing.

Psalm 34:18-22

Key
erse
¹⁸The LORD is near to the
   brokenhearted,
   and saves the crushed in spirit.
¹⁹Many are the afflictions of the
   righteous,
   but the LORD rescues them
      from them all.
²⁰He keeps all their bones;
   not one of them will be
      broken.
²¹Evil brings death to the wicked,
   and those who hate the
      righteous will be
      condemned.
²²The LORD redeems the life of his
   servants;
   none of those who take refuge
      in him will be condemned.

¹⁰The lions may grow weak and hungry,
   but those who seek the LORD lack no good
      thing.

Psalm 34:18-22

¹⁸The LORD is close to the brokenhearted   Key
   and saves those who are crushed in spirit.   Verse

¹⁹A righteous man may have many troubles,
   but the LORD delivers him from them all;

²⁰he protects all his bones,
   not one of them will be broken.

²¹Evil will slay the wicked;
   the foes of the righteous will be
      condemned.

²²The LORD redeems his servants;
   no one who takes refuge in him will be
      condemned.

UNDERSTANDING THE SCRIPTURE

Psalm 34. This poem is set in the form of an acrostic, based on the Hebrew alphabet. Normally, each verse in an acrostic begins with one of the twenty-two letters of the alphabet, arranged in consecutive order. We lose that symmetry, of course, in our English translation. Psalm 34 is not quite a perfect acrostic, however. For some reason the author leaves out one letter, then adds one at the end.

The notation before the psalm tells us that David wrote this song "when he feigned madness before Abimelech." Since all the notations, known as *superscriptions*, in the Psalms were added after they were originally written, they are always open to question. Nevertheless, they represent ancient traditions, so they deserve atten-

tion. In this case the question of historical accuracy arises because the Philistine king before whom David pretended to be mad is named Achish (1 Samuel 21:10-15), but it is possible that "Abimelech" was a dynastic name among the Philistines.

Much of the teaching in this psalm of individual thanksgiving is rooted in the Wisdom literature tradition. The basic point is that things will go well for the righteous person who will not lack anything, for "the eyes of the LORD are on the righteous" (Psalm 34:15). In contrast, the wicked person will be punished (Psalm 34:16).

Psalm 34:1. This verse, which is not included in our printed portion, along with verses 2 and 3, forms a hymn of praise to God. The phrase "bless the LORD" shows recognition of God's authority over all of life.

Psalm 34:2. When the writer uses the term "soul," he is not simply making a spiritual reference, but is describing the total person.

Psalm 34:3. We find frequent references in the Psalms to the name of the Lord. The Hebrews laid great store by names; even as used with humans, they represented the essence of one's character. The name of the Lord had far greater significance. To call on God's name was to call on God's very person and power.

Psalm 34:4. This verse recounts the psalmist's experience of God's deliverance.

Psalm 34:5. The psalmist uses a figure of speech similar to our own "losing face" when he promises that if we will look to God our "faces shall never be ashamed."

Psalm 34:6. Although the reference to "poor" may be economic, it seems more likely to refer to someone's total experience. The "poor soul" is one who has come to the end of the rope and is now acknowledging his or her utter helplessness and dependence on God.

Psalm 34:7. The term "angel of the LORD" is used only twice in the Psalms, here and in 35:5-6. Although the concept of "guardian angels" has recently become popular among secular as well as religious people, it was no mere fad with the psalmist. He was very sure of God's care and intervention in his time of need.

Psalm 34:8. "Happy" is translated "blessed" in many versions; the two words are interchangeable. The blessed life is the happy life, as described in Psalm 1:1 and in the Beatitudes (Matthew 5:3-12).

Psalm 34:9. In scriptural references, the word "fear" refers to godly fear, reverence, and a sense of humility before God; it does not have the negative connotation that we have given to that word.

Psalm 34:10. For the psalmist, living closer to nature than we do, this figure of speech was more powerful. What creature could be more secure than the offspring of the lion? But even the young lions are not as fortunate as those "who seek the Lord."

Psalm 34:11-17. In verse 11, the psalmist invites children to come and be taught about God. The home was the place of instruction; hence, the reference to children. Wisdom literature of the ancient Near East was commonly addressed to "sons."

Psalm 34:18-19. These verses remind us of Psalm 51. Although we may feel spiritually crushed and totally lacking in inner resources, God will preserve the righteous.

Psalm 34:20. The poet is thinking of the whole person—much the way we do when we speak of someone being "broken" by a particular experience. This verse may be the reference concerning Jesus quoted by the gospel writer in John 19:36.

Psalm 34:21-22. In contrast to the Lord's deliverance of the righteous person, wicked persons are destroyed as a result of evil.

INTERPRETING THE SCRIPTURE

A Call to Praise

Usually we expect the praise of God to be an end in itself, but in Psalm 34 it leads to godly instruction. The writer tells us with wondrous excitement of his desire to bless the Lord, after which he gives us his testimony; and with that he instructs us like children (Psalm 34:11) to live in such a way that we, too, will see the mercy and deliverance of God.

The author of this psalm is wonderfully

candid about himself. He has suffered a trial of faith and of existence, and he has survived, so he is not timid now about telling his story. He speaks from experience, and as the late Roy L. Smith, in one of his editorials in the *Christian Advocate* once said, the person who has an experience with God has something beyond the reach of any argument. We can't know for sure what the writer's specific experience has been, but of one thing we are sure: he knows he has been delivered by God.

I read the newspaper accounts of a professional athlete who had a near-death experience in an auto accident. In his first public statement, he said that he would spend the rest of his life differently, as a result of coming so close to death. Time will tell if his resolve will hold; I pray so. Many of us know someone with a similar experience, and probably a similar vow. We know, too, that some have, indeed, become different as a result of their experience, while others have settled back to their old life. The psalmist wants to be sure not only that he himself remains changed, but also that he will influence others to change their ways. He wants to teach us, a common feature of the Wisdom literature tradition, so that we will know how God deals with the righteous and the wicked.

Usually the psalms are very specific; they name places, persons, and events. In this case, however, the report is quite general. I wish the writer had told us more, but perhaps if he had we wouldn't so easily apply his witness to our own lives. When he speaks of his fears, troubles, and wants, he includes all of us. What do we do with trouble?

How did David handle his trouble? He tells us simply that he "sought the LORD (Psalm 34:4)." If he had left us there, we might rejoice in his religious experience but we wouldn't be helped as specifically as we might. The first step in his deliverance is that he was saved from his fears. This testimony is psychologically sound.

We must deal with our fears early because until we get fear out of the way, we're not able to cope with anything else. We sometimes hear the phrase, "paralyzed by fear." It is an appropriate figure of speech. Fear can make it impossible for us to act.

But it's interesting, isn't it, that in Psalm 34:4 fear is an enemy from which to be delivered, while in Psalm 34:9, it is a recommended outlook on life. This reminds us that fear is itself a neutral quality; it is good or evil depending on its cause and use. We teach our children to fear a hot stove, a busy street, or suspicious strangers. In such instances, fear is an instinct for survival. But when they face a school test, an athletic competition, or a job interview, we work earnestly to absolve their fears.

As we note elsewhere, the fear of the Lord has the quality of reverence. Nevertheless, fear is still the operative word, and we shouldn't be so uneasy with the word that we miss its value. Someone has said that the person who fears God need not fear anything or anyone else. I find that quality in Madeleine L'Engle's comment when she tells of the automobile accident that nearly took her life, then left her hospitalized in great pain for weeks. She tells of her constant use of the "Jesus Prayer," then rejoices in "the lack of fear." Somehow she knew that "whatever happened all would be well." A right fear of God allays all other fears.

David was also delivered from shame. Shame is one of the most devastating emotions; modern psychology is only recently coming to understand its power. It doesn't necessarily have anything to do with our condition or conduct; rather, it is something others impose upon us. Trouble is itself bad enough, but it is generally followed by a sense of shame: "what will others think of me?" We know how valid this man's testimony is when he moves from the issue of his fears to that of his shame. Shame is an almost inevitable companion of trouble. Shame isn't always logical, but who ever said that life is rational? Perhaps it is simply that when we're in trouble our spiritual resistance is broken; in that condition we are susceptible to shame and self-doubt. But David is not only delivered from shame, his face has become "radiant" (Psalm 34:5). There could hardly be a more dramatic turnaround than a face that goes from the blush of shame to the glow of radiance.

A Testimony from Experience

After issuing his call to praise and telling how he sought the Lord and found deliverance, David speaks of his experience. First, there is the admission of need. He identifies himself as a "poor soul" (Psalm 34:6). When I was young, a loan officer told me that the worst part of his job was having to reject the applicants who most needed loans. I'm very grateful God operates on a different principle! God reaches out to those who are in need. David testifies that he was poor, that he cried (not a very dignified approach!), and that God heard. A critic might say that the formula is too simple, too pat, but those who have tried it will smile gratefully and say, "You'll have to find out for yourself." Which is the very point of the matter as the psalmist sees it. He tells us that the Lord delivers the poor from their troubles, and more than that, "the angel of the LORD encamps around those who fear him" (Psalm 34:7), as if to assure us of continuing care. So now he invites others to discover the truth that has blessed his life: "O taste and see that the LORD is good" (Psalm 34:8). In other words, the psalmist calls us to experience God for ourselves. There may be exceptions to the rule, but generally speaking, in religion, experience precedes knowledge. We believe because we have been convinced within. Knowledge can clear away prob-

lems, making experience more accessible, but on the whole it is the tasting—the experience—that leads to the seeing—the knowledge.

The psalmist goes on to assure us that those persons who do choose to take refuge in the Lord will find themselves happy or blessed. The reason for their happiness is that they will be cared for by God. They will, in the psalmist's words, "lack no good thing" (Psalm 34:10).

Remembering God's Faithfulness

Don't think, however, that this ancient saint sees his relationship with God as a permanent hedge against problems. Even though the angel of the Lord protects those who fear God, they will still suffer many afflictions. Some of the writers of the psalms speak of their righteousness as if they anticipate that it may in some way stand to their credit, but this writer knows otherwise. The righteous will experience afflictions. They will endure mental pain serious enough to destroy their own inner resources. Such pain will break their hearts and crush their spirits. That's the bad news. The good news is this: that "the LORD rescues them from them all" (Psalm 34:19). Name the number, and it will repeat itself: fifty-one afflictions, fifty-one rescues.

The bad news shouldn't really surprise us. We live in a world that has been marred by sin, and one can't be part of such a world without suffering from the fallout. We are, of course, susceptible to sickness, death, disappointment, and economic depression. But the good news is surprising: we will be rescued. Every time. God is willing and able to do that for us. No matter what our trouble or problem is we can rest assured that God is our refuge. No wonder the psalmist calls us to bless and praise the Lord!

SHARING THE SCRIPTURE

PREPARING TO TEACH

In one sense, this lesson will be easy to teach, because it deals with a common human experience. The problem you will face will be to keep discussion to the point of the lesson. It will be very easy to wander into humorous, sentimental stories that will not advance the lesson. Review the "Previewing the Lesson" portion so that you will be able to help the class stay focused on the intent of the lesson.

As you read the scripture lesson, think about our typical human experiences of trouble. Be especially sensitive to your knowledge of the troubles suffered by your class members. Remember that in many instances the troubles we know about are like the tip of the iceberg; far more troubles lie hidden beneath the visible ones. For that reason, this subject should be approached carefully, though with touches of humor. In truth, most of us have done some of our best laughing when we've been in hard places. You may want to talk briefly with your class about the importance of laughing when the going is tough, and how laughter can be an element of faith.

Review your own life, too, to see to what degree your own experience corroborates Psalm 34. Has God delivered you? Can you say that you have tasted and seen that God is good? It's important to think through these issues before you present the lesson to the class, or else your own experience may subtly undercut what you're teaching.

Remember that the ultimate mood of this lesson is one of victory. The psalmist is realistic; he knows that even the righteous suffer. But he has himself been delivered by God from troubles, and he is utterly confident that others will have the same experience. This mood should inform everything you say.

Have greeting cards available if you

choose to use them under "A Call to Praise."

If you plan to do the written activity under "A Testimony from Experience," have paper and pencils on hand.

Be sure to have hymnals available if you plan to close with a song of praise.

LEADING THE CLASS

Introduction

You might want to start this lesson by saying: "Today's lesson is about trouble. Is there anyone here without enough experience to discuss this subject?" Perhaps then you will want to discuss the fact that persons of every age have troubles. Trouble is part of the human condition. At one time or another, in an astonishing variety of ways, we are acquainted with trouble. Our concern in this lesson is to see how a person of faith has experienced trouble, been delivered from that trouble by God, and emerged from this experience with a song.

Note that our main questions for today are: **What can we do when trouble comes? What can we expect God to do?**

A Call to Praise

Choose someone to read aloud Psalm 34:2-3.

Point out to the class that many psalms begin with a complaint or with a passionate cry for help. This one begins as exultantly as can be imagined. The writer has found something to boast about, and it is the kind of boasting that will bring joy to the humble. His gladness is so great that he wants his solo to become a grand chorus: "O magnify the LORD with me!" (Psalm 34:3). Encourage class members to think of a time when the burden of a trouble they were carrying was lifted. Then ask:

?

(1) How did you feel?

(2) What response did you make privately to God?

(3) Did you tell anyone else about how you were feeling and invite that person to praise God with you? If the class is large, you may want to have partners or small teams discuss these questions.

Note that the apostle tells us we should rejoice with those who rejoice and weep with those who weep (Romans 12:15). Provide some time for the class to briefly share their joys and concerns. Pray for these persons some time during the class. If possible, have on hand some greeting cards that can be sent to absent members or other persons known by most of the class who are experiencing distress (such as illness, bereavement, loss of a job, family crisis) or joy (such as the birth of a child or marriage).

A Testimony from Experience

Select a volunteer to read Psalm 34:4-10.

Help the class to identify some patterns in these verses. Verses 4 and 5 are coupled, as are verses 6 and 7. Verses 4 and 6 are personal biographical statements, while verses 5 and 7 call for the larger company to join in the experience. Note the balance between the poor soul's action and God's response. Write these words on a chalkboard or newsprint:

sought	answered, delivered
cried	heard, saved
fear	angel of the Lord encamps, delivers

Ask class members to state in a sentence or two what the psalmist's testimony tells them they can expect from God, especially during difficult times in their own lives.

If the class enjoys creative activities, provide a few moments for them to rewrite Psalm 34:4-7 (in either paragraph form or as a psalm) using their own experience. To do this activity, students will need to think

of a time when they sought the Lord and state how God healed or rescued them. After a few minutes, invite several volunteers to read the testimonies they have written.

Note that persons who have been able to "taste and see that the LORD is good" (Psalm 34:8) may want to share that experience with other persons. Ask the class to think of ways that they can reach out to others who are in need to help them experience God's love and care. Brainstorm a list of situations where concerned Christians could help others in their time of need. Ideas might include volunteering to work in a hospice, hospital, crisis counseling center or hot line, shelter for the homeless or abused, church support group, or a soup kitchen. Personal care can also be given to neighbors, friends, and family.

Point out that just as we encourage other persons to experience God, so too friends support us in our time of need, often through their prayers, gifts, and service. Provide a few moments of silence. Ask students to think of someone who really helped them during a difficult period and to thank God for this person's love and support.

Remembering God's Faithfulness

Ask a student to read the conclusion of Psalm 34, verses 18-22.

Focus first on the key verse, Psalm 34:18. Ask the class: **Why is the Lord so near to the brokenhearted?** (You might also want to ask: Is it because we allow God to come closer when we are broken?) This question may spark responses by several persons who have experienced God's comforting presence during an especially difficult time. Note that God has the resources to rescue us, even when we are so crushed in spirit that we cannot help ourselves.

Refer to Psalm 34:19. Point out that this verse indicates that the righteous will suffer afflictions. Contrary to some Chris-

?

tians' beliefs that the godly should never suffer, difficult experiences—bereavement, disappointment in some human relationships, or mistreatment by other persons— are common to us all. Discuss the degree to which students feel "the righteous" are better off. Emphasize, especially, God's promise of deliverance.

You may want to close today's lesson by singing a hymn that praises God for faithfulness, such as "Great Is Thy Faithfulness" (*The United Methodist Hymnal*, page 140).

HELPING CLASS MEMBERS ACT

Ask every class member to think of someone who is currently in trouble, and to pledge to pray for that person this week. If possible, extend some kindness to that individual. A card, phone call, baked good, or some special assistance (such as mowing the grass) can be a real uplift to someone who feels overwhelmed by the circumstances of his or her life.

Challenge class members who themselves are carrying a heavy burden to praise God each day. One way would be to read Psalm 34:1-10 and 18-22 at a regular time each day. Another way would be to sing a hymn of praise each day. A third way would be to tell someone else something good that God has done for you that day.

Encourage students to find situations (such as those brainstormed in the activity under "A Testimony from Experience") where they can help persons facing difficulties. Ask them to contact an agency and make a commitment, if they are in a position to volunteer. One of the agencies may be your own church, for many churches offer support groups for the bereaved or terminally ill.

Suggest that students phone or write a thank you note to someone who helped them through a difficult period to let that person know how much his or her love and support meant to them.

PLANNING FOR NEXT SUNDAY

Next week's lesson is from one of the most beautiful of all psalms, 139. Ask your class members, as they read it, to think of ways God has been with them at every imaginable juncture of life.

NEVER ALONE

PREVIEWING THE LESSON

Lesson Scripture: Psalm 139:1-14, 23-24
Background Scripture: Psalm 139
Key Verse: Psalm 139:23

Focus of the lesson:
God's constant presence and care

Main question(s) of the lesson:
(1) How do I experience God's intimate, ever present relationship in my own life?

This lesson will enable adult learners to:
(1) comprehend that God has intimate knowledge of each person
(2) appreciate God's abiding presence in their lives
(3) respond by becoming more aware of God's presence.

Today's lesson may be outlined as follows:
(1) Introduction
(2) You Know Everything About Me (Psalm 139:1-6)
(3) Sometimes I Wish You Didn't (Psalm 139:7-12)
(4) You Had a Head Start in Knowing Me (Psalm 139:13-14)
(5) Please, Know Me Even Better! (Psalm 139:23-24)

FOCUSING ON THE MAIN QUESTION

In a lifetime of reading the Psalms, this psalm is undoubtedly one of my three or four absolute favorites. I am drawn to it partly by the sheer beauty of language; but more than that, the magnificent theme reminds me that God is always with me. I am never alone. What good news!

I doubt that there is any human being who has not at some time felt alone or lonely. The potential for loneliness is built into our human condition, not only because we are sometimes isolated from one another by distance or personal insensitivity, but also because there is a kind of loneliness in the universe. We may look up at the heavens on a certain kind of night and long to feel that there is Someone there who cares, Someone with whom there can be conversation. Psalm 139 tells us, in dramatic, powerful poetry that we are never alone. Someone is there, and that Someone is the God of the universe.

While the assurance we are never alone may be very comforting, we may also find it to be a threat at times. Human beings don't always want God on their trail. The all-seeing eye of God unnerves us when we feel we are falling short of the divine purpose, or when we—like Jonah—are fleeing from God. Francis Thompson saw God as "The Hound of Heaven," and said that he "fled Him, down the nights and down the days," running "[f]rom those strong Feet that followed, followed after." The psalmist had tried to run from God; and only after being found by the Eternal did he discover that the threat is at last the ultimate blessing. He comes to know this because he has tried to escape.

As the psalmist learned, the God who watches over us even as we are being formed in our mother's womb never allows us to be alone. The knowledge that God is always present and all knowing strikes us as a two-edged sword: God's intimacy with us is both a cause for gladness and a reason for fear.

This exquisite record of the psalmist's recognition of God's constant presence causes us to ask: **How do I experience God's intimate, ever present relationship in my own life?**

READING THE SCRIPTURE

NRSV
Psalm 139:1-14
1 O LORD, you have searched me
    and known me.
2You know when I sit down and
    when I rise up;
you discern my thoughts from
    far away.
3You search out my path and my
    lying down,
    and are acquainted with all my
    ways.
4Even before a word is on my
    tongue,
    O LORD, you know it
    completely.
5You hem me in, behind and
    before,
    and lay your hand upon me.
6Such knowledge is too wonderful
    for me;
    it is so high that I cannot
    attain it.

7Where can I go from your spirit?
    Or where can I flee from your
    presence?
8If I ascend to heaven, you are
    there;
    if I make my bed in Sheol,

NIV
Psalm 139:1-14
1 O LORD, you have searched me
    and you know me.
2You know when I sit and when I rise;
    you perceive my thoughts from afar.

3You discern my going out and my lying
    down; you are familiar with all my ways.

4Before a word is on my tongue
    you know it completely, O LORD.

5You hem me in—behind and before;
    you have laid your hand upon me.

6Such knowledge is too wonderful for me,
    too lofty for me to attain.

7Where can I go from your Spirit?
    Where can I flee from your presence?

8If I go up to the heavens, you are there;
    if I make my bed in the depths, you are
    there.

you are there.
⁹If I take the wings of the
      morning
   and settle at the farthest limits
      of the sea,
¹⁰even there your hand shall lead
      me,
   and your right hand shall hold
      me fast.
¹¹If I say, "Surely the darkness
      shall cover me,
   and the light around me
      become night,"
¹²even the darkness is not dark to
      you;
   the night is as bright as the
      day,
   for darkness is as light to you.

¹³For it was you who formed my
      inward parts;
   you knit me together in my
      mother's womb.
¹⁴I praise you, for I am fearfully
      and wonderfully made.
   Wonderful are your works;
   that I know very well.

Psalm 139:23-24
²³Search me, O God, and know
      my heart;
      test me and know my
         thoughts.
²⁴See if there is any wicked way
      in me,
   and lead me in the way
      everlasting.

⁹If I rise on the wings of the dawn,
   if I settle on the far side of the sea,

¹⁰even there your hand will guide me,
   your right hand will hold me fast.

¹¹If I say, "Surely the darkness will hide me
   and the light become night around me,"

¹²even the darkness will not be dark to you;
   the night will shine like the day,
   for darkness is as light to you.

¹³For you created my inmost being;
   you knit me together in my mother's
      womb.

¹⁴I praise you because I am fearfully and
      wonderfully made;
   your works are wonderful,
   I know that full well.

Psalm 139:23-24
²³Search me, O God, and know my heart;
   test me and know my anxious thoughts.

²⁴See if there is any offensive way in me,
   and lead me in the way everlasting.

Key Verse

UNDERSTANDING THE SCRIPTURE

Psalm 139. This psalm is traditionally ascribed to David. We have no proof of authorship, of course, only the witness of ancient tradition. When one considers the intimacy of David's faith and its frequent struggles, it is easy to believe that he could have written these beautiful words. The psalm is divided into four sections: God is all knowing (verses 1-6); God is ever present (verses 7-12); God has intimate knowledge of the psalmist because of God's own creative power (verses 13-18); and the psalmist seeks God's help in vindicating him (verses 19-24).

Psalm 139:1-2. God's knowledge of us is complete. God's greatness is measured by attention to little things—a knowledge of our most routine sittings and risings. It is the same point Jesus makes in saying that the very hairs of our head are numbered (Matthew 10:30). The greatness of God is revealed not only in the vastness of the universe but also in the capacity for infinite detail.

Psalm 139:3. The Hebrew word translated as "search" refers to a thorough examination. The reference to "path" and "lying down" makes us think of a traveler who journeys and then rests. God is constantly on the journey with us, even when we are at rest.

Psalm 139:4. The Wisdom literature of the Old Testament makes much of the importance of right speech, so when the psalmist speaks of God knowing a word before it even reaches his tongue, he is dealing with a solemn matter.

Psalm 139:5. Is the writer complaining or rejoicing when he says God has hemmed him in? Either response is possible, depending on his state of faith.

Psalm 139:6. God's knowledge is "wonderful" not simply in its degree, but in its quality; it is a "high" knowledge.

Psalm 139:7-8. The psalmist recognizes that there is nowhere that he can hide from God, not even in Sheol. At this point in Israel's history, Sheol was generally thought of simply as the abode of the dead, rather than as a hell. The idea that God is in Sheol, as well as in heaven, is new to Israel's thought.

Psalm 139:9-10. David imagines God as filling the entire universe. The source of the image "wings of the morning" is unknown, but the image may be understood as a personification of dawn as a winged creature. When the writer speaks of fleeing to "the farthest limits of the sea" and finding God there, we may think of the prophet Jonah's experience in running from God and his assignment in Nineveh.

Psalm 139:11-12. The psalmist cannot hide in the dark because God's presence is light.

Psalm 139:13. The psalmist is so caught up in his adoration of God that when he thinks of his conception and birth, he loses sight of his human parents and thinks only of God's creative activity. "Inward parts" is literally "kidneys." The Hebrews thought of the kidneys as the innermost center of the body, much as we might speak of the heart. The kidneys were believed to be the organ responsible for thought. "Knit" is a particularly expressive word.

Psalm 139:14. When the writer speaks of being "wonderfully made," the phrase carries the idea of being distinguished. It is as if he sees himself as the handiwork of a sublime artist. When he says that he knows God's works are wonderful, he confesses that he has been convinced of this fact by observing his own person. Humans are walking marvels, products of the Supreme Artist.

Psalm 139:15-18. These verses, which do not appear in the printed portion, continue to consider God's care. Before his birth, God wrote the psalmist's number of days in a book of life (see also Psalm 40:7). Such limitless knowledge is incomprehensible to the author.

Psalm 139:19-22. In these verses, which are also not included in the printed portion, the psalmist equates his own personal enemies with the enemies of God. He prays for deliverance and the destruction of the wicked.

Psalm 139:23. The psalmist wants to enter into a still more awesome relationship with the One who knows him so well; therefore, he asks for the searching and testing that will draw him yet closer to God.

Psalm 139:24. The psalmist knows himself (and human nature) well enough to realize his capacity for evil. Thus, he appeals for God to search him, test him, and lead him in the way everlasting.

INTERPRETING THE SCRIPTURE

You Know Everything About Me

When theologians speak of the attributes of God, they traditionally speak of God's omniscience, omnipresence, and omnipotence; that is, God is all-knowing, always present, and all-powerful. The writer of Psalm 139 is expressing a similar idea, but not in the sometimes sterile language of the scholar. For him, these divine qualities are spelled out in his experiences. Is God omniscient? Absolutely. God knows my thoughts before the words shape on my tongue. Is God omnipresent? Yes, indeed. I find God in heaven and in Sheol. Is God omnipotent? No question about it. God makes the night as bright as day.

It is one thing (and an honorable one) to study God in the library, but the author of this profound psalm has encountered God in the dust of daily life, in experiences that range from getting out of his chair to fleeing to the ends of the earth. He knows by his experiences, both negative and positive, that we humans are never alone. God is with us all the time and knows us more intimately than we know ourselves.

Those of us who have tried in our imperfect way to walk with God have our own memories of God's nearness at all times. I was a nineteen-year-old hitchhiker on a lonely stretch of road in northern Missouri. Hitchhiking was not only legal in those days, it was a major form of transportation for students, servicemen, and the unemployed, ranking close behind the train and bus as a means of getting somewhere. But it was dark and terribly lonely on that road, and no cars were in sight. Then, the presence of God reassured me. God had searched out my path: I was not alone.

Half a lifetime later, I was in an intensive care unit of a hospital following surgery. I was awakened repeatedly by a furor over a shooting victim who had just been brought in. Everything about my curtained-off area was so unreal in those nighttime hours, half-fogged as I was with medication. At times it was almost surrealistic. But one thing was absolutely real, absolutely certain: God was with me. There could be no doubt of that.

I remember my pastoral calls on an elderly woman who lived in a rather forlorn two-room house, alone, as she had been all of her adult life. I was young, and her setting seemed to me to be desolate. "Are you sometimes lonely?" I asked. "Never," she smiled. "I'm not alone. I've never been alone. The Lord is with me." The psalmist said it more eloquently, but not better. Each was speaking from real experience, beyond challenge.

I have read the statements of scholars and public personalities concerning their experiences with God, and I am grateful for such expressions. But my most memorable hearings have come from people, like this elderly woman, in the daily run of life—the world of downsittings and uprisings. Your class will be a cornucopia of wonder if its members will feel free to tell of some of those occasions when God proved to be very near. An average adult class has enough experiences of God's omnipresence to fill a very large book. And it would be good reading.

Sometimes I Wish You Didn't

It's popular to speak of our human search for God. But the great twentieth-century Christian apologist, C. S. Lewis, said that speaking of our search for God is a little like speaking of a mouse's search for the cat; our frequent inclination is to flee from God. We may seek God while we're hunkered down in foxholes during despairing moments of life. At other times, though, our inclinations are decidedly mixed.

"Hide and seek" may be an accurate description of our relationship with God. Maybe we were told during our childhood that God knows everything we say and do. Whoever intoned these words may have said them to frighten us so that we would behave—and they were probably successful! We've been looking over our shoulder ever since to see where God is lurking so that we can hide. We didn't invent this game, though. Ever since Adam and Eve were portrayed as hiding from God while God was seeking them, humans have experienced this seesawing desire to run from the divine Presence one minute and seek God the next.

This desire persists until we are found! Then we never tire of telling how God found us. No stories of faith are more moving and awesome than the stories of our flight from God, God's faithful pursuit, and our eventual reunion. Jesus celebrates the theme when he tells of a shepherd finding a sheep that has been lost, and calling the whole community to rejoice with him (Luke 15:3-7).

The psalmist simply exults in the realization of the wondrous knowledge and nearness of God. When he flees "to the farthest limits of the sea" (Psalm 139:9), God hunts him out. Even in the darkness of night, God is present. The psalmist recognizes that there is no place to run.

You Had a Head Start in Knowing Me

God's knowledge of us is so intimate and presence with us is so constant because God knew us even before we were born. God presided over our creation. In recent years, science has unlocked profound secrets about our human makeup. We marvel at the intricacies of our genetic code, the capacities of our brains for thought and creativity, and the amazing resiliency of our bodies to with-

stand transplants of major organs. David may not have had such scientific knowledge, but his awe of God and his innate insight into human nature helped him see what remarkable creatures we are. He knew, even as our scientific advances confirm, that we humans are "fearfully and wonderfully made" (Psalm 139:14). David saw us as products of God's creative hand, a hand that "knit [us] together" (Psalm 139:13) in our mother's womb. Since God has been involved in making us who we are, God's knowledge of us is beyond compare.

Please, Know Me Even Better!

It seems to me that the prayer with which the psalm ends reflects the psalmist's concern lest he has spoken too forcefully in verses 19-22 (which are not part of our printed portion). Obviously, he is troubled by the evil he sees and calls for vindication. While we may not like the language he uses, we can nevertheless learn from his passion for what is right. Perhaps he realizes that even the passion for God and for goodness can easily slip into a "wicked way." So he pleads to God in verses 23-24 to examine his heart and his thoughts (those thoughts again!) to be sure that he has not done wrong.

In a sense, this closing prayer is the best of the psalmist's expression. At an early point in the psalm, he confessed that it was impossible to flee from God, though it seems very clear that he had tried to do so. Then, in the heart of the psalm, he rejoices in God's constant presence, even as he marvels at it. He is awestruck by the fact that God knows him from his very conception; no wonder, then, that he cannot hide from God!

In contrast, the psalmist now pleads for God's constant presence to continue. He knows that this inescapable God is his only guarantee of freedom from evil. The presence, which at some times may have seemed oppressive, is perceived now as unmitigated blessing. The writer wants this God who knows him so well to search him and test him. He senses that there may be some evil ways in him of which he is not conscious, so he wants them revealed and rooted out before they cause harm.

Some readers might consider this a mor-bid prayer, too painfully introspective. In truth, it is a prayer that leads to true interior goodness. Having learned the profound depth of God's knowledge, the psalmist now embraces it and pleads for it to continue. Search more deeply, he cries. He wants to be sure, utterly sure, that he is never, never alone.

SHARING THE SCRIPTURE

PREPARING TO TEACH

From a theological point of view, today's lesson deals with many significant aspects of the doctrine of God, especially God's total knowledge of us (omniscience) and God's constant presence with us (omnipresence). But it does so from the vantage point of human experience. Psalm 139 is no dry-as-dust statement, but the awesome story of one person's spiritual pilgrimage. As such, it deals with the human problem of aloneness. "It's a lonely universe," someone says. But the psalmist tells us otherwise. As you prepare to teach, examine your own experiences with loneliness, both in human relationships and in your walk with God. One way to do this is to read Psalm 139 at least once each day. As you do, ask God to let this psalm illuminate your own understandings.

Spend some time this week recalling experiences of some members of the class. Has anyone ever testified to feelings of being pursued by God? Is there someone in the class you know to be an especially lonely or bereft person? Be particularly sensitive to life situations such as these as you do your planning this week. Make a special effort to pray for class members.

Have hymnals on hand if you plan to ask the class to choose a song.

Have paper and pencils available if you plan to do the spiritual journal activity under "Please, Know Me Even Better!"

LEADING THE CLASS

Introduction

Read or retell the information in the "Focusing on the Main Question" section.

Lead a discussion on the major themes of Psalm 139 by asking these questions:
(1) **Can you think of a time when you were grateful for God's abiding presence?** *(Students may give generic answers, such as illness or death of a loved one. A few may want to give more personal stories.)*
(2) **Can you think of times when you have run—or wanted to run—from God?** *(Spend some time discussing the ambivalence most of us feel about God's constant presence with us. The students' responses can be used for points of comparison with the psalmist's reactions as the lesson progresses.)*

Point out the main question: **How do I experience God's intimate, ever present relationship in my own life?** Allow students a few moments to ponder this question silently.

Invite class members to suggest hymns that are especially meaningful in reassuring them of God's presence. If possible, sing one of their selections.

You Know Everything About Me

Direct the group's attention to Psalm 139:1-6.

Ask class members to remember a time when someone was trying to learn more about them. Perhaps they were teenagers or courting their future spouses then. Suggest that they call out words or phrases to describe how they felt about someone wanting to know all about them. List their ideas on a chalkboard or newsprint. Be open to both positive responses (we want to be known) and negative ones (we recoil from too much intimacy).

Continue the discussion by translating those feelings, as much as possible, to the wonder that God cares to search and know us. Ask: **How does God's desire for such an intimate relationship with you make you feel?**

Invite your class to paraphrase verses 2 and 3 to give further insight into the way God knows the routine details of our lives. Here are some examples to help the class get started: You know where I like to shop . . . my favorite restaurant . . . what kinds of clothes I like to wear. You may want to have students work alone, but they would probably enjoy doing this activity with a partner or in a small team. After a few moments, ask students to share their paraphrases.

Sometimes I Wish You Didn't

Select volunteers to each read one verse of Psalm 139:7-12.

Remind the class of your opening discussion regarding our ambivalence about God's constant presence and intimate knowledge of us. Ask the students: **How many of you have childhood memories of someone frightening you into good behavior by telling you God was watching everything you did?** A few persons may be willing to share some brief anecdotes.

Move the discussion to the present by asking:

(1) To what degree has that feeling that God is watching your every move carried over into adult life?

(2) In what ways is that a desirable feeling, in that it helps keep us from doing wrong?

(3) In what ways is that a negative feeling, in that we want to avoid God because we are afraid?

Conclude this segment by asking: **In what ways do we, or others we know, try to run from God?** Some persons may remind the class of the story of Jonah or Adam and Eve. Others may suggest habits (such as alcohol or drug abuse) or activities in which people try to escape from God by becoming totally immersed (such as work, sports, music, even volunteer work at the church). Still others may respond with personal examples if they did not do so during the discussion of "Focusing on the Main Question."

You Had a Head Start in Knowing Me

Choose someone to read Psalm 139:13-14.

Ask class members the following questions: **(1) Although David did not have the benefit of our scientific knowledge, he certainly had a keen appreciation for God's creative role as our maker. What scientific discoveries in your own lifetime have made you more in awe of God's gift of our bodies?** (2) How might God's intimate knowledge of us influence the way we treat our bodies?

Depending on the composition of your class, some students may want to engage in a discussion concerning the implications of these verses as they relate to the abortion issue. If so, be sure to set a time limit, keeping in mind that our main concern in this lesson is God's presence with us and knowledge of us.

Please, Know Me Even Better!

Read Psalm 139:23-24 aloud yourself in short phrases. Ask class members to prayerfully repeat each phrase after you.

You may want to read or retell the information in this section under "Interpreting the Scripture." Note that poor religion makes us think that we are superior to others, but good religion makes us realize how fallible we are and how capable we are of doing wrong. This sensitivity is our best safeguard against sin. David wisely prays that God will search him and test him, because he wants to be led "in the way everlasting."

Provide some time for quiet meditation on these two closing verses. Point out that true Christian introspection leads to grace, forgiveness, and a new start. Some students will simply want to think silently. Others may want to write their thoughts as they would in a spiritual journal. Have paper and pencils available.

Close the session by leading the class in prayer. Conclude with words of thanksgiving that we are "never alone."

HELPING CLASS MEMBERS ACT

Encourage students to spend some time thinking this week about childhood images they had of God. Ask them to take a hard look at ones, such as the heavenly police officer who is waiting to catch them red-handed, that put barriers between themselves and God. Have them pray, seeking greater intimacy with a loving Friend who wants to be with them.

Suggest that students think of one step they can take to do something to overcome a social evil. Or ask them to help an individual they know personally who is the victim of an unjust situation to deal with that problem.

Ask students to be more aware of the constant presence of God in their own lives this week. As they make decisions about where they will go and what they will do, challenge them to ask themselves what Jesus might do in this situation.

PLANNING FOR NEXT SUNDAY

Next Sunday's lesson deals with another favorite psalm, Psalm 40, and with another common human experience, trust in God. Ask your class, as they read this psalm, to be aware of how it fits some of their own past experiences. This lesson, which begins the final unit of summer, will shift our focus from praising God to responding to God.

TRUST IN GOD

PREVIEWING THE LESSON

Lesson Scripture: Psalm 40:1-5, 9-11, 16-17
Background Scripture: Psalm 40
Key Verse: Psalm 40:4

Focus of the lesson:
the happiness of persons who put their trust in God

Main question(s) of the lesson:
(1) How do I put my trust in God, especially when I feel myself sinking in a perilous pit?

This lesson will enable adult learners to:
(1) identify trust in God as a source of happiness
(2) affirm their willingness to trust God in all situations
(3) respond by witnessing to someone else with a word of praise about God's trustworthiness.

Today's lesson may be outlined as follows:
(1) Introduction
(2) I Was Delivered (Psalm 40:1-2)
(3) Now I Am Happy (Psalm 40:3-5)
(4) I'm Telling Others of My Joy (Psalm 40:9-11)
(5) I Continue to Trust (Psalm 40:16-17)

FOCUSING ON THE MAIN QUESTION

I pity the person who has never been in one of life's pits. If you haven't been in a pit of some sort, you haven't had a chance to trust—really trust!—God.

For trust, you see, is a word that implies peril. It has little significance if something is not at risk. When we say, "I trust my doctor," we're thinking of those instances where our health is threatened. Banks have trust officers to oversee estate matters; if they are not capable of handling such business, the estate is in peril. If someone's conduct is in question, those of us who believe in the person will say, "I trust him absolutely"—but the statement would not need to be made if there were no issue.

As we might expect, a psalm concerning trust in God will be set in a hard and trying place. This setting reflects the difficult situation in which the psalmist finds himself. He has experienced life in a desolate pit and writes about how God, who is trustworthy, delivered him from this miry bog.

When I said at the outset that I was sorry for anyone who had never been in one of life's pits, I didn't really expect to have any takers rushing to agree with me. I'm not pessimistic when I say that; quite the opposite. As I look at my own life, I'm so grateful for where I am just now that I might easily forget some of the pits through which I passed to get here. Pits are a part of life, and to deny their existence is to diminish life rather than to exalt it. Our pits differ in size and severity, of course,

and so does our perception of them. What one person sees as a devastating place might hardly be acknowledged by another as more than a slight decline. But the pits exist, and biblical religion recognizes the reality of such experiences. Better yet, our biblical faith shows the way out.

We want to find that way and we can do so by trusting in God. As we study David's words of thanksgiving and lament in Psalm 40, we are prompted to ask ourselves: **How do I put my trust in God, especially when I feel myself sinking in a perilous pit?**

READING THE SCRIPTURE

NRSV
Psalm 40:1-5
1 I waited patiently for the LORD;
　　he inclined to me and heard
　　　　my cry.
²He drew me up from the
　　　　desolate pit,
　　out of the miry bog,
and set my feet upon a rock,
　　making my steps secure.
³He put a new song in my mouth,
　　a song of praise to our God.
Many will see and fear,
　　and put their trust in the
　　　　LORD.

NIV
Psalm 40:1-5
1 I waited patiently for the LORD;
　　he turned to me and heard my cry.

²He lifted me out of the slimy pit,
　　out of the mud and mire;
he set my feet on a rock
　　and gave me a firm place to stand.

³He put a new song in my mouth,
　　a hymn of praise to our God.
Many will see and fear
　　and put their trust in the LORD.

Key Verse

⁴Happy are those who make
　　the LORD their trust,
who do not turn to the proud,
　　to those who go astray after
　　　　false gods.
⁵You have multiplied, O LORD
　　　　my God,
　　your wondrous deeds and your
　　　　thoughts toward us;
　　none can compare with you.
Were I to proclaim and tell of
　　　　them,
　　they would be more than can
　　　　be counted.

⁴Blessed is the man
　　who makes the LORD his trust,
who does not look to the proud,
　　to those who turn aside to false gods.

⁵Many, O LORD my God,
　　are the wonders you have done.
The things you planned for us
　　no one can recount to you;
were I to speak and tell of them,
　　they would be too many to declare.

Ke Ve

Psalm 40:9-11
⁹I have told the glad news of
        deliverance
    in the great congregation;
see, I have not restrained my
        lips,
    as you know, O LORD.
¹⁰I have not hidden your saving
        help within my heart,
    I have spoken of your
        faithfulness and your
        salvation;
I have not concealed your
        steadfast love and your
        faithfulness
    from the great congregation.

¹¹Do not, O LORD, withhold
    your mercy from me;
let your steadfast love and your
        faithfulness
    keep me safe forever.

Psalm 40:16-17
¹⁶But may all who seek you
    rejoice and be glad in you;
may those who love your
        salvation
    say continually, "Great is the
        LORD!"
¹⁷As for me, I am poor and
        needy,
    but the Lord takes thought for
        me.
You are my help and my
        deliverer;
    do not delay, O my God.

Psalm 40:9-11
⁹I proclaim righteousness in the great
        assembly;
    I do not seal my lips,
    as you know, O LORD.

¹⁰I do not hide your righteousness in my heart;
    I speak of your faithfulness and salvation.
I do not conceal your love and your truth
    from the great assembly.

¹¹Do not withhold your mercy from me,
        O LORD;
    may your love and your truth always
        protect me.

Psalm 40:16-17
¹⁶But may all who seek you
    rejoice and be glad in you;
may those who love your salvation
        always say,
    "The LORD be exalted!"

¹⁷Yet I am poor and needy;
    may the Lord think of me.
You are my help and my deliverer;
    O my God, do not delay.

UNDERSTANDING THE SCRIPTURE

Psalm 40. This psalm is traditionally attributed to David, but we are given no details of the circumstances under which it might have been written. The poem contains two different psalm forms: a psalm of thanksgiving (verses 1-11) and a psalm of lament (verses 12-17). Some commentators believe these two sections may have been written separately and later combined by an editor. The fact that Psalm 40:13-17 is nearly identical to Psalm 70 seems to support this idea.

Psalm 40:1. When David says that he "waited patiently," he is describing a mood that rarely appears in the Psalms. So many of these prayers are anxious and insistent. "Inclined (un)to me" (NRSV, KJV), "turned to hear me" (NIV), and "stooped to me" (New Jerusalem) describe God's tender care. God is positioned to listen; no wonder God hears the cry.

Psalm 40:2. "Desolate" could also be translated "pit of tumult." A "miry bog" makes one think of quicksand. "Rock" provides a vivid contrast. We are not told how the psalmist fell into the pit, but God is clearly responsible for lifting him out of it and setting him on solid rock.

Psalm 40:3. On the day when Charles Wesley, perhaps the greatest hymn writer of Christendom, was converted, he was impressed by the verse, "I will put a new song into thy mouth." Although that phrasing comes from another place in the Psalms, Wesley's first hymn after this experience indicates that he felt he was delivered from a pit.

Psalm 40:4. Trust usually comes to its best strength in hard places; it makes for extraordinary happiness. This verse emphasizes that fact. Persons who are happy (blessed) are neither arrogant nor seeking after idols. They trust completely in God.

Psalm 40:5. We are on God's mind—and just now David feels that God has "multiplied" thoughts and deeds toward him. A recitation of God's deeds was a major component of the Old Testament covenant renewal ceremony. An old Sunday school hymn urges us to "count your blessings," assuring us that it will then "surprise" us to see what God has done. David has tried to do that and concluded that God's favors to him are simply beyond counting.

Psalm 40:6-8. These verses, which are not included in our printed portion, speak of the offerings that the covenant worshipers are to bring. The usual types of offerings and sacrifices, which are listed,

are not necessary. What God yearns for is worshipers who present themselves ("Here I am."), desiring to do God's will according to the law that is written on each worshiper's heart. In other words, obedience is more important than sacrifice.

Psalm 40:9. The "great congregation" no doubt refers to the assembled people of God. The psalmist may well be thinking of a feast day, when people are thronging to the house of God for celebration.

Psalm 40:10. Some things should be kept secret, but not the faithfulness, salvation, and steadfast love of God. These matters should be shared widely.

Psalm 40:11. Notice that "steadfast love" and "faithfulness," which appeared in verse 10, are both repeated here. These words are the closest approximation to "grace" in the Hebrew Scriptures. The term "steadfast love," a very important attribute of God, occurs 172 times in the Old Testament (NRSV). "Faithfulness" occurs 71 times. The two terms are often linked to describe God's care for people.

Psalm 40:12-15. These verses, omitted from the printed portion, are part of a lament in which the psalmist pours out his difficulties unto God. He pleads for deliverance from his enemies.

Psalm 40:16. We think of "salvation" in a spiritual, eternal sense, but for this writer it was more of a present, physical matter. In contrast to those who seek the psalmist's life and verbally mock him (verses 14-15), persons who seek God sing words of praise to God.

Psalm 40:17. At the beginning of this psalm, David said he was waiting "patiently," but now he speaks with urgency: "do not delay." At this moment, his needs seem to overwhelm him. He reiterates the idea, which appears in verse 5, that God "takes thought" of him, but he wants that thought to eventuate in action.

INTERPRETING THE SCRIPTURE

I Was Delivered

When I was a boy, almost every evening service included time for testimonies—an opportunity for people to report God's working in their lives. I realize that there was usually a sameness to these testimonies and that they didn't always reflect as much personal growth as they might; nevertheless, I miss them. They provided an occasion for people to recount the goodness of God, as personally experienced. I have a feeling that part of the appeal of Alcoholics Anonymous (and its related groups) is that such personal "witnessing" is part of their meetings.

The person who wrote this psalm has a story to tell, and he remembers it well. He was once in a "desolate pit," a "miry bog," and God brought him out to "a rock." Now he has to sing. He doesn't get specific about the nature of his pit. It may have been poverty or sickness, or perhaps some broken human relationship; the possibilities are as wide as our human experience. Whatever it was, it was a time of utter extremity; and whatever it was, God was sufficient to deliver. The psalmist's emphasis is more on the deliverance than on the pit.

As a young person, I thought some people had it made; they seemed to me to be beyond failure or defeat. After I was a pastor for a few years, I learned that the very opposite is true. If we come to know any person well enough, we will discover that there has been, or currently is, some desolate pit in his or her life.

In such pits we come to know the wonder of God's grace. In another place a psalmist writes that it is those who go "down to the sea in ships" who see "the deeds of the LORD, his wondrous works in the deep" (Psalm 107:23-24). The Israelites —not a seafaring people—realized that in the peril of that foreign world of the sea there was special opportunity for seeing the glory of God. Only a masochist would seek for a pit, but if and when one comes, we can be sure that it will be a setting for a revelation of God's grace.

Now I Am Happy

After such an experience, a person not only knows how wonderful it is to trust God, but also wants others to have the same experience. For David, it is a song to be sung, a song of praise to God. As a result of his praise, he hopes that many persons will "see and fear" God. More particularly, the psalmist wants those who hear his testimony to be converted, so they too will "put their trust in the LORD" (Psalm 40:3).

He wants others to experience the same kind of relationship with God the deliverer that he has experienced because he's sure that this is the way to live! This is the happy life, a life of trust. As we learn later in the psalm, the writer's troubles did not end when he was delivered from the pit; he concludes with an appeal for another deliverance. But living in trust is living in happiness. As someone has said, when you trust in God nothing really, ultimately bad can ever happen to you. Bad things can happen, yes; but not in a final, irrevocable way. For those who trust in God, the final score has to be a winning one. No wonder, then, that those who "make the LORD their trust" (Psalm 40:4) are happy!

David was assured in his trusting because he believed he was in God's thoughts. As I pondered that wondrous fact—that the Intelligence behind all of the universe had reserved thinking-room for me—I discovered that I was humming a hymn to myself. That happens to those of us who have lived long and lovingly with the music of the church. But I couldn't recall when I had last heard the hymn, so I hardly knew where to begin searching for it. At last I located it in one of the tattered hymnbooks I keep on my shelves. It was written in 1885 by E. D. Mund, and the chorus catches the mood of our psalm:

> Thou thinkest, Lord, of me;
> What need I fear when Thou art near,
> And thinkest, Lord, of me.

Such was the psalmist's assurance. If I am in God's thoughts, why should I fear? I knew a pastor once who prided himself on being able to type while he carried on telephone conversations of a routine kind. One day I phoned him when I was in a decidedly non-routine state, hoping for his attention and counsel. As I tried to tell him what was on my mind, I heard his typewriter going and sensed that his responses were perfunctory—and I knew I was not in his thoughts, even though we were on the phone. Sometimes I am slow in perceiving God's responses, but I know I am always—as David said—in God's thoughts. And that is good reason to trust.

I'm Telling Others of My Joy

When the psalmist has been delivered, he wastes no time in telling this joyous news to the entire congregation. He wants everyone to know of God's faithfulness and salvation. But David, like all humans, is an ambivalent creature. We fluctuate in our trust. Within almost the breath of our announcement of trust, we sometimes ask for reassurance, just as David did. He calls out: "Do not, O LORD, withhold your mercy from me" (Psalm 40:11). Why should he even raise such an appeal, when he knows that he is in God's thoughts, and when he recalls how God has watched over him in the past? Because he's a human being, that's why! Don't blame David for his wavering; take heart, because you and I waver at times, too.

I Continue to Trust

When we waver, struggling with issues of trust, we should take hold of the unchanging truth of the character of God, which remains constant despite our fluctuations. Wonderful as our religious experiences may be, they are not the ultimate foundation. The foundation for our trust is rooted in the character of God. David considers again, as he appeals for help, that God's character is one of steadfast love and faithfulness, and that "the LORD takes thought for me" (Psalm 40:17). The hymn to which I referred earlier assures us of this truth in simple but certain terms:

> Let shadows come, let shadows go,
> Let life be bright or dark with woe,
> I am content, for this I know,
> Thou thinkest, Lord, of me!

What an amazing idea: the Lord of the universe, acclaimed by the congregation with the cry "Great is the LORD" (Psalm 40:16) cares about you and me, "poor and needy" as we are (Psalm 40:17). Surely we can trust this great God to be our deliverer. Have no doubt about it. We will live better—far better—if we trust God. We will sing more, with the kind of new song that comes to those who are trusting. We will be a better witness, too, because we will have so many experiences to witness about when we learn how to trust God, even in the risky situations. When we enjoy a trusting relationship with God, we will find ourselves living on a reasonably even keel, not because life is so regular and not because we are so stable, but because we are trusting a good foundation: the character of God.

SHARING THE SCRIPTURE

PREPARING TO TEACH

All of our lessons this quarter are down-to-earth and practical because both James and Psalms are such daily life kinds of books. This lesson is no exception. Most people know what it is to have life experiences where trust is put to the test, and where they learn how to trust.

As you read the scripture lesson and the material under "Focusing on the Main Question," consider how big a part trust plays in your own life. Marriage, business, the whole political system, all human relationships, in fact, are built on trust.

As you plan this week, consider how the erosion of trust in our government, institutions (including the church), and interpersonal relationships has rent a tear in our social fabric. Ponder how this lack of trust in persons and institutions affects our ability to trust God.

Have hymnals available if you plan to sing.

Have paper and pencils on hand.

LEADING THE CLASS

Introduction

Begin today's session by noting that this lesson meets us where we live because trust is an issue in everyday life.

If your class prefers a lecture, read or retell the information under "Focusing on the Main Question," being sure to refer to such common terms as "trust officer" and "I trust you." Include comments in your lecture on the role trust plays in our personal, social, political, and economic lives, and seek to establish a connection with the trust we have in God.

If the class enjoys discussion, ask these questions: **(1) When you think of the word "trust," what words or phrases come to mind? (2) Although trust plays a major role in our personal, social, political, and economic lives, many persons would argue that the level of trust in other persons and institutions has greatly eroded in our society. Do you agree with that perception? Give reasons to support your answer.**

Link your lecture or discussion with the scripture lesson by pointing out that while our human experiences with trust may not be completely satisfactory, the psalmist assures us that we can always trust God, even when we are sinking in a pit of despair. In fact, our trust in God is very often shaped and reinforced by our experiences in life's pits.

Be sure to state today's main question: **How do I put my trust in God, especially when I feel myself sinking in a perilous pit?**

I Was Delivered

After reading the two opening verses of today's psalm as a class, see if anyone might recall a song ("He Brought Me Out"), which now rarely appears in hymnbooks, the chorus of which is built on verses two and three of Psalm 40: "He bro't me out of the miry clay, He set my feet on the Rock to stay." Perhaps someone who is familiar with the hymn could sing what he or she remembers of it.

Ask the class to list kinds of pits they have known, or that they have seen in the lives of others. Help students to recognize that we learn to trust in God as we see God meet our needs in the everyday experiences of life.

As noted under "Understanding the Scripture," in Psalm 40:2 there is a sharp difference between the consistency of the miry bog and the rock. This figurative difference is reflected in our feelings when we are in and out of life's pits as well. Ask the class members to complete these two sentence stems, either in writing or by talking with a partner or small group:

(1) When I am in the pit of confusion or despair, I feel . . . .

(2) When I have been delivered from such a pit, I feel . . . .

Now I Am Happy

Ask a student to read Psalm 40:3-5.

Note that the psalmist responded to his deliverance with a song. Religious experience, whether that of an individual believer or an entire congregation in the midst of a spiritual renewal, almost always leads to singing. Ask your class to name a hymn that is related to some special memory of God's faithfulness in their lives. If possible in your setting, you may want to sing one verse of one or more of these hymns.

If your class enjoys creative activities, challenge them to select a familiar hymn tune and write their own songs of praise to fit the tune. This work could be done alone, but it may be easier and more meaningful if students work with partners or small groups. Perhaps one person in each group could polish the hymn and have it reproduced so as to be available next week for the class to sing.

Note the word "happy" (or "blessed") in today's key verse, Psalm 40:4. The psalmist, who a short time ago was living in a pit, now is standing on a rock and is happy. All persons who trust in the Lord have reason for happiness as well. Ask the class: **(1) How would you rate the level of joy in contemporary Christianity? On what observations do you base your answer? (2) If Christians seem unhappy, what might be at the root of their unhappiness?** (A key to this answer is also in verse 4: Those who put their trust in the Lord are neither arrogant nor seeking after false gods.)

I'm Telling Others of My Joy

Choose someone to read Psalm 40:9-11.

Ask students to rate their answers to the following questions on a scale of one to five, with one meaning "I completely disagree" and five meaning "I completely agree." Provide paper and pencils if you want class members to write the questions and record their answers.

(1) I tend to be rather cautious about sharing my faith with others.

(2) I feel more comfortable talking about my favorite team or soap opera than I do about witnessing to the love and faithfulness of God.

(3) My attitude toward sharing my faith with others has been influenced by friends or family members who have shared their faith with me.

(4) My attitude toward sharing my faith has been influenced by strangers, especially persons who come knocking on my door.

These matters are private, so do not ask for students to discuss their answers. Conclude this activity by asking class members to consider this week how they might become more comfortable in sharing their faith with others if they do not feel confident in doing so now.

Discuss these questions with the class as a whole, or in small groups:

(1) How does one share the joy of answered prayer without seeming self-righteous?

(2) What can the church do to help us feel more confident about sharing our faith?

(3) Without mentioning names, describe someone from your experience whose faith is so radiant that it is persuasive. Why does this person seem so persuasive?

(4) Since we are told that the redeemed of the Lord should say so, does our caution in speaking of our redemption raise questions as to its reality and effectiveness in our lives?

I Continue to Trust

Direct the class's attention to Psalm 40:16-17.

Point out that the Christian life is a journey, not a single event. Sometimes our emphasis on religious experience makes it seem that once we've had some notable experience, nothing afterward matters, or at least that it will all take care of itself. We might have gotten such an impression from the opening portion of this psalm if it were not for its conclusion. The psalmist again needs to be delivered, this time from his enemies. He calls upon God because he trusts God to deliver him. David is once again confessing his poverty and his need in Psalm 40:17. God's thought for him to which he testified in verse 5 is now an expression of hope and faith.

Ask the class: **How would you distinguish between "trust" and "faith"?** This question is difficult because the two words are close kin. Here is one way to draw a distinction: A seminary professor used to remind us that faith is a noun; it has no verb form. "Trust" is the best verb for "faith"; trust, so to speak, is faith in action. When I trust you, I'm putting faith in you. When we trust God, it is an act of faith.

Focus on the issue of our continuing need to trust God, especially as new problems present themselves and old ones recur. Provide an opportunity for persons to share brief stories of instances where an answer to prayer was followed by another appeal—either a recurrence of the old need, or a completely new problem. Ask the class: **(1) Did this additional problem cause a crisis of faith? (2) Is something wrong with our faith when we have to deal with problems a second or third time?**

Close this segment with a prayer that emphasizes seeking God's help for those whose difficult circumstances compel them to trust in special ways.

HELPING CLASS MEMBERS ACT

Urge class members to find an opportunity in the coming week to speak of their trust in God, preferably to a friend.

Invite students to make a list of pits they have been in during the last year or so. Have them consider how God delivered (or is in the process of delivering) them from these pits. How did these experiences increase their trust in God? Suggest that students record their thoughts in a spiritual journal.

Challenge class members to think about David's observation that they are in God's thoughts and to consider the difference this knowledge of God's concern for them makes in their daily routine. Have students try to call this point to mind when they are in the midst of a difficult situation.

PLANNING FOR NEXT SUNDAY

Next week's lesson is from the longest chapter in the Bible, Psalm 119. Challenge your class to read the entire 176 verses, and to notice that every verse (with just two exceptions) refers specifically to the law of God and its importance in our lives. Our lesson will focus on Psalm 119:1-16, 45, 105, and 129-130.

VALUING GOD'S WORD

PREVIEWING THE LESSON

Lesson Scripture: Psalm 119:1-16, 45, 105, 129-130
Background Scripture: Psalm 119:1-16, 45, 105, 129-130
Key Verse: Psalm 119:105

Focus of the lesson:
the happiness of persons who treasure and obey God's Word

Main question(s) of the lesson:
(1) What value does the Bible have in our own lives?

This lesson will enable adult learners to:
(1) believe that God's Word is the foundation for true happiness
(2) affirm the value of the Bible in their own lives
(3) respond by committing themselves to reading and acting upon God's Word.

Today's lesson may be outlined as follows:
(1) Introduction
(2) The Happy Way (Psalm 119:1-3)
(3) The Steadfast Way (Psalm 119:4-8)
(4) The Way of Purity (Psalm 119:9-16)
(5) The Way of Freedom (Psalm 119:45)
(6) A Way that Makes Sense (Psalm 119:129-130, 105)

FOCUSING ON THE MAIN QUESTION

John Bunyan, that remarkable, self-taught tinker and itinerant mender who gave literature one of its enduring classics in *Pilgrim's Progress*, said of the Bible, "I have sometimes seen more in a line of the Bible than I could well tell how to stand under, yet at another time the whole Bible hath been to me as dry as a stick." With those words Bunyan effectively summarized our mixed response to this book for which people over the ages have given their lives. Although buyers keep it on the world's best-seller list, few of them seem to read the Bible regularly. In countries where it has been virtually forbidden for more than a generation, people go to any lengths to get a copy, but in many homes it is taken off the shelf only on ceremonial occasions.

How much do we value God's Word? Some unknown ancient writer—or perhaps several writers—spent a great deal of time putting together a poem that is dedicated to the praise of God's Word.

Those writers may have had in mind only the first five books of what we now call the Old Testament, known as the Pentateuch, or books of the Law. But when my fifth grade Sunday school teacher required us to memorize a verse from that psalm—"Thy word have I hid in mine heart, that I might not sin against thee" (119:11, KJV)—she intended us to think of the whole Bible, including the New Testament. I don't think she was wrong in doing so, and I suggest that as we study this lesson together, we do the same. The beauty that the long-ago psalmist found especially in the books of the Law is found for many of us throughout the sixty-six books of the Bible. This book has blessed and nourished us, and guided us through life. We're confident it will do the same for any who will read it seriously and faithfully.

As we approach this week's lesson, we will want to ask ourselves: **What value does the Bible have in our own lives?**

READING THE SCRIPTURE

NRSV
Psalm 119:1-16

1 Happy are those whose way is
        blameless,
    who walk in the law of the
        LORD.
2 Happy are those who keep his
        decrees,
    who seek him with their whole
        heart,
3 who also do no wrong,
    but walk in his ways.
4 You have commanded your
        precepts
    to be kept diligently.
5 O that my ways may be steadfast
    in keeping your statutes!
6 Then I shall not be put to
        shame,
    having my eyes fixed on all
        your commandments.
7 I will praise you with an upright
        heart,
    when I learn your righteous
        ordinances.
8 I will observe your statutes;
    do not utterly forsake me.

9 How can young people keep
        their way pure?
    By guarding it according to
        your word.

NIV
Psalm 119:1-16

1 Blessed are they whose ways are
        blameless,
    who walk according to the law of the LORD.

2 Blessed are they who keep his statutes
    and seek him with all their heart.

3 They do nothing wrong;
    they walk in his ways.
4 You have laid down precepts
    that are to be fully obeyed.

5 Oh, that my ways were steadfast
    in obeying your decrees!
6 Then I would not be put to shame
    when I consider all your commands.

7 I will praise you with an upright heart
    as I learn your righteous laws.

8 I will obey your decrees;
    do not utterly forsake me.

9 How can a young man keep his way pure?
    By living according to your word.

¹⁰With my whole heart I seek you;
    do not let me stray from your
       commandments.
¹¹I treasure your word in my
     heart,
    so that I may not sin against
     you.
¹²Blessed are you, O LORD;
    teach me your statutes.
¹³With my lips I declare
    all the ordinances of your
     mouth.
¹⁴I delight in the way of your
     decrees
    as much as in all riches.
¹⁵I will meditate on your precepts,
    and fix my eyes on your ways.
¹⁶I will delight in your statutes;
    I will not forget your word.

Psalm 119:45
⁴⁵I shall walk at liberty,
    for I have sought your
     precepts.

Psalm 119:105

Key Verse

¹⁰⁵Your word is a lamp to my feet
    and a light to my path.

Psalm 119:129-130
¹²⁹Your decrees are wonderful;
    therefore my soul keeps them.
¹³⁰The unfolding of your words
     gives light;
    it imparts understanding to the
     simple.

¹⁰I seek you with all my heart;
    do not let me stray from your commands.
¹¹I have hidden your word in my heart
    that I might not sin against you.

¹²Praise be to you, O LORD;
    teach me your decrees.
¹³With my lips I recount
    all the laws that come from your mouth.
¹⁴I rejoice in following your statutes
    as one rejoices in great riches.

¹⁵I meditate on your precepts
    and consider your ways.
¹⁶I delight in your decrees;
    I will not neglect your word.

Psalm 119:45
⁴⁵I will walk about in freedom,
    for I have sought out your precepts.

Psalm 119:105
¹⁰⁵Your word is a lamp to my feet
    and a light for my path.

Psalm 119:129-130
¹²⁹Your statutes are wonderful;
    therefore I obey them.
¹³⁰The unfolding of your words gives light;
    it gives understanding to the simple.

UNDERSTANDING THE SCRIPTURE

Psalm 119. Some of the most remarkable features of Psalm 119 (the longest chapter in the Bible) are lost to us in translation. Many of our Bibles have headings throughout this psalm, and virtually all show the psalm in eight-verse segments. These headings (*aleph, beth, gimel* and so on) are the twenty-two letters of the Hebrew alphabet.

If we were reading the Hebrew, we would see that each of the eight verses in the first unit begin with *aleph,* while each of the next eight begin with *beth,* and so on through the alphabet. In other words, this psalm is a very complete acrostic.

The theme of this psalm, as we have already noted, is the Word of God; specifically, the Law. Each of the 176 verses, with the exception of verses 122 and 132, has some synonym for law—such as word, statute, commandment, or judgment. It's difficult to find a common sub-theme within any part of the psalm, but there's no doubt about its overriding emphasis: a loving testimony to the beauty of God's law.

Psalm 119:1. Happy (or blessed) is established in Psalm 1 as the key word of the Psalms. The first psalm declares that the secret of such happiness is in walking in the way of righteousness rather than in the counsel of the ungodly. In Psalm 119 the writer tells us the secret of the right way: the law of the Lord. Law is understood to mean guidance or teaching or instruction. The verb "walk" is the very symbol of steady, unspectacular progress, and is often used as a symbol of the life of faith.

Psalm 119:2-8. The word "law" is used in verse 1, but notice the variety of synonyms in the verses that follow in the first stanza (*aleph*): decrees, ways, precepts, statutes, commandments, and ordinances.

Psalm 119:9-16. The second stanza continues the theme of the first by asking God's help in observing the Law aright.

Psalm 119:9. Some commentators have reasoned that this psalm was written by a young person because of the reference in this verse. It seems more likely, however, that it was written by an older person as a manual of instruction for the young. It appears to reflect a lifetime of thinking on the Law.

Psalm 119:10. The Bible uses "heart" not so much as the seat of the emotions, as we do, but more as the total person, involving particularly the mind. When the Hebrews spoke of the emotions, they used the terms bowels or kidneys. You see the wisdom of their language when you think of a phrase we often employ when something affects us deeply; we say, "It hit me right in the pit of my stomach."

Psalm 119:45. "At liberty" can also be translated "at large." The psalmist sees the godly life as one that leads a person into wide, large places. "Large" is used several times in the Bible to describe the good life, emphasizing its abundance and freedom.

Psalm 119:105. This verse, which is today's key verse, is probably one of the most memorized in the Bible. Describing God's Word as a "lamp to my feet and a light to my path" is a most appropriate figure of speech for the Holy Land, where every step is in the midst of sand, rocks, and stones. Without light, not a single step is safe.

Psalm 119:129. The psalmist praises the Law. He observes God's decrees because they are wonderful. This verse is the first one in the stanza entitled with the Hebrew letter *pe*. It includes not only praise for the Law but also a prayer for deliverance from enemies.

Psalm 119:130. The psalmist uses the image of light, and with it a definition for light: understanding. To understand, in a biblical sense, is more than simply having knowledge; it includes the inward grasping of data, followed by a pattern of conduct that is changed by the knowledge.

INTERPRETING THE SCRIPTURE

The Happy Way

I confess that I have had a lifelong love affair with the Bible. As with many love affairs, part of it is sentiment. I picture the Bible that was in the living room in my childhood, and the one I earned as a nine- or ten-year-old by memorizing Bible verses; I remember Laura Oslo, the Sunday school teacher who gave it to me.

Beginning at age eleven, when I read the Bible through for the first time, and in the fifty-plus years since then, the Bible has won its place in my heart by its power, its beauty, and its unceasing inspiration. I won't tell you that I love Ezekiel's measurements of the temple (Ezekiel 40) as much as I do Paul's Letter to the Philippians, but I treat those measurements with respect because I have seen the impact of the Bible on my own life and on the lives of ten thousands of others—many of them my personal friends and untold others known to me through history or correspondence.

So I'm ready to say amen to all the affirmations of Psalm 119. I do, indeed, value God's Word.

It may be a little harder, however, to grasp fully the psalmist's enthusiasm for the portion of God's Word that he particularly cherished, the Law of the Lord. Who falls in love with a law book, other than those who make their living by the law? How can a person feel such a flow of gladness over statutes, commandments, and decrees? Why would he or she (or they) want to write 176 verses in an intricate acrostic form in order to say how much God's law means to them?

From a purely pragmatic point of view, the writer is convinced that God's law is the way to happiness. "Happy are those," he begins, "whose way is blameless," and he knows that such a blameless quality is possible only for those "who walk in the law of the LORD." The Psalmist underlines that conviction in the second verse: "Happy are those who keep his decrees."

The Steadfast Way

The notion that one who keeps God's law is happy is heard skeptically by a generation that has lived on a rather steady diet of self-indulgence. Discipline is not one of the favorite words of our time. But the psalmist clearly has a point. Life is so much more manageable when it has boundaries. Without stoplights and speed limits, travel would be virtually impossible. Restraints guide us, keep us on track, direct our powers, and prevent disaster. A

coach says of a young athlete, "He'll be a better player when he's more disciplined." The poet becomes more productive when he or she learns the rules of structure. We need boundaries, for the sake of both the other party and for our own sense of worth and fulfillment.

When we cross those boundaries, we sin. The psalmist was clearly aware of that danger. He knew, for one thing, that sin would in time put him "to shame" (Psalm 119:6), a state the ancients despised more fiercely than we do. But far worse, sin would separate him from God; above all he wanted to be sure that God would not "utterly forsake" him (Psalm 119:8). His relationship with God was so essential that he wanted nothing to interfere with it.

The Way of Purity

To guard against a breach in his relationship with God, the psalmist asks: "How can young people keep their way pure?" (Psalm 119:9). Purity probably seems like an old-fashioned word to many, but when we think of the numerous kinds of conduct, conversation, reading matter, and entertainment that corrupt our minds, it's easy to see that purity is not only worth pursuing, it is difficult to obtain. To the psalmist, the pursuit is not only worthwhile, but it brings him "delight" (Psalm 119:14). He seeks God with his whole being: fixing his eyes on God's way, treasuring God's words in his heart, declaring them with his lips, and meditating on them in his mind.

The Way of Freedom

The pure way is liberating, as well as delightful. The psalmist recognizes that the Law does not, at its best, bind us, but that it sets us "at large." Reading Psalm 119:45, one thinks of George Matheson's hymn lines: "Make me a captive, Lord, and then I shall be free." All of us are under some dominion or other—fads, public opinion, glands, ambition—and most of these forces are not consciously chosen; they simply grow around us or are imposed by others. The person who chooses—really chooses—to be a disciple of God and of the Word has a wonderful sense of liberty. If we are captives, it is by choice, and that makes all the difference. H. L. Mencken, probably the most notable curmudgeon of this century, was speaking somewhat cynically when he said, "Say what you like about the Ten Commandments, you must always come back to the pleasant truth that there are only ten of them." He was wiser than he knew. Those who try to live outside God's law find themselves bound by ten thousand confusions and frustrations because they are missing the point of living.

The psalmist sensed, as did the prophets in another way, that there is an order in our universe, and if we cooperate with it, we have a much happier time of life. It's when we insist on flying in the face of this order that life becomes irrational and unbearable. Sadly, proof of this precept is all around us as we see lives shattered by persons who insisted that they "do it my way."

A Way That Makes Sense

The various writers of the Psalms were realistic about life. They confess that life is at times a struggle, and they are distressed that the wicked prosper while the godly seem sometimes to suffer. In other words, they acknowledge that life on this earth is often difficult. When Norman Vincent Peale was criticized for his emphasis on positive thinking, his defense was that since this is such an awful world, and we're stuck with it, he was just simply trying to help people make the best of it. In this psalm, the writer is convinced that the surest way to "make the best of it" was by immersing himself in God's Word, particularly the Law. The pathway through this world is often enough confusing, but the law will give light, and it will impart "understanding to the simple" (Psalm 119:130).

The psalmist is no doubt a scholar in his own right. He shows as much by his love of the Law as by the artistry with which he writes about it. But he studies the Law, not as a scholar but as a hungry soul. He wants nourishment for his whole being. The ultimate value of the Law, he knows, is not in being able to quote its precepts but in being nourished by its truth.

On occasions I have lectured about the importance of the Bible in the shaping of Western literature, and its influence upon art and law and public policy. It's an easy case to make, and one that our ultra secular society needs to hear. But I have come to realize that the ultimate importance of the Scriptures has little to do with their literary value as such; their role is to transform and nurture life, and to lead readers into that which is eternal. I think the writer of this psalm understood that.

The people of Israel had a sense of community that is almost unknown to us. They saw themselves as part of a people rather than simply as individuals. That's why it is all the more significant that today's key verse, Psalm 119:105, is written in the first person singular: "a lamp to my feet and a light to my path." There is a great deal of the first person singular throughout the book of Psalms, but I think a point can rightly be made here. As important as the Scriptures are to the preservation of society as a whole, their significance begins with us as individuals. It is my feet and my path, and your feet and your path to which we must give attention. If each of us renews and sustains his or her commitment to the Scriptures, and if we allow the Book to work effectively in our lives, its influence will eventually be felt in the nation as a whole. But the valuing of God's Word must begin with you and me. Not in classrooms or legal decisions or the media, important as all these are, but in our individual lives. The transformation begins in us—in you and in me.

SHARING THE SCRIPTURE

PREPARING TO TEACH

If you are to teach a lesson on valuing God's Word, you need to begin by looking at your own attitude toward the Scriptures. Ask yourself: How important is the Bible in my life? How much do I read it? How regularly? Do I understand and share the excitement the psalmist feels as he speaks of God's Word? How would I describe my own personal history with God's Word?

If you have a book of quotations, you might want to look up some quotations about the Bible. One that reflects something of the mood of Psalm 119 would be especially meaningful to the class; it might seem to bring the psalm up to date. If you do not have such a book, consider using the quote from John Bunyan under "Focusing on the Main Question," or this quotation by the eighteenth-century German philosopher, Immanuel Kant: "The existence of the Bible is the greatest blessing which humanity has ever experienced."

Last week we urged the class to read not simply the assigned verses, but the entire chapter—all 176 verses! You'll want to do so too. Since the whole psalm is on the same theme, it may at times seem repetitive; I urge you to read slowly and meditatively so that you will be captured by the devotion and excitement of the psalmist.

Decide whether you will stage the debate as suggested under "A Way That Makes Sense."

If the hymnals you have include Psalm 119 with a sung response, consider using it in an appropriate place in the lesson. Portions of this psalm, with sung responses from verses 45 and 105, are found on pages 840-843 in *The United Methodist Hymnal*.

LEADING THE CLASS

Introduction

Announce the main question for today's lesson: **What value does the Bible have in our own lives?**

Ask students to think about their own personal history with the Bible. If the class is small, invite each one to tell when they got their first Bible, and from whom. If the class is large, ask them to share that information with the person next to them. Then invite several persons with "special" stories to share with the class as a whole.

Now read several of the quotations you've found to show how others have felt about the Bible. Class members may want to respond to these quotations.

Our generation is blessed with a wide variety of translations; see how many you have in your class today. Some students may want to say why they prefer a particular translation.

Note that despite the Bible's continuing best-seller status, many persons feel that people today don't know the Bible as well as their parents and grandparents did. Ask the class: **Do you agree? If so, why do you think this is so?**

Use the information under "Understanding the Scripture" to talk about the background of Psalm 119, its structure, and its emphasis on the love of God's Word, particularly the Law.

The Happy Way

Invite the class to brainstorm words or phrases to complete this sentence as they think most Americans would: Happy people are ones who _____.
List their answers on a chalkboard or newsprint.

Direct the class's attention to Psalm

119:1-3. Ask the class: **How does the psalmist define happiness?** Now ask them to review the list they made and put an asterisk next to definitions that the writer of Psalm 119 would find acceptable. Ask the class: **(1) What conclusions can you draw as you compare these lists? (2) Would you say your own understanding of happiness is more defined by modern society or by the Bible?**

The Steadfast Way

Select a volunteer to read Psalm 119:4-8.

Note that the psalmist recognized that his chance for being steadfast lay in keeping God's statutes. He relied on the Word of God as his sole criterion for determining his attitudes and actions. Point out that we often find our ideas swayed by opinion polls, the media, and current fads. Ask the class:

(1) What criteria do you use to determine whether a certain behavior or attitude is acceptable for you as a Christian?

(2) How do you deal with persons who try to convince you to follow the latest trends which, in your mind, amount to the same old sins?

(3) How does the Bible enable you to remain steadfast in God's way?

The Way of Purity

Choose someone to read Psalm 119:9-16.

Spend a few moments thinking about the psalmist's concern with purity in Psalm 119:9. Note that in verses 14 and 16 he uses the word "delight" to describe his response to this pure, disciplined living.

Point out that the pure way is a clearly focused way. If time permits, ask the class to look at Matthew 6:19-21. Ask the students: **In what ways does Jesus' teaching reflect the psalmist's single-minded approach to the things of God?** (You may want to note the use of the words "treasure" and "heart" in both passages. We treasure in our hearts that which is important to us.)

The Way of Freedom

Direct the class's attention to Psalm 119:45.

Ask the group to list some of the phrases and philosophies common to our time that suggest that freedom is to be found in self-centered living. Answers may include terms like, "I'm number one," "Just do it," or "If you've got it, flaunt it." List their ideas on a chalkboard or newsprint. Then ask: **(1) In contrast to the message of total freedom for the individual, what liberty is to be found in abiding by the law of God? (2) How can we make disciplined living attractive to modern young people—or to adults, for that matter?**

A Way That Makes Sense

Look at Psalm 119:129-130 and the key verse, 105.

Note that the people of Israel were devoted to wisdom, but their idea of wisdom was not theoretical knowledge. Instead, they prized a very practical kind of wisdom that manifested itself in effective daily living. Ask the class:

(1) What value does the Bible have for you personally in guiding your daily living?

(2) Does it provide you with the wisdom you need to live in today's world?

(3) Give some examples of this wisdom that are especially valuable to you.

Spend a few moments allowing class members to read or recite favorite scripture passages. If time permits, let each one say a few words about why this verse is so helpful to them.

If your class enjoys creative activities, you may want to stage an informal debate on this topic: The teachings of the Bible are outmoded and therefore do not provide light for us today. (*Note that this topic is phrased negatively because class members are more likely to find themselves in situations where persons are questioning the continuing validity of the Bible, rather than perceiving its life-giving value. Having to deal with this issue from the negative point of view may help class members develop their own witnessing skills as they think of arguments against this view.)*

Psalm 119:105 speaks of God's Word as a lamp and a light. Ask the class: **In your own faith journey (or walk of faith), how does God's Word light the way for you?**

If you have access to *The United Methodist Hymnal*, use pages 840-843 in the Psalter section. Note that of the three sung responses, two use verse 105 and the other uses verse 45. This reading would be an appropriate way to close today's session.

HELPING CLASS MEMBERS ACT

Ask your class members to make a commitment to read the Bible every day in the coming week. Some students will already do this, but others may find they can continue this spiritual discipline if they start with a very short-term commitment of seven days.

Challenge class members to keep track of instances during the week when they were tempted to compromise their own values and beliefs. Ask them to be aware of who or what (perhaps a movie or TV show) initiated the temptation, how they dealt with it, and how God's Word enabled them to avoid this snare.

Encourage class members to think of a child or other person who would enjoy receiving a Bible and to give one to that person. Suggest that they spend some time with this person helping him or her to value the Bible as much as they do.

PLANNING FOR NEXT SUNDAY

Next week's lesson is based on what is probably the best known penitential prayer in all of literature. Encourage your class to read Psalm 51. Ask them to consider what importance they attach to repentance and to believing that they are forgiven.

SEEKING FORGIVENESS

PREVIEWING THE LESSON

Lesson Scripture: Psalm 51:1-13, 17
Background Scripture: Psalm 51
Key Verse: Psalm 51:10

Focus of the lesson:
the human longing to seek forgiveness and live repentantly before God

Main question(s) of the lesson:
(1) How do we seek forgiveness?

This lesson will enable adult learners to:
(1) understand their need of forgiveness and God's desire for persons to repent and
    be forgiven
(2) experience the joy of God's forgiveness and salvation
(3) respond by seeking and offering forgiveness.

Today's lesson may be outlined as follows:
(1) Introduction
(2) I Know My Transgressions (Psalm 51:1-9)
(3) Restore to Me the Joy of Your Salvation (Psalm 51:10-12)
(4) Then Will I Teach Transgressors Your Ways (Psalm 51:13)
(5) A Broken and Contrite Heart (Psalm 51:17)

FOCUSING ON THE MAIN QUESTION

Some say that sin is an outdated subject. They haven't listened to the evening news, or read the morning paper! No subject is so close to our daily lives as sin, and probably no subject is such an issue to our deepest peace of mind. Sin affects our relationship with God, with our fellow human beings, with society at large, and with our own souls. It would be hard to find a more comprehensive problem than that!

Our generation has been particularly adept at finding synonyms for sin that seem to us to be less offensive. As candid as we are about many subjects, this is one that we try to avoid or to treat at a distance. But by whatever name we call it—mistake, error, lapse, poor choice, bad judgment—sin is our problem and we have to face it and cope with it.

How do we do so? Many centuries ago a great soul came up with as insightful and poignant a statement as we're ever likely to find. It's our privilege to study that statement this week. I say "privilege" because as we read Psalm 51 we are not only looking at one of the great masterpieces of literature, we are also being ushered into the private places of a human soul. More important still, as we enter this sacred space, we discover that it is familiar territory. The ancient writer is describing experiences with which we are both painfully and wonderfully familiar. He found his answer in the experience of forgiveness. Modern mental health practice agrees that forgiveness is an essential element in a wholesome outlook on life. Generally, secular attitudes toward mental health are concerned with our ability to forgive ourselves, and as far as this goes, it is a proper concern. But Christian theology—and the Hebrew Scriptures, too—teaches that we aren't ready to forgive ourselves until we sense that God has forgiven us. The question, the huge question, we want to discuss this week is this: **How do we seek forgiveness?**

READING THE SCRIPTURE

NRSV
Psalm 51:1-13
1 Have mercy on me, O God,
     according to your steadfast
          love;
     according to your abundant
          mercy
     blot out my transgressions.
²Wash me thoroughly from my
          iniquity,
     and cleanse me from my sin.

³For I know my transgressions,
     and my sin is ever before me.
⁴Against you, you alone, have I
          sinned,
     and done what is evil in your
          sight,
     so that you are justified in your
          sentence
     and blameless when you pass
          judgment.
⁵Indeed, I was born guilty,
     a sinner when my mother
          conceived me.

⁶You desire truth in the inward
          being;
     therefore teach me wisdom in
          my secret heart.
⁷Purge me with hyssop, and I
          shall be clean;

NIV
Psalm 51:1-13
1 Have mercy on me, O God,
          according to your unfailing love;
according to your great compassion
          blot out my transgressions.

²Wash away all my iniquity
          and cleanse me from my sin.

³For I know my transgressions,
          and my sin is always before me.
⁴Against you, you only, have I sinned
          and done what is evil in your sight,
so that you are proved right when
               you speak
          and justified when you judge.
⁵Surely I was sinful at birth,
          sinful from the time my mother
               conceived me.

⁶Surely you desire truth in the inner parts;
          you teach me wisdom in the inmost place.

⁷Cleanse me with hyssop, and I will be clean;
          wash me, and I will be whiter than snow.

wash me, and I shall be whiter
than snow.
⁸Let me hear joy and gladness;
let the bones that you have
crushed rejoice.
⁹Hide your face from my sins,
and blot out all my iniquities.

⁸Let me hear joy and gladness;
let the bones you have crushed rejoice.

⁹Hide your face from my sins
and blot out all my iniquity.

¹⁰Create in me a clean heart,
O God,
and put a new and right spirit
within me.

¹⁰Create in me a pure heart, O God,
and renew a steadfast spirit within me.

Key
Verse

¹¹Do not cast me away from your
presence,
and do not take your holy
spirit from me.
¹²Restore to me the joy of your
salvation,
and sustain in me a willing
spirit.
¹³Then I will teach transgressors
your ways,
and sinners will return to you.

¹¹Do not cast me from your presence
or take your Holy Spirit from me.

¹²Restore to me the joy of your salvation
and grant me a willing spirit, to sustain me.

¹³Then I will teach transgressors your ways,
and sinners will turn back to you.

Psalm 51:17
¹⁷The sacrifice acceptable to God
is a broken spirit;
a broken and contrite heart,
O God, you will not
despise.

Psalm 51:17
¹⁷The sacrifices of God are a broken spirit;
a broken and contrite heart,
O God, you will not despise.

UNDERSTANDING THE SCRIPTURE

Psalm 51. This psalm of lament is traditionally believed to have been written by David after the prophet Nathan confronted him concerning his adultery with Bathsheba (see 2 Samuel 12:1-25). Some scholars question this belief, though they identify no other author. One thing is very sure: this psalm is the deep cry of some repentant soul, a person who has been profoundly moved by a sense of wrongdoing, and has come to a feeling of divine acceptance and forgiveness.

Psalm 51:1. David builds all his case on the basis of God's steadfast love. This term is the closest the Hebrew Scriptures come to the Christian concept of grace.

Psalm 51:1-2. Notice that the psalmist uses three different nouns for his sin (transgressions, iniquity, sin) and three different verbs in his appeal for God to deal with his sins (blot out, wash, cleanse). Each word has specific significance. Transgression is literally rebellion; iniquity means that which is twisted or bent; and sin means missing a mark. So, too, with the verbs of redemption. Blot out means to erase or remove writing (as in an indictment); wash carries the idea of kneading or beating garments; and cleanse is the technical word for the priestly act of ceremonial purity.

Psalm 51:3-4. David laments his sin, seeking repentance. He recognizes the control that sin has over his life, acknowledges that sin is committed against God, and assumes responsibility for his actions.

Psalm 51:5. David's saying that he was "born guilty" is more a statement of emotion than of theology. He feels his sin so deeply that it seems to him that sin has been part of him from the very moment of his conception. At the same time, let it be said that our conduct is a fact of heredity; from our conception we have "human tendencies" and traits that get us in trouble. Call it what you will, we are born with problems.

Psalm 51:6. The psalmist sees wisdom as part of his solution. This reminds us again of the biblical concept of wisdom as the ability to use life effectively. It is operative, not theoretical, wisdom.

Psalm 51:7. The reference to hyssop was especially significant to a Jew, since the hyssop weed was used in the Passover event, to sprinkle the blood of the lamb on the doorpost (Exodus 12:22). Hyssop was also used in cleansing ceremonies for lepers (Leviticus 14:6). In this psalm, hyssop is used metaphorically, not literally, to cleanse the sinner.

Psalm 51:8-9. David wants to hear the "joy and gladness" of the temple worship. He continues to ask for forgiveness as he pleads with God not to look upon his sins. Whereas the hiding of God's face is usually a sign of divine anger, that metaphor is used here in a positive sense as a sign of God's forgiveness and grace.

Psalm 51:10. When the psalmist asks that God "create" a clean heart for him, the word used is the same one as in Genesis 1:1 at the creation of the heavens and the earth. The Hebrew word indicates creating something out of nothing.

Psalm 51:11. The term "holy spirit" is used in the Hebrew Scriptures only here and in Isaiah 63:10-11. It is not used as Christians would, in referring to the Trinity, but it is a kind of forerunner of that teaching.

Psalm 51:12. Salvation is not used in the New Testament sense, but it surely suggests the beginning of that wondrous concept, including the factor of joy. References such as these in Psalm 51 let us see how some of the Hebrew Scriptures were beginning to anticipate the message of the New Testament.

Psalm 51:13. No one is more likely to "teach transgressors" than the person whose own transgressions have been forgiven. David expects that sinners will return to God when they know God's ways.

Psalm 51:14-15. The psalmist is anxious to sing and praise God when he has been transformed from a state of guilt ("bloodguilt" or "bloodshed") to one of salvation.

Psalm 51:16-17. Here again the writer anticipates a kind of spirituality beyond the system of sacrifices and offerings. I don't think he is suggesting, at this point, that such sacrifices be abandoned, but simply that the issue is in the attitude of the heart more than in the animal sacrifice.

Psalm 51:18-19. These verses were written in the days of the Babylonian exile or the post-exilic period. The walls of the Temple would need to be rebuilt because they had been destroyed by King Nebuchadnezzar's troops in 587-586 B.C.E. Some commentators argue that these verses were a later addition to the psalm, whereas others believe that the entire psalm was written during this period, rather than at the time of David.

INTERPRETING THE SCRIPTURE

I Know My Transgressions

Cyril Connolly, the twentieth-century British critic and essayist, described a great many modern people when he wrote: "Those of us who were brought up as Christians and who have lost our faith have retained the Christian sense of sin without the saving belief in redemption." Psalm 51 is a corrective to that state; it confronts sin with profound seriousness, but it goes on to forgiveness and redemption.

Forgiveness has no meaning, of course, unless there is a sense of wrongdoing. Why seek forgiveness if nothing is wrong, if no harm is done? A good deal of contemporary secular thought has tried to put an end to the concept of sin, but something deep within us knows better. Call it what you will, we know we fall short, or miss the mark, or are twisted, to use some of the biblical words for sin. When we are honest with ourselves, we recognize that all of us are at times guilty of conduct that needs forgiveness. A person who denies this fact is both spiritually dull and personally unbearable.

If our sense of wrongdoing leads only to remorse and soul agony, it has done no real good; in fact, the problem is only compounded. The Christian gospel, when truly presented, leads to both a sense of need and a way of salvation and forgiveness.

The sense of sin in Psalm 51 is intense. If, as tradition says, it was written by David after his sin with Bathsheba and his confrontation by the prophet Nathan, we have some context for understanding the language; David was guilty of adultery, murder, and deception. He had violated not only the lives of Uriah and Bathsheba and his own family, but also the trust of the nation of which he was the adored king. He had reason, indeed, to feel profound remorse.

Anyone who takes life, people, and God seriously has known some comparable feelings of remorse; that's why so many of us read this psalm with a very real sense of ownership. In a sense, there's no other way to read it; it would seem a sacrilege to look at it in a purely academic way. This document is dominated by the first person singular; it is full of the words I, my, and me. A true sense of sin will make us painfully aware of our very own shortcomings before God; as the spiritual puts it, "Not my brother, not my sister, but it's me, O Lord, standing in the need of prayer." Often we attempt to lessen the impact of our sin. If we offer a confession and then look at our neighbor and say, "He's guilty, too," we haven't yet gotten to the heart of the matter. It is not self-centeredness that makes David use the first person singular, but a proper sense of his own guilt. When we realize we are away from God, we know that our only business is to set that relationship right.

Restore to Me the Joy of Your Salvation

This recognition of sin is a huge factor in finding forgiveness; as a matter of fact, we aren't likely to seek forgiveness unless we have a sense of having done wrong. But another element is probably just as important, namely, the desire to mend a relationship. All through this psalm we find woven David's hunger for restored communion with the Almighty. I know of no greater pathos than David's cry, "do not take your holy spirit from me" (Psalm 51:11). He wants one thing above all else: his tie with God.

When we cherish a relationship deeply, we will seek forgiveness even if we aren't fully sure we are at fault. Most of us can think of a time when, in a human relationship, we thought that probably the friend or family had wronged us, but we nevertheless sought their forgiveness. "I really don't care who's right or who's wrong," a man said of a misunderstanding with his aged father. "I only know that I don't want our love to be broken. My feelings about being right aren't worth it." He was correct, of course. I've known some people (as you have, too) who went to their graves being "right," but cut off from someone they once loved.

Of course there's no likelihood, in our relationship with God, that we are right and God is wrong. But sometimes we're upset enough to think so. The driving impulse in seeking forgiveness is the realization that nothing—absolutely nothing—is so important as keeping that communion intact. "Please don't take your Holy Spirit from me," we cry. God wouldn't do that anyway, but we can seem to make it so by our own rebellion or by our self-righteousness.

The goal is "a clean heart" (Psalm 51:10) and with it a relationship in which we have the full "joy of [your] salvation" (Psalm 51:12). We are sometimes reminded that the root meaning of "religion" is "to bind back" or to reunite. When we repent of our wrongdoing, we are bound back to God; and in the process, we are bound back to our own selves. One of our most difficult assignments is to forgive ourselves. Long after God has forgiven us, we must accept ourselves even in our failed state. We frequently demand more of ourselves than God demands of us. This is a perverse kind of pride; we won't allow ourselves to acknowledge that we're not perfect, so we simply won't forgive ourselves. Clinging to this prideful attitude, we can easily miss the joy of our salvation. Too many believers walk about with a heaviness of spirit, almost as if the grace of God were not for them. Too bad! To be forgiven by God is to forgive others—including ourselves.

Then Will I Teach Transgressors Your Ways

If we experience the joy of salvation, we will quite naturally and inevitably share the goodness with transgressors and sinners—people who, like ourselves, have been burdened with guilt. No one is so persuasive of the goodness of God as the person who has accepted that goodness and found it effective. The more we know the joy of forgiveness, the more naturally we share it with others.

Unfortunately, many things prevent our faith-witnessing. Probably the most significant deterrent is an unconscious feeling that we haven't that much to share. I expect this is why those who experience the most dramatic conversions are the most likely to tell others. Persons who grow up in the faith and whose transformation is gradual and even routine are sometimes not certain they have anything to say. If a stranger should ask, "Of what have you been forgiven?" they aren't sure what they would answer. But if we will search our souls, including the places we sometimes hide from even ourselves, we will find abundant reasons to give thanks for the forgiveness we have received. We will realize that it is no small gift.

A Broken and Contrite Heart

Psalm 51:17 reminds us that a right state of heart is an indispensable element in the experience of forgiveness. We are always tempted to think that some ritual or some religious ceremony will restore our communion with God. David pondered the practices of his time and concluded that only one factor really mattered—"a broken and contrite heart." I once heard an evangelist say that religious motions, without righteous emotions, make unacceptable devotions. In other words, there is no secret formula for doing business with God, but only a simple longing—a longing so deep that it seems to break the heart. God finds such human longing irresistible. It is foolish to seek forgiveness without it.

SHARING THE SCRIPTURE

PREPARING TO TEACH

Once again our lesson has to do with a common human experience—one as old, I venture, as the human race. Perhaps this is where our race could first be identified as being human, when we sensed that there was a divine standard of which we had fallen short. The apostle Paul said that we all have sinned, and that not one can claim to be good (see Romans 3:10-12). We have sinned, so we need forgiveness.

Our preparation again begins with some inner searching. Meditate on these questions. If you keep a spiritual journal, you may want to write your responses there. (1) What do I know about forgiveness? (2) What do I remember about feeling forgiven—by God or by a human being? (3) How would I describe that special relief that comes when a broken relationship is re-established?

Reread the story of David and Bathsheba (2 Samuel 11 and 12). Since tradition links Psalm 51 with the prophet Nathan's confrontation of David after his adultery with Bathsheba, we will be helped by recalling the story. Consider especially that David, as an ancient king, could easily have destroyed Nathan when the prophet encountered him. What does David's response say about his willingness to face his shortcomings? How do we respond when someone points out our faults? How does David's reaction relate to the whole experience of forgiveness? Can a person experience forgiveness without acknowledging guilt?

A tremendous amount of human psychology is woven into Psalm 51: the experience of guilt, the need for forgiveness, the hunger for a restored relationship, and the very nature of sin. Think on these subjects, not so much from the point of view of academic psychology but from your experience as a human being and from your knowledge of the experiences of other people.

If you plan to read Psalm 51 responsively, have hymnals available. If you have *The United Methodist Hymnal*, you will find it on pages 785-786. Either sung response would be appropriate.

Have paper and pencils available if you choose to have students write a psalm of lament.

LEADING THE CLASS

Introduction

Begin the class by asking: **Is there anyone here who has never felt guilty?** Perhaps you will want to note that sometimes guilt is imposed upon us and that we at times feel unhealthy guilt, but this experience shouldn't prevent our dealing with the kind of guilt that comes from having done wrong. Guilt, like fear, is an emotion that is intended—if used rightly—to benefit us.

Ask the class about the changing attitudes toward sin. Some of us remember a time when the definition of sin was pretty simple, limited as it was to a few very measurable items. Jesus taught us to look at deeper levels. Ask: **(1) What is happening to the definition of sin in our increasingly secular culture? (2) What are some terms that secular society now uses as substitutes for sin?** Remind the class that though we use different words, the realities remain the same.

Then introduce the concept of forgiveness. Look at both the human and the divine experiences of forgiveness, and also at the issue of forgiving ourselves.

Close this segment by noting that sin is a universal human experience, and that every person needs to experience forgiveness. Our main question for today is: **How do we seek forgiveness?** To answer that

475

question, we will look at one of the most beloved passages of scripture, Psalm 51.

I Know My Transgressions

Look at Psalm 51:1-9. If you have hymnbooks that include a Psalter, read this portion of the psalm responsively.

Note that when David says, "my sin is ever before me" (Psalm 51:3), he describes the kind of experience Edgar Allan Poe used in his story "The Telltale Heart." See if a class member recalls this story, or a novel or play like it which portrays a person unable to escape the memory of a wrongdoing. Ask the class: **How does such a sense of sin and guilt affect us mentally and spiritually?**

Direct the class's attention to the nouns and verbs used in Psalm 51:1-2 to describe sin and its remedy. Use the information under "Understanding the Scripture" to help students understand the nuances of meaning the psalmist uses.

Point out that David is earnestly seeking forgiveness. All of us have had such experiences. The most important of course is our forgiveness from God, but each experience of human forgiveness is in its own way a picture of the divine experience. Ask your class to remember some experience—perhaps from childhood, with a parent or teacher—where a wrongdoing was followed by forgiveness. Recall how the pain of the wrongdoing, and the separation it caused, were healed by someone's act of forgiveness. You may want to do this activity as a silent meditation. Or, you may want to ask volunteers to tell the entire class some brief anecdotes about experiences of forgiveness. If the class is large, invite a class member to share with a partner or small group.

If the class enjoys creative activities, provide a few moments for them to begin working individually on their own psalm of lament. You may need to provide paper and pencils. Set a time limit. Suggest that they finish these psalms at home and use them this week during their devotional time.

Restore to Me the Joy of Your Salvation

Direct the class to look at Psalm 51:10-12.

Note that David is deeply concerned that his relationship with God is broken. He is truly in pain and wants to be restored to the joyful relationship he had once known. To do this, he prays that God will create a clean heart in him. The word "create" used here is the same word used in Genesis 1. The psalmist is not speaking of some minor rearrangement of his spiritual life but of a brand new inner life. Ask the class: **(1) What qualities or characteristics do you think God would put in this new heart? (2) What does the idea of absolute newness of heart—of starting over from scratch—say to you about the power of God's forgiveness?**

Draw a vertical line in the center of a chalkboard or sheet of newsprint. On the left write: I Have Sinned; on the right write: I Am Forgiven. Ask the class to brainstorm ideas as to how they feel in each of these situations. On the left, they will likely list such emotions as guilt, pain, and alienation. On the right, they may use words such as joy, relief, reconciled, or feeling as if a weight has been lifted from me.

Then Will I Teach Transgressors Your Ways

Look at Psalm 51:13, a verse that deals with David's promise to witness.

You may want to read or retell in your own words the information in this section under "Interpreting the Scripture." Note especially reasons suggested for our reluctance to witness. Ask the class: **Why do you or people you know find it difficult to tell other persons about the ways of God?**

Brainstorm with the class some points that they might want to share about God with other persons. You may want to list their ideas on a chalkboard or newsprint. Note that this psalm alone includes many ideas that could be shared, such as:

- the mercy of God
- our sinfulness
- God's desire to forgive and cleanse us
- God's willingness to teach us
- the joy that we feel about our relationship with God
- the importance of sharing God's ways with others

A Broken and Contrite Heart

Look at Psalm 51:17.

In its discussion of Psalm 51, *The Interpreter's One Volume Commentary of the Bible* defines a broken spirit as "one in which the self-assertive craving for autonomy has been shattered and replaced by conformity to God's will." You may want to paraphrase this definition by saying something such as: A broken spirit is one that no longer wants to do things my way but only God's way. Ask the class: **(1) Do you agree with this definition? (2) If you do agree, what does the idea of offering a broken spirit as a sacrifice to God say to us about what God expects from us?**

HELPING CLASS MEMBERS ACT

Challenge students to consider the state of their relationship with God. During their devotional time this week, ask them to pray especially for illumination concerning their sins and to seek God's forgiveness for them.

Ask class members to think of someone from whom they are estranged. Encourage them to offer forgiveness to that person. Such an act will bring joy to both parties.

Encourage each person to share a word of witness to someone who needs to know of God's love and forgiveness.

PLANNING FOR NEXT SUNDAY

Next Sunday will be our last lesson in the book of Psalms. Ask the class to read Psalm 96, and to see what hymns they can recall that reflect a comparable quality of joyful worship.

WORSHIP AND WITNESS

PREVIEWING THE LESSON

Lesson Scripture: Psalm 96
Background Scripture: Psalm 96
Key Verse: Psalm 96:2

Focus of the lesson:
worship and witness as responses to God

Main question(s) of the lesson:
(1) What do the words "worship" and "witness" mean to us?
(2) How can we worship and witness effectively?

This lesson will enable adult learners to:
(1) grasp the importance of both worship and witness
(2) explore their own attitudes toward worship and witness
(3) respond by committing themselves to witness and to participate regularly in worship.

Today's lesson may be outlined as follows:
(1) Introduction
(2) Worship the Lord (Psalm 96:1-9)
(3) Say Among the Nations, "The Lord Is King!" (Psalm 96:10-13)

FOCUSING ON THE MAIN QUESTION

The Christian life is built on three main elements: worship, witness, and service. Not many of us would say we do enough by way of service, but in truth we understand service better than worship or witness. Perhaps it is our activist spirit, or something of our Protestant tradition; in one way or another we are better at grasping the idea of doing something for others (and for God) than at telling others about the goodness of God or engaging ourselves in the worship and adoration of the Almighty.

Although this lesson deals with two of the major elements of the daily Christian life—worship and witness—this is not the familiar and comfortable ground we might expect it to be. That's unfortunate. Worship unlooses qualities in us human beings that cannot be touched in any other way. It is often said that humans are worshiping animals—that is, worship is what makes us different from the rest of the animal kingdom. It is without a doubt our most distinctively human act and also our highest human endeavor. It comes to us so naturally that even a little child or a person of the most limited intelligence can worship. Yet we never grow wise or sensitive enough to comprehend the highest levels of worship. Worship transforms life. Those who worship most faithfully will also, inevitably, serve because when we are closest to God we are most sensitive to all of God's creatures.

When we witness to our faith we honor God and we bless others. A good witness is the most generous of acts because with it we make available to others what has become our dearest treasure, our secret of fulfilled living. Some witnesses have given their lives in order to share the faith they have found; we call them martyrs. But every true act of witnessing bears that quality in some small measure because when we witness we give others a share of our very being.

Worship and witness: What do these words mean to us? How can we worship and witness effectively? These are our main questions for today's study.

READING THE SCRIPTURE

NRSV
Psalm 96
1 O sing to the LORD a new song;
　　sing to the LORD, all the earth.
2 Sing to the LORD, bless his
　　　　name;
　　tell of his salvation from day
　　　　to day.
3 Declare his glory among the
　　　　nations,
　　his marvelous works among all
　　　　the peoples.
4 For great is the LORD, and
　　　　greatly to be praised;
　　he is to be revered above all
　　　　gods.
5 For all the gods of the peoples
　　　　are idols,
　　but the LORD made the
　　　　heavens.
6 Honor and majesty are before
　　　　him;
　　strength and beauty are in his
　　　　sanctuary.

7 Ascribe to the LORD, O families
　　　　of the peoples,
　　ascribe to the LORD glory and
　　　　strength.
8 Ascribe to the LORD the glory
　　　　due his name;

NIV
Psalm 96
1 Sing to the LORD a new song;
　　sing to the LORD, all the earth.
2 Sing to the LORD, praise his name;
　　proclaim his salvation day after day.

3 Declare his glory among the nations,
　　his marvelous deeds among all peoples.

4 For great is the LORD and most worthy of
　　　　praise;
　　he is to be feared above all gods.

5 For all the gods of the nations are idols,
　　but the LORD made the heavens.

6 Splendor and majesty are before him;
　　strength and glory are in his sanctuary.

7 Ascribe to the LORD, O families of
　　　　nations,
　　ascribe to the LORD glory and strength.

8 Ascribe to the LORD the glory due his name;
　　bring an offering and come into his courts.

Key
Verse

AUGUST 25

⁹Worship the LORD in holy
        splendor;
    tremble before him, all the
        earth.

¹⁰Say among the nations, "The
        LORD is king!
    The world is firmly
        established; it shall never
        be moved.
    He will judge the peoples with
        equity."
¹¹Let the heavens be glad, and let
        the earth rejoice;
    let the sea roar, and all that
        fills it;
¹²let the field exult, and
        everything in it.
Then shall all the trees of the
        forest sing for joy
¹³before the LORD; for he is
        coming,
    for he is coming to judge the
        earth.
    He will judge the world with
        righteousness,
    and the peoples with his truth.

bring an offering, and come
        into his courts.
⁹Worship the LORD in the splendor of his
        holiness;
    tremble before him, all the earth.

¹⁰Say among the nations, "The LORD reigns."
    The world is firmly established, it cannot
        be moved;
    he will judge the peoples with equity.

¹¹Let the heavens rejoice, let the earth be glad;
    let the sea resound, and all that is in it;

¹²let the fields be jubilant, and everything
        in them.
Then all the trees of the forest will sing for joy;

¹³they will sing before the LORD, for he comes,
        he comes to judge the earth.
    He will judge the world in righteousness
        and the peoples in his truth.

UNDERSTANDING THE SCRIPTURE

Psalm 96. This psalm has no particular problems of scholarship and no difficulties of interpretation. It is a straightforward expression of praise to God that would have been used as a hymn of worship. Psalm 96 is referred to as an enthronement or coronation psalm because it celebrates the sovreignty of God. We have no tradition as to its authorship or its circumstances of writing, but it appears almost exactly in 1 Chronicles 16:23-33 as the song Asaph and his family sang at the re-installation of the Ark of the Covenant in Israel.

Psalm 96:1. A new day and new revelations of the glory of God call for a new song. This verse, along with verses 2 and 3, calls the people to worship God.

Psalm 96:2. We often use the name of God to bless others, as when we say, "God bless you"; here the psalmist blesses God. It is quite awesome to think that we human beings can "bless" the Eternal; it puts a high value on our praise and on our person. The psalmist also calls us to proclaim God's salvation.

Psalm 96:3. Most of the coronation psalms—that is, those that praise God as King—celebrate God's reign over Israel. This psalm includes all the nations of the earth in its scope. The word for nations or peoples conveys the idea of all persons, including Gentiles.

Psalm 96:4. The Hebrew Scriptures readily acknowledged that there are many gods—as many as people choose to worship. However, Israel's God is to be revered above all others.

Psalm 96:5. "Idols" is sometimes translated "nothings." Isaiah uses this term often in his writings (see for example, Isaiah 40:18-20). The psalmist is drawing a dramatic parallel when he notes that the foreign gods are idols whereas the Lord made the heavens; he is saying that the other gods are themselves created things (made by those who worship them) while the Lord is the Creator.

Psalm 96:6. Honor, majesty, strength, and beauty are pictured as servants standing in the presence of the Lord. A commentator has noted that "strength and beauty are often separated in our disordered world," but in a perfect world they are joined and blended.

Psalm 96:7. All the "families of the peoples" are commanded to glorify God. When we "ascribe to the LORD glory and strength," we are recognizing God as supreme.

Psalm 96:8. This use of the "name" of the Lord reminds us again that the name of the Lord is synonymous with the divine character. The people are commanded to come into the temple and worship. They are to not to come empty-handed but to bring offerings. An offering is a necessary element of worship.

Psalm 96:9. Persons are to come to worship in "holy splendor," meaning that they are to be wearing ceremonial garments. Not only is humanity to worship the Lord; the created universe is to offer praise as well.

Psalm 96:10. "The LORD is king!" is the cry of the coronation psalm that is now proclaimed to all nations. Because of the Hebrew belief in the justice of God, one of the major reasons for worshiping God was judgment. God's judgments, the writer reminds us, are "with equity."

Psalm 96:11-13. Now the writer enlarges his scope still further, calling on all of nature—heavens, earth, sea, fields, trees—to declare the glory of the Eternal King. At this point the psalm takes on a kind of millennial quality, as all of creation joins in the recognition and joyous praise of God. The psalmist returns to the theme of the Lord as judge; he finds great joy in noting that God will "judge the earth," and this judgment will be with righteousness and truth.

INTERPRETING THE SCRIPTURE

Worship the Lord

Psalm 96 calls all persons—indeed the entire creation—to sing praises of worship unto the Lord. It also summons those who know God to witness to God's glory. These are critically important matters for us. Yet, when we try to discuss such themes as worship and witness, we are up against a serious problem because the terms are so poorly understood. The words are common enough, of course, but most people—including many churchgoers—have few real pictures in their minds.

For vast numbers of people, almost anything seems to pass for worship. Novelist Aldous Huxley said of his father that he "considered a walk among the mountains as the equivalent of church-going." You can add to Huxley's number the people who think a Sunday morning on the golf course or on a trout stream to be a religious experience.

Some feel that way about the symphony, or a poetry reading, or an evening with friends. I surely don't want to discredit any of these wonderful experiences, some of which mean a great deal to me personally; but I want to be sure we don't make the tent of worship so broad that it becomes meaningless. Our times are inclined that way—probably because we know so little about worship in its truest, highest form.

Worship is more than simply feeling good; it is more even than a sense of awe. It involves our relationship to God, and anything less misses the point entirely. The late great Archbishop of Canterbury, William Temple, has suggested that in worship our consciences are made sensitive to the holiness of God, our minds are nourished with God's truth, our imaginations are purged by God's beauty, and our wills are directed to God's purposes. In other words, God is the issue, not my emotions or my sense of the aesthetic. Worship ought surely to lead to nobler, more purposeful living. Its main purpose is to declare the glory of God, for the focus of our worship is God.

See the excitement and the gladness in Psalm 96! This writer has experienced God in such a way that he insists on a new song; no old song will do. His joy is so great that he can hardly find words or concepts to convey it. Forgive him if he seems to put down the gods of other nations; he simply can't imagine being satisfied with a god you must carve from a tree when his God carves the heavens out of nothingness. And if you're wanting a processional worthy of such a God, the psalmist sees honor, majesty, strength, and beauty marching into the sanctuary.

His exuberance is so great that he turns at last to nature, sensing that nature has a voice more varied than his own. I once heard a major symphony orchestra play Beethoven's "Ode to Joy," with an opera chorus singing. That scene and sound come to mind as the psalmist marshals his

concert: the earth rejoicing, the sea roaring, the fields exulting, the trees of the forest singing—can you imagine such a concert? The unknown writer imagines it because he is desperate to find a scene that will seem worthy of the worship of the Lord of the universe.

In the past decade or two we have seen a number of new emphases on worship. They range all the way from the freedom of the charismatic to those who are returning to ancient Catholic or Orthodox rituals in hope of adding new dimensions to their worship. I honor the hunger that inspires such a quest, and I'm glad for those instances where fulfillment is found. But with it all I remind myself that the most significant elements in worship have little to do with liturgy or the other trappings, beautiful as they might be. The ultimate issue of our worship of God has to do with the state of our souls.

Worship is not simply a matter of the soul's goodness or righteousness. Sometimes we seek God best when we are most conscious of our shortcomings (as we sensed in our study of Psalm 51), and we enter most fully into the adoration of God when we are most conscious of the degree to which we have been forgiven, like the woman who washed the feet of Jesus with her tears (Luke 7:36-50). In any event, the most crucial element in effective worship is our desire for God and our hunger to worship and adore. No ritual, no choir, no incense or processional or elements of beauty can take the place of this.

Say Among the Nations, "The Lord Is King!"

If we are unsure how to worship as we ought, we are equally uncertain about the call to witness. Our problem with witnessing probably springs from instances where we think it has been done badly, and we are so anxious to avoid such a style of witnessing that we do not witness at all.

At their best, the Israelites knew that they were to tell the whole world of the glory of God. Like us, they didn't always succeed. Often they became so obsessed with maintaining their purity and isolation, that they seemed at times to look upon their role as a chosen people as a favor to be enjoyed rather than a calling to be fulfilled. But now and again they recognized that they were to tell the entire earth of the Lord God. Psalm 96 is one of those occasions.

The writer doesn't think of his responsibility as a burden; indeed, it has caused him to "sing . . . a new song" (Psalm 96:1). Witnessing is something he wants to do "from day to day" (Psalm 96:2), and he wants especially to declare God's glory "among the nations" and "among all the peoples" (Psalm 96:3)—that is, among the non-Jews, the peoples who do not know of God or are even opposed to what little they know. The psalmist's goal is that the Lord shall "be revered" (Psalm 96:4) and because his own experience with God is so fulfilling, he's confident that others will be equally enthusiastic once they discover that this is "the LORD [who] made the heavens" (Psalm 96:5).

Now and again some of us defend our failure to speak of our faith by saying that we simply live a life that will tell the story. We probably don't realize how arrogant such a statement is; not many of us live with such dramatic beauty that others will find themselves drawn to God by our example. In truth, no spoken witness is of much worth unless the life from which it comes is consistent; but on the other hand, even the best life needs a verbal accompaniment. If a person lives a particularly exemplary life, those observing it are likely to give him or her credit without thinking of the role God has played in the goodness.

Besides, there is more to the glory of God than the life of some individual—or indeed, of a whole body of people. Much of God's glory—such as nature, history, and justice—must be told by those who have come to appreciate it, else others will observe it without realizing what they are seeing. The psalmist, for instance, sees the wonder of God in acts of judgment and justice; neighboring nations won't understand this unless the psalmist explains it.

So it is in our day. Now and again secular poets and novelists catch a glimpse of the work of God in our world, for God finds a witness everywhere. But the main burden of witnessing rests upon those of us who believe. We are called to share the gladness, beauty, and truth we have found. When we fail to do so, we not only dishonor God, we also cheat our neighbors. Their chances of hearing are very slight unless those who believe will tell the story. That's why we are called to witness. The person who wrote Psalm 96 understood this. So must we.

SHARING THE SCRIPTURE

PREPARING TO TEACH

Often during this quarter I have emphasized the importance of the inner preparation of the teacher. I must do so again. Spend some time this week examining your own practices of worship and faithfulness in witnessing. We aren't expected to be perfect, so we shouldn't lay such an impossible burden on ourselves. But we should feel the importance of both worship and witness, and should have a commitment to do our best in both areas if we are to handle this lesson adequately.

Read Psalm 96 several times, allowing yourself to feel the excitement of the writer. Allow your imagination to be especially caught up with the pictures he evokes: honor, majesty, strength, and beauty in procession before God; nations hearing of God's glory; and nature bursting forth in celebration and song.

Think for a moment of some especially memorable experiences of worship, and try to recall what made those occasions so wonderful. Then, recall instances where you have witnessed to your faith. Perhaps you've done so in a formal setting, when you've spoken to a religious or secular group; but think especially of times you have shared your beliefs quite naturally in some conversation, or in a letter, or a greeting card. Try to imagine how many ways one can witness.

Your class may well be uneasy with both the issues of today's lesson. Anticipate this possibility, but don't be troubled by it. Simply be prepared.

If you plan to do the Psalter reading, have hymnals available. Psalm 96 is found on pages 815-816 of *The United Methodist Hymnal*.

If you plan to have someone read a hymn for one of the activities under "Worship the Lord," contact that person early in the week and suggest the hymn(s) you would like.

If you have persons in the class or congregation who are knowledgeable about other world religions, such as Buddhism, Islam, Hinduism, or Judaism, ask them to be prepared to give an overview of the religion they know.

LEADING THE CLASS

Introduction

Introduce today's lesson by noting that you are going to discuss two "W" words that are both familiar yet, in their own way, strange to us. Note that these two words—worship and witness—represent two-thirds of our basic calling, along with service.

Present the main questions for today: **What do the words worship and witness mean to us? How can we worship and witness effectively?**

Invite one or two volunteers to tell of some especially memorable experience of worship. It's quite likely that someone will mention a solitary experience with nature. If so, note that most of us have such a memory, and that probably the reason it stands out in our minds is because we don't expect God to break in upon us outside the stated worship services—and that, for the same reason, we can easily take our church worship experiences for granted. We expect to meet God in the sanctuary, so we only rarely recall these week-after-week events. Save the issue of witness until later in the lesson because it is a subject that can easily lead into side tracks.

Worship the Lord

If you have access to a hymnal with a Psalter, read Psalm 96 responsively. Use a sung response if that is appropriate in your classroom setting. Think of a different way to divide the class for the reading. Perhaps persons born between January and June could read the leader's portion and those born between July and December, the congregation's part. Encourage joyous, enthusiastic reading as a means of worshiping God at this moment.

Read or retell paragraphs two and three under this heading in the "Interpreting the Scripture" portion. Ask the class these questions: **(1) Where do you feel closest to God?** (Note that we can feel close to God in any setting.) **(2) If one can feel close to God anywhere, why is attendance at worship in the sanctuary important?** (Note that the psalmist calls the people to "bring an offering and come into his courts," that is, the temple. While private devotions are important, they cannot replace corporate worship by the community of faith.)

Read aloud William Temple's ideas on worship as printed in the fourth paragraph of this section under "Interpreting the Scripture." Provide an opportunity for class members to talk, preferably in small groups, about how they would define worship.

Call on someone whom you contacted prior to class to read a hymn that speaks of nature and the worship of God—such as "All Things Bright and Beautiful" or "For the Beauty of the Earth." Ask class members to recall some instance where they have especially felt the glory of God in nature—a time, for example, when it seemed that one could almost feel the joy in the fields, or the praise of God in the song of a bird.

If your church or denomination has recently adopted a new hymnal or new orders of worship, talk with the class about these changes by asking:

(1) **How has the opportunity to sing new songs and experience worship in a new way helped you to feel more excited about attending church?**

(2) **What changes or new hymns do you particularly like?**

(3) **What changes are you having difficulty adapting to? Can you identify why these changes are difficult for you?** (If concerns surface that would be helpful for the pastor to know, be sure to pass them along.)

Spend some time brainstorming words or phrases to complete this sentence: If I were in charge of worship in this church, I would _____. Invite students to call out answers as you record them on newsprint. You may want to give the paper to the pastor or a church leader (if you have a worship committee) as friendly suggestions from the class. Some ideas may be appropriate for implementation by the pastor, music director, ushers, altar guild, or other persons responsible for worship.

Say Among the Nations, "The Lord Is King!"

Introduce this segment by noting that the psalmist speaks disparagingly of the gods of other nations. We are often told nowadays that we should not consider our beliefs superior and that we should be sensitive to the beliefs of others. That is sage advice when we look around a constantly

shrinking world and see the strife caused by religious differences, but it need not prevent us from witnessing. Ask the class these questions: **(1) How can we respect other beliefs, yet share what is meaningful in our lives? (2) How do we speak of our own deep convictions without putting down others?**

If you have knowledgeable resource persons in the church whom you have contacted during the week, provide time for them to share brief reports on major world religions. Then ask the class: **What unique things does Christianity have to offer to a world where there are many different beliefs?** You may want to list their ideas on a chalkboard or newsprint.

Read or retell paragraphs three through six under this heading in the "Interpreting the Scripture" portion. This information may challenge the understanding that many Christians have that we only need to live an exemplary life to be witnesses for God. Ask the class:

(1) **Why must we directly witness to our faith?**

(2) **How can we do this, especially in the midst of our everyday life and conversation?**

(3) **What difference might our verbal witness make to someone else, to the church, to God, to ourselves?**

Note that in Psalm 96:11-12, even nature bears witness to God. It too rejoices in the Lord. Ask the class: (1) What is our responsibility in terms of caring for God's creation? (2) How can we be good stewards of all of creation so that it may continue to witness to the power of God?

Point out that in the closing verse, Psalm 96:13, the psalmist speaks of God coming to "judge the world with righteousness." Discuss these questions: **(1) What responsibility does that foreknowledge of judgment place on persons who know God to share the good news? (2) How can we proclaim that message in such a way that listeners understand that we are not judging them?**

HELPING CLASS MEMBERS ACT

Challenge class members who attend Sunday school, but not worship, to make a commitment to become regular participants in the worship service.

Encourage class members to pay particular attention to the elements of worship in your service. These may include acts such as prayer, confession, verbal and sung praise, thanksgiving, words of assurance, call to worship, affirmation of faith, proclamation of the Word, and Bible reading. Ask students to consider which of these are most meaningful in helping them to worship. Consider which aspects are the most difficult or challenging and try to discern why this is so.

To help adults gain a better perspective on the diversity of beliefs and cultures that exists within our world, encourage them to seek out news articles that show clashes among persons of different religious faiths. Ask them to try to identify the differences in belief that are causing problems. Also ask them to consider whether or not ecumenical dialogue might make any difference in these situations.

Encourage class members to make one commitment toward better stewardship of the earth. Perhaps they could begin recycling, or use more energy efficient lighting, or buy produce that has been organically grown. Whatever they choose to do, help them see that their efforts will help God's creation.

PLANNING FOR NEXT SUNDAY

Next Sunday we enter a new quarter of studies entitled "God's People Face Judgment." This study will deal with the period in Israel's history from the fall of Samaria in 722 B.C.E. to the fall of Jerusalem in 587 B.C.E. To prepare for next week's class, ask the students to read 2 Kings 18-20. Our lesson will focus on Hezekiah's steadfast faith as seen in 2 Kings 18.

Please turn now to the Quarterly Evaluation form on pages 487-88. Complete this form for the Fourth Quarter.

Evaluation of the *New International Lesson Annual*

Your comments are extremely important in shaping future editions of the *New International Lesson Annual*. Kindly take a few moments to complete this survey and return it to:

> Dr. Nan Duerling
> Abingdon Press
> The United Methodist Publishing House
> P.O. Box 801
> Nashville, TN 37202

---

ease respond to each statement below by circling the number that best describes your action according to this scale:
STRONGLY DISAGREE   2 DISAGREE   3 NEUTRAL   4 AGREE   5 STRONGLY AGREE

---

he New International Lesson Annual (NILA)
erally helps me to understand the scripture
is the basis for the lesson.   1   2   3   4   5

LA provides concrete examples to relate
achings of the scripture to the lives of my
nts.   1   2   3   4   5

ILA offers a variety of ideas for teaching the
ns that I find useful in my own class.   1   2   3   4   5

he "Previewing the Lesson" portion of *NILA*
s me to see at a glance where the lesson is
g and what it is trying to accomplish.   1   2   3   4   5

generally use ideas in the "Helping Class
mbers Act" section to challenge my students
espond to the teachings of the lesson.   1   2   3   4   5

Design features like boxes, boldtype questions,
stion marks, and page size help me prepare and
ch each lesson.   1   2   3   4   5

---

ease tell something about your class by checking the appropriate answers to these uestion

---

7) T' class members have a student book.   ....Yes   ....No   ....Maybe

(The students generally read the scripture
and lesson book if used) in advance.   ....Yes   ....No   ....Maybe

(9) My class mostly includes students who are   ....under 35 35-60

                                                             ....over 60   ....mixed ages

(10) Our weekly attendance averages   ....fewer than 10 11-25

                                                            26-50 51-75

                                                            76-100   ....over 10(

(11) My class enjoys (check all that apply)   ....discussion   ....lecture

                                                             ....small group work

                                                             ....creative activities (e.g.,
                                                                      debate, journaling)

Please tell us something about yourself by checking the answers to the follo
questions:

---

(12) I consider myself to be a ....novice, ...somewhat experienced, or ....very experi
teacher of adults.

(13) On average, I spend ....less than 1 hour, ...1-3 hours, ...4-6 hours, ...more than
hours per week preparing my lesson.

(14) I usually teach ....every week, ...several times per month, ...on a quarterly basi
....just a few weeks each year.

(15) To continue growing in my own faith and knowledge, I (check all that apply)
    ....regularly attend worship.
    ....attend Bible studies led by the pastor or other persons in my own church.
    ....attend denominationally or ecumenically sponsored studies.
    ....attend prayer meetings.
    ....am involved in hands-on mission and/or social justice activities.
    ....practice spiritual disciplines (e.g., prayer, meditation, tithing).
    ....regularly study the Bible on my own.

Comments or suggestions you'd care to make about this resource:

Thank you very much for your helpful responses.